**SERIES ON
INTERNATIONAL
LAW AND
DEVELOPMENT**

# Emerging Principles of International Environmental Law

**SUMUDU A. ATAPATTU**

 *Transnational Publishers*

Published and distributed by Transnational Publishers, Inc.
Ardsley Park
Science and Technology Center
410 Saw Mill River Road
Ardsley, NY 10502

Phone: 914-693-5100
Fax: 914-693-4430
E-mail: info@transnationalpubs.com
Web: www.transnationalpubs.com

*Library of Congress Cataloging-in-Publication Data*

Atapattu, Sumudu A.
    Emerging principles of international environmental law /
Sumudu A. Atapattu.
        p. cim.
    Includes bibliographical references and index.
    ISBN 1-57105-182-1
    1. Environmental law, International.    2. Sustainable development—
Law and legislation.

K3585.A86 2006
344.04'6—dc22
                                                                    2006045554

Manufactured in the United States of America

*To My "Future Generation"*
*—Praveena and Prasangi—*
*With Undying Love*

# CONTENTS

# FOREWORD

It is a pleasure to welcome to the *International Law and Development Series* of Transnational Publishers, Inc., the present work by Dr. Sumudu Atapattu, *Emerging Principles of International Environmental Law.*

The publication of Dr. Atapattu's comprehensive analysis of environmental issues facing the global community comes at an auspicious time. Never before have these issues commanded the attention of so many governments, non-governmental organizations, lawyers and students. And for good reasons—the tremendous environmental stresses that accompany economic growth and the fundamental question about the sustainability of the present nature of development. Dr. Atapattu's book goes to a key issue: what principles are emerging in international environmental law to deal with these stresses and the sustainability question? Her careful scholarship explains relations among economic, political, scientific and legal factors and thus possesses an appropriate and admirable interdisciplinary flavor.

Dr. Atapattu begins with the concept of sustainable development (Chapters 1 and 2)—how it originated, what it means and who and what it impacts. She thereby lays a strong foundation for what follows. In subsequent chapters, she discusses the key emerging principles in international environmental law: the precautionary principle (Chapter 3), environmental impact assessments (Chapter 4), common but differentiated responsibility (Chapter 5) and polluter pays (Chapter 6). She concludes (in Chapter 7) with an engaging consideration of the future of sustainable development law. Thus, she brings her analysis full circle.

Throughout the book, she operates effectively and adroitly at the levels of theory and practice in a flowing, accessible style attractive to seasoned veterans and newcomers. All in all, *Emerging Principles of International Environmental Law* is a book that masterfully ties together years of contemplation and work by a world-class scholar. May I add, Dr. Atapattu, who has lived and worked in developing and developed countries, is especially positioned, and passionately committed to, international environmental law.

Without doubt, Dr. Atapattu's book fits squarely within the mission of the *International Law and Development Series.* That mission is to publish books on the intersection between international law and Third World development. The relevant fields of international law include trade, commerce, foreign direct investment, banking, securities regulation, labor, the environment, business associations, competition policy, public law, human rights and jurisprudence. The relevant aspects of development include legal, economic or political progress in one or more poor countries. Books in the *Series* explore the relationship between doctrines in one of these fields and real-world events. They also may focus on comparative aspects of their subject, including discussions of structures and trends in one or more developed countries.

Thus, books in the *International Law and Development Series* are for a global audience of legal practitioners, policymakers and academicians. Dr. Atapattu's timely work is sure to be of interest.

Raj Bhala
Rice Distinguished Professor
The University of Kansas School of Law
Lawrence, Kansas

# ACKNOWLEDGMENTS

This project started from a telephone conversation with Professor Raj Bhala (now the Rice Distinguished Professor at the University of Kansas School of Law), then on the faculty of George Washington University Law School where I had spent my sabbatical time as a Fulbright scholar. He encouraged me to consider writing a book for a series that he was editing on International Law and Development for Transnational Publishers, New York. Without his encouragement and guidance throughout the long process of research and writing, this publication would not have been possible, and I would like to thank him wholeheartedly.

I would like to sincerely thank Heike Fenton of Transnational Publishers for her patience with this publication and for the faith put in me. I am particularly grateful to her for being flexible with deadlines. I would also like to thank Maria Angelini who so efficiently prepared the text for publication. I am particularly grateful to Maxine Idakus for meticulously editing the book. She greatly impressed me with her thoroughness and pertinent questions. She was very friendly and easy to work with, and she made sure that the final product was reader-friendly.

I am indebted to the University of Wisconsin-Madison Law School and particularly the Institute for Legal Studies for welcoming me with open arms and providing me space and facilities to carry out my research. I was given access to their excellent library resources and the opportunity to interact with their highly qualified and world renowned faculty. Special thanks are due to Professor Howard Erlanger, Director of the Institute, Pam Hollenhorst, Associate Director, for her ready smile and for always being willing to help, and Dianne Sattinger who never failed to greet me and inquire about my work and offer words of encouragement, particularly during the long, cold days of winter. I would also like to thank the other members of the "ILS family" for their camaraderie.

The UW-Madison Law School also gave me the opportunity to teach my pet subject—International Environmental Law—which enabled me to test my ideas with the students and to keep alive my love of teaching. I would like to thank all my students—past and present—for their rich ideas and their input into the seminar, which made it so interesting to teach. To Professor Chuck Irish, Director of the East Asian Studies Center, I owe a special debt, for sponsoring my course at the Law School. I am very grateful to Professors Alta Charo and John Kidwell who encouraged me to develop a seminar on International Environmental Law and for their advice and encouragement throughout my stay at the Law School. I would also like to sincerely thank Professors Richard Bilder, Greg Schaffer, Peter Carstensen, Art McEvoy and Dave Trubek who helped me in numerous ways.

I would also like to thank my colleagues at the Center for International Sustainable Development Law in Montreal, Canada, for keeping the debate on sustainable development alive and for providing me a springboard to test my ideas. The Center also gave me the opportunity to work on cutting edge issues such as poverty and human rights within a framework of international sustainable development law.

To my family I owe a special word of gratitude for being patient with me during the rather "messy" stages of writing. I would like to thank my daughters, Praveena and Prasangi, for being patient with me and not complaining when Mummy could not spend all her spare time with them. A big thank you is due to my husband, Dhammika, who encouraged me throughout my career and helped me reach goals that at times seemed unattainable. I remember affectionately my mother's love of books (a prolific writer herself), which I probably inherited! I would also like to thank all my friends for their good humor and for keeping cultural ties alive in a country far away from our motherland and my sister and two brothers as well as my extended family for their constant love and support.

I would like to mention two people *in memorium.* My father who passed away ten years ago and Dr. Neelan Tiruchelvam, Director of the Law & Society Trust, Colombo (among many other titles he held) under whom I had the privilege of working for several years. His untimely death in 1999 left a huge vacuum in academic and civil society circles in Sri Lanka. Both my father and Neelan would have been very happy to see this publication.

I will always be indebted to my teachers and advisors in Sri Lanka and Cambridge who guided and taught me how to think critically and to be innovative in approaching international law issues.

Needless to say, of course, that any errors in this publication are all mine.

Sumudu Atapattu
March 2006
University of Wisconsin-Madison Law School
Wisconsin, USA

# ABOUT THE AUTHOR

*Sumudu Anopama Atapattu* teaches *Selected Problems in Environmental Law: International Environmental Law* as a lecturer at the University of Wisconsin-Madison Law School and was recently appointed as the Associate Director of the Global Legal Studies Initiative of the Law School. She is also a visiting scholar at the Law School's Institute for Legal Studies. She holds an LL.M. in Public International Law and a Ph.D. in International Environmental Law from the University of Cambridge, U.K., and is an Attorney-at-Law of the Supreme Court of Sri Lanka.

Ms. Atapattu has received numerous awards and scholarships for academic excellence, including a Cambridge Commonwealth Trust scholarship and a Benefactor Studentship awarded by St. John's College, Cambridge. In 2000, she was awarded a Senior Fulbright Scholarship and carried out research on "Environmental Rights and Human Rights" at the New York University Law School and the George Washington University Law School as a visiting scholar.

From August 1995 to January 2002, Ms. Atapattu worked as an Associate Professor at the Faculty of Law, University of Colombo, Sri Lanka, where she taught Environmental Law and Public International Law and was instrumental in introducing a course on environmental law to the law school curriculum. She also taught International Organizations for the LL.M. Degree and the Public International Law component of the M.A. in International Relations course, both at the University of Colombo, Sri Lanka.

Ms. Atapattu has also worked as a Senior Consultant to the Law & Society Trust, a human rights non-governmental organization in Colombo, Sri Lanka. She was the editor of *Sri Lanka: State of Human Rights 2002*, and the consultant editor of *Sri Lanka: State of Human Rights 2003*, an annual publication on the human rights situation in Sri Lanka. In 2003 she was appointed the Lead Counsel for Human Rights and Poverty Eradication of the Center for International Sustainable Development Law based in Montreal, Canada, and also serves on the Advisory Board of the *McGill International Journal of Sustainable Development Law and Policy*.

Ms. Atapattu has also worked on several projects as an independent consultant, and, in 2001, she served on a panel of experts on liability and compensation issues for the World Health Organization's Framework Convention on Tobacco Control.

Ms. Atapattu is the author and editor of several publications on issues relating to Public International Law, Human Rights Law and International Environmental Law. Her publications include "Sustainable Development, Myth or Reality?: A Survey of Sustainable Development under International Law and Sri Lankan Law," 14 *Georgetown International Environmental Law Review* 265 (2001); "The Right to a Healthy Life or the Right to Die Polluted? The Emergence of a Right to a Healthy Environment under International Law," 16 *Tulane Environmental Law Journal 65* (2002); "The Public Health Impact of Global Environmental Problems and the Role of International Law," *American Journal of Law and Medicine* (2004); Sustainable Development and Terrorism: International Linkages and a Case Study of Sri Lanka, 30 *William & Mary Environmental Law and Policy Review* 273 (2006), as well as several book chapters. She also served as consultant editor of *Infrastructure Development in Sri Lanka: Regulation, Policy and Finance* (Euromoney Publications, Jersey: 1997).

# LIST OF ABBREVIATIONS

| | |
|---|---|
| AIDS | Acquired Immuno-Deficiency Syndrome |
| ASEAN | Association of South East Asian Nations |
| CBD | Convention on Biological Diversity |
| CDM | clean development mechanism |
| CDR/CBDR | common but differentiated responsibility principle |
| CFCs | chlorofluorocarbons |
| CIEL | Center for International Environmental Law |
| CITES | Convention to Regulate International Trade in Endangered Species of Flora and Fauna |
| COPs | Conference of Parties |
| CSD | Commission on Sustainable Development |
| CTE | Committee on Trade and Environment |
| DSB | Dispute Settlement Body |
| EA | environmental assessment |
| EAP | Environmental Action Plan |
| EIA | environmental impact assessment |
| EC | European Community |
| ECE | Economic Commission for Europe |
| EEZ | Exclusive Economic Zone |
| ENMOD | Convention on the Prohibition of Military or other Hostile use of Environmental Modifications Techniques |
| ETS | European Treaty Series |
| FAO | Food and Agricultural Organization |
| FIELD | Foundation for International Environmental Law and Development |
| GA | General Assembly |
| GATT | General Agreement on Tariff and Trade |
| GEF | Global Environment Facility |
| GMOs | genetically modified organisms |
| HIV | Human Immuno-Deficiency Virus |
| HRC | Human Rights Committee |
| IAEA | International Atomic Energy Agency |
| ICCPR | International Covenant on Civil and Political Rights |
| ICESCR | International Covenant on Economic, Social and Cultural Rights |
| ICJ | International Court of Justice |
| ICLQ | International and Comparative Law Quarterly |
| IEL | international environmental law |

| IFC | International Finance Corporation |
|---|---|
| IHRL | international human rights law |
| ILA | International Law Association |
| ILC | International Law Commission |
| ILM | International Legal Materials |
| ILO | International Labor Organization |
| ILR | International Law Reports |
| IMO | International Maritime Organization |
| IPCC | Inter-Governmental Panel on Climate Change |
| ISDL | international sustainable development law |
| ISO | International Standards Organization |
| ITLOS | International Tribunal for the Law of the Sea |
| IUCN | International Union for the Conservation of Nature and Natural Resources |
| IWC | International Whaling Commission |
| LMOs | living modified organisms |
| LNTS | League of Nations Treaty Series |
| MEAs | Multilateral Environmental Agreements |
| MFN | most-favored-nation obligation |
| NEIO | new international economic order |
| NGOs | non-governmental organizations |
| OAS | Organization of American States |
| OECD | Organization for Economic Cooperation and Development |
| OHCHR | Office of the High Commissioner for Human Rights |
| PCB | polychlorinated biphenyl |
| PCIJ | Permanent Court of International Justice |
| PIC | prior informed consent |
| POPs | persistent organic pollutants |
| PPM | production and process methods |
| PPP | polluter pays principle |
| RECIEL | Review of European Community and International Environmental Law |
| RIAA | Reports of International Arbitral Awards |
| SEA | strategic environmental assessment |
| SIA | social impact assessment |
| SPS Agreement | WTO Agreement on the Application of Sanitary and Phytosanitary Measures |
| TRIPS Agreement | Agreement on Trade Related Aspects of Intellectual Property Rights |
| UDHR | Universal Declaration of Human Rights |
| UN | United Nations |

| | |
|---|---|
| UNCED | United Nations Conference on Environment and Development |
| UNCLOS | United Nations Convention on Law of the Sea |
| UNDP | United Nations Development Program |
| UNECE | United Nations Economic Commission for Europe |
| UNEP | United Nations Environment Program |
| UNESCO | United Nations Education, Scientific and Cultural Organization |
| UNFCC | United Nations Framework Convention on Climate Change |
| UNTS | United Nations Treaty Series |
| UST | U.S. Treaties and Other International Agreements |
| WCED | World Commission on Environment and Development |
| WHO | World Health Organization |
| WMO | World Meteorological Organization |
| WSSD | World Summit on Sustainable Development |
| WTO | World Trade Organization |

# INTRODUCTION

Much water has flowed under the "environmental" bridge 30 years since the Stockholm Conference on the Human Environment[1] and certainly ten years since the Rio Conference on Environment and Development.[2] The Johannesburg Summit on Sustainable Development[3] convened to mark the tenth anniversary of the Rio Conference was yet another important watershed in the history of international environmental law. There is no doubt that the last 30 years have witnessed a remarkable upsurge in the activities relating to environmental protection. While many strides have been taken, there is an unfinished agenda and many environmental issues remain, very much similar to other issues, embroiled in political controversy.[4] Human poverty, which is a serious obstacle to achieving sustainable development, is at alarming levels: about 1.2 billion people in the world today survive on less than U.S. $1.00 a day[5] and more than 2 billion people live on less than U.S. $2.00 a day.[6] Approximately 44 percent of the world's poor live in South Asia.[7] The alarming rate of poverty led the UN Secretary-General Kofi Annan to declare that absolute poverty "is an affront to our common humanity"[8] and called upon states to take steps to halve the number of the poor by 2015.[9] Thus, sustainable development[10]

---

[1] UN Doc. A/CONF.48/PC.17, June 16, 1972. The Stockholm Declaration adopted at this conference is available at 11 ILM 1416 (1972).

[2] The Rio Declaration on Environment and Development, UN Doc. A/CONF.151/26, *reprinted in* 31 ILM 874 (1992), *available at* http://www.un.org/documents/ga/conf121/aconf15126-1annexl.htm adopted at this conference.

[3] See UN Doc. A/CONF.199/20, *available at* http://www.johannesburgsummit. org/.

[4] The controversy surrounding climate change is a good example. *See,* DAVID HUNTER, JAMES SALZMAN & DURWOOD ZAELKE, INTERNATIONAL ENVIRONMENTAL LAW AND POLICY 588 (2002) [hereinafter HUNTER ET AL.].

[5] *World Development Report 2000/2001: Attacking Poverty* (World Bank), *available at* http://web.worldbank.org/WBSITE/EXTERNAL/TOPICS/EXTPOVERTY/.

[6] *Id.*

[7] *Id.*

[8] *We the Peoples: The Role of the United Nations in the 21st Century,* Millennium Report of the Secretary General of the United Nations, Executive Summary (2000), *available at* http://www.un.org/millennium/sg/ report/ [hereinafter The Millennium Report].

[9] *Id.*

[10] *See* the discussion in Chapter 2.

advocated by the World Commission on Environment and Development[11] in 1987 and reinforced by the Rio Declaration on Environment and Development in 1992 and reiterated by the Johannesburg Declaration on Sustainable Development in 2002, has remained elusive to much of the international community.

International environmental law (IEL) has come a long way since the Stockholm Conference on the Human Environment. This conference, which was the turning point in the history of IEL, laid the foundation for many of the developments that took place during the subsequent years. Indeed, some of the principles contained in the Stockholm Declaration, particularly Principle 21, have since become part of customary international law.[12] According to Principle 21:

> States have, in accordance with the Charter of the United Nations and the principles of international law, the sovereign right to exploit their own natural resources pursuant to their own environmental policies, and the responsibility to ensure that activities within their jurisdiction or control do not cause damage to the environment of other states or of areas beyond the limits of national jurisdiction.[13]

Principle 21 thus constitutes the cornerstone of modern international environmental law. A rather limited version of this principle was applied many decades ago in the *Trail Smelter Arbitration*[14] between the United States and Canada. While affirming the sovereign right of states to exploit their natural resources, Principle 21 subjected this right to a very important limitation: this right ended the moment it had the capacity to harm the environment of other states or the environment of global commons. This provision has had a profound effect on the evolution of international environmental law. Often referred to as the principle of harm prevention, Principle 21 was applied principally to transboundary environmental damage. IEL has since evolved to encompass the prevention of environmental harm even in the absence of any extra-territorial impact: IEL now regulates activities that would have traditionally fallen within the domestic jurisdic-

---

[11] OUR COMMON FUTURE, REPORT OF THE WORLD COMMISSION ON ENVIRONMENT AND DEVELOPMENT (1987).

[12] *See* PATRICIA BIRNIE & ALAN BOYLE, INTERNATIONAL LAW & THE ENVIRONMENT 110 (2d ed. 2002); PHILIPPE SANDS, PRINCIPLES OF INTERNATIONAL ENVIRONMENTAL LAW 246 (2d ed. 2002); HUNTER ET AL., *supra* note 4, at 177.

[13] Principle 21, Stockholm Declaration, *supra* note 1.

[14] 3 RIAA 1905 (1941).

tion of states,[15] and this phenomenon of "internationalization" of environmental protection will be discussed in more detail later.

IEL has also witnessed the emergence of several new principles and/or concepts that have greatly influenced the developments in the field. While some of these principles have been in existence for several decades, others are of recent origin. The relatively "old" principles include: the principle of good neighborliness[16] stemming from the principle of sovereignty itself, notification and assistance in the event of transboundary environmental harm,[17] prior consultation and negotiation,[18] common heritage of mankind[19] and providing redress in the event harm occurs to other states.[20] The principles/concepts of recent origin include: sustainable development;[21] the precautionary principle;[22] the polluter pays principle;[23] common concern of mankind;[24] common but differentiated responsibility

---

[15] Protection of biodiversity, preparation of environmental assessments are two examples. *See* the discussion in Chapter 1, Section A.1.

[16] *See* HUNTER ET AL., *supra* note 4, at 428.

[17] This issue came to the forefront in the aftermath of the Chernobyl nuclear accident in 1986. Two international conventions were adopted under the auspices of the IAEA in response to the lacuna in the law: 1986 Convention on Early Notification of a Nuclear Accident, 25 ILM 1370 (1986), signed Sept. 26, 1986, entered into force Oct. 27, 1986, *available at* http://www.iaea.org/Publications/Documents/Infcircs/Others/inf335.shtml, and 1986 Convention on Assistance in the Case of a Nuclear Accident or Radiological Emergency, 25 ILM 1377 (1986), signed Sept. 26, 1986, entered into force Feb. 26, 1987, *available at* http://www.iaea.org/Publications/Documents/Infcircs/Others/inf336.shtml. However, the adoption of international conventions after such a catastrophic incident highlighted the reactionary nature of environmental law. This react-after-the event approach has been heavily criticized and has since then given way to an anticipate-and-prevent approach in relation to environment issues. *See*, in this regard, the action taken in relation to the depletion of the ozone layer, *in* HUNTER ET AL., *supra* note 4, at 526.

[18] *See* HUNTER ET AL., *supra* note 4, at 430.

[19] The legal status of this concept is rather controversial. *See id.* at 389.

[20] *See* SANDS, *supra* note 12, at 869.

[21] *See* discussion in Chapter 2.

[22] Codified in Principle 15 of the Rio Declaration, *supra* note 2. *See* discussion in Chapter 3.

[23] Codified in Principle 16 of the Rio Declaration, *supra* note 2. *See* discussion in Chapter 6.

[24] This concept emerged partly as a response to the controversy surrounding the common heritage principle. The common concern of mankind concept has been included in the Preamble to the UN Framework Convention on Climate Change, 31 ILM 849 (1992), 1771 UNTS 107, signed May 9, 1992, entered into force Mar. 21, 1994, *available at* http://www.unfccc.ea/; and the Preamble to the Convention on Biological

principle;[25] global partnership;[26] inter-generational equity principle;[27] and environmental impact assessment[28] and procedural rights.[29]

Five such principles/concepts[30] have been selected for discussion in this publication: sustainable development; the precautionary principle; environmental impact assessment process and procedural rights; the common but differentiated responsibility principle; and the polluter pays principle. These principles/concepts were chosen because of their tremendous impact on international environmental law as well as national law and because some of these concepts are at the verge of attaining normativity. In these chapters the methodology adopted has been to trace the historical evolution of a particular concept or principle, evaluate the treaties and other international instruments that embody it, and discuss how tribunals and other organizations have applied that concept or principle. The underlying notion for the whole publication is sustainable development, and other principles or concepts discussed in this publication are evaluated in terms of their relationship with sustainable development. In other words, sustainable development—which the writer believes to be the single most issue that has influenced international environmental law as no other concept or principle has—informs the whole publication.

Chapter 1 places the discussion in its historical context and discusses the emergence of international sustainable development law (ISDL) from its early origins of international IEL. IEL, which emerged in response to cross-border pollution issues, had to adapt itself to deal with global environmental issues such as global warming and ozone depletion. The phenomenon of internationalization of environmental protection, which is a significant development in international law, is also discussed. Chapter 1 discusses several issues that have emerged in the international environmental law discourse: human rights and good governance and a right to a

---

Diversity, 31 ILM 822 (1992), 1760 UNTS 79, *available at* http://www.biodiv.org/.

[25] Codified in Principle 7 of the Rio Declaration, *supra* note 2. *See* discussion in Chapter 5.

[26] *Id.*

[27] Principle 3 of the Rio Declaration, *supra* note 2, refers to the needs of present and future generations in the context of the right to development.

[28] Codified in Principle 17 of the Rio Declaration, *supra* note 2. *See* discussion in Chapter 5.

[29] Codified in Principle 10 of the Rio Declaration, *supra* note 2. *See* discussion in Chapter 4, Section F.

[30] The words "principles" or "concepts" are used in a broad sense and do not seek to convey any legal significance unless indicated otherwise.

healthy environment; globalization and international trade; health and human rights; poverty; state responsibility and global partnership; development assistance; World Bank environmental strategy and the Global Environment Facility.

Chapter 2 is the heart of the publication and discusses sustainable development from its emergence to the present status. It looks at various definitions and parameters of sustainable development and discusses the Report of the Experts Group appointed by the UN Commission on Sustainable Development, which elaborates on the components of sustainable development. It also discusses how it has been operationalized in treaties and other instruments and how it has been applied by different bodies. Particular attention is paid to the *Case Concerning the Gabcikovo Nagymaros Project* and the separate opinion of Judge Weeramantry. Chapter 2 then discusses obstacles to sustainable development including poverty and good governance and evaluates the legal status of sustainable development.

The precautionary principle, an important tool that has influenced the decision-making process and how it has evolved over the years is discussed in Chapter 3. It surveys the international instruments embodying the precautionary principle and how it has been applied by different international bodies. It then discusses the relationship between prevention, precaution and environmental impact assessment as well as its relationship with sustainable development and finally evaluates its legal status.

Environmental impact assessment (EIA) and procedural rights is the subject of Chapter 4. Having discussed the emergence at the international level, it surveys international instruments that embody provisions on EIA as well as how it has been applied by various international bodies. Particular attention is paid to the Espoo Convention on EIA in a transboundary context. Strategic environmental assessment (SEA), another emerging tool is also discussed in this chapter. It then discusses procedural rights in relation to EIA and particular attention is paid to the Aarhus Convention on Access to Information, Public Participation and Access to Remedies.[31] How to facilitate public participation and the difficulties of public participation are discussed followed by a discussion on the legal status of EIA and procedural rights.

Another concept that has emerged in recent years is the common but differentiated responsibility principle. Although controversial, this concept has greatly influenced international environmental law and has been incorporated in many treaties. The rationale for the principle, the role of equity and its relationship with the principle of sovereign equality is discussed fol-

---

[31] 38 ILM 517 (1999), signed June 25, 1998, entered into force Oct. 30, 2001.

lowed by a survey of international instruments embodying the concept. It then discusses its relationship with other concepts such as the inter-generational equity principle, sustainable development and the polluter pays principle followed by a discussion of its legal status.

The final substantive chapter discusses the polluter pays principle, an economic tool originally adopted by the Organization for Economic Cooperation and Development (OECD) but included in the Rio Declaration in 1992. Having discussed the evolution of this principle, Chapter 6 discusses its application outside the OECD, exceptions to the principle, how it has been operationalized and its relationship with other concepts and principles including liability for damage and international trade. It is concluded with a discussion of its legal status.

The final chapter summarizes the conclusions of the publication and offers some thoughts on how these concepts and principles will evolve under international sustainable development law.

CHAPTER 1

# FROM STOCKHOLM TO JOHANNESBURG VIA RIO: THE EMERGENCE OF INTERNATIONAL SUSTAINABLE DEVELOPMENT LAW

We stand now where two roads diverge. But unlike the roads in Robert Frost's familiar poem, they are not equally fair. The road we have long been traveling is deceptively easy, a smooth superhighway on which we progress with great speed, but at its end lies disaster. The other fork of the road—the one "less traveled by" —offers our last, our only chance to reach a destination that assures the preservation of our earth.

The choice, after all, is ours to make.

*Rachel Carson, Silent Spring (1962)*[1]

## A. INTERNATIONALIZATION OF ENVIRONMENTAL PROTECTION AND THE EROSION OF THE DOMESTIC JURISDICTION CLAUSE

A few decades ago, public international law was not concerned with environmental protection and, indeed, no separate branch of international law called "international environmental law" even existed. No textbook on international law discussed this subject, and it was even harder to find any writings in academic journals. The reason for this apathy may have been due either to the ignorance of the existence of environmental problems or because other pressing issues caught the attention of states. Thus, in the aftermath of the second world war, much attention was paid to the protection of human rights and, although in the 1960s environmental problems were beginning to emerge, it was not until the UN Conference on the Human Environment of 1972[2] (commonly referred to as the Stockholm Declaration) that the international community began to pay attention to environmental issues.

---

[1] RACHEL CARSON, SILENT SPRING 277 (1962).

[2] UN Doc. A/CONF. 48/14, June 16, 1972, *reprinted in* 11 ILM 1416 (1972).

## 1. Emergence of International Environmental Law and Cross-Border Environmental Issues

With the emergence of cross-border pollution issues such as in the *Trail Smelter Arbitration*[3] or the *Lac Lanoux Arbitration*,[4] however, it was realized by the international community that international law should ensure that activities within one state did not cause damage to the environment of other states. The response of the international community was to adapt existing international law principles, such as territorial sovereignty and state responsibility, to cover these emerging cross-border pollution issues.

The first threat to this rather complacent attitude was the phenomenon of acid rain, which was beginning to show signs of destruction in Europe, particularly in the Scandinavian states, as a result of accelerated industrialization taking place in this region.[5] This issue could not be addressed through traditional norms of international law, as the sources of pollution were difficult to ascertain and it was often the cumulative impact of the activities of several, if not all, states in the region that gave rise to the problem. The Stockholm Conference of 1972, convened at the agitation of the Scandinavian states, succeeded in putting environmental issues on the international agenda.[6] The Stockholm Declaration adopted at the Conference urged states to develop principles of international environmental law in relation to liability and compensation for the victims of pollution caused by activities within the jurisdiction or control of states.[7]

The journey of evolution, which thus began in 1972, culminated in 1992 with the adoption of the Rio Declaration on Environment and Development (Rio Declaration) by which time international environmental law had changed its course to encompass the concept of sustainable development. Sustainable development was advanced by the World Commission on Environment and Development which was established by the UN General Assembly in 1983 to find ways to reconcile the increasingly polarizing debate on economic development and environmental protection.[8] During this period global environmental issues, such as the depletion of the ozone layer

---

[3] 3 RIAA 1905 (1941).

[4] 24 ILR 119 (1961).

[5] *See* DAVID HUNTER., JAMES SALZMAN & DURWOOD ZAELKE, INTERNATIONAL ENVIRONMENTAL LAW AND POLICY, 513 (2d ed. 2002).

[6] *Id.* at 177.

[7] *See* Principle 22 of the Stockholm Declaration, *supra* note 2.

[8] *See* OUR COMMON FUTURE, REPORT OF THE WORLD COMMISSION ON ENVIRONMENT AND DEVELOPMENT (1987) and discussion in Chapter 2, Section B.3.

and the greenhouse effect, were also emerging, further reinforcing the argument for specific principles governing environmental issues.

Even with the sophistication that international environmental law has achieved during its rather short journey of evolution, it had had to grapple with traditional international law principles, such as non-intervention in internal affairs of states (called the "domestic jurisdiction clause"),[9] which often posed an obstacle to achieving an integrated approach to environmental protection. With the realization, however, that many internal policies of states could have an undesirable impact on the environment, it became necessary for international law to step in, once again, to ensure that unsustainable activities *within* states were regulated. The obligations of states in relation to biodiversity and the environmental impact assessment (EIA) process, as well as the concept of sustainable development itself, are good examples of this development. This has resulted in a gradual erosion of the domestic jurisdiction clause culminating in the new phenomenon of "internationalization" of environmental protection.[10]

The *Trail Smelter Arbitration*[11] represents the oldest dispute relating to transboundary air pollution and involved the damage caused in the territory of the United States by a smelter in Canada. These fumes were carried across the border by wind and caused damage to human health and property in the United States. In the ensuing arbitration between the parties, the arbitrator noted:

> Under principles of international law, as well as the law of the United States, no state has the right to use or permit the use of territory in such a manner as to cause injury by fumes in or to the territory of another or the properties or persons therein, when the case is of serious consequence and the injury is established by clear and convincing evidence.[12]

This principle of harm prevention has been endorsed by the International Court of Justice (ICJ) in several cases. In the *Corfu Channel* case[13] the ICJ reiterated every state's obligation not to allow knowingly its territory to be used for acts contrary to the rights of other states.[14] In its advi-

---

[9] Codified in art. 2(7) of the UN Charter.

[10] *See* discussion in Section A.3.

[11] *See supra* note 3.

[12] *Id.*

[13] 1949 ICJ 4, at 22.

[14] *Id.*

sory opinion in the *Legality of the Threat or Use of Nuclear Weapons*,[15] the World Court specifically endorsed this principle in relation to environmental issues:

> The existence of the general obligation of states to ensure that activities within their jurisdiction and control *respect* the environment of other states or of areas beyond national control is now part of the corpus of international law relating to the environment.[16]

The choice of words used by the ICJ in the above passage differs somewhat from the formulation in Principle 21 of the Stockholm Declaration. The ICJ refers to a general obligation of states to *respect* the environment of other states and the environment of global commons, rather than to the obligation not to cause damage to the environment of other states, which is a stronger formulation. While on the first reading of it, the ICJ seems to have affirmed Principle 21 of the Stockholm Declaration as having become part of customary international law, a closer look reveals that the wording used by the ICJ does not fully coincide with Principle 21. The ICJ seems to have diluted the effect of Principle 21 by using the word "respect" rather than the stricter formulation in Principle 21.[17]

This obligation of harm prevention is now a well-established principle of customary international law relating to environmental protection.[18] While the origin of this principle can be traced to the *Trail Smelter Arbitration*,[19] its ambit is wider than the Trail Smelter formulation, which made no reference to environmental protection *per se*. Its expanded and modern version is embodied in Principle 21 of the Stockholm Declaration, which can be considered as the foundation of modern international environmental law.

Principle 21 has been embodied in almost all subsequent instruments on the environment, whether binding or non-binding. This principle was reiterated, 20 years later, in the Rio Declaration albeit with a minor, yet rather significant, adjustment:

---

[15] 1996 ICJ 226.

[16] *Id.*, para. 29 (emphasis added).

[17] *See* Edith Brown Weiss, *Opening the Door to the Environment and to Future Generations, in* INTERNATIONAL LAW, THE INTERNATIONAL COURT OF JUSTICE AND NUCLEAR WEAPONS, 338, at 340 (Laurence Boisson de Chazournes & Philippe Sands eds., 1999).

[18] *See* HUNTER ET AL., *supra* note 5, at 404; PHILIPPE SANDS, PRINCIPLES OF INTERNATIONAL ENVIRONMENTAL LAW 246 (2d ed. 2003); PATRICIA BIRNIE & ALAN BOYLE, INTERNATIONAL LAW & THE ENVIRONMENT, 109 (2d ed. 2002).

[19] *See supra* note 3.

Under principles of international law and the UN Charter, every state has the right to exploit their natural resources according to their environmental *and developmental* policies, and the responsibility to ensure that activities within their jurisdiction or control do not cause damage to the environment of other states or of areas beyond the limits of national jurisdiction.[20]

While the Rio Declaration and particularly Principle 2 has been critiqued for its reference to developmental policies, thereby upsetting the delicate balance achieved at the Stockholm Conference,[21] as well as for adopting an anthropocentric approach to environmental protection,[22] the Rio Declaration does reflect the developments that have taken place since the adoption of the Stockholm Declaration. The main development, of course, relates to sustainable development.[23]

During its journey of evolution, international environmental law has traversed many paths; having started from purely cross-border issues, it changed its course to embrace other environmental issues. During the 1980s, different kinds of environmental issues started emerging, namely, global environmental issues. It was during this time that the international community heard of possible consequences of ozone depletion and global warming. These phenomena resulted from internal activities of states but had a global impact: in order to arrest these global phenomena, these internal activities had to be regulated. Traditional principles of international environmental law, based primarily on territorial sovereignty and state responsibility, could not accommodate these second-generation environmental issues. This resulted in the adoption of international conventions on the subject: Vienna Convention for the Protection of the Ozone Layer (1985)[24] and the Montreal Protocol on Substances that Deplete the Ozone Layer (1987)[25] adopted under it, and the UN Framework Con-

---

[20] Principle 2, Rio Declaration UN Doc. A/CONF.151/26, *reprinted in* 31 ILM 874 (1992), *available at* http://www.un.org/documents/gal/conf151/aconf15126-1annex1.htm (emphasis added).

[21] *See* Marc Pallemaerts, *International Environmental Law From Stockholm to Rio: Back to the Future? in* GREENING INTERNATIONAL LAW 1, 5 (Philippe Sands ed., 1994).

[22] *Id.* at 12.

[23] The significance of this development is discussed in Chapter 2, particularly Sections J and K.

[24] 26 ILM 1529 (1985); 1513 UNTS 293, signed Mar. 22, 1985, entered into force Sept. 22, 1988.

[25] 26 ILM 1541 (1987), 1522 UNTS 3, signed Sept. 16, 1987, entered into force Jan. 1, 1989, *available at* http://www.unep.org/ozone/index.html (amended several times since its adoption).

vention on Climate Change (1992)[26] and the Kyoto Protocol (1997)[27] adopted under it. These global phenomena resulted from the activities of each and every state in the international community, although admittedly, their contributions vary and, when taken individually, may not be significant. In the same vein, all states can become victims of these global phenomena. The international community responded by evolving new principles to address these issues. The polluter pays principle, the precautionary principle, the environmental impact assessment process, sustainable development and inter-generational equity, as well as procedural principles relating to participation and information, are some of these principles that have been developed to govern the emerging and increasingly complex environmental issues that the international community is now facing. The proliferation of multilateral environmental agreements is a significant feature of recent years.

## 2. From Global to Internal

It was against this background that the Rio Declaration was adopted in 1992. The main feature of the Rio Declaration was that it endorsed the concept of sustainable development proposed by the World Commission on Environment and Development (WCED)[28] in 1987, which defined sustainable development as "development which meets the needs of the present without compromising the ability of future generations to meet their own needs."[29] The Rio Declaration, however, does not contain a definition of sustainable development. Instead, it elaborates on it by adopting various principles and concepts which are considered the components of sustainable development.[30]

The third stage of the evolution of international environmental law reflects the influence of the concept of sustainable development. Some even contend that a new branch of international law has emerged called

---

[26]  31 ILM 849 (1992), 1771 UNTS 107, signed May 9, 1992, entered into force Mar. 21, 1994, *available at* http://www.unfccc.int/.

[27]  FCCC/CP/1997/L.7/Add.1, signed Dec. 11, 1997, entered into force Feb. 16, 2005, *reprinted in* 36 ILM 22 (1998), *available at* http://www.unfccc.int/.

[28]  The WCED was appointed by the UN General Assembly 1983 with the mandate of finding ways to reconcile economic development with environmental protection. Their report entitled *Our Common Future* was published in 1987 and received wide publicity. *See supra* note 8.

[29]  *Id.* at 43.

[30]  Sustainable development is generally considered an umbrella embodying both substantive and procedural elements. *See* HUNTER ET AL., *supra* note 5, at 205; and Sumudu Atapattu, *Sustainable Development, Myth or Reality?: A Survey of Sustainable Development under International Law and Sri Lankan Law*, 14 GEO. INT'L ENVTL. L. REV. 265, 273 (2001).

the "international law of sustainable development."[31] The significance of this development is that, despite doubts cast on its normative quality, the concept of sustainable development mandates states to integrate environmental protection into the economic development process and to evaluate the environmental impact of development activities through the environmental impact assessment process. This clearly is a new phenomenon: we have come to a stage where international law is actually dictating how states should conduct their internal affairs, *irrespective* of their impact on the global environment. This is a remarkable development, particularly given the fact that we have been grappling with the general prohibition under customary international law—also reflected in Article 2(7) of the UN Charter—that states must refrain from interfering in the internal affairs of other states. This principle, generally referred to as the domestic jurisdiction clause, was a major obstacle to the development of both human rights law and environmental law, where no cross-border element was present. Fortunately, however, the international community has worked towards narrowing the ambit of the domestic jurisdiction clause and activities, which hitherto fell legitimately within its scope, have now become subject to international scrutiny. The significance of this development should not be underestimated.

## 3.   "Internationalization" of Environmental Protection

The internationalization of environmental protection is a recent development. By this it is meant that international law has stepped in to regulate activities that traditionally fell *within* the internal affairs of states. A few years ago, this development would have been unthinkable. The significance of this development, of course, is that international law now regulates the very development process by mandating that development activities should be evaluated for their environmental impact. It requires states to develop in a sustainable manner so that future generations will be left with sufficient resources and options to develop in a similar manner. The fact that international law now regulates activities, which hitherto fell within internal affairs, also means the gradual erosion of the concept of sovereignty and particularly of the domestic jurisdiction clause. In other words, states are no longer able to rely on this "escape valve" which, in the past, provided a ready excuse to exclude international scrutiny.[32] It is obvious that the process of internationalization is a victory for international law and partic-

---

[31] *See* Philippe Sands, *International Law in the field of Sustainable Development*, 65 BRIT. Y.B. INT'L L. 303 (1994). *See also* SUSTAINABLE DEVELOPMENT LAW: PRINCIPLES, PRACTICES & PROSPECTS (Marie-Claire Cordonier Segger & Ashfaq Khalfan eds., 2004).

[32] In the aftermath of the Chernobyl nuclear accident in 1986, the government of the USSR argued that it was an internal issue, despite the obvious consequences experienced thousands of miles away. *See* PHILIPPE SANDS, CHENOBYL: LAW AND COMMUNICATION (1988).

ularly for human rights law and environmental law, which rely on international scrutiny of states' activities for implementation of obligations under these regimes. More international scrutiny means greater transparency and accountability on the part of states. The less states are able to invoke the domestic jurisdiction clause, the better it is for international law. With regard to the process of internationalization, de Chazournes and Sands note as follows:

> To a great extent than ever international law regulates many matters which would previously have been considered to remain within an exclusively domestic setting, such as human rights, environmental standards and the treatment of investments. And it does so with increasing sophistication. This has led commentators to identify a tendency towards specialisation and fragmentation.[33]

Perhaps the most successful regime of international scrutiny has been established in relation to international human rights law, although that regime is not without its own problems. International environmental law has not yet achieved the level of sophistication achieved by international human rights law; the approach adopted by the former is rather different from that of the latter, thus making a comparison difficult. While international human rights law has developed in the direction of establishing treaty bodies, submission and scrutiny of country reports and individual complaints procedures,[34] international environmental law has opted for a rather "soft" form of international scrutiny—establishing conferences of parties and the submission of periodic reports. It lacks the enforcement powers of international human rights law. No individual complaints procedure has been adopted in relation to environmental issues, although admittedly, an environmental issue can be the subject of an individual complaint under the International Covenant on Civil and Political Rights (ICCPR) or other human rights treaty.[35]

This divergence in approach in relation to international scrutiny and supervision also reflects the different nature of international human rights law and international environmental law: while the former is individual in nature, the latter is very much a collective issue. While it is possible to speak

---

[33] *See* Laurence Boisson de Chazournes & Philippe Sands, *Introduction, in* INTERNATIONAL LAW, *supra* note 17, at 7. *See also* TUOMAS KUOKKANEN, INTERNATIONAL LAW AND THE ENVIRONMENT: VARIATIONS ON A THEME 101 (2002).

[34] *See* CHRISTIAN TOMUSCHAT, HUMAN RIGHTS BETWEEN IDEALISM AND REALISM (2003).

[35] *See* the discussion in Section B.1.

in terms of an individual's right to a clean environment,[36] the protection of the environment cannot be considered solely in terms of humankind alone: states must take action to protect the environment irrespective of its utility to humankind.[37] The environment itself and other species of fauna and flora warrant protection in their own right inasmuch as the need to protect it for the survival of humankind.[38]

## B. OTHER RELATED DEVELOPMENTS

Inasmuch as the developments in the environmental field, several developments in other fields also have had an impact on the former. These include human rights and good governance; globalization and international trade; health and environmental protection; and poverty and the environment. In addition, there is an emerging right to a healthy environment, which could provide another avenue to seek redress for environmental wrongs. These issues will be discussed in this section, as they have a direct bearing on the development of international environmental law.

### 1. Human Rights, Good Governance and the Environment

One of the significant developments at the international level is the convergence between human rights law and environmental law.[39] This development can be seen at the national level too, particularly in South Asia.[40] The increasingly clear relationship between environmental protection and economic, social and cultural rights, as well as civil and political rights, has led to two developments: firstly, the call for a distinct right to a healthy environment, and secondly, the invocation of human rights machinery to seek redress for environmental harms.

Thus, for example, the right to health[41] and the right to an adequate standard of living[42] are some of the economic and social rights invoked in

---

[36]  *See* the discussion in Section B.1.a & b.

[37]  *See* the World Charter for Nature, adopted by the UN General Assembly in 1982, GA Res. 37/7, *reprinted in* 22 ILM 455 (1983). The Preamble notes that "Every form of life is unique, warranting respect regardless of its worth to man, and, to accord other organisms such recognition, man must be guided by a moral code of action."

[38]  *Id.*

[39]  *See* Sumudu Atapattu, *The Right to a Healthy Life or the Right to Die Polluted?: The Emergence of a Human Right to a Healthy Environment Under International Law*, 16 TULANE ENVTL. L. REV. 65 (2002).

[40]  *Id.*

[41]  Protected under Article 12 of the International Covenant on Economic, Social and Cultural Rights (ICESCR), *available at* http://www.unhchr.org.

[42]  Protected under Article 11 of the ICESCR, *supra* note 41.

relation to environmental issues. Of the civil and political rights that have been invoked, the right to life,[43] the right to privacy[44] and the right to equality[45] take precedence. The absence of a specific international machinery to seek redress for environmental harm has led to this development. The problem with this approach, of course, is the need to establish the causal nexus between the environmental issue in question and the human right that is being invoked. It may not be easy to establish this link in every case.

Moreover, not every human rights issue is related to an environmental issue and *vice versa*. How do we deal with such issues? There are no doubts problems associated with the human rights approach to environmental protection. On the other hand, absent specific machinery on environmental protection, there may not be many options available to victims of environmental harm to seek redress.

The human rights approach also has its limitations: it is anthropocentric in nature; it is remedial in nature; and damage to other species or to the environment itself will go uncompensated. Thus, a human rights approach can never replace an ecocentric approach to environmental protection. Rather, the former must complement the latter.[46]

Similar to the link between human rights and the environment, there is an increasing tendency to link environmental protection (and particularly sustainable development) with issues of good governance. Good governance constitutes another example where international law has impinged upon the internal affairs of states by stipulating how a country should be governed. That basic principles of transparency, accountability and participation must be followed, and that the rule of law must be upheld and human rights be protected, are no longer disputed. Good governance is also vital for the realization of sustainable development.[47] The World Bank, in particular, has advocated the necessity of good governance in relation to

---

[43] Protected under Article 6 of the International Covenant on Civil and Political Rights (ICCPR), *available at* http://www.unhchr.org.

[44] Protected under Article 17 of the ICCPR, *supra* note 43.

[45] Protected under Article 14 of the ICCPR, *supra* note 43.

[46] *See* Atapattu, *supra* note 39.

[47] *See*, in this regard, John C. Dernbach, *Sustainable Development as a Framework for National Governance*, 49 CASE W. RES. L. REV. 1 (1998) where he articulates that unless sustainable development is incorporated into governance at the national level, nothing much can be achieved: "Sustainable development provides a powerful and attractive set of tools for reinvigorating governance."

development aid.[48] Although it has not been articulated as imposing a conditionality, those in developing countries have viewed the linking of good governance with development aid with much trepidation and apprehension. The World Bank defines good governance as a "public service that is efficient, a judicial system that is reliable and an administration that is accountable."[49]

The former UN Secretary-General, Boutros-Boutros Ghali, identified the following as the principles of good governance: sensible economic and social policies, democratic decision making, adequate governmental transparency, financial accountability, creation of a market-friendly environment for development, measures to combat corruption and respect for the rule of law and human rights.[50] In his report on the work of the United Nations, he noted that "Good governance, democracy, participation, an independent judiciary, the rule of law and civil peace create conditions necessary to economic progress."[51] Thus, there is a clear link between good governance and economic development as well as between good governance and sustainable development.

Sustainable development is also considered to include access to information, participation and transparency as its components.[52] Sustainable development cannot be achieved in a country plagued by secrecy and corruption. Thus, in order to achieve sustainable development, embracing and upholding principles of good governance becomes imperative for any society at whatever level of economic development.[53] As Kamal Hossain noted:[54]

---

[48] *See* Mark E. Wadrzyk, *Is It Appropriate For The World Bank To Promote Democratic Standards in a Borrower Country?* 17 WIS. INT'L L.J. 553 (1999).

[49] Referred to in Amado S. Tolentino, *Good Governance through Popular Participation in Sustainable Development, in* SUSTAINABLE DEVELOPMENT AND GOOD GOVERNANCE 137 (Konrad Ginter et al. eds., 1995).

[50] Boutros Boutros-Ghali, *An Agenda for Peace,* United Nations, New York (1992) para. 59, referred to in SUSTAINABLE DEVELOPMENT AND GOOD GOVERNANCE, *supra* note 49, at 1.

[51] Boutros Boutros-Ghali, Report on the Work of the Organization from the 46th to the 47th session of the General Assembly, UN, New York (1992), referred to in SUS-TAINABLE DEVELOPMENT AND GOOD GOVERNANCE, *supra* note 49, at 2.

[52] These are the procedural components of sustainable development. *See* discussion in Chapter 2, Section F and Chapter 4, Section F.

[53] *See* Atapattu, *supra* note 30, 285.

[54] *See* Kamal Hossain, *Evolving Principles of Sustainable Development and Good Governance, in* SUSTAINABLE DEVELOPMENT AND GOOD GOVERNANCE, *supra* note 49, at 15, 20.

Inherent in the concept of sustainable development is the need for a political system which provides for effective citizen participation in decision-making and for good governance, i.e. institutions for policy-making, decision-making and their implementation which are responsive to the objectives of sustainable development.

Good governance in the context of the goal of sustainable development would mean respecting the principles of the Rio Declaration in designing development projects and programmes. Thus narrow economic appraisals of the cost-benefit of development projects and programmes would clearly not be sufficient for this purpose. There must be an assessment of the environmental and social impact of projects and programmes, and their implications for the goals of sustainable development.[55]

Furthermore, reducing corruption[56] is a particular need in developing countries where already limited choices have been further restricted by large-scale corruption and lack of transparency. Strengthening civil society is an important element in achieving sustainable development and good governance. Corruption has led to severe problems in developing countries where funds earmarked for development and particularly poverty alleviation have ended up in private bank accounts of public authorities.[57] Thus, the public must be mobilized to fight against corruption, and a legal framework must be adopted to deal with those who are engaged in corrupt activities.

It is, therefore, clear that a close relationship exists between sustainable development and good governance. Both require access to information (transparency), participation in the decision-making process and accountability (lack of corruption). Thus, sustainable development cannot be achieved in a society that does not respect basic principles of good governance.

The Rio Declaration, while not specifically endorsing good governance, refers to some of its components in Principle 10:

Environmental issues are best handled with the participation of all concerned citizens, at the relevant level. At the national level, each

---

[55] *Id.* at 21.

[56] Corruption has been defined as the abuse of public power for private profit, *see id.* at 22.

[57] *See* Ambika Sathkunanathan, *Bribery and Corruption, in* SRI LANKA: STATE OF HUMAN RIGHTS 2001 (Law & Society Trust, Colombo, 2001).

individual shall have appropriate access to information concerning the environment that is held by public authorities, including information on hazardous materials and activities in their communities, and the opportunity to participate in decision-making processes. States shall facilitate and encourage public awareness and participation by making information widely available. Effective access to judicial and administrative proceedings, including redress and remedy, shall be provided.[58]

Principle 10 embodies several important features. First, public authorities must make information affecting the environment available and the public has the right to access such information. Second, each individual must be given the opportunity to participate in the decision-making process. Third, states are required *to facilitate and encourage* public awareness and participation. The mere provision of information is not sufficient to fulfill this obligation. Finally, *effective* access to judicial and administrative remedies must be provided. Here again, the mere availability of remedies is not sufficient: access to such remedies must be effective. Thus, in effect, Principle 10 endorses principles of transparency, accountability, participation and access to remedies, all of which are essential components of good governance.

The draft articles on Environment and Development proposed by the International Union for the Conservation of Nature and Natural Resources (IUCN)[59] endorses these in terms of "rights." Draft Article 15 provides: "All persons have the right to information concerning the environment" and Draft Article 18 provides: "All persons have the right to active, free and meaningful participation in planning and decision-making activities and processes that may have an impact on the environment and development. This includes the right to a prior assessment of the environmental, developmental and human rights consequences of proposed actions." Draft Article 20 embodies the right to effective remedies and redress in administrative and judicial proceedings.

Both the Political Declaration[60] and the Plan of Implementation of the World Summit on Sustainable Development[61] specifically refer to good gov-

---

[58] Principle 10, Rio Declaration, *supra* note 20.

[59] *See* IUCN, DRAFT INTERNATIONAL COVENANT ON ENVIRONMENT AND DEVELOPMENT (2d ed. 2001).

[60] UN Doc. A/CONF.199/20 (2002).

[61] World Summit on Sustainable Development, Plan of Implementation, Sept. 4, 2002, *id.*

ernance. The Political Declaration states that the parties undertake to strengthen and improve governance at all levels for the effective implementation of Agenda 21, the Millennium Development Goals and the Plan of Implementation of the Summit.[62] The Plan of Implementation, in turn, provides that good governance *within each country* and at the *international level* is essential for sustainable development.[63] It notes the following features as components of good governance: sound environmental, social and economic policies; democratic institutions responsive to the needs of people; rule of law; anti-corruption measures; gender equality; and an enabling environment for investment.[64] These components are wider than those traditionally associated with good governance. Hence, ensuring a sound environment for investment seems more associated with globalization than with good governance, which seems to indicate the convergence between globalization and good governance. The reference to gender equality, important as it is, is narrower than the usual formulation of respect for human rights. However, the latter is listed separately as a necessary pre-condition for sustainable development along with peace, security and stability.[65]

While a right to good governance seems to be emerging in public international law, it is by no means a "new right." International human rights law has long recognized the right to participation and access to information, as well as access to effective remedies. It is only recently that a link has been made between these principles, on the one hand, and environmental protection and sustainable development, on the other. Article 19 of the ICCPR, for example, provides that: "Everyone shall have the right to freedom of expression; this right shall include freedom to seek, receive and impart information and ideas of all kinds, regardless of frontiers." Article 25 endorses the right of every citizen to take part in the conduct of public affairs, directly or through freely chosen representatives.

The Draft Earth Charter,[66] too, endorses these principles in relation to environmental issues. Draft Article 13 is pertinent in this regard:

    a.   Uphold the right of everyone to receive clear and timely information on environmental matters and all development plans and activities which are likely to affect them or in which they have an interest.

---

[62] *Id.*, para. 30.

[63] *Id.*, para. 4.

[64] *Id.*

[65] *Id.*, para. 5.

[66] *Available at* http://www.earthcharter.org/earthcharter/charter.htm. The Earth Charter was, unfortunately, never adopted.

    b.   Support local, regional and global civil society, and promote the meaningful participation of all interested individuals and organizations in decision making.

    c.   Protect the rights to freedom of opinion, expression, peaceful assembly, association, and dissent.

    d.   Institute effective and efficient access to administrative and independent judicial procedures, including remedies and redress for environmental harm and the threat of such harm.

    e.   Eliminate corruption in all public and private institutions.[67]

Thus, a clear link has been made between corruption and sustainable development and the need to strengthen democratic institutions at all levels; provide transparency and accountability, inclusive participation in decision making and access to justice. As will be discussed in Chapter 2, these procedural rights are also components of sustainable development, which indicates that, without implementing these rights, sustainable development cannot be achieved.

It is, therefore, clear that democratic (good) governance is a crucial requirement for environmental protection and sustainable development. There is no doubt that the right to information, the right to participate in the decision-making process and the right to effective remedies are now part of international environmental law. The rights to information and participation crept into environmental law mainly through the environmental impact assessment (EIA) process. The EIA documents are normally public documents, and the public has a right to make their comments on the document to the relevant agency, thereby participating in the decision-making process. Outside the EIA process, however, access to information and participation has been rather limited. Yet, Principle 10 of the Rio Declaration, discussed above, clearly shows that these rights are not confined to the EIA process. Thus, states must facilitate access to government-held environmental information and provide a forum for the public to participate in the decision-making process. The Convention on Access to Information, Public Participation in Decision-making and Access to Justice in Environmental Matters,[68] opened for signature in 1998, assumes significance in this light. Despite being geographically limited,[69] it is the first international instrument to embody environmental procedural rights. It also recognized a fundamental right to a clean environment.[70] Access to information is the

---

   [67]  Draft art. 13.

   [68]  38 ILM 517 (1999) [hereinafter The Aarhus Convention].

   [69]  The Aarhus Convention is open for signature only to the states of the ECE region, although other states can accede to it. *See* the discussion in Chapter 4.

   [70]  Art. 1(1) of the Aarhus Convention, *supra* note 68. *See* discussion in Section B.1.b.

core right embodied in the Convention upon which the other rights depend: without information, participation will be reduced to a meaningless exercise. Conversely, without a proper forum to air the grievances, mere access to information would be meaningless.[71] Giving effect to the twin rights of information and participation is an important feature of the Convention. It is hoped that an international instrument of universal application would be adopted in the near future along the lines of the Aarhus Convention. The twin rights of information and participation promote transparency and accountability, essential in a democratic society.[72] However, it is important to note the relevance of *timely* information and participation. Very often, information is divulged when proposals have already been accepted by the relevant agency. The EIA process has been criticized for coming too late in the decision-making process and for using it to justify decisions that have already been made.[73] Such actions negate the very purpose of participatory rights. Indeed as pointed out by one writer:

> Opportunities for participation are also sometimes offered late in the decision-making process when proposals are already developed and accepted by the relevant agency. Indeed, a major problem of environmental policy is how to properly mobilize individual initiative at the right time in the collective interest for sustainable development.[74]

There is no doubt that the Convention breaks new ground in international environmental law. It embodies "environmental procedural rights" that have hitherto remained in soft law instruments. Although these rights are established rights under international human rights law, the Convention has extended these rights to cover environmental issues.

There can no longer be any doubt that environmental procedural rights are now part of contemporary international law. While individual states may decide to apply these procedural rights in relation to proposed activities likely to have a significant impact on the environment (which is usually tied to the EIA process), if individuals seek information on a particular aspect of

---

[71] *See* Tolentino, *supra* note 49, at 141 where he notes: "A condition precedent to effective popular participation is the availability of adequate information in public inputs."

[72] *See* Atapattu, *supra* note 39.

[73] *See* Marceil Yeater & Lal Kurukulasuriya, *Environmental Impact Assessment Legislation in Developing Countries, in* UNEP'S NEW WAY FORWARD: ENVIRONMENTAL LAW AND SUTSAINABLE DEVELOPMENT 257, at 261 (Sun Lin & Lal Kurukulasuriya eds., 1995).

[74] *See* Tolentino, *supra* note 49, at 142.

the environment, it would be very difficult to deny such information, unless, of course, security or other compelling reasons are present.[75]

### a. *Right to a Healthy Environment* [76]

Discussing rights in terms of different "generations" has become a common practice in human rights parlance.[77] Thus, while civil and political rights are considered first generation rights, economic, social and cultural rights are considered second generation rights. Increasingly, there is a tendency to refer to third generation rights—these rights are neither first generation nor second generation rights but are emerging rights that involve groups or peoples as a whole. Frequently cited examples are minority rights, right to development, right to peace and the right to a healthy[78] environment.

However, whether third generation rights actually fall within the realm of human rights has been hotly debated. While some have argued that time is ripe for the acceptance of third generation rights,[79] others have cau-

---

[75] The Aarhus Convention contains a fairly lengthy list of grounds on which information can be denied. *See* art. 4(3) and (4).

[76] There is a wealth of material on this. *See generally* HUMAN RIGHTS APPROACHES TO ENVIRONMENTAL PROTECTION (Alan Boyle & Michael Anderson eds., 1996); PAUL GORMLEY, HUMAN RIGHTS AND ENVIRONMENT: THE NEED FOR INTERNATIONAL CO-OPERATION (1976); THE RIGHT OF THE CHILD TO A CLEAN ENVIRONMENT (Agata Fijalkowski & Malgosia Fitzmaurice eds, 2000); ANTONIO TRINDADE, HUMAN RIGHTS, SUSTAINABLE DEVELOPMENT AND THE ENVIRONMENT (2d ed. 1995); PRUE TAYLOR, AN ECOLOGICAL APPROACH TO INTERNATIONAL LAW: RESPONDING TO CHALLENGES OF CLIMATE CHANGE (1998); Dinah Shelton, *What Happened in Rio to Human Rights?*, 3 Y.B. INT'L ENVTL. L. 75 (1992); Human Rights, Health & Environmental Protection: Linkages in Law & Practice, A Background paper for the World Health Organization (2002); John Lee, *The Underlying Legal Theory to Support a Well-Defined Human Right to a Healthy Environment as a Principle of Customary International Law*, 25 COLUM. J. ENVTL. L. 283 (2000); Joshua Eaton, *The Nigerian Tragedy, Environmental Regulation of Transnational Corporations, and the Human Right to a Healthy Environment*, 15 B.U. INT'L L.J. 261 (1997); Justine Thornton & Stephen Tromans, *Human Rights and Environmental Wrongs: Incorporating the European Convention on Human Rights: Some Thoughts on the Consequences for UK Environmental Law*, 11 J. ENVTL. L. (1999); Prudence E. Taylor, *From Environmental to Ecological human Rights: A New Dynamic in International Law?*, 10 GEO. INT'L ENVTL L. REV. 309 (1998); Timothy Schorn, *Drinkable Water and Breathable Air: A Livable Environment as a Human Right*, 4 GREAT PLAINS NAT. RES. J. 121 (2000).

[77] *See* TOMUSCHAT, *supra* note 34, at 24.

[78] What the adjective should be has been subject to debate in recent times. Thus, healthy, sound, decent, and adequate and viable have been used to qualify the word environment. *See* Atapattu, *supra* note 39.

[79] *See* Stephen Marks, *Emerging Human Rights: A New Generation for the 1980s?*, 33 RUTGERS L. REV. 435 (1980–81).

tioned against accepting new rights, thereby diluting the existing rights.[80] Admittedly, one has to exercise caution in expanding the notion of rights, as not every issue will become a fundamental human right. However, the argument that the acceptance of new rights will have the effect of diluting the existing ones does not carry much weight. This also gives the impression that human rights are static rights and cannot evolve further. As experience has shown, human rights are dynamic and essentially depend on how they are interpreted and given content to over time. By their very nature, they must evolve with time. Otherwise, they run the risk of becoming redundant or outdated.

Third generation rights are different from the other two rights at least in one respect: they are group rights as opposed to individual rights. This does not, however, mean that the other two generation rights comprise exclusively individual rights. On the contrary, many of the established rights are exercised collectively. For example, freedom of association or freedom of assembly, well-established first generation rights, can be exercised only collectively. Similarly, the right to an adequate standard of living, food and clothing or right to housing, while being an individual right, could also be construed (and implemented) as a collective right. Conversely, the rights in the third generation category are almost exclusively exercised collectively. The right to environment can be considered both an individual right as well as a collective right depending on the number of people who are affected by a particular issue.

It is against this background that the present debate on the right to environment must be evaluated. At the outset, the terminology used must be defined. By a right to environment, we mean a substantive right to a healthy environment. Environmental rights, by contrast, are procedural rights that have been "borrowed" from international human rights law.[81] These include the right to information and the right to participate in the decision-making process.[82] There is hardly any debate whether these form part of contemporary international law. Whether international law accepts a distinct right to a healthy environment has been a more controversial issue.

---

[80] *See* Philip Alston, *Conjuring Up New Human Rights: A Proposal for Quality Control,* 78 AM. J. INT'L L. 607 (1984); and Philip Alston, *A Third Generation of Solidarity Rights: Progressive Development or Obfuscation of International Human Rights Law?,* 29 NETH. INT'L L. REV. 307 (1985).

[81] *See* Dinah Shelton, *Human Rights, Environmental Rights and Right to Environment,* 28 STAN. J. INT'L L. 103 (1991).

[82] *See* the discussion *supra* note 68 and accompanying text and also Chapter 4, Section F.

Another approach has been to use existing substantive human rights law (in addition to procedural rights) for the vindication of environmental wrongs. Thus, for example, rights to life, privacy, adequate standard of living and health have been used in relation to environmental issues. These, by themselves, do not imply that a distinct right to environment exists in international law. While they do demonstrate the flexibility of human rights, problems have arisen with the issue of causation—establishing that the environmental issue in question resulted in a violation of the protected right. It may not be possible to make this link in every case. Thus, the recognition of a distinct right to environment becomes attractive in such situations.

Nonetheless, there are several problems inherent in a human rights approach to environmental protection. Firstly, what is the definition of the right to environment? Secondly, who are the beneficiaries of this right? Is it an individual right or a collective right or both? Thirdly, given the undeniable anthropocentric nature of the right, how can other species and ecosystems be protected through a human rights approach? Finally, who are the protectors of the right? It is proposed to deal with each of these issues separately.

## i.    What Are the Parameters of the Right to Environment?

A mere right to environment, without any further qualification, would be meaningless. Thus, several adjectives have been used by writers to make this right more meaningful. The frequently cited examples are: clean, adequate, sound, healthy or a combination of these. It is submitted here that the right to a healthy environment is the best option to adopt as it is the easiest to establish. It circumvents the usual problem of establishing the causal link—that a particular environmental issue caused the damage in question. All one needs to establish is that the pollution levels in his locality have exceeded the levels for a healthy environment. The victim does not have to establish that as a result of high levels of pollution, his health has been impaired. This approach also circumvents problems associated with *locus standi*. It, however, presupposes the existence of threshold levels for a healthy environment. All other formulations run the risk of being too subjective or too difficult to establish in practice.

## ii.    Who Are the Beneficiaries of the Right?

Whether a right to environment, if accepted, should be considered an individual right or a solidarity right is another debated issue. Like other human rights, a right to environment should be considered an individual right, although in some instances, the issue can affect many individuals or a group of individuals. Some human rights related actions too have the potential to affect groups of individuals (like retrenchment or genocide). It is submitted that the right to environment should not be considered a third generation right as these have problems inherent in the very debate. Moreover, the fact that environmental procedural rights now form part of contemporary international law gives currency to this argument. The question, however, arises where this right should be placed in the human rights debate.

### iii.   The Anthropocentric Nature of the Right to Environment

A right to environment, like all other human rights, is anthropocentric in nature—it accrues to human beings. However, it must be stressed that an anthropocentric approach to environmental protection can (and should) never replace an ecocentric approach to environmental protection. It can only complement, not replace, an ecocentric approach. It is submitted that the recognition of a right to environment would be a useful tool to seek redress for environmental harm *in addition to* other measures to protect the environment as a whole (this includes other species).

In the absence of a specific right to environment, victims have resorted to existing human rights law, with varying degrees of success.[83] Some of the failed actions may have been successful if international law had recognized a specific right to environment, as it is not always possible to make a link between a particular environmental issue and the protected right that is being invoked.

Obviously, a human rights approach to environmental protection cannot ensure protection for other species. Other species and ecosystems have a right to be protected irrespective of their worth to human beings. Thus, the World Charter for Nature provides thus: "every form of life is unique, warranting respect regardless of its worth to man, and, to accord other organisms such recognition, man must be guided by a moral code of action."[84] Article 1 further provides that "nature shall be respected and its essential processes shall not be impaired."[85]

### iv.   Who Are the Protectors of the Right?

As with other human rights, the protector or the guarantor of a right to environment would be the state. An interesting debate that is taking place in human rights circles is whether human rights can also be applied horizontally—i.e., whether they can be enforced *vis-à-vis* other individuals.

---

[83]   *See* the discussion of cases in Atapattu, *supra* note 39.

[84]   Preamble, *supra* note 60.

[85]   *Id.*

The South African Constitution is perhaps the only Constitution that provides for this possibility.[86] In contemporary international law, states remain the primary guarantors of human rights. States would, however, incur responsibility for their failure to control the activities of private individuals, which result in human rights violations or for their failure to investigate or stop such activities from escalating or recurring.[87]

### b. Emergence of a Right to Environment Under International Law

Whether contemporary international law recognizes a substantive right to environment is a hotly debated issue. Judging by state practice on the issue, the answer seems to be in the negative. While such a right seems to be emerging, it does not have the necessary state practice to crystallize it into a customary international law principle. Procedural environmental rights, on the other hand, seem firmly grounded in international law.

International instruments have endorsed the right to environment in varying degrees. While many make the link between the environment and human rights, only a few documents actually go as far as endorsing a distinct right to environment. The Stockholm Declaration seems to be a good starting point to survey the international instruments. While the Preamble clearly noted the link between the environment and human rights,[88] the formulation in Principle 1 is rather ambiguous and does not endorse a specific human right to a healthy environment:

> Man has the fundamental right to freedom, equality and adequate conditions of life, in an environment of a quality that permits a life of dignity and well-being, and he bears a solemn responsibility to protect and improve the environment for present and future generations.[89]

---

[86] *See* art. 8.2 of the Constitution of the Republic of South Africa, 1996, *available at* http://www.polity.org.za/html/govdocs/constitution/saconst.html?rebookmark=1.

[87] *See* Case of Velasquez Rodriguez, Inter-American Court of Human Rights, July 29, 1988, *reprinted in* 28 ILM 294 (1989) where the Court articulated that:

The State has a legal duty to take reasonable steps to prevent human rights violations and to use the means at its disposal to carry out a serious investigation of violations committed within its jurisdiction, to identify those responsible, to impose the appropriate punishment and to ensure the victim adequate compensation (325, para. 174).

[88] It provides that: "Both aspects of man's environment, the natural and the man-made, are essential to his well-being and to the enjoyment of basic human rights—even the right to life itself."

[89] Principle 1, Stockholm Declaration, *supra* note 2.

Principle 1 notes that an environment of a particular quality is necessary for man to enjoy his rights: freedom, equality and adequate conditions of life. The Preamble recognizes that even the right to life—the most sacred right of all—can be undermined as a result of environmental degradation. Furthermore, Principle 1 refers to "man" instead of the standard language in human rights instruments of "human being."

The World Charter for Nature understandably does not endorse a right to environment: to do so would have been contrary to the very nature of the Charter. It, however, affirms procedural rights of information and participation as well as environmental impact assessment. It stresses the need to protect the environment irrespective of its worth to human beings, thus endorsing an ecocentric approach to environmental protection.

The Rio Declaration, by contrast, is human centered. Article 1 clearly articulates this. Despite this, however, it did not endorse a specific right to environment.[90] Its clear emphasis on sustainable development has made it more human centered than the Stockholm Declaration,[91] which has led some writers to critique it on the ground that environmental protection has been lost in favor of development.[92] They further point out that the Rio Declaration is "frankly anthropocentric in nature."[93] This critique is not disputed but can be defended. While not advocating an anthropocentric approach to environmental protection, there is no denying that human beings are the most influential species on earth. Not only do they have the ability to destroy the earth beyond repair, it is only they who can take action to protect the earth from such destruction. Furthermore, without economic development, as experience with developing countries has clearly shown, it becomes futile to speak of environmental protection. In other words, the period between Stockholm and Rio clearly demonstrated the necessity for sustainable development. It is not surprising, therefore, that

---

[90] *See* David Wirth, *The Rio Declaration on Environment and Development: Two Steps Forward and One Back or Vice Versa?*, 29 GA. L. REV. 599 (1994) who notes that:

Although Principle 1 of the Rio Declaration obliquely addresses a substantive standard requiring a minimally acceptable environment, that provision stops well short of enunciating such a right. Instead, the Rio Declaration as a whole rejects what can be regarded as a balance in the Stockholm Declaration between a nascent right to environment on the one hand and attention to development imperatives on the other.

*See also* Dinah Shelton, *What Happened at Rio to Human Rights?*, 3 Y.B. INT'L ENVTL. L. 75 (1992).

[91] *See* Wirth, *supra* note 90 who is of the view that Principle 1 of Rio implies that people's needs drive environmental policies.

[92] *See* Pallermaerts, *supra* note 21.

[93] *Id.*

the Rio Declaration places so much emphasis on the need to achieve sustainable development that, no doubt, is human centered.[94]

Principle 1 of the Rio Declaration provides: "Human beings are at the centre of concerns for sustainable development. They are entitled to a healthy and productive life in harmony with nature."[95] This formulation falls even shorter of a right to environment than that in Principle 1 of the Stockholm Declaration.

None of the international human rights treaties recognizes a right to environment. Apart from the Convention on the Rights of the Child,[96] there is hardly any reference to environmental protection in international human rights treaties. Despite the clear link between the environment and the enjoyment of human rights and the fact that a degraded environment can even violate the most basic human right—right to life—international human rights law and machinery has been slow in recognizing this link.

It has been articulated that there are three human rights approaches to environmental protection: mobilizing existing rights in relation to environmental issues; reinterpreting existing rights to include environmental issues; and creating a new right to environment.[97]

Several jurisprudential bases have been articulated in relation to the right to environment.[98] First, it can be said that it is a norm that is already embedded in legal systems through common law, through concepts such as nuisance and the good neighborly principle. Therefore, the right to environment should be considered a general principle of international law under Article 38(1)(c) of the ICJ Statute. Secondly, it can be argued that the right to environment is a logical outcome of other human rights, such as the right to life and the right to property. Thirdly, it can be contended that it is emerging as a customary international law principle as a result of the increasing number of national Constitutions guaranteeing a right to environment as well as the increasing number of treaties on environmen-

---

[94] *See* Wirth, *supra* note 90 who argues that the Rio Declaration as a whole is considerably more anthropocentric than its earlier counterpart.

[95] Principle 1, Rio Declaration, *supra* note 20.

[96] *See* art. 24(2)(c) of the Convention on the Rights of the Child, 1989, *available at* http://www.unhchr.org.

[97] *See* Michael Burger, *Bi-polar and Polycentric Approaches to Human Rights and the Environment*, 28 COLUM. J. ENVTL. L. 371 (2003).

[98] *Id.*

tal protection. Finally, an argument can be made that such a right should be created through treaty, given its importance.[99]

However, not all writers are in favor of recognizing such a right. While some writers have enthusiastically espoused the existence of a right to environment,[100] others have given it a lukewarm reception.[101] The link between environmental protection and the enjoyment of human rights is clear enough. Despite this, some have argued that the practical utility of recognizing a human right to environment is not evident:[102]

> Certainly there are conceptual and practical difficulties in defining, implementing, and enforcing an individual human right to an environment of a minimum quality. Even if an international legal right to a minimally acceptable environment were widely acknowledged, the precise content of that right would be very difficult to define and its application to particular cases would be a formidable task. . . . The practical utility of a human right to a *minimally* adequate environment is not immediately evident, and the right certainly has not been realized in practice in many of the places where it is purportedly guaranteed. But the Rio Declaration, because it does not even approach the question of a substantive individual right to environment or a duty of states to provide a minimally tolerable environment, implicitly rejects such a notion as a matter of principle.[103]

While there is some merit to this argument, particularly in relation to the scope and the definition of a right to environment,[104] to argue that its utility is limited would be to ignore the developments that have taken place

---

[99] *Id.*

[100] *See* Marks, *supra* note 79; Jennifer A. Downs, *A Healthy and Ecologically Balanced Environment: An Argument for a Third Generation Right*, 3 DUKE J. COMP. & INT'L L. 351 (1993).

[101] *See* Gunther Handl, *Human Rights and Protection of the Environment: A Mildly "Revisionist" View, in* HUMAN RIGHTS, SUSTAINABLE DEVELOPMENT AND THE ENVIRONMENT (Antonio Trindade ed., 1992); Wirth, *supra* note 90; Pallermaerts, *supra* note 21.

[102] *See* Wirth, *supra* note 90.

[103] *Id.* (emphasis added). What is postulated is not a minimally adequate environment for human beings, but an environment adequate for the health and well-being of human beings or the right to a healthy environment.

[104] *See* the discussion in Section B.1.b. Lack of a proper definition is not a major obstacle as the jurisprudence relating to human rights has clearly shown us. Many of the rights have been given content by the judiciary—examples include due process, torture, freedom of expression and right to privacy. Without such interpretation, many of these human rights would not have achieved the level of sophistication that they enjoy today.

since the adoption of the Rio Declaration, particularly the application of human rights machinery to environmental abuses. Certainly the developments in some countries, particularly India,[105] point to the growing recognition of a human right to environment. As discussed earlier, the right can be defined in such a way that it can be invoked by victims of environmental abuse. At present environmental issues do not enjoy the same status as human rights issues, probably because they have not been endorsed in the same way by the United Nations. Recognition of a right to environment would elevate it to the status of a protected right and will give it seriousness of purpose, in addition to giving victims another avenue of redress. In an effort, perhaps, to ascertain the feasibility of a right to environment, the UN Sub-Commission on Prevention of Discrimination and Protection of Minorities (now called the Sub-Commission on Minorities) appointed Mrs. Fatma Zohra Ksentini as Special Rapporteur on Human Rights and the Environment in 1990.[106] The reports submitted by the Special Rapporteur will be discussed next.

### c.  *Ksentini Reports*[107]

Of particular significance is the appointment of a Special Rapporteur on Human Rights and the Environment in 1990 who submitted four reports to the Sub-Commission together with a set of draft articles on the subject for adoption. Although the Sub-Commission and the UN Commission on Human Rights have adopted a few resolutions, and the subject appears on their agenda every year, their progress in this area can hardly be considered groundbreaking.

During her tenure as Special Rapporteur, Mrs. Ksentini submitted four reports (in 1991,[108] 1992,[109] 1993[110] and 1994[111]) and a Note[112] on the sub-

---

[105]  *See* Vijayashri Sripati, *Toward Fifty Years of Constitutionalism and Fundamental Rights in India: Looking Back to See Ahead (1950–2000)*, 14 AM. U. INT'L L. REV. 413 (1998).

[106]  *See* UN Doc. E/CN.4/Sub.2/1991/8, 1 (1990).

[107]  For a detailed discussion of the Special Rapporteur's reports, *see* Neil Popovic, *In Pursuit of Environmental Human Rights: Commentary on the Draft Declaration of Principles on Human Rights and the Environment*, 27 COLUM. HUM. RTS. L. REV. 487 (1996),

[108]  Preliminary Report Prepared by Mrs. Fatma Zohra Ksentini, Special Rapporteur, UN Doc. E/CN.4/Sub.2/1991/8 (1991).

[109]  First Progress Report Prepared by Mrs. Fatma Zohra Ksentini, Special Rapporteur, UN Doc. E/CN.4/Sub.2/1992/7 and Add. 1 (1992).

[110]  Second Progress Report Prepared by Mrs. Fatma Zohra Ksentini, Special Rapporteur, UN Doc. E/CN.4/Sub.2/1993/7 (1993).

[111]  Final Report Prepared by Mrs. Fatma Zohra Ksentini, Special Rapporteur, UN Doc. E/CN.4/Sub.2/1994/9 (1994).

[112]  Note Prepared by Mrs. Fatma Zohra Ksentini pursuant to Sub-Commission decision 1989/108, UN Doc. E/CN.4/Sub.2/1990/12 (1990).

ject. The draft articles on human rights and the environment culminated in an Experts' Group meeting convened by the Sierra Club at the request of the Special Rapporteur. These were appended to the final report of the Special Rapporteur[113] and reflect both *lex lata* and *lex ferenda*. The draft articles provide that:

1.  Human rights, an ecologically sound environment, sustainable development and peace are interdependent and indivisible.
2.  All persons have the right to a secure, healthy and ecologically sound environment. This right and other human rights, including civil, cultural, economic, political and social rights, are universal, interdependent and indivisible.
3.  All persons shall be free from any form of discrimination in regard to actions and decisions that affect the environment.
4.  All persons have the right to an environment adequate to meet equitably the needs of present generations and that does not impair the rights of future generations to meet equitably their needs.[114]

The draft articles embody both substantive and procedural rights in relation to the environment. The substantive rights include the right to a secure, healthy and ecologically sound environment;[115] the right to be free from pollution;[116] and inter- and intra-generational equity.[117] Procedural rights include the right to information,[118] the right to hold and express opinions,[119] the right to participate in the decision-making process,[120] the right to effective remedies[121] and the freedom of association.[122] The procedural rights are established rights under international human rights law and the specific articulation in the environment context is unnecessary, although reiteration in the context of environmental protection is helpful.

---

[113] *Supra* note 111.

[114] Draft Articles on Human Rights and the Environment, appended to the Final Report, *supra* note 111, Part I.

[115] *Id.*, Part I.1.

[116] *Id.*, Part II.5.

[117] *Id.*, Part I.4.

[118] *Id.*, Part III.15.

[119] *Id.*, Part III.16.

[120] *Id.*, Part III.18.

[121] *Id.*, Part III.20.

[122] *Id.*, Part III.19.

Rights that are *lex ferenda* include: the right to a secure environment;[123] the right to protection and preservation of the air, soil, water, sea-ice, etc.;[124] and the right to freedom from pollution.[125] In addition, the draft articles include a right to environmental and human rights education,[126] which although included with other procedural rights, cannot be categorized as such. Most of the other rights included in the draft articles are protected rights under international human rights law,[127] and a separate articulation of them in the context of environmental protection, although helpful, is unnecessary as these are already binding on those states that have ratified the treaties embodying those rights.

Despite the wealth of material in the Ksentini reports and the effort put into the draft articles, no further action has been taken by the United Nations in this regard.[128] Granted some of the provisions in the reports, particularly the assertion that "the demand for a healthy and balanced environment has facilitated the transition from environmental law to the right to the environment,"[129] are flawed, given, however, the crucial link between the environment and human rights, these reports should not have been relegated to the back burner, which unfortunately conveys the message that the right to environment is not important. If, on the other hand, the United Nations took this one step further and recognized its importance, it would have put the right to environment on par with other human rights.

The subject of environment and human rights has also received the attention of the Office of the High Commissioner for Human Rights (OHCHR). Together with UNEP, OHCHR convened a meeting of experts on the subject in January 2002 pursuant to a decision by the Commission on Human Rights.[130] Six background papers were pre-

---

[123] *Id.*, Part I.2.

[124] *Id.*, Part II.6.

[125] *Id.*, Part II.5. It can, however, be argued that if a right to a healthy environment is recognized under international law, it will automatically include a right to be free from pollution and a separate articulation of the latter right then becomes redundant.

[126] *Id.*, Part III.17.

[127] These include the right to food and water (Part II.8); the right to health (Part II.7); the right to a safe and healthy working environment (Part II.8); and the right to adequate housing (Part II.10).

[128] *See* Karrie Wolfe, *Greening the International Human Rights Sphere? Environmental Rights and the Draft Declaration of Principles on Human Rights and the Environment*, 9 APPEAL: REVIEW OF CURRENT LAW AND LAW REFORM 45 (2003).

[129] UN Doc. E/CN.4/Sub.2/1990/12.

[130] Decision 2001/111. The Commission on Human Rights invited OHCHR and

pared[131] to facilitate the work of the Experts Group, which included government representatives, civil society and international organizations.

At the meeting of experts it was recognized that many important developments have taken place nationally as well as internationally in this area:

> They indicate a growing inter-connectedness between the fields of human rights and environmental protection. The overall context for these developments is the concept of sustainable development, which requires that different societal objectives be treated in an integrated manner.[132]

It is thus obvious that the developments in relation to sustainable development have further reinforced the integration of human rights and the environment. This is also reflected in the Draft Principles on Human Rights and the Environment,[133] which recognizes that "sustainable development links the right to development and the right to a secure, healthy and ecologically sound environment."[134] The Experts Group also found that Principle 10 of the Rio Declaration[135] has played an important role in integrating human rights and environmental protection at national and international levels.[136]

---

UNEP to organize a joint expert seminar "to review and assess progress achieved since the United Nations Conference on Environment and Development in promoting and protecting human rights in relation to environmental questions and in the framework of Agenda 21," *Introduction, available at* http://www.unhchr.ch/environment/index.html.

[131] *See* Dinah Shelton, *Human Rights and Environment Issues in Multilateral Treaties Adopted Between 1991 and 2001*, Background Paper No. 1, Joint UNEP-OHCHR Expert Seminar on Human Rights and the Environment (2002); Dinah Shelton, *Human Rights and the Environment: Jurisprudence of Human Rights Bodies*, Background Paper No. 2; Adriana Fabra, *The Intersection of Human Rights and Environmental Issues: A Review of Institutional Developments at the International Level*, Background Paper No. 3; Jona Razzaque, *The Environment: The National Experience in South Asia and Africa*, Background Paper No. 4; Jonas Ebbesson, *Information, Participation and Access to Justice: The Model of the Aarhus Convention*, Background Paper No. 5; Adriana Fabra & Eva Arnal, *Review of Jurisprudence on Human Rights and the Environment in Latin America*, Background Paper No. 6.

[132] Final Text, Meeting of Experts on Human Rights and the Environment (2002), *available at* http://www.unhchr.ch/environment/conclusions.html.

[133] *Supra* note 111.

[134] *Id.* Preamble.

[135] Principle 10 embodies provisions on access to information, participation and effective remedies.

[136] *Supra* note 111, para. 6.

In assessing the practice of international organizations, developments at the national level as well as internationally, the Experts Group noted:

> The experts recognized that respect for human rights is broadly accepted as a precondition for sustainable development, that environmental protection constitutes a precondition for the effective enjoyment of human rights protection, and that human rights and the environment are interdependent and interrelated. These features are now broadly reflected in national and international practices and developments.[137]

The Experts Group articulated that further steps should be taken, *inter alia*, to affirm the link between human rights and environmental protection as an essential tool to eradicate poverty; to achieve sustainable development and to treat economic, environmental and human rights in an integrated manner; to recognize the environmental dimension in human rights protection and *vice versa* in part by developing rights-based approaches to environmental protection and sustainable development; and to support the growing recognition of a right to a secure, healthy and ecologically sound environment, either as a constitutionally guaranteed right or a guiding principle of national and international law.[138] This latter recommendation seems to dilute the importance of the recognition of a distinct right to environment, as it refers to it as a "guiding principle" and not as a protected right under international human rights law. Despite recognizing the integration between human rights and environmental protection and that environmental protection constitutes a pre-condition for the effective enjoyment of human rights, the Experts Group does not actually call upon the international community to adopt the right to a healthy environment as a distinct and separate right under international human rights law. The reason for this assertion is not very clear. The Experts Group also articulated that both UNEP and OHCHR should ensure that the subject of human rights and the environment is fully addressed at the World Summit on Sustainable Development. Unfortunately, however, the World Summit, while affirming its commitment to sustainable development, did not deal with the issue of integrating human rights and the environment.

## d. Regional Instruments

Developments in this area have taken place mainly at the regional level. Two regional human rights regimes specifically recognize the right to environment, while a regional environmental treaty too has endorsed this.

---

[137] *Id.*, para. 12.

[138] *Id.*

The African Charter on Human and Peoples' Rights of 1981[139] was the first binding instrument to articulate a right to environment: "All peoples shall have the right to a general satisfactory environment favourable to their development."[140] The wording here suggests that the right to environment is a collective right rather than an individual one. Moreover, it implies that a satisfactory environment is necessary only in order to achieve economic development. Despite being in existence for two decades, it is only recently that any jurisprudence has emerged from the African Commission on Human and Peoples' Rights.

*The Social and Economic Rights Action Center and the Center for Economic and Social Rights v. Nigeria*[141] involved the disposal of oil wastes into the environment and local waterways in Nigeria. The African Commission on Human and Peoples' Rights held that this amounted to a violation of the rights to life, health, property, the right to free disposal of natural resources, freedom from discrimination and the right to a healthy environment.[142] This case involved the environmental degradation and health problems among the *Ogoni* People caused by oil production, disposing of toxic wastes into the environment and local waterways in violation of environmental laws. The Communication of the complainants noted that "the resulting contamination of water, soil and air has had serious short and long-term health impacts, including skin infections, gastrointestinal and respiratory ailments and increased risk of cancers, and neurological and reproductive problems."[143] It further alleged that the government had not required the oil companies to carry out basic health and environmental impact studies despite the obvious health and environmental crisis in *Ogoniland.* Furthermore, the government has destroyed *Ogoni* food sources, which were caused by the soil and water contamination. The complainants alleged that the Nigerian government violated the right to health and the right to a clean environment protected under Articles 16 and 24 of the African Charter.

The Commission noted that "these rights recognize the importance of a clean and safe environment that is closely linked to economic and social rights in so far as the environment affects the quality of life and safety of the individual."[144]

---

[139] African Charter on Human and Peoples' Rights, *reprinted in* BASIC DOCUMENTS ON HUMAN RIGHTS 557 (Ian Brownlie ed., 1992).

[140] Art. 24 of the African Charter.

[141] *Available at* http://www.umn.edu/humanrts/Africa/comcases/155-96.html.

[142] Communication 155/96, *referred to in* SUSTAINABLE DEVELOPMENT LAW, *supra* note 31, at 208.

[143] *Id.*

[144] *Id.*, para. 51.

The right to a general satisfactory environment, as guaranteed under Article 24 of the African Charter or the right to a healthy environment, as it is widely known, therefore imposes clear obligations upon a government. It requires the State to take reasonable and other measures to prevent pollution and ecological degradation, to promote conservation, and to secure an ecologically sustainable development and use of natural resources.[145]

The Commission also noted that pollution and environmental degradation to a level humanly unacceptable has made living in *Ogoniland* a nightmare. As a result, the Commission held that the Republic of Nigeria was in violation of Articles 2,[146] 4,[147] 14,[148] 16,[149] 18(1),[150] 21[151] and 24[152] of the African Charter on Human and Peoples' Rights and appealed to the Nigerian government to ensure protection of the environment, health and livelihood of the people by: stopping all attacks on *Ogoni* communities; ensuring adequate compensation to victims; ensuring that appropriate environmental and social impact assessments are prepared for any future oil development; and providing information on health and environmental risks and meaningful access to regulatory bodies.

This case clearly links environmental degradation with human rights violations. It was, however, facilitated by the fact that the African Charter does, in fact, recognize a right to a satisfactory environment.[153]

The significance of this case is summarized by Dinah Shelton as follows:

The decision not only sees environmental degradation as leading to the violation of other rights, but as a human rights violation in itself because of its impact on the quality of life. . . . This suggestion of a broadly justiciable right to environment is reinforced by the Commission's final suggestion that all rights in the Charter may be applied and enforced. The Commission gives the right to environment meaningful content by requiring the state to adopt

---

[145] *Id.*, para. 52.

[146] The non-discrimination clause.

[147] The right to life.

[148] The right to property.

[149] The right to health.

[150] The right to family life.

[151] The right to dispose of natural resources.

[152] The right to environment.

[153] Protected under Article 24 of the Charter.

various techniques of environmental protection, such as environmental impact assessment, public information and participation, access to justice for environmental harm, and monitoring of potentially harmful activities. The result offers a blueprint for merging environmental protection, economic development, and guarantees of human rights.[154]

The next instrument to endorse a right to environment was the Additional Protocol to the American Convention on Human Rights of 1988.[155] Article 11 provides:

1.  Everyone shall have the right to live in a healthy environment and to have access to basic public services.
2.  The States Parties shall promote the protection, preservation and improvement of the environment.

While the Protocol provides for the submission of periodic reports on the measures taken in relation to the rights therein, the right of individual petition was not recognized in the Protocol. Despite being adopted in 1988, it did not enter into force until 1999; this can be attributed to the lack of interest in economic, social and cultural rights including the right to environment. Only time will tell whether the Protocol had any positive impact on the protection of economic, social and cultural rights, including the right to environment.[156]

A significant development in relation to environmental rights is the adoption of the Aarhus Convention on Access to Information, Public Participation in Decision-making and Access to Justice in Environmental Matters[157] in 1998 under the auspices of the UN Economic Commission for Europe (ECE). Although regional in its application, it is the first binding international environmental instrument to embody environmental proce-

---

[154] Dinah Shelton, *International Decisions: Decision Regarding Communication 155/96 (Social and Economic Rights Action Center/Center for Economic and Social Rights v. Nigeria)*, 96 AM. J. INT'L L. 937 (2002). *Case No ACHPR/COMM/A044/1, at* http://www.umn.edu/humanrts/africa/comcases/allcases.html.

[155] Additional Protocol to the American Convention on Human Rights in the Area of Economic, Social and Cultural Rights, Nov. 14, 1988, *reprinted in* 28 ILM 156 [hereinafter Protocol of San Salvador].

[156] No similar counter-part instrument exists in Europe, although several cases have been brought before the European Court invoking existing rights. *See* Richard Desgagne, *Integrating Environmental Values into the European Convention on Human Rights*, 89 AM. J. INT'L L. 263 (1995).

[157] Aarhus Convention, *supra* note 68.

dural rights in a comprehensive manner. Furthermore, it embodies a substantive right to a healthy environment. The objective of the Convention is as follows:

> In order to contribute to the protection of the right of every person of present and future generations to live in an environment adequate to his or her health and well-being, each Party shall guarantee the rights of access to information, public participation in decision-making and access to justice in environmental matters in accordance with the provisions of this Convention.[158]

This provision makes it clear that the objective of embodying procedural rights is to ultimately give effect to the substantive right to environment. In other words, the procedural rights guaranteed in the Convention will feed into the substantive right to environment. The Preamble, too, endorses a right to environment:

> Recognising also that every person has the right to live in an environment adequate to his or her health and well-being, and the duty, both individually and in association with others, to protect and improve the environment for the benefit of present and future generations.

With regard to the issue whether a substantive right to environment should be recognized, Birnie and Boyle note as follows:

> What is less clear is whether, over and above existing international human rights, there is any need for a separate, generic right in international law to a decent, viable or satisfactory environment, or for the re-conceptualization of international environmental law into the international law of environmental rights. The strongest argument in favour of qualitative environmental rights is that other human rights are themselves dependent on adequate environmental quality, and cannot be realized without governmental action to protect the environment.[159]

The assertions here are somewhat puzzling as nowhere have the advocates of a right to environment articulated the need to reconceptualize international environmental law into an *international law of environmental rights*. The importance of the recognition of a distinct right to environment is mainly

---

[158] *Id.*, art. 1.

[159] *See* BIRNIE & BOYLE, *supra* note 18, at 266.

two-fold: it will elevate environmental protection to a status that is now lacking in international human rights law; and, it will be recognized as a separate right that need not be linked to any existing protected rights in order to seek redress. In other words, it will give individual victims of environmental abuse an additional avenue to seek redress, rather than having to rely on existing human rights that has not proven to be very successful in the past. Environmental law cannot go down the same path as human rights law for several reasons: it encompasses a much wider range of actors than human rights; environmental issues have the potential to affect future generations; and some environmental problems are global in dimension. As repair is more expensive than prevention, the primary approach of environmental law would be regulation. Moreover, for environmental issues with a transboundary dimension, it would be difficult to invoke a human rights approach because the victims may be in a different state from the source of the pollution, unless, states are willing to harmonize their laws and relax procedural obstacles. However, there is nothing to stop the international community from adopting a basket approach by providing for different levels of strategies in relation to environmental issues.

While definitional problems remain, they are by no means insurmountable. Moreover, many of the existing human rights also suffer from definitional problems; this does not mean that they should cease to be recognized as human rights. Many of the human rights have achieved the sophistication that they presently enjoy as a result of a long process of judicial interpretation and refinement by the international community. It seems unjust to deny the right to environment, which by far is more fundamental than any of the protected rights in existence today, the same chance to achieve a level of refinement simply on the ground that it lacks a proper definition.

## 2. Globalization, International Trade and the Environment

Globalization, like sustainable development, has become one of the catch phrases of the 20th century. Similar to sustainable development, it is hard to find a single definition of globalization that captures its essence.[160] The World Bank defines it as the "growing integration of

---

[160] *See generally Globalization, Growth, and Poverty: Building an Inclusive World Economy*, A World Bank Policy Research Report (2002) *available at* www.econ.worldbank.org/; *From Globalization to Sustainable Development: UNEP's Work on Trade, Economics, and Sustainable Development*, Background Paper No. 1, submitted by UNEP to the Commission on Sustainable Development, DESA/DSD/PC4/BP1; Dinah Shelton, *Symposium: Globalization & the Erosion of Sovereignty in Honor of Professor Lichtenstein: Protecting Human Rights in a Globalized World*, 25 B.C. INT'L & COMP. L. REV. 273 (2002); Alberto Bernabe-Riefkohl, *"To Dream the Impossible Dream": Globalization and Harmonization of Environmental Laws*, 20 N.C. J. INT'L & COMP. REG. 205 (1995).

economies and societies around the world."[161] It recognizes that globalization is a complex process that affects many aspects of our lives from the ter-
rorist attacks of September 11, 2001, to the rapid growth and poverty
reduction in China, India and many other countries, from the development of the Internet, easier transportation and communication, to the
spread of AIDS.[162] It is so complex that a single definition will not probably do it justice.

One of the main features of globalization is the integration of societies
and economies around the world: "Integration is the result of reduced
costs of transport, lower trade barriers, faster communication of ideas, raising capital flows, and intensifying pressure for migration."[163] On the other
hand, it has also generated fears about increasing inequality, shifting power
and cultural uniformity.[164] We can also see the increased role that non-state
actors are playing in the global market, while the role that states are playing is significantly decreasing, particularly in developed countries.

It is generally considered that globalization with increased mobility of
products and services (including labor) provides a solution to the economic problems of developing countries. While this may be true in theory,
what has happened in reality is quite different. Those who are supposed to
benefit from globalization—the poor—have become poorer and marginalized; there is little doubt now that the beneficial effects of globalization
are not trickling down to those who really need it.[165]

While it is contended that globalization generally reduces poverty
because more integrated societies tend to grow faster, and integration
reduces the gap between the rich and the poor, in many poor countries the
true picture is quite different. Some countries have been left out of the
globalization process altogether because of internal policies, weak governance structures and outdated laws and institutions.[166] Yet others have been
affected by poor geographical location or disease.[167] Global growth also
threatens the environment. While some environmental issues require

---

[161] *See* Foreword, *Globalization, Growth, and Poverty, supra* note 160.

[162] *Id.*

[163] *Id.*

[164] *Id.*

[165] *See Globalization and its Impact on the Full Enjoyment of Human Rights,* Progress
Report Submitted by J. Oloka-Onyango & Deepika Udagama, E./CN.4/Sub.2/2001/10,
Aug. 2, 2001.

[166] *See Globalization, Growth, and Poverty, supra* note 160.

[167] *Id.*

action at the local level, others require a global response.[168] Although some have predicted a "race to the bottom," there is no evidence that this is in fact happening.[169] The World Bank highlights the emergence of a global civil society for the first time in history: "This can become a powerful impetus to global collective action, both for improving the environment and for reducing poverty."[170]

The Johannesburg Declaration on Sustainable Development,[171] while reconfirming the commitment to sustainable development, also refers to the effects of globalization. Discussing the different challenges facing the international community in the form of poverty, consumption patterns, managing the natural resource base, continued deterioration of the global environment and the increasing gap between developing and developed countries, the Declaration notes that globalization has added a new dimension to these challenges:

> The rapid integration of markets, mobility of capital and significant increases in investment flows around the world have opened new challenges and opportunities for the pursuit of sustainable development. But the benefits and costs of globalization are unevenly distributed, with developing countries facing special difficulties in meeting this challenge.[172]

The Plan of Implementation also adopted at the World Summit for Sustainable Development (WSSD) further notes that while many opportunities have arisen as a result of globalization, there remain serious challenges, particularly for developing countries and countries with economies in transition.[173] In order to meet these challenges, it is necessary to continue to promote a multilateral trading and financial system that benefits all countries in the pursuit of sustainable development; enhances the capacities of developing countries; actively promotes corporate responsibility and accountability based on Rio principles; and strengthens regional trade and cooperation agreements.[174]

---

[168] *See* Rudolf Dolzer, *Global Environmental Issues: The Genuine Area of Globalization,* 7 TRANSNAT'L L. & POL'Y 157 (1998).

[169] *See* HUNTER ET AL., *supra* note 5.

[170] *See Globalization, Growth, and Poverty, supra* note 160.

[171] Adopted at the World Summit for Sustainable Development in 2002, UN Doc. A/CONF.199/20 (2002).

[172] *Id.,* para. 14.

[173] Plan of Implementation, *supra* note 60, para. 47.

[174] *Id.*

On the one hand, globalization has increased the movement of people, whether as migrants, students, workers or simply tourists. This has increased the interaction between different cultures, ethnic groups and religions thereby improving the respect for human rights. However, the question has been raised whether globalization has improved the situation of traditionally marginalized groups such as women, indigenous people or peasants. The Special Rapporteurs on Globalization and Human Rights note that:

> The world today can be characterized by what one observer has described as "the concurrence of globalization and marginalization." While one section of humanity is growing and developing—literally basking in the glow of globalization—the other wallows in increasing despondency and despair. The processes most closely associated with globalization are rife with contradictions. . . . Although globalization is closely associated with the notion of free trade, many developed countries such as the United States and the members of the European Union (EU) maintain protectionist regimes and subsidies as basic instruments of economic policy. Developing countries, on the other hand, are being pressured to open up and liberalize their own economies.[175]

While globalization is generally viewed as an economic issue, it has implications in every sphere of social activity, be it social, cultural, environmental or political. Thus, its impacts are felt in virtually every sphere. The Special Rapporteurs point out that while international economic law has been largely involved in the process of globalization, it has not, unfortunately, paid much attention to international human rights law.[176] An area where considerable tension has arisen between globalization and human rights has been in the field of intellectual property rights. It is necessary to pay attention to the negative effects of globalization where poverty has been exacerbated, livelihoods have been affected or where social imbalances have been further distorted, while at the same time trying to improve the benefits of globalization.

The link between trade and environment has become a hotly debated issue in recent times. In 1994 the WTO established a Committee on Trade and Environment (CTE) pursuant to the adoption of the Ministerial

---

[175] *Globalization and its Impact on the Full Enjoyment of Human Rights,* E/CN.4/Sub.2/2001/10, Aug. 2, 2001, *available at* http://documents-dds-ny.un.org/doc/UNDOC/GEN/G01/148/01/pdf/G0114801.pdf?OpenElement.

[176] *Id.*

Decision on Trade and Environment.[177] The Ministerial Decision was adopted at the end of the Uruguay Round, which called for the establishment of a Committee on Trade and Environment.[178]

The Ministerial Decision refers to the Rio Declaration, Agenda 21, the work of the Group on Environmental Measures and International Trade, the Committee on Trade and Development and the Council of Representatives.[179] The Preamble refers to the need to raise the living standard of people, "expanding the production of and trade in goods and services, while allowing for the optimal use of the world's resources in accordance with the objective of sustainable development, seeking both to protect and preserve the environment and to enhance the means for doing so in a manner consistent with their respective needs and concerns at different levels of economic development."[180] The Decision further notes that there should not be any policy contradiction between upholding an equitable multilateral trading system and protecting the environment and promoting sustainable development. In other words, the Decision articulates that there should be no conflict between promoting trade, on the one hand, and protecting the environment, on the other. Given that sustainable development should inform both these processes—trade and environment—in theory at least, there should be no contradiction. In practice, however, the story has been quite different.[181]

The Doha Ministerial Declaration of 2001 also refers to trade and environment.[182] Noting that international trade can play a major role in the promotion of economic development and the alleviation of poverty, the Declaration reaffirms the commitment to the objective of sustainable development:

---

[177] http://www.wto.org/english/tratop_e/envir_e/envir_e.htm.

[178] Marrakesh Agreement Establishing the WTO, *available at* http://www.wto.org/english/docs_e/legal_e/04-wto.doc.

[179] *Id. See* Vicente Paolo B. Yu III, *Briefing Paper on the WTO Committee on Trade and Environment* (2002), *available at* http://www.tradeobservatory.org/library.cfm?refID =25583.

[180] http://www.wto.org/english/tratop_e/envir_e/envir_e.htm.

[181] *See* the discussion, *infra* in relation to the tension between environmental measures and trade measures. *See also* High Level Symposium on Trade and Environment (1999) and the Symposium on Trade and Sustainable Development held in October 2005, *available at* http://www.wto.org/english/tratop_e/envir_e/sym_oct05_e/.

[182] *Available at* http://www.wto.org/english/thewto_e/minist_e/min01/mindecl_e. htm. *See* Ved P. Nanda, *Sustainable Development, International Trade and the Doha Agenda for Development*, 8 CHAP. L. REV. 53 (2005).

We are convinced that the aims of upholding and safeguarding an open and non-discriminatory multilateral trading system, and acting for the protection of the environment and the promotion of sustainable development can and must be mutually supportive. . . . We recognize that under WTO rules no country should be prevented from taking measures for the protection of human, animal or plant life or health or of the environment at the levels it considers appropriate.[183]

However, the Declaration notes that such measures should not be applied in a manner that would constitute a means of arbitrary or unjustifiable discrimination between countries where the same conditions prevail or there is a disguised restriction on international trade.[184]

Within the trade and environmental debate, several issues have arisen. Firstly, if measures taken on environmental grounds directly or indirectly affect international trade, is it a violation of trade obligations under international law? Secondly, are trade provisions in international environmental treaties incompatible with trade obligations under the WTO agreements? Thirdly, what is the relationship between environmental policies, trade policies and sustainable development? The answers to these questions have, unfortunately, given rise to much controversy.

While the Stockholm Declaration does not have specific provisions on trade and environment, the Rio Declaration deals specifically with this:

States should cooperate to promote a supportive and open international economic system that would lead to economic growth and sustainable development in all countries, to better address the problems of environmental degradation. Trade policy measures for environmental purposes should not constitute a means of arbitrary or unjustifiable discrimination or a disguised restriction on international trade. Unilateral actions to deal with environmental challenges outside the jurisdiction of the importing country should be avoided. Environmental measures addressing transboundary or global environmental problems should, as far as possible, be based on an international consensus.[185]

---

[183] *Id.*

[184] *Id.*

[185] Principle 12, Rio Declaration, *supra* note 20.

Several features of this Principle should be noted here. It employs hortatory language—the word "should" as opposed to "shall" and the phrase "as far as possible" are used diluting the effect of Principle 12.[186] It calls upon states to promote an open international economic system to facilitate economic growth and sustainable development. It also articulates that trade measures for environmental purposes should not cause discrimination or be considered a disguised restriction on international trade. Furthermore, it cautions against the use of unilateral measures that have effects outside the jurisdiction of that state. Finally, measures taken to address transboundary or global environmental problems should be based on consensus.

The key argument against liberalized trade has been the fear that in order to gain market access, states will relax their environmental standards, which may cause a "race to the bottom."[187] It is argued that companies will relocate to places with lax environmental standards, as they will have a comparative advantage in the international market and that domestic producers will lobby for lower environmental standards.[188] Whether this has actually happened is debatable.[189]

Industries, on the one hand, argue that strict environmental regulation will "give away markets" to foreign firms operating in places with lax environmental standards, and some have argued that this amounts to a subsidy.[190] Environmentalists, on the other hand, fear that international trade bodies (the WTO) would strike down national environmental regulations as protectionist trade barriers.[191]

### a.  *Trade Measures in Multilateral Environmental Treaties*

One of the most effective ways that environmental treaties have dealt with the issue of non-compliance is through the use of trade measures.[192] The first multilateral environmental treaty to do so was the Convention to

---

[186] Granted that the whole Declaration is of a non-binding nature. However, within the Declaration itself, it is possible to see differentiation in language—for example, Principles 5, 7, 11, 15 18, 19 embody the word "shall" while Principles 8, 9, 12 14 embody the word "should."

[187] *See* HUNTER ET AL., *supra* note 5, at 1133.

[188] *Id.*

[189] *Id.*

[190] *Id.*

[191] *Id.*

[192] *See* "MEA Database: Matrix on Trade Measures Pursuant to Selected Multilateral Environmental Agreements (MEAs)," *at* http://www.wto.org/english/tratop_e/envir_e/mea_database_e.htm for a discussion on trade measures in environmental treaties.

Regulate International Trade in Endangered Species of Flora and Fauna (CITES).[193] The Convention has three appendices. Appendix I includes all species threatened with extinction that may be affected by trade. Trade in these species should be authorized in exceptional circumstances. Appendix II includes all species that are not yet facing extinction but may become so unless trade in them is regulated.[194] Appendix III includes all species that parties have identified as being subject to regulation within its jurisdiction. The Convention provides that trade in species included in Appendix I, II and III cannot take place except in accordance with the provisions of the Convention.

The Convention operates on the basis of export and import permits to be issued by a scientific authority and a management authority. Article X applies to trade with non-parties to the Convention. According to this provision, where export, re-export or import is from a non-party to the Convention, comparable documentation issued by the competent authorities in that country, which substantially conforms with the requirements in the Convention, may be accepted.

This provision is a departure from the approach found in the later treaties that specifically prohibit trade with non-parties. The Montreal Protocol on Substances that Deplete the Ozone Layer,[195] for example, requires parties to ban the import of controlled substances[196] from any non-party within one year of the entry into force of the Protocol.[197] Furthermore, beginning January 1, 1993, no party may export any controlled substances to any non-party.[198] It further calls upon parties to discourage the export of technology for producing or utilizing controlled substances to non-parties.

The Basel Convention on the Control of Transboundary Movements of Hazardous Wastes and Their Disposal[199] adopts an approach similar to the Montreal Protocol and provides that "A Party shall not permit hazardous wastes or other wastes to be exported to a non-Party or to be imported from a non-Party."[200]

---

[193]   12 ILM 1085 (1973), entered into force July 1, 1975.

[194]   *Id.*, art. II.

[195]   1522 UNTS 3, entered into force Jan. 1, 1989.

[196]   "Controlled substances" are defined in Article 1 of the Protocol.

[197]   Art. 4, Montreal Protocol.

[198]   *Id.*

[199]   1673 UNTS 57, signed in 1989, entered into force May 5, 1992.

[200]   *Id.*, art. 4(5).

Thus, the question is whether these trade measures in environmental treaties would constitute a violation of the parties' trade obligations under the General Agreement on Tariff and Trade (GATT) instruments. Thus, for example, if a party and a non-party are both GATT members, the provisions in the Montreal Protocol could violate GATT's most-favored-nation (MFN) requirement.[201] In the event of a challenge, which obligations should prevail—environmental or trade? Which forum is best suited to hear such challenges? It has been repeatedly noted that the WTO is not an environmental body, and as such it should not hear disputes of an environmental nature.[202] On the other hand, given the close relationship between trade and environment, the question arises whether they can actually be divorced from one another. To date this issue has not been resolved.

As trade rules and environmental protection rules have developed on separate tracks, in many cases, their provisions may conflict with one another.[203] This issue also demonstrates the danger of compartmentalizing issues into separate labels and points to the urgent need to harmonize these obligations, as the fulfillment of obligations under one treaty should not result in the violation of obligations under another.

### b. The Use of Environmental Measures as Barriers to International Trade

It is with the application of unilateral environmental measures to trade issues that the trade and environment debate has come to the forefront.[204] Several cases have been brought before the WTO dispute settlement machinery challenging such measures. In order to discuss these challenges, a brief discussion of the core principles of the GATT/WTO is necessary.

Three basic principles form the foundation of the GATT: the MFN obligation, which prohibits discrimination between the products of different importing states;[205] the national treatment obligation, which prohibits

---

[201] *See* HUNTER ET AL., *supra* note 5, at 1178.

[202] *See* the WTO Web site, *at* http://www.wto.org.

[203] *See* Ryan L. Winter, *Reconciling the GATT and WTO with Multilateral Environmental Agreements: Can We Have Our Cake and Eat it Too?*, 11 COLO. J. INT'L ENVTL. L. & POL'Y 223 (2000).

[204] *See* Daniel Bodansky, *What's So Bad about Unilateral Action to Protect the Environment?*, 11 EUR. J. INT'L L. 339 (2000); and Laurence Boisson de Charzournes, *Unilateralism and Environmental Protection: Issues of Perception and Reality of Issues*, 11 EUR. J. INT'L L. 315 (2000).

[205] GATT art. 1. 55 UNTS 194, signed Oct. 30, 1947, *available at* http://www.wto.org. This provision seeks to ensure equal treatment and prevents offering favored treatment to trading partners. It applies to "like products" which has given rise to interpretation difficulties. *See* HUNTER ET AL., *supra* note 5 at 1159.

discrimination between imported and domestically produced goods;[206] and prohibition on quantitative restrictions, which covers restrictions to trade such as bans, quotas and licenses on exported and imported products.[207] It must be noted that to the extent that products are different, discrimination is justified. The issue of "like product" has given rise to controversy, with environmentalists arguing that discrimination should be allowed on the basis of how they are produced[208] while the trade community has argued that this would interfere with the sovereignty of the exporting state thereby undermining trade.[209]

In *Tuna/Dolphin I Case*,[210] the WTO panel adopted a restrictive meaning of "like products," arguing that likeness should be determined on the basis of physical characteristics and not by reference to the process by which it is produced. When Mexico challenged U.S. restrictions on imports of tuna, which were caught using methods that harmed dolphins, the panel was of the view that "regulations governing the taking of dolphins incidental to the taking of tuna could not possibly affect tuna as a product" and, therefore, the measure discriminated between like products and was contrary to the obligations under GATT.[211]

While developing countries may support this interpretation, environmentalists argue that production and process methods (PPMs) are important: in other words, environmental policies require distinguishing between products according to how they are produced.[212] They argue that the present international trade system prevents countries from favoring sustainably produced goods and services.[213] Hunter notes:

> The challenge is to find an interpretation of 'like products' that ensures developing countries have continued access to export markets whilst allowing industrialized countries to address unsustainable consumption patterns.[214]

---

[206] GATT art. III, *supra* note 205. It requires foreign products to be treated no less favorably than domestic "like products" and seeks to prevent measures to protect domestic industry.

[207] GATT art. XI, *supra* note 205.

[208] *See* Jennifer Schultz, *The GATT/WTO Committee on Trade and the Environment—Toward Environmental Reform*, 89 AM. J. INT'L L. 423 (1995).

[209] *See* HUNTER ET AL., *supra* note 5, at 1160.

[210] *Available at* http://www.wto.org.

[211] *Id.*

[212] *See* Schultz, *supra* note 208.

[213] *Id.*

[214] *See* HUNTER ET AL., *supra* note 5, at 1161.

This very strict literal approach has been modified in the *Asbestos Case*[215] where the WTO Appellate Body has taken a less rigid approach to the interpretation of like products. Pointing out that "no one approach would be appropriate for all cases," the Appellate Body stated that four general criteria must be employed to analyzing likeness: (1) the properties, nature and quality of the products; (2) the end-uses of the products; (3) consumers' tastes and habits; and (4) the tariff classification of the products.[216] These are not treaty-mandated criteria that will determine the legal characteristics of a product. The kind of evidence necessary to assess likeness will depend on the particular products and the legal provision at issue.[217]

Despite this less rigid approach to like products, this debate is likely to continue in the WTO. Harmonization of domestic environmental laws through agreed international standards is often suggested as an alternative to trade sanctions for addressing environmentally harmful production processes.[218] If these standards are comparable, there is a less likelihood for international disputes to arise.[219]

Article XX of the GATT provides an exception to GATT obligations:

> Subject to the requirement that such measures are not applied in a manner which would constitute a means of arbitrary or unjustifiable discrimination between countries where the same conditions prevail, or a disguised restriction on international trade, nothing in this Agreement shall be construed to prevent the adoption or enforcement . . . of measures: . . .
>
> (b) necessary to protect human, animal or plant life or health; . . .
>
> (g) relating to the conservation of exhaustible natural resources.[220]

These exceptions have been subject to several WTO decisions. Article XX allows countries to take measures that would otherwise be in conflict with

---

[215] European Communities-Measures Affecting Asbestos and Asbestos-Containing Products, AB-2000-11, WT/DS135/AB/R, Mar. 12, 2001, *available at* http://www.wto. org/english/tratop_e/ dispu_status_e.htm#58 (referred to as the *Asbestos Case*).

[216] *Id.*

[217] *Id.*

[218] *See* HUNTER ET AL., *supra* note 5 at 1162.

[219] *Id. See also The Relationship Between Trade and MEAs, at* http://www.wto.org/english/tratop_e/envir_e/envir_backgrnd_e/c5s1_e.htm.

[220] Art. XX, *available at* http://www.wto.org.

GATT obligations if those measures are "necessary" to protect "human, animal or plant life or health." Earlier GATT decisions gave a narrow interpretation to the term "necessary." In the *Tuna/Dolphin I Case,*[221] the panel stated that the party invoking Article XX(b) must show that no other GATT-consistent measures were reasonably available.[222] In later cases, the Appellate Body seems to have adopted a balancing test in which trade restrictive measures were weighed along with other factors.[223] This approach was later reaffirmed by the Appellate Body in the *Asbestos Case.*[224]

> In this case, the objective pursued by the measure is the preservation of human life and health through the elimination, or reduction, of the well-known, and life-threatening, health risks posed by asbestos fibres. The value pursued is both vital and important in the highest degree. The remaining question, then, is whether there is an alternative measure that would achieve the same end and that is less restrictive of trade than a prohibition.[225]

In this case, there does not seem to be a doubt that preservation of human life and health from the hazards posed by asbestos falls under Article XX(b). However, the real issue is whether any alternative measures are available that would achieve the same result. This is the test that a claimant under Article XX(b) will have to satisfy.[226] In the *Gasoline Case*[227] the WTO Appellate Body stated that the General Agreement should not be read in "clinical isolation" from public international law.[228] It is interesting to see whether the Appellate Body would be willing to favor an interpretation that takes into account principles of international law, including sustainable development that forms part of the objectives of the WTO.

---

[221] *Available at* http://www.wto.org/english/tratop_e/envir_e/envir_backgrnd_e/c5s1_e.htm.

[222] *See* HUNTER ET AL., *supra* note 5, at 1164.

[223] Korea-Measures Affecting Imports of Fresh, Chilled and Frozen Beef, WT/DS169/AB/R, Dec. 11, 2000, *available at* http://www.wto.org/english/tratop_e/dispu_status_e.htm#58 (referred to as Korea-Beef Case). *See also* HUNTER ET AL., *supra* note 5, at 1164.

[224] *See supra* note 215.

[225] *See* HUNTER ET AL., *supra* note 5, at 1165.

[226] *See* Paige J. Brock, *A Change in the "Trade-Winds:" World Trade Organization Places Human Health Before Free-Trade,* COLO. J. INT'L. ENVTL. L. & POL'Y 85 (2000).

[227] United States—Standards for Reformulated and Conventional Gasoline, WT/DS2/AB/R. May 20, 1996, *available at* http://www.wto.org/english/tratop_e/dispu_status_e.htm#58.

[228] *Id.*

Another hurdle to be cleared under the exception is the *chapeau* to Article XX. It requires that measures should not be an arbitrary or unjustifiable discrimination between countries or a disguised restriction on international trade. The Appellate Body noted in the *Gasoline*[229] and *Shrimp-Turtle Case*[230] that the purpose of the *chapeau* is to ensure that Article XX exceptions are not abused.

In the *Gasoline* case, the Appellate Body concluded that U.S. measures did not satisfy the requirements in the *chapeau*. It noted that the United States had a number of alternative ways to apply the Clean Air Act Amendments that did not discriminate between foreign and domestic suppliers. The Appellate Body was concerned over the coercive effect of the U.S. measures on the policies of other governments. It further referred to the failure of the U.S. government to undertake sufficient negotiations with the complainants noting that the United States negotiated seriously with some but not with others, indicating that their behavior was discriminatory.[231] In the *Shrimp-Turtle Case*,[232] the Appellate Body discussed the role of the *chapeau* and pointed out that the task of interpreting and applying the *chapeau* is a delicate one of marking out a line of equilibrium between the right of a member to invoke the exception in Article XX and the rights of other members to rely on the substantive provisions of the GATT. The interpretation adopted should not cancel out the competing rights and impair the balance of rights and obligations under the Agreement. However, this line of equilibrium is not fixed and depends on the facts of each case.[233] With regard to the Appellate Body decision on unilateral environmental measures and trade, it has been noted that:

> Most important for the purposes of this analysis, however, the Appellate Body suggested that the outcome of the case might have differed had the United States sought protection of the turtles through bilateral or multilateral negotiations. In dictum, the Appellate Body indicated that measures derived from multilateral negotiations, such as those contained in MEAs, are preferable to purely unilateral environmental measures. It went so far as to cite international instruments to show that conservation measures call

---

[229] *Supra* note 227.

[230] United States—Import Prohibition of Certain Shrimp and Shrimp Products, AB-1998-4, WT/DS58/AB/R, Oct. 12, 1998, *available at* http://www.wto.org/english/tratop_e/dispu_status_e.htm#58 (referred to as *Shrimp-Turtle Case*).

[231] *Supra* note 227.

[232] *Supra* note 230.

[233] *See* Winter, *supra* note 203.

for cooperative efforts, not unilateral measures. Again, if future WTO tribunals choose to follow this interpretation it could have important implications for MEAs.[234]

It is interesting to discuss the *amicus* brief presented to the Appellate Body by several non-governmental organizations led by the Center for International Environmental Law, based in Washington DC.[235] The *amicus* brief stresses that the WTO agreements must be interpreted in the light of international law principles that support and define sustainable development for several reasons: sustainable development forms part of the object and purpose of the WTO agreements; "international law principles of sustainable development comprise part of the international law relations among the parties which forms another important guide to the interpretation of Article XX under the Vienna Convention."[236] Finally, the brief argues that "interpreting WTO Agreements in light of international sustainable development principles promotes the development of a coherent system of international law."[237] The brief also refers to the various multilateral commitments and "customary laws of sustainable development,"[238] which obliges states, *inter alia*, to protect migratory marine resources, to control unsustainable consumption, to prevent extra-territorial environmental harm and to observe the precautionary principle.[239] It is not clear which of these principles form part of customary international law, although the brief does seem to indicate that these principles are part of both multilateral commitments and customary law. The multilateral conventions referred to in the brief include the CITES, the UN Convention on the Law of the Sea,[240] the UN Convention on Biological Diversity[241] and the Convention on the Conservation of Migratory Species of Wild Animals.[242] In addition, the brief refers to Agenda 21 and the 1995 FAO Code of

---

[234] *Id.* (footnotes omitted).

[235] *Available at* http://www.ciel.org.

[236] *Id.*

[237] *Id.*

[238] *Id.* As discussed in Chapter 2, Section J, sustainable development has not entered the portals of sustainable development, although some of its components are already part of customary international law.

[239] *Id.*

[240] 21 ILM 1261 (1982), 1833 UNTS 3, signed Dec. 10, 1982, entered into force Nov. 16, 1994, *available at* http://www.un.org/Depts/los/index.htm.

[241] 31 ILM 822 (1992), 1760 UNTS 79, *available at* http://www.biodiv.org/.

[242] 19 ILM 15 (1980).

Conduct for Responsible Fisheries.[243] Concluding that the sea turtle conservation measures flow from fundamental principles of sustainable development embodied in environmental treaties and customary law principles, the brief argued that, as U.S. measures were carefully guided by international consensus, they should be given considerable deference, including a presumption that they fall within Article XX(g) of the GATT.[244] It further noted that U.S. measures have been applied consistently with the fundamental principles of sustainable development that are embodied in international law and the Preamble to the GATT. The brief concluded by urging the Appellate Body to interpret Article XX in the light of sustainable development and the commitment of the WTO to enhance the means for protecting the environment, and to determine that the sea turtle conservation measures are within the protection of Article XX.[245]

The tendency of the WTO adjudication bodies to rule against unilateral environmental measures has been criticized by environmentalists as imposing an unreasonable burden on governments seeking to protect the environment.[246] While being concerned about the potential use of environmental measures as protectionism, some are urging that the PPM issue must be addressed.[247] There is no doubt that multilateral solutions to trade-environmental problems are preferable to unilateral measures.[248] The criteria that should be used by panels and the Appellate Body, when determining what kinds of unilateral measures should be permitted under Article XX, must be adopted, preferably by the WTO Committee on Trade and Environment.

### c. Intellectual Property Issues and Indigenous Knowledge

Another controversy that has arisen within the trade/environmental debate relates to intellectual property issues and biodiversity.[249] Within the

---

[243] *Available at* http://www.fao.org/documents/show_cdr.asp?url_file=/DOCREP/005/v9878e/v9878e00.htm.

[244] *See* the discussion in Section B.2.b.

[245] *Supra* note 235.

[246] *See* Winter, *supra* note 203.

[247] *See* HUNTER ET AL., *supra* note 5, at 1160–63.

[248] *See* Winter, *supra* note 203. *See also* Bodansky, *supra* note 204 and de Charzournes, *supra* note 204.

[249] *See Globalization and Its Impact on the Full Enjoyment of all Human Rights, Preliminary Report of the Secretary-General*, A/55/342, 55th Session of the UN General Assembly, Aug. 31, 2000, para. 19.

WTO, the TRIPS Agreement[250] plays an important role in patenting inno-
vations. Unfortunately, this has led to patenting traditional knowledge by
multi-national companies resulting in what environmentalists call "bio
piracy."[251] Traditional knowledge of indigenous groups, passed from generation to generation, in relation to agriculture and medicinal use of plants
has been tapped by multi-national companies for bioprospecting and then
subjecting it to intellectual property rights. Traditional knowledge has usually been treated as common heritage[252] to be used and enjoyed by everybody in the community. The UN Convention on Biological Diversity, unlike
the TRIPS Agreement which opts for exclusive rights, uses the concept of
benefit sharing in relation to access to genetic resources.[253] Thus, as can be
seen, the private rights regime under the TRIPS agreement, and the community rights (or the benefit sharing regime) under the Convention on
Biological Diversity have collided with each other, causing much concern
in developing countries.[254] This is another example of two regimes of international obligations that have the potential to conflict with one another.

Given the current debate on trade and environment issues, there is no
doubt that the international community will have to work out some rules
to overcome these conflicts, both in relation to the compatibility of unilateral environmental measures as an exception under Article XX as well as
the possible conflict of trade measures in environmental treaties with
GATT obligations. It is likely that these disputes would increase before the
WTO Dispute Settlement Bodies in the years to come, as it is, so far, the
only compulsory dispute settlement machinery available under international law.

## 3. Health, Environmental Protection and Human Rights

That environmental degradation has a serious impact on human
health is no longer disputed. The adverse consequences of ozone depletion,[255] predicted consequences of global warming[256] and even day-to-day

---

[250] Agreement on Trade-Related Aspects of Intellectual Property Rights, 1994, *available at* http://www.wto.org/english/tratop_e/trips_e/t_agm0_e.htm.

[251] *See* HUNTER ET AL., *supra* note 5, at 965.

[252] *Id.*

[253] Art. 15(7), *supra* note 241. This provision refers to the sharing, in a fair and equitable way, the results of research and development and the benefits arising from the
commercial and other utilization of genetic resources.

[254] *See* HUNTER ET AL., *supra* note 5, at 964–69.

[255] *See* OUR COMMON FUTURE, *supra* note 8, at 3.

[256] *Id.*

pollution have a negative impact on human health. Thus, the close link between environmental protection and human health has led many organizations involved in health issues to deal also with environmental issues and *vice versa*. It is envisaged that sustainable development will also promote better human health. Environmentalists also argue for the health of other species, including the health of ecosystems.[257] It can be argued that by incorporating environmental protection into the development process, the healthy survival of other species and ecosystems can be achieved.

International human rights law is also relevant in this regard. While not making the link between environmental degradation and human health (except, perhaps in relation to children[258]), international human rights law recognizes a human right to health. Thus, Article 12 of the ICESCR provides that: "The States parties to the present Covenant recognize the right of everyone to the enjoyment of the highest attainable standard of physical and mental health."[259] The steps to be taken by the parties to achieve this right include those necessary to improve "all aspects of environmental and industrial hygiene."[260] In addition, international human rights law endorses the right to an adequate standard of living. Article 11 of the Covenant stipulates the "right of everyone to an adequate standard of living for himself and his family, including adequate food, clothing and housing, and to the continuous improvement of living conditions."[261] It is clear that neither the right to health nor the right to an adequate standard of living can be realized in a degraded or polluted environment. While international human rights law has been slow to make the link between environmental protection and human rights, this void seems to have been addressed by General Comment No. 14 of the UN Committee on Economic, Social and Cultural Rights.[262] Noting the interdependence of human rights, the General Comment stresses that food and nutrition, housing, access to safe and potable water and adequate sanitation, safe

---

[257] *See* the World Charter for Nature, *supra* note 37.

[258] *See* the Convention on the Rights of the Child, 1989, *supra* note 96.

[259] International Covenant on Economic, Social and Cultural Rights, 1966, *available at* http://www.unhchr.org/. *See* Katrina Tomasevski, *Health Rights* in ECONOMIC, SOCIAL AND CULTURAL RIGHTS, 125 (Asbjorn Eide, Catarina Krause & Allan Rosas eds., 1995).

[260] Art. 12, ICESCR, *id.*

[261] *Id.*, art. 11. *See* Asbjorn Eide, *The Right to an Adequate Standard of Living Including the Right to Food, in* ECONOMIC, SOCIAL AND CULTURAL RIGHTS, 89 (Asbjorn Eide, Catarina Krause & Allan Rosas eds., 1995).

[262] Economic, Social Council E/C.12/2000/4, CESCR General Comment No. 14, July 4, 2000, "The Right to the Highest Attainable Standard of Health," *available at* http://www.unhchr.org/.

and healthy working conditions and a healthy environment are indispensable for the realization of the right to health.[263] The Committee has, thus, clearly recognized the link between human health and environmental protection.

The Comment interpreted the right to health as an inclusive right, including not only access to health care but also the underlying causes of ill health. While the international recognition of the right to health does not mean that people have a right to be healthy,[264] it does mean that states have certain obligations toward its people. The core obligations in respect of the right to health are:

> (a) to ensure the right of access to health facilities, goods and services on a non-discriminatory basis. . . ; (b) to ensure access to the minimum essential food which is nutritionally adequate and safe . . . ; (c) to ensure access to basic shelter, housing and sanitation, and an adequate supply of safe and potable water; (d) to provide essential drugs; (e) to ensure equitable distribution of all health facilities, goods and services; and (f) to adopt and implement a national health strategy.[265]

While human rights treaties have been slow to link health and environmental conditions, environmental instruments have been much more forthcoming. They have consistently made the link between environmental protection and human health. Starting with the Stockholm Declaration, many of the instruments make this link explicitly. Indeed, protecting public health is an objective of many of these environmental treaties.[266] Principle 1 of the Stockholm Declaration, for example, provides that: "Man has the fundamental right to freedom, equality and adequate conditions of life, in an environment of a quality that permits a life of dignity and well-being."

---

[263] *Id.*

[264] *See* NIHAL JAYAWICKRAMA, THE JUDICIAL APPLICATION OF HUMAN RIGHTS, 883 (2002).

[265] *Id.* at 884.

[266] *E.g.,* the Convention on Long-Range Transboundary Air Pollution, 18 ILM 1442 (1979), states in Article 2 that the parties are determined to protect man and his environment against air pollution and air pollution is defined by reference to human health; the Vienna Convention for the Protection of the Ozone Layer, which refers to the "potentially harmful impact on human health and the environment through modification of the ozone layer" (Preamble); similarly, the Basel Convention on the Control of Transboundary Movement of Hazardous Wastes and Their Disposal refers to the "risk of damage to human health and the environment caused by hazardous wastes and other wastes and the transboundary movement thereof" (Preamble).

Principle 1 thus makes a clear link between the quality of the environment and man's well-being.[267] Furthermore, Principle 7 makes a specific link between marine pollution and hazards to human health.[268]

Similarly, the Rio Declaration provides: "Human beings are at the centre of concerns for sustainable development. They are entitled to a healthy and productive life in harmony with nature."[269] Again falling short of a right to a healthy environment, it does make a link between a healthy life and nature.

Many international organizations and specialized agencies, too, have studied the relationship between environmental protection and human health. The World Health Organization (WHO), for example, has consistently studied the impact of environmental factors on human health, particularly, on children. In a 2002 study by the WHO[270] it has been identified that 4.7 million children under five years of age died in the year 2000 as a result of environment-related health problems; 1.3 million from diarrhoea; 2 million from acute respiratory infections; 1 million from malaria and other infectious diseases; and 400,000 from injuries.[271] Stating that "unhealthy environments are a major killer of children"[272] this report notes:

> Environmental hazards are on the rise. Increasing industrialization, explosive urban population growth, lack of pollution control, unabated waste dumping, non-sustainable consumption of natural resources and unsafe use of chemicals affect the environment in which today's children live. Preliminary estimates suggest that almost one third of the global burden of disease (for all ages) can be attributed to environmental risk factors.[273]

---

[267] However, the reference to "man" rather than "human beings" has been interpreted as embodying non-rights language. It is thus contended that Principle 1 does not embody a right to environment, despite its reference to "fundamental." The wording adopted in the Principle also suggests that an environment of a particular quality is required for the enjoyment of other rights. *See also* the discussion on right to environment in Section B.l.a and b.

[268] Principle 7 provides: "States shall take all possible steps to prevent pollution of the seas by substances that are liable to create hazards to human health, to harm living resources and marine life, to damage amenities or to interfere with other legitimate uses of the sea."

[269] Principle 1.

[270] "Brundtland starts new movement to address environmental crisis affecting children's health," *at* http://www.who.int/mediacentre/news/releases/who66/en/.

[271] *Id.*

[272] *Id.*

[273] *Id.*

An unhealthy environment also affects adults. However, children are more vulnerable to disease, as their level of resistance is not as high as in adults. The above report notes that "one in five children in the poorest parts of the world will not live beyond their fifth birthday to a large extent because of environment-related diseases."[274] Even if they survive, they would be impaired for life either physically or mentally. According to the WHO, each year, at least 3 million children under the age of five die due to environment-related diseases.[275] Acute respiratory infections, about 60 percent of which are related to environmental factors, kill about 2 million children under the age of five annually; in addition, diarrhoeal diseases kill nearly 2 million children every year.[276]

The subjects on the WHO's agenda under environment include water and sanitation, food safety, solid wastes, noise, climate, occupational health, air, ultraviolet radiation, chemicals and children.[277] Of these, the WHO has paid particular attention to the issue of climate change, which is considered to have a severe impact on human health. In a report on climate and health, the WHO noted:

> Human societies are very vulnerable to climate extremes (droughts, floods, wind storms). A changing climate would entail changes in the frequency and/or intensity of such extremes. This is a major concern for human health. To a large extent, public health depends on safe drinking water, sufficient food, secure shelter, and good social conditions. All these factors can be affected by climate change.[278]

The Office of the High Commissioner for Human Rights (OHCHR), too, has studied the link between human health and the environment, more in terms of the right to health. Under its work on environment and human rights, an experts' meeting was convened to study the relationship between the two fields.[279] These reports were discussed in relation to the right to a healthy environment.[280]

---

[274] *Id.*

[275] *See Children's Environmental Health, available at* http://www.who.int/ceh/en/.

[276] *Id.*

[277] *See* http://www.who.int/.

[278] Climate and Health, Fact Sheet No. 266, Dec. 2001, *available at* http://www.who.int/inf-fs/en/fact266.html.

[279] *Available at* http://www.unhchr.org.

[280] *See* discussion in Section B.l.b.

UNEP has also dealt with the issue of environment and human health.[281] In its report on "A framework for Action on Health and the Environment"[282] prepared for the World Summit on Sustainable Development, the report addressed the key issues and challenges relating to health and the environment.[283] It pointed out that "health is both an indicator of as well as a resource for sustainable development."[284] It further noted that "at least a quarter of the global burden of disease may be attributable to poor environmental conditions. Many infectious diseases are associated with poor environmental quality and lack of access to basic services such as clean water or household energy."[285]

The report further highlighted the link between poverty and ill health, which is exacerbated by environmental conditions. It identified rapid urbanization as a major factor and notes that pollution, lack of sanitation, growing migration from the country to cities and extreme poverty have made many cities unhealthy.[286] Moreover, infectious and parasitic diseases, which account for around 25 percent of total deaths in the world, are intimately linked to environmental conditions and poverty. These diseases are the world's leading killer of children and young adults.[287]

The Plan of Implementation adopted at the WSSD is another document that recognizes the link between human health and the environment. It noted that "the provision of clean drinking water and adequate sanitation is necessary to protect human health and the environment."[288] In addition, it contains a separate section on health and sustainable development. Section VI pointed out that "the goals of sustainable development can only be achieved in the absence of a high prevalence of debilitating diseases, while obtaining health gains for the whole population requires poverty eradication."[289] In the same way that environmental pollution can cause health problems, those with health problems unrelated to the environment, such as HIV/AIDS, can hinder the achievement of sustainable development. Thus, a healthy population is vital for sustainable development.[290]

---

[281] *See Children in the New Millennium: Environmental Impact on Health, available at* http://www.unep.org/ceh/.

[282] WEHAB Working Group, Aug. 2002.

[283] *Id.*

[284] *Id.* at 7.

[285] *Id.*

[286] *Id.*

[287] *Id.* at 8.

[288] Para. 7, *supra* note 60.

[289] Para. 46, *supra* note 60.

[290] *See* Sumudu Atapattu, *Sustainable Development and the Right to Health, in* SUSTAIN-

The link between health and water has been identified by the UN Committee on Economic, Social and Cultural Rights in the context of the right to water. In 2002, the UN Committee adopted General Comment No. 15 declaring water as a human right: "Water is fundamental for life and health. The human right to water is indispensable for leading a healthy life in human dignity. It is a pre-requisite to the realization of all other human rights."[291] The Committee was of the opinion that the right to water is clearly implicit in the rights contained in the ICESCR, particularly Article 11, which contains a right to an adequate standard of living.

There is no doubt that human rights law, environmental law and sustainable development law are all designed to protect, *inter alia*, human beings and human health. In addition to this objective, environmental law (and arguably sustainable development law, although this objective may not be immediately apparent) seeks to protect other species and ecosystems irrespective of their worth to human beings. While some may argue that the objective of protecting ecosystems and other species is ultimately for the benefit of human beings, environmentalists strongly oppose this anthropocentric view of environmental protection. It cannot be denied, however, that the human being is the only species that has the potential to change the environment irrevocably; conversely, it is the human being alone who can take measures to protect the environment. Thus, it is no wonder that most environmental laws are aimed at controlling the activities of human beings.

## 4. Poverty and Environmental Protection

Poverty is seen as a major obstacle to many issues. Whether it is in the context of health, environment, human rights or sustainable development, poverty is a major obstacle to achieving any of these objectives. Thus, for example, when people are poor, they tend to resort to unsustainable practices, thereby leading to environmental degradation. When people are poor, their health suffers. Furthermore, they are unable to realize any of the socio-economic rights recognized in international human rights law. They may be vulnerable to other abuses too. In short, poverty poses a particular challenge to achieving sustainable development.

However, poverty is not the only factor that poses an obstacle to sustainable development. Over-consumption of resources also causes environmental degradation, health problems and unsustainable practices.[292]

---

ABLE JUSTICE: RECONCILING ECONOMIC, SOCIAL AND ENVIRONMENTAL LAW, 355 (Marie-Claire Cordonier Segger & C.G. Weeramantry eds., 2005).

[291] Adopted in Dec. 2002, *available at* http://www.unhchr.ch/html/menu2/6/gc15.doc.

[292] The WCED addressed the issue of over-consumption in the context of sustainable development. *See* OUR COMMON FUTURE, *supra* note 8, at 95.

While the world today produces sufficient food to feed the entire population, this is not evenly distributed.[293] Thus, when one-half of the globe faces starvation and suffers from malnutrition and even death, the other half of the globe suffers from obesity and related diseases. Unequal distribution of resources and their over-exploitation and over-consumption have also created many environmental problems in their wake. It is estimated that developed countries, with about 26 percent of the world's population, utilize 80 percent of commercial energy.[294] It is here that the principle of intra-generational equity assumes importance. While poverty is being blamed for all evils, hardly anything is being said about over-consumption of resources by the rich. The Rio Declaration is one of the few instruments that recognize poverty as well as over-consumption as obstacles to sustainable development:

> All States and all people shall cooperate in the essential task of eradicating poverty as an indispensable requirement for sustainable development, in order to decrease the disparities in standards of living and better meet the needs of the majority of the people of the world.[295]

Principle 8 deals with consumption patterns: "To achieve sustainable development and a higher quality of life for all people, States should reduce and eliminate unsustainable patterns of production and consumption and promote appropriate demographic policies."[296] On a comparison between the two provisions, one cannot help but notice the difference in language adopted: while Principle 5 uses the word "shall," thereby indicating a level of compulsion, Principle 8 uses the word "should."[297] Whether or not the drafters intended to convey different levels of compulsion by using different words, one thing is clear: both poverty and over-consumption must be addressed if sustainable development is to be achieved. It is also a matter of equity: developed countries should refrain from engaging in wasteful practices, merely because they have access to more resources. By sustainable development, we are not advocating a Western-type lifestyle for everybody in the whole world. That itself would be unsustainable. What is being advocated is a decent standard of living, access to sufficient food

---

[293] *Id.*, ch. 5.

[294] *Id.* at 33.

[295] Principle 5, *supra* note 20.

[296] Principle 8, *supra* note 20.

[297] Of course, the document itself is a non-binding one. However, the difference in language adopted even within the various principles is striking.

and safe drinking water, a shelter above the head, the ability to give a decent education to children, access to proper health care and the right to live in a healthy environment, necessary to lead a healthy life. Once these basic amenities are in place for everybody, one may then perhaps speak of luxuries that those in developed countries take for granted. Unfortunately, the majority of the world's population does not enjoy even these basic amenities.[298]

The UN Millennium Declaration adopted at the UN Millennium Summit[299] is also relevant in this regard. In his report to the United Nations, the UN Secretary-General declared that "extreme poverty is an affront to our common humanity."[300] The international community pledged in the Millennium Declaration to halve, by the year 2015, the proportion of the people whose income is less than $1 a day.[301] The international community further declared that:

> We will spare no effort to free our fellow men, women and children from the abject and dehumanizing conditions of extreme poverty, to which more than a billion of them are currently subjected. We are committed to making the right to development a reality for everyone and to freeing the entire human race from want.[302]

The Johannesburg Declaration also recognized the twin threat of poverty and consumption and production patterns: "We recognize that poverty eradication, changing consumption and production patterns and protecting and managing the natural resource base for economic and social development are overarching objectives of and essential requirements for sustainable development."[303] Poverty eradication "is the greatest global challenge facing the world today and an indispensable requirement

---

[298] More than 1 billion people in the world today live on less than U.S. $1 a day. More than double that number lack access to basic sanitation. *See* World Bank, *World Development Report 2000/01* (World Bank, 2001). *See also* Atapattu, *supra* note 290, at 307.

[299] UN Millennium Declaration, A/Res/55/2, *available at* http://www.un.org/millennium/declaration/ares552e.htm.

[300] Kofi Annan, "We the Peoples: The Role of the United Nations in the 21st Century" (New York, 2000), *available at* http://www.un.org/millennium/sg/report/full.htm.

[301] Millennium Declaration, *supra* note 299, para. 19.

[302] *Id.*, para. 11.

[303] UN Doc. A/CONF.199/20, para. 11, *available at* http://www.johannesburgsummit.org/.

for sustainable development."[304] The Plan of Implementation further stressed the important role of concerted action while noting the primary responsibility of each country to eradicate poverty. This would include action at all levels to: halve, by the year 2015, the proportion of people whose income is less than $1 a day;[305] establish a world solidarity fund to eradicate poverty and promote social and human development in developing countries; develop national programs for sustainable development; promote women's equal access to and full participation in decision making at all levels, eliminating all forms of violence and discrimination against women, deliver basic health services, ensure that children everywhere have access to education; increase food availability and affordability; combat desertification; provide clean drinking water and adequate sanitation to protect human health and the environment; improve rural infrastructure; and improve access by indigenous people to economic activities.[306]

Five years after the adoption of the Millennium Declaration and the Millennium Development Goals, the UN Secretary-General submitted his follow-up report to the General Assembly.[307] He noted that "more than one billion people still live below the extreme poverty line of one dollar per day, and 20,000 die from poverty each day."[308] Drawing a link between poverty, development and conflict, the Secretary-General noted that "we will not enjoy development without security, we will not enjoy security without development, and we will not enjoy either without respect for human rights."[309] During the past 25 years, the world has experienced the most dramatic reduction in extreme poverty, partly due to the progress in China and India, yet dozens of countries have become poorer.[310] We need to see the Millennium Development Goals as part of an even larger development agenda. The Secretary-General noted that extreme poverty has many causes, "ranging from adverse geography through poor or corrupt governance (including neglect of marginalized communities) to the ravages of conflict and its aftermath."[311]

---

[304] Plan of Implementation, *supra* note 60, para. 7.

[305] This is one of the Millennium Development Goals.

[306] Plan of Implementation, *supra* note 60.

[307] "In Larger Freedom: Towards Development, Security and Human Rights For All," A/59/2005, *available at* http://www.un.org/.

[308] *Id.*, para. 9.

[309] *Id.*, para. 17.

[310] *Id.*, paras. 25 and 26.

[311] *Id.*, para. 12.

International human rights law recognizes the basic right of everyone to an adequate standard of living;[312] however, this basic right has eluded the majority of the world's community.[313] Poverty is a major violator of human rights as well as a major polluter—it leads to the violation of other rights relating to health, education, work and privacy and causes environmental degradation. Poverty also leads to the denial of procedural rights, as those who are poor will not be interested in participating in the decision-making process, obtaining relevant information or to have access to justice.[314] Thus, poverty is a condition that cuts across a wide spectrum of issues and requires a holistic approach.

The draft Earth Charter[315] noted in its Preamble that:

> The dominant patterns of production and consumption are causing environmental devastation, the depletion of resources, and a massive extinction of species. Communities are being undermined. The benefits of development are not shared equitably and the gap between rich and poor is widening. Injustice, poverty, ignorance, and violent conflict are widespread and the cause of great suffering.[316]

Part III of the Charter deals with social and economic justice. Draft Principle 9(a) stresses the need to "guarantee the right to potable water, clean air, food security, uncontaminated soil, shelter, and safe sanitation, allocating the national and international resources needed."[317] Draft Principle 10(a) stresses the need to promote the equitable distribution of wealth both *within* and *among* nations. The need to realize intra-generational equity—i.e., equity among those who form part of the present generation—is extremely important.[318] The present generation tends to get left out in the discussion on inter-generational equity—i.e., equity among generations.

---

[312] Art. 11, ICESCR, *supra* note 259.

[313] This part is drawn from Atapattu, *supra* note 290.

[314] *Id.* at 308.

[315] The Earth Charter, *available at* http://www.earthcharter.org/earthcharter/charter.htm.

[316] *Id.*

[317] *Id.*

[318] For a discussion of inter and intra-generational equity, *see* EDITH BROWN WEISS, IN FAIRNESS TO FUTURE GENERATIONS: INTERNATIONAL LAW, COMMON PATRIMONY AND INTERGENERATIONAL EQUITY (1989).

It is only recently that poverty was seen through the human rights lens. In human rights parlance, eradicating poverty really means addressing, economic, social and cultural rights of people. Urgent attention should be paid to the progressive realization of these rights. While there is increasing recognition that these rights are justiciable,[319] it is necessary to give attention to alternative mechanisms, such as national human rights commissions, as courts can be expensive and, therefore, out of the reach for the majority of people.[320]

## 5.  From State Responsibility to the Principle of Global Partnership

The cornerstone of public international law is the principle of territorial sovereignty of states: all states are sovereign and equal.[321] The converse of this principle means that in the same way that states are sovereign within their territory, they must refrain from undertaking or authorizing activities that may cause damage to the territory of other states.[322] This notion of territorial sovereignty, consisting of rights and obligations, forms the basic foundation of international law. It follows that in the event the sovereignty of another state is violated, reparations must be made.[323] This forms the basic foundation of the principles of state responsibility,[324] which also constituted the foundation of traditional international environmental law as reflected in cases such as the *Trail Smelter Arbitration*,[325] *Lac Lanoux Arbitration*,[326] the *Nuclear Tests* cases[327] and the *Gut Dam Arbitration*.[328] This principle is codified in the Stockholm Declaration:

---

[319]  *See* Albie Sachs, *Enforcing Socio-Economic Rights, in* SUSTAINABLE JUSTICE, *supra* note 290, at 57.

[320]  *See* Atapattu, *supra* note 290, at 309.

[321]  Art. 2(1) of the UN Charter.

[322]  *See* the Island of Palmas Case, 2 HCR 84 (PCA 1928).

[323]  *See* Chorzow Factory Case (Jurisdiction), 1927 P.C.I.J. (ser. A), No. 9, at 21 and Corfu Channel Case (U.K. v. Albania), 1949 ICJ 4, 23.

[324]  For a detailed discussion of state responsibility, *see* IAN BROWNLIE, SYSTEM OF THE LAW OF NATIONS: STATE RESPONSIBILITY—PART I (1983) and the work of the International Law Commission on which subject it has been working almost since its inception, and draft articles adopted in 2001, *available at* http://www.un.org/ law/ilc/texts/ State_responsibility/responsibility_articles(e).pdf.

[325]  USA v. Canada, 3 RIAA 1907 (1941).

[326]  France v. Spain, 24 ILR 101 (1957).

[327]  Australia v. France and New Zealand v. France, 1974 ICJ 253 (Dec. 20).

[328]  8 ILM 118 (1969). In addition, the *Corfu Channel Case* (*supra* note 323) is often cited in relation to state responsibility for environmental damage, although the case did not involve an environmental problem. Its significance lies in the endorsement of the principle of harm prevention—i.e., the obligation not to use one's territory knowingly for acts contrary to international law.

States have, in accordance with the Charter of the United Nations and the principles of international law, the sovereign right to exploit their own resources pursuant to their own environmental policies, and the responsibility to ensure that activities within their jurisdiction or control do not cause damage to the environment of other States or of areas beyond the limits of national jurisdiction.[329]

However, principles of state responsibility are not suitable for modern environmental issues for several reasons.[330] Firstly, state responsibility arises only after an obligation has been breached.[331] In the environmental context, where prevention is more important than repair, a regime of state responsibility cannot offer a meaningful solution. Moreover, it cannot offer any solution in a situation where a species or an ecosystem has been irrevocably lost. Secondly, while state responsibility can be useful in a bilateral relationship where the author of the damage and the victim/s are readily identifiable, it is not so useful in relation to complex environmental problems, such as global warming or ozone depletion that are global in dimension and affect the entire international community. Thirdly, establishing causation necessary to bring a claim against another state is virtually impossible in relation to global environmental issues, as there could be as many victims as there are perpetrators. Fourthly, traditional forms of remedies associated with state responsibility, such as restitution or compensation,[332] may not be suitable for environmental damage.[333] Fifthly, connected to the issue of causation, environmental damage is often cumulative and long term. When significant damage finally manifests itself, it may be too late to take remedial action. Finally, the operations giving rise to environmental damage are often undertaken by private entities. As a general principle, a state is not liable for the activities of private individuals, unless it can be established that the state failed to control the activities of the private individual. Thus, establishing imputability can give rise to problems.[334] Even when all the criteria of state responsibility can be established, there has been a general reluctance on the part of states to bring a claim against another state for the damage caused by environmental issues.[335] The Chernobyl incident of 1986 provides a good example of

---

[329] Principle 21, Stockholm Declaration, *supra* note 2.

[330] *See* Jutta Brunnee, *Of Sense and Sensibility: Reflections on International Liability Regimes as Tools for Environmental Protection*, 53 ICLQ 351 (2004).

[331] *See* ILC Draft arts. 1 and 2, *supra* note 324.

[332] ILC Draft arts. 34–37, *supra* note 324.

[333] The ICJ recognized this in the *Case Concerning the Gabcikovo Nagymaros Project. See* discussion in Chapter 2.

[334] *See* ILC Draft Articles on rules of attributability; BROWNLIE, *supra* note 324, at 159.

[335] *See* IAN BROWNLIE, THE RULE OF LAW IN INTERNATIONAL AFFAIRS, 189 (1998) who

this.[336] Despite the rather clear-cut nature of the incident, the existence of quantifiable damage at least in the immediate term, the ability to establish the causal link, and the obvious failure on the part of the Soviet government to provide information of the accident, provided a rich ground for a possible claim against the Soviet Union by several states. Yet, in reality, this did not happen.

Brownlie notes the deficiencies in the state responsibility regime as follows:

> Chernobyl and its aftermath casts doubt on the efficacy of the approach to environmental disasters by way of state responsibility. States clearly did not regard the legal approach as being especially relevant. The State responsibility, or liability, approach is about allocation of losses and reparation. It is thus *retrospective*. In the case of the protection of the environment it is prospective and prevention action which is called for.[337]

Consequently, international environmental law has moved away from a confrontational approach based on state responsibility to a more regulatory approach. Indeed, modern environmental problems, which require the concerted efforts of each and every member of the international community, cannot be addressed without international cooperation. A single non-cooperating state has the potential to undermine the efforts of the entire international community. International environmental law, for the most part, consists of treaty law based on mutual cooperation. Many treaties provide for the establishment of a Conference of Parties (COP) to oversee the implementation of the treaty in question.[338]

The Stockholm Declaration recognized the need for international cooperation as early as 1972:

> To achieve this environmental goal will demand the acceptance of responsibility by citizens and communities and by enterprises

---

noted in relation to state responsibility and the environment: "Apart from the finding of a cause of action, the requirement of damage as a necessary condition of claim bears an uneasy relation to the scientific proof of a certain threshold of damage caused by an overall rise in radiation or other forms of pollution and problems of multiple causation then arise."

[336] *Id.* at 190.

[337] *Id.* at 192–93 (emphasis in original). Nevertheless, its value as a tool to seek remedies for environmental damage in a bilateral relationship still remains.

[338] *E.g.*, art. 7, UN Framework Convention on Climate Change, 1771 UNTS 107 (1992) and art. 6, Vienna Convention for the Protection of the Ozone Layer, *supra* note 24.

and institutions at every level; all sharing equitably in common efforts. . . . Local and national governments will bear the greatest burden for large-scale environmental policy and action within their jurisdictions. International co-operation is also needed in order to raise resources to support the developing countries in carrying out their responsibilities in this field. A growing class of environmental problems, because they are regional or global in extent or because they affect the common international realm, will require extensive co-operation among nations and action by international organizations in the common interest.[339]

Principle 24 further strengthened the call for international cooperation:

International matters concerning the protection and improvement of the environment should be handled in a co-operative spirit by all countries, big and small, on an equal footing. Co-operation through multilateral or bilateral arrangements or other appropriate means is essential to effectively control, prevent, reduce and eliminate adverse environmental effects resulting from activities conducted in all spheres, in such a way that due account is taken of the sovereignty and interests of all States.[340]

Furthermore, present day environmental problems require a substantial allocation of resources—both money and technology—which can be beyond the reach of many developing countries. Thus, faced with the prospect of non-cooperation due to lack of resources, which can undermine efforts by other countries, the only viable option is to ensure technology transfer etc., through international cooperation. The international fund established under the framework of the Montreal Protocol is an innovative method to ensure compliance and will be discussed in Chapter 5.

The Rio Declaration has taken the notion of international cooperation one step forward by adopting the notion of global partnership. The Declaration refers to "the goal of establishing *a new and equitable global partnership* through the creation of new levels of cooperation among states, key sectors of societies and people."[341] and calls upon states to "cooperate in a spirit of global partnership to conserve, protect and restore the health and integrity of the Earth's ecosystem."[342]

---

[339] Stockholm Declaration, Preamble, *supra* note 2.

[340] *Id.*, art. 24.

[341] Preamble, Rio Declaration, *supra* note 20 (emphasis added).

[342] *Id.*, Principle 7.

Admittedly, the formulation adopted in the Rio Declaration is wider than that in the Stockholm Declaration. The former requires cooperation in order to achieve a global partnership between various groups of entities. The concept of global partnership is now breaking new ground in international environmental law, particularly in relation to sustainable development. It is increasingly being realized by states and other entities alike that without such partnership, it is difficult to achieve sustainable development. Many obstacles to this partnership, however, remain, including how to operationalize it, its parameters and its legal effect.

The UN Secretary-General urged the international community to develop a global partnership between rich and poor countries in order to eradicate poverty,[343] which he noted was reaffirmed and elaborated at the International Conference on Financing for Development, Monterrey[344] and the WSSD. He stated that "it is worth recalling the terms of that historic compact" but regretted that this promise had not been delivered:

> Each developing country has primary responsibility for its own development—strengthening governance, combating corruption and putting in place the policies and investments to drive private-sector-led growth and maximize domestic resources available to fund national development strategies. Developed countries, on their side, undertake that developing countries which adopt transparent, credible and properly costed development strategies will receive the full support they need, in the form of increased development assistance, a more development-oriented trade system and wider and deeper debt relief.[345]

The notion of global partnership is tied to the common but differentiated responsibility principle in Principle 7 of the Rio Declaration. Many developed countries view this principle with much suspicion. They feel that an unfair and disproportionate burden is placed on their shoulders while developing countries reap benefits from the technology and wealth of developed countries. This argument, however, does not take the historical context into account. Many developed countries achieved their present day wealth and advancement by creating much of the world's pollution. The phenomena of global warming and acid rain are good examples. Thus, developing countries feel that if they are to fulfill their obligations under international treaties, developed countries should bear a greater share of

---

[343] In Larger Freedom, *supra* note 307, para. 32.

[344] *See* http://www.un.org/esa/ffd/.

[345] *Id.*, para. 32.

the burden, as they are the main contributors to the present situation. They feel that it is a matter of equity, and that a global partnership is necessary to redress the pre-set imbalance in international society. Indeed, the common but differentiated responsibility principle stems from the principle of equity and will be discussed in Chapter 5.

How does global partnership relate to sustainable development? The term "global partnership" appeared for the first time in the Rio Declaration on Environment and Development. The Preamble is instructive in this regard. It provides: "with the goal of establishing a new and equitable global partnership through the creation of new levels of cooperation among States, key sectors of societies and people." According to Principle 7, "States shall cooperate in a spirit of global partnership to conserve, protect and restore the health and integrity of the Earth's ecosystem." The Preamble indicates that global partnership is an expanded version of the principle of cooperation but also that cooperation is not confined to traditional actors of international law. It clearly extends to non-state actors and individuals. However, cooperation is not synonymous with global partnership, for the simple reason that the word "partnership" clearly implies much more than mere cooperation. The Preamble refers to the need to create "a new and equitable global partnership"; thus, global partnership seems to be based on two concepts: equity and cooperation. By extending this to encompass non-state actors, the Rio Declaration has acknowledged the rapidly changing nature of international law, particularly in relation to protecting the environment. By including this in the section on common but differentiated responsibility principle, the Declaration seems to convey the message that a more equitable level of cooperation is necessary between developing and developed countries. Developing countries are clearly not in a position to implement their environmental obligations or to fulfill their aspirations without the assistance of developed countries, whether by way of technology transfer or transfer of funds.

Agenda 21 is also relevant in this regard. It noted that "In order to meet the challenges of environment and development, States have decided to establish a new global partnership."[346] It further noted that in order to do so, confrontation must be overcome, and a climate of genuine cooperation and solidarity must be fostered. It is thus clear that the Rio Conference envisaged a new kind of international cooperation based on a global partnership.

---

[346] Agenda 21, UN Doc. A/CONF.151/26, *reprinted in* 31 ILM 874 (1992), para. 2.1.

## 6. Environment, Armed Conflict and Sustainable Development

There are several other developments that are related to environmental protection and sustainable development but which will not be discussed in detail here. One such development is the environmental impact of armed conflict; given the current debate on global terrorism, many are drawing a link between terrorism and sustainable development.[347] There is no doubt that wars and armed conflicts cause environmental degradation. Two international conventions address this issue: Environment Modifications Convention of 1977[348] addresses the issue of using the environment as a weapon and Protocol I Additional to the Geneva Conventions of 1949[349] prohibits methods and means of warfare that are likely to cause widespread, long-term and severe damage to the natural environment.[350] In this context, it has become necessary to discuss both environmental impact of armed conflict as well as environmental factors giving rise to conflict.[351] In addition, conflict as a cause of unsustainable development has also received international attention. The WCED points out how environmental stress has caused conflicts in many parts of the world, particularly in Africa, giving rise to a new category of refugees—environmental refugees.[352] Moreover, global environmental problems, such as global warming, can pose a security threat and can lead to conflict as states compete for fewer resources.[353]

Similarly, armed conflict and terrorism lead to unsustainable development as they make a huge dent on scarce resources, particularly in developing countries.[354] While not undermining the importance of national security, it does not justify the colossal amount of money spent today on arms and wars. It is also a cause for concern that military spending has increased substantially not only developed countries (with the United

---

[347] *See* NORMAN MYERS, ULTIMATE SECURITY (1993); Sumudu Atapattu, *Sustainable Development and Terrorism: International Linkages and a Case Study of Sri Lanka*, 30 WILLIAM & MARY ENVTL. L. & POL'Y REV. 273 (2006).

[348] ENMOD Convention, 1108 UNTS 151 (1977).

[349] Protocol I Additional to the Geneva Conventions of 12 August 1949 and Relating to the Protection of Victims of International Armed Conflicts, Dec. 12, 1977, 1125 UNTS 3 (1977).

[350] *Id.*, art. 35. *See also id.*, art. 55.

[351] *See* UNEP, *Understanding Environment, Conflict and Cooperation* (2004), *available at* http://www.unep.org/PDF//ECC.pdf.

[352] OUR COMMON FUTURE, *supra* note 11, at 291.

[353] *Id.* at 294.

[354] *See* Atapattu, *supra* note 347.

States being at the top of the list) but also in many developing countries.[355] The large amounts of money expended on military activities leave governments with little to spend on essential services, such as health care, education and poverty alleviation programs, giving rise to a vicious cycle of "poverty breeding conflict and conflict breeding poverty."[356]

## 7.  Development Assistance and Environmental Protection

Whether development assistance should promote environmental protection or support environmentally unsound development projects has become a hotly debated issue in recent times. Although donor agencies did not earlier take into account the environmental impact of their development assistance, due to many disasters in developing countries, they have generated a code of practice, as well as environmental guidelines, which must be complied with in relation to development assistance. The World Bank, which has been criticized in the past for its bad environmental record,[357] has developed an impressive body of environmental guidelines, and the preparation of an environmental impact assessment is mandatory for many Bank supported projects.[358] In addition, it supports environmental protection projects and sustainable development features high on its agenda. What brought about such a change?

Many other international bodies, as well as official development assistance and donor agencies, now require the environmental assessment of development activities that they support. Resistance to the inclusion of environmental protection to development assistance was based on the suspicion that it will constitute a conditionality that will be used to withhold aid. Experience has, however, shown that including environmental appraisal in the project design itself has led to many success stories in developing countries. The Bank has funded many unsustainable projects in the past, the most controversial perhaps being the Narmada valley project in India.[359] There is no doubt, however, that, as a result of many disasters and protests, donor agencies have become increasingly environmentally and socially conscious, which is reflected in their policy documents and guide-

---

[355] *See* SIPRI YEARBOOK 2003: ARMAMENTS, DISARMAMANET & INTERNATIONAL SECURITY (2003), *available at* http://editors.sipri.se/pubs/yb03/aboutyb.html.

[356] *See* Atapattu, *supra* note 347.

[357] *See* Jacob Werksman, *Greening Bretton Woods, in* GREENING INTERNATIONAL LAW 65 (Philippe Sands ed., 1994).

[358] *See* the discussion in Chapter 4, Section C.6. *See also* http://www.worldbank.org/.

[359] *See* Werksman, *supra* note 357, at 73.

lines. The Bank, in particular, because of its link with both environmental protection and human rights, has increasingly become interested in poverty eradication and supports many programs toward this end.[360]

## 8. World Bank Environmental Guidelines and the Environmental Strategy

While the track record of the World Bank in relation to environmentally sound projects left a lot to be desired,[361] the World Bank has shifted its focus to environmental protection and sustainable development in relation to its development assistance. According to the operational policies of the Bank, the Bank requires the environmental assessment of projects to ensure that they are environmentally sound and sustainable.[362] The *Manual* further provides that the Bank favors preventive measures over mitigatory or compensatory measures, whenever possible. The environmental assessment (EA) takes into account the natural environment, human health and safety, social aspects and transboundary and global environmental aspects.

The borrower is responsible for carrying out an EA. For purposes of evaluating the environmental impact, projects are categorized into four groups: category A are those projects that are likely to have a significant adverse environmental impact; category B are those projects whose impact on the environment is less than those in category A; category C are those projects likely to have minimal or no adverse environmental impacts; and category FI are those projects that involve investment through a financial intermediary in sub-projects that may result in adverse environmental impacts.

The *Operational Manual* has several provisions on public participation. It provides that for all category A and B projects, during the environmental assessment process, the borrower is required to consult groups that may be affected by the project and local NGOs about the project's environmental aspects and take their views into account. The borrower is required to initiate such consultations as early as possible. For category A projects, the borrower is required to consult these groups *at least twice*.[363] In addition, the borrower is required to consult these groups throughout the project implementation process as necessary.[364]

---

[360] *See* http://worldbank.org/ for its activities on sustainable development.

[361] *See* Werksman, *supra* note 357, at 69.

[362] The *World Bank Operational Manual, Operational Policies, Environmental Assessment* OP 4.01 (Jan. 1999).

[363] *Id.* These instances are: (1) shortly after environmental screening and before the terms of reference for the EA are finalized; and (2) once a draft EA has been prepared (para. 15)

[364] *Id.*

In order to facilitate consultations, the borrower is required to provide relevant material in a timely manner. This must be in a form and language that are understandable and accessible to the groups being consulted.[365] For category A projects, the borrower is required to make the draft EA report available at a public place accessible to affected groups and NGOs.[366]

In addition, the Bank has prepared many handbooks and guidelines, including the *Pollution Prevention and Abatement Handbook*.[367] This handbook describes prevention and abatement measures and emission levels that are acceptable to the Bank. It contains provisions on the environmental factors to be taken into account in project design and implementation.

The environmental themes that the Bank is involved in include: biodiversity, forests and forestry, land resources management, natural resources management, water resources management, pollution management, global climate change, Montreal Protocol and ozone depleting substances, environmental assessment and the Global Environmental Facility.[368]

Prepared in 2001, the *Environment Strategy* of the Bank is considered as informing all environmental aspects of Bank's work.[369] According to the *Executive Summary*, the report is "based on an understanding that sustainable development, built on a balance of economic growth, social cohesion, and environmental protection, is fundamental to the Bank's core objective of lasting poverty alleviation—a link that has been recognized by international environmental conventions and in the International Development Goals (IDGs) set forth in the United Nations Millennium Declaration in 2000."[370]

With regard to environmental issues, the Bank applies following principles in their work:

- focus on the positive linkages between poverty reduction and environmental protection
- focus first on local environmental benefits, and build on the overlaps with regional and global benefits

---

[365] *Id.*, para. 16.

[366] *Id.*, para. 17.

[367] *Available at* http://www.worldbank.org/.

[368] *Id.*

[369] *Available at* http://www.worldbank.org/.

[370] *Executive Summary, Making Sustainable Commitments—An Environment Strategy for the World Bank* xvii (2001).

- address the vulnerability and adaptation needs of individual developing countries
- facilitate transfer of financial resources to client countries to help them meet the costs of generating global and environmental benefits not matched by national benefits
- stimulate markets for environmental public goods.[371]

## 9. The Global Environment Facility

Along with the UN Development Program (UNDP) and the UN Environment Program (UNEP), the World Bank is an implementing agency of the Global Environment Facility (GEF). The GEF was established in 1991 initially to fund activities in relation to ozone depletion. It has since been expanded to support projects in six focal areas: biodiversity; climate change; ozone depletion; international waters; land degradation; and persistent organic compounds.[372]

According to the GEF Web site, biodiversity makes up nearly half of all GEF projects. It is the financial mechanism for the Convention on Biological Diversity and receives guidance from the Conference of Parties (COP) on policy, strategy, program priorities and eligibility criteria. Projects generally deal with one or more of four critical ecosystem types: arid and semi-arid zones; coastal, marine and freshwater resources; forests; and mountains.[373] Between 1991 and 2004, the GEF has allocated $1.89 billion in grants and mobilized an additional $3.8 billion in co-financing.[374]

The GEF is also the financial mechanism for the UN Framework Convention on Climate Change (UNFCCC) and receives guidance from the COP. Climate change projects are designed to reduce risks of global climate change while providing energy for sustainable development. These programs are organized into four areas: (1) removing barriers to energy efficiency and energy conservation; (2) promoting the adoption of renewable energy by removing barriers and reducing implementation costs; (3) reducing the long-term costs of low greenhouse gas emitting energy technologies; and (4) supporting the development of sustainable transport.[375] During the period of 1991–2004, GEF has allocated $1.74 billion to climate change with more than $9.29 billion in co-financing.[376]

---

[371] http://Inweb18.worldbank.org/ESSD/essdext.nsf/41ByDocName/Environmental Themes.

[372] GEF Focal Areas, *at* http://www.gefweb.org/Projects/Focal_Areas/focal_areas/html.

[373] *Id.*

[374] *Id.*

[375] *Id.*

[376] *Id.*

With regard to international waters, three categories have been identified for funding: water bodies; integrated land and water projects; and contaminants. GEF projects seek to reverse the degradation of international waters and enable countries to learn more about water-related issues that they share, find ways to cooperate and identify the need to make domestic changes to solve problems. During the period 1991–2004, GEF allocated $767 million to international water initiatives and generated additional co-financing of $2.11 billion.[377]

With regard to ozone depletion, GEF has been working in partnership with the Montreal Protocol to fund projects that enable the Russian Federation and Eastern Europe and Central Asian countries to phase out their use of ozone depleting substances. Between 1991 and 2004, the GEF had allocated more than $177 million to projects to phase out ozone depleting substances and generated additional co-financing of $182 million.[378]

Due to its link to biodiversity and other global environmental problems, land degradation was identified as a new focal area in 2002 and in September 2003, GEF was designated as the official financial mechanism for the UN Convention to Combat Desertification. Between 2002–2004, GEF has funded projects for more than $72 million focusing primarily on deforestation and desertification and spent an additional amount of $155 million in co-financing.[379]

In 2002 the GEF Assembly approved the addition of persistent organic pollutants (POPs) as a new focal area, and the Stockholm Convention on POPs named the GEF as its interim financial mechanism, pending its entry into force. POPs are highly stable compounds that circulate globally and accumulate in the tissue of living organisms causing numerous problems. They are also a threat to biodiversity and from 2001 to 2004, GEF has funded more than $141 million projects with co-financing of $91 million.[380]

Since its modest inception in 1991, the GEF has firmly established itself as the official funding mechanism of the United Nations in relation to major environmental issues. It is likely that the current list of six focal areas would grow, encompassing all global environmental problems. This mechanism has ensured the participation of developing countries in environmental treaties, which has proven to be crucial to the success of these treaty regimes.

---

[377] *Id.*

[378] *Id.*

[379] *Id.*

[380] *Id.*

While it seems that the Bank is actively involved in environmental protection and promoting sustainable development, this has not always been the case. The Bretton Woods Institutions, of which the Bank is a member, have been soundly criticized for funding ecological and economic disasters in developing countries.[381] It is only recently that the Bank has got involved in social issues, including environmental issues, although it has consistently shied away from attaching conditionalities to development aid. Although it was established to rebuild Europe after the Second World War, it has got increasingly involved in social issues, including good governance, judicial reform and more recently, sustainable development. Despite these efforts, particularly on the part of the Bank, there are still ardent critics of the Bank.[382] With regard to the progress made by the Bank in integrating environment with development, it has been pointed out:

> Although the Bank can be said to have made significant progress in establishing policies that are designed to promote sustainable development and environmental protection, and to establish institutional structures within the Bank for monitoring the implementation of these policies, the conclusions of UNCED suggest that the degree to which these policies are implemented and enforced will depend on deeper institutional reforms that open the Bank's governance to accountability to those outside the Bank.[383]

To be fair, the Bank has tried hard to reform itself and to make itself more environment-conscious. One major criticism of its work has constantly been that the Bank does not provide for public participation in relation to its projects. This has been remedied, to a certain extent, by providing for mandatory public participation in relation to projects that undergo the environmental impact assessment process. The borrower is also required to provide information in a timely manner.

The establishment of an Inspection Panel by the World Bank in 1993 is significant in this regard. The primary purpose of the Panel, consisting of three members, is to:

> address the concerns of the people who may be affected by Bank projects and to ensure that the Bank adheres to its operational policies and procedures during design, preparation and implementation phases of projects.[384]

---

[381] *See* Werksman, *supra* note 357.

[382] *Id.*

[383] *Id.* at 71.

[384] http://web.worldbank.org/WBSITE/EXTERNAL/EXTINSPECTIONPANEL/ 0,,menuPK:64129249~pagePK:64132081~piPK:64132052~theSitePK:380794,00.html.

This is the first time that an international organization has established a procedure to entertain concerns by people who may be affected by projects funded by it. It provides a forum to private citizens to forward a complaint if their rights have been violated by the activities of the Bank. At a minimum, complainants must establish that:

- They live in the project area (or represent people who do) and are likely to be affected adversely by project activities.
- They believe that actual or likely harm results from failure by the Bank to follow its policies and procedures.
- Their concerns have been discussed with Bank management and they are not satisfied with the outcome.[385]

It is significant that aggrieved parties can be represented by another party in relation to the complaint. Since its inception in 1993, 27 complaints have been referred to the Panel and its reports are publicly available.[386]

The very establishment of a panel of this nature is a significant development in relation to the World Bank, particularly given the criticism that Bank's activities are not transparent and no public participation is envisaged for projects funded by the Bank.

## C. CONCLUSION

There is no doubt international environmental law has come a long way since the Stockholm Conference in 1972. It is even possible to talk of another sub-branch called international sustainable development law.

Having surveyed the development of international environmental law and other related developments, such as good governance, human rights and development assistance, it is now proposed to look more closely at some of these "principles" that have influenced the development of international environmental law in recent years. While many of these principles have not yet entered the sacred portals of customary international law, and many will remain so for many years to come, they have undoubtedly influenced the decision-making process in relation to the environment and are essential components of sustainable development. Sustainable development, defined and discussed in detail in Chapter 2, informs the entire discussion in this publication. It is envisaged that the other concepts selected for discussion here—the precautionary principle, environmental assessment and participatory rights, the common but differentiated responsibil-

---

[385] http://web.worldbank.org/WBSITE/EXTERNAL/EXTINSPECTION-PANEL/0,,contentMDK:20173251~menuPK:64129467~pagePK:64129751~piPK:64128378~theSitePK:380794,00.html.

[386] *Id.*

ity principle, and the polluter pays principle—all facilitate the progress toward sustainable development. Their ultimate objective is to achieve sustainable development, which is not strictly a principle, but a goal. In addition to the principles selected for this study, other principles have also emerged. Some of these are: the principle of global partnership and the principle of prior informed consent (PIC).

The principle of global partnership and the prior informed consent principle are both based on the principle of cooperation and information. Cooperation in good faith forms one of the core principles of international law.[387] Tribunals have frequently referred to this principle[388] as do many international instruments.[389] In the *Case Concerning the Gabcikovo Nagymaros Project*, the ICJ said that the parties were under an obligation to negotiate a settlement in good faith.

The general obligation to cooperate has been translated into many specific obligations such as the obligation to provide information; ensure public participation; notification, exchange of information and consultation in relation to potential transboundary environmental issues; provision of information and assistance in the event of emergencies; and environmental impact assessment procedures.[390]

Prior informed consent has emerged in response to hazardous activities, such as trade in hazardous waste and persistent organic compounds. The conventions adopted in this regard[391] have taken the principle of notification and consultation one step further by actually requiring the consent

---

[387] *See* Article 1 of the UN Charter, which lays down the purposes of the United Nations. One of the purposes is "to achieve international co-operation in solving international problems of an economic, social, cultural or humanitarian character." Art. 1.3. *See also* SANDS, *supra* note 18, at 249.

[388] *See* North Sea Continental Shelf Cases, 1969 ICJ 3; MOX Case, Application Oct. 25, 2001, which was filed before the International Tribunal for the Law of the Sea (ITLOS) where Ireland claimed that the United Kingdom failed to cooperate as required by Articles 123 and 197 of the UN Law of the Sea Convention.

[389] *E.g.*, arts. 123 and 197 of the UN Law of the Sea Convention, 21 ILM 1261 (1992), 333 UNTS 3; art. 2(2) of the Vienna Convention on the Protection of the Ozone Layer, *supra* note 24; art. 5 of the Convention on Biological Diversity, *supra* note 241; Principle 24 of the Stockholm Declaration, *supra* note 7; Principles 7 and 27 of the Rio Declaration, *supra* note 20.

[390] *See* SANDS, *supra* note 18, at 250.

[391] *E.g.*, Rotterdam Convention on Prior Informed Consent Procedure for Certain Hazardous Chemicals and Pesticides in International Trade, 38 ILM 1 (1999), signed Sept. 11, 1998, entered into force Feb. 24, 2004; and Basel Convention on the Control of Transboundary Movement of Hazardous Wastes and Their Disposal, *supra* note 199.

of the recipient state. Prior informed consent has three important components: information must be provided well in advance of the activity—in
other words, information must be timely; in deciding whether to give consent or not, proper information of the activity is necessary; finally, consent
for the activity must be expressly given. Information must be sufficiently
detailed to enable the recipient to come to a conclusion about the activity
in question. Information not provided in a timely manner is not considered
proper information. Woven into this is the requirement for consultations
and negotiations in good faith prior to giving consent. The issue whether
consent can be implied could arise in practice, and while the answer may
depend on the circumstances in a given case, the better approach may be
to say that consent has to be expressly given. Implied consent can give rise
to many difficulties.

There is no doubt that many new principles and concepts will continue
to emerge in response to environmental and developmental problems. It
is hoped that the analysis in this publication will facilitate and inform the
process of developing new norms and principles to address increasingly
complex environmental problems that human beings will no doubt continue to create.

CHAPTER 2

# SUSTAINABLE DEVELOPMENT:
# EMERGENCE AND APPLICATION

Humanity stands at a defining moment in history. We are confronted with a perpetuation of disparities between and within nations, a worsening of poverty, hunger, ill health and illiteracy, and the continuing deterioration of the ecosystems on which we depend for our well-being. However, integration of environment and development concerns and greater attention to them will lead to the fulfillment of basic needs, improved living standards for all, better protected and managed ecosystems and a safer, more prosperous time. No nation can achieve this on its own; but together we can—in a global partnership for sustainable development.

Preamble, Agenda 21[1]

## A. INTRODUCTION

Compared to international environmental law, the modern notion of sustainable development has a shorter history. Nonetheless, it can be argued that sustainable development is as old as civilization itself. Historic evidence suggests that ancient people led a very sustainable way of life.[2] Sustainable development seeks to provide a solution to both environmental problems and developmental problems facing the international community today.

The roots of modern sustainable development can be found in the World Conservation Strategy drafted by the International Union for the Conservation of Nature and Natural Resources (IUCN) in 1980.[3] It was not until 1987, however, that it gained popularity, with the publication of the much acclaimed report of the World Commission on Environment and

---

[1] Preamble, Agenda 21, UN Doc. A/CONF.156/26, *reprinted in* 31 ILM 874 (1992), adopted at the UN Conference on Environment and Development, 1992.

[2] *See* the Separate opinion of Judge Weeramantry in the *Case Concerning the Gabcikovo Nagymaros Project (Hungary v. Slovakia)* 1997 ICJ 7, discussed later in the chapter.

[3] IUCN, *World Conservation Strategy, 1980.* For a synopsis, *see* http://www.unep.org/geo/geo3/english/049.htm.

Development (WCED).[4] The WCED was appointed by the UN General Assembly in 1983 with the specific mandate to reconcile the increasingly polarizing debate on environmental protection versus economic development between developing and developed countries, which was hampering environmental protection measures proposed by international bodies.[5] The reason for this polarization was due to the difference of approach between developed countries and developing countries. While developing countries felt that environmental protection was a luxury they could ill afford, developed countries felt that time was already running out in relation to environmental issues. Developing countries also felt that it was unfair of developed countries to insist on environmental protection, which they felt would be at the expense of economic development. They argued that it was developed countries that had caused these environmental problems, so why should developing countries spend their limited resources on environmental protection when they had more pressing issues to deal with such as poverty and malnutrition?

The report of the WCED, published in 1987, identified both under-development and over-consumption as challenges to sustainable development.[6] In an effort to reconcile the debate on environmental protection versus economic development, the WCED put forward the notion of sustainable development, which was defined as "development which meets the needs of the present generation without compromising the ability of the future generations to meet theirs."[7] It is ironic that the definition that was advocated as a solution to environmental problems makes no reference to environmental protection at all. Its emphasis on development was welcomed by developing countries that wanted an endorsement of their development agenda. The definition of sustainable development encompasses both inter-generational and intra-generational equity aspects of development.[8] The only way inter-generational equity can be achieved is by ensuring that natural resources are exploited in an optimal manner and ensuring that future generations have at least the same choices that we enjoy today. The above definition of sustainable development also addresses the issue of intra-generational equity. The vast disparity today between

---

[4] *See* OUR COMMON FUTURE, REPORT OF THE WORLD COMMISSION ON ENVIRONMENT AND DEVELOPMENT (1987).

[5] *See id.* 4 at ix, for the mandate given to the WCED by the UN General Assembly.

[6] *See id.*, Overview.

[7] *Id.* at 43.

[8] For the seminal work on inter-generational equity, *see* EDITH BROWN WEISS, IN FAIRNESS TO FUTURE GENERATIONS: INTERNATIONAL LAW, COMMON PATRIMONY AND INTERGENERATIONAL EQUITY (1989).

developing countries and developed countries and between the rich and the poor even in developed countries shows that the distribution of resources and wealth in the world today is not equitable.[9] While some people live in luxury and abundance, others live in squalor and poverty. As noted in Chapter 1, about 1 billion people in the world today live on less than $1 a day.[10] Extreme poverty is a major obstacle to achieving sustainable development.[11]

## B.   EMERGENCE OF SUSTAINABLE DEVELOPMENT AND ITS SIGNIFICANCE

While the WCED is credited with the modern notion of sustainable development, it is with the Rio Declaration on Environment and Development[12] adopted at the Rio Conference in 1992 that sustainable development acquired some legal status. It is the first international instrument of universal acceptance, albeit non-binding, to elaborate on sustainable development. It has been noted that "Not until the UN Conference on Environment and Development met at Rio in 1992, however, did sustainable development secure general support as the leading concept of international environmental policy."[13]

The Rio Declaration, does not, however, provide a definition of sustainable development. Rather, it seems to embody components of and the conditions necessary to achieve sustainable development. It is proposed to trace the evolution of sustainable development since the adoption of the Stockholm Declaration in 1972. The other milestones that will be discussed here are: the World Commission on Environment and Development (WCED); Rio Declaration and Agenda 21 of 1992; and the World Summit on Sustainable Development and the Plan of Implementation of 2002.

### 1.   Stockholm Declaration

The Stockholm Declaration adopted at the UN Conference on the Human Environment[14] does not contain any reference to sustainable development as it pre-dates the WCED report. However, it is generally accepted

---

[9]   *See supra* note 1, at 5–6.

[10]   WORLD DEVELOPMENT REPORT 2000/01 (World Bank, 2001).

[11]   *See* discussion in Chapter 1, Section B.4.

[12]   UN Doc. A/CONF.151/26, *reprinted in* 31 ILM 874 (1992), *available at* http://www.un.org/documents/ga/conf121/aconf15126-lannexl.htm.

[13]   *See* PATRICIA BIRNIE & ALAN BOYLE, INTERNATIONAL LAW & THE ENVIRONMENT 41 (2d ed. 2002) [hereinafter BIRNIE & BOYLE].

[14]   11 ILM 1416 (1972).

that it laid the foundation for sustainable development, and, indeed, some of the principles there specifically endorse the components of sustainable development, as we understand them today.

Thus, the Preamble to the Declaration specifically identifies the link between under-development and environmental problems. It notes:

> In the developing countries most of the environmental problems are caused by under-development. Millions continue to live far below the minimum levels required for a decent human existence, deprived of adequate food and clothing, shelter and education, health and sanitation. Therefore, developing countries must direct their efforts to development, bearing in mind their priorities and the need to safeguard and improve the environment.[15]

The Preamble endorsed inter-generational equity in the following terms: "To defend and improve the human environment for present and future generations has become an imperative goal of mankind."[16] Principle 2 also endorsed the inter-generational equity principle in relation to the exploitation of natural resources of the earth.[17]

Principles 13 and 14 are the most important for the present discussion. Principle 13 advocates for an integrated approach and provides:

> In order to achieve a more rational management of resources and thus to improve the environment, States should adopt an integrated and co-ordinated approach to their development planning so as to ensure that development is compatible with the need to protect and improve environment for the benefit of their population.[18]

Principle 14 notes that "rational planning constitutes an essential tool for reconciling any conflict between the needs of development and the need to protect and improve the environment."[19]

---

[15] Preamble, Stockholm Declaration, UN Doc. A/CONF.48/14, June 16, 1972, *reprinted in* 11 ILM 1416 (1972).

[16] *Id.*

[17] According to Principle 2, *id.*, "The natural resources of the earth including the air, water, land, flora and fauna and especially representative samples of natural ecosystems must be safeguarded for the benefit of present and future generations through careful planning or management, as appropriate."

[18] Principle 13, *id.*

[19] Principle 14, *id.*

Principles 13 and 14, taken together, laid the foundation for sustainable development. The only element lacking in this formulation is a reference to future generations; this is, however, included in Principle 2 of the Declaration. Thus, it can be argued that the Stockholm Declaration is a visionary document that laid the foundation for sustainable development, although the term itself is not mentioned there. Balancing environment with development, rational planning and an integrated approach are all components of sustainable development.[20]

## 2. World Conservation Strategy

The Strategy was drafted by the IUCN, an organization devoted to the protection of natural resources.[21] It is based in Gland, Switzerland, and has as its members, governments, environmental NGOs as well as individuals. The aim of the strategy is to "help advance the achievement of sustainable development through the conservation of living resources."[22] The strategy further notes that until a new international economic order is achieved, a new environmental ethic adopted and sustainable modes of development become the rule, the relationship between human beings and the environment would continue to deteriorate. Adopting an integrated approach to development,[23] the Strategy notes that "Among the prerequisites for sustainable development is the conservation of living resources."[24]

While a specific definition of sustainable development is not provided in the Strategy, it does seem to adopt the principle of integration. Thus, the Strategy provides that the most effective way for society to avoid ecological damage (which, in turn, gives rise to economic and social damage) is to integrate conservation into the development process from the initial stages to its implementation.[25] It proposes the adoption of anticipatory environmental policies and of a cross-sectoral conservation policy. The Strategy further calls upon states to adopt measures elaborated there, in relation to their development plans, in order to achieve equitable sustainable development.[26]

---

[20] *See* the discussion in Section E.

[21] *See* http://www.iucn.org.

[22] IUCN, WORLD CONSERVATION STRATEGY (1980).

[23] The Strategy stresses that its goal is the integration of conservation and development.

[24] *Supra* note 22, at 1.

[25] *Id.*

[26] *Id.*

## 3.   World Commission on Environment and Development

After the Stockholm Conference in 1972 developing and developed countries became increasingly polarized on the issue of environmental protection. On the one hand, developed countries, which were acutely aware of the ill effects of industrialization, felt that polluting activities must be decreased and more attention should be paid to environmental protection. Developing countries, which had witnessed the ill effects of poverty and under-development for too long, felt that more attention be paid to economic development, on the other. These countries felt that any emphasis on environmental protection would detract attention from their main objective of economic development and that it was unfair of developing countries to request them not to develop. This polarization led to the further deterioration of the environment. Thus, the UN General Assembly appointed the WCED, in 1983, to find ways to reconcile environmental protection with economic development. The mandate given to the WCED was to:

- Propose long-term environmental strategies for achieving sustainable development by the year 2000 and beyond;
- Recommend ways concern for the environment may be translated into greater co-operation among developing countries and between countries at different stages of economic and social development and lead to the achievement of common and mutually supportive objectives that take account of the interrelationships between people, resources, environment, and development;
- Consider ways and means by which the international community can deal more effectively with environmental concerns; and
- Help define shared perceptions of long-term environmental issues and the appropriate efforts needed to deal successfully with the problems of protecting and enhancing the environment, a long-term agenda for action during the coming decades, and aspirational goals for the world community.[27]

The mandate given to the Commission was by no means easy. Despite this monumental mandate, its report is now acclaimed as the "bible" of sustainable development. Given its importance, a discussion of its salient features is imperative.

The Commission discussed the issues under three main headings: common concerns, common challenges and common endeavors. The message of the Commission is clear enough: concerted global action is necessary to arrest the present trends of environmental degradation. No state can

---

[27]   Chairman's Foreword, OUR COMMON FUTURE, *supra* note 4, at ix.

achieve this alone. Furthermore, the report highlights the threat that poverty and international inequality pose to environmental protection:

> Poverty is a major cause and effect of global environmental problems. It is therefore futile to attempt to deal with environmental problems without a broader perspective that encompasses the factors underlying world poverty and international inequality.[28]

The Commission's mandate was based on three main objectives:

- To re-examine the critical environment and development issues and to formulate realistic proposals for dealing with them;
- To propose new forms of international cooperation on these issues that will influence policies and events in the direction of needed changes; and
- To raise the levels of understanding and commitment to action of individuals, voluntary organizations, businesses, institutes, and governments.[29]

The report recognized that the present development trends have left many people poor and vulnerable as well as with a degraded environment.[30] It further points out that the inequality in the world is the planet's main environmental problem as well as its development problem.[31]

The Commission's definition of sustainable development implied limits. Unlimited economic growth is no longer considered a viable option. We need to ensure that our children, grandchildren and generations to come have at least the same options that we enjoy today, if not more. If we develop now without any heed for the environment, the people who will suffer would be the generations to come who had no say in the matter. Thus, the issue becomes one of equity and fairness: does the present generation have the right to damage the environment irrevocably at the expense of the future generations, who have no say in the matter? Viewed in this light, sustainable development becomes even more urgent and imperative.

The central theme of the report is *change*.[32] It calls upon affluent states to change their lifestyle of waste and over-consumption. It calls upon devel-

---

[28] OUR COMMON FUTURE, *supra* note 4, at 3.

[29] *Id.* at 3–4.

[30] *Id.* at 4.

[31] *Id.* at 6.

[32] *Supra* note 4, at 23: "We are unanimous in our conviction that the security, well-being and very survival of the planet depend on such changes, *now*." (Emphasis added.)

oping states to change their unsustainable practices. In the same way that poverty causes environmental degradation, over-consumption and waste too has a severe impact on the environment. Change is also required with regard to institutions and policies that are often fragmented and polarized. Developed countries with about 20 percent of the world's population consume about 80 percent of the world's energy.[33] Thus, over-consumption of resources poses a real challenge to environmental protection today.

The report also highlights the vast disparity between developing countries and developed countries.[34] It demonstrates the urgent need to achieve intra-generational equity while at the same time trying to achieve inter-generational equity. In other words, states must seek to achieve equity in the short term as well as in the long term.

The report also critiqued the react-after-the-event approach adopted thus far by states and their institutions in relation to environmental protection. Instead, it called upon states to anticipate and prevent environmental damage.[35] Thus, the ecological dimensions of policy must be considered along with economic, trade, energy and other dimensions.[36] The Commission noted that the reorientation from a reactive to a preventive approach is one of the main institutional challenges of the 1990s. It further noted that all countries—rich and poor, big and small—must change, as must international agencies dealing with, *inter alia*, development aid, trade regulation and economic development.[37]

The Commission considered the following inter-connected issues specifically in its report: population; food security; loss of species and genetic resources; energy; industry; and the urban challenge.[38] It called upon states to adopt new approaches to environment and development. It stressed that "environment and development are not separate challenges; they are inexorably linked.[39] . . . They are linked in a complex system of cause and effect"[40] in several ways:

---

[33] *Id.*

[34] *Id.* at 32.

[35] *Id.* at 39.

[36] *Id.* at 10.

[37] *Id.* at 11.

[38] *Id.* These issues were termed "common challenges" in the report and a separate chapter was devoted to each issue.

[39] *Id.* at 37.

[40] *Id.*

- Environmental issues are linked to one another, which means that several different issues must be dealt with simultaneously.
- Environmental issues and economic development are linked to one another: "Thus economics and ecology must be completely integrated in decision-making and lawmaking processes not just to protect the environment, but also to protect and promote development."[41]
- Environmental and economic issues are linked to social and political factors.
- Systemic features operate not only within but also between nations.

Thus, international cooperation and political commitment are necessary to tackle the myriad of interwoven problems that the international community is facing today. These problems transcend traditional economic, environmental, social and political boundaries and together form part of the one gigantic problem facing the world today: survival. Sustainable development also requires the integration of environment and development in all countries and requires changes in domestic and international policies of every state. Furthermore, as no country can develop in isolation, it requires a new orientation of international relations. The report is based on the basic premise that every human being has the right to a decent life.

The report further provides that sustainable development contains within it two key concepts: the concept of *needs* and the idea of *limitations*.[42] It is necessary to meet the needs of everybody, particularly the poor, but it also implies limitations on development. As the report further highlights:

In essence, sustainable development is a process of change in which the exploitation of resources, the direction of investments, the orientation of technological development, and institutional change are all in harmony and enhance both current and future potential to meet human needs and aspirations.[43]

Thus, unless this process of change is initiated at every level—local, national, regional and international/global—the goal of sustainable development would remain unattainable.

The report was received with mixed reactions by the international community. While some considered that sustainable development was the blue-

---

[41] *Id.*

[42] *Id* at 43.

[43] *Id.* at 46.

print for the eradication of poverty and the path for prosperity,[44] others, particularly environmentalists, were more cautious. They felt that undue emphasis was given to economic development at the expense of environmental protection. They argued that sustainable development was anthropocentric in nature and ignored the rights of other species.[45]

## 4. Rio Declaration and Agenda 21

The Rio Declaration was adopted at the 1992 UN Conference on Environment and Development (UNCED).[46] It was in response to the report of the WCED,[47] and it was the first time that the international community had actually adopted an instrument[48] endorsing sustainable development. Although UNCED was held to mark the 20th anniversary of the Stockholm Conference, it was not a mere sequel to it.[49] Changing the prior approach to development, sustainable development called for the addition of a fifth element to development[50]—protecting the environment.

---

[44] *See generally* Dan Turlock, *Ideas Without Institutions: The Paradox of Sustainable Development*, 9 IND. J. GLOBAL LEGAL STUD. (2001); Nicholas A. Robinson, *Legal Structure and Sustainable Development: Comparative Environmental Law Perspectives on Legal Regimes for Sustainable Development*, 3 WID. L. SYMP. J. 247 (1998); Mary Pat Williams Silveira, *International Legal Instruments and Sustainable Development: Principles, Requirements, and Restructuring*, 31 WILLAMETTE L. REV. 239 (1995). *See also* Alhaji B.M. Marong, *From Rio to Johannesburg: Reflections on the Role of International Legal Norms in Sustainable Development*, 16 GEO. INT'L ENVTL. L. REV. 21 (2003); Graham Mayeda, *Where Should Johannesburg Take Us? Ethical and Legal Approaches to Sustainable Development in the Context of International Environmental Law*, 15 COLO. J. INT'L ENVTL. L. & POL'Y 29 (2004).

[45] *See* Michael McCloskey, *The Emperor Has No Clothes: The Conundrum of Sustainable Development*, 9 DUKE ENVTL. L. & POL'Y F. 153 (1999); Marc Pallemaerts, *The Future of Environmental Regulation: International Environmental Law in the Age of Sustainable Development: A Critical Assessment of the UNCED Process*, 15 J.L. & COM. 623 (1996); Jude L. Fernando, *Rethinking Sustainable Development: Preface: The Power of Unsustainable Development: What is to be Done?*, 590 ANNALS 6 (2003); and John S. Applegate & Alfred C. Aman, Jr., *Syncopated Sustainable Development*, 9 IND. J. GLOBAL LEGAL STUD. (2001).

[46] *Supra* note 12.

[47] OUR COMMON FUTURE, *supra* note 4.

[48] Although the instrument itself falls into the category of soft law, it has made a great impact on international environmental law, similar to the Stockholm Declaration adopted 20 years earlier.

[49] *See* John C. Dernbach, *Sustainable Development as a Framework for National Governance*, 49 CASE W. RES. L. REV. 1 (1998).

[50] The earlier approach had four elements to development: peace and security, economic development, social development and supportive national governance. *See* Dernbach, *supra* note 49, who argues that development must be understood in a more broad sense.

Several binding and non-binding instruments were adopted at the Rio Conference: while the Rio Declaration on Environment and Development, Agenda 21[51] and Forest Principles[52] fall into the category of soft law, the UN Framework Convention on Climate Change[53] and the UN Convention on Biological Diversity[54] are the two binding instruments adopted at the Rio Conference.

Principle 1 of the Rio Declaration, discussed in Chapter 1, provides that "Human beings are at the centre of concerns for sustainable development. They are entitled to a healthy and productive life in harmony with nature."[55] This formulation, together with its reference to sustainable development, has been soundly criticized for being too anthropocentric in nature.[56] On the other hand, it has been contended that because of the reference to "in harmony with nature" in Principle 1, simultaneous progress must be made toward environmental protection and economic development.[57]

It is hard to deny that the notion of sustainable development is anthropocentric in nature. However, its reference to future generations seeks to ensure that development remains within acceptable levels. The only way to ensure this would be to exploit natural resources in a sustainable manner and by adopting a holistic approach to development. Thus, although environmental protection is not explicitly mentioned in the definition of sustainable development, in an indirect manner, sustainable development promotes environmental protection. The essential task is to strike a *balance* between environmental protection and economic development. States have to find ways to integrate environmental protection into the development

---

[51] *Agenda 21: A Blueprint for Action for Global Sustainable Development into the 21st Century* (1992).

[52] Non-Legally Binding Authoritative Statement of Principles for a Global Consensus on the Management, Conservation and Sustainable Development of All Types of Forests (1992), A/CONF.151/26 (Vol III), *available at* http://www.un.org/documents/ga/conf151/aconf15126-3annex3.htm.

[53] 31 ILM 849 (1992), 1771 UNTS 107, signed May 9, 1992, entered into force Mar. 21, 1994, *available at* http://www.unfccc.ed/.

[54] 31 ILM 822 (1992), 1760 UNTS 79, *available at* http://www.biodiv.org.

[55] Principle 1, Rio Declaration.

[56] *See* Marc Pallermaerts, *International Environmental Law From Stockholm to Rio: Back to the Future?, in* GREENING INTERNATIONAL LAW 1, 9 (Philippe Sands ed., 1994). *See also* Robert John Araujo, *Rio+10 and the World Summit on Sustainable Development: Why Human Beings are at the Center of Concerns,* 2 GEO. J.I. & PUB. POL'Y 201 (2004).

[57] *See* Dernbach, *supra* note 49.

process. Thus, the principle of integration[58] is an important component of sustainable development.

The concept of sustainable development proposed in the WCED report was taken to its logical conclusion in the Rio Declaration on Environment and Development adopted at the Rio Conference in 1992. Agenda 21, also adopted at the Rio Conference, is the blueprint to implement sustainable development.[59] Again, while not binding, Agenda 21 is an important document and represents a political commitment: "The success or failure of UNCED, in short, ultimately depends on implementation of Agenda 21."[60]

The Rio Declaration, instead of trying to define sustainable development, seeks to give it content. Principle 2 endorsed Principle 21 of the Stockholm Declaration, albeit with a reference to "development," which clearly shows how the environmental protection discourse started at Stockholm has changed to embrace development goals at Rio:

> States have, in accordance with the Charter of the United Nations and the principles of international law, the sovereign right to exploit their own resources pursuant to their own environmental *and developmental policies*, and the responsibility to ensure that activities within their jurisdiction or control do not cause damage to the environment of other states or of areas beyond the limits of national jurisdiction.[61]

Principle 3 seeks to strike a balance between environmental protection and the right to development and also introduces an inter-generational element to development.[62] This is the first time that the right to development was articulated in a universal instrument adopted by consensus. It is also the first time that the right to development was brought into the discourse on sustainable development.[63] While the right to development was reaf-

---

[58] *See* Philippe Sands, *International Environmental Law: An Introductory Overview, in* GREENING INTERNATIONAL LAW, *supra* note 56, at xv, xxviii, who contends that the UNCED launched the period of integration in international law—that "environmental concerns be integrated into and fully taken account of in all relevant activities."

[59] *See* Dernbach, *supra* note 49.

[60] *Id.*

[61] Principle 2, Rio Declaration, *supra* note 12 (emphasis added).

[62] Principle 3, *id.*, provides that "The right to development must be fulfilled so as to equitably meet developmental and environmental needs of present and future generations."

[63] *See* discussion in Section C.1.a.

firmed by the international community, no corresponding claim was made regarding a right to a healthy environment.[64] In other words, the right to environment did not reach the level of a right under international law,[65] similar to other rights proclaimed by the international community.

The Rio Declaration, on the whole, seeks to elaborate on the concept of sustainable development, whether by expanding on its components, or by identifying tools to achieve sustainable development or by identifying other areas that have an impact on it. The principles contained in the Rio Declaration can be classified into four categories: principles that contain substantive elements of sustainable development (Principles 2, 3, 4); those that contain procedural elements of sustainable development (Principles 10, 18, 19); tools that can be utilized to achieve sustainable development (Principles 15, 16, 17); and issues that are related to and integrated with sustainable development (Principles 5, 6, 7, 8, 12, 23, 24, 25).

Furthermore, the Rio Declaration contains several other procedural principles that are important in the context of sustainable development: notification and assistance in the event of emergencies;[66] and notification and consultation in good faith in relation to activities likely to have a significant transboundary impact.[67] These principles derive from general international law, and the Rio Declaration embodies them in the context of sustainable development. These principles and concepts would no doubt provide guidance in the march toward sustainable development.

However, the Rio Declaration has been subject to much criticism, precisely because of its emphasis on sustainable development.[68] The opponents argue that the Declaration gives development preference over environmental protection. Moreover, they argue that the delicate balance that was struck at the Stockholm Conference has been upset by the Rio Declaration by its undue emphasis on development.[69]

It is contended that these criticisms are unjustified and do not give sufficient credence to the positive elements of sustainable development. The polarization between developing and developed countries occurred pre-

---

[64] *See* Dernbach, *supra* note 49.

[65] *Id.*

[66] Principle 18 of the Rio Declaration, *supra* note 12.

[67] Principle 19 of the Rio Declaration, *supra* note 12.

[68] *See* Pallermaerts, *supra* note 56.

[69] *Id.*

cisely because of the perceived notion after the Stockholm Conference that undue emphasis was placed on environmental protection at the expense of economic development. Thus, the reconciliation between environment and development in the notion of sustainable development paved the way for a new era of international environmental law—international law of sustainable development or international sustainable development law (ISDL). Indeed, the Rio Declaration does not refer to international environmental law at all. Instead, it calls upon states *and people* to cooperate in good faith to fulfill the principles in the Declaration and "in the further development of *international law in the field of sustainable development.*"[70] It would seem that international environmental law has changed its course to embrace the concept of sustainable development and that a new body of law called international law of sustainable development, which draws on international environmental law, international human rights law, and international trade law has emerged.[71] It has been articulated that sustainable development has become the "leading concept of international environmental policy."[72] Considering that this development took place within a relatively short period of time, this is a major achievement for the proponents of sustainable development. Opponents could, of course, argue that concepts carry no legal weight. While this is true, there is no denying that sustainable development is the most discussed and debated concept of recent times, and it has definitely influenced the activities of states and non-state actors alike.

Agenda 21, called the blueprint for action for global sustainable development, embodies a very ambitious set of guidelines and action plans to implement sustainable development at both the national level and the international level. Agenda 21 is divided into four broad categories: social and economic dimensions; conservation and management of resources for development; strengthening the role of major groups; and means of implementation.[73] It also identified program areas for each of these broad categories.

Stating that "humanity stands at a defining moment in history,"[74] Agenda 21 noted that the world is confronted with the vast disparities between and within nations, worsening poverty, hunger, ill health and the continuing

---

[70] Principle 27, *supra* note 12 (emphasis added).

[71] *See* SUSTAINABLE DEVELOPMENT LAW 103 (Marie-Claire Cordonier Segger & Ashfaq Khalfan eds., 2004).

[72] *See* BIRNIE & BOYLE, *supra* note 13, at 41.

[73] Agenda 21, *supra* note 1.

[74] *Id.*, Preamble, para. 1.1.

deterioration of ecosystems. However, integration of environment and development will lead to the fulfillment of basic needs and lead to a more prosperous future: "No nation can achieve this on its own; but together we can—in a global partnership for sustainable development."[75]

For each program area identified, objectives, activities and means of implementation are described in Agenda 21. It further notes that Agenda 21 is a dynamic program and will be carried out by the various actors according to the different situations, capacities and priorities: "This process marks the beginning of a new global partnership for sustainable development."[76] Some of the program areas identified in Agenda 21 are: protecting the atmosphere; combating deforestation; conservation of biological diversity; protection of oceans; promoting human health, combating poverty, changing consumption patterns; toxic chemicals; and radioactive waste.

The Commission on Sustainable Development[77] was established to monitor the implementation of Agenda 21. Given the sheer volume of Agenda 21, it is doubtful whether one organization (and a newly established one at that) would be in a position to supervise the implementation of the entire document.

## 5. World Summit on Sustainable Development and Plan of Implementation

The latest milestone in the history of international environmental law was the World Summit on Sustainable Development (WSSD) held in Johannesburg, South Africa to mark the 30th anniversary of the Stockholm Conference. Again, attended by many heads of state and thousands of delegates, WSSD marked yet another watershed in the evolution of international environmental law.[78]

It is interesting to note that the nomenclature of the conferences also reflects the direction that international environmental law has taken during the period 1972 to 2002. In 1972, the conference dealt with "the human environment." Twenty years later, faced with many developmental issues, the conference dealt with "environment and development" while in 2002, the dominant issue was, without doubt, sustainable development. It seems that there is now no going back and that sustainable development is here to stay.

---

[75]  *Id.*

[76]  *Id.*, para. 1.6.

[77]  *See* http://www.un.org/esa/sustdev/csd/review.htm.

[78]  World Summit on Sustainable Development, UN Doc. A/CONF.199/20.

Unlike at the two previous events, however, WSSD did not adopt a formal declaration embodying principles. What was adopted was called a political declaration with a commitment to sustainable development and a Plan of Implementation similar to Agenda 21. It outlined the grave problems facing the international community from illicit drugs to HIV/AIDS. These issues were identified as threats to sustainable development. Specific global environmental problems identified in the declaration include, loss of biodiversity, depletion of fish stocks, desertification, air and water pollution, and climate change. Of course, while none of these issues are new, some of them were identified as global problems only recently. A good example is the loss of biodiversity, which requires action at both the international and domestic level. It is also a good example of an environmental issue that has become "internationalized" in the recent years. Biodiversity was considered a purely domestic issue (hence outside the reach of international law) until issues relating to biopiracy, etc., came to the forefront.

To those who were waiting for another declaration to shape international environmental law principles, or to refine the principles of sustainable development, the adoption of a political declaration would have come as a deep disappointment. To those who oppose strict environmental regulation, this outcome would have been a welcome step. Yet others would have had mixed feelings. A political declaration coupled with a Plan of Implementation is, of course, better than no declaration at all. On the other hand, both Stockholm and Rio produced two important declarations, albeit non-binding, which were important milestones in the history of international environmental law. There is no doubt that these two declarations greatly shaped the course of international environmental law and some of the principles have, since then, become part of customary international law.[79] From this point of view, a political declaration devoid of any principles was indeed disappointing.

The fact that no formal declaration similar to Stockholm or Rio was adopted can be interpreted in two ways: it is possible to argue that yet another declaration with new principles was not necessary; what was necessary is a commitment to the existing principles, and that is precisely what the political declaration and the Plan of Implementation did. What is necessary is precision and the consolidation of existing principles (or emerging ones), not yet another set of vague principles. From this point of view, the WSSD declaration can be considered a success. On the other hand, it could be interpreted that there was no consensus on what should be

---

[79] Principle 21 of the Stockholm Declaration, *supra* note 15, is generally considered to have become part of customary international law. *See* discussion in Chapter 1, Section A.1.

included in a formal declaration. Whichever way one looks at the outcome of the WSSD, one thing is clear: sustainable development has come of age, and whatever its legal status is under international law, states can no longer deny its significance. The political declaration reiterated the commitment to sustainable development and the Plan of Implementation referred to the three pillars of sustainable development as economic development, environmental protection and social development and noted that they were "interdependent and mutually reinforcing" pillars.[80] The Copenhagen Declaration on Social Development[81] was the first document to identify these three pillars of sustainable development.

## C. DEFINITION AND PARAMETERS OF SUSTAINABLE DEVELOPMENT

Apart from the WCED definition referred to above, it is hard to find a comprehensive definition of sustainable development. Writers have instead used it as an umbrella term encompassing several components, both substantive and procedural.[82] Sands, for example, posits the following as its components: rights of future generations; sustainable use of natural resources; equitable use of natural resources; and the integration of environment and development.[83] While these can be considered the substantive elements of sustainable development, it is generally accepted that it contains procedural elements also. These are: the right to have access to information concerning the environment, the right to participate in the decision-making process and the right to seek remedies.[84] It is generally accepted that without ensuring these procedural rights, sustainable development cannot be achieved. These are also closely intertwined with principles of good governance. Thus, sustainable development cannot be achieved in a society that is corrupt and that does not uphold principles of transparency and accountability. As the *World Bank Operational Manual* pro-

---

[80] Plan of Implementation, UN Doc. A/CONF199/20, *available at* http://www.johannesburgsummit.org/, at 8.

[81] Copenhagen Declaration was adopted at the World Social Summit in 1995, *available at* http://www.visionoffice.com/socdev/wssdco-0.htm.

[82] *See* Vaughn Lowe, *Sustainable Development and Unsustainable Arguments, in* INTERNATIONAL LAW AND SUSTAINABLE DEVELOPMENT: PAST ACHIEVEMENTS AND FUTURE CHALLENGES 26 (Alan Boyle & David Freestone eds., 1999); Sumudu Atapattu, *Sustainable Development, Myth or Reality?: A Survey of Sustainable Development under International Law and Sri Lankan Law,* 14 GEO. INT'L ENVTL. L. REV. 265, 273 (2001).

[83] PHILIPPE SANDS, PRINCIPLES OF INTERNATIONAL ENVIRONMENTAL LAW, 256 (2d ed. 2003).

[84] These rights are also related to the environmental assessment process and will be discussed in Chapter 4, Section F.

vides, the provision of timely information is vital.[85] Outdated information, by implication, amounts to not providing information at all. It can be seen that the components of sustainable development overlap heavily with the right to environment, as discussed in Chapter 1.

The lack of a proper definition has been one of the main criticisms of sustainable development.[86] Yet, this has not stopped international organizations, national institutions and non-governmental organizations from seeking to implement it. As Birnie and Boyle point out in discussing the indeterminacy problem in relation to the right to environment:

> Much the same problems [definitional] affect international attempts to define sustainable development, yet this has not rendered futile the UN's efforts to promote sustainability as the central objective of international environmental policy, or its use by international courts and inter-governmental bodies as a legal principle which can influence their decisions. Indeterminacy is thus a problem, but not necessarily an insurmountable one.[87]

Given the nuances to the concept of sustainable development, striving to adopt a precise definition of it may prove futile. Instead, identifying and giving content to its components might prove more instructive. As noted above, sustainable development encompasses both procedural and substantive elements.[88] Birnie and Boyle note that the substantive elements of sustainable development are set out in Principles 3–8 and 16 of the Rio Declaration, while the procedural elements are found in Principles 10–17.[89] Thus, according to this interpretation, the substantive elements are the principle of integration (Principle 4),[90] the right to development (Principle 3),[91] sustainable utilization and conservation of natural resources, inter-

---

[85] *World Bank Operational Manual on Environmental Assessment*, OP4.01, Jan. 1999, *available at* http://wbln0018.worldbank.org/Institutional/Manuals/OpManual.nsf/toc2/9367A2A9D9DAEED38525672C007D0972?OpenDocument.

[86] *See* Dernbach, *supra* note 49.

[87] *See* BIRNIE & BOYLE, *supra* note 13, at 257.

[88] *Id.* at 86.

[89] *Id.*

[90] *Id* at 87. They believe that integration is a well established feature of environmental regulation. However, its real implications may be for developing countries which have not historically integrated environmental concerns into development planning.

[91] *See* the discussion *infra*. Birnie and Boyle note that this is the first occasion that the international community has fully endorsed this controversial concept, *supra* note 13, at 87.

generational equity (Principle 3), intra-generational equity (Principle 3)[92] and the polluter pays principle (Principle 16). The procedural elements, which facilitate implementation at the national level are: environmental impact assessment (Principle 17), access to information (Principle 15) and public participation in decision making (Principle 15). Together, these procedural principles have been referred to as "environmental democracy."[93]

Several groups have discussed the concept of sustainable development, its parameters and status under international law. The Foundation for International Environmental Law and Development (FIELD), for example, convened a Group of Experts to discuss the issue. They identified several core elements of sustainable development:

- the idea that the needs of present and future generations must be taken into account;
- the need to ensure that renewable and non-renewable environmental resources are conserved and not exhausted;
- the requirement that access to and use of natural resources must take equitable account of the needs of all peoples; and
- a recognition that issues of environment and sustainable development must be treated in an integrated manner.[94]

The participants noted that although sustainable development is not yet a clearly defined legal concept; it has certain legal implications. Moreover, they pointed out that international law in the field of sustainable development does not replace or supersede international environmental law:

In sum, sustainable development must be considered in relation to institutional arrangements, procedural requirements and substantive standards, obligations and norms, including in particular those in the field of human rights.[95]

The report also addressed procedural aspects of sustainable development.

Others have taken the view that rather than trying to come up with a definition of sustainable development, it is important to note that it has

---

[92]  The Rio Declaration endorses the intra and inter generational equity principle in the context of the right to development.

[93]  *See* SUSTAINABLE DEVELOPMENT LAW, *supra* note 71.

[94]  *Report of a Consultation on Sustainable Development: The Challenge to International Law,* convened by the Foundation for International Environmental Law and Development (FIELD), 2:4 RECIEL r1, r5 (1993).

[95]  *Id.* at r6.

implications at the domestic level.[96] As with any international obligation, the success of sustainable development lies if it is incorporated into national legislation and policy and given effect at the national level. In order to do so, however, it is necessary to understand what sustainable development is:

> Sustainable development is something of a mystery to domestic policy makers, economists, lawyers and academics, who tend to be separated from their international colleagues by a lack of common language, knowledge and experience. Whatever reasons explain the lack of progress . . . progress cannot occur unless we first understand sustainable development.[97]

In order to do so, it has been proposed to focus on sustainable development as a framework for national governance and that it provides a powerful set of tools to reinvigorate governance:[98]

> Sustainable development affirms the importance of social and economic development goals in governance but adds another goal, protection of natural resources and the environment, and emphasizes that these goals must be furthered for the sake of future generations.[99]

Thus, the essence of sustainable development is that it provides us with a long-term view of development, which will sustain this earth for years to come. The present Westphalian model of development has not been successful in protecting the environment or providing us with a vision for future development. At best, the present development model is distorted with developing countries lagging far behind developed countries. Developed countries, on the other hand, consume far too many resources than they need to lead a comfortable lifestyle, resulting in wasteful practices. Thus, both developing countries and developed countries have pursued unsustainable development by polluting the environment and exploiting natural resources unsustainably. Developing countries have done so because of poverty and lack of resources and technology. Developed countries have done so because of their ever expanding needs as a result of having too many resources at their disposal. Distribution of wealth and resources in the world today is anything but equitable.[100]

---

[96] *See* Dernbach, *supra* note 49.

[97] *Id.*

[98] *Id.*

[99] *Id.*

[100] *Id.* John Dernbach points out that "sustainable development would result in greater equity within and among nations."

It has been articulated that the traditional development model, which basically equated development with economic development,[101] has failed for two main reasons: poverty and environmental degradation.[102] As noted in Chapter 1, more than 1 billion people in the world today live in abject poverty, and more than double that number lack access to safe water and sanitation. Millions die from preventable diseases. This is exacerbated by a deteriorating environment[103] and is further complicated by the increasing globalization of the economy.[104]

## 1.  Report of the Experts Group

An Expert Group was convened by the Commission on Sustainable Development in 1995 to identify the principles of international law for sustainable development. Its report issued in 1996 identifies an extensive array of principles that constitutes part of sustainable development.[105] While some of these components may be subject to some controversy, others have been generally accepted as components of sustainable development. These principles can be summarized as follows:

1.  Principle of interrelationship and integration.
2.  Principles and concepts relating to environment and development:
    (i)    right to development;
    (ii)   right to a healthy environment;
    (iii)  eradication of poverty;
    (iv)   equity;
    (v)    sovereignty over natural resources and the responsibility not to cause damage to other states;
    (vi)   sustainable use of natural resources;
    (vii)  prevention of environmental harm;
    (viii) precautionary principle.
3.  Principles relating to international cooperation:
    (i)    duty to cooperate in a spirit of global partnership;

---

[101] John Dernbach points out that development in the past half-century included four related concepts: peace and security, economic development, social development and national governance that secured peace and development, *id.*

[102] *Id.*

[103] *Id.* John Dernbach articulated that "The global scale and severity of environmental degradation and poverty are unprecedented in human history."

[104] *Id.*

[105] *Report of the Expert Group Meeting on Identification of Principles of International Law for Sustainable Development*, Geneva, Sept. 1995 and prepared by the Division for Sustainable Development for the Commission on Sustainable Development, 4th sess., 1996, *available at* http://www.un.org/gopher-data/esc/cn17/1996/background/law.txt. [hereinafter Experts Group Report].

      (a)   common concern of mankind;
      (b)   common but differentiated responsibility principle;
      (ii)   common heritage of mankind;
      (iii)  cooperation in a transboundary context;
      (iv)  equitable use of transboundary natural resources;
      (v)   environmental impact assessment in a tranboundary context;
      (vi)  prior informed consent;
      (vii) cooperation to prevent relocation of harmful activities.

4. Principle of participation, decision-making and transparency:
      (i)   public participation;
      (ii)   access to information;
      (iii)  environmental impact assessment and informed decision-making.

5. Dispute avoidance, resolution procedure, monitoring and compliance:
      (i)   peaceful settlement of disputes;
      (ii)   national compliance of international commitments;
      (iii)  monitoring of compliance with international commitments.[106]

This long list of components does not include the polluter pays principle, considered an important tool to achieve sustainable development.[107] Originally an economic concept, the Organization for Economic Cooperation and Development (OECD) was instrumental in developing it as a general principle of international environmental law. It has, since then, found its way into legal instruments.[108]

It has been pointed out that several elements of the definition of sustainable development are critical to understanding it: the concept applies to both developing and developed countries:[109] secondly, it attempts to reconcile economic growth and environmental protection rather than viewing them as trade-offs; thirdly, it is strongly anthropocentric. In other words, human needs must be met in order to address environmental problems.[110]

---

[106] *Id.*

[107] Discussed in Chapter 6.

[108] Principle 16 of the Rio Declaration, *supra* note 12.

[109] Norman J. Vig, *Introduction: Governing the International Environment, in* THE GLOBAL ENVIRONMENT: INSTITUTIONS, LAW AND POLICY 6 (Regina S. Axelrod et al., eds., 2004).

[110] This, however, is problematic. Formulated this way, it implies that economic development comes first and then, environmental protection. It is doubtful whether this is the correct interpretation of sustainable development, although there is no doubt that sustainable development is anthropocentric in nature.

Fourthly, limits to growth are social and technological; and finally, the concept is extremely vague and does not specify who has the responsibility to achieve it.[111]

The Experts Group identified the principle of interrelationship and integration[112] as playing an important role in sustainable development. It further noted that sustainable development will be enhanced if competing legal rules strive towards compatibility and mutual support. Conflicts between rules should be settled in accordance with Vienna Convention on Law of Treaties.[113] According to the Experts Group, the principle of interrelationship and integration forms the backbone of sustainable development.[114] Principles 3 and 4 of the Rio Declaration integrate "not only the concepts of environment and development, but also the needs of generations, both present and future."[115] Principle 25 of the Rio Declaration notes the interrelationship between sustainable development and other areas: peace, development and environmental protection.[116] Agenda 21 also addresses the principle of interrelationship and integration.[117] Another example of this interrelationship is the three pillars of sustainable development: economic development, social development and environmental protection.[118] Some examples of this principle in treaty law are: the UN Convention on the Law of the Sea,[119] which states "the problems of the ocean space are closely interrelated and need to be considered as a whole"[120] and the UN Convention to Combat Desertification[121] which

---

[111] *Id.* at 7. The writer contends that this vagueness was deliberate. *See also* SUSTAINABLE DEVELOPMENT LAW, *supra* note 71, at 4, where it is noted that "The vagueness in the concept of sustainable development may have been appropriate in 1992, for it allowed the idea to be adopted almost universally."

[112] *See* Experts Group Report, *supra* note 105.

[113] *Id.*, para.13.

[114] *Id.*, para 15.

[115] *Id.*

[116] According to Principle 25, *supra* note 12, "Peace, development and environmental protection are interdependent and indivisible."

[117] *See* ch. 8 of Agenda 21, *supra* note 1, which deals with integrating environment and development in decision making.

[118] *See* Experts Group Report, *supra* note 105, para. 15.

[119] 21 ILM 1261 (1982), 1833 UNTS 3, signed Dec. 10, 1982, entered into force Nov. 16, 1994, *available at* http://www.un.org/Depts/los/index.htm.

[120] *Id.*, Preamble.

[121] UN Convention to Combat Desertification in Countries Experiencing Serious Drought and/or Desertification, Particularly in Africa, 33 ILM 1328 (1994), 1954 UNTS 3, signed Oct. 14, 1994; entered into force Dec. 26, 1996.

stresses the importance of an integrated approach to desertification.[122]

Each of the components of sustainable development as identified by the Experts Group will be discussed next.

### a. The Right to Development

While development has been on the UN agenda since its inception,[123] it did not get crouched in human rights parlance until the 1980s. In 1986, the UN General Assembly adopted the Declaration on Right to Development amidst much controversy.[124] The North-South divide here was obvious. The Declaration provided that:

> [t]he right to development is an inalienable human right by virtue of which every human person and all peoples are entitled to participate in, contribute to, and enjoy economic, social, cultural and political development, in which all human rights and fundamental freedoms can be fully realized.[125]

It has been argued that the basic elements of the right to development are contained in the International Bill of Rights[126] which includes, *inter alia*, the rights to an adequate standard of living,[127] education,[128] housing,[129] work[130] and food.[131] The Experts Group contended that right to development is the synthesis of existing human rights.[132] Not everybody, however,

---

[122]  *Id.*, Preamble.

[123]  Article 55 of the UN Charter calls upon the United Nations to promote "higher standards of living, full employment, and conditions of economic and social progress and development."

[124]  GA Res. 41/128, Dec. 4, 1986. The United States did not endorse the Declaration. When signing the Rio Declaration, the U.S. government attached an interpretative statement reiterating its long-standing opposition to the right to development. *See* DAVID HUNTER, JAMES SALZMAN & DURWOOD ZAELKE, INTERNATIONAL ENVIRONMENTAL LAW AND POLICY, 388–89 (2d ed. 2002).

[125]  Art. 1, Declaration on the Right to Development, *supra* note 124.

[126]  International Bill of Rights comprises the UDHR, ICCPR and the ICESCR.

[127]  Art. 11, ICESCR, 1966, *available at* http://www.unhchr.org.

[128]  Art. 13, ICESCR, *id.*

[129]  Art. 11, ICESCR, *id.*

[130]  Arts. 6 and 7, ICESCR, *id.*

[131]  Art. 11, ICESCR, *id.*

[132]  *See* Experts Group Report, *supra* note 105, para. 21.

accepts this argument. The right to development has been controversial since its inception, and many feel that it has no place in international human rights law. No binding international instrument of universal application embodies this right yet[133] and the Rio Declaration, another non-binding instrument, is the first document adopted by consensus to refer to right to development, this time in the context of sustainable development.[134] Other instruments include the Vienna Declaration on Human Rights,[135] Copenhagen Declaration on Social Development[136] and the Beijing Declaration and Platform for Action,[137] all of which are non-binding instruments. It is regrettable that the General Assembly resolution on the right to development does not refer to sustainable development at all. This is even more disturbing given that another parallel commission appointed by the General Assembly—World Commission on Environment and Development—was working during the same period on ways to reconcile environmental protection with developmental issues.[138]

Despite the controversy surrounding the right to development, the UN General Assembly has continued its work on it, and, in 1998, the Economic and Social Council endorsed the recommendation of the Commission on Human Rights to establish a dual mechanism of an open ended Working Group on the right to development and an Independent Expert on the right to development.[139] The mandate of the open-ended Working Group is to:

---

[133] The African Charter on Human and Peoples' Rights, 1981, *reprinted in* BASIC DOCUMENTS ON HUMAN RIGHTS 557 (Ian Brownlie ed., 1992) is the only binding instrument, albeit regional, to embody this right. According to Article 22:

1. All peoples shall have the right to their economic, social and cultural development with due regard to their freedom and identity and in the equal enjoyment of the common heritage of mankind.

2. States shall have the duty, individually or collectively, to ensure the exercise of the right to development.

[134] Principle 3 notes that the right to development must be fulfilled so at to equitably meet developmental and environmental needs of present and future generations.

[135] Vienna Declaration and Program of Action, adopted at the World Conference on Human Rights, 1993 A/CONF.157/23, *available at* http://www.unhchr.ch/huridocda/huridoca.nsf/(Symbol)/A.CONF.157.23.En?OpenDocument.

[136] *Supra* note 81.

[137] Beijing Declaration and Platform for Action, Fourth World Conference on Women, 1995, *available at* http://www.unhchr.ch/.

[138] *See* Sumudu Atapattu, *The Right to a Healthy Life or the Right to Die Polluted?: The Emergence of a Human Right to a Healthy Environment under International Law*, 16 TULANE ENVTL. L.J. 65, 117 (2002).

[139] Decision 1998/269.

- monitor and review progress made in the promotion and implementation of the right to development;
- review reports and other information submitted by states and international or non-governmental organizations;
- submit a sessional report to the Commission on Human Rights.[140]

Recently the Commission renewed the mandate of the Working Group for one year, and also established a high-level task force on the implementation of the right to development.[141] Several reports have been issued within this mandate,[142] as has the Independent Expert. In his third report on the right to development, the Independent Expert noted that a country can develop by many different processes. However, this process must be linked to the realization of human rights and social development: "It is only that process of development 'in which all human rights and fundamental freedoms can be fully realized' that can be a universal human right which is the entitlement of every person."[143] In other words, the right to development implies a process of development that also achieves the full realization of human rights:

> The right to development is not just the sum total of all the different rights that can be realized individually or in isolation from other rights. As constituent elements of the right to development, these individual rights have to be realized in a manner that takes into account their interdependence with all other rights, does not detract from the realization of the other rights and does not ignore the requirements of the sustainability of the whole process of realizing all the rights.[144]

He has also pointed out that the right to development is not just an umbrella right or the sum of other rights.[145] He described the right to development as a vector composed of various elements including the right to food, right to health, right to housing, etc., as well as civil and political

---

[140] *Available at* http://www.unhchr.ch/development/right-03.html.

[141] Res. 2004/7, Commission on Human Rights, *available at* http://www.unhchr.org. Res. 2005/4, *id.*

[142] *See Report of the Working Group on the Right to Development on its Sixth Session,* E/CN.4/2005/25, Mar. 3, 2005.

[143] *Third Report of the Independent Expert on the Right to Development,* Mr Arjun Sengupta, submitted in accordance with Commission Res. 2000/5, E/CN.4/2001/WG.18/2, Jan. 2, 2001.

[144] *Id.,* para. 8.

[145] *Id.,* para. 9.

rights. Each element of the vector is a human right, as well as the vector itself is a human right.[146] Moreover, all the elements are interdependent to the extent that the realization of one right may depend on the level of realization of other rights. Because all human rights are inviolable and none is superior to the other, the improvement of one right cannot lead to the deterioration of another.[147]

It is interesting to note that the Independent Expert refers to sustainability as a requirement for the realization of the right to development.[148] While this is a welcome development, it is a pity that a more comprehensive analysis of the need for sustainable growth or sustainable development within the context of the right to development has not been made either by the Independent Expert or the Working Group.[149]

Although, at the time the resolution was adopted, the sustainable development movement had not gained momentum, it was precisely at the same time that another General Assembly appointed commission was looking into the relationship between environment and development. The fact that no reference whatsoever was made to this process gives the impression that there is lack of coordination among various institutions, which gives rise to compartmentalizing issues and looking at them in isolation, not as a whole. It took the right to development discourse several years to acknowledge the discourse on sustainable development and incorporate it into its process.

Both the Vienna Declaration on Human Rights and the Copenhagen Declaration on Social Development adopt a more expansive definition of the right to development and seek to balance that with sustainable development. Thus, the Vienna Declaration, adopting language similar to the Rio Declaration stresses that the right to development must be fulfilled so as to equitably meet developmental and environmental needs of present and future generations.[150] The Copenhagen Declaration adopts almost identical language—the only difference being the addition of the word "social" into the above equation.[151]

---

[146] *Id.*, para. 10.

[147] *Id.*

[148] *Id.*

[149] Report of the Working Group on the Right to Development, *supra* note 143, where only a passing reference is made to "sustainability."

[150] Vienna Declaration, *supra* note 135, para. 11.

[151] Copenhagen Declaration, *supra* note 81.

There are several problems with right to development: it is not clear what the parameters of the right are; it is also not clear who the beneficiaries of the right are—are they individuals, groups of individuals or states? The Declaration lists all three categories as beneficiaries. Under general human rights law, states are the guardians of these rights, not beneficiaries. Does this mean that in relation to the right to development, states are both beneficiaries and guardians of the right at the same time? This can lead to confusing results, to say the least.

An important aspect of the international human rights machinery is the remedies that are available to victims in the event of a violation of a protected right. Thus, the question arises as to how a violation of the right to development can be established. In the absence of an acceptable definition of this right, as well as a beneficiary group, it would be hard to establish a violation.

Many academics are not convinced of the utility of adopting the right to development as an inalienable right of people.[152] They argue that development cannot be expressed in human rights parlance. Human rights are usually individual in nature and while some human rights are exercised collectively,[153] it is not clear whether the right to development can be exercised individually or collectively. While there is no doubt that lack of development would impinge adversely on the enjoyment of protected rights, whether development itself is a "human right" has been hotly debated.[154] As one writer has noted:

> If it achieves any significance, the right to development will divert attention from the pressing issues of human dignity and freedom, obfuscate the true nature of human rights, and provide increasing resources and support for the state manipulation (not to say repression) of civil society and social groups. It will keep the international and diplomatic community engaged for many years in useless and feigned combat on the urgency and parameters of this right.[155]

---

[152] *See* the authorities cited in *infra* notes 156 and 158.

[153] Freedom of Assembly, freedom of association are examples, while genocide is the collective violation of the right to life.

[154] *See* HUNTER ET AL., *supra* note 124, at 388.

[155] *See* Yash Ghai, *Whose Human Right to Development?* Human Rights Unit Occasional Paper, 5–6 (Commonwealth Secretariat, Nov. 1989), *referred to in* Isabella D. Bunn, *The Right to Development: Implications for International Economic Law*, 15 AM. U. INT'L L. REV. 1425 (2000).

The right to development falls into the category of third generation rights. While some writes have advocated for a right to development,[156] others have warned of devaluing existing rights by expanding the notion of rights.[157] Many of the opponents have pointed to the lack of a philosophical basis, a lack of a proper definition and the issue of non-justiciability.[158] While there is no reason why new human rights should not be recognized and indeed there is a need for dynamism, much work remains to be done before the right to development can attain the degree of specificity or concreteness that would make it operable in practice.[159]

Third generation rights are attributed to Karel Vasak who articulated the need for solidarity rights.[160] Included in this category are right to development, right to peace, right to a healthy environment and the right to common heritage of mankind.[161] There is no consensus on the existence of these rights, and although the General Assembly adopted the Declaration on Right to Development in 1986, the actual text is vague and inconsistent, and there was no political consensus in relation to the right to development.[162] It has been, however, argued that "during the past decades it [right to development] has been transformed from a concept focused on economic development of states to a multi-dimensional human right aimed at contributing to the promotion of economic, social and cultural rights, as well as civil and political rights."[163]

---

[156] *See* Stephen Marks, *Emerging Human Rights: A New Generation for the 1980s?*, 33 RUTGERS L. REV. 435 (1980–81); Christopher Weeramantry, *Right to Development*, 25 INDIAN J. INT'L L. 482 (1985); Ronald Rich, *The Right to Development as an Emerging Human Right*, 23 VA. J. INT'L L. 287 (1983).

[157] Philip Alston, *A Third Generation of Solidarity Rights: Progressive Development or Obfuscation of International Human Rights Law*, 29 NETHERLANDS INT'L L. REV. 307 (1985).

[158] *See* Philip Alston, *Making Space for New Human Rights: The Case of the Right to Development*, HARVD. HUM. RTS. Y.B. 3 (1988). *See also* Philip Alston, *Conjuring up New Human Rights: A Proposal for Quality Control*, 78 AM. J. INT'L L. 607 (1984); RIGHTS OF PEOPLES (James Crawford ed., 1988); Anja Lindroos, *The Right to Development*, The Erik Castren Institute of International Law and Human Rights Research Reports 2/1999 (Helsinki, 1999). *See also* Upendra Baxi, *The Development of the Right to Development, in* HUMAN RIGHTS: NEW DIMENSIONS AND CHALLENGES 99 (Janusz Symonides ed., 1998); Weeramantry, *supra* note 156; and James C.N. Paul, *The United Nations Family: Challenges of Law and Development: The United Nations and the Creation of an International Law of Development*, 36 HARV. INT'L L.J. 307 (1995)

[159] *Id.*

[160] *See* Alston, *supra* note 157.

[161] *See* Lindroos, *supra* note 158.

[162] *Id.*

[163] *Id.*

As pointed out, the right to development suffers from definitional problems. Part of the problem is that there is no consensus on what is meant by "development." Does it refer to economic development, human centered development or sustainable development?[164] The earlier notion of development being synonymous with economic development has given way to a much broader notion of development—sustainability.[165] The new ideology dictates that without environmental sustainability, development is meaningless.[166] Does this mean that right to development means "a right to sustainable development?"[167] Furthermore, other problems remain: Is it a new right or is it a synthesis of other human rights?[168] Who is the holder of the right—is it individual or collective?[169] What is the content of the right? Who has the correlative duty in relation to this right?[170] The answers to these questions are far from clear. These issues will have to be resolved before we can talk about a "right to development." Despite these difficulties, the United Nations has made a tremendous effort to promote the realization of this right.[171] It has been referred to in many UN World Conferences,[172] the mandate of the UN High Commissioner for Human Rights and was the subject of a global consultation.[173] Many development agencies, including the UNDP and the World Bank have embraced human rights within their mandates, and the UNDP, in particular, has set forth a policy to integrate human rights with sustainable development.[174] As dis-

---

[164] *Id.*

[165] *See* Dernbach, *supra* note 49.

[166] *See* the 1992 Rio Declaration, 1987 Report of the World Commission on Environment and Development and the 2002 Plan of Implementation of the World Summit for Sustainable Development.

[167] It is interesting to note in this regard that during the negotiations of the Rio Declaration, developing countries strongly opposed the amalgamation of Principles 3 and 4 on the ground that the right to development should not be transformed into a right to sustainable development. *See* HUNTER ET AL., *supra* note 124, at 388.

[168] The Experts Group takes the view that it is a synthesis of existing human rights. *See* discussion *supra* notes 63–64 and accompanying text.

[169] It has been argued that some third generation rights such as the right to development may contain an individual element. *See* Allan Rosas, *So-called Rights of the Third Generation, in* ECONOMIC, SOCIAL AND CULTURAL RIGHTS 244 (Asbjorn Eide, Catarina Krause & Allan Rosas eds., 1995).

[170] *Id.*

[171] *See* Bunn, *supra* note 156.

[172] The Rio Conference on Environment and Development, The Copenhagen Summit on Social Development are examples.

[173] *See* http://www.unhchr.org.

[174] *Id.*

cussed in Chapter 1, poverty violates many human rights and the argument that "development" would "cure all evils" makes sense in this context. However, everything depends on the articulation of this right in operable terms.

Controversial as it may be, it is encouraging to observe that the debate on the right to development has taken note of other international developments, such as the debate on sustainable development. Thus, reconciling the two discourses, it is possible to contend that the right to development in actual terms means the right to sustainable development.[175] However, neither of the terms is sufficiently established to be elevated to the status of a legal right as their definition (as well as conceptual foundation in relation to the right to development) is far from clear. In their comments submitted to the Working Group on the Right to Development, the U.S. government pointed out that there is still no consensus on the precise meaning of the right to development.[176] However, it would continue to support further discussion, which would help member states of the United Nations to reach the shared goal of sustainable development and noted the relevance of good governance.[177]

In its 2005 report on the right to development, the Working Group endorsed the conclusions of the Task Force and agreed that the implementation of the right to development requires growth with equity.[178] Development must be grounded in economic policies that foster growth with social justice. The Working Group noted that the right to development incorporates human rights and principles of transparency, equality, participation, accountability and non-discrimination into the development process at both national and international levels.[179] It further recognizes the multi-faceted nature of the right to development and that a rights-based approach to economic growth is necessary, which contributes to the realization of the right to development.[180] While the Working Group made several recommendations, which included references to the unsustainable

---

[175]  *Cf.*, the argument made by developing countries during the negotiations of the Rio Declaration, *supra* note 167.

[176]  U.S. Comments to the Right to Development Working Group (Feb. 25–Mar. 8, 2002), *at* http://www.state.gov/s/1/38654.htm.

[177]  *Id.*

[178]  *Right to Development, Report of the Working Group on the Right to Development on its Sixth Session,* E./CN.4/2005/25, Mar. 3, 2005.

[179]  *Id.*

[180]  *Id.*, para. 46.

[181]  *Id.*, para. 54(a).

debt burden,[181] the role of donor countries in realizing the Millennium Development Goals,[182] the successful conclusion of the Doha Round of trade negotiations,[183] independent assessment of trade agreements, participation of women and including a gender perspective,[184] no reference was yet again made to sustainable development or environmental protection. This continued lack of reference to the most crucial issue facing the international community today is indeed disturbing and seems to reinforce the view that sustainable development and environmental protection are secondary to economic development.

Judging from the contents of the above report, it is not clear what the right to development discourse adds to the rights-based approach to development. There is no longer any doubt that development has to be rights-based. In other words, if development does not take place within a framework of human rights, it is accepted that there is no development at all. Moreover, there is some consensus on the three pillars of sustainable development as economic development, social development and environmental protection;[185] one without the other is not considered sustainable. So what does the debate on the right to development add to the discussion on sustainable development?

### b. The Right to a Healthy Environment

This issue received attention in Chapter 1. It must be noted here that as compared with the right to development, the right to a healthy environment has received only step-motherly treatment by the UN General Assembly. No resolution akin to the one on the right to development was ever adopted by the General Assembly in relation to the right to environment. The closest the General Assembly has come to endorsing a right to environment was its resolution in 1990, which welcomed the decision of the Commission on Human Rights and the Sub-Commission on Minorities to study the relationship between human rights and the environment and noted that "all individuals are entitled to live in an environment adequate for their health and well-being."[186] Although this resolution endorsed the relationship between environmental degradation and enjoyment of human

---

[182]   *Id.*, para. 54(c).

[183]   *Id.*, para. 54(d).

[184]   *Id.*, para. 54(f).

[185]   *See* Plan of Implementation adopted at the WSSD.

[186]   GA Res. 45/94, UN GAOR, 45th sess., at 2, UN Doc. A/RES/45/94 (1991).

[187]   *See* Atapattu, *supra* note 138.

rights, it fell short of adopting a human right to a healthy environment.[187] Similarly, the draft articles on Human Rights and the Environment adopted by the Sub-Commission on Minorities have remained gathering dust in the UN archives.[188]

The Experts Report on Sustainable Development traces the evolution of this right and refers to the Stockholm Declaration.[189] However, its reference to the Convention on Biological Diversity in this context is rather strange.[190] Unfortunately, the Experts Report does not refer either to the Ksentini reports or to the regional instruments that specifically endorse a right to a healthy environment.[191] In conclusion, it noted: "The right to a healthy environment provides a focus to guide the integration of environment and development. Development is sustainable where it advances or realizes the right to a healthy environment."[192]

Some may find fault with this argument. It is not strictly necessary to adopt a right to environment in order to achieve sustainable development. As noted earlier, sustainable development embodies several components, both substantive and procedural, and the right to environment is not one of these components. What the recognition of a right to environment does is to give victims of environmental abuse an additional forum to seek redress and the ability to resort to the international human rights machinery.[193] If everybody has the opportunity to live in a healthy environment, it could mean that development has been sustainable—this, however, is the end result. The mere recognition of a right to environment does not, by itself, mean that sustainable development has been achieved. That would mean equating environmental protection with sustainable development. We now know that environmental protection is but one pillar of sustainable

---

[188] *See* Karric Wolfe, *Greening the International Human Rights Sphere? Environmental Rights and the Draft Declaration of Principles on Human Rights and the Environment*, 9 APPEAL 45 (2003).

[189] *See* Experts Group Report, *supra* note 105.

[190] The Report notes that the Convention recognizes in its Preamble the "intrinsic value of biological diversity." *Id.* at para. 29.

[191] As discussed in Chapter 1, these regional instruments are: the African Charter on Human and Peoples' Rights and the San Salvador Protocol to the American Convention on Human Rights.

[192] Experts Group Report, *supra* note 105, at para. 31.

[193] *See* Caroline Dommen, *Claiming Environmental Rights: Some Possibilities Offered by the United Nations' Human Rights Mechanisms*, 11 GEO. INT'L. ENVTL. L. REV. 1 (1998).

[194] *See* discussion in Section B.5, *supra* note 80 and accompanying text.

development.[194] People could live in a pristine environment without enjoying a good standard of living. This does not mean sustainable development has been achieved.

Three approaches have been suggested in adopting a right to environment: first, "greening" existing human rights; second, proclaiming a substantive, distinct right to environment; and finally, adopting environmental procedural rights.[195] In this regard, it must be noted that the first approach has already been tested, particularly at the national level.[196] At the international level, too, this trend can be seen.[197] This amounts to invoking protected rights such as the right to life, the right to health, the right to an adequate standard of life, etc., to seek redress for environmental wrongs.[198] The third approach can be considered as part of international law, given that the procedural rights of information, participation and access to remedies, are part of international human rights law and increasingly applied in relation to environmental issues. The Aarhus Convention on Access to Information[199] is a good example of this trend. The second approach is rather contentious and reflects some of the criticisms aimed at the debate on the right to development.[200]

Some have even contended that a rights-based approach to environment is unsuitable for several reasons: the right to environment cannot be considered as vested in humans alone; an environmental right is not based on morality but on the need for survival; and the element of universality did not exist as it cannot be said that all cultures in the world would demand it, whatever the economic cost.[201] Others have contended that it cannot be termed as an inalienable human right, as it will be subject to derogation.[202] It is hard to agree with this contention. Except for a few

---

[195] *See* Dinah Shelton, *Human Rights, Environmental Rights and Right to Environment*, 28 STAN. J. INT'L L., 103 (1991). *See also* Michael Burger, *Bi-Polar and Polycentric Approaches to Human Rights and the Environment*, 28 COLUM. J. ENVTL. L. 371 (2003).

[196] *See* Atapattu, *supra* note 138.

[197] *Id. See also* Shelton and Burger, *supra* note 195.

[198] *See* Atapattu, *supra* note 138 for a discussion of some of these cases.

[199] Convention on Access to Information, Public Participation in Decision-Making and Access to Justice in Environmental Matters, 1998, 38 ILM 517 (1999). *See* discussion in Chapter 4.

[200] *See* Section C.1.a on the right to development.

[201] *See* Noralee Gibson, *The Right to a Clean Environment*, 54 SASK. L. REV. 5 (1990).

[202] *See* Gunther Handl, *Human Rights and Protection of the Environment: A Midly Revisionist View, in* HUMAN RIGHTS, SUSTAINABLE DEVLEOPMENT AND THE ENVIRONMENT (Antonio Trindade ed., 1992).

rights, such as the right to life and the right against torture, almost all other rights are derogable.[203] It is not contended that the proposed right to environment should be either absolute or non-derogable. Courts have generally adopted a balancing of interests test in relation to environmental issues,[204] and no doubt this trend will continue even if a distinct right to environment is adopted.

One of the advantages of adopting a distinct right to environment is that activities of states will become subject to international scrutiny both through the submission of country reports, as well as through individual petitions, if such a right is recognized. While there is some level of international scrutiny under certain international environmental treaties,[205] the process of scrutiny differs from that under international human rights treaties. Moreover, individuals may be able to make use of the individual complaints procedure available under the First Optional Protocol to the ICCPR,[206] depending on how the right is placed in the human rights discourse.

### c. Eradicating Poverty

Sustainable development and poverty eradication go hand in hand. If a society is plagued with poverty, it would be hard to achieve sustainable development. Poverty also leads to the violation of human rights such as the right to health, the right to an adequate standard of living, the right to a livelihood, the right to food, the right to housing, etc. Thus, poverty has received the attention of the international community in the recent years particularly in relation to sustainable development. It is also closely related to the North-South divide in relation to development and environmental protection.

Several environmental treaties also refer to the need to eradicate poverty. The UN Framework Convention on Climate Change,[207] for exam-

---

[203] *See* art. 4 of the ICCPR, *available at* http://www.unhchr.org.

[204] *See* the *Case of Powell and Rayner v. UK*, 172 Eur. Ct. H.R. (ser. A) (1990) where it was held that while the aircraft noise from the Heathrow airport amounted to a violation of the petitioner's right to privacy, it was justified on the ground of greater benefit to the community. A similar conclusion was reached in the *Skarby Case*, 180-B Eur. Ct. H.R. (ser. A) (1990). *See also* Richard Desgagne, *Integrating Environmental Values into the European Convention on Human Rights*, 89 AM. J. INT'L. L. 263 (1995).

[205] Most environmental treaties establish a Conference of Parties (COPs), which monitors the implementation of the treaty.

[206] First Optional Protocol to the ICCPR, *available at* http://www.ohchr.org, recognizes the right of individual petition to the Human Rights Committee for a violation of the provisions of the ICCPR, provided domestic remedies have been exhausted. *See* art. 2 of the First Optional Protocol.

[207] *Supra* note 53.

ple, noted that "responses to climate change should be coordinated with social and economic development in an integrated manner with a view to avoiding adverse impacts on the latter, taking into account the legitimate priority needs of developing countries for the achievement of sustained economic growth and the eradication of poverty."[208] Similarly, the Convention on Biological Diversity[209] points out that "economic and social development and poverty eradication are the first and overriding priorities of developing countries."[210] The UN Desertification Convention[211] provides another example and links desertification with poverty, poor health and nutrition, lack of food security, as well as issues relating to migration and displacement.[212] It further provides that the parties shall integrate strategies for poverty eradication into efforts to combat desertification.[213] The Desertification Convention is probably the only convention to embody provisions on poverty eradication as a general obligation; the other two conventions merely refer to poverty eradication in the Preambles, without embodying any specific obligations.

The World Summit for Social Development held in Copenhagen in 1995 and follow-up action is important in this regard. The parties noted in the Copenhagen Declaration in relation to sustainable development and social development that:

> We are deeply convinced that economic development, social development and environmental protection are interdependent and mutually reinforcing components of sustainable development, which is the framework for our efforts to achieve a higher quality of life for all people. . . .[214]

> We recognize, therefore, that social development is central to the needs and aspirations of people throughout the world and to the responsibilities of Governments and all sectors of civil society.[215]

---

[208]  *Id.*, Preamble.

[209]  *Supra* note 54.

[210]  *Id.*, Preamble.

[211]  1994 UN Convention to Combat Desertification in Countries Experiencing Serious Drought and/or Desertification, Particularly in Africa, *supra* note 121.

[212]  *Id.*, Preamble.

[213]  *Id.*, art. 4(2)(c).

[214]  Copenhagen Declaration, *supra* note 81, para. 6.

[215]  *Id.*, para. 7.

One of the commitments that the parties made is to eradicate poverty in the world through decisive national actions and international cooperation.[216] To this end, the parties have identified the need to address the root causes of poverty and to provide for the basic needs of all. At the international level, the parties have committed to ensure that the international community and international organizations, particularly multilateral financial institutions, assist developing countries to achieve the goal of poverty eradication.[217]

The Declaration adopted on the tenth anniversary of the World Summit for Social Development[218] stressed that policies and programs designed to achieve poverty eradication should include measures to foster social integration, including by providing marginalized groups with equal access to opportunities.[219] The report also includes the conclusions of a high-level round table on the eradication of poverty, which notes that the current levels of global poverty cannot be tolerated and that coordinated national and global action was needed.[220] The wide-ranging root causes of poverty were categorized into three groups: unequal distribution of assets; insecurity and vulnerability; and social exclusion and powerlessness.[221] Not only is it necessary to identify the root causes of poverty, it is also necessary to see whether these root causes were appropriately addressed. Equity and equality dimensions have to be incorporated into national strategies and programs on poverty eradication. The report points out that poverty exists in both developed and developing countries, and the world needed to assume collective responsibility for its eradication. It also notes that the promotion of good governance and the rule of law are an essential precondition for combating poverty.[222]

## d. Equity

Equity is considered a general principle of international law and has received the attention of the International Court of Justice (ICJ) on several

---

[216] *Id.*, Commitment 2.

[217] *Id.*

[218] Declaration on the Tenth Anniversary of the World Summit for Social Development, Commission for Social Development, Report on the Forty-Third Session, E/2005/26, E/CN.5/2005/7.

[219] *Id.*, para. 3.

[220] *Id.*, Annex I.

[221] *Id.*

[222] *Id.*

occasions. In the *North Sea Continental Shelf Cases*,[223] the ICJ referred to the application of "equitable principles."[224] Similarly, in the *Tunisia-Libya Continental Shelf Case*,[225] the ICJ noted that the judicial application of equitable principles means that a court should render justice in the concrete case, by means of a decision shaped by and adjusted to the "relevant factual matrix of that case."[226] The Court emphasized "equitable solutions" and noted that each continental shelf dispute should be considered on its own merits.[227] Equity has played an important role in de-limiting maritime zones, and in allocating fishery resources.[228] It received extensive treatment by Judge Weeramantry in his separate opinion in the *Jan Mayen Case*.[229] He identified the uses of equity as: a basis for individualized justice; introducing considerations of fairness, reasonableness, and good faith; a basis for certain specific principles of legal reasoning; offering standards for the allocation and sharing of resources and benefits; and to achieve distributive justice.[230] The methods of operation of equity included the balancing of interests of the parties; the equitable interpretation of the rule of law; tempering the application of strict rules; filling gaps in the law; and through the use of judicial discretion.[231]

In the present context equity has played an important role in relation to sustainable development. Equity underlies several concepts that have emerged in this area: inter- and intra-generational equity and the common but differentiated responsibility principle originated from the principle of equity.[232] It can indeed be argued that equity underlies the whole debate on sustainable development, which seeks to ensure that people have a decent standard of living in a healthy environment; they have access to resources and to information relating to their environment; they have the opportunity to participate in the decision-making process; the disparity

---

[223] 1969 ICJ 3.

[224] *Id.*, para. 50.

[225] 1982 ICJ 18.

[226] *Id.*, para. 4.

[227] *Id.*

[228] *See* INTERNATIONAL LAW: CASES AND MATERIALS 131 (Lori Damrosch et al. eds., 4th ed. 2001).

[229] *Maritime Delimitation in the Area Between Greenland and Jan Mayen (Denmark and Norway)*, 1993 ICJ 38.

[230] *Id.*

[231] *Id.*

[232] *See* Chapter 5 for a discussion of the common but differentiated responsibility principle.

between the rich and the poor is addressed; poverty is eradicated; and unsustainable patterns of consumption and production are addressed. Many other components can be added to this list.

Inter- and intra-generational equity is an important component of sustainable development. It seeks to ensure that there is equity among generations as well as equity in the present generation itself. In other words, it seeks to ensure that future generations will have at least the same options that are available to the present generation and that the members of the present generation have the same opportunity to access resources. It is generally argued that each generation constitutes a continuum and that all generations form a partnership and must be treated in a non-discriminatory manner.[233] Edith Brown Weiss is considered the architect of the inter-generational equity principle.[234] The WCED definition of sustainable development specifically embodies an inter-generational dimension.[235]

Many environmental treaties also refer to the need to protect future generations. The International Convention for the Regulation of Whaling[236] and the Convention for the Protection of World Cultural and Natural Heritage[237] are examples of earlier treaties while the UN Climate Change Convention, the Convention on Biological Diversity, as well as non-binding instruments, such as the Rio Declaration, all refer to the inter-generational equity principle.

It is interesting to note, in this regard, the provisions in the recently concluded Convention on the Protection and Promotion of the Diversity of Cultural Expressions under the auspices of UNESCO.[238] The Convention notes that "cultural diversity creates a rich and varied world, which increases the range of choices and nurtures human capacities and values, and therefore is a mainspring for sustainable development for communities,

---

[233] Experts Group Report, *supra* note 105, para 48.

[234] *See* WEISS, *supra* note 8.

[235] *See* OUR COMMON FUTURE, *supra* note 4.

[236] 161 UNTS 72, 10 UST 952, signed Dec. 2, 1946, entered into force Nov. 10, 1948. The Preamble states that the parties recognize "the interest of the nations of the world in safeguarding for future generations the great natural resources represented by the whale stocks."

[237] Signed in 1972 under the auspices of UNESCO, *available at* http://www.wcmc. org.uk/igcmc/convent/wh/wh_atls.html. Article 4 of the Convention refers to future generations.

[238] Signed Oct. 2005, *available at* http://www.unesco.org/culture/culturaldiversity/ convention_en.pdf/.

peoples and nations."[239] The Convention further provides in relation to sustainable development that:

> Cultural diversity is a rich asset for individuals and societies. The protection, promotion and maintenance of cultural diversity are an essential requirement for sustainable development for the benefit of present and future generations.[240]

It is interesting how the Convention makes a link between sustainable development and cultural diversity. Cultural diversity is defined in the Convention as referring to "the manifold ways in which the cultures of groups and societies find expression."[241] Parties are required to provide appropriate information to UNESCO on measures taken to protect and promote cultural diversity within their territory and at the international level.[242] The parties must endeavor to integrate culture in their development policies at all levels for the creation of conditions conducive to sustainable development.[243] Furthermore, parties must endeavor to support cooperation for sustainable development and poverty reduction through, *inter alia*, the strengthening of cultural industries in developing countries.[244]

As with many other environmental concepts, problems remain with the implementation of the inter-generational equity principle. It is not clear what this principle adds to the legal concept of standing or, since future generations have no voice in the decision-making process, it is not clear how their interests should be secured. When the consequences of many of the environmental problems created by the present generations become manifest, the decision makers of the present generation will not be available to be held accountable. That is why it is important to ensure that the decisions and activities of the present generation do not cause damage to the future generations and that this is factored into the decision-making process. Other principles/concepts of international environmental law, such as the precautionary principle, the principle of prevention and environmental impact assessment process are also significant in ensuring that damage will not be caused to future generations as a result of activities today.

---

[239] *Id.*, Preamble.

[240] *Id.*, art. 2(6).

[241] *Id.*, art. 4(1).

[242] *Id.*, art. 9(a).

[243] *Id.*, art. 13.

[244] *Id.*, art. 14.

The ICJ made a reference to future generations in its Advisory Opinion on *The Legality of the Threat or Use of Nuclear Weapons*,[245] where the Court said that "the environment is not an abstraction but represents living space, the quality of life and the very health of human beings, including generations unborn."[246] In his dissenting opinion in the *Nuclear Tests Case*,[247] Judge Weeramantry noted that this case raised, as no case has done before, the principle of inter-generational equity. He pointed out that as the characteristics of radioactive material is such that its consequences can extend to over 20,000 years, the issues raised in this case are "too serious to be dismissed as lacking in importance merely because there is no precedent."[248] The rights of the people of New Zealand include the rights of generations unborn. He pointed out that "Those are rights which a nation is entitled, and indeed obliged, to protect."[249] Referring to Principle 1 of the Stockholm Declaration, which refers to the solemn responsibility to protect and improve the environment for present and future generations, Judge Weeramantry noted:

> This Court has not thus far had occasion to make any pronouncement on this developing field. The present case presents it with a pre-eminent opportunity to do so, as it raises in pointed form the possibility of damage to generations yet unborn.[250]

In the case of *Minors Oposa v. Secretary of the Department of Environment and Natural Resources*,[251] the Philippines Supreme Court held that the plaintiffs had standing to represent their unborn posterity. This case was brought by a group of minors representing their generation as well as generations yet unborn. They argued that the deforestation of rainforests, caused by the existing timber licenses in the country, violated their right to a balanced and healthful ecology. The Court pronounced in this regard that:

> The case, however, has a special and novel element. Petitioners minors assert that they represent their generation as well as generations yet unborn. We find no difficulty in ruling that they can,

---

[245]  1996 ICJ 226.

[246]  *Id.*, para. 226.

[247]  Request for an Examination of the Situation in Accordance with Paragraph 63 of the Court's Judgment of 20 December 1974 in the Nuclear Tests (New Zealand v. France) Case, 1995 ICJ 228.

[248]  *Id.*, Dissenting Opinion, Judge Weeramantry.

[249]  *Id.*

[250]  *Id.*

[251]  *Reprinted in* 33 ILM 173 (1994).

for themselves, for others of their generation and for the succeeding generations, file a class suit. Their personality to sue in behalf of the succeeding generations can only be based on the concept of intergenerational responsibility insofar as the right to a balanced and healthful ecology is concerned. Such a right, as hereinafter expounded, considers the "rhythm and harmony of nature." . . . Needless to say, every generation has a responsibility to the next to preserve that rhythm and harmony for the full enjoyment of a balanced and healthful ecology. Put a little differently, the minors' assertion of their right to a sound environment constitutes, at the same time, the performance of their obligation to ensure the protection of that right for the generations to come.[252]

While this case is a clear expression of the acceptance of the inter-generational equity principle, to what extent it can be operationalized is doubtful. Thus, for example, would the future generations be bound by this decision? While it is important from the point of view of laying down the obligation of the present generation to protect the environment for the benefit of future generations, beyond this recognition, its significance is rather limited.[253]

The principle of equity also dictates that those who created a particular environmental problem should be held accountable for that action, while at the same time ensuring that there is global participation in treaties. This has resulted in the adoption of the common but differentiated responsibility principle, which acknowledges that given the different contribution to global environmental problems by developed and developing states, they bear a common but differentiated responsibility in dealing with those global problems.[254] Many environmental treaties have operationalized this principle by adopting different compliance regimes for different countries based on their level of development.[255] The Global Environment Facility (GEF) also facilitates this process by giving financial assistance to developing countries to implement their obligations under various treaties.[256]

The other principles of sustainable development discussed by the Experts Group include the sovereignty over natural resources and the

---

[252] *Id.*

[253] *See* Lowe, *supra* note 82.

[254] Principle 7 of the Rio Declaration, *supra* note 61, embodies this principle. This is discussed in Chapter 5.

[255] *See* the instruments discussed in Chapter 5, Section C.2.

[256] The Montreal Protocol, the Climate Change Convention, the Convention on Biological Diversity are some examples. *See also* Chapter 5.

obligation not to cause extra-territorial damage;[257] sustainable use of natural resources;[258] prevention of environmental harm;[259] and the precautionary principle.[260] As these principles have received attention in various chapters of this publication, they will not be discussed here.

### e.  Duty to Cooperate in a Spirit of Global Partnership

The Experts Group Report also discussed principles and concepts of international cooperation and referred to the duty to cooperate as a well-established principle of international law.[261] The duty to cooperate in good faith is tied to the procedural components of sustainable development and often requires prior information, consultation and negotiation.[262] The duty to negotiate a settlement in good faith was articulated by the ICJ in the *Case Concerning the Gabcikovo Nagymaros Project.*

It is not exactly clear what is meant by the principle of global partnership, although it does seem an extension of the duty to cooperate but seeks to convey more. It seems to apply to global environmental problems or to global issues, such as poverty or terrorism. The Expert Groups Report points out that the principle of cooperation in a spirit of global partnership should also be extended to non-state entities. The Report has further subdivided this principle into three major components: (1) common concern of mankind; (2) common but differentiated responsibility principle; and (3) special treatment of developing countries, small island states and countries with economies in transition.[263] It is not clear on what criteria this subdivision was done. Certainly, components (2) and (3) have roots in the principle of equity, and while the principle of cooperation may give rise to certain procedural requirements, it is unlikely that it has any substantive components such as the common but differentiated responsibility. The distinction between (2) and (3) is also not clear and seem to overlap in content.

---

[257]  *See* Experts Group Report, *supra* note 105.

[258]  *Id.*

[259]  *Id. See also* Chapter 3.

[260]  *Id.*

[261]  *Id.*

[262]  Principle 18 of the Rio Declaration, *supra* note 12, requires states to immediately notify other states of any natural disasters or other emergencies while Principle 19 requires states to provide prior and timely notification and relevant information to potentially affected states. It also requires the parties to enter into consultations in good faith.

[263]  Experts Group Report, *supra* note 105, para. 81.

Principle 27 of the Rio Declaration also refers to the need to cooperate in a spirit of partnership. The word "global" is missing here. Was this omission an oversight or deliberate? Does this mean that while Principle 7 applies to global issues, Principle 27 applies to all issues? Principle 27 calls upon states and people to cooperate in good faith and in a spirit of partnership in the fulfillment of the principles embodied in the Declaration and in the "further development of international law in the field of sustainable development."[264] The main distinction between the two principles seems to be that while Principle 7 applies to states, Principle 27 encompasses non-state actors within its ambit.

### f. Common Concern of Mankind

According to the Experts Group, this principle finds roots in the principle of cooperation. If a particular issue is categorized as a common concern of mankind, it seems to imply that there is a duty to cooperate in addressing that issue. Thus, climate change[265] and protection of biological diversity[266] are considered as common concerns of mankind. It must be pointed out that the notion of common concern originated as a response to the controversy surrounding the concept of common heritage of mankind.[267] The legal ramifications of such designation or the parameters of this concept are not very clear, aside from elevating a particular issue to international scrutiny. While it has avoided the controversy surrounding the common heritage of mankind concept, it does not seem to carry any legal implications. According to the Experts Group, however:

> The concept of common concern of humankind interlinks with a number of others relating to global environmental and resources issues. Most prominent among them are the fundamental right to an environment conducive to a life in dignity, and the principle of inter-generational equity. It can, however, also be viewed as a specific manifestation of the overarching duty to cooperate, which constitutes the very anchor of international law.[268]

It is difficult to see how the concept of common concern of mankind is related to the right to environment and the inter-generational equity

---

[264] Principle 27, Rio Declaration, *supra* note 12.

[265] *See* the Preamble to the UN Framework Convention on Climate Change, *supra* note 53.

[266] *See* the Preamble to the Convention on Biological Diversity, *supra* note 54.

[267] *See* HUNTER ET AL., *supra* note 124, at 396.

[268] Experts Group Report, *supra* note 105, para 88.

principle. While, of course, sustainable development may be the link that brings every strand (in this case, every concept or principle) together, it is difficult to conceptualize how common concern relates to the other two principles.

The Experts Report further notes that the word "humankind" establishes a link between the present and future generations, underlying a long-term temporal dimension.[269] "Common" connotes solidarity in protecting the global environment and a spatial dimension in matters of importance to the biosphere as a whole.[270]

### g.   Common Heritage of Mankind

This principle applies mainly to natural resources and has been applied in the context of exploitation of fisheries and marine resources. The UN Convention on the Law of the Sea, for example, declares that the international seabed area is the common heritage of mankind:

> Desiring by this Convention to develop the principles embodied in resolution 2749 (XXV) of 17 December 1970 in which the General Assembly of the United Nations solemnly declared *inter alia* that the area of the sea-bed and ocean floor and the subsoil thereof, beyond the limits of national jurisdiction, as well as its resources, are the common heritage of mankind, the exploration and exploitation of which shall be carried out for the benefit of mankind as a whole, irrespective of the geographical location of States.[271]

Similarly, the Convention points out that "The Area and its resources are the common heritage of mankind."[272] Article 137 elaborates on the legal status of the Area and its resources. Accordingly, no state can make any claims of sovereignty over the Area or its resources, nor can any part of it be appropriated. All rights in the resources of the Area are vested in mankind as a whole. The Authority shall act on its behalf. Article 140 notes that activities in the Area must be carried out for the benefit of mankind as a whole irrespective of the geographical location of states. The Authority shall provide for the equitable sharing of financial and other economic benefits derived from activities in the Area on a non-discriminatory basis. It further provides that non-peaceful activities cannot be carried out in the Area.

---

269   *Id.*, para. 84.

270   *Id.*

271   Preamble, *supra* note 119.

272   *Id.*, art. 136.

Thus, these provisions indicate that if an area is subject to the common heritage principle, any benefits that arise from peaceful activities in that area should be equitably shared on a non-discriminatory basis. This is the essence of the common heritage principle. That is precisely why it has been controversial.[273] Those states that invest heavily in exploration or exploitation activities do not want to share the benefits arising from such activities in an equitable manner on an equal basis. According to the Experts Group, "the common heritage of humankind principle implies, among other things, regulated access to resources, non-alienation, sharing of benefits, reservation for peaceful purposes and due regard to the interests of future generations."[274] While benefit sharing has been included in the Convention on Biological Diversity,[275] the common heritage label has been discarded in favor of a common concern of mankind label[276] in order to avoid the controversies of the former. However, apart from elevating an issue to the international level, it is not clear what the legal consequences of common concern of mankind are.

## h.  Cooperation in a Transboundary Context

The Experts Group Report notes that cooperation in solving international problems is one of the purposes of the United Nations and points out that while Chapter IX of the UN Charter refers to "international economic and social cooperation," this should also include environmental cooperation.[277] A general obligation to cooperate in environmental matters was recognized in Article 8 of the WCED Principles.[278] From a historical perspective, cooperation in relation to transboundary environmental issues preceded the concern for cooperation in relation to global environmental issues. The report notes that the duty to cooperate in a transboundary context includes five main components:

- equitable and reasonable use of transboundary natural resources;
- notification to and consultations with neighboring and potentially affected states;

---

[273] *See* HUNTER ET AL., *supra* note 124, at 393.

[274] Experts Group Report, *supra* note 105, para. 104.

[275] Art. 15(7), *supra* note 54.

[276] Preamble, *supra* note 54.

[277] Para. 105, *supra* note 105.

[278] ENVIRONMENTAL PROTECTION AND SUSTAINABLE DEVELOPMENT: LEGAL PRINCIPLES AND RECOMMENDATIONS adopted by the Experts Group on Environmental Law of the World Commission on Environment and Development, 27 (R.D. Munro & J.G. Lammers eds., 1986).

- environmental impact assessment in a transboundary context;
- prior informed consent;[279] and
- cooperation to discourage or prevent the relocation and transfer of activities and substances that cause severe environmental degradation or are harmful to human health.[280]

## 2. New Delhi Principles on Sustainable Development

The New Delhi Principles on Sustainable Development[281] adopted by the International Law Association (ILA) have also been utilized as the foundation for the discussion on sustainable development principles.[282] These principles include both substantive and procedural elements of sustainable development. The principles enumerated in the Declaration are: the duty of states to ensure sustainable use of natural resources; the principle of equity and the eradication of poverty; the principle of common but differentiated responsibilities, the principle of the precautionary approach to human health, natural resources and ecosystems; the principle of public participation and access to information and justice; the principle of good governance; and the principle of integration and interrelationship, in particular in relation to human rights and social, economic and environmental objectives. As can be seen, some of these principles overlap with the principles identified by the Experts Group.

In its 2002 report, the ILA points out that "some general and some specific principles of international law are at the core of international law of sustainable development. Taken together, they may well be viewed as a framework of an international law in the filed of sustainable development."[283] The general principles of international law identified by the ILA are: the rule of law in international relations, including international economic relations; the duty to cooperate; the duty to observe human rights; and the principle of integration. The specific principles of international

---

[279] It must be pointed out that prior informed consent is required only in very specific contexts (e.g., hazardous substances) and is not generally required under the principle of cooperation.

[280] Para. 106, *supra* note 105. Other principles referred to in the Experts Group Report, such as the precautionary principle, participatory rights and environmental impact assessment are not discussed here as they are discussed in other chapters in this publication.

[281] International Law Association, *New Delhi Declaration of Principles of International Law Relating to Sustainable Development*, Res. 3/2002. *See* http://www.ila-hq.org.

[282] *See* SUSTAINABLE DEVELOPMENT LAW, *supra* note 71.

[283] International Law Association, New Delhi Conference, *Legal Aspects of Sustainable Development* (2002). *See* http://www.ila-hq.org.

sustainable development law are: sovereignty over natural resources;[284] the duty to ensure sustainable use of natural resources; principle of intergenerational equity; principle of common but differentiated responsibilities; common heritage of humankind;[285] the precautionary principle; public participation and access to information and justice; and good governance including democratic accountability.

Discussing examples of the principle of integration, Cordonier Segger and Khalfan identify four categories of instruments that give effect to this principle: separate spheres; parallel yet interdependent; partially integrated spheres; and highly integrated new regimes.[286] The examples that are cited for the last category are: the UN Convention to Combat Desertification in Countries Experiencing Serious Drought and/or Desertification, Particularly in Africa, the Cartegena Protocol on Biosafety,[287] and the International Plant Genetic Resources Treaty.[288] These treaties seek to balance developmental issues with environmental and social issues, and the integration of these issues is reflected during the negotiation process, as well as in the final document itself. Thus, according to the Desertification Convention, "desertification and drought affect sustainable development through their interrelationships with important social problems such as poverty, poor health and nutrition, lack of food security, and those arising from migration, displacement of persons and demographic dynamics."[289] The Convention also notes that desertification is caused by "complex interactions among physical, biological, political, social, cultural and economic factors."[290] Among the general obligations under the Convention is the obligation to "adopt an integrated approach addressing the physical, biological and socio-economic aspects of the processes of desertification and drought."[291] It also requires the parties to integrate strategies for poverty eradication into efforts to combat desertification and mitigate the effects of drought.[292] Clearly, the Desertification Convention is a good example of an integrated approach to sustainable development.

---

[284] One would have expected this to be included in the general principles category.

[285] The ILA notes that this principle is currently called the common concern of humankind. *Cf.*, the discussion in Section E.1.e.

[286] *Supra* note 71, at 106–09.

[287] 39 ILM 1027 (2000), *available at* http://www.biodiv.org/.

[288] International Treaty on Plant Genetic Resources for Food and Agriculture, 2001, not yet in force, *available at* http://www.fao.org/biodiversity/cgrfa/.

[289] Preamble, *supra* note 121.

[290] *Id.*

[291] *Id.*, art. 4.

[292] *Id.*

The Convention on Biological Diversity notes the importance of conservation of biodiversity while at the same time endorsing that economic and social development and poverty eradication are the overriding priorities of developing countries.[293] It also calls upon parties to integrate consideration of sustainable use of biological resources into the national decision-making process.[294]

Thus, highly integrated sustainable development law treaties and instruments are now emerging.[295] Another example of an integrated approach is the UN Framework Convention on Climate Change, which notes that "Parties have a right to, and should promote sustainable development."[296] Policies and measures to protect against human-induced climate change should be integrated with national development programs. It further provides that economic development is essential for adopting measures to address climate change.[297] The Preamble also refers to the need for an integrated approach:

> [r]esponses to climate change should be coordinated with social and economic development in an integrated manner with a view to avoiding adverse impacts on the latter, taking into full account the legitimate priority needs of developing countries for the achievement of sustained economic growth and the eradication of poverty.[298]

Having discussed the 2002 New Delhi Principles on Sustainable Development, Cordonier Segger and Khalfan conclude that they are a good starting point and that they appear frequently in many instruments:

> It will be important, over the next decades, to monitor their development, operationalization and recognition by States as sustainable development law becomes better defined and implemented.[299]

This is sound advice, as much depends on state practice over the next few years to see how states and non-state actors alike apply these norms in their activities. In an increasingly gloablized world, states are no longer the only

---

[293] Preamble, *supra* note 54.

[294] *Id.*, art. 10.

[295] SUSTAINABLE DEVELOPMENT LAW, *supra* note 71, at 108.

[296] Art. 3, *supra* note 53.

[297] *Id.*

[298] Preamble, *supra* note 53.

[299] SUSTAINABLE DEVELOPMENT LAW, *supra* note 71, at 171.

actors in the international realm and non-state actors have greatly influenced the international legal process, be it economic law, human rights law or environmental protection.

## D. OPERATIONALIZING SUSTAINABLE DEVELOPMENT

Despite conceptual and ideological differences, numerous attempts have been made to translate sustainable development into policy initiatives. Examples of two such attempts are the Rio Declaration and Agenda 21 in 1992, and the Political Declaration and Plan of Implementation in 2002. An example of the adoption of an institutional framework for sustainable development is the establishment of the Commission on Sustainable Development by the UN General Assembly to monitor the implementation of Agenda 21. However, despite these initiatives, many have expressed disappointment regarding the implementation of Agenda 21.[300] Thus, it was pointed out that: "A sense of pessimism thus pervaded the World Summit on Sustainable Development (WSSD) held in Johannesburg on the tenth anniversary of UNCED."[301] Whether it was dealt with in a piece-meal fashion, many policies and projects at the national level have implications for the entire international community.[302] Many have argued that sustainable development is too "slippery" a concept to have meaning and, therefore, is a failure.[303]

It has also been argued that because sustainable development attempted to marry two incompatible ideas, the resulting formulation has no consequences.[304] Because the concept is so vague, any action can be justified as the practice of sustainable development.[305] However, it has been articulated that sustainable development contains three core ideas:

---

[300] "It was hardly a secret that the progress in implementing sustainable development has been extremely disappointing . . . with poverty deepening and environmental degradation worsening." George (Rock) Pring, *The 2002 Johannesburg World Summit on Sustainable Development: International Environmental Law Collides with Reality, Turning Jo'Burg Into Joke'Burg*, 30 DENV. J. INT'L L. & POL'Y 410 (2002).

[301] *Id.* at 7.

[302] *Id* at 14.

[303] David Hodas, *The "Rio" Environmental Treaties Colloquium: The Climate Change Convention and Evolving Legal Models of Sustainable Development*, 13 PACE ENVTL. L. REV. 75 (1995).

[304] Tarlock, *supra* note 44.

[305] *Id.* This is similar to David Hoda's (*supra* note 303) idea that anything can be justified as sustainable as long as a few jobs are created in the process.

(1) acceptance of limitations on the exploitation and consumption of many resources, (2) the recognition that present generations owe conservation duties to future generations, and (3) the necessity to integrate these duties into individual as well as public choices.[306]

Environmental sustainable development adds a fourth criterion to this: development must be far less environmentally destructive than in the past.[307] These core ideas are inherent in the concept of sustainable development. It implies limits to growth, that the present generation must take a long-term view of development (in other words, it must evaluate the impact of activities at least on the next generation) and that these duties must be implemented by both individuals and public bodies. The fourth element would be automatically implemented if the first three elements are properly implemented.

Some developing country advocates have argued that sustainable development is an attempt by developed countries to impose a no growth policy on developing countries.[308] Some have also argued that sustainable development, with its Brundtland definition, applies only to developing countries, as developed countries are already "developed."[309] Both these arguments do not hold much credence. Sustainable development refers to a particular kind of "development"—development that meets the needs of the present generation. The only caveat is that development should be pursued in such a way that the right of future generations to meet their needs is not jeopardized. Unsustainable consumption patterns clearly fall within this definition. If consumption patterns are unsustainable, not only future generations but also some members of the present generation will not be able to meet their needs, given how finite resources are. This is how sustainable development applies to developed countries. States have to compromise between environment and economic growth:

> Whatever else it means therefore, sustainable development need not imply a policy of no growth. . . . A more plausible interpretation is that sustainable development entails a compromise between the natural environment and economic growth. Some element of compromise is undoubtedly part of the concept. . . . The integration of environmental protection and economic development was

---

[306] *Id.*

[307] *Id.*

[308] *See* HUNTER ET AL., *supra* note 124, at 188.

[309] *Id.*

for that reason an important objective of the UNCED Conference, expressed in Principle 4 of the Rio Declaration.[310]

The underlying notion of sustainable development is equity, both inter-generational and intra-generational, seeking to benefit developing countries, particularly those who are poor and marginalized and seeks to allocate costs and benefits across generations:[311]

> Thus, "sustainable development" is intended to serve not simply the needs of the environment, but entails a reorientation of the world's economic system in which the burdens of environmental protection will fall more heavily on the developed Northern States and the economic benefits will accrue more significantly to the underdeveloped south, for the common benefit of all.[312]

Birnie and Boyle note that sustainable development is as much about processes as about outcomes, and for lawyers this may be a key issue.[313] It is also an inherently complex notion and requires policymakers to reorient themselves and seek a balance between social, political, economic and environmental choices.[314] Despite the importance of sustainable development, it is worth remembering that there is more to international environmental law than sustainable development. Other principles also play an important role.

It is also important to note the role that institutions will play in implementing sustainable development.[315] Institutions at both national and international levels are at best fragmented and fraught with bureaucracy. It is important to reform these institutions in order to ensure a holistic, coordinated approach to development and environmental protection. The Brundtland Report also referred to the importance of institutional reform.[316] Despite these calls, not much seems to have been done by way of reforming existing institutions. Instead, the international community seems to be establishing more and more new institutions. Thus, for example, instead of reforming UNEP to make sustainable development its main focus, the UN General Assembly created the Commission on Sustainable

---

[310] *See* BIRNIE & BOYLE, *supra* note 13, at 44, 45.

[311] *Id.* at 45

[312] *Id.*

[313] *Id.* at 47.

[314] *Id.*

[315] *Id.*

[316] *See* OUR COMMON FUTURE, *supra* note 4, at 308.

Development after the Rio Conference to oversee the implementation of Agenda 21. Was this step necessary?

## E.  SUBSTANTIVE ELEMENTS OF SUSTAINABLE DEVELOPMENT

As identified above, the substantive elements of sustainable development comprises the following: the principle of integration, inter- and intra-generational equity (based on the more general principle of equity), and non-exhaustion of natural resources. Other possible principles are: international cooperation and global partnership; and common but differentiated responsibility principle (again, based on the principle of equity). The precautionary principle, the polluter pays principle, and environmental assessment are tools that can be used to achieve sustainable development. These are discussed in separate chapters of the book.

### 1.  Principle of Integration

One of the basic norms of sustainable development and indeed the main message of the Brundtland Commission, is that environmental concerns must be integrated into the development process.[317] The principle of integration is codified in Principle 4 of the Rio Declaration: "In order to achieve sustainable development, environmental protection shall constitute an integral part of the development process and cannot be considered in isolation from it."[318] The failure to give effect to this basic tenet of environmental law has resulted in present-day environmental problems.

The principle of integration now constitutes one of the basic principles of environmental law and a core element of sustainable development. Several tools have been developed to give effect to this principle: the environmental impact assessment process, discussed in Chapter 4 is one such tool. Other tools include the licensing of industries, internalizing of environmental costs, pollution permits and the precautionary principle.

While the principle of integration assumed greater significance and prominence after the WCED Report and later the Rio Declaration, it is not a new principle. The Stockholm Declaration was perhaps the first instrument to embody the principle of integration, although no reference was made to the concept of sustainable development:

> In order to achieve a more rational management of resources and thus to improve the environment, States should adopt an integrated

---

[317]  *Id.* at 5.

[318]  Principle 4, Rio Declaration, *supra* note 12.

and co-ordinated approach to their development planning so as to ensure that development is compatible with the need to protect and improve environment for the benefit of their population.[319]

Principle 14 of the Stockholm Declaration provides a tool to achieve this: rational planning. "Rational planning constitutes an essential tool for reconciling any conflict between the needs of development and the need to protect and improve the environment."[320] Although, again, no reference was made to sustainable development, Principle 14 provides that in order to reconcile development with environment (in other words, to achieve sustainable development), it is necessary to adopt rational planning as a tool. To this can be added the need to adopt an integrated approach to rational planning. However, this is precisely what is lacking in many developing countries.

The environmental assessment process is an important tool to integrate environmental protection and economic development. It has been utilized at the national level for several decades and is now being used in relation to transboundary environmental damage. Environmental assessment is also related to participatory rights and will be discussed in Chapter 4. Other tools that play an important role in achieving sustainable development—the precautionary principle, the polluter pays principle and the common but differentiated responsibility principle—are discussed in later chapters in this publication.

## 2. Principle of Integrated Decision Making

It has been suggested that since sustainable development is an umbrella term, encompassing several principles, rather than a principle in its own right (it is more a process and a goal),[321] the strand that keeps all these components together is *integrated decision making*.[322] It has been pointed out that "the biggest challenge for sustainable development in coming decades will be to operationalize it."[323]

---

[319] Principle 13, Stockholm Declaration, *supra* note 15.

[320] Principle 14, Stockholm Declaration, *supra* note 15.

[321] *See* John C. Dernbach, *Symposium: Globalization and Governance: The Prospects for Democracy: Part II" Globalization, Democracy and Domestic Law: Achieving Sustainable Development: The Centrality and Multiple Facets of Integrated Decisionmaking,"* 10 IND. J. GLOBAL LEG. STUD. 247 (2003) where he notes that "sustainable development is widely recognized as a framework of concepts and principles, rather than a single concept or principle."

[322] *Id.*

[323] *Id.*

To operationalize sustainable development, we need to recognize that one principle—integrated decisionmaking—holds the other principles together. Integrated decisionmaking would ensure that environmental considerations and goals are integrated or incorporated into the decisionmaking processes for development, and are not treated separately or independently. Of all the principles contained in the sustainable development framework, integrated decisionmaking is perhaps the principle most easily translated into law and policy tools.[324]

There is much merit in this argument. Integrated decision making means taking an integrated approach to decision making and not compartmentalizing decisions into economic, social, environmental or security issues. Peace and security issues often impinge on environmental issues and *vice versa*—therefore, it is necessary to adopt an integrated approach to decision making, at both national and international levels. We are all too familiar with lack of integrated decision making. For example, trade issues and environmental issues are dealt with in isolation from one another despite its obvious impact on the other. At the national level issues are compartmentalized into various ministries (most often for convenience or personal preference than on any rational basis) which work in isolation. It is only recently that inter-ministerial committees or commissions have been established to deal with cross-cutting issues, such as sustainable development. However, the end result has been rather disappointing. It has been pointed out that the major reason for the lack of progress toward sustainable development is the failure to translate the plans and principles into specific action.[325]

As the Johannesburg Summit on Sustainable Development pointed out, sustainable development rests on three pillars: economic development, social development and environmental protection.[326] As a result, all three pillars have to be integrated into decision making. In other words, fragmented decision making will result in one-sided decisions being taken without any consideration of the impact on other pillars. Such decisions, needless to say, are unsustainable and will defeat the very purpose of sustainable development.

The principle of integration is not new to environmental protection. It requires that environmental considerations be integrated into the develop-

---

[324] *Id.*

[325] *Id.*

[326] Plan of Implementation, *supra* note 80, para. 2.

ment process.[327] By the same token, integrated decision making requires that environmental issues be taken into consideration when taking decisions (whether they are economic, security or social in nature). As the World Commission on Environment and Development noted almost 20 years ago, "economics and ecology must be completely integrated in decision-making and lawmaking processes not just to protect the environment, but also to protect and promote development."[328] The report notes that environment and development are linked in a complex system of cause and effect. First, environmental stresses are linked to one another. Second, environment and development are linked to one another. Third, environmental and economic problems are linked to many social and political factors. Finally, the systemic features operate not merely within but also between nations.[329] A good example of how these factors relate to one another is the issue of the climate change. Climate change is inextricably linked to ozone depletion and energy use. It is also linked to agricultural policy, population growth, deforestation and transport policy. Because it is linked to energy and the use of fossil fuels, it is also a political issue, given the present relations between states. It is also a global issue, given that every nation in the international community is contributing to the problem and is a potential victim. It has also strained relations between states because international law requires developed states to cut down on their carbon dioxide emissions.[330] It is also a human rights issue because it has the potential to displace communities, inundate some low-lying cities and give rise to migration resulting in an influx of environmental refugees.[331] This, in turn, can undermine international security and also cause conflict when more and more people compete for scarce resources.[332] This is a prime example of an instance that requires integrated decision making, both at the national level as well as at the international level. It has brought to the forefront the issue of developed nations

---

[327] This was recognized as early as the Brundtland Report in 1987. *See* OUR COMMON FUTURE, *supra* note 4, at 37, where the WCED noted that "Environment and development are not separate challenges; they are inexorably linked. . . . These problems cannot be treated by fragmented institutions and polices. They are linked in a complex system of cause and effect."

[328] *Id.* at 37

[329] *Id.* at 37–38.

[330] The legal framework is provided by the Framework Convention on Climate Change, *supra* note 55. The Kyoto Protocol FCCC/CP/1997/L.7/Add.1, signed Dec. 11, 1997, entered into force Feb. 16, 2005, *reprinted in* 36 ILM 22 (1998), *available at* http://www.unfccc.de/, embodies binding obligations for Annex I countries (defined in the Convention).

[331] *See* OUR COMMON FUTURE, *supra* note 4, at 176.

[332] *Id.*, ch. 11.

versus developing nations. Noting that ecological dimensions of policy be considered at the same time as economic, trade, energy, agricultural and other dimensions, the WCED urged that:

> What is required is a new approach in which all nations aim at a type of development that integrates production with resource conservation and enhancement, and that links both to the provision for all of an adequate livelihood base and equitable access to resources.[333]

It can thus be seen that integrated decision making is a fundamental principle of sustainable development without which sustainable development becomes meaningless. As John Dernbach notes it "provides the glue that holds the other principles together, and is the principle on which other principles depend,"[334] and without integrated decision making, "sustainable development is simply an odd assortment of unrelated principles."[335]

A procedural tool that has evolved over the years, which gives effect to the principle of integration, is the environmental impact assessment process. Although the law may differ from nation to nation, common elements include the need to assess the environmental impact of a given project before deciding whether to permit the project or not and opening the process to public participation. Public participation is an important component of integrated decision making[336] and also promotes transparency and good governance.[337]

John Dernbach raises a very important issue relating to integration. He notes that integrated decision making has a temporal quality.[338] In other

---

[333] *Id.* at 40.

[334] *See supra* note 49.

[335] *Id.* It is interesting to note that HUNTER ET AL., *supra* note 124, at 179, makes the same argument in relation to sustainable development:

> All this treaty-making clearly indicated that the field of international environmental law had come of age. But the field had (and still has) an *ad hoc* quality, consisting primarily of separate conventions. . . . As the number and scope of environmental treaties expanded, observers hoped to be able to superimpose some order on the emerging field, by placing international environmental law in the context of some broader organizing concept—to some extent at least, they found that organizing conceptual framework in the concept of sustainable development.

[336] *See supra* note 49.

[337] *See* the discussion in Chapter 1, Section B.1.

[338] *See supra* note 49.

words, because of the principle of inter-generational equity, one must take into consideration the long-term impact of decisions taken today.[339] He notes that "without temporal integration, sustainable development cannot succeed. . . . What temporal integration suggests is the need to look at the longer-term consequences of decisions. Such an approach is also consistent with intergenerational equity."[340]

Temporal integration (although the terminology is new, the concept is not) is not always easy to achieve. It is often difficult to predict the long-term consequences of actions today.[341] Moreover, our decisions today may be limited by scientific uncertainty. Here the precautionary principle plays an important role. As discussed in Chapter 3, the precautionary principle calls upon states not to use scientific uncertainty as an excuse to postpone action, if there is a likelihood of significant environmental damage. This "principle" was included in the Rio Declaration as a specific reaction to the international community's response to global warming.

The environmental impact assessment process is also helpful in identifying the long-term impact of development activities, although how far into the future one must look is an issue to be resolved. The continuous assessment and monitoring of activities[342] would be necessary to ensure that unexpected problems are swiftly dealt with and that the project is constantly under review. This would be particularly relevant for major projects with a significant impact on the environment.

As Judge Weeramantry noted in his separate opinion in the *Case Concerning the Gabcikovo Nagymaros Project:*

> I wish in this opinion to clarify further the scope and extent of the environmental impact principle in the sense that environmental impact assessment means not merely an assessment prior to the commencement of the project, but a continuing assessment and evaluation as long as the project is in operation. This follows from the fact that EIA is a dynamic principle and is not confined to a pre-project evaluation of possible environmental consequences. As long as a project of some magnitude is in operation, EIA must con-

---

339  *Id.*

340  *Id.*

341  *Id.*

342  *See* the *Case Concerning the Gabcikovo Nagymaros Project,* 1997 ICJ 88, where Judge Weeramantry referred to the principle of continuous environmental assessment in his separate opinion.

tinue, for every such project can have unexpected consequences; and considerations of prudence would point to the need for continuous monitoring.

The greater the size and scope of the project, the greater is the need for a continuous monitoring of its effects, for EIA before the scheme can never be expected, in a matter so complex as the environment, to anticipate every possible environmental danger.[343]

Judge Weeramantry advanced the principle of continuous environmental assessment, which is usually referred to as monitoring under national law. Once a project has been approved and is being implemented, it must be constantly under review to ensure that unexpected and unforeseen issues are dealt with, with minimum impact on the environment. It is also necessary to ensure that the conditions and emission standards on which approval was granted are in fact being met in project implementation.

Another challenge to temporal integration is that human beings lack the willingness or the ability to plan for events that are far into the future.[344] Climate change is a prime example of an environmental issue that could have implications for generations to come. Whether the present-day decision makers are in a position to plan so far ahead is doubtful given the present level of scientific knowledge on the subject.[345] It has thus been suggested that we plan for the next 50 years, as it represents about two human generations.[346] It would be necessary to design and implement policies with a much longer time frame than that is customarily used.

## F.  PROCEDURAL ELEMENTS OF SUSTAINABLE DEVELOPMENT

As noted above, sustainable development encompasses both substantive and procedural elements. There is general consensus that the procedural elements of sustainable development are the right to have access to information relating to the environment; the right to participate in the decision-making process; and the right to have access to remedies in the event of any damage.[347] These are universally accepted human rights[348] that have been extended to environmental issues more recently. As the discus-

---

[343]  *Id.*

[344]  *Id.*

[345]  *See* the discussion in Chapter 3, Section C.1.

[346]  *See* Dernbach, *supra* note 49.

[347]  These are codified in the Aarhus Convention, discussed in Chapter 4.

[348]  *See* arts. 19 and 25 of the ICCPR, *supra* note 203.

sion in chapter 1 shows, there is a heavy overlap between the components of sustainable development and the right to environment, particularly in relation to their procedural elements.

A particularly important development in relation to procedural elements is the adoption in 1998 of the Aarhus Convention on Access to Information, Public Participation in Decision-Making and Access to Justice in Environmental Matters[349] under the auspices of the Economic Commission for Europe (ECE). This is the first time that environmental procedural rights have been embodied in a binding convention. While these rights are already part of international human rights law, the Aarhus Convention has put these rights firmly within the discourse on environmental protection. Despite being geographically limited, the significance of the Convention should not be under-estimated. The Convention also endorsed the right to environment and stressed that the objective of the Convention in endorsing procedural rights is in reality to give effect to the right to environment:

> In order to contribute to the protection of the right of every person of present and future generations to live in an environment adequate to his or her health and well-being, each Party shall guarantee the rights of access to information, public participation in decision-making, and access to justice in environmental matters in accordance with the provisions of this Convention.[350]

The Rio Declaration endorses the significance of procedural rights as:

> Environmental issues are best handled with the participation of all concerned citizens, at the relevant level. At the national level, each individual shall have appropriate access to information concerning the environment that is held by public authorities, including information on hazardous materials and activities in their communities, and the opportunity to participate in decision-making processes. States shall facilitate and encourage public awareness and participation by making information widely available. Effective access to judicial and administrative proceedings, including redress and remedy, shall be provided.[351]

---

[349] 38 ILM 517, signed June 25, 1998, entered into force Oct. 30, 2001. *See also* Chapter 4, Section F.1.

[350] *Id.*, art. 1.

[351] Principle 10, *supra* note 12.

While Principle 10 embodies important principles of sustainable development, it embodies soft language. Thus, for example, it notes that environmental issues are "best handled" with the participation of all concerned citizens "at the relevant level." With regard to information, Principle 10 refers to "appropriate access," while states are required to "facilitate and encourage" public awareness and participation. It does not require states to provide for public participation.[352]

It has been noted that the right to participate has two components: the right to be heard and the right to influence decisions.[353] If there is no way to influence the decision—in other words, where the exercise is for cosmetic purposes only—public participation becomes meaningless. It is important to let the public know that their comments will be considered in the decision-making process.[354] Otherwise, they will lose faith and not get involved in future events.

While public participation as a concept or goal is accepted at the international level, exact modalities of how this should be done have not been worked out. Civil society groups have participated in international fora with varying degrees of success, but this has not been institutionalized. Thus, for example, human rights groups have participated in the Human Rights Committee (HRC), often submitting shadow reports, but there is no formal process for this to happen. While the HRC regularly scrutinizes these shadow reports, there is no obligation for them to do so. In the environmental field, too, civil society groups have participated in influencing the decision-making process; again, however, this is done on an *ad hoc* basis.

In this context, the adoption by the ECE of the Aarhus Convention is significant. It establishes minimum standards for civil society participation. Much of its provisions are addressed to states to be implemented at the national level. Although a regional instrument, "it is nonetheless useful as one model of minimum standards for public participation, as it was one of the first international efforts to give concrete content to the concept."[355]

---

[352] *See* Chapter 4, Section F for a more detailed discussion of this provision.

[353] *See* Alexandre Kiss, *The Right to the Conservation of the Environment, in* LINKING HUMAN RIGHTS AND THE ENVIRONMENT 31, 36 (Romania Picolatti & Jorge Daniel Taillant eds., 2003).

[354] *Public Participation in Making Local Environmental Decisions, The Aarhus Convention Newcastle Workshop, Good Practice Handbook* (2000), *available at* http://www.unece.org/env/pp/ecases/ handbook.pdf.

[355] *See supra* note 353, at 59.

It has been articulated that participation rights "find some support in international human rights instruments."[356] It must be pointed out that that is precisely where these rights originated from. Rather than the environmental discourse informing the human rights discourse, it is really the human rights discourse that developed these rights. Applying participatory rights to environmental issues is of more recent origin. The Special Rapporteur on Human Rights and the Environment also identified participatory rights in the draft principles on human rights and the environment:[357]

> All persons have the right to information concerning the environment. This includes information, howsoever compiled, on actions or courses of conduct that may affect the environment and information necessary to enable effective public participation in environmental decision-making. The information shall be timely, clear, understandable and available without undue financial burden to the applicant.[358]

Draft Article 18 endorsed public participation:

> All persons have the right to active, free and meaningful participation in planning and decision-making activities and processes that may have an impact on the environment and development. This includes the right to a prior assessment of the environmental, developmental and human rights consequences of proposed actions.[359]

Draft Article 20 endorsed the right to remedies in the environmental context. These provisions endorse existing law, more or less. One innovation is the prior assessment of *environmental, developmental and human rights* consequences of proposed actions. While social impacts are usually included in environmental assessments (for example, whether people will be displaced as a result of the proposed project, where they will be relocated and whether their livelihood will be affected as a result of relocation etc.), what is meant by developmental consequences of actions is not clear.

There is no doubt that procedural rights of information, participation and access to remedies now form part of contemporary international law

---

[356] *Id.*

[357] Draft art. 15. Draft Principles on Human Rights and the Environment, appended to the Final Report Prepared by Mrs. Fatma Zohra Ksentini, Special Rapporteur, UN Doc. E/CN.4/Sub.2/1994/9 (1994).

[358] Draft art. 15, *id.*

[359] Draft art. 18, *id.*

governing environmental protection. Since they also form part of sustainable development, it can be concluded that at least the procedural elements of sustainable development form part of customary international law.

At the national level, these rights are generally tied to the EIA process that is implemented in many countries.[360] EIA process usually applies to activities likely to have a significant impact on the environment. No such limitation is placed on these rights by Principle 10 of the Rio Declaration. The Johannesburg Declaration on Sustainable Development adopted at the World Summit on Sustainable Development also endorsed these rights: "We recognize sustainable development requires a long-term perspective and broad-based participation in policy formulation, decision-making and implementation at all levels."[361]

Access to information, the right to participate and the right to remedies now form part of general principles governing environmental issues.

## G. SURVEY OF INTERNATIONAL INSTRUMENTS THAT INCORPORATE SUSTAINABLE DEVELOPMENT

The Bergen Ministerial Declaration was the first international environmental instrument, albeit non-binding, adopted after the publication of the WCED Report to refer to the term sustainable development. After a rather slow start, its evolution after the Rio Conference has been remarkable, and almost every document, binding and non-binding, adopted since the WCED Report refers to sustainable development, the sustainable exploitation of resources or the sustainable use of natural resources. The influence of the WCED Report on the development of international environmental law and particularly of sustainable development as a principle has been remarkable. While a thorough examination of all these instruments would be beyond the scope of this work, a survey of main instruments is necessary, particularly in order to ascertain its legal scope.

It is noteworthy that neither the Vienna Convention for the Protection of the Ozone Layer nor the Montreal Protocol on the Substances that Deplete the Ozone Layer embody the term sustainable development, although reference is made to the need to adopt precautionary measures

---

[360] *See* HUNTER ET AL., *supra* note 124, at 36, where it is noted that over 70 percent of countries have adopted EIA requirements for certain types of projects. EIA is also incorporated in many international treaties.

[361] Johannesburg Declaration, *supra* note 80, para. 26.

to protect the ozone layer.[362] This is not surprising because both these instruments pre-date the WCED Report.

The UN Convention on Law of the Sea (UNCLOS) deals with, *inter alia*, the conservation of living resources in the Exclusive Economic Zone (EEZ). It requires coastal states to ensure, through proper conservation and management measures, that the maintenance of living resources is not endangered by over-exploitation.[363] Such measures shall also be designed to maintain or restore populations of harvested species at levels that produce the maximum sustainable yield, as qualified by relevant environmental and economic factors.[364] Similar provisions apply to the conservation of living resources of the High Seas.[365]

The UN Framework Convention on Climate Change (UNFCC) not only specifically endorses sustainable development, it also seems to endorse it in rights language. According to the Convention:

> *The parties have a right to, and should, promote sustainable development.* Policies and measures to protect the climate system against human-induced change should be appropriate for the specific conditions of each Party and should be integrated with national development programs, taking into account that economic development is essential for adopting measures to address climate change.[366]

Again, the hortatory nature of the language used here must be noted. The Preamble too refers to the need for developing countries to achieve sustainable social and economic development. The Kyoto Protocol does not refer specifically to sustainable development; rather it endorses Article 3 of the UNFCC, which refers to sustainable development. The Protocol refers to sustainable development in the context of the clean development mechanism. Establishing a clean development mechanism, Article 12 of the Protocol notes that the purpose of the mechanism is to assist parties not included in Annex 1 in achieving sustainable development and to assist Annex 1 parties in achieving compliance with their obligations under Article 3.

The Straddling Fish Stocks and Highly Migratory Fish Stocks Convention[367] refers to the need to "ensure the long-term conservation and sus-

---

[362] Preamble, Vienna Convention, 26 ILM 1529 (1985), 1513 UNTS 293, signed Mar. 22, 1985, entered into force Sept. 22, 1988; and the Preamble, Montreal Protocol, 26 ILM 1541 (1987), 15 UNTS 3, signed Sept. 16, 1987, entered into force Jan. 1, 1989, *available at* http://www.unep.org/ozone/index.html.

[363] Art. 61, UNCLOS Convention, *supra* note 119.

[364] *Id.*

[365] *Id.*, art. 119.

[366] Art. 3.4, *supra* note 53 (emphasis added).

[367] United Nations Conference on Straddling Fish Stocks and Highly Migratory Fish

tainable use of straddling fish stocks and highly migratory fish stocks."[368] Article 2 provides that the objective of the Convention is to ensure the long-term conservation and sustainable use of these fish stocks through the effective implementation of the Convention. One of the general principles embodied in the Convention is to "adopt measures to ensure long-term sustainability of straddling fish stocks and highly migratory fish stocks and promote the objective of their optimum utilization."[369] It also refers to the "maximum sustainable yield" and the need to apply the precautionary approach in accordance with Article 6 of the Convention.

Another instrument that refers to sustainable use is the 1996 Protocol to the Convention on the Prevention of Marine Pollution by Dumping of Wastes and Other Matter.[370] It stresses the need to protect the marine environment and to promote the sustainable use and conservation of marine resources.[371] The Protocol also endorses the precautionary principle and the polluter pays principle.[372]

The UN Convention on the Law of the Non-navigational uses of International Watercourses[373] refers to the promotion of the optimal and sustainable utilization of the international watercourses for the present and future generations.[374] It also refers to the importance of international cooperation and good neighborliness. Part II embodies general principles that include the equitable and reasonable utilization of an international watercourse, the obligation not to cause significant harm and the general obligation to cooperate.[375] Article 5 of the Convention requires watercourse states to utilize an international watercourse in an equitable and reasonable manner. Such a watercourse shall be used and developed by watercourse

---

Stocks: Agreement for the Implementation of the Provisions of the United Nations Convention of the Law of the Sea of 10 December 1982, Relating to the Conservation and Management of Straddling Fish Stocks and High Migratory Fish Stocks, UN Doc. A/CONF.164/37, *reprinted in* 34 ILM 1542 (1995), signed Aug. 4, 1995, entered into force Dec. 11, 2001.

[368] *Id.*, Preamble.

[369] *Id.*, art. 5.

[370] 36 ILM 1 (1997), signed Nov. 7, 1996, *available at* http://www.londonconvention.org and http://www.imo.org.

[371] *Id.*, Preamble.

[372] *Id.*, art. 3.

[373] UN Doc. A/51/1869, signed May 21, 1997, *reprinted in* 36 ILM 700 (1997).

[374] *Id.*, Preamble.

[375] *Id.*, arts. 5, 7 and 8 respectively.

states with a view to attaining optimal and sustainable utilization. They shall participate in the use, development and protection of an international watercourse in an equitable and reasonable manner. The factors to be taken into consideration in doing so are listed in Article 6. These include the geographic and ecological factors of a natural character; the socio-economic needs of the watercourse state; the population dependent on the watercourse; conservation, protection, development and economy of use of water; and the availability of alternatives.

While the 1979 Geneva Convention on the Long-Range Transboundary Air Pollution,[376] the framework convention adopted in response to acid rain in Europe, makes no reference to sustainable development, the Protocol on Further Reduction of Sulphur Emissions[377] adopted within the framework convention in 1994 affirms "the need to ensure environmentally sound and sustainable development"[378] in its Preamble. It also refers to the precautionary principle.[379]

The 1992 Convention on the Protection and Use of Transboundary Watercourses and International Lakes[380] also refers to the need for sustainable water management, conservation of water resources and environmental protection and the role of the UN Economic Commission for Europe (UNECE) in promoting international cooperation for the prevention, control and reduction of transboundary water pollution and sustainable use of transboundary waters. The parties have undertaken to be guided by the following principles: the precautionary principle, the polluter pays principle and that the water resources shall be managed so that the needs of the present generation are met without compromising the ability of future generations to meet their own needs.[381] In other words, Article 2 has endorsed sustainable development.

A Protocol on Water and Health[382] to the 1992 Convention on the Protection and Use of Transboundary Watercourses and Lakes was adopted

---

[376] 18 ILM 1442 (1979), 1302 UNTS 217, *available at* http://www.unece.org/env/lrtap.

[377] Protocol to the 1979 Convention on Long-range Transboundary Air Pollution on Further Reduction of Sulphur Emissions (Oslo Protocol), 33 ILM 1540 (1995), signed June 14, 1994, entered into force Aug. 5, 1998.

[378] *Id.*

[379] *See* the discussion in Chapter 3.

[380] 31 ILM 1312 (1992), signed Mar. 17, 1992, entered into force, Oct. 6, 1996, *available at* www.unece.org/env/water/.

[381] *Id.*, art. 2(5).

[382] UN Doc. UNEP/POPS/CONF/4, signed May 22, 2001, *reprinted in* 38 ILM 1708 (1999), *available at* www.unece.org/env/water/. Not yet in force.

by the ECE in 1999. Its Preamble notes that water is essential to sustain life and "the availability of water in quantities, and of a quality, sufficient to meet basic human needs is a prerequisite both for improved health and for sustainable development."[383] Article 1 of the Protocol lays down its objective as the promotion of, at all appropriate levels, the protection of human health and well-being within a framework of sustainable development, through improving water management, including the protection of water ecosystems, and through preventing, controlling and reducing water-related diseases. Article 4 calls upon states to take all appropriate measures to prevent, control and reduce water-related disease within a framework of integrated water management systems aimed at sustainable use of water resources. The parties are also required to take into account the implications for human health, water resources, and sustainable development when designing such measures.[384]

The principles and approaches to be adopted in implementing this Protocol are embodied in Article 5. These include the precautionary principle, the polluter pays principle, the obligation not to cause environmental damage, equitable access to water, water resources to be managed so that the needs of future generations are also taken into account, the principle of prevention, access to information and public participation and equitable access to water.[385]

The Rotterdam Convention on Prior Informed Consent Procedures for Certain Hazardous Chemicals and Pesticides in International Trade[386] is another instrument that refers to sustainable development in the Preamble. It recognizes that trade and environmental policies should be mutually supportive with a view to achieving sustainable development.[387] Interestingly, the Stockholm Convention on Persistent Organic Pollutants,[388] while embodying a similar provision, does not refer to sustainable development. The only reference to sustainable development is in relation to the Program of Action for Sustainable Development of Small Island Developing States.[389]

---

[383] *Id.*, Preamble.

[384] *Id.*, art. 4(4).

[385] It is clear that components of sustainable development are included in this provision, particularly the reference to future generations.

[386] 38 ILM 1 (1999), signed Sept. 11, 1998, entered into force Feb. 24, 2004.

[387] *Id.*, Preamble.

[388] UN Doc. UNEP/POPS/CONF/4, *reprinted in* 40 ILM 532 (2001), signed May 22, 2001, entered into force May 17, 2004.

[389] *Id.*, Preamble.

The Convention on Biological Diversity[390] refers to the conservation of biological diversity as a common concern of humankind and notes that parties are determined to conserve and sustainably use biological diversity for the benefit of present and future generations.[391] The objectives of the Convention, as embodied in Article 1, are the conservation of biological diversity, the sustainable use of its components and the fair and equitable sharing of benefits arising out of utilization of genetic resources. "Sustainable use" is defined as "the use of components of biological diversity in a way and at a rate that does not lead to the long-term decline of biological diversity, thereby maintaining its potential to meet the needs and aspirations of present and future generations."[392] Under Article 6 parties are required to develop national strategies, plans or programs for the conservation and sustainable use of biological diversity. Article 10 requires parties to integrate consideration of conservation and sustainable use of biological diversity into national decision making.

Regional conventions also endorse sustainable development. Thus, for example, the Convention for the Protection of the Marine Environment and the Coastal Region of the Mediterranean[393] refers to the responsibility to preserve and sustainably develop the Mediterranean sea area for the benefit and enjoyment of present and future generations.[394] It refers to this area as a common heritage. The Preamble further notes that the Mediterranean Action Plan adopted in 1975 has contributed to the process of sustainable development in the Mediterranean region. Among the general obligations of the parties is the obligation to protect and enhance the marine environment so as to contribute to sustainable development. Towards this end, the parties shall apply the precautionary principle and the polluter pays principle; undertake environmental impact assessment of activities likely to cause a significant impact on the marine environment; commit themselves to the integrated management of the coastal zones; and to promote cooperation among states. The parties have also undertaken to take fully into account the recommendations of the Mediterranean Commission on Sustainable Development established under the Action Plan in implementing the objectives of sustainable development.

---

[390] *Supra* note 54.

[391] *Id.*, Preamble.

[392] *Id.*, art. 2.

[393] 15 ILM 290 (1976), formerly known as the Barcelona Convention, amended extensively (including the name), signed on Feb. 16, 1976, entered into force Feb. 12, 1978, *available at* http://www.oceanlaw.net/texts/unepmap.htm and www.unep.ch/regionalseas/.

[394] *Id.*, Preamble.

Another example of a regional instrument is the Convention for the Protection of the Marine Environment of the North-East Atlantic.[395] The Preamble refers to the need for concerted action at national, regional and global levels to prevent and eliminate marine pollution and to achieve sustainable management of the maritime area and to manage human activities in such a manner that the marine ecosystem will continue to sustain the legitimate uses of the sea and will continue to meet the needs of present and future generations.[396] Among the principles that the parties are required to apply are the precautionary principle and the polluter pays principle.[397]

Soft law instruments also endorse sustainable development. While the Stockholm Declaration does not contain the term sustainable development, many of its principles contain its elements. As discussed earlier, Principles 13 and 14 of the Declaration refer to the need for an integrated and coordinated approach to development and endorse the importance of rational planning. Principle 13 uses hortatory language and provides that states "should" adopt an integrated approach to development planning.

The Bergen Ministerial Declaration of 1990, on the other hand, refers specifically to sustainable development and endorses the WCED definition of sustainable development. It further links sustainable development with the precautionary principle, discussed in Chapter 3. It is also the first instrument to have specifically adopted the precautionary principle.

In order to achieve sustainable development, policies must be based on the precautionary principle. Environmental measures must anticipate, prevent and attack the causes of environmental degradation. Where there are threats of serious or irreversible damage, lack of full scientific certainty should not be used as a reason for postponing measures to prevent environmental degradation.[398]

The Declaration deals with common challenges, economics of sustainability, sustainable energy use, sustainable industrial activities, awareness raising and public participation.

---

[395] 32 ILM 1068 (1993), *available at* http://www.ospar.org, signed Sept. 22, 1992, entered into force Mar. 25, 1998.

[396] *Id.*, Preamble.

[397] *Id.*, art. 2.2.

[398] Principle 7, Ministerial Declaration on Sustainable Development in the ECE Region United Nations Economic Commission for Europe Conference on Action for a Common Future, Bergen, Norway, May 15, 1990.

Perhaps the most notable instrument embodying "principles" of sustainable development is the Rio Declaration, although it does not contain a definition of sustainable development. Not only is it replete with references to sustainable development, it also seeks to give it content. It was the first universal instrument adopted since the publication of the report of the WCED to endorse sustainable development. The Principles in the Declaration can be characterized into at least four groups: substantive components of sustainable development; procedural components of sustainable development; tools to achieve sustainable development; and linkages.

The substantive components of sustainable development mentioned in the Declaration are: the inter-generational equity principle,[399] the principle of integration[400] and the common but differentiated responsibility principle.[401] The procedural components include cooperation in a spirit of global partnership,[402] public participation and access to information,[403] access to remedies,[404] notification of natural disasters or other emergencies[405] and timely notification and provision of information to potentially affected states of transboundary environmental damage.[406] The tools to achieve sustainable development are: the precautionary principle,[407] the polluter pays principle[408] and environmental assessment.[409]

The Rio Declaration also embodies several general principles. These are the principle of sovereignty,[410] the obligation not to cause environmental damage,[411] the right to development,[412] a possible human right to environment[413]

---

[399] Principle 3, *supra* note 12.

[400] Principle 4, *supra* note 12.

[401] Principle 7, *supra* note 12.

[402] Art. 7, *supra* note 12. *See also* Principle 12 which calls upon states to promote a supportive and open international economic system.

[403] Principle 10, *supra* note 12.

[404] *Id.*

[405] Principle 18, *supra* note 12.

[406] Principle 19, *supra* note 12.

[407] Principle 15, *supra* note 12.

[408] Principle 16, *supra* note 12.

[409] Principle 17, *supra* note 12.

[410] Principle 2, *supra* note 12.

[411] *Id.*

[412] Principle 3, *supra* note 12. *See* the discussion in Section C.1.a.

[413] Principle 1. The word "possible" is added here because Principle 1 does not

and the peaceful settlement of disputes.[414] The Rio Declaration is important as it endorses the principle of integration and interrelatedness and draws links with other areas that have an impact on sustainable development. The linkages embodied in the Declaration are: the eradication of poverty,[415] eliminating unsustainable patterns of production and consumption,[416] promoting appropriate demographic policies,[417] trade,[418] warfare[419] and peace.[420]

In addition, the Declaration calls upon states to enact effective environmental legislation,[421] and to further develop international law in the field of sustainable development.[422] It is not clear what international law in the field of sustainable development means, although the Declaration seems to indicate that it is separate and distinct from international environmental law. Some writers argue that a separate branch of international law called international sustainable development law (ISDL) has emerged,[423] hence the reference to "international law in the field of sustainable development" in Principle 27.

It is true that international environmental law has changed its course to embrace international sustainable development law. Or it may be that it is a separate branch of international law altogether, encompassing features from international human rights law and international economic law has emerged. The Johannesburg Declaration on Sustainable Development seems to indicate that the latter is correct. Again, no definition of sustain-

---

specifically mention a right to environment although some might interpret it that way. It does not embody rights language although it does link human rights with environment (or rather, nature).

[414] Principle 26, *supra* note 12.

[415] Principle 5, *supra* note 12.

[416] Principle 8, *supra* note 12.

[417] Principle 9, *supra* note 12.

[418] Principle 12, *supra* note 12.

[419] Principle 24, *supra* note 12.

[420] Principle 25, *supra* note 12.

[421] Principle 11, *supra* note 12.

[422] Principle 27, *supra* note 12.

[423] *See* SUSTAINABLE DEVELOPMENT LAW, *supra* note 71; Philippe Sands, *International Law in the Field of Sustainable Development*, 65 BRIT. Y.B. INT'L. L. 303 (1994); Graham Mayeda, *Where Should Johannesburg Take Us?, supra* note 44; Alhaji B.M. Marong, *From Rio to Johannesburg, supra* note 44. *Cf.* Nicholas Robinson, *Legal Structure and Sustainable Development, supra* note 45, who noted in 1998 that "There is, of course, no "field" of law yet denoted as "Sustainable Development Law."

able development is to be found, but the international community has made a firm commitment to sustainable development.[424] Referring to both Stockholm and Rio Declarations, the Johannesburg Declaration notes that "the Rio Conference was a significant milestone that set a new agenda for sustainable development."[425] While also endorsing the need to eradicate poverty, change consumption and production patterns, the Johannesburg Declaration refers to something that the Rio Declaration does not: good governance.[426]

As noted, the Plan of Implementation adopted at the Johannesburg Summit endorses the three components of sustainable development as economic development, social development and environmental protection.[427] It refers to these as interdependent and mutually reinforcing pillars. If sustainable development encompasses economic development, social development and environmental protection, then international sustainable development law must embody components of international environmental law, international economic law and international human rights law. It would thus be safe to assume that this new branch of law called "International Sustainable Development Law" is the area of overlap between these three areas of international law.[428]

The instruments that were surveyed above have embraced sustainable development. These instruments deal with various aspects of the environment, ranging from the atmosphere to the oceans, from Antarctica to the high seas. Some of these instruments are binding while others are not. This survey goes to demonstrate to what extent sustainable development has influenced international environmental law—to such an extent that a separate branch of law called international sustainable development law seems to be emerging.

## H. APPLICATION OF SUSTAINABLE DEVELOPMENT BY INTERNATIONAL BODIES

### 1. International Court of Justice

The International Court of Justice (ICJ) did not have occasion to deal with sustainable development until recently. While the Court's jurisprudence contains several principles that can be applied in relation to envi-

---

424 Para. 1, *supra* note 80.

425 Para. 8, *supra* note 80.

426 Para. 4 of the Plan of Implementation, *supra* note 80.

427 Para. 5 of the Declaration and para. 2 of the Plan of Implementation, *supra* note 80.

428 *See* SUSTAINABLE DEVELOPMENT LAW, *supra* note 71, Chapter 4 and particularly 103.

ronmental issues,[429] and the *Nuclear Tests Cases* of 1974 clearly raised environmental concerns, the Court did not directly pronounce on these issues until the 1990s when several cases and requests for advisory opinions were brought before the Court that clearly implicated environmental issues.

### a. Nuclear Tests Case

In the *Nuclear Tests Case*[430] New Zealand sought to reopen the case filed in 1974.[431] It found jurisdiction on paragraph 63 of the 1974 judgment:

> Once the Court has found that a State has entered into a commitment concerning its future conduct it is not the Court's function to contemplate that it will not comply with it. However, the Court observes that if the basis of this Judgment were to be affected, the Applicant could request an examination of the situation in accordance with the provisions of the Statute.[432]

New Zealand argued that by virtue of treaty undertakings and customary international law, France had an obligation to conduct an environmental impact assessment before carrying out any further tests. It further contended that France's conduct was illegal because it caused the introduction, into the marine environment, of radioactive material and that it was under an obligation to provide evidence, before carrying out such tests, that they did not result in introducing such material into the environment in accordance with the precautionary principle "very widely accepted in contemporary international law."[433]

The Court, however, held that since its 1974 judgment related to atmospheric nuclear testing, New Zealand cannot bring a claim under paragraph 63 of that judgment in relation to underground nuclear testing. Therefore, New Zealand's request was dismissed. Several judges appended

---

[429] *E.g.*, the principle in the *Corfu Channel Case*, which referred to the state's obligation not to allow knowingly its territory to be used for acts contrary to international law.

[430] Request for an Examination of the Situation in Accordance with Paragraph 63 of the Court's Judgment of 20 December 1974 in the Nuclear Tests (New Zealand v. France) Case, 1995 ICJ 288.

[431] Nuclear Test Case (New Zealand v. France) 1974 ICJ 457, which related to atmospheric nuclear testing by France that the Court found became moot as a result of the unilateral undertaking given by France to stop such testing. An identical case filed by Australia [(Nuclear Test Case (Australia v. France), 1974 ICJ 253)] was taken together.

[432] *Supra* note 430, para. 3.

[433] *Id.*, para. 5.

dissenting opinions.[434] It is interesting to note Judge Weeramantry's discussion of inter-generational rights in this case, because it is a substantive component of sustainable development.[435] He noted that this case raised the principle of inter-generational equity, "an important and rapidly developing principle of contemporary environmental law."[436]

### b.   Case Concerning Gabcikovo Nagymaros Project

A similar opportunity presented itself in 1994 in the form of the *Case Concerning the Gabcikovo Nagymaros Project.*[437] This can be considered the first "true" environmental case to come before the ICJ. While the Court did refer to sustainable development and other environmental obligations of states, many commentators felt that the Court missed yet another golden opportunity to develop international environmental law.[438] Despite the clear environmental nature of the dispute, the Court seemed to have been more concerned with principles of state responsibility, law of treaties and state succession, than international environmental law. The separate opinion of Judge Weeramantry, albeit non-binding, is far more instructive and insightful and provides rich ideas for future discussion and development in this area, although from a legal point of view, is a little troubling.

### i.   Background to the Case

On September 16, 1977, Hungary and Czechoslovakia entered into a treaty for the construction and operation of the "Gabcikovo-Nagymaros System of Locks" as a joint investment. It was aimed at the production of hydroelectricity, the improvement of navigation on the Danube and the protection of the areas along the banks against flooding. The parties also undertook to ensure that the quality of water in the Danube would not be impaired. This treaty entered into force on June 30, 1978. However, the project generated intense criticism in Hungary, and the Hungarian government decided to suspend the works at Nagymaros on May 13, 1989. On October 27, 1989, Hungary decided to abandon the works at Nagymaros.

---

[434] Judges Weeramantry and Koroma and *ad hoc* judge Sir Geoffrey Palmer appended dissenting opinions.

[435] *See* discussion in Section C.1.d. His elucidation of other principles of international environmental law such as the precautionary principle and environmental assessment will be discussed in those chapters.

[436] Dissenting Opinion, Judge Weeramantry, *supra* note 429, at 341.

[437] 1997 ICJ 7.

[438] *See* A. Khavari & D.R. Rothwell, *The ICJ and the Danube Dam Case: A Missed Opportunity for International Environmental Law?*, 22 MELB. U. L. REV. 507, 534 (1998).

In the meantime, Czechoslovakia was investigating alternatives and, in November 1991, it embarked on a project called "Variant C," which entailed a unilateral diversion of the Danube. Although discussions continued between the parties, on May 19, 1992, Hungary transmitted a verbal note to the Czech government terminating the 1977 treaty. The latter, however, continued work on Variant C and, starting on October 23, proceeded to dam the river. The parties entered into a Protocol in 1989 whereby they agreed to accelerate the completion of the work on the Gabcikovo-Nagymaros project.

The Commission of the European Communities offered to mediate, and during a meeting held in 1992, the parties entered into a series of interim undertakings. They agreed that the dispute would be submitted to the ICJ, that a tripartite fact-finding mission should report on Variant C and that a tripartite group of independent experts would submit suggestions as to the emergency measures to be taken.[439]

Slovakia became an independent state on January 1, 1993. In April, the parties decided by Special Agreement to submit the dispute to the ICJ.[440] After several aborted attempts, the parties finally agreed on a temporary water management regime for the Danube pending the decision of the ICJ.

For its part, Hungary contended that it was relying on "a state of ecological necessity"[441] when it suspended the operation of the 1977 Treaty. Some of the reasons given by Hungary for the existence of an ecological necessity were: silting of the Danube, a result of which was that the quality of water would have been impaired; with regard to surface water, eutrophication would have arisen; and fluvial fauna and flora would have become extinct.[442]

Hungary also contended that its conduct should not be evaluated solely in relation to the law of treaties. Although it contended that the provisions of the Vienna Convention on the Law of Treaties could not be applied to a treaty entered into in 1977, as the Vienna Convention entered into force only in 1980, Hungary did accept that the Vienna Convention embodied, for the most part, customary international law relating to treaties. Further, Hungary stressed the need to adopt a cautious attitude.[443]

---

[439] *Supra* note 437, para. 24.

[440] This Agreement was entered into on Apr. 7, 1993.

[441] *Supra* note 437, para. 40.

[442] *Id.*

[443] *Id.*, para. 42.

Slovakia, on the other hand, argued that the suspension or termination of treaties was governed by the law of treaties. While the provisions of the Vienna Convention could not be applied to the 1977 treaty, the Vienna Convention, particularly the provisions relating to the termination and suspension of treaties, reflected customary international law. It further argued that the law of treaties did not recognize a state of necessity as a ground for either terminating or suspending a treaty. Moreover, it cast doubt whether ecological necessity or ecological risk could, under the law of state responsibility, constitute a circumstance precluding wrongfulness. In any event, Slovakia denied that a state of ecological necessity existed either in 1989 or subsequently, as contended by Hungary.[444]

The Court, in its decision, had no difficulty in separating the law of treaties from the law relating to state responsibility and noted that the Vienna Convention on the Law of Treaties governed the instances in which a treaty could be lawfully terminated or suspended. Whereas the law of state responsibility governed the situation that arose if a treaty was not lawfully terminated or suspended. Under the principles of state responsibility, the Court noted, the parties were entitled to invoke circumstances precluding wrongfulness as defined by the International Law Commission (ILC), which the parties agreed reflected customary international law.[445]

### ii. State of Necessity

One of the grounds on which an obligation can be deviated from is a state of necessity; this, the Court noted, could be ecological in nature—the ILC too seems to have recognized this possibility in its commentary to Draft Article 33 adopted on first reading.[446] The parties agreed that the state of necessity must be evaluated in the light of the criteria laid down in Draft Article 33. While the Court was of the view that a state of ecological necessity could indeed be a circumstance precluding wrongfulness for purposes of state responsibility, the Court pointed out that, in the instant case, the criteria necessary to establish an imminent, grave peril have not been established by Hungary. The Court had no difficulty in acknowledging that the concerns expressed by Hungary for its natural environment related to an "essential interest" of that state within the meaning of Draft Article 33. Moreover, the Court noted that even if such a danger existed, Hungary had

---

[444] *Id.*, paras. 43 and 44.

[445] *Id.*, para. 47.

[446] ILC noted in its commentary to Article 33 that "a grave danger to . . . ecological preservation of all or some of [the] territory [of a state]" could be a ground for invoking a state of necessity. It noted further that safeguarding the ecological balance has come to be considered an essential interest of states. *Id.*, para. 53.

other means available to it to respond to that situation, without terminating the treaty. Thus, while accepting the defense of ecological necessity (which is a victory for environmental law), the Court was of the view that it did not apply to the circumstances in the present case, as the ecological dangers were neither grave nor imminent. The fact that Hungary had other options also made the defense of ecological necessity unavailable.

The Court referred to its advisory opinion in the *Legality of the Threat or Use of Nuclear Weapons*[447] and noted that it attached "great significance" to the respect for the environment. Moreover, Hungary had referred several times to the uncertainties as to the ecological impact of this project, which is why it asked for new scientific studies be carried out.[448] The Court, however, noted that:

> Serious though these uncertainties might have been they could not, alone, establish the objective existence of a "peril" in the sense of a component element of a state of necessity. The word "peril" certainly evokes the idea of a "risk"; that is precisely what distinguishes "peril" from material damage. But a state of necessity could not exist without a "peril" duly established at the relevant point in time; the mere apprehension of a possible "peril" could not suffice in that respect. It could hardly be otherwise, when the "peril" constituting the state of necessity has at the same to be "grave" and "imminent." "Imminence" is synonymous with "immediacy" or "proximity" and goes far beyond the concept of "possibility."[449]

Does this mean that even if a grave peril has been established, if the risk is not immediate, then a state of necessity (and by implication a state of ecological necessity) cannot be invoked? What is the relationship between a state of necessity and the precautionary principle? The precautionary principle requires us not to invoke scientific uncertainty as a defense if there is evidence of serious environmental damage.[450] Thus, if there is scientific uncertainty as to a particular issue and evidence suggests serious environmental damage,[451] but the damage is not imminent (in other words, could take place several years later), it would seem that a state of necessity cannot be invoked.

---

[447] *Supra* note 437, para. 29.

[448] This can be a reference to the precautionary principle.

[449] *Supra* note 437, para. 54.

[450] *See* Chapter 3, Section C.

[451] *See* Daniel Dobos, *The Necessity of Precaution: The Future of Ecological Necessity and the Precautionary Principle*, 13 FORDHAM ENVTL. L.J. 375 (2002).

### iii. Developments in International Environmental Law

The Court also examined the contention put forward by Hungary that the developments in relation to international environmental law subsequent to the conclusion of the 1977 treaty precluded the performance of the treaty: "The previously existing obligation not to cause substantive damage to the territory of another State had, Hungary claimed, evolved into an *erga omnes* obligation of prevention of damage pursuant to the 'precautionary principle.'"[452] Slovakia, on the other hand, contended that none of the developments in environmental law gave rise to norms of *jus cogens* that would override the Treaty.[453]

However, since neither party had contended that a peremptory norm of environmental law had emerged since the conclusion of the 1977 treaty, the Court did not examine the scope of Article 64 of the Vienna Convention on the Law of Treaties.[454] Nonetheless, the Court noted that new norms of environmental law were relevant to the performance of the treaty, and the parties could, by agreement, incorporate these norms into the 1977 treaty. Several provisions of the treaty required the parties to ensure that the quality of water in the Danube is not impaired, that nature is protected and to "take new environmental norms into consideration when agreeing upon the means to be specified in the Joint Contractual Plan."[455]

The Court further pointed out that the treaty is not static and is open to adapt to emerging norms of international law. Since there was joint responsibility to do so, there must be a mutual willingness to discuss, in good faith, actual and potential environmental risks: "The awareness of the vulnerability of the environment and the recognition that environmental risks have to be assessed on a continuous basis have become much stronger in the years since the Treaty's conclusion."[456] While the parties agreed on the need to take environmental concerns seriously and to take required precautionary measures, they disagreed on the consequences this had for the joint project.[457]

---

[452] *Supra* note 437, para. 97. In addition, Hungary invoked material breach (Article 60 of the Vienna Convention on Treaties), supervening impossibility of performance (Article 61), and fundamental change of circumstances (Article 62) as justification for its conduct.

[453] *Supra* note 437, para. 97.

[454] *Id.*, para. 112.

[455] *Id.*

[456] *Id.*

[457] *Id.*, para. 113.

Hungary further maintained that any mutually accepted long-term discharge regime must be capable of avoiding damage, particularly damage to biodiversity prohibited by the 1992 Convention on Biological Diversity. Moreover, it argued that "a joint environmental impact assessment of the region and of the future of Variant C structures in the context of sustainable development of the region" should be carried out.[458]

### iv. State Responsibility and Reparation

Hungary claimed reparation from Slovakia for the damage in connection with the operation of Variant C, including: damage to the environment; *restitutio in integrum*; damage to the fauna, flora, soil, sub-soil, the groundwater and the aquifer; damage suffered by the Hungarian population due to the increase in uncertainties; damage arising from the unlawful use of installations; and the cessation of the unlawful acts as well as a guarantee that these actions will not be repeated.[459] Slovakia, on the other hand, called upon Hungary to put an end to its unlawful conduct and cease to impede the application of the 1977 treaty.[460] Slovakia contended that Hungary must make reparation for the deleterious consequences of its failure to comply with its obligations and that compensation should be in the form of *restitution in integrum*.[461] It also requested a guarantee against non-repetition.

The Court noted that the project's impact on the environment is a key issue to be taken into consideration.[462] In order to evaluate the environmental risks, current standards must be taken into consideration: "The Court is mindful that, in the field of environmental protection, vigilance and prevention are required on account of the often irreversible character of damage to the environment and of the limitations inherent in the very mechanism of reparation of this type of damage."[463]

The Court then went on to discuss the notion of sustainable development without, however, discussing either its legal status or its definition. Moreover, it failed to indicate whether sustainable development was part of the new norms of international environmental law that must be taken into account by the parties when renegotiating the treaty:

---

[458] *Id.*, para. 125.

[459] *Id.*, para. 127.

[460] *Id.*, para. 128.

[461] *Id.*, para. 129.

[462] *Id.*, para. 140.

[463] *Id. See* Jutta Brunnee, *Of Sense and Sensibility: Reflections on International Liability Regimes as Tools for Environmental Protection*, 53 ICLQ 351 (2004).

The Court is mindful that, in the field of environmental protection, vigilance and prevention are required on account of the often irreversible character of damage to the environment and of the limitations inherent in the very mechanism of reparation of this type of damage. . . . Throughout the ages, mankind has, for economic and other reasons, constantly interfered with nature. In the past, this was often done without consideration of the effects upon the environment. Owing to new scientific insights and to a growing awareness of the risks for mankind—for present and future generations—of pursuit of such interventions at an unconsidered and unabated pace, new norms and standards have been developed, set forth in a great number of instruments during the last two decades. Such new norms have to be taken into consideration, and such new standards given proper weight, not only when States contemplate new activities but also when continuing with activities begun in the past. *This need to reconcile economic development with protection of the environment is aptly expressed in the concept of sustainable development.*[464]

The Court said that for the purposes of the present case, this means that the "Parties together should look afresh at the effects on the environment of the operation of the Gabcikovo power plant."[465] Noting that both parties had violated the 1977 treaty, which entitled both to claim reparation from each other, the Court called upon the parties to renegotiate the 1977 treaty, which the parties had not performed for several years. The Court said that in doing so, new norms of environmental law and the principles of the law of international watercourses must be taken into consideration by the parties. The Court did not, however, indicate what these new norms of international environmental law are or whether sustainable development formed part of them.

Thus, the Court endorsed the principle of integration in relation to sustainable development, which the Court seems to have equated with sustainable development. While reference has been made earlier in the quotation to rights of future generations, the Court made no attempt to define the concept of sustainable development or clarify its legal status content merely to equate it with the principle of integration.

On the positive side, the Court accepted that environmental concerns play an important role in this case; that a state of ecological necessity could

---

[464] *Supra* note 437, para 140 (emphasis added).

[465] *Id.*

be invoked in certain circumstances; that new norms of international environmental law must be taken into consideration by the parties; and that sustainable development seeks to reconcile economic development with environmental protection. The Court also accepted that principles of responsibility and reparation do not play a significant role in cases of this nature; that vigilance and precaution must be exercised; and that the environmental impact of this project is the key issue to be taken into consideration in this case.

## v.    Separate Opinion of Judge Weeramantry

If environmental law and norms played a relatively minor role in the Court's judgment, it constituted the major reason for at least one judge of the Court. In appending a separate opinion to the majority decision, Judge Weeramantry drew extensively from international environmental law, particularly, sustainable development. He discussed three issues in relation to the case: (1) the role played by the principle of sustainable development; (2) the principle of continuing environmental impact assessment; and (3) the appropriateness of the use of *inter partes* legal principles for the resolution of problems with an *erga omnes* character, such as environmental damage. His discussion of the principle[466] of sustainable development will be dealt with here.

Judge Weeramantry noted that if the case involved only environmental considerations, the contention of Hungary would have been conclusive. However, there are other factors to be taken into consideration, particularly, the importance of the project to Slovakia from a developmental point of view. In order to strike a balance between environmental considerations and developmental considerations, the principle of sustainable development must be applied. He pointed out that sustainable development is a principle fundamental to the determination of the competing claims in this case and is likely to play a major role in determining environmental disputes in the future:

> When a major scheme, such as that under consideration in the present case, is planned and implemented, there is always the need to weigh considerations of development against environmental

---

[466] The difference in nomenclature in relation to sustainable development was not accidental. It is noteworthy that the majority opinion referred to sustainable development as a "concept," whereas Judge Weeramantry referred to it as a "principle"; the implication of this is obvious for purposes of its legal status. Judge Weeramantry specifically referred to this in his opinion: "The Court has referred to it as a concept in paragraph 140 of its Judgment. However, I consider it to be more than a mere concept, but as a principle with normative value which is crucial to the determination of this case."

considerations, as their underlying juristic bases—the right to development and the right to environmental protection—are important principles of current international law.[467]

This is the first time that the right to development and the right to environmental protection have received attention by the ICJ, albeit in a separate opinion that, of course, has no binding value. Judge Weeramantry further noted that both these rights formed part of contemporary human rights doctrine and enjoy wide support of the international community. As discussed earlier in this chapter, neither the right to development, nor the right to environment, has received "overwhelming" international support as contended by Judge Weeramantry. On the contrary, they have been criticized for being too vague, not conducive to being considered a "human right" and lacking normative status, etc. It is generally believed that neither the right to development nor the right to environment is part of contemporary human rights.[468]

Judge Weeramantry noted that each principle—right to development and right to environment—cannot be given free rein. Noting that the principle of reconciliation, in this instance, is the principle of sustainable development, Justice Weeramantry pointed out that this case offered a unique opportunity to apply that principle.

Judge Weeramantry was of the view that the concept of sustainable development can be traced to events even before the Stockholm Conference. He cited as examples the Founex meeting of experts in June 1971 and the conference on environment and development in Canberra in 1971. The concept received "a powerful impetus" in Principle 11 of the Stockholm Declaration.[469] He further noted that "since then, it has received considerable endorsement from all sections of the international community, and at all levels."[470] Whether in relation to multilateral treaties, international declarations, foundation documents of international organizations, the practice of international financial institutions, regional decla-

---

[467] Separate Opinion of Judge Weeramantry, 1997 ICJ 88, at 89.

[468] *See* discussion in Chapter 1, Section B.1.a and Chapter 2, Section C.1.a.

[469] Principle 11 of the Stockholm Declaration reads as follows: "The environmental policies of all States should enhance and not adversely affect the present or future development potential of developing countries, nor should they hamper the attainment of better living conditions for all, and appropriate steps should be taken by States and international organizations with a view to reaching agreement on meeting the possible national and international economic consequences resulting from the application of environmental measures."

[470] Separate Opinion of Judge Weeramantry, *supra* note 467, at 93.

rations and planning documents or state practice, he noted that there is wide and general recognition of sustainable development. At the end of this survey he noted that:

> The concept of sustainable development is thus a principle accepted not merely by the developing countries, but one which rests on a basis of worldwide acceptance. . . . The principle of sustainable development is thus a part of modern international law by reason not only of its inescapable logical necessity, but also by reason of its wide and general acceptance by the global community.[471]

He then proceeded to discuss ancient practices relating to sustainable development and chose several examples for this exercise: ancient irrigation system and Buddhist doctrine in Sri Lanka (Ceylon as it was then known); Sonjo and Chagga, two tribes in Tanzania; *qanats* of Iran; irrigation works in China; Inca civilization; practices of indigenous people including American Indians; and rules of Islamic law.

He further noted that several traditional principles can be of assistance to develop modern environmental law, particularly, the trusteeship of earth resources; the principle of inter-generational rights; and the principle that development and environmental protection must be integrated.

## vi.   Analysis

While no one would argue with the wisdom of Judge Weeramantry's separate opinion from an environmental point of view, the conclusion reached by him in relation to the legal status of sustainable development is troubling. Contrary to his opinion, the general consensus is that sustainable development lacks yet the normative quality necessary for it to become part of customary international law.[472]

This does not, however, mean that sustainable development is devoid of any effect. There is no doubt that sustainable development has come a long way since its proclamation by the World Commission on Environment and Development in 1987. Since then, it has been included in almost every instrument, whether binding or otherwise, and is probably the single-most issue that has attracted the attention of policymakers, academics, environmentalists, economists, states as well as international and regional organizations in recent years. Amidst this overwhelming attention to the concept

---

[471]   *Id.* at 94.

[472]   *See* Lowe, *supra* note 82.

of sustainable development, there is also considerable criticism aimed against it. Thus, its legal status is subject to some controversy.

It is also noteworthy that sustainable development has not been totally rejected by any state. On the contrary, it seems to have been endorsed by all states and seems to be a good tool that has influenced decision making. Thus, the fact that it has not been rejected by states has a bearing on its legal status. Whether states are under a legal obligation to give effect to sustainable development is a more difficult issue, however. The answer can be evaluated in terms of *the failure* to give effect to it. Would a state incur international responsibility if it failed to implement the "principle" of sustainable development? To the extent that there is no treaty governing the issue in question, which specifically requires the state to apply the principle of sustainable development, the failure to do so will not give rise to state responsibility under contemporary international law. It is in this light that Justice Weeramantry's conclusion in the above case becomes troubling. While it is true that it is an important principle and offers a solution to the traditional dichotomy between environmental protection and economic development, it suffers from definitional problems.

The modern approach is to consider it as an umbrella term encompassing both substantive and procedural elements.[473] There seems to be wide acceptance at least with regard to its procedural components. Moreover, the principle of integration has gained wide support, which is usually implemented through the environmental impact assessment process. That the present day decision makers should evaluate the impact of their decisions on future generations is also gaining ground now. Thus, the principle of sustainable development is not as vague as some would argue.

While contemporary international law does not recognize sustainable development as a binding principle, it would be wrong to assume that it is a mere concept totally lacking in substance or effect. On the contrary, most development decisions are evaluated against this principle, and all international organizations, including non-traditional environmental organizations like the World Bank, have adopted it as a guiding principle. This is an important development and its impact should not be underestimated.

c.   *Advisory Opinion on the Legality of the Threat or Use of Nuclear Weapons*[474]

In 1994 the UN General Assembly requested an Advisory Opinion from the ICJ on the following question: "Is the threat or use of nuclear

---

[473]  *See* discussion in Section C.

[474]  1996 ICJ 226.

weapons in any circumstances permitted under international law."[475] While this case did not raise issues in relation to sustainable development, the Court did pronounce on environmental law. Some states in their written and oral statements argued that the use of nuclear weapons would be unlawful by reference to the existing norms relating to the safeguarding and protection of the environment, "in view of their essential importance."[476] Specific reference was made to the ENMOD Convention,[477] Additional Protocol 1 to the 1977 Geneva Conventions,[478] Principle 21 of the Stockholm Declaration and Principle 2 of the Rio Declaration. Other states had questioned the binding legal quality of these provisions. In this regard the Court noted:

> The Court recognizes that the environment is under daily threat and that the use of nuclear weapons could constitute a catastrophe for the environment. The Court also recognizes that the environment is not an abstraction but represents the living space, the quality of life and the very health of human beings, including generations unborn. The existence of the general obligation of States to ensure that activities within their jurisdiction and control respect the environment of other States or of areas beyond national control is now part of the corpus of international law relating to the environment.[479]

The Court, however, pointed out that these treaties were not intended to deprive a state of the exercise of the right of self-defense under international law because of its obligations to protect the environment: "Nonetheless, States must take environmental considerations into account when assessing what is necessary and proportionate in the pursuit of legitimate military objectives. Respect for the environment is one of the elements that go to assessing whether an action is in conformity with the principles of necessity and proportionality."[480] The Court noted that this approach is supported by Principle 24 of the Rio

---

[475] Res. 49/75 K, Dec. 15, 1994.

[476] *Id.*, para. 27.

[477] Convention on the Prohibition of Military or other Hostile Use of Environmental Modification Techniques, 1108 UNTS 151, signed May 18, 1977, entered into force Oct. 5, 1978.

[478] Protocol Additional to the 1949 Geneva Conventions Relating to the Protection of Victims of International Armed Conflicts, 16 ILM 1391, signed June 8, 1977, entered into force Dec. 7, 1978.

[479] *Supra* note 475, para. 29.

[480] *Id.*

Declaration, which calls upon states to respect international environmental law during armed conflict.[481]

The Court pointed out that while existing environmental law does not specifically prohibit the use of nuclear weapons, it indicates important environmental factors that must be taken into account during an armed conflict. The Court also noted that nuclear weapons had unique characteristics, which included the release of immense quantities of heat and energy as well as prolonged radiation. "The destructive power of nuclear weapons cannot be contained in either space or time. They have the potential to destroy all civilization and the entire ecosystem of the planet."[482] The Court noted that the radiation released could not only affect human health, agriculture and natural resources, but also pose a serious danger to future generations: "Ionizing radiation has the potential to damage the future environment, food and marine ecosystem, and to cause genetic defects and illness in future generations."[483]

i.    Dissenting Opinion of Judge Weeramantry

Judge Weeramantry appended a dissenting opinion in this case. He paid particular attention to the issue of rights of future generations and noted that, given the potential damage that nuclear weapons could cause (this could extend to thousands of years), "no one generation is entitled, for whatever purpose, to inflict such damage on succeeding generations."[484] He further noted:

> This Court, as the principal judicial organ of the United Nations, empowered to state and apply international law with an authority matched by no other tribunal must, in its jurisprudence, pay due recognition to the rights of future generations. If there is any tribunal that can recognize and protect their interests under the law, it is this Court.[485]

He was of the view that the principle of inter-generational equity and the rights of future generations has been elevated to the level of a binding state obligation:

---

[481] According to Principle 24, "Warfare is inherently destructive of sustainable development. States shall therefore respect international law providing protection for the environment in times of armed conflict and cooperate in its further development, as necessary."

[482] *Supra* note 475, para. 35.

[483] *Id.*

[484] Dissenting Opinion, Judge Weeramantry, *supra* note 474.

[485] *Id.*

When incontrovertible scientific evidence speaks of pollution of the environment on a scale that spans hundreds of generations, this Court would fail in its trust if it did not take serious note of the ways in which the distant future is protected by present law.[486]

He noted further that the ideals of the UN Charter is not limited to the present generation, but extends to succeeding generations. The possibility of the impairment of the environment over an infinite time span would be sufficient for the Court to apply protective principles of international law.

### d. Legality of the Use by a State of Nuclear Weapons in Armed Conflict

A similar advisory opinion requested by the World Health Organization (WHO) on the *Legality of the Use by a State of Nuclear Weapons in Armed Conflict*[487] was dismissed by the ICJ in 1996 on the ground that the question requested by the WHO did not relate to a question that arises within the scope of the activities of that organization under Article 96(2) of the UN Charter.[488] The question put to the Court was "In view of the health and environmental effects, would the use of nuclear weapons by a State in war or other armed conflict be a breach of its obligations under international law including the WHO Constitution?"[489] Given the specificity of the question put to the Court, it is hard to understand how the Court came to the conclusion that the question did not come within the scope of the activities of the WHO.

Again, Judge Weeramantry appended a dissenting opinion. He discussed extensively the effects of nuclear weapons on health, short-term, intermediate and long-term, and noted the importance of prevention. With regard to state obligations relating to the environment, Judge Weeramantry referred to Principle 21 of the Stockholm Declaration and Principle 2 of the Rio Declaration both of which "may be said to be articulations, in the context of the environment, of general principles of customary law."[490] He also referred to the general obligation of states referred to in the *Corfu Channel Case:* every state is under an "obligation not to allow knowingly its territory to be used for acts contrary to the rights of other States."[491]

---

[486] *Id.*

[487] 1996 ICJ 66.

[488] *Id.*, para. 31.

[489] Res. WHA46.40, May 14, 1993.

[490] Dissenting Opinion, Judge Weeramantry, 1996 ICJ 101.

[491] United Kingdom v. Albania, 1949 ICJ 22.

Judge Weeramantry also referred to the evolution of international environmental law:

> From rather hesitant and tentative beginnings, environmental law progressed rapidly under the combined stimulus of ever more powerful means of inflicting irreversible environmental damage and an ever increasing awareness of the fragility of the global environment. Together these have brought about a universal concern with activities that may damage the global environment, which is the common inheritance of all nations, great and small.[492]

Judge Weeramantry noted that not only is there a negative obligation on the part of states to refrain from causing environmental damage, but there is a positive obligation to improve the environment. He noted that in relation to environmental obligations, these are duties owed *erga omens* and the rights are assertible *erga omnes.*[493] He also discussed at length the obligations of states in protecting public health and the role of the WHO in relation to public health and noted that the WHO had a legitimate interest in the question referred to the Court; there are state obligations in relation to international health that can be violated by the use of nuclear weapons; there are state obligations in relation to the international environment that can be violated by the use of nuclear weapons; and there are state obligations under international law with regard to the WHO Constitution that can be violated by the use of nuclear weapons.

## 2. World Bank and Sustainable Development[494]

When the World Bank was established after the Second World War, its main aim was to rebuild Europe after the devastation caused by the War.[495] Environmental protection, human rights or social development were not on its agenda, and over the years, the Bank has funded a few "disastrous" projects that led to an outcry over Bank activities.[496] Nonetheless, in recent years, the Bank has not only changed its focus by embracing environmental protection, including environmental assessment for Bank projects,[497] it

---

[492] Dissenting Opinion, Judge Weeramantry, *supra* note 490.

[493] *Id.*

[494] *See* Gunther Handl, *The Legal Mandate of Multilateral Development Banks as Agents for Change Toward Sustainable Development,* 92 AM. J. INT'L L. 642 (1998).

[495] *See* Jorge Daniel Taillant, *A Rights-based Approach to Analysing International Financial Institutions, in* SUSTAINABLE JUSTICE, *supra* note 71, at 469.

[496] *See* Jacob D. Werksman, *Greening Bretton Woods, in* GREENING INTERNATIONAL LAW, *supra* note 57, at 65, 73.

[497] *See* the discussion in Chapter 4, Section C.6.

has become an ardent advocate for sustainable development.[498] According to the Bank, its goal is reducing poverty through sustainable development.[499] In 2001, the Bank adopted its environmental strategy to guide its work.[500] In 2004, the Bank published its first sustainability review focusing on the private sector as well as on its own work.[501] It noted that this review underlines its commitment to sustainable development. Furthering its commitment to sustainable development, the Bank created a vice presidency for sustainable development in 1998.[502]

According to the Bank, "development in the 21st century is a multi-dimensional concept which combines five perspectives, all of which are key to making development sustainable:"[503] financial capital, physical capital, human capital, social capital and the natural capital.[504]

The Environment Strategy outlines how the Bank will work with client countries to address their environmental challenges and ensure that the Bank's projects and programs integrate principles of environmental sustainability.[505] The Strategy stresses that it is based on an understanding that sustainable development is fundamental to the Bank's core objective of poverty alleviation. Sustainable development requires the balancing of economic growth, social cohesion and environmental protection.[506]

The strategy links poverty, environment and development and notes that this link becomes clearer when poverty is viewed as a multi-dimen-

---

[498] *See* the World Bank Web site—www.worldbank.org. *See also* Charles E. Di Leva, *International Environmental Law and Development*, 10 GEO. INT'L ENVTL. L. REV. 501 (1998) and HUNTER ET AL., *supra* note 124, at 1474.

[499] *Id.*

[500] *Making Sustainable Commitments: An Environment Strategy for the World Bank* (2001), *available at* www.worldbank.org.

[501] World Bank, *Focus on Sustainability 2004* (2004), *available at* http://Inweb18.worldbank.org/ESSD/ sdvext.nsf.

[502] World Bank, *Sustainable Development (ESSD) Vice Presidency, Reference Guide. See* Ko-Yung Tung, *Sustainable Development and the Global Role of International Financial Institutes, in* SUSTAINABLE JUSTICE, *supra* note 71, at 449.

[503] World Bank, *Sustainable Development in the 21st Century, available at* http://Inweb18.worldbank.org/ESSD/ sdvext.nsf.

[504] *Id.*

[505] *See supra* note 500.

[506] Executive Summary, *Making Sustainable Commitments, supra* note 500. *See also* Rudolf Dolzer, *The World Bank and the Global Environment: Novel Frontiers?, in* LIBER AMICORUM IBRHIM F.I. SHIHATA: INTERNATIONAL FINANCE AND DEVELOPMENT LAW 141 (Sabine Schlemmer-Schulte & Ko-Yung Tung eds., 2001).

sional phenomenon rather than simply a matter of income.[507] This is reflected in the UN Millennium Development Goals for 2015.[508] Noting that the environmental problems of the world are vast, the Bank can best contribute to their solution by focusing on those areas where it can achieve particular results. To help achieve these goals, the Strategy adopts a three-fold approach: learning and applying lessons; adapting to a changing world; and deepening the commitment by ensuring that environmental concerns are fully internalized throughout the Bank.

The Strategy notes that sustainable development calls for a more comprehensive, integrated, systematic approach that takes a long-term view of development and balances its different dimensions—economic growth, social equity and long-term environmental stability.[509] It further notes that these goals have been incorporated in the Millennium Declaration and have been accepted as key indicators of sustainable development. Achieving them requires a concerted effort by governments, civil society and development partners.[510]

Sustainability is a long-term concept but is directly affected by short-term financial and political considerations. Major international development institutions have been working on a common set of international development goals that focus on key aspects of human well-being.[511] There are seven broadly agreed goals: eradicate poverty and hunger; achieve universal primary education; reach gender equality and empower women; reduce child mortality; combat HIV/AIDS, malaria and other diseases; and ensure environmental sustainability.[512]

While there are many win-win situations, sometimes there can be tradeoffs between sustainable resource use and environmental protection.[513] Balancing the various objectives and tradeoffs requires value judgments. They have to be informed choices, made with the participation of affected stakeholders.[514] As

---

[507] *See supra* note 500.

[508] Adopted at the UN Millennium Summit. *See* discussion in Section I.1.

[509] Chapter 1, "Development, Poverty and the Environment—Tracing the Connections," *supra* note 500.

[510] *Id.*

[511] *Id.* These are identified as: poverty reduction, education, gender equality, health and sustainable development.

[512] *Id.*

[513] *Id.*

[514] *Id.*

discussed earlier, this provision gives effect to the principle of participation, an integral component of sustainable development.[515]

The strategy notes that three broad factors underlie many decisions and strategies concerning environmental problems: the tradeoffs between present and future generations; equitable access to resources; and the perceived lack of overlap between actions that address local and global environmental issues.[516]

The strategy identifies the links between environmental protection and economic development as: quality of life, quality of growth and the quality of the regional and global commons.[517] The poorest countries are often the ones that are most affected by the environmental degradation of the global commons. Climate change is a good example. It is expected to increase hunger and famine in world's poorest areas, displace millions of people from small island states and low-lying cities, increase vector-borne diseases and lead to loss of biodiversity and livelihoods.[518] This will also have a huge impact on the global economy.

In its report prepared for the Johannesburg Summit in 2002, the Bank notes that the WSSD must lay the foundations for sustainable development while shrinking the ranks of the poor.[519] It notes that poverty and sustainable development are at the core of the Summit. The Millennium Development Goals represent a program for sustainable development. The report notes that while increased growth will be key, the benefits of growth must be widely spread, and must be environmentally and socially sustainable.[520] It further notes that if the vision of a world without poverty is to be realized, sustainable growth is the key.[521] Some of the challenges within this goal are: achieving sustainable rural development and agricultural growth; sustainable energy; sustainable water services, health, human and social capital; and technology. It is also necessary to build stronger partnerships.[522]

---

[515] *See* discussion in Section F and Chapter 4, Section F.

[516] *Id.*

[517] *Id.*

[518] *Id.*

[519] World Bank, *Johannesburg and Beyond: An Agenda for Action* (2002).

[520] *Id.*

[521] *Id.*

[522] *Id.*

The report further notes that consensus is emerging on the elements of implementing a sustainable development agenda: poverty reduction; long-lasting partnerships between private and public sectors and with civil society; strong policies and transparent institutions; a vibrant private sector that must adopt corporate social responsibility as a guiding principle.[523]

## 3. UN Environment Program (UNEP)

UNEP enjoys the unique position of being the first ever inter-governmental organization on environmental protection. While there are other organizations that deal with some aspect of the environment, such as the WHO (environmental health), WMO (weather, climate change), ILO (environmental hygiene of the work place), IMO (marine pollution), UNDP (development, poverty and more recently, sustainable development), FAO (agriculture) and IAEA (atomic energy, radiation), UNEP is the first true international environmental agency. It was established in 1973 following the Stockholm Conference by General Assembly Resolution 2997.[524]

The mission of UNEP was to "facilitate international co-operation in the environmental field; to keep the world environmental situation under review so that problems of international significance receive appropriate consideration by Governments; and to promote the acquisition, assessment and exchange of environmental knowledge."[525] It was not established as a UN specialized agency, but rather as a program, as its name indicates. UNEP was established as a coordinating body and not as an executive or regulatory agency. This has proven to be a major obstacle to its work in the later years. Despite this, and a financial crisis affecting its continuity, UNEP has been successful in many areas, particularly, ozone depletion, biodiversity and environmental assessment. Its regional seas program now includes more than 30 treaties and numerous action plans.[526]

UNEP's focus areas are: biodiversity; business and industry; chemicals; civil society and NGOs; energy; environmental assessment; freshwater; governance and law; land; marine and coastal areas; ozone layer; sustainable consumption; and urban issues.[527] Voluntary contributions by governments to the Environment Fund are the main source of UNEP's funding. The per-

---

[523] *Id.*

[524] GA Res. 2997 (1972).

[525] *See* HUNTER ET AL., *supra* note 124, at 219.

[526] *See* SANDS, *supra* note 83, at 83.

[527] *See* http://www.unep.org.

ception that UNEP was badly managed led to the breakdown of confidence in the organization on the part of the donor countries.[528] Although many proposals were made for reform, by and large, no far-reaching reforms have been carried out to either its structure or the mandate.

Despite the criticisms made against UNEP, it boasts of significant achievements and has contributed to the development of international environmental law as no other international organization has. Not only did it manage to put environmental protection on the international agenda, it was also responsible for the negotiation of more than 40 multilateral treaties[529] and many soft law instruments[530] including guidelines.[531] Some of its achievements include: the global international waters assessment; Montreal Protocol on Substances that Deplete the Ozone Layer; sound management of hazardous chemicals and the negotiation of an instrument on Prior Informed Consent Procedure for Certain Hazardous Chemicals and Pesticides in International Trade; administering the Convention to Regulate International Trade in Endangered Species of Flora and Fauna (CITES) and Convention on Biological Diversity (CBD); Adoption of the Rotterdam Convention with cooperation of the Food and Agricultural Organization (FAO); promoting the preparation of the Global Biodiversity Assessment; promoting the Global Reporting Initiative for voluntary reporting by companies worldwide; and preparing a global set of guidelines for corporate sustainability.[532]

As can be seen from the above discussion, UNEP's activities fall within the broad category of environmental protection. During the last ten years, it has changed its focus to include sustainable development in keeping with international developments, although this is not its main focus. The UNDP, on the other hand, has a sustainable development agenda, given that its main focus is economic development and alleviation of poverty.[533]

---

[528]  *See* HUNTER ET AL., *supra* note 124, at 220.

[529]  *Id.* at 222.

[530]  The World Charter for Nature, GA Res. 37/7 (1982), *reprinted in* 22 ILM 455 (1983) is a good example.

[531]  Some of the well-known guidelines include the ones on: management of shared natural resources; environmental assessment; and marine pollution from land-based sources. *See* http://www.unep.org for a list of these guidelines.

[532]  *See* http://www.unep.org.

[533]  The UNDP describes itself as the UN's global development network. *See* http://www.undp.org/

Both Agenda 21 and WSSD Plan of Implementation made suggestions for UNEP's reform. Agenda 21 notes that in the follow-up to the UNCED conference, there will be a need for an enhanced and strengthened role for UNEP and its governing council. It lays down certain priority areas on which UNEP should concentrate on, including: strengthening its catalytic role in promoting environmental activities throughout the UN system; promoting international cooperation in the environmental field; environmental monitoring and assessment; coordination and promotion of relevant scientific research; dissemination of environmental information and data to governments and to the UN system; raising awareness on environmental protection through collaboration with the general public, NGOs and inter-governmental institutions; further development of international environmental law; and provision of technical, legal and institutional assistance to governments.[534] This list contains 14 priority areas for UNEP activities, which do not seem to be different from activities that UNEP has always been engaged in. The question also arises whether 14 priority areas are too many.

Agenda 21 notes that:

In order to perform all of these functions, while retaining its role as the principal body within the United Nations system in the field of environment and taking into account the development aspects of environmental questions, UNEP would require access to greater expertise and provision of adequate financial resources and it would require closer cooperation and collaboration with development organs and other relevant organs of the UN system. . . . UNEP should take steps to reinforce and intensify its liaison and interaction with UNDP and the World Bank.[535]

The question has also arisen whether the creation of yet another organization in 1992 was necessary. Granted that the mandate of the Commission on Sustainable Development is different from that of UNEP;[536] however, there is no doubt that there is a heavy overlap between the activities of the two organizations. Given the direction that international environmental law has evolved over the years to encompass international

---

[534] Agenda 21, ch. 38, *supra* note 1.

[535] *Id.*, para. 38.23.

[536] The Commission on Sustainable Development was created to monitor the implementation of Agenda 21. *See* Agenda 21, para. 38.11, *supra* note 1: "A high-level Commission on Sustainable Development should be established in accordance with Article 68 of the Charter of the United Nations."

sustainable development law, it is highly unlikely that UNEP would have been able to carry out its mandate without impinging on the toes of the Commission on Sustainable Development (CSD) or at least touching on sustainable development. Given the successful role that the UNDP has played in implementing programs on sustainable development, it can be questioned whether the implementation of Agenda 21 could have been entrusted to the UNDP, without creating yet another bureaucracy.[537]

The Plan of Implementation adopted at the World Summit on Sustainable Development in 2002 also discusses the institutional framework for sustainable development. It notes that "an effective institutional framework for sustainable development at all levels is key to the full implementation of Agenda 21 and other sustainable development activities."[538] It also notes that good governance is essential for sustainable development and that a vibrant and effective UN system is fundamental to the promotion of international cooperation for sustainable development. In this context, the Plan discusses the role of the General Assembly,[539] the Economic and Social Council[540] and the Commission on Sustainable Development,[541] but it is surprisingly silent on the role of UNEP, except to say that it should strengthen its contribution to sustainable development programs.[542] It discusses other international institutions in some detail, such as the WTO, the GEF, the UNDP and financial institutions. The reference to UNEP is almost as an afterthought and does not augur well for the main UN body dealing with environmental protection.

### 4.  UN Development Program (UNDP)

According to the UNDP Web site, it is the "UN's global development network, an organization advocating for change and connecting countries to knowledge, experience and resources to help people build a better life."[543] World leaders have pledged to achieve the Millennium Development Goals,[544] which include the goal of reducing poverty in half by

---

[537] *See* BHARAT H. DESAI, INSTITUTIONALIZING INTERNATIONAL ENVIRONMENTAL LAW 223 (2004).

[538] Plan of Implementation, para. 137, *supra* note 80.

[539] *Id.*, para. 143.

[540] *Id.*, para. 144.

[541] *Id.*, para. 145.

[542] *Id.*, para. 155.

[543] *See* http://www.undp.org.

[544] Adopted at the UN Millennium Summit.

2015. The UNDP seeks to coordinate global and national efforts to reach these goals. It works in five focus areas: democratic governance; poverty reduction; crisis prevention and recovery; energy and environment; and HIV/AIDS.[545] The UNDP encourages the protection of human rights and the empowerment of women in all its activities.[546]

As can be seen, the UNDP can easily pass off for an organization with a sustainable development mandate, similar to the Commission on Sustainable Development. The UNDP's focus areas show that it has adopted a broad approach to development, encompassing within its mandate issues such as governance, crisis prevention and HIV/AIDS, which are not traditional "developmental" issues, but which nonetheless have a direct bearing on development. Thus, for example, a society plagued with the HIV/AIDS pandemic will not be able to achieve development, as its labor force will not be productive. Similarly, a society that does not promote democratic governance will not be able to achieve development, as decisions will be taken behind closed doors, no public participation will be possible and access to information will be a myth. Similarly, gender equality and protection of human rights play an important role in the development process. Moreover, a society plagued by violence or conflict will find it difficult to achieve development.[547] It is obvious that the kind of development that the UNDP envisages is sustainable development. Its activities in relation to energy and environment amply demonstrate this:

> Energy and environment are essential for sustainable development. The poor are disproportionately affected by environmental degradation and lack of access to clean, affordable energy services. These issues are also global as climate change, loss of biodiversity and ozone layer depletion cannot be addressed by countries acting alone. UNDP helps countries strengthen their capacity to address these challenges at global, national and community levels, seeking out and sharing best practices, providing innovative policy advice and linking partners through pilot projects that help poor people build sustainable livelihoods.[548]

Some of the priority areas under the Energy and Environment Program are: frameworks and strategies for sustainable development; effective water governance; access to sustainable energy services; sustainable land

---

[545] *Id.*

[546] *Id.*

[547] *See* NORMAN MYERS, ULTIMATE SECURITY (1993).

[548] *See* http://www.undp.org.

management to combat desertification and land degradation; and conservation and sustainable use of biodiversity.[549] Again, there is a heavy overlap between the activities of UNEP, the UNDP and the CSD. In order to cut down on unnecessary duplication and wastage, it is necessary to coordinate the activities of these organizations so that they can complement one another, rather than duplicate work. Resources are scarce, and most organizations constantly face financial cut backs. It is, therefore, important to ensure that there is no duplication of activities in these institutions.

### 5. Commission on Sustainable Development (CSD)

The CSD was established after the Rio Conference to oversee the implementation of Agenda 21.[550] As may be recalled, Agenda 21 was the blueprint for sustainable development action adopted at the Rio Conference. It identified the need to establish a high-level Commission on Sustainable Development under Article 68 of the UN Charter, which would report to the Economic and Social Council.[551] The mandate of the Commission would be to ensure the effective follow-up of the Conference, enhance international cooperation, rationalize inter-governmental decision-making capacity for the integration of environment and development issues; and examine the progress in the implementation of Agenda 21 at national, regional and international levels.[552]

The functions of the Commission include:

- reviewing progress at the international, regional and national levels in the implementation of recommendations contained in Agenda 21 and the Rio Declaration;
- elaborating policy guidance and options for future activities on the Johannesburg Plan of Implementation;
- building partnerships for sustainable development with governments, the international community and groups, such as women, youth, indigenous peoples, NGOs, local authorities, workers and trade unions, business and industry, the scientific community and farmers.[553]

---

[549]  *Id.*

[550]  *See* http://www.un.org/esa/sustdev/csd/csd_mandate.htm.

[551]  Agenda 21, ch. 38, para. 38.11, *supra* note 1.

[552]  *Id.*

[553]  *See* http://www.un.org/esa/sustdev/csd/csd_mandate.htm.

The CSD Web site lists 41 items as sustainable development issues that are on the CSD agenda.[554] Dealing with 41 items is no easy feat for any organization, high-level or otherwise. Again, issues that are dealt with by other organizations are also listed here—no doubt because of its relevance to sustainable development, but it must be accepted that CSD cannot possibly deal with all the issues identified in this list. Indeed, there is no need for it to do so, as other organizations are dealing with these issues. Thus, for example, health is handled by the WHO, while mountains, land management, desertification and drought, and forests are handled by the FAO. Out of this long list, only two or three items will fall exclusively within the CSD mandate: integrated decision making, international cooperation and national sustainable strategies. All other areas are handled by other agencies. If the CSD was only meant to coordinate the sustainable development activities of other organizations, to what extent this has been achieved is questionable.

The Plan of Implementation notes that the CSD should continue to be the high-level commission on sustainable development within the UN system and serve as a forum to integrate the three dimensions of sustainable development. While its original mandate remains valid, the Commission needs to be strengthened. It should place more emphasis on implementation at all levels, including promoting partnerships between governments, international organizations and relevant stakeholders for the implementation of Agenda 21. The Plan of Implementation also recommended that the CSD should limit the number of themes addressed in each session, focus on cross-sectoral aspects of sectoral issues and provide a forum for their integration.[555] It also recommended that the Commission take into account significant legal developments in the field of sustainable development.[556]

## I. OBSTACLES TO ACHIEVING SUSTAINABLE DEVELOPMENT

### 1. Poverty and Sustainable Development[557]

That there is a clear link between poverty and sustainable development needs no special emphasis. Suffice it to note that in a society saddled with a

---

[554] *Id.*

[555] *Id.*, para. 147. *See also Follow-up to Johannesburg and the Future Role of the CSD—The Implementation Track*, Report of the Secretary-General, E/CN.17/2003/2, Feb. 18, 2003.

[556] *Id.* With regard to the work of the WTO in relation to trade and sustainable development, *see* Chapter 1.

[557] This section is drawn from the author's publication entitled *International Human Rights Law and Poverty Eradication, in* SUSTAINABLE JUSTICE, *supra* note 71, at 305.

heavy burden of poverty and deprivation, achieving sustainable development is no easy feat. However, that is precisely the challenge that we must meet.

Despite the technological advances of the world today, which have surpassed anybody's wildest dreams, 1.2 billion people today live in absolute poverty (on less than $1 a day) and a further 2 billion people live on less than $2 a day.[558] While over-consumption is the norm in many developed countries manifested by wasteful practices and obesity, squalor and starvation signify many developing countries. Thus, abject poverty, on the one hand, and over-consumption of resources, on the other, pose a significant challenge to achieving sustainable development.

Starting with the Stockholm Declaration, the link between environmental protection (and later sustainable development) and poverty is recognized in many international instruments.[559] The Rio Declaration, for example, has made this link explicitly:

All States and all people shall cooperate in the essential task of eradicating poverty as an indispensable requirement for sustainable development, in order to decrease the disparities in standards of living and better meet the needs of the majority of the people of the world.[560]

Furthermore, Principle 6 of the Rio Declaration refers specifically to the needs of developing countries, particularly the least developed and the most environmentally vulnerable. The issue of eradicating poverty is closely related to the notion of intra-generational equity, an important component of sustainable development.

The vicious circle of poverty and environmental protection must be recognized and addressed: in a world plagued by poverty, environmental protection cannot be achieved. When there is extreme poverty, unsustainable practices abound. As it is very difficult to achieve environmental protection if people are extremely poor, economic development is imperative. This, however, does not mean that any kind of development is acceptable.

---

[558] World Bank, *World Development Report 1999/2000* (2000).

[559] *See* the United Nations Framework Convention on Climate Change *supra* note 53, the Convention on Biological Diversity, *supra* note 54, the UN Millennium Declaration, UN Doc. A/RES/55/2 (2000), *available at* http://www.un.org/millenium/declaration/ares55c.htm and the 2005 World Summit Outcome, A/RES/60/1, Oct. 24, 2005, *available at* http://www.un.org/summit2005/documents.html.

[560] Principle 5, *supra* note 12.

The contemporary thinking is to ensure that states achieve sustainable development, which would be an answer to the issue of eradicating poverty.

The basic right to an adequate standard of living, recognized more than 50 years ago by the international community,[561] has remained elusive to the majority of the world's community. Twenty years later, states parties recognized in a binding instrument "the right of everyone to an adequate standard of living for himself and his family, including adequate food, clothing and housing, and to the continuous improvement of living conditions."[562] Despite these noble statements, millions of poor people continue to live in poverty without adequate food and water and without adequate housing and sanitation. Many people have become poorer and marginalized, and the reference to the "continuous improvement of living conditions" has become a non-starter, as many millions of people in the world today live in squalor and starvation.[563]

There is no doubt that *poverty is the biggest violator of human rights,* as it leads to the deprivation of other rights enshrined in international human rights instruments, particularly the right to health,[564] the right to education,[565] the right to a livelihood,[566] the right to privacy,[567] as well as other procedural rights such as the right to participate in the decision-making process[568] and the right to information.[569] It is also a violation of the principle of equality,[570] a fundamental tenet of international human rights law, and of the principle of intra-generational equity, which is generally considered a component of sustainable development.[571]

---

[561] Principle 25, Universal Declaration of Human Rights, *available at* http://www.unhchr.org.

[562] Art. 11, ICESCR, *supra* note 127.

[563] As noted, 1.2 billion people in the world today live on less than U.S. $1 a day. *See World Development Report 2000/01* (World Bank) and UN Secretary General's Millenium Report (2000) presented to the UN General Assembly's Millenium Summit.

[564] Protected under Article 12 of the ICESCR, *supra* note 127.

[565] Protected under Article 13 of the ICESCR, *supra* note 127.

[566] Protected under Article 6 of the ICESCR, *supra* note 127.

[567] Protected under Article 17 of the ICCPR, *supra* note 203.

[568] Protected under Article 25 of the ICCPR, *supra* note 203.

[569] Protected under Article 19 of the ICCPR, *supra* note 203. *See* HUMAN RIGHTS IN THE TWENTY-FIRST CENTURY: A GLOBAL CHALLENGE (Kathleen E. Mahoney & Paul Mahoney eds., 1993).

[570] Protected under Article 26 of the ICCPR, *supra* note 203.

[571] *See* discussion, in Section C.1.d.

*Poverty is also the biggest polluter.* Many people live in dire poverty, which has exacerbated environmental degradation, as poor people often have no choice but to resort to unsustainable practices in order to eke out a meager living. The international community recognized the link between poverty and sustainable development and proclaimed in the 1992 Rio Declaration on Environment and Development:

> All states and all people shall cooperate in the essential task of eradicating poverty as an indispensable requirement for sustainable development, in order to decrease the disparities in standards of living and better meet the needs of the majority of the people of the world.[572]

*Poverty is also a developmental issue.* It is clear that lack of economic development has led to the present problems associated with poverty. Thus, the UN General Assembly Resolution on the Right to Development[573] recognized thus:

> The right to development is an inalienable human right by virtue of which every human person and all peoples are entitled to participate in, contribute to, and enjoy economic, social, cultural and political development, in which all human rights and fundamental freedoms can be fully realized.

Thus, poverty has the ability to cut across a wide spectrum of issues—social, economic and environmental—and, as a result, requires an integrated approach.[574] It is here that international sustainable development law—understood as the intersection between economic, social and environmental law—plays a significant role.[575]

While enormous strides have been made with regard to international protection of human rights, in practice, a huge gap exists between civil and

---

[572] Principle 5 of the Rio Declaration, *supra* note 61.

[573] GA Res. 41/128, Dec. 4, 1986. It must be recognized, however, that this Declaration is a soft law instrument and that the notion of right to development has attracted much criticism in literature. It is also of concern that the debate on the right to development has not integrated the parallel developments in relation to sustainable development. *See* discussion in Section C.1.a.

[574] *See* Joe Oloka-Onyango, *Human Rights and Sustainable Development in Contemporary Africa: A New Dawn, or Retreating Horizons?*, 6 BUFF. HUM. RTS. L. REV. 39 (2000).

[575] *See* SUSTAINABLE DEVELOPMENT LAW, *supra* note 71; HUMAN RIGHTS, SUSTAINABLE DEVELOPMENT AND THE ENVIRONMENT (Antonio Trindade ed., 1992); and INTERNATIONAL LAW AND SUSTAINABLE DEVELOPMENT: PAST ACHIEVEMENTS AND FUTURE CHALLENGES (Alan Boyle & David Freestone eds., 1999).

political rights on the one hand, and economic, social and cultural rights, on the other.[576] This also reflects the North-South divide on the issue. This has contributed to the marginalization of the poor, and the time has come to bridge the gap between these two sets of right, which despite the official UN position that all rights are indivisible, inter-dependent and inter-related, in practice, a clear divide does exist between these two sets of rights. The progressive realization of economic, social and cultural rights is imperative, if the present plight of the poor is to be ameliorated. In addition, governance issues have exacerbated the problems faced by the poor, as societies in which governments are corrupt and do not respect the rule of law or fundamental rights of peoples tend to further marginalize the poor.[577]

The issue of poverty received particular attention at the Millenium Summit of the United Nations at which the UN Secretary-General noted that "The combination of extreme poverty with extreme inequality between countries and often also within them, is an affront to our common humanity."[578] He called upon all states to take action to reduce extreme poverty by half in every part of the world before 2015.[579]

Development assistance institutions, such as the World Bank, have also taken a keen interest in poverty alleviation and sustainable development.[580] Its approach to poverty has varied over time. According to its operational directive, in the 1960s, the Bank has focused on economic growth as the key to poverty reduction while, in the 1970s, attention shifted from redistribution with growth to the satisfaction of basic human needs. In the 1990s, the Bank adopted "Assistance Strategies to Reduce Poverty," which reaffirmed its commitment to poverty reduction.[581] According to the Operational Directive, "Sustainable poverty reduction is the Bank's overarching objective."[582] It further notes that "Maintaining the environment is critical if gains in poverty reduction are to be sustained and if future increases in poverty are to be avoided."[583]

---

[576] ECONOMIC, SOCIAL AND CULTURAL RIGHTS (Asbjorn Eide, Catarina Krause & Allan Rosas eds., 1995).

[577] SUSTAINABLE DEVELOPMENT AND GOOD GOVERNANCE (Konrad Ginther, Erik Denters & Paul J.I.M. de Waart eds., 1995).

[578] *We the Peoples: The Role of the United Nations in the 21st Century*, Millennium Report of the Secretary-General of the United Nations (2000), Executive Summary.

[579] *Id.*

[580] *See* discussion in Section H.2.

[581] World Bank, *Operational Manual, Operational Directive—Poverty Reduction*, OD 4.15 (Dec. 1991).

[582] *Id.*

[583] *Id.*

## 2. Good Governance and Sustainable Development

That sustainable development and good governance are inter-linked is increasingly accepted at both national and international levels. In other words, it is generally accepted that in a society that does not respect principles of good governance, it is hard to achieve sustainable development. Good governance and sustainable development also share similar features.

While the elements of good governance are subject to some debate, transparency, accountability, upholding the rule of law and respecting human rights are generally considered as principles of good governance.[584] In addition, an independent judiciary, democratic decision making, sensible economic and social policies, creation of a market-friendly environment for development and measures to combat corruption are considered principles of good governance.[585] In 1993 the UN Secretary-General noted that "without development, long-term enjoyment of human rights and democracy will prove illusory, for good governance, democracy, participation, an independent judiciary, the rule of law and civil peace create conditions necessary to economic progress."[586]

Whatever the components of good governance are, it is clear that it shares common elements with sustainable development. Sustainable development embodies participatory rights—access to information, participation in the decision-making process and access to remedies. These principles promote transparency and accountability. Good governance requires, *inter alia*, accountability and transparency. Thus, there is a clear link between sustainable development and good governance.[587] As was noted by the Supreme Court of Sri Lanka, publicity, transparency and fairness are essential if the goal of sustainable development is to be achieved.[588]

The link between sustainable development and good governance has been identified as:

Inherent in the concept of sustainable development is the need for a political system which provides for effective citizen participation in decision-making and for good governance, i.e. institutions for

---

[584] SUSTAINABLE DEVELOPMENT AND GOOD GOVERNANCE, *supra* note 577, at 1, *quoting* BOUTROS BOUTROS-GHALI, AN AGENDA FOR PEACE (United Nations, 1992).

[585] *Id.*

[586] *Id.* at 2.

[587] *See* Atapattu, *supra* note 81, at 285.

[588] *Gunaratne v. Homagama Pradeshiya Sabha,* 5 S. ASIAN ENVTL. L. REP. 28 (1998).

policy-making, decision-making and their implementation which are responsive to the objectives of sustainable development.[589]

It has been further articulated that "good governance in the context of the goal of sustainable development would mean respecting the principles of the Rio Declaration in designing development projects and programmes."[590] A mere cost-benefit analysis of a project will not suffice for this purpose. The environmental and social impact of projects and programs must be evaluated together with their implications for the goals of sustainable development. It is also necessary to combat corruption[591] that results from lack of transparency and accountability. Strengthening the role of civil society institutions is necessary to promote sustainable development.[592]

Whether good governance also means democratic governance has also been questioned. If one looks at the principles of good governance, it becomes obvious that it is impossible to achieve those principles in a system that is not democratic. Thus, it seems that authoritarian, one-party states cannot promote principles of good governance. This may be why some developing countries have argued that good governance is another ploy invented by developed countries to impose conditionalities on developing countries.[593] While violations of human rights can occur in any regime, it is no secret that such violations are rampant in authoritative and autocratic regimes. In a democratic regime, checks and balances are available if violations of human rights do take place, and remedies are available for victims of such violations.

## 3. The Present Institutional Framework and Lack of Coordination

The institutional structure governing international environmental issues was discussed earlier. The main institutions are the UNEP, the CSD, the UNDP, and the World Bank. In addition, the mandate of many other organizations and specialized agencies can have an impact on the environment and sustainable development. Thus, for example, the FAO deals with sustainable agriculture, the impact of pesticides and fertilizer, plant

---

[589] *See* Kamal Hossain, *Evolving Principles of Sustainable Development and Good Governance, in* SUSTAINABLE DEVELOPMENT AND GOOD GOVERNANCE, *supra* note 577, at 15, 20.

[590] *Id.* at 21.

[591] *Id.* at 22. Corruption is defined as the abuse of public power for private profit.

[592] *Id.*

[593] *See* Pearson Nherere, *Conditionality, Human Rights and Good Governance: A Dialogue of Unequal Partners, in* SUSTAINABLE DEVELOPMENT AND GOOD GOVERNANCE, *supra* note 577, at 289.

genetic resources, etc.[594] In addition, its focus on food security has a direct bearing on poverty and human health. It also deals with fisheries, forestry and forest products, and marine products.

The World Health Organization's (WHO) primary function is protection of human health. As such, it has a direct bearing on environmental degradation. In 1990, it established the WHO Commission on Health and Environment[595] and has issued many reports on environmental health, including children's environmental health.[596] It has established standards for foodstuffs, emission standards for pollutants, etc.[597]

The World Meteorological Organization (WMO) with regard to climate, the International Labor Organization (ILO) with regard to occupational hygiene, the International Maritime Organization (IMO) with regard to marine pollution and protecting the marine environment, UN Education, Scientific and Cultural Organization (UNESCO) in relation to protection of cultural property and world heritage sites as well as children's issues and the International Atomic Energy Agency (IAEA) with regard to nuclear safety all have impinged on environmental protection and sustainable development. In addition, there are other global (such as the IUCN) and regional organizations (OECD, European Union (EU), ECE, Organization of American States (OAS), Association of South East Asian Nations (ASEAN), etc.) as well as non-governmental bodies that have an environmental agenda.

Given the plethora of these institutions, how can one ensure coordination? It is obvious that overlap of activities cannot be avoided altogether, although it can be minimized given the lack of resources and the need to minimize waste. The CSD was established with the specific objective of coordinating the activities of all these organizations and agencies. A strong institutional mechanism at both the national and international levels is imperative to achieve sustainable development.

It has been articulated that international law has three interrelated challenges:[598] first, to ensure that all states are able to participate in the international community in relation to a growing range of environmental challenges that require an international response; second, to strengthen the role of international organizations and their effectiveness, by rational-

---

[594]   *See* http://www.fao.org.

[595]   *See* SANDS, *supra* note 83, at 99.

[596]   *See* the discussion on health in Chapter 1, Section B.3.

[597]   *See* http://www.who.int.

[598]   *See* SANDS, *supra* note 83, at 120.

izing their activities; third, to ensure that the role of non-state actors is properly harnessed.[599]

It has been noted in relation to the proliferation of institutions that:

> The proliferation of organizations, including treaty-based environmental organizations, has brought with it a proliferation of secretariats, most of which would be able to function far more efficiently if they could share experiences and expertise. Rationalization would allow the functions of the organizations and the secretariats to be more efficiently undertaken, and might then provide them with a stronger basis to engage in the sorts of activities which are clearly needed, for which they are well equipped.[600]

Thus, there is a clear need to identify priorities, increase coordination between the various institutions that deal with some aspect of environmental protection and to minimize the proliferation of institutions that has become unwieldy in the field of environmental protection.

## J.  LEGAL STATUS OF SUSTAINABLE DEVELOPMENT

The most important issue to be resolved in our discussion on sustainable development is whether it has any legal status under international law. Writers are divided on this issue. Many argue that the legal status is closely related to the issue of definition: if the concept lacks a proper definition, how can it have any binding effect?[601] The issue is more complex, however. As the above discussion revealed, sustainable development is an umbrella term that contains both substantive and procedural components. In order to decide whether sustainable development has any normative effect, it is necessary to evaluate the status of each and every component that comes under the umbrella. If this approach were taken, it becomes obvious that some strands of sustainable development do indeed have normative effect.

Before we draw any conclusions as to the legal status of sustainable development, it is necessary to discuss the relevance of provisions of Article 38(1) of the ICJ Statute. According to this provision, two components are

---

[599]  *Id.*

[600]  *Id.* at 121.

[601]  As Vaughn Lowe has noted the vagueness of the concept is "incompatible with it having a 'norm-creating character' and precludes it becoming a primary rule of law." *See* Lowe, *supra* note 82, at 34. He also noted that no clear meaning can be ascribed to sustainable development and it is subject to considerable uncertainty as to its meaning and scope. *id.* at 29.

necessary to establish custom: state practice and *opinio juris* (conviction that a practice is binding). Both these elements are necessary to establish a customary international law principle. Although it seems simple enough, this requirement has given rise to a number of questions:[602] What constitutes state practice? How much state practice is necessary? For how long should such practice have existed? Is universal or consistent practice necessary? How is *opinio juris* to be established? It is generally accepted that universal adherence to a practice is not necessary but consistent practice is—deviations from the practice are treated as breaches rather than the emergence of a new practice. The Court looks at various events, statements, diplomatic notes, how states have voted before UN bodies, etc., in order to establish state practice, but the difficult issue has been to establish *opinio juris*. In the *North Sea Continental Shelf Cases*[603] the ICJ stressed that the practice in question should be of a fundamentally norm-creating character in order to generate a customary international law principle.[604]

Thus, does the concept of sustainable development have a "fundamentally norm creating character"? As argued earlier, perhaps some of the different components that make up the umbrella may satisfy this test. With regard to the substantive components, it can be argued that at least the principle of integration has received sufficient state practice to be considered normative. The principle of integration (referred to in Principle 4 of the Rio Declaration) has been included in many international environmental treaties[605] and has been implemented at the national level in the form of environmental impact assessments (EIAs) in many countries.[606] The main purpose of an EIA is to evaluate the environmental consequences of a given

---

[602] *See* INTERNATIONAL LAW: CASES AND MATERIALS, *supra* note 228, at 59.

[603] *North Sea Continental Shelf Cases* (Federal Republic of Germany v. Denmark, Federal Republic of Germany v. Netherlands), 1969 ICJ 3.

[604] *Id.*

[605] *E.g.*, the Preamble to the Convention on Environmental Impact Assessment in a Transboundary Context, 30 ILM 800 (1991), where it is noted that parties are aware of the interrelationship between economic activities and their environmental consequences; art. 3 of the UN Framework Convention on Climate Change, *supra* note 53, states: "The Parties have a right to, and should, promote sustainable development. Policies and measures to protect the climate system from human induced change should be appropriate for the specific conditions of each Party and should be integrated with national development programs, taking into account that economic development is essential for adopting measures to address climate change" and the Preamble to the UN Convention to Combat Desertification in Countries Experiencing Serious Drought and/or Desertification, Particularly in Africa, *supra* note 121.

[606] *See* HUNTER ET AL., *supra* note 124, at 36 who notes that over 70 percent of world's nations have domestic provisions on environmental impact assessment. *See also* CHRISTOPHER WOOD, ENVIRONMENTAL IMPACT ASSESSMENT: A COMPARATIVE REVIEW (1995).

activity in order to ensure that the impact on the environment will remain within acceptable levels. In other words, the development activity will continue with environmental safeguards in place.[607] This is the essence of the principle of integration. The EIA process seeks to implement this principle. The principle of integration is the best known component of sustainable development, and it is no wonder that some have used this synonymously with sustainable development. Indeed, it was precisely how the ICJ interpreted sustainable development in the *Case Concerning the Gabcikovo Nagymaros Project.*[608]

The procedural components of sustainable development, on the other hand, have already attained normative status, being part of international human rights law. Thus, access to information, participation in the decision-making process and the right to remedies in relation to environmental issues are now considered as being part of customary international law.[609]

Thus, what does this say about the legal status of sustainable development itself? While it has definitely influenced the decision-making process at both the international and national levels, it is difficult to accept the notion that it has achieved customary status. It has been articulated that "according to the orthodox account of customary international law, few principles of international environmental law qualify as customary."[610] Advocating that there is "declarative law," Daniel Bodansky notes that:

> In my view, the focus by scholars on verbal practice is not merely methodological; it represents a fundamentally different ontology of international law—one that is discursive rather than behavioral in orientation. International environmental norms reflect not how states regularly behave, but how states speak to one another. They represent the evaluative standards used by states to justify their actions and to criticize the actions of others. Writers persist in characterizing these norms as "customary," the catch-all term generally applied to any non-treaty norm, but it would be more accurate to distinguish this type of norm from custom.[611]

---

[607] *See* the discussion in Chapter 4, Section B.

[608] *See* the discussion in Section H.1.b.

[609] *See* discussion in Chapter 4, Sections F and G.

[610] *See* Daniel Bodansky, *Customary (and Not so Customary) International Environmental Law*, 3 IND. J. GLOBAL LEGAL STUD. 105 (1995).

[611] *Id.*

He further contended that these norms do not depend on their legal status. Rather, "they will set the terms of international discussions and serve as the framework for negotiations."[612] Thus, according to this argument, these norms will play an important role even if they lack customary international law status in the strict sense of the term. This is rather similar to the argument that Vaughn Lowe makes with regard to modifying norms. Vaughn Lowe has eloquently noted that:

> How does the concept of sustainable development match up to the requirement that it be of a fundamentally norm-creating character? At this point, the looseness with which I have so far referred to the concept can no longer be concealed. Sustainable development cannot be a norm-constraining behaviour. Any such norm must be couched in normative terms.[613]

He, however, noted that it is not devoid of any impact at the international level and stated that it is a meta-principle:

> Sustainable development can properly claim a normative status as an element of the process of judicial reasoning. It is a meta-principle, acting upon other legal rules and principles—a legal concept exercising a kind of interstitial normativity, pushing and pulling the boundaries of true primary norms when they threaten to overlap or conflict with each other. If I read Judge Weeramantry's Opinion correctly, this (or something close to it) is the kind of normativity that he asserts is now possessed by sustainable development.[614]

He then advanced the notion of "modifying norms" that, according to him, do not depend on state practice or *opinion juris* for their legal status but can be applied by tribunals. These norms are free agents and may be combined with other primary rules to modify those rules. Sustainable development, according to him, is a modifying norm:

> Modifying norms are concepts. Legal concepts do not depend upon state practice or *opinio juris* for their status, in the way that primary legal norms do. . . .[615]

---

[612] *Id.*

[613] *See* Lowe, *supra* note 82, at 24.

[614] *Id.* at 31.

[615] *Id.* at 33.

The process of developing a precise and coherent concept of sustainable development has a way to go before it is well suited to application by tribunals as a component of judicial reasoning. Yet even now it is possible to discern some threads common to the majority of the formulations of the concept. These threads seem to be more of a procedural than of a substantive character.[616]

Lowe believes that "sustainable development is potentially a tool of great power in the hands of decision-makers"[617] and decision makers "need not wait on state practice and *opinio juris* to develop the concept of sustainable development in the way that a primary rule of international law would be developed."[618] Thus, Lowe indicates that sustainable development is not a primary rule of international law and, therefore, does not depend on state practice and *opinio juris* for its legal status. As noted above, it can be considered a modifying norm that can be applied in conjunction with other primary norms to modify the effect of the primary norm.

Noting the relationship between development and environmental protection, Lowe pointed out that: "Neither development nor environmental protection can be pursued to its logical conclusion. Neither alone, is a sustainable goal; but both must find a place in the international system."[619] He seemed to indicate that sustainable development will be the modifying norm, reconciling development with environmental protection.

While Lowe believes that the vagueness of the concept stands in the way of it achieving normative status,[620] Hunter et al. are of the view that it has been accepted by states because of its ambiguity: "Partly because of its brilliant ambiguity, the concept of sustainable development has received nearly universal acceptance among every sector of international society."[621] While this seems to indicate that sustainable development has received "universal acceptance," it does not actually state that it has normative quality.

Thus, it can be concluded that sustainable development is neither a concept nor a principle but falls somewhere between the two. It is more

---

[616] *Id.* at 36.

[617] *Id.* at 37.

[618] *Id.*

[619] *Id.* at 37.

[620] *Id.* at 34.

[621] *See* HUNTER ET AL., *supra* note 124, at 180.

than a mere concept for the reason that states increasingly look to it in relation to development activities and it has greatly influenced the decision-making process. However, it is not a principle because it lacks normative quality. If it were a legal principle, the failure would result in the invocation of state responsibility. The better approach is to consider sustainable development as a goal rather than a principle and apply its components in order to achieve sustainable development. To the extent that the components of sustainable development have acquired normative status—and some components have—the failure to give effect to them could entail responsibility.

It has been articulated that sustainable development has been "accepted as a global policy."[622] It appears in many treaties and declarations as an objective. As Cordonier Segger and Khalfan point out:

> It is not clear that "sustainable development," as such, can be accurately described as a single emerging principle of international environmental law, or a customary norm that will eventually be accepted binding on all States.[623]

There are several reasons for this: sustainable development is not only about protecting the environment; there is no consistent state practice; there is little *opinio juris* to support the contention that sustainable development is part of customary international law. "As such, it is difficult, at present to describe 'sustainable development' as a binding international legal principle in the traditional sense."[624] However, the sheer volume of documents that refer to sustainable development does not allow us to dismiss the concept lightly, as it is not accurate to describe it "simply a vague international policy goal, void of normative value."[625]

Cordonier Segger and Khalfan argue that sustainable development can be understood through the combination of two complementary approaches: first, it can be seen as an emerging area of international law in its own right; second, it may serve as a different type of norm, one that requires a reconciliation between three areas of international law—economic development, environmental protection and social development.[626] It is contended that both these approaches are correct and have to be applied in combination. While sustainable development may never display a "funda-

---

[622] *See* SUSTAINABLE DEVELOPMENT LAW, *supra* note 71, at 45.

[623] *Id.*

[624] *Id.* at 46.

[625] *Id.*

[626] *Id.* at 49.

mentally norm creating character," its significance lies in the fact that it is not only a great tool in the hands of the decision makers,[627] but that it applies to the intersection between three areas of international law that can often be seen as conflicting with one another: economic development, environmental protection and social development. Thus, sustainable development can be seen as a new modifying norm, and, as Lowe pointed out, we may not even need to travel the traditional path of customary law to evaluate state practice and *opinio juris* in order to ascertain its legal status.[628]

In evaluating the status of sustainable development, Philippe Sands refers to it as a "legal term":

> Sustainable development is a *legal term* which refers to processes, principles and objectives, as well as to a large body of international agreements on environment, economics and civil and political rights. . . . International law in the field of sustainable development describes a broad umbrella accommodating the specialized field of international law which aims to promote economic development, environmental protection and respect for civil and political rights. It is not an independent and free-standing body of principles and rules and it is still emerging. As such, it is not coherent or comprehensive, nor is it free from ambiguity or inconsistency. It endorses on behalf of the whole of the international community an approach requiring existing principles, rules and institutional arrangements to be treated in an integrated manner.[629]

It is not at all clear what is meant by a "legal term" here. Sands seems hesitant to refer to sustainable development as a legal principle, yet he does not seem to want to label it as a concept either. He seems to indicate that the legal status of sustainable development is unclear but falls somewhere between a legal norm and a concept. His reference to a "legal term," however, is rather unhelpful. He notes that it is not a free-standing body of principles but requires us to apply the existing principles, rules and institutional arrangements in an integrated manner.

Birnie and Boyle, noting that sustainable development secured near universal endorsement at Rio, point out that the most far-reaching aspect of sustainable development is that "for the first time it makes a state's man-

---

[627] *See* Lowe, *supra* note 82, at 37.

[628] *Id.*

[629] *See* Philippe Sands, *International Law in the Field of Sustainable Development*, 65 BRIT. Y.B. INT'L L. 303, 379 (1994) (emphasis added).

agement of its own domestic environment a matter of international concern in a systematic way."[630] In other words, Birnie and Boyle refer to the phenomenon of internationalization of environment protection discussed in Chapter 1. They point out that this will have implications for the future development of national and international human rights law.[631]

According to Birnie and Boyle there are fundamental uncertainties about the nature of sustainable development which has a direct bearing on whether it can be considered a legal principle:

> If it is a principle to be interpreted, applied and achieved primarily at national level, by individual governments, there may be only a limited need for international definition and oversight. If, however, it is intended that states should be held internationally accountable for achieving sustainability, whether globally or nationally, then the criteria for measuring this standard must be made clear, as must the evidential burden for assessing the performance of individual states.[632]

Birnie and Boyle thus make an important distinction here: is sustainable development essentially an internal principle or policy, which influences the decision-making process at the national level, or is it an international principle, which seeks to influence the behavior of states at the international level? It can be argued that it contains both features in that it is an international principle, which seeks to influence decision making at the national level. Essentially, sustainable development must be achieved at the national level, although international legal norms can guide this process. This is what sustainable development seeks to do. According to Birnie and Boyle, if sustainable development is considered an internal principle, international law need only provide a basic definition. If, on the other hand, states are to be held internationally responsible, then the parameters have to be identified, criteria for measuring it must be laid down as well as the evidential burden for assessing state practice.

That sustainable development provides a framework for national governance has been advanced by John Dernbach.[633] According to him, the starting point is to recognize that sustainable development has implications at the national level. In order to do so, however, it is necessary to under-

---

[630] *See* BIRNIE & BOYLE, *supra* note 13, at 85.

[631] *Id.*

[632] *Id.* at 85.

[633] *See* Dernbach, *supra* note 49.

stand what sustainable development means. He addresses the issue of the meaning of sustainable development in three ways: by synthesizing Agenda 21, the Rio Declaration and other texts into a conceptual framework for national governance;[634] secondly, he argues that sustainable development provides a powerful set of tools to reinvigorate governance; and finally, he identifies unresolved issues in the sustainable development framework, such as comparative responsibilities of developing and developed countries, the role of international trade, etc.[635] He contends that "sustainable development must be realized primarily through national actions, or not at all."[636] While it is true that sustainable development must be realized at the national level, international law does have a role to play. It seeks to ensure that standards are harmonized and that certain common denominators are identified for action at the national level. This is the role played by documents such as the Rio Declaration and Agenda 21.

Whether international law requires that all development should be sustainable is a difficult question to answer. Probably no state in the international community today would openly argue that development should not be sustainable: "What is lacking is any comparable consensus on the meaning of sustainable development, or on how to give it concrete effect in individual cases."[637]

Birnie and Boyle believe that "normative uncertainty, coupled with the absence of justiciable standards for review, strongly suggest that there is as yet no international legal obligation that development must be sustainable, and that decisions on what constitutes sustainability rest primarily with individual governments."[638] They, however, accept that this is not the end of the matter. They articulate that a more plausible argument is that international law does require development decisions to be the outcome of a process that promotes sustainable development.[639] Thus, if a state fails to carry out an EIA for a given activity, does not subject it to public participation, does not integrate environmental factors into the decision-making process, that state would have failed to implement the main features of sustainable devel-

---

[634] *Id.* John Dernbach notes that these texts define sustainable development as a bundle of related concepts. Thus, he is in agreement with the view that sustainable development is an umbrella term.

[635] *Id.*

[636] *Id.*

[637] *See* BIRNIE & BOYLE, *supra* note 13, at 95.

[638] *Id.* at 96.

[639] *Id.*

opment as contained in the Rio Declaration.[640] Granted that the Rio Declaration itself is a non-binding document, but there is there is much state practice to support the normative status of most of these elements. In other words, this approach concentrates on the *components* of sustainable development rather than on the concept itself:[641]

> As Lowe convincingly demonstrates sustainable development and its components are very relevant when courts or international bodies have to interpret, apply or develop, the law. That is perhaps the most important lesson to be drawn from the ICJ's references to sustainable development in the Gabcikovo-Nagymaros Case and from the WTO Appellate Body's decision in the Shrimp-Turtle Case. Whether or not sustainable development is a legal obligation, and as we have seen this seems unlikely, it does represent a goal which can influence the outcome of cases, the interpretation of treaties, and the practice of states and international organizations, and it may lead to significant changes and developments in the existing law. In that very important sense, international law does appear to require states and international bodies to take account of the objective of sustainable development, and to establish appropriate processes for doing so.[642]

Thus, the best approach to take is not to waste time in evaluating whether sustainable development has normative quality or try and come up with a workable definition. The drafters of the Rio Declaration did not attempt to do so. Instead, the Rio Declaration elaborated on its components, identified tools to achieve sustainable development and also identified interrelated issues that have an impact on sustainable development. As Birnie and Boyle point out, to merely dismiss sustainable development as a concept that lacks a proper definition or normative quality is to ignore the larger picture and disregard the developments that have taken place during the last 30 years. Sustainable development cannot be dismissed lightly; it has acquired a distinct quality under international law—a norm that is different from those we are familiar with. It is a broad goal and, as such, cannot be more than a policy. However, some of its components have acquired normativity and, in that sense, the broad policy goal of sustainable development will continue to influence international law in the years to come.

---

[640] *Id.*

[641] That the components of sustainable development must be evaluated for normative status is also accepted by Lowe, *supra* note 82 and Dernbach, *supra* note 49.

[642] *See* BIRNIE & BOYLE, *supra* note 13, at 96–97.

In this regard, it is necessary to point out that the traditional international lawmaking procedures seem to have undergone profound change and given rise to new ways of making law, at least in relation to environmental issues. International environmental law, whose history spans a short space of 30 (odd) years since the Stockholm Declaration, no longer relies on traditional international law sources such as customary international law. It is heavily dominated by treaty law. Given that many of these environmental issues are complex, technical and often interacting with one another, adopting highly specific treaties seems to be the only way to deal with them. However, traditional treatymaking procedure is also cumbersome, very time consuming and expensive. International environmental law seems to have opted for consensus[643] and developed its own mechanisms to overcome traditional difficulties in adopting treaties.

It has been articulated that "one of the most significant developments in international law during the twentieth century has been the expanded role played by multilateral treaties addressed to the common concerns of states."[644] Similarly, international organizations have also assumed greater significance. Due to the global nature of environmental problems, the international community has faced the "need to develop universal norms to address global concerns."[645] This highlights the importance of establishing norms to control activities of all nations, regardless where the activities take place:

> To solve such problems, it may be necessary to establish new rules that are binding on all subjects of international law regardless of the attitude of any particular state. For unless all states are bound, an exempted recalcitrant state could act as a spoiler for the entire international community. Thus, states that are not bound by international law designed to combat universal environmental threats could become havens for the harmful activities concerned. . . . Consequently, for certain circumstances it may be incumbent on the international community to establish international law that is binding on all states regardless of any one state's disposition.[646]

Thus, Jonathan Charney highlights the importance of adopting universal norms to protect the global environment, as even one non-partici-

---

[643] *See* Jonathan I. Charney, *Universal International Law*, 87 AM. J. INT'L L. 529 (1993). Consensus is defined as the lack of expressed objections which amounts to tacit consent.

[644] *Id.*

[645] *Id.*

[646] *Id.*

pating state can undermine the entire legal regime. A good example is the United States and the Kyoto Protocol. It is, however, acknowledged that a traditional international legal system based on the principle of sovereignty appears "to work against ability to legislate universal norms."[647] Moreover, he points out that traditional customary law formation may have been sufficient for an international community of states with a small number of states and with a relatively small number of issues to deal with. Today, not only the number of states has increased dramatically, but also the issues that are being regulated by international law have increased in both complexity and in number. As a result, traditional international law formation has been relegated to the background in favor of a more structured method of lawmaking. In this regard, Jonathan Charney argues that "Rather than state practice and *opinion (sic) juris*, multilateral forums often play a central role in the creation and shaping of contemporary international law."[648] Important issues are debated in these multilateral forums where states may express their support to the rule under discussion. Often decisions are adopted by consensus, which is considered as tacit consent. Charney, however, is mindful of the limitations of multilateral forums:

> I do not intend to suggest, however, that multilateral forums have independent legislative authority. They do not. . . . Nor do I intend to suggest that all generally applicable treaty texts become *ipso facto* and *ab initio* customary international law upon adoption or entry into force. Rather, the products of multilateral forums substantially advance and formalize the international lawmaking process. They make possible the rapid and unquestionable entry into force of normative rules if the support expressed in the forum is onfirmed.[649]

Inasmuch as these multilateral forums have played a critical role in international lawmaking, soft law instruments have played an equally important role in the development of international environmental law. It can be said that there is a clear link between these two mechanisms. Indeed, the document that laid the foundation for modern international environmental law—the Stockholm Declaration—is itself a soft law instrument. The Rio Declaration—the first universal document to specifically incorporate sustainable development and to elaborate on its components— is another soft law instrument that profoundly influenced the development

---

[647] *Id.*

[648] *Id.*

[649] *Id.*

of sustainable development. These soft law instruments have had a major impact on the development of international environmental law.[650]

International environmental law has also developed other mechanisms to deal with one of the traditional problems that vexed the international community—the adoption of the lowest common denominator.[651] This resulted from seeking to accommodate the wishes of different states in the international community, which is heterogeneous and displays vast differentiation. Despite the juridical notion of sovereign equality of states, international environmental law had to respond to a situation where states are anything but equal and to adopt obligations that took account of this differentiation. Thus, the principle of common but differentiated responsibility principle was born, and the international community no longer had to adopt the lowest common denominator in relation to their environmental obligations.

## K. CONCLUSION: INTERNATIONAL LAW OF SUSTAINABLE DEVELOPMENT?

While some have contended that sustainable development is an "inoperable concept,"[652] or "a dangerous slippery concept,"[653] others insist that despite its shortcomings, sustainable development cannot be easily dismissed.[654] Some have contended that the emergence of the concept of sustainable development characterizes the intersection of the discourse on economic development and the development of international environmental law and policy.[655] The Copenhagen Declaration on Social Development, later endorsed by the World Summit for Sustainable Development, added a third dimension to this discussion: social development.[656] Thus, it is now

---

[650] *See* Geoffrey Palmer, *New Ways to Make International Law,* 86 AM. J. INT'L L. 259 (1992). *See also* Oscar Schachter, *United Nations Law,* 88 AM. J. INT'L L. 1 (1994).

[651] *See* Palmer, *supra* note 650, where he argues that "one of the biggest obstacles that must be overcome in international negotiations is the rule of unanimous consent. This rule impels each negotiating body to search for the lowest common denominator."

[652] *See* Jude Fernando, *Rethinking Sustainable Development: Preface: The Power of Unsustainable Development: What is to be Done?,* 590 THE ANNALS OF THE AMERICAN ACADEMY OF POLITICAL AND SOCIAL SCIENCE 6 (2003) *quoting* TIMOTHY O'RIORDAN, NEW ENVIRONMENTALISM AND SUSTAINABLE DEVELOPMENT (1987).

[653] *See* Robert John Araujo, *Rio+10 and the World Summit on Sustainable Development: Why Human Beings Are at the Center of Concerns,* 2 GEO. J.L. & PUB. POL'Y 201 (2004).

[654] *Id. See also* SUSTAINABLE DEVELOPMENT LAW, *supra* note 71.

[655] Peter Malanczuk, *Sustainable Development: Some Critical thoughts in the Light of the Rio Conference, in* SUSTAINABLE DEVELOPMENT AND GOOD GOVERNANCE, *supra* note 577, at 23.

[656] Plan of Implementation, WSSD, para. 2, *supra* note 80.

accepted that the three components of sustainable development are: economic development, environmental protection and social development, which are "interdependent and mutually reinforcing pillars."[657]

As the above discussion revealed, sustainable development is not totally devoid of content or meaning. It has greatly influenced the international (as well as national) environmental law and policy discourse. The fact that it has been included in almost all the instruments adopted since the publication of the Brundtland Report must account for something. No state, whether developing or developed, has specifically rejected it. The best way to approach it is as an umbrella term encompassing both substantive and procedural elements. As one writer points out:

> When international agreements address problems on an ad hoc basis, they create a patchwork of legal solutions that is merely reactive to environmental crises. Although economic concerns are always a variable in these agreements, international law has not created a systematic framework within which environmentally sound sustainable development decisions can be made in the daily activity of the world. This paper suggests that the conceptual approaches to environmental law and international law do not lead to a workable international law of sustainable development.

> Instead, the law must be reformulated to reflect the laws of ecology, biology, physics and chemistry on the one hand, and economic principles on the other. . . . An international law of sustainable development must provide a framework that balances the privilege of sovereign action with the responsibility for that action. To do this, the law must internalize adverse environmental effects into economic development decisions.[658]

It has been argued that as long as a project provides some additional jobs and economic gains, any development activity will be considered sustainable, despite possible adverse effects on human health and the environment.[659] This argument overlooks the fundamental components of sustainable development, which are the principles of integration, equity and prevention of environmental damage, including environmental assessment. Sustainable development requires us to adopt practices that are economically, socially and environmentally sound. A development project,

---

[657] *Id.*

[658] *See* Hodas, *supra* note 303.

[659] *Id.*

which merely provides additional jobs, will not be considered sustainable, unless it is also environmentally sound. Thus, the above argument does not hold much merit and overlooks the constituent elements of sustainable development.

Tracing the development of international law from Stockholm to Rio, Hunter et al. point out that while all the treatymaking indicated that the field of international environmental law has come of age, it had an *ad hoc* quality without a broader framework guiding its development:[660]

> As the number and scope of environmental treaties expanded, observers hoped to be able to superimpose some order on the emerging field, by placing international environmental law in the context of some broader organizing concept—to some extent at least, they found that organizing conceptual framework in the concept of sustainable development.[661]

Thus, sustainable development provides the broad framework within which international environmental treatymaking should be placed. Some writers give a more expanded role for sustainable development: "Sustainable development provides a framework for reconciling and simultaneously furthering the broad goals of peace and security, economic development, social development and environmental protection."[662] The traditional development model did not include environmental protection, and the idea was that environmental degradation was the price to pay for economic development. This model is no longer accepted, and the development model accepted today is the sustainable development model that includes peace and security, economic development, social development and environmental protection.

Dernbach questions whether sustainable development actually protects the environment—although companies and others claim that they are engaged in sustainable development, the environment continues to deteriorate[663] and poor people seem to be getting poorer. He points out that some skeptics have suggested that sustainable development should be abandoned because it ultimately undermines environmental protection.[664]

---

[660]  *See* HUNTER ET AL., *supra* note 124, at 179.

[661]  *Id.*

[662]  *See* John C. Dernbach, *Targets, Timetables and Effecting Implementing Mechanisms: Necessary Building Blocks for Sustainable Development*, 27 WM. & MARY ENVTL. L & POL'Y REV. 79 (2002).

[663]  *Id.*

[664]  *Id.* It is interesting that one of the authors that Dernbach quotes for this argument

Sustainable development is the only internationally accepted framework for making the broad goals of development mutually reinforcing as well as the only framework for responding to environmental degradation around the world and the growing gap between the rich and the poor.

Dernbach is of the view that the present framework needs to be improved by filling in the gaps. According to him, one critical set of gaps is the absence of specific internationally agreed goals for environmental protection and social well-being.[665] In addition, national actions to establish and implement goals are more likely to succeed than those without such goals. Targets and timetables accompanied by political and legal commitments and resources to achieve them are necessary: "targets, timetables, and implementing machinery are a crucial component of sustainable development."[666] Furthermore, appropriate national and international governance structures are necessary to achieve sustainable development.

Sustainable development is premised on the interdependence and essential equality of economic development, social well-being, peace and security and environmental protection.[667] Sustainable development has modified the traditional definition of development and progress, and it seeks to protect and restore the environment while achieving economic development. Five conclusions are offered on the relationship between environmental protection and sustainable development: environmental protection is what makes sustainable development different from conventional development. Second, our understanding of environmental protection will determine whether we actually protect the environment. Third, we will have taken steps to protect the environment over a much longer period of time than we generally apply to other activities. Fourth, the objectives of environmental protection within sustainable development will shift over time. Finally, environmental protection cannot be separated from poverty

---

is the present author herself (*Sustainable Development: Myth or Reality, supra* note 82). This, however, seems to be a misunderstanding (or a misrepresentation) of the argument made in that article. The present author argued in that article that despite the problems inherent in the concept of sustainable development, it has the potential to become an important concept and has, in fact, influenced the decision-making process in countries. Furthermore, no country in the world has expressly rejected sustainable development.

[665] *Id.*

[666] *Id.*

[667] Dernbach seems to advocate *four* pillars of sustainable development: he has added peace and security to the three pillars mentioned in the Johannesburg Plan of Implementation of 2002. This is significant and reflects the present reality that without peace and security, it is difficult to achieve sustainable development. *See* Sumudu Atapattu, *Sustainable Development and Terrorism: International Linkages and a Case Study of Sri Lanka*, 30 WILLIAM & MARY ENVTL. L. REV. 273 (2006), which looks at the link between terrorism and sustainable development.

alleviation. Developing countries will require reassurance that priority will be given to environmental problems that most directly interfere with economic development in these countries.[668]

Without targets and timetables, goals will simply remain aspirational and with no incentive to achieve them. The strongest targets and timetables have no escape clauses. Dernbach argues that the establishment of targets and timetables can accomplish at least six tasks: it can identify priorities, force decision makers to clarify objectives, demonstrate a commitment to sustainable development, give operational meaning to sustainable development, clarify the role of law and provide benchmarks for progress.[669] However, targets and timetables should also be realistic and would be country-specific in most instances. It is unlikely that targets and timetables in a given situation in one country would work in another country, particularly if the latter is a developing country. Even in developed countries, priorities would be different, and so would targets and timetables. In developing countries, identifying priorities is particularly important, given the limited resources available at hand. It is also important to involve civil society in these tasks, as often they have particular expertise that the government could use. Unfortunately, there are many needs and problems particularly in developing countries and it is impossible for any government to deal with them at once. The core objective of sustainable development is to reverse the trends toward global environmental problems and to reduce the gap between the rich and the poor.[670] If Agenda 21 is to be taken as an indication of a blueprint for future action, then it shows just how much work is necessary to achieve sustainable development. Agenda 21 requires national governments to develop their own priorities and programs.[671] However, virtually all countries experience degrading environments and worsening poverty. Thus, the immediate task would be to stop further environmental degradation and worsening of poverty.

Some countries and regions have indeed prepared sustainable development strategies, and the EU is an example of this.[672] Its priorities are global warming, public health, poverty, aging population, loss of biodiversity and transport congestion.[673] These were identified through an analyti-

---

[668] *See* Dernbach, *supra* note 662.

[669] *Id.*

[670] *Id.*

[671] Agenda 21, ch. 37, *supra* note 1.

[672] *EU Sustainable Development Strategy: A Test Case for Good Governance* (2001), *available at* http://europa.eu.int/comm/env/forum/susdevstra.pdf.

[673] *Id.*

cal process that focused on three criteria: severity of the problem, the extent to which future generations would be affected and the extent to which the problem is common to EU members.[674] Thus, the first step was to identify the problems and set priorities. Once priorities have been identified, it is easier to set timetables and targets. However, for some of these priorities, such as climate change or poverty, action would be long term. It is also necessary to identify benchmarks or targets to measure success. While this will have to done at the international level for global issues, such as climate change, country-specific targets and benchmarks would also be necessary.

While identifying priorities is important, setting goals is necessary in order to ensure that progress can be measured and the goals can be achieved within the time specified and that these goals are realistic. Sometimes goals to protect the environment are linked to public health— for example, air quality standards or water quality standards are set so that there is no harm to pubic health. Thus, for example, under the Clean Air Act of the United States, air quality standards are to be established at a level that is necessary to protect public health. Under the Clean Water Act, water quality standards must be established to protect public health or welfare and enhance the quality of water. Thus, the achievement of these standards would be the goal to meet, and the absence of public health problems would indicate that these goals are, in fact, being met.

Thus, the Convention on Long-range Transboundary Air Pollution of 1979[675] notes in Article 2 that the parties are determined to protect man and the environment against air pollution and have undertaken to gradually reduce air pollution. The Protocol of 1984 on Reduction of Sulphur Dioxide[676] is more specific in this regard and establishes actual goals and timetables in order to protect human health and the environment. According to Article 2:

> The Parties shall control and reduce their sulphur emissions in order to protect human health and the environment from adverse effects, in particular acidifying effects, and to ensure, as far as possible, without entailing excessive costs, that depositions of oxidized compounds in the long term do not exceed critical loads for sulphur given, in annex I, as crucial sulphur despositions, in accordance with present scientific knowledge.

---

[674] *Id.*

[675] 18 ILM 1442 (1979).

[676] 33 ILM 1540 (1995).

As a first step, the Parties shall, as a minimum, reduce and maintain their annual sulphur emissions in accordance with the timing and levels specified in annex II.

Perhaps the best example of timetables and targets can be found in the legal regime governing ozone depletion. The Vienna Convention for the Protection of the Ozone Layer of 1985 notes that the parties are "determined to protect human health and the environment against adverse effects resulting from modifications of the ozone layer"[677] but being an umbrella treaty, does not contain any specific targets and timetables. The Montreal Protocol, on the other hand, is based on timetables and targets and has been revised periodically to reflect scientific evidence as and when it becomes available. Specific commitments are embodied in Article 2, and calculation of control levels is embodied in Article 3.

The Kyoto Protocol of 1997 also contains some targets and timetables. These are, however, not as comprehensive as the ones found in the Montreal Protocol on Substances that Deplete the Ozone Layer. Given the scientific uncertainty surrounding these issues, it is important to realize that the targets and timetables adopted at a given time are temporary in nature and will have to be revised as and when scientific evidence becomes available.[678] The ozone regime is a prime example of this exercise.[679]

Other international conventions also adopt targets and timetables. While these international targets and timetables are necessary to ensure consistency and coherence, they need to be translated into domestic action too. Otherwise, these targets and timetables at the international level become meaningless. In other words, while an international framework is necessary, domestic action is crucial.[680]

According to Dernbach, "targets and timetables are particularly important when there are many public and private decision makers whose activities need to be coordinated or, at least, consistent."[681] He fur-

---

[677] Preamble, Vienna Convention for the Protection of the Ozone Layer, *supra* note 362.

[678] *See also* the discussion on the precautionary principle in Chapter 3.

[679] The Montreal Protocol has been amended many times to bring the obligations up to date with scientific developments.

[680] *See* Dernbach, *supra* note 662, who notes that "international targets and timetables help ensure that individual nations are working together and motivated by a common objective. While national targets and timetables are also necessary, particular countries or groups of countries cannot successfully address global problems such as climate change or the loss of biodiversity by themselves."

[681] *Id.*

ther notes that specificity is important and reduces any confusion or mis-understanding.[682]

Another advantage of having targets and timetables is that they provide a way to measure progress or lack of progress toward achieving a particular goal. The failure to achieve these targets embodied in a binding instrument would result in a breach of that obligation and hence in non-compliance. The failure to achieve targets in a non-binding instrument will not, by itself, amount to non-compliance.

It is quite probable that there now exists a distinct field of international law called international sustainable development law which is separate from international environmental law. It is likely to evolve as a distinct branch of international law or at least as a sub-branch of international environmental law and will continue to challenge the traditional norms of international law in the years to come.

---

[682] *Id.*

# CHAPTER 3
# THE PRECAUTIONARY PRINCIPLE

In order to protect the environment, the precautionary approach
shall be widely applied by States according to their capabilities.
Where there are threats of serious or irreversible damage, lack of
full scientific certainty shall not be used as a reason for postponing
cost-effective measures to prevent environmental degradation.

Principle 15, Rio Declaration
on Environment and Development[1]

## A. INTRODUCTION

The evolution of international environmental law can be compartmentalized into at least three stages. During stage one, repairing environmental damage was the norm, and no real attempt was made to prevent
such damage. When the adverse effects of acid rain were felt all over
Europe and in North America,[2] however, the realization slowly dawned on
states that another approach was necessary to deal with environmental
issues, some of which have wide-ranging and long-term consequences.
Thus, during stage two, repairing damage gave way to an anticipatory
approach to environmental protection. Under this approach, states were
required to anticipate and prevent environmental damage. Various techniques were devised to do so, the environmental impact assessment process[3]
being the tool that was applied most. This approach, however, was limited
by existing scientific knowledge on a particular issue, and the time soon
came where the necessary scientific knowledge was insufficient to predict
the consequences of some environmental problems—a case in point is

---

[1] Rio Declaration on Environment and Development adopted at the UN Conference on Environment and Development, 1992, UN Doc. A/CONF.151/26, *reprinted
in* 31 II.M 874 (1992), *available at* http://www.un.org/documents/ga/conf151/
aconf15126-1annex1.htm.

[2] Acid rain is mainly caused by sulfur emissions from industrial plants that come
back to the earth in the form of sulfur dioxide, which is very acidic. Acid rain has caused
considerable damage in Europe causing historic buildings to erode and lakes and waterways to become very acidic killing aquatic life. *See* US Environmental Protection Agency,
Acid Rain, *at* http://www.epa.gov/airmarkets/acidrain/index.html, and DAVID HUNTER,
JAMES SALZMAN & DURWOOD ZAELKE, INTERNATIONAL ENVIRONMENTAL LAW AND POL-
ICY 513 (2d ed. 2002).

[3] *See* the discussion in Chapter 4, Sections A and B.

global warming. Here, while there was sufficient evidence to suggest that global warming was taking place, scientific certainty was lacking. Several states made this an excuse not to take preventive measures. They argued that scientific evidence was inconclusive to warrant taking measures that were expensive.[4] It is in response to this argument that the precautionary principle was born.

Put simply, the precautionary principle requires states to take measures to protect the environment, where there is evidence of serious environmental damage, even if scientific certainty is lacking. It must be noted that Principle 15 of the Rio Declaration does not limit the application of the precautionary principle to global environmental problems. The wording in Principle 15 is sufficiently broad to cover any kind of environmental damage, including those without an extra-territorial impact, provided that the criteria therein are satisfied. The present tendency is to apply the precautionary principle in relation to global environmental issues. The wording in Principle 15 is much broader and is of general application.

Environmental damage is often long-term and could take years (sometimes even decades) to materialize. Very often those who created (or at least contributed to) the environmental problem do not suffer its consequences. It is the next generation that has to bear the brunt of irresponsible action taken by the previous generation. Here the inter-generational equity principle becomes important. This principle requires states to evaluate the impact of their decisions on future generations too. How far into the future must we look has also arisen, and it has been contended that we must seek to evaluate our activities for the next 50 years as it represents about the next two human generations.[5]

It has also been contended that it is necessary to evaluate the impact of the precautionary principle through a sector-by-sector analysis, as it is easier to predict the human activity on some sectors than others.[6]

## B. EVOLUTION OF THE PRECAUTIONARY PRINCIPLE

While the evolution of the precautionary principle in international law began in the early 1980s, some domestic legal systems have considered it a legal principle since the 1970s.[7] West Germany and Sweden are exam-

---

[4] *See* HUNTER ET AL., *supra* note 2, at 612.

[5] *See* John Dernbach, *Achieving Sustainable Development: The Centrality and Multiple Facets of Integrated Decisionmaking,* 10 IND. J. GLOBAL LEGAL STUD. 247 (2003).

[6] *See* SIMON MARR, THE PRECAUTIONARY PRINCIPLE IN THE LAW OF THE SEA: MODERN DECISION MAKING IN INTERNATIONAL LAW 3 (2003).

[7] For a discussion of the emergence of the precautionary principle, *see* Scott

ples.[8] Several international agreements, such as the Convention of the High Seas Fisheries of the North Pacific[9] and the Convention on International Trade in Endangered Species of Wild Flora and Fauna (CITES)[10] are also cited as examples of the precautionary approach.[11] With regard to the marine environment, the principle attracted attention at the first North Sea Conference in 1984, and, at the end of the decade, several binding instruments had incorporated the principle.[12] Its main function is to provide guidance to environmental decision makers in situations where policymakers face scientific uncertainty. Two international instruments specifically incorporate the precautionary principle—the Cartegena Protocol on Biosafety[13] and the Stockholm Convention on Persistent Organic Pollutants.[14] Simon Marr observes that "in today's political sphere, the precautionary principle enjoys a wide, unprecedented recognition."[15] He further notes that:

> The precautionary principle has become of such tremendous importance because in many cases, the scientific establishment of cause and effect is a difficult task sometimes approaching a fruitless investigation of an infinite series of events.[16]

Not everyone, however, is enamored by the precautionary principle. While environmentalists believe that it provides the basis for early international action,[17] critics argue that it has the potential for over-regulation, limiting human activity.[18] Given the different nuances and the formulations of the precautionary principle in different texts, it is useful to make some distinctions: although preventive in nature, the precautionary principle

---

Lafranchi, *Surveying the Precautionary Principle's Ongoing Global Development: The Evolution of an Emergent Environmental Management Tool*, 32 B.C. Envtl. Aff. L. Rev. 678 (2005).

[8] *See* MARR, *supra* note 6, at 5.

[9] *Available at* http://www.oceanlaw.net/texts/nphs.htm.

[10] 12 ILM 1085 (1973), 993 UNTS 243, signed Mar. 3, 1973, entered into force July 1, 1975, *available at* http://www.cites.org/.

[11] *See* MARR, *supra* note 6, at 5.

[12] *Id.*

[13] 39 ILM 1027 (2000), signed Jan. 29, 2000, entered into force Sept. 11, 2003, *available at* http://www.biodiv.org.

[14] UN Doc. UNEP/POPS/CONF/4, signed May 22, 2001, entered into force May 17, 2004, *available at* http://www.pops.int/.

[15] *See* MARR, *supra* note 6, at 6.

[16] *Id.*

[17] *Id.*

[18] *Id.* at 7.

must be distinguished from the preventive principle: the latter requires states to prevent foreseeable environmental harm. Principle 21 of the Stockholm Declaration embodies the principle of prevention in a transboundary context.[19]

The precautionary principle, by contrast, mandates environmental action at an earlier stage. It provides for the situation where there is a potential hazard, but due to scientific uncertainty, a proper prediction cannot be made as to the environmental impact. The precautionary principle also differs from the assimilative capacity approach, which assumes that the environment has the capacity to absorb a certain amount of pollution.[20] The problem with the assimilative capacity approach is that "it cannot protect the environment until harm is evident."[21] The era of sustainable development has given way to a paradigm shift whereby there is a broader concern for the global environment "in which its intrinsic value and its intergenerational implications are given much greater significance than before."[22] Simon Marr distinguishes between two forms of precaution: action-guiding approach and the deliberation-guiding approach.[23]

> In the face of scientific uncertainties the action-guiding approach requires action to prevent possibly damaging effects of human practice that may be damaging the environment. The deliberation-guiding approach does not expressly call for action but stipulates that lack of evidence shall not be used as a reason to postpone action against a potentially damaging practice.[24]

In this sense, the latter formulation is less stringent than the former.

It has been contended that precaution is a "unique legal technique for addressing some of contemporary society's environmental and public health challenges."[25] Four constitutive elements have been identified as appearing in international legal instruments: risk, damage, scientific uncer-

---

[19] UN Doc. A/CONF.48/14, June 16, 1972, in 11 ILM 1416 (1972). For a discussion of the principle of prevention and Principle 21, *see* discussion in Section F.

[20] *See* MARR, *supra* note 6, at 10.

[21] *Id.* at 11.

[22] *Id.* quoting Alan Boyle, *Protecting the Marine Environment: Some Problems and Developments in the Law of the Sea*, 16 MARINE POL'Y 79–85, 84–85 (1992).

[23] *Id.* at 11.

[24] *Id.* (footnotes omitted).

[25] Laurence Boisson de Chazournes, *The Precautionary Principle in Precaution from Rio to Johannesburg*, Proceedings of a Geneva Environment Network Roundtable (2002).

tainty and differential capabilities.[26] By its very nature, risk is uncertain, and precaution has been defined in relation to ecological risk.[27] International law does not provide any answers as to how risk is to be assessed and damage is linked to risk, but the threshold of irreversibility or seriousness must be established. Scientific uncertainty is considered as the *sine qua non* for the application of the precautionary principle.[28] Moreover, it represents the difference between precaution and prevention.[29] Finally, it has been argued that the capacities of the state in question must be taken into account when deciding what precautionary measures must be applied to a given issue. In other words, "States of different levels of development cannot be subjected to the same requirements regarding the implementation of precautionary measures."[30] It is interesting that the precautionary measures have been linked to the common but differentiated responsibility principle.[31] It can be contended that the Montreal Protocol and the Kyoto Protocol are examples of the link between precautionary measures and the common but differentiated responsibility principle.

The precautionary principle is essentially related to the decision-making process and responds to an important problem in decision making—how to take decisions when complete scientific information concerning the environment is not available.[32] If reliance is made only on available information, it is likely that environmental damage would occur, sometimes irreparably:[33]

> Instead of assuming that important natural systems are resilient or invulnerable, the precautionary principle presumes their vulnerability. By giving the benefit of the doubt to the environment when there is scientific uncertainty, the precautionary principle would shift the burden of proof from those supporting natural systems to those supporting development. The principle is premised on the

---

[26] *Id.*

[27] *Id.* However, it must be noted that risk is not confined to ecological risk. Risk is defined in relation to human health as well. In the EU, particularly, precaution is applied to a wide range of issues including food safety. *See* discussion in Section E.2.

[28] *See* de Chazournes, *supra* note 25.

[29] *Id.*

[30] *Id.*

[31] *See* discussion in Chapter 5, Sections A and B.

[32] *See* John C. Dernbach, *Sustainable Development as a Framework for National Governance,* 49 CASE W. RES. L. REV. 1 (1998).

[33] *Id.*

preference of preventing pollution to subsequent remediation, the relevance of scientific data to governmental decision-making and the obligation to take precautionary measures that are in proportion to the potential damage.[34]

Although reference is made to prevention of "pollution" in the above quotation, reference to "environmental damage" would have been preferable, as the precautionary principle is not confined to pollution issues. It further emphasizes the importance of scientific data to decision making, as well as the necessity to take measures that are proportionate to the potential damage. In other words, only proportional measures are necessary. This requirement of proportionality would dispel the fears of critics of the precautionary principle who contend that its application would result in an excessive burden on states.[35]

It is contended that the law generally uses two methods for dealing with uncertainties: evidentiary presumptions and the burden of proof to allocate the risk of uncertainty.[36] Simon Marr argues that a number of precautionary measures are included in the precautionary principle: the obligation to conduct an environmental assessment prior to the activity; the obligation to apply the best available technology; and the obligation to apply environmental quality standards that are set at a level below the threshold likely to be hazardous to the environment.[37] Moreover, some treaties adopt the "prior justification procedure" under which an activity or a substance can be prohibited unless evidence can be produced that the activity is not detrimental to the environment.[38] This is the most rigorous application of the precautionary principle.[39]

## C. COMPONENTS AND APPLICATION OF THE PRECAUTIONARY PRINCIPLE

While it was the Rio Declaration that codified the precautionary approach at the global level, it has been noted that the formulation in

---

[34] *Id.* (footnotes omitted).

[35] *See* Frank B. Cross, *Paradoxical Perils of the Precautionary Principle*, 53 WASH & LEE L. REV. 851 (1996).

[36] *See* MARR, *supra* note 6, at 15, *quoting* Daniel Bodansky, *New Developments in International Environmental Law*, 85 AM SOC. INT'L L. PROC. 413, at 414 (1991).

[37] *Id.*

[38] The Convention on the Prior Informed Consent Procedure for Certain Hazardous Chemicals and Pesticides in International Trade, 1998 (Rotterdam Convention), 38 ILM 1 (1999), signed Sept. 11, 1998, entered into force Feb. 24, 2004, is an example.

[39] *See* MARR, *supra* note 6, at 15, *quoting* David Freestone, *Implementing Precaution Cautiously, in* DEVELOPMENTS IN INTERNATIONAL FISHERIES LAW 287 at 306 (Ellen Hey ed., 1999).

Principle 15 is "less forward looking than many of its predecessors."[40] In particular, it has been pointed out that the qualification that the application of the precautionary approach should be according to the capabilities of individual states does not appear in the models for Principle 15.[41]

The real importance of Principle 15 comes in the face of scientific uncertainty. It requires states to act with caution if it is not clear what kind of repercussions would accrue to their actions. The debate on genetically modified organisms (GMOs) is a case in point.[42] While it seems that GMOs could provide the answer to the present-day food crisis, particularly in Africa, there is insufficient evidence about their long-term impact on human health and the environment.[43]

Principle 15 lays down several criteria for the application of the precautionary principle: (1) states are to take precautionary measures according to their capabilities; (2) threats to the enviornment must be serious or irreversible; and (3) the measures that the precautionary approach mandates must be cost-effective. Thus, a plain reading of Principle 15 seems to indicate that to the extent that one does not have the necessary capability (presumably, technology as well as the funds), one does not have to take precautionary action. This interpretation, however, ignores the other principles of the Rio Declaration, particularly, the principle relating to common but differentiated responsibility principle,[44] which calls upon developed countries to take the lead role in relation to environmental problems. Other relevant principles may be Principle 2 of the Rio Declaration, Principle 21 of the Stockholm Declaration, and the principle of prevention, discussed later in this chapter.

Clearly, Principle 15 indicates that some degree of seriousness of environmental damage must be present in order to trigger the application of the precautionary principle. In other words, the precautionary principle will not be applicable either where the damage in question is less than serious, or where there is scientific certainty as to the level of damage that would ensue. Here the question arises as to what kind of environmental damage would amount to serious damage. Irreversible damage in this respect would be easier to define. Less clear is what amounts to serious damage, although,

---

[40] *See* David Wirth, *Rio Declaration on Environment and Development: Two Steps Forward and One Back or Vice Versa?*, 29 GA. L. REV. 599 (1995)

[41] *Id.*

[42] *See* HUNTER ET AL., *supra* note 2, at 84.

[43] *Id.*

[44] Principle 7, Rio Declaration, *supra* note 1. Discussed in Chapter 5, Sections A and B.

no doubt, this would depend on the circumstances in each case and would require the establishment of standards and threshold levels.

Finally, even if other two criteria are satisfied, only cost effective measures need to be taken by states. This addition to the criteria was at the insistence of the United States, which consistenly argued (in relation to global warming) that preventive measures may prove to be futile if the predicted environmental damage does not materialize.[45] As such, it does not warrant taking measures that are so expensive that it constitutes an unnecessary burden on states. While many developing countries, which are particularly vulnerable to the effects of global warming, called upon developed countries, particularly the United States—the biggest contributor of carbon dioxide to the atmosphere[46]—to take preventive measures, many states seem to have taken refuge behind the "scientific uncertainty" defense.

Principle 15 formulation of the precautionary principle is not without criticism. Its threshold requirements of the level of damage and cost-effectiveness of measures are considered as controversial.[47] A definition of the precautionary principle, which would be applicable in all instances, has been formulated as: "Where threats of harm to the environment exist, scientific uncertainty will not be used as a reason to postpone the taking of measures for the protection of human life or health or the environment."[48] Does this mean that the precautionary principle will be applicable to any issue, regardless of the magnitude of the proposed harm? While it would be beneficial if the precautionary principle can be applied generally, it must be noted that every human action produces *some* threat of harm to the environment, some of which could be shrouded in scientific uncertainty. Given the controversy even the rather muted down version of Principle 15 has evoked, it seems unlikely that the international community would be willing to adopt a general version of the precautionary principle, as formulated above, without any threshold requirements.

Despite the fact that the precautionary approach has been described as "the most important new policy approach in international enviornmental cooperation,"[49] and the Indian Supreme Court has held that the pre-

---

[45] *See* Jonathan B. Wiener & Michael D. Rogers, *Comparing Precaution in the United States and Europe*, 5(4) J. RISK RESEARCH 317 (2002).

[46] *See* HUNTER ET AL., *supra* note 2, at 612.

[47] *See* Jaye Ellis & Alison FitzGerald, *The Precautionary Principle in International Law: Lessons from Fuller's Internal Morality*, 49 MCGILL L.J. 779 (2004).

[48] *Id.*

[49] *See* David Freestone, *The Precautionary Principle, in* INTERNATIONAL LAW AND GLOBAL CLIMATE CHANGE 21, at 36 (Robin Churchill & David Freestone eds., 1991).

cautionary principle is part of customary international law,[50] "the invocation of the principle as a basis for global risk management remains controversial."[51] It has also been articulated that the precautionary principle "is deeply perverse in its implications for the environment and human welfare"[52] and that it is "a marvelous piece of rhetoric."[53]

## 1. The Role of Science

Several issues have arisen in the context of the application of the precautionary principle. For example, is the precautionary principle only applicable when there is not enough scientific evidence? What is the situation where there is contradictory scientific evidence? What is the degree of scientific certainty necessary? As can be seen, the precautionary principle seeks to bridge the gap between science, on the one hand, and policy and law, on the other.[54]

It has been articulated that the precautionary principle includes contradictory scientific evidence under the category of "uncertainty."[55] While it would be unlikely to find a sector relating to the enviornment that does not require any scientific expertise, most scientific information contains an element of uncertainty, particularly in relation to environmental issues. Global warming, depletion of the ozone layer, genetically modified food crops, long-term effects of marine pollution, are all shrouded in some degree of uncertainty. Simon Marr notes that scientific error can occur from five sources: the variables chosen; the measurements made; the samples drawn; the models employed; and the causal relationships inferred.[56] The present debate surrounding global warming is a good example of contradictory scientific evidence. While the International Panel on Climate Change (IPCC) has increasingly taken the view that global warming is indeed taking place as a result of the accumulation of greenhouse gases in the atmoshpere due to human activity,[57] industry and some government

---

[50] Vellore Citizens Welfare Forum v. Union of India, AIR 1996 SC 2715.

[51] *See* Peter Sand, *The Precautionary Principle: A European Perspective*, 6 HUM. & ECOLOGICAL RISK ASSESSMENT 445 (2000). He notes that sometimes the precautionary principle has led to the breakdown of negotiations, for example, in relation to the Biosafety Protocol where disagreements on precautionary measures was a contributing factor.

[52] *See* Cross, *supra* note 35.

[53] *Id.*, *quoting* AARON WILDAVSKY, BUT IS IT TRUE? 428 (1995).

[54] *See* Gregory D. Fullem, *The Precautionary Principle: Environmental Protection in the Face of Scientific Uncertainty*, 31 WILLAMETTE L. REV. 495 (1995).

[55] *See* MARR, *supra* note 6, at 25.

[56] *Id.*

[57] *See* Intergovernmental Panel on Climate Change, *Climate Change 2001: Synthesis*

leaders have disputed this—they seem to take the view that the present warming trend is part of a natural process, and there is insufficient evidence on the causal link between greenhouse gases and global warming.[58]

With regard to the degree of scientific certainty needed to trigger the application of the precautionary principle, it has been posited that "a balance needs to be struck between absolute certainty, reasonable certainty and no rational basis in sound scientific data at all."[59] It must be pointed out that if there is absolute scientific certainty on the causal link between the activity and the result, there is no need for the precautionary principle.[60] As noted above, the precautionary principle applies only in the face of scientific uncertainty.[61]

With regard to the definition of the precautionary principle, one writer points out that the second sentence of Principle 15 contains a triple negative.[62] The wording has been rephrased by the writer to make the triple negative more obvious:

> Where there are threats of serious or irreversible damage, the fact that authorities do not have full scientific certainty shall not be

---

*Report, Summary for Policy Makers, available at* http://www.ipcc.ch/pub/un/syreng/spm.pdf. [hereinafter IPCC Report].

[58] The present U.S. administration is a good example. Although it signed the Kyoto Protocol under the Clinton administration, the Bush administration made it very clear that they will withdraw from the Protocol. This led to the deadlock of negotiations under Kyoto, but with the ratification of the Protocol by Russia, the Protocol entered into force in February 2005. Kyoto Protocol to the United Nations Framework Convention on Climate Change, FCCC/CP/1997/L.7/Add.1, signed Dec. 11, 1997, entered into force Feb. 16, 2005, *reprinted in* 36 ILM 22 (1998), *available at* http://www.unfccc.de/. *See* SEBASTIAN OBERTHUR & HERMANN E. OTT, THE KYOTO PROTOCOL: INTERNATIONAL CLIMATE POLICY FOR THE 21ST CENTURY (1999) and Jutta Brunnee, *The United States and International Environmental Law: Living with an Elephant,* 15 EUROPEAN J. INT'L L. 617 (2004).

[59] *See* MARR, *supra* note 6, at 25.

[60] *See* Joel Tickner, Carolyn Raffensperger & Nancy Myers, THE PRECAUTIONARY PRINCIPLE IN ACTION: A HANDBOOK (1st ed. 1999) who note that: "If there is certainty about cause and effect, as in the case of lead and children's health, then acting is no longer precautionary, although it might be preventive."

[61] *Id.* "In essence, the precautionary principle provides a rationale for taking action against a practice or substance in the absence of scientific certainty."

[62] *See* Laurent A. Ruessmann, *Reflections on the WTO Doha Ministerial: Conference: Putting the Precautionary Principle in Its Place: Parameters for the Proper Application of a Precautionary Approach and the Implications for Developing Countries in Light of the Doha WTO Ministerial,* 17 AM. U. INT'L L. REV. 905 (2002).

used as a reason for not taking prompt cost-effective measures to prevent environmental degradation.[63]

It has been contended that the precautionary principle is based on two fundamental principles of sound adminsitration: a government authority must give adequately reasoned justification for its action; and it must not take arbitrary action.[64] While this contention is beyond reproach, there is nothing in Principle 15 to suggest that it is confined to government authorities. On the contrary, as the following discussion reveals, Principle 15 suggests that it should be applied by everybody faced with a threat of serious or irreversible environmental damage, even in the absence of full scientific certainty. It has been contended that reflecting the classic adage that it is better to be safe than sorry, "the precautionary principle suggests that government should take precautions to protect public health and the environment, even in the absence of clear evidence of harm and *notwithstanding the costs of such action.*"[65] It must be pointed out that this is a misinterpretation of the precautionary principle: the Rio Declaration clearly states that only cost-effective measures should be taken. Moreover, this interpretation is contrary to the principle of proportionality—if the costs of taking precautionary measures are prohibitive and is not in proportion to the threat of harm, then the Rio formulation does not require states to take precautionary measures.[66]

In a study done for the Science and Environmental Health Network,[67] the following are identified as the components of the precautionary principle:

- Taking precautionary action before scientific certainty of cause and effect;
- Setting goals;
- Seeking out and evaluating alternatives;
- Shifting the burden of proof—This requires the proponents of an activity to prove that their activity will not cause undue harm to human health and the environment.[68]

---

[63]  *Id.*

[64]  *Id.*

[65]  *See* Cross, *supra* note 35 (emphasis added).

[66]  *Cf.* Ellis & FitzGerald, *supra* note 47 who do not agree with the requirement of taking cost-effective measures.

[67]  *See* Tickner et al., *supra* note 60.

[68]  *See* Section C.5 on the burden of proof.

- Developing more democratic and thorough decision-making criteria and methods. This requires the affected public to be involved in the decision-making process.[69]

However, as noted earlier, some level of seriousness of damage must be evident before it triggers the application of the precautionary principle. If this threshold level is not present, Principle 15 does not require the application of the precautionary principle.

There is a close relationship between the precautionary principle and the environmental impact assessment (EIA) process. Requiring the proponent to show that his project or development activity does not cause significant damage to the environment is not a reversal of the burden of proof, but rather its normal application.[70] By conducting an environmental impact assessment, the proponent will be able to show the impact of his project on the environment and the measures he proposes to mitigate such impact. The EIA process, however, is limited by existing scientific knowledge. If scientific knowledge is lacking on a particular issue, the precautionary principle will come into play. Whether this means a total prohibition unless scientific certainty is proven, depends on the circumstances in each case. The above study notes the existence of a spectrum of precautionary action ranging from weak to strong measures.[71] Additionally, it identifies several tools that have been used in relation to the precautionary principle:

- bans and phase-outs—used in relation to highly toxic substances;
- clean production and pollution prevention;
- alternatives assessment;
- health-based occupational exposure limits;
- reverse onus chemical listing;
- pre-market or pre-activity testing requirements;
- ecosystem management.[72]

## 2.   Risk Assessment Methods

In order to apply the precautionary principle, which is a risk management tool, a risk assessment has to be carried out. There are several methods used at present, including quantitative risk assessment methods, environ-

---

[69] *See* discussion in Chapter 2, Section F, on procedural aspects of sustainable development and Chapter 4, Section F, on Public Participation and EIA.

[70] *See* discussion in Section C.5.

[71] *See supra* note 60.

[72] *Id.*

mental impact assessment, etc. While there is no recognized method of risk assessment yet,[73] the problem is that risk assessment methods can be highly subjective and complex:[74]

> The origins of this debate lie in the approach to risk assessment. On the one hand, some scientists argue that risk assessment is inherently subjective due to the fact that danger and threat are not products of physical and natural processes, but also of our minds and cultures. According to them there is no such thing as "real risk" or objective risk. Subjectivity can influence the decision making process at every stage.[75]

It has been articulated that "the extreme focus on environmental risks means that other and larger risks are routinely ignored"[76] and that the precautionary principle is about making worse decisions than we need to.[77] This seems a harsh critique of the precautionary principle. As we shall note, the precautionary principle is not confined to environmental risks. It has been applied equally to risks to human health[78] and food safety. Thus, the argument that the precautionary principle focuses only on environmental risks is unwarranted. It is also hard to see how it is possible to make a worse decision by relying on the precautionary principle; the only way this may possibly happen is in relation to economics. However, the definition in Principle 15 makes it clear that only cost-effective measures need to be taken under the precautionary principle. Another critique of the precautionary principle contends that "Applied fully and logically, the precautionary principle would cannibalize itself and potentially obliterate all environmental regulation."[79]

---

[73] *Cf.* the European Commission Directive 93/67/EEC of 1993, which lays down four criteria for risk assessment: hazard identification; dose—response assessment; exposure assessment; and risk characterization. A similar approach has been adopted in the Communication of the European Commission on the Precautionary Principle; *see* discussion in Section E.2.

[74] *See* MARR, *supra* note 6, at 31.

[75] *Id.*

[76] *See* MARR, *supra* note 6, at 32, *quoting* BJORN LOMBORG, THE SCEPTICAL ENVIRONMENTALIST, MEASURING THE REAL STATE OF THE WORLD 338, 350 (2001).

[77] *Id.*

[78] Hans-Joachim Priess & Christian Pitschas, *Protection of Public Health and the Role of the Precautionary Principle Under WTO Law: A Trojan Horse Before Geneva's Walls?*, 24 FORDHAM INT'L L.J. 519 (2000).

[79] *See* Cross, *supra* note 35.

The precautionary principle is a step forward from risk assessment that, together with the cost benefit analysis, formed part of the tools of decision-making during the 1980s. Risk assessment is highly reliant on scientific assumptions.[80] It also assumes "assimilative capacity" of the environment—that the environment can render a certain amount of pollution harmless. While this is true, it could result in stretching this limit beyond the assimilative capacity of the environment—the point at which the resilience of the environment is lost. The following have been identified as the major drawbacks of the risk assessment approach:

- It focuses on quantifying and analyzing problems than solving them.
- It allows dangerous activities to continue under the guise of "acceptable risk."
- It is undemocratic—risk assessment does not traditionally involve the public in the decision-making process.
- It puts responsibility in the wrong place—it assumes that society as a whole must deal with environmental harm, not those who created the harm.
- It creates a false dichotomy between economic development and environmental protection.[81]

The study, however, notes that despite these drawbacks, risk assessment can play a useful role in implementing the precautionary principle:

Instead of using risk assessment to establish "safe" levels of exposure, levels that are fundamentally unknowable, it can be used to better understand the hazards of an activity and to compare options for prevention. . . . But the underlying basis for policy and decision-making must be precaution and prevention, rather than risk.[82]

In tracing the origin of the precautionary principle, David Freestone refers to the German principle of *Vorsorgeprinzip* that, according to him, is regarded as one of the most fundamental principles of German environmental policy.[83] However, it is also termed "an elusive concept"[84] and its legal status remains controversial.

---

[80] *See* MARR, *supra* note 6, at 13.

[81] *Id.* at 13–15.

[82] *Id.* at 15.

[83] *See* Freestone, *supra* note 49, at 21.

[84] *Id.*, *quoting* Loather Gundling, *The Status in International Law of the Principle of*

Like other useful principles, the precautionary principle, too, has both benefits and pitfalls.[85] Its capacity for both aspects becomes apparent only when it is invoked in a particular context:

> Like all good and useful principles that are pitched at a high level of generality—some others include reasonableness, good faith, best interests of the child, and state sovereignty—the precautionary principle has its benefits and pitfalls, but these cannot readily be understood in the abstract. The principle's capacity both for good and evil can become truly apparent only when it is invoked, discussed, criticized, and—in some form or another—applied or avoided in a particular context. Furthermore, contributions of the principle to the resolution of disputes and problems depend much more on the processes in which it is taken up than on its inherent features.[86]

It is worth remembering that the precautionary principle does not tell decision makers what to do.[87] Neither does it reverse the burden of proof, although, in a given situation, it could: "What it does do is propose a course of action to be followed in instances where the impact of a given substance or activity on human health or the environment gives rise to questions or concerns, but where the cause-effect linkage between the substance or activity and harm cannot be identified with certainty."[88]

The role of the precautionary principle has been summarized as follows:

> The precautionary principle is an overarching framework of thinking that governs the use of foresight in situations characterised by uncertainty and ignorance and where there are potentially large costs to both regulatory action and inaction. . . .

> The procedures for dealing with the situations of risk, uncertainty and ignorance need to be fair, transparent and accountable, key elements of the (sic) 'good governance' which is needed to regain public confidence in policy-making on technologies, their benefits and potential hazards."[89]

---

*Precautionary Action, in* THE NORTH SEA: PERSPECTIVES ON REGIONAL ENVIRONMENTAL CO-OPERATION 23–30 (David Freestone & T. Ijlstra eds., 1990).

[85]   *See* Ellis & FitzGerald, *supra* note 47.

[86]   *Id.*

[87]   *Id.*

[88]   *Id.*

[89]   *See* THE PRECAUTIONARY PRINCIPLE IN THE 20TH CENTURY 216–17 (Poul Harremoes et al. eds., 2002).

The level of proof that is necessary depends on the size and nature of the potential harm, the benefits and available alternatives and the cost of being wrong in both directions.[90] "Military intelligence has long adopted similar precautionary approaches to uncertainty and high stakes, where the costs of being wrong can be catastrophic."[91] Having discussed 12 case studies ranging from PCB's to benzene, from radiation to fisheries, from asbestos to the mad cow disease, writers have identified several "late lessons from early warnings:"[92] acknowledge and respond to ignorance, as well as uncertainty and risk, in technology appraisal and public policymaking; provide adequate long-term environmental and health monitoring and research into early warnings; reduce blind spots and gaps in scientific knowledge; reduce interdisciplinary obstacles to learning; systematically scrutinize the benefits with potential risks; evaluate alternatives; ensure the use of local knowledge; reduce institutional obstacles; avoid "paralysis by analysis" by reducing potential harm when there are grounds for concern.[93]

The writers while highlighting the benefits of adopting a precautionary approach[94] also caution against over-precaution that can be expensive in terms of lost opportunities for innovation and by stifling scientific inquiry.[95] What is necessary, then, is to strike a balance between the level of uncertainty, potential for significant harm to human health and the environment, on the one hand, and the proposed benefits of the activity, on the other, with a careful analysis of economic considerations for both sides of the equation.

## 3. The Role of the Principle of Proportionality

It has been posited that the principle of proportionality could "serve as a general limiting factor to the precautionary principle."[96] The principle of proportionality is a general principle of international law and is applicable to a variety of issues whether it is in relation to humanitarian law, use of force or environmental protection. It is not really a limiting factor—rather,

---

[90]  *Id.* at 218.

[91]  *Id.*

[92]  *Id.*

[93]  *Id.* at 218–19.

[94]  *Id.* at 219. The benefits include the chances of anticipating costly impacts, achieving a better balance between pros and cons and minimizing the costs of unpleasant surprises. It can also stimulate more innovation via technology diversity and better science.

[95]  *Id.*

[96]  *See* MARR, *supra* note 6, at 35.

it is a test used to evaluate the appropriateness of the response to a certain event. Thus, in the field of self-defense, the principle of proportionality is applied to evaluate whether the measures used in self-defense are proportionate to the threat.[97] If not, the plea of self-defense would fail. This argument was used in relation to the use of nuclear weapons—that its use cannot be proportionate to the threat. As noted by the ICJ in its advisory opinion:

> The Court does not consider that the treaties in question could have intended to deprive a State of the exercise of its right of self-defence under international law because of its obligations to protect the environment. Nonetheless, States must take environmental considerations into account when assessing what is necessary and proportionate in the pursuit of legitimate military objectives. Respect for the environment is one of the elements that go to assessing whether an action is in conformity with the principles of necessity and proportionality.[98]

Judge Weeramantry, in appending a dissenting opinion, noted that environmental law incorporates a number of principles that are violated by the use of nuclear weapons: the inter-generational equity principle; common heritage of mankind principle; the precautionary principle; the principle of trusteeship of earth resources; and the polluter pays principle.[99] With regard to a nuclear response to a nuclear attack, he pointed out that "we are in territory where the principle of proportionality becomes devoid of meaning."[100]

Some national laws also incorporate the proportionality principle. For example, under the German administrative law, four factors must be taken into consideration: the intended measures must serve the public interest; the measure must be suitable to the desired objective; the measure needs to be necessary; and the measure and desired object must be proportionate to each other.[101]

Two other factors play an important role in relation to the precautionary principle: the duty to monitor and the preparation of a cost-benefit

---

[97] *See* LORI F. DAMROSCH ET AL., INTERNATIONAL LAW: CASES AND MATERIALS 923 (4th ed. 2001).

[98] *Legality of the Threat or Use of Nuclear Weapons*, Advisory Opinion, 1996 ICJ 2. The Court also referred to the principle of proportionality in the context of reprisals, para. 46.

[99] Dissenting Opinion, Judge Weeramantry, 1996 ICJ 2, para. 57.

[100] *Id.* para. 66.

[101] *See* MARR, *supra* note 6, at 37.

analysis. With regard to the former, it must be noted that the measures envisaged under the precautionary principle are considered to be provisional—until such time that there is sufficient scientific evidence. The cost-benefit analysis will enable us to weigh pros and cons of applying the precautionary principle and would facilitate the application of the principle of proportionality. In addition, socio-economic considerations must be taken into account.

It is accepted that every human activity will have some impact on the environment. While it is impossible to avoid *any* impact on the environment, the present environmental crisis is due to the irresponsible, short-sighted activities of human beings carried out for short-term gain. In the process of accumulating wealth and strategic advantage, we have created many environmental problems, and the consequences of some of them are still unknown. The question is should we continue to do so? Can the environment survive this onslaught?

The first explicit reference to the precautionary principle at the international level is considered to be the Declaration issued by the participants at the Second International North Sea Conference (called the 1987 London Declaration) held in November 1987. The Declaration stated that:

> In order to protect the North Sea from possibly damaging effects of the most dangerous substances, a precautionary approach is necessary which may require action to control inputs of such substances even before a causal link has been established by absolutely clear scientific evidence.[102]

The most rigorous application of the precautionary principle—prior justification procedure[103]—was adopted in relation to dumping and incineration of industrial waste at sea by the Oslo Commission in 1989.[104] According to this decision, which is binding on the parties, those wishing to dump industrial waste at sea must show that it is not harmful to the marine environment.[105]

There are varying levels of the definition of the precautionary principle, depending on the view point of the person defining it. Its definition can be considered on a continuum—at the lower end of the spectrum, the

---

[102] *Referred to in* Freestone, *supra* note 49, at 23.

[103] *See* Freestone, *supra* note 49, at 25.

[104] *Id.* at 25.

[105] *Id.*

precautionary principle is equated with the principle of prevention,[106] while at the other end of the spectrum, the precautionary principle is similar to the prior justification procedure requiring the prior informed consent.[107] The Principle 15 version of the principle adopts the "middle ground" avoiding any reference to either extreme.[108] However, the precise definition of the precautionary principle is subject to some controversy.[109]

The principle of harm prevention, as endorsed by Principle 21 of the Stockholm Declaration, requires states to take action to prevent environmental harm beyond its territorial boundaries. Such action, however, is limited by existing scientific knowledge in that the obligation in Principle 21 extends only to environmental harm or risk of harm that is already established. The precautionary principle, on the other hand, requires states to take measures to prevent environmental harm, even in the absence of scientific certainty, provided a certain level of risk of harm already exists. This is the main distinction between the principle of harm prevention and the precautionary principle. Similarly, the environmental impact assessment process, an invaluable tool toward achieving sustainable development, is also limited by scientific knowledge. Coupled with the precautionary principle, these mechanisms go a long way in achieving sustainable development.

Noting that contemporary international law requires states to take measures beyond simple prevention where there is a "significant risk" of extraterritorial harm, Freestone notes that the requirement of foreseeability is not a passive obligation:

Against this background, the precautionary principle may not be such a radical departure from existing international principles. The innovative aspect of its formulation is the requirement that action should be taken to control or abate possible environmental interference even when there is scientific uncertainty as to the effects of the activities.[110]

He further points out that "the threshold of significant risk has become easier to cross and once a *prima facie* case is made that a risk exists, then sci-

---

[106] *See* Freestone, *supra* note 49, at 30. *See also* Section F on the relationship between the precautionary principle, prevention and environmental assessment.

[107] *Id.*

[108] *Id.*

[109] As noted in Chapter 2, Section C, a similar controversy exists in relation to sustainable development.

[110] *See* Freestone, *supra* note 49, at 32.

entific uncertainty works against the potential polluter rather than, as in the past, in his favour."[111] Thus, the precautionary approach envisages the development and adoption of clean technologies and rejects the traditional assimilative capacity approach.[112]

Despite definitional problems, it is noteworthy that the precautionary principle has found its way into many international instruments, both binding and non-binding. The Bergen Ministerial Declaration on Sustainable Development, one of the first instruments to refer to the precautionary principle, explicitly makes the link between sustainable development and the precautionary principle:

> In order to achieve sustainable development, policies must be based on the precautionary principle. Environmental measures must anticipate, prevent and attack the causes of environmental degradation. Where there are threats of serious or irreversible damage, lack of full scientific certainty should not be used as a reason for postponing measures to prevent environmental degradation.[113]

This provision makes it clear that the precautionary principle is a tool to achieve sustainable development. It further emphasizes the importance of an anticipatory approach[114] to environmental protection, even where scientific certainty is lacking (which is the essence of the precautionary principle). The rationale behind this approach is that it is not always possible to have scientific certainty—in other words, when scientific certainty is achieved, it may be too late to take preventive measures. Moreover, it is generally the future generations who will have to bear the brunt of the

---

[111] *Id.*

[112] *Id.*

[113] Ministerial Declaration on Sustainable Development in the ECE Region—United Nations Economic Commission for Europe Conference on Action for a Common Future, Bergen, Norway, May 15, 1990, A/CONF.151/PC/10, Aug. 6, 1990, art. 1.7.

[114] It may be recalled that the approach to environmental protection during the 1970s (and prior to that) and early 1980s was based on a reactive approach, rather than an anticipatory one. A good example is the (in)action in relation to the problem of acid rain in Europe. Despite the existence of the problem as early as the Stockholm Conference, a framework convention to deal with the issue was adopted only in 1979. Specific pollution control measures took several more years with the adoption of a protocol in 1985. *See* Protocol on the Reduction of Sulphur Emissions or their Transboundary Fluxes by at least 30 per cent, entered into force Sept. 2, 1987; Protocol Concerning the Control of Emissions of Volatile Organic Compounds or their Transboundary Fluxes, entered into force Sept. 29, 1997; and The 1988 Protocol concerning the Control of Nitrogen Oxides or their Transboundary Fluxes, entered into force February 14, 1991. These instruments are *available at* http://www.unece.org/env/lrtap.

actions taken by the present generations: the issue thus becomes one of equity and fairness.

The controversy surrounding the phenomenon of global warming is a case in point. It is predicted that if the present emission levels of greenhouse gases continue unabated, sea levels would rise causing the submergence of existing low-lying cities such as Bangkok, Dhaka, and perhaps causing the disappearance of states such as the Maldives.[115] In addition, global warming is considered to cause epidemiological problems,[116] as well as desertification in Africa.[117] Global warming is not just another environmental problem—the very survival of certain states and peoples could depend on the action taken now. Thus, it is also a human rights issue—among the rights that can be adversely affected are the right to life,[118] the right to health,[119] the right to an adequate standard of living,[120] the freedom of movement,[121] the right to choose one's residence,[122] the right to a livelihood,[123] the right to privacy[124] and possibly the right to live in a healthy environment at least for those states that are parties to the African Charter and the San Salvador Protocol.[125] All these rights and many more can be jeopardized as a result of global warming. Moreover, global warming with its predicted economic consequences[126] has the potential to affect all three pillars of sustainable development—economic development, social development and environmental protection.[127] In short, global warming and climate change will undermine sustainable development.

---

[115] *See* IPCC Report, *supra* note 57.

[116] *Id. See also* Paroma Basu, *Third World Bears Brunt of Global Warming Impacts*, *available at* http://www.news.wisc.edu/11878.html.

[117] *Id.*

[118] Protected under Article 6, ICCPR, *available at* http://www.unhchr.org.

[119] Protected under Article 12, 1966, ICESCR, *available at* http://www.unhchr.org.

[120] Protected under Article 11, ICESCR, *id.*

[121] Protected under Article 12, ICCPR, *supra* note 118.

[122] Protected under Article 12, ICCPR, *supra* note 118.

[123] Protected under Article 6, ICESCR, *supra* note 119.

[124] Protected under Article 17, ICCPR, *supra* note 118.

[125] Discussed in Chapter 1, Section B.1.d.

[126] *See* IPCC Report, *supra* note 57 and OUR COMMON FUTURE, REPORT OF THE WORLD COMMISSION ON ENVIRONMENT AND DEVELOPMENT 172 (1987).

[127] The Plan of Implementation adopted at the WSSD referred to the three pillars of sustainable development as economic development, social development and environmental protection, para. 2. *See* discussion in Chapter 2, Section B.5.

While present trends point towards global warming, there is by no means scientific certainty on the issue. On the other hand, waiting for scientific certainty may well sound the death knell for certain states and people and could cause problems for the entire international community. Already, above-average warm temperatures and failing food crops point toward a warming earth.[128] Thus, how do we strike a balance between the need to take anticipatory measures and the need to avoid expensive action that may later prove to be futile? The importance of the precautionary principle should be viewed in this light. It tells policymakers *when* action should be taken, rather than *what* kind of action is necessary.[129] Thus, the essence of the precautionary principle lies in its *timing*.[130] David Freestone and Ellen Hey note that the precautionary approach entails the following:

> 1) clean production methods, best available technology and best environmental practices must be applied; 2) comprehensive methods of environmental and economic assessment must be used in deciding upon methods to enhance the quality of the environment; 3) research, particularly scientific and economic research, that contributes to a better understanding of long-term options available must be stimulated; and 4) legal, administrative and technical procedures that facilitate the implementation of this approach must be applied and, where not available, developed.[131]

While it seems that the existence of a significant risk of environmental harm would trigger the application of the precautionary principle, writers have grappled with the issue of operationalizing the principle. In other words, some level of credible evidence of an environmental problem is necessary in order to trigger the application of the precautionary principle. However, it has been contended that the formulation of the precautionary principle in Principle 15 of the Rio Declaration contains two requirements that are not ubiquitous features of the precautionary principle: the reference to serious harm and the reference to cost-effective measures.[132] A baseline version of the principle is articulated as "Where threats of harm to the environment exist, scientific uncertainty will not be used as a reason to

---

[128] *See* IPCC Report, *supra* note 57.

[129] *See* Ellis & FitzGerald, *supra* note 47.

[130] *See* David Freestone & Ellen Hey, *Origins and Development of the Precautionary Principle, in* THE PRECAUTIONARY PRINCIPLE AND INTERNATIONAL LAW: THE CHALLENGE OF IMPLEMENTATION 13 (David Freestone & Ellen Hey eds., 1996).

[131] *Id.*

[132] *See* Ellis & FitzGerald, *supra* note 47.

postpone the taking of measures for the protection of human life or health or the environment."[133]

This baseline version of the precautionary principle indicates that states are required to adopt a precautionary approach where there is a threat of *any* harm to the environment. While this approach is certainly beneficial for environmental protection and protection of human health, it is doubtful whether states would be willing to apply the precautionary principle in such a general manner, in the absence of a threat of significant damage to the environment, given the controversy that arose when Principle 15 was debated. It must be pointed out that even the environmental assessment process is generally mandated for activities likely to have a *significant impact* on the environment.[134] The second requirement—cost-benefit measures—was included in Principle 15 at the insistence of the United States, which continues to refute that global warming is taking place.[135] It is indeed in relation to the issue of global warming and climate change that the precautionary principle has been most hotly debated. In a report issued by the IPCC[136] it is established that the global average surface temperature has increased over the 20th century by about 0.6 degrees centigrade; globally it is very likely that the 1990s was the warmest decade and 1998 was the warmest year on record; snow cover and ice extent have decreased; and global average sea level has risen and ocean heat content has increased.[137] It further notes that emissions of greenhouse gases and aerosols due to human activities continue to alter the atmosphere in ways that are expected to affect the climate. According to the report, atmospheric concentrations of carbon dioxide has increased by 31 percent since 1750 and about three-fourths of the anthropogenic emission of carbon dioxide to the atmosphere during the past 20 years is due to fossil fuel burning while the rest is due to land-use change, especially deforestation.[138] In addition, atmospheric concentrations of methane, nitrous oxide, halocarbon gases and ozone have also increased.[139] It is thus clear

---

[133] *Id.*

[134] *See* discussion in Chapter 4, Section B and C.

[135] *Cf.* Fullem, *supra* note 54, who contends that the precautionary principle has been part of the U.S. environmental law since the early 1970s. *See also* Wiener & Rogers, *supra* note 45, who contend that "neither the EU nor the US can claim to be 'more precautionary' than the other."

[136] *See* IPCC Report, *supra* note 57.

[137] *Id.*

[138] *Id.*

[139] *Id.*

that anthropogenic emissions of certain gases are interfering with climate, and while all the predicted consequences of global warming may not materialize, the present trends seem sufficiently grave to warrant taking precautionary measures.

What kind of evidence is necessary to trigger the application of the precautionary principle is also contested. One issue that must be highlighted is the hostile attitude of scientists belonging to different groups—this has been evident in relation to the debate on global warming: while one group of scientists paints a very gloomy picture of the repercussions of global warming, another group refutes these findings and paints a very different picture of the global scenario. Policymakers, who rely heavily on the scientific community for guidance, are torn between two (sometimes more) groups and tend to adopt the opinion of the group that is politically and economically favorable to them. Needless to say, this approach is detrimental to environmental protection. While it may reap short-term benefits, it cannot bring in long-term benefits. By their very nature, the consequences of many environmental issues are hard to predict. It is impossible to have scientific certainty about them, particularly when so many variables are involved. Thus, requiring scientific certainty about something as complex as global warming may be well-neigh impossible. The international community has been willing to take precautionary measures in the absence of scientific certainty in the past. The measures taken in relation to ozone depletion are a good example. When the United States banned the domestic use of CFCs in the 1970s,[140] there was hardly any scientific evidence that linked CFCs to the thinning of the ozone layer. Even when the Montreal Protocol was adopted in 1987, there was no definitive evidence of this link. It was only in 1988 that the Ozone Trends Panel[141] issued its report with the first solid data linking halons and CFCs with ozone depletion.[142] This goes to show that at the time when emission reductions and phase-out timetables were agreed upon in the Montreal Protocol, there was no hard evidence linking CFCs to ozone depletion. Yet, the international community was willing to take action to protect the ozone layer. Why is there a difference in approach with regard to global warming? There are several reasons for this: the United States, the nation at the forefront in relation to ozone depletion, is backing out on binding targets in relation to global warming.

---

[140] *See* HUNTER ET AL., *supra* note 2, at 535. In 1978 the Environmental Protection Agency of the United States banned the use of CFC aerosol propellants for all but essential uses. It was followed by similar bans in Sweden, Canada and Norway.

[141] This Panel was established with over 100 scientists from ten different countries to inform governments of the present state of science. *See* http://www.atmosp.physics. utoronto.ca/SPARC/SPARCReport1/ 0_Summary/Summary.html.

[142] *See* HUNTER ET AL., *supra* note 2, at 549.

Without the United States, which is the largest contributor of carbon dioxide into the atmosphere, it may not be possible to have a successful regime in relation to global warming. It was really the domestic controls in the United States that spurred international action in relation to ozone depletion. The second reason is industry. Unlike in relation to ozone depletion where industry backed the adoption of international controls,[143] in relation to global warming, industry is actually advocating against binding obligations or timetables.[144] The third reason is that global warming is much more complex than ozone depletion encompassing day-to-day activities, such as driving (vehicular emissions), farming (methane) and the use of energy (fossil fuels). Ozone depletion and global warming are also related to one another.[145] Ultimately, however, everything boils down to politics.

Whether or not the precautionary principle informs our decisions, states and individuals take various decisions everyday that contain an element of risk. Weighing various decisions in the face of risk has become part of our daily activities. The question is to what extent the precautionary principle should influence these decisions when faced with an element of risk. When an element of uncertainty is added to this equation, decisions become a little more difficult to take. When the potential victim is the international community as a whole, the decisions become even harder. The environment itself involves many uncertainties. According to Ellis and FitzGerald, "A decision taken in accordance with the precautionary principle will ultimately be one that pays close attention to preferences and priorities. Different states will, therefore, ultimately have to tolerate laws and policies that they do not agree with or that differ from their own."[146] Furthermore, once a decision is taken through the application of a precautionary approach, states must be capable of providing well-reasoned justifications for the decision.[147]

With regard to the issue whether the precautionary principle should be applied to tourism in the Antarctic, it has been noted that any uncertainty about the environmental impacts of tourist activities should not automatically lead to its prohibition.[148] It is further contended that such an interpretation of the precautionary principle would transform it into an

---

[143]  *Id.* at 535.

[144]  *Id.* at 536.

[145]  Ozone is also a greenhouse gas. *See* OUR COMMON FUTURE, *supra* note 126, at 37.

[146]  *See* Ellis & FitzGerald, *supra* note 47.

[147]  *Id.*

[148]  *See* Kees Bastmeijer & Ricardo Roura, *Current Development: Regulating Antarctic Tourism and the Precautionary Principle*, 98 AM. J. INT'L L. 763.

absolute norm, which is not the way it has developed under international environmental law: "Its aim is to ensure that "uncertainties" about the impacts of an activity (or set of activities) are weighed in the decision-making process."[149] Thus, not only socio-economic advantages and the environmental impact of a project are taken into consideration, but also any gaps in knowledge. Applying the precautionary principle to Antarctic tourism may mean imposing certain conditions on activities as a whole, and specific restrictions on particular regions or sites. It may also mean banning certain activities (or suspending them) for a particular period of time from ecologically sensitive areas until more information is available on the human impact on this fragile ecosystem. While environmental monitoring is a good tool to identify potential environmental impacts, such tools are necessarily limited by existing knowledge. If there are gaps in current scientific knowledge, these tools become ineffective. It is here that a precautionary approach becomes valuable.

### 4. The Process in Applying the Precautionary Principle

Several practical steps have been identified in applying the precautionary principle. This process may differ slightly depending on whether it is a new activity or an existing one. For new activities, the proponents will have to show that the activity will not be harmful and also that they have considered alternatives to the activity.[150] Here the precautionary principle goes hand in hand with the EIA process. For existing activities, action must be taken before proof of harm, and the proponent has the burden of proof. The steps to be taken have been identified as follows:[151]

(1) Identify the possible threat and characterize the problem—
Under this, several questions arise, such as what is the potential scale of the threat? What is the full range of potential impacts? What is the intensity of possible impacts? What is the temporal scale of the threat?[152] And how reversible is the threat?

(2) Identify what is known and what is not known about the threat—This is a useful exercise because it enables both the proponent and the decision maker to identify the limits of knowledge and get a better picture of uncertainties involved. Under

---

[149] *Id.*

[150] *See* Tickner et al., *supra* note 60.

[151] This section is drawn from Tickner et al., *supra* note 60.

[152] There are two issues to consider here: the time lapse between a threat and harm (immediate, near future, future generations) and the persistence of impacts, *See* Tickner et al., *supra* note 60, at 7.

this, several questions have to be addressed: Can the uncertainty be reduced by more study or data? Are we dealing with something about which we are highly ignorant? If there is high uncertainty about a particular activity and its impact, it may be a good reason not to proceed with it. Does the fact that something is claimed to be safe mean that it has not been proven to be dangerous yet? Making a chart with known and unknown facts will enable us to get a better grasp of the issue.

(3) Reframe the problem to describe what needs to be done—The goal is to understand what purpose the proposed activity serves. For existing activities, this may or may not be the case.

(4) Step four in this process is to assess alternatives that are available—The approach will differ depending on whether it is a proposed activity or continuing activity.

(5) In either case, the assessment of alternatives is a multi-stage process. Under this, it is necessary to identify alternatives that are available, then rule out ones that seem impossible. Then it is necessary to identify options that are politically, technically and economically feasible. In relation to the equation on economics, one needs to add possible harm to the environment, health costs, cost of using environmental goods for the project, such as water, land, etc. These are rarely included. One then needs to consider potential unintended consequences of the proposed alternatives.

(6) Determine the course of action—Once all the above information is gathered, it is necessary to analyze the information to decide how much precaution is necessary. The options available are: not proceeding with the activity; demanding alternatives; or demanding modifications to reduce potential impacts.

(7) Monitoring and follow-up—The final step of the process is to monitor the activity to identify expected and unexpected results. This step, of course, presupposes that the activity has proceeded with or without modifications.

The procedure that is discussed above is remarkably similar to the procedure that is usually followed in relation to environmental impact assessments, discussed in Chapter 4. Thus, what is the distinction between precaution and EIAs? As noted above, the environmental impact assessment process will be conducted based on the available scientific evidence and information, although, increasingly, international instruments require parties to identify gaps in knowledge when conducting an environmental impact assessment.[153] The main distinction between the two tools would be

---

[153] Several examples are discussed in Chapter 4, Section C.2.

the element of scientific uncertainty—otherwise, both the precautionary principle and the environmental impact assessment process are based on the broad principle of prevention.

Of course, as with any innovative principle or approach, there are critics too. Many, particularly those from industry, have argued that the precautionary approach puts an end to technological advance.[154] Some have also argued that it fails to take science into account.[155] Yet others contend, similar to the presumption of innocence, that technology is safe until proved otherwise. In other words, unless we can prove that a particular product or technology is unsafe or dangerous, we need to accept them as safe despite any gaps in our knowledge. What the precautionary approach does is to place the burden of proof on the person who alleges something: if there is uncertainty as to the safety of a product or technology, then the manufacturer of that product or technology must prove that it is safe. Thus, uncertainty works in consumers' interest, not against them as in the past.[156] As discussed later, however, this does not amount to a reversal of the burden of proof.

However, the precautionary principle does not provide us with a magic formula to deal with all environmental problems:

> The precautionary principle does not provide us with an algorithm for decision making. We still have to seek the best scientific evidence we can obtain and we still have to make judgements about what is in the best interest of ourselves and our environment. Indeed, one of the advantages of the principle is that it forces us to face these issues; we cannot ignore them in the hope that everything will turn out for the best whatever we do. The basic point, however, is that it places the burden of proof firmly on the advocates of new technology. It is for them to show that what they are proposing is safe. It is not for the rest of us to show that it is not.[157]

It is argued that the precautionary principle does not require industry to provide absolute proof that a new technology or product is safe.[158] The precautionary principle does not deal with absolute certainty. Indeed,

---

154 *See* Peter Saunders, *Use and Abuse of the Precautionary Principle, at* http://www.rati-cal.org/co-globalize/MaeWanHo/PrecautionP.html.

155 *Id.*

156 *See* Freestone, *supra* note 49.

157 *See* Saunders, *supra* note 154.

158 *Id.*

it would be impossible to provide absolute proof, given the environmental changes that are taking place everyday. The precautionary principle is "specifically intended for circumstances in which there is no absolute certainty. . . . The requirement is to demonstrate, not absolutely but beyond reasonable doubt, that what is being proposed is safe."[159] Comparing the precautionary principle to the presumption of innocence, Saunders argues that due to the inequality between the defense and the prosecution, they are not on equal footing. The defendant does not have to prove his innocence. The prosecution must establish, beyond reasonable doubt, that the defendant is guilty. The inequality is due to the uncertainty of the situation and the consequences of taking a wrong decision.[160] The same applies to the precautionary principle. Faced with uncertainty, it is natural that mistakes will be made. Our objective should be to minimize the damage that will occur in such situations and to ensure that our decisions are based on the precautionary principle.

It has been pointed out that "The precautionary principle is so obviously common sense that we might expect it to be universally adopted."[161] Unfortunately, the reality is different. Although in day-to-day activities we say "it is better to be safe than sorry," we are far from accepting the precautionary principle as a legally binding principle. The underlying premise for this principle—if there is uncertainty, we must weigh that into the decision-making process—is indeed sound. Whether our decisions can be legally challenged if the precautionary principle is not taken into consideration, however, is not clear. What is clear is that it should inform our decision-making process, when faced with scientific uncertainty.

## 5. Precautionary Principle and the Burden of Proof

It has also been contended that the precautionary principle is about the burden of proof, a concept that underlies every legal system. It is generally accepted that those who contend something must prove it, unless the court takes judicial notice of that fact or where there is a presumption in favor of that person. Thus, for example, if I allege that my neighbor stole my plants, I have to prove that fact. My neighbor does not have any burden of proof. Similarly, if a person alleges that a particular product or technology is safe, he has to establish that fact. Those who contend otherwise do not have to establish that it is, in fact, unsafe. This is the principle that underlies the precautionary principle.

---

[159] *Id.*

[160] *See supra* note 154.

[161] *Id. Cf.* Cross, *supra* note 35, who critiques the common sense approach on the ground that it is contrary to science which requires proof and "is not a common sense activity."

This does not mean that the precautionary principle actually reverses the burden of proof, as contended by some writers.[162] It simply applies the burden of proof in its normal context, as shown in the above example: those who contend something must establish that fact. In other words, if somebody alleges that a particular product or technology is safe and does not cause harm to public health or the environment, that person must establish that fact. Society at large does not have to prove that such product or technology is not safe. *This* would be a reversal of the burden of proof.

According to Simon Marr:

The precautionary principle suggests that behavior should be subject to regulation before harm is demonstrated. Thereby it suggests a departure from the traditional, tort-oriented approach which precludes the presumption of harm as a result of an activity of another until a party can show damage and causation. Thus, it shifts the burden of proving harmlessness to the party who wishes to engage in the environmentally sensitive activity. The wider implication of the reversal of the burden of proof is that it implies that human action should be assumed to be harmful to the environment unless proven otherwise, giving the environment or the resources the benefit of the doubt.[163]

Marr actually refers to two issues here: the fact that the party who wishes to engage in an environmentally sensitive activity has to show that there is no significant environmental damage does not mean that the burden of proof is reversed; as discussed above, the party that asserts a fact, simply has to prove it. The second issue relates to the presumption that an activity is harmful unless proven otherwise. Here the complainant has the benefit of a presumption in his favor and has no initial burden of proof. The proponent of the activity has the burden of proof to show that his activity has no detrimental effects on the environment. Here the burden of proof is reversed because of the presumption. This approach is adopted in relation to activities that are considered extremely hazardous in nature.[164]

The precautionary principle can also be applied in relation to existing industries or technologies.[165] Some examples are cigarettes, CFC's and lead

---

[162] *See* MARR, *supra* note 6, at 16.

[163] *Id.* at 17.

[164] An example of this approach is GA Res. 44/225, Dec. 22, 1989, which recommended a total ban on large-scale drift-net fishing in the absence of scientific consensus on the long-term impact and until shown *otherwise, see* MARR, *supra* note 6, at 17.

[165] *See* Saunders, *supra* note 154.

in petrol. In these instances, more research work is necessary,[166] and we should continuously assess the impact of these technologies or products to ensure that public health and safety is not jeopardized. When research reveals an impact on public health, it is then necessary for intervention through legal measures.

Writing on the standard of the burden of proof, Saunders notes:

> The principle does not, as some critics claim, require industry to provide absolute proof that something new is safe. That would be an impossible demand and would indeed stop technology dead in its tracks, but it is not what is being demanded. The precautionary principle does not deal with absolute certainty. On the contrary, it is specifically intended for circumstances in which there is no absolute certainty. It simply puts the burden of proof where it belongs, with the innovator. The requirement is to demonstrate, not absolutely but beyond reasonable doubt, that what is being proposed is safe.[167]

## 6. The Position of Industries

While the precautionary principle makes common sense, unfortunately, it is not universally adopted. Arguing that the strict application of the precautionary principle would thwart all innovation, industries have resisted its adoption. Their argument is simple: let us benefit from the profits, and let somebody else (usually, society at large) and perhaps future generations be responsible for any losses that may be incurred. Put this way, it is not hard to understand why this position is so resisted by environmentalists.

While it may not be necessary to legislate on the precautionary principle, its application is required to ensure that public safety and the environment are not jeopardized. On the other hand, precisely because of the resistance of industry, it may be necessary to give it legal content—otherwise, it may not have any effect at all. What are the costs of not implementing the precautionary principle? Greater incidence of carcinoma and other health problems with increased expenditure for healthcare, not to mention environmental degradation are some of these costs. How can one value human life? How can one value damage to the environment or species loss? These are some of the questions that industry as well as policymakers are facing today.

---

[166]  *Id.*

[167]  *Id.*

## D. SURVEY OF INTERNATIONAL INSTRUMENTS THAT EMBODY THE PRECAUTIONARY PRINCIPLE

Almost all the instruments adopted since the Rio Declaration now refer to the precautionary principle at least in the Preamble. It is not the intention of this section to discuss each and every instrument in which reference is made to the precautionary principle. This has been done in earlier works.[168] Instead, only the more prominent ones will be discussed and a particular trend noted.

The first reference to the content of the precautionary principle is found in the World Charter for Nature although the term itself is not mentioned there. Principle 11 of the Charter provides as follows:

Activities which might have an impact on nature shall be controlled, and the best available technologies that minimize significant risks to nature or other adverse effects shall be used; in particular:

(a) Activities which are likely to cause irreversible damage to nature shall be avoided;

(b) Activities which are likely to pose a significant risk to nature shall be preceded by an exhaustive examination; their proponents shall demonstrate that expected benefits outweigh potential damage to nature, and *where potential adverse effects are not fully understood, the activities should not proceed;*

(c) Activities which may disturb nature shall be preceded by assessment of their consequences, and environmental impact studies of development projects shall be conducted sufficiently in advance, if they are to be undertaken, such activities shall be planned and carried out so as to minimize potential adverse effects.[169]

Thus, according to the World Charter, the burden of proving that an activity does not pose a significant threat to nature is on the proponent of

---

[168] *See* ARIE TROUWBORST, EVOLUTION AND STATUS OF THE PRECAUTIONARY PRINCIPLE IN INTERNATIONAL LAW 55–156 (2002). *Cf.* Sumudu Atapattu, *Evolution and Status of the Precautionary Principle in International Law by Arie Trouwborst,* Book Review, 96 AM. J. INT'L L. 1016 (2002). Some of the examples provided by Trouwborst are of the environmental impact assessment process rather than of the precautionary principle. *See also* Section F on the relationship between the principle of prevention, environmental impact assessment and the precautionary principle.

[169] Principle 11, World Charter for Nature, adopted in 1982, GA Res. 37/7, *reprinted in* 22 ILM 455 (1983) (emphasis added).

that activity; the proponents must show that benefits outweigh potential damage to nature; where adverse effects are not fully understood, the activities shall not proceed. In other words, if there is uncertainty, the benefit of that uncertainty should be given to nature. Principle 11, however, makes it clear that these requirements apply only to activities that are likely to cause a significant risk to nature. Any activity falling short of this threshold is not subject to these requirements. In that respect, Principle 11 of the World Charter is similar to Principle 15 of the Rio Declaration. However, the other requirement in Principle 15—that measures should be cost-effective—is not present in Principle 11. Principle 11 also imposes a moratorium on activities where their adverse effects are not yet understood and requires the proponent of the activity to show that the benefits from the implementation of the activity outweigh the damage to nature. If one compares Principle 11 of the World Charter with Principle 15 of the Rio Declaration, it seems obvious that the former adopts a much stricter version of the precautionary principle than the latter.

The provisions of the Bergen Ministerial Declaration and those of the Rio Declaration were noted earlier. The UN Framework Convention on Climate Change (UNFCCC) and the Convention on Biological Diversity and many other instruments adopted since the Rio Conference embody the precautionary principle. The Forest Principles[170] also adopted at the Rio Conference, while making extensive reference to sustainable development,[171] do not refer to the precautionary principle.

It is widely accepted that the measures taken in relation to ozone depletion is a true example of the precautionary approach[172] although the Vienna Convention of 1985 does not actually refer to this approach. This is hardly surprising. The precautionary approach or the precautionary principle appeared in an international instrument only in 1987 and it was really in the Rio Declaration that the precautionary approach made an entrance. In fact, most instruments adopted after the Rio Declaration embody this approach.

The Montreal Protocol on Substances that Deplete the Ozone Layer refers to precautionary measures in the Preamble, according to which the Parties are determined "to protect the ozone layer by taking precautionary

---

[170] Non-legally Binding Authoritative Statement of Principles for a Global Consensus on the Management, Conservation and Sustainable Development of All Types of Forests, A/CONF.151/26, *available at* http://www.un.org/documents/ga/conf151/aconf15126-3annex3.htm.

[171] Thus, the Preamble notes: "The guiding objective of these principles is to contribute to the management, conservation and sustainable development of forests and to provide for their multiple and complementary functions and uses."

[172] *See* HUNTER ET AL., *supra* note 2, at 541.

measures to control equitably total global emissions of substances that deplete it, with the ultimate objective of their elimination on the basis of developments in scientific knowledge, taking into account technical and economic considerations."[173] The parties have also noted that precautionary measures have already been taken at national and regional levels to control the emission of certain chlorofluorocarbons.[174] Although the Protocol refers to precautionary measures, it does not refer to taking action in the face of scientific uncertainty. Measures should be taken to protect the ozone layer on the basis of developments in scientific knowledge, taking into account technical and economic considerations.[175] Thus, it seems that although reference is made to the need to adopt precautionary measures, the Protocol does not explicitly refer to the need to take action in the face of scientific uncertainty. It is well known that measures to protect the ozone layer were taken amidst much scientific uncertainty,[176] and thus both the Vienna Convention and the Montreal Protocol are good examples of the precautionary approach whether or not it is actually mentioned in these instruments.

The UN Framework Convention on Climate Change, by contrast, specifically refers to taking precautionary measures in the face of scientific uncertainty:

> The Parties should take precautionary measures to anticipate, prevent or minimize the causes of climate change and mitigate its adverse effects. Where there are threats of serious or irreversible damage, lack of full scientific certainty should not be used as a reason for postponing such measures, taking into account that policies and measures to deal with climate change should be cost-effective so as to ensure global benefits at the lowest possible cost.[177]

It must be noted that this provision uses the word "should" as opposed to "shall" indicating the hortatory nature of the "principle." Neither does the Convention refer to it as the precautionary principle. It calls upon par-

---

[173] Preamble, 26 ILM 1541 (1987), 15 UNTS 3, signed Mar. 22, 1985, entered into force Sept. 22, 1988.

[174] *Id.*

[175] *Id.*

[176] *See supra* notes 140 and 141 and accompanying text.

[177] 31 ILM 849 (1992), 1771 UNTS 107, signed May 9, 1992, entered into force Mar. 21, 1994, *available at* http://www.unfccc.de/, art. 3(3). The *chapeau* to Article 3 states that the parties "shall" be guided by the following, which includes the precautionary approach.

ties to take precautionary measures to anticipate, prevent or minimize the adverse effects of climate change and to ensure that policies and measures that they adopt are cost effective. To achieve this, the Convention calls upon the parties to ensure that their policies and measures take into account different socio-economic contexts; are comprehensive; cover all relevant sources, sinks and reservoirs of greenhouse gases; and comprise all economic sectors.[178]

Similar to the formulation in the Rio Declaration, the UNFCCC has been careful about laying down the parameters of the precautionary principle. Thus, only cost-effective measures are envisaged, and the parties are also required to take into account different socio-economic contexts when taking precautionary measures.

It is interesting to note that the Convention on Biological Diversity does not specifically embody the term "precautionary principle or precautionary approach" but states that "where there is a threat of significant reduction or loss of biological diversity, lack of full scientific certainty should not be used as a reason for postponing measures to avoid or minimize such a threat."[179] The question arises as to why this Convention does not specifically endorse the precautionary principle while the UNFCCC does.

The Cartegena Protocol on Biosafety[180] adopted within the framework of the Convention on Biological Diversity is the first international treaty to specifically endorse and adopt Principle 15 of the Rio Declaration. It reaffirms "the precautionary approach contained in Principle 15 of the Rio Declaration on Environment and Development."[181] Article 1 of the Protocol reinforces the precautionary approach by providing that its objective is to contribute to an adequate level of protection in relation to the safe transfer, handling and use of living modified organisms resulting from biotechnology, in accordance with the precautionary approach contained in Principle 15 of the Rio Declaration. By including the precautionary approach in the operative part of the Protocol, the Protocol has given a new impetus to the precautionary approach.[182] It also makes a specific link

---

[178]  *Id.*

[179]  Preamble, 31 ILM 822 (1992), 1760 UNTS 79, *available at* http://www.biodiv.org/.

[180]  *Supra* note 13.

[181]  Preamble, *supra* note 13.

[182]  *See* Carolina Lasen Diaz, *Biotechnology and the Cartagena Protocol, in* de Chazournes, *supra* note 25, where it is articulated that "The Cartegena Protocol makes the precautionary principle "operational." *Cf.*, Deborah Katz, *The Mismatch Between the Biosafety Protocol and the Precautionary Principle*, 13 GEO. INT'L ENVTL. L. REV. 949 (2001), who

with the Rio Declaration by adopting the same definition given in the Rio Declaration to the precautionary approach. Thus, by endorsing the provisions hitherto contained in a soft law instrument, the Biosafety Protocol has elevated the precautionary approach to a more substantive level.[183] None of the earlier instruments refer to Principle 15 of the Rio Declaration, although almost identical wording has been used. It has been pointed out that the Cartagena Protocol adopts a significantly lower threshold level for damage than Principle 15, as it refers to potential adverse effects.[184] It was precisely the precautionary approach that gave rise to controversy during the negotiations.[185]

Several other provisions of the Biosafety Protocol are of interest here. It contains provisions on risk assessment[186] and risk management[187] and Annex III to the Protocol elaborates on risk assessment. Article 15 of the Protocol requires parties to carry out risk assessments in a scientifically sound manner in accordance with Annex III. Such assessments shall be based on information provided under Article 8 and other scientific evidence available. According to Annex III, the objective of risk assessment is to identify and evaluate the potential adverse effects of living modified organisms on biodiversity as well as risks to human health. Annex III also contains several general principles relevant to risk assessment: it should be carried out in a scientifically sound and transparent manner; lack of scientific knowledge or scientific consensus should not be interpreted as indicating a particular level of risk, an absence of risk or an acceptable risk; and it should be carried out on a case-by-case basis. It also contains the methodology to be followed in the process of risk assessment. Article 16 requires parties to impose measures based on risk assessment to the extent necessary to prevent adverse effects on biological diversity and human health within its territory. Although Article 16 does not specifically refer to the precautionary principle, it can be argued that the precautionary approach should inform any action taken under the Protocol given that the precautionary approach forms part of the objective of the Protocol.

---

argues that "strict embodiments of the precautionary principle are appropriate only for situations in which the risks of the activity outweigh the benefits."

[183] This also means, however, that the deficiencies in Principle 15 have also been endorsed by the Cartagena Protocol. Thus, it must be noted that the wording there refers to "should" as opposed to "shall" conveying a degree of discretion on states.

[184] *See* Lasen Diaz, *supra* note 182.

[185] *Id.* It is noted that given the differences in the position of negotiating countries with regard to the precautionary principle, progress has been slow.

[186] Art. 15, *supra* note 13.

[187] Art. 16, *supra* note 13.

What does this mean for the legal status of the precautionary principle? At least with regard to the parties to the Biosafety Protocol, the precautionary approach has become a binding provision. In other words, parties must adopt a precautionary approach as defined under Principle 15 of the Rio Declaration in relation to living modified organisms (LMOs).[188] The Protocol applies to "the transboundary movement, transit, handling and use of all living modified organisms that may have adverse effects on the conservation and sustainable use of biological diversity, taking also into account risks to human health."[189]

Article 5 makes it clear that the Protocol does not apply to the transboundary movement of LMOs, which are pharmaceuticals for humans that are covered by other international agreements or organizations. Thus, the precautionary approach does not apply to the transboundary movement of LMOs for pharmaceutical purposes. If the international conventions that apply to pharmaceuticals do not cover this aspect, does that mean that such activities are outside the scope of the Cartegena Protocol or that Article 5 restriction does not apply as that situation is not covered by the convention in question? To the extent that the precautionary principle is not part of customary international law,[190] it seems that the precautionary approach does not apply to pharmaceuticals. In the interest of protecting the environment and human health, it is better to apply the precautionary approach to LMOs used for pharmaceutical purposes.

The Stockholm Convention on Persistent Organic Pollutants recognizing the health concerns resulting from local exposure to persistent organic pollutants and the need to take global action, acknowledges that precaution underlies the concerns of all parties and is embedded within the Convention.[191] This Convention adopts an approach similar to the Cartegena Protocol and endorses Principle 15 of the Rio Declaration, although the difference in language used in the two instruments must be highlighted here. The objective of the Convention is to protect human health and the environment from persistent organic pollutants, "*mindful of* the precautionary approach as set forth in Principle 15 of the Rio Declaration on Environment and Development."[192] This, unfortunately, is not very strong language and does not convey a binding obligation to apply the

---

[188] Defined in art. 3(g), *supra* note 13, as "any living organism that possesses a novel combination of genetic material obtained through the use of modern biotechnology.

[189] Art. 4.

[190] *See* discussion, in Section II.

[191] Preamble, *supra* note 14.

[192] *Id.*, art. 1.

precautionary approach. Although the Preamble acknowledges that precaution is embedded within the Convention, under Article 1 the parties are only required to be "mindful" of the precautionary approach. Although reference is made to the precautionary approach, this is an example of a "soft provision" in a hard document.[193]

The most extensive provisions on the precautionary principle are found in the Agreement on the Conservation and Management of Straddling Fish Stocks and Highly Migratory Fish Stocks of 1995.[194] Article 6 of the Agreement calls upon states to apply the precautionary approach to conservation, management and exploitation of straddling fish stocks and highly migratory fish stocks in order to protect the living marine resources and preserve the marine environment. It calls upon states to be more cautious when information is uncertain, unreliable or inadequate. The absence of adequate scientific information *shall not be* used as a reason for postponing or failing to take conservation and management measures. It must be pointed out here that no reference is made to taking cost-effective measures. This, by far, is the most stringent application of the precautionary approach.

The Convention further provides that when implementing the precautionary approach states shall improve decision making by obtaining and sharing the best scientific information available and implementing improved techniques for dealing with risk and uncertainty;[195] apply the guidelines in Annex II and determine stock-specific reference points and action to be taken if they are exceeded; take into account uncertainties relating to the size and productivity of stocks; and develop data collection and research programs.[196] It further provides that where the status of target stocks is of concern, states are required to subject them to enhanced monitoring in order to review their status and the efficacy of conservation and management measures. They shall revise those measures regularly in the light of new information. Annex II contains guidelines for the application of precautionary reference points in conservation and management of straddling fish stocks and highly migratory fish stocks. Annex II notes that two types of precautionary reference points should be used: conservation (or limit) reference points and management (or target) reference points.

---

[193] *Cf.* Bo Wahlstrom, *Precaution and the Stockholm Convention, in* de Chazournes, *supra* note 25, who argues that "the Stockholm Convention refers to precaution explicitly but also incorporates it implicitly as an overarching principle throughout the text."

[194] UN Doc. A/CONF.164/37, *reprinted in* 34 ILM 1542 (1995), signed Dec. 4, 1995, entered into force Dec. 11, 2001.

[195] *Id.*, art. 6.

[196] *Id.*

It is noteworthy that throughout the text, reference is made to the precautionary approach and not the precautionary principle. It departs from the definition of the precautionary approach in Principle 15 of the Rio Declaration by not requiring the measures taken to be cost-effective. Combining Articles 5 and 6, it is clear that the precautionary approach is adopted in order to achieve sustainability. Article 6(2) also indicates that no threshold level is required to apply the precautionary principle. The formulation adopted in this Agreement is very close to the baseline definition proposed by Ellis and FitzGerald.[197]

The Protocol on Environmental Protection to the Antarctic Treaty[198] adopted in 1991 has extensive provisions on protecting the Antarctic ecosystem. The parties have committed themselves to the comprehensive protection for the Antarctic environment and dependent and associated ecosystems and have designated Antarctica as a natural reserve, devoted to peace and science. While the parties are required to carry out an environmental impact assessment of activities as set out in Annex I to the Protocol,[199] there is no mention of the precautionary principle. Under Article 3, activities in the Antarctic Treaty Area shall be planned and conducted so as to limit adverse impacts on the Antarctic environment. The parties are also required to assess the cumulative impacts of activities both by themselves and in combination with other activities in the area. Regular monitoring is to take place and priority should be accorded to scientific research. Article 8 embodies provisions on environmental impact assessment. Given the fragile nature of the Antarctic environment, and the uncertainty involved in relation to the impact of activities there, it is a pity that the precautionary principle is not part of the Protocol.

The debate continues as to whether reference should be made to the precautionary principle, precautionary approach or precautionary measures.[200] The majority of the international treaties surveyed above seem to refer to the precautionary approach. None of the treaties surveyed above actually refer to the precautionary principle.

---

[197] *See* Ellis & FitzGerald, *supra* note 47.

[198] 30 ILM 1461 (1991), entered into force Jan. 14, 1998.

[199] *Id.*, art. 8.

[200] *See* discussion in Section II.

## E. APPLICATION OF THE PRECAUTIONARY PRINCIPLE BY DIFFERENT BODIES

### 1. The ICJ[201]

While a few "environmental" cases have been filed before the ICJ, it has failed to endorse the precautionary principle in any of these cases. In two cases, the issues were ripe for a decision based, *inter alia*, on this principle, but the Court failed to make any reference to it. The *Nuclear Tests Case*[202] and the *Case Concerning the Gabcikovo Nagymaros Project*[203] involved a rich array of issues relating to environmental protection, but to the disappointment of many, the Court did not rise to the occasion. In both these cases, several judges appended separate or dissenting opinions; those of Judge Weeramantry are of particular interest to the present discussion.

### a. *Nuclear Tests Case*

In the *Nuclear Tests Case*,[204] New Zealand requested the Court to examine the situation pursuant to paragraph 63 of the 1974 Decision,[205] which, New Zealand contended, gave it the "right" to request the resumption of the case filed in 1973. The main contentions of New Zealand were as follows:

- By virtue of both treaty law and customary international law, France has an obligation to conduct an environmental impact assessment before carrying out any further nuclear tests;
- France's conduct was illegal as it caused the introduction of radioactive material into the marine environment;
- In accordance with the precautionary principle, France is under an obligation to provide evidence that new underground nuclear tests will not result in introducing radioactive

---

[201] *See* Philippe Sands, *International Courts and the Precautionary Principle, in* de Chazournes, *supra* note 25.

[202] Request for an Examination of the Situation in Accordance with Paragraph 63 of the Court's Judgment of 20 December 1974 in the Nuclear Tests (New Zealand v. France) Case, 1995 ICJ 288.

[203] Hungary v. Slovakia, 1997 ICJ 7.

[204] *See* Prudence Taylor, *Testing Times for the World Court: Judicial Process and the 1995 French Nuclear Tests Case*, 8 COLO. J. INT'L ENVTL. L. POL'Y 199 (1997).

[205] This provided as follows:

Once the Court has found that a State has entered into a commitment concerning its future conduct it is not the Court's function to contemplate that it will not comply with it. However, the Court observes that if the basis of this Judgment were to be affected, the Applicant could request an examination of the situation in accordance with the provisions of the Statute.

material into the environment. According to New Zealand, the precautionary principle is "very widely accepted in contemporary international law."[206]

New Zealand further contended that by virtue of the precautionary principle, "the burden of proof fell on a State wishing to engage in potentially damaging environmental conduct to show in advance that its activities would not cause contamination."[207] New Zealand further referred to a "significant development" that has a direct bearing on the application of rules in the environmental field. Under the traditional approach to establishing violations, the burden of proof normally rests on the complainant, unless access to evidence was within the control of the respondent, as is the case with French nuclear testing. In the environmental field, a widely accepted and operative principle referred to as the "precautionary principle" has emerged whereby, in the event of potential significant environmental damage, the burden of proof is placed upon the party seeking to carry out the conduct to show that the conduct will not give rise to environmental damage. New Zealand quoted from Philippe Sands' book on environmental law:[208]

> The precautionary principle provides guidance in the development and application of international environmental law where there is scientific uncertainty. . . . The precautionary approach has been relied upon in relation to measures to protect . . . environmental media, especially the marine environment. The Preamble to the 1984 Ministerial Declaration of the International Conference on the Protection of the North Sea reflected a consciousness that States 'must not wait for proof of harmful effects before taking action,' since damage to the marine environment can be irreversible or remediable only at considerable expense and over long periods.[209]

New Zealand also referred to the Bergen Ministerial Declaration and the 1989 UNEP Governing Council decision, which recommended that all governments adopt the principle of precautionary action as a basis for their policy with regard to the prevention and elimination of marine pollution.

---

[206] *Supra* note 202, at para. 5.

[207] *Id.* at para. 34.

[208] *See* PHILIPPE SANDS, PRINCIPLES OF INTERNATIONAL ENVIRONMENTAL LAW (2d ed. 2003).

[209] *Id.* at 208–10.

New Zealand also based its arguments on the French Law No 95-101 of February 2, 1995, which refers to the precautionary principle "according to which the absence of certainty, having regard to scientific and technical knowledge at the time, should not hold up the adoption of effective and proportionate measures with a view to avoiding a risk of serious and irreversible damage to the environment at an economically acceptable cost."[210] New Zealand thus argued that before France can carry out underground nuclear tests, it must provide evidence that the tests will not result in the introduction of any radioactive material to the environment. In order to do this, argued New Zealand, a full environmental impact assessment in accordance with international standards must be carried out.[211]

Unfortunately, the Court agreed with the French contention that the 1974 decision dealt exclusively with atmospheric testing and, therefore, New Zealand could not make a request to reopen the former case in relation to any other form of nuclear testing—in this instance, underground testing. Therefore, the Court did not address the important issues raised by New Zealand, particularly in relation to environmental impact assessment and the precautionary principle. Perhaps fearing being branded as "anti-environment" the Court was careful to stress that its order was "without prejudice to the obligations of States to respect and protect the natural environment, obligations to which both New Zealand and France have in the present instance reaffirmed their commitment."[212] While the Court seems to have decided the issue on a triviality (similar to how they dealt with the case in 1974), the reference to the obligations of parties in relation to environmental protection (without, of course, specifying what they were) is a somewhat positive sign. Unfortunately, however, the Court failed to make use of this opportunity to further develop principles of international environmental law.

i.   Dissenting Opinion of Judge Weeramantry

As usual, it fell upon the dissenting judges to refer to international environmental law concepts. In a fairly lengthy dissenting opinion, Judge Weeramantry referred to several emerging principles of international environmental law, particularly, the concept of inter-generational rights, the precautionary principle, the environmental impact assessment principle and the principle that damage must not be caused to other states. With regard to inter-generational rights, Judge Weeramantry referred to the

---

[210] New Zealand's written pleadings, *available at* http://www.icj.org, para. 107.

[211] *Id.*, para. 108.

[212] *Id.*, para. 64.

works of Edith Brown Weiss[213] and noted that New Zealand's complaint alleged that France's conduct affected the rights of not only the present generation, but those of unborn posterity. He further pointed out that the World Court must regard itself as the trustee of those rights similar to a domestic court, which is the trustee of minors under domestic law. Pointing out that the Court has not made any pronouncements on this developing field, Judge Weeramantry articulated that this case gave it an opportunity to do so and that it raised issues of possible of harm to generations yet unborn.[214]

Judge Weeramantry referred to the precautionary principle essentially as an evidentiary principle, rather than a substantive one. He noted that when one party claims that another is causing irreversible environmental damage, very often the necessary information with regard to such damage is largely in the hands of the party causing such damage, thereby posing an evidentiary problem to the victim state. The principle that has evolved to meet this difficulty is the precautionary principle, which, according to Judge Weeramantry, is "gaining increasing support as part of the international law of the environment."[215]

He also referred to the Bergen Ministerial Declaration of 1990 as well as several international treaties embodying the precautionary principle[216] and noted that "It is a principle of relevance to New Zealand in its application to this Court and one which inevitably calls for consideration in the context of this case."[217] He noted that referring to the Maastricht Treaty, which incorporates the precautionary principle as the basis for EU policy on the environment, that principle would be applicable to European activity in relation to global threats. Judge Weeramantry also referred to Principle 15 of the Rio Declaration, which forms the basis of our present discussion.

---

[213] *See* EDITH BROWN WEISS, IN FAIRNESS TO FUTURE GENERATIONS: INTERNATIONAL LAW, COMMON PATRIMONY AND INTERGENERATIONAL EQUITY (1989) and FUTURE GENERATIONS AND INTERNATIONAL LAW (Emmanuel Agius et al. eds. 1998).

[214] Dissenting Opinion, Judge Weeramantry, *supra* note 202, at 341–42.

[215] *Id.* at 342. In this regard he relied on Philippe Sands' book, *supra* note 208.

[216] Again he referred to Philippe Sands, *supra* note 208, at 343. The treaties referred to are: 1992 Baltic Sea Convention; 1992 Maastricht Treaty which states that EU's policy on the environment "shall be based on the precautionary principle;" and 1992 Convention for the Protection of the Marine Environment of the North-East Atlantic (OSPAR Convention)—"the parties are required to report to the OSPAR Commission on the results of scientific studies which show that any potential dumping operations would not result in hazards to human health, harm to living resources or marine ecosystems, damage to amenities or interfere with other legitimate uses of the sea."

[217] *Supra* note 202, at 343.

It must be pointed out that the present day application of the precautionary principle does not confine it to the realm of an evidentiary rule. The definition adopted by Judge Weeramantry in this case is a rather limited one and departs from the accepted definition (to the extent that there is consensus on this issue). While its main function is procedural, it cannot be confined to the evidentiary realm—it is closely related to the burden of proof as well. Judge Weeramantry refers to the burden of proof in his dissenting opinion, but not in the context of the precautionary principle. He refers to it in the context of the obligation not to cause damage to the environment of other states. In this respect, Judge Weeramantry noted that the principle that damage must not be caused to other states is a fundamental principle of modern environmental law, and two approaches can be used regarding it: One approach is to place the burden of proof on the complainant (in this case, New Zealand) to show that it has established a *prima facie* case of dangers complained of. The second approach would be to "apply the principle of environmental law" under which, where environmental damage is threatened, the burden of proving that it will not cause damage will shift on to the author of the damage (in this case, France). According to Judge Weeramantry, the second approach is sufficiently well established in international law for the Court to act upon it. The principle of environmental law that he refers to here is not very clear. This is a variation of the precautionary principle, although Judge Weeramantry does not apply it in that context. He admonished the Court for having taken a strict literal interpretation and dismissing the case:

> On the basis of this strict and inflexible construction, matters of critical importance to the global environment are passed by without the benefit of a preliminary examination. . . .[218]

> I regret that the Court has not availed itself of the opportunity to enquire more fully into this matter and of making a contribution to some of the seminal principles of the evolving corpus of international environmental law. The Court has too long been silent on these issues and, in the words of ancient wisdom, one may well ask "If not now, when?"[219]

### ii. Dissenting Opinion of Judge Palmer

Sentiments similar to Judge Weeramantry were expressed by *ad hoc* judge Sir Geoffrey Palmer. In appending a dissenting opinion, Sir Geoffrey Palmer noted that the application before the Court appears to be unique.

---

[218] *Id.* at 361.

[219] *Id.* at 362.

He discussed the evolution of international environmental law and the new principles that have emerged in this field. Particular mention was made of the precautionary principle and the environmental impact assessment process.

New Zealand requested the Court to adjudge and declare that (1) conducting nuclear tests will constitute a violation of rights under international law of New Zealand and other states; and (2) it is unlawful for France to conduct such tests before it had undertaken an environmental impact assessment according to accepted international standards.[220] The New Zealand request refers to increasing scientific concern about the possible environmental impacts of underground nuclear testing and the radioactive contamination of the marine environment, including marine natural resources. While the Court was not in a position to make conclusions on scientific evidence on the basis of the material before it, the true question is the assessment of the level of risk, and the two states to the dispute have very different approaches.

Sir Geoffrey pointed out that there are several factors to be weighed in deciding whether New Zealand has satisfied a *prima facie* standard: these include the ultrahazardous nature of nuclear explosions; length of time that some nuclear materials remain hazardous; the fragile nature of the atoll structure; the high number of tests concentrated in a small area; the proximity to the marine environment; and the risks of radiation entering the food chain. He was in no doubt that France had engaged in activities that have substantially altered the natural environment of the test sites: "The nature of the risks inherent in the activity itself would suggest caution to be appropriate. Some means of calculating those risks is necessary to arrive at a determination of whether New Zealand has satisfied the test."[221] Some of these elements are: the magnitude of the recognizable risk of harm by nuclear contamination; the probability of risk materializing; and the costs of the measures needed to avert the risk.[222] Sir Geoffrey articulated that the Court should apply a risk-benefit analysis, balancing the risks of the activity and the probability of harm, on the one hand, and the utility of the activity and the measures needed to eliminate the risk, on the other:

> The gravity of the radiation harm if it occurs is likely to be serious for the marine environment. The magnitude of the risk that the harm will occur must be regarded as significant given the destruc-

---

[220] Dissenting Opinion, Sir Geoffrey Palmer, *supra* note 202, at 401.

[221] *Id.* at 404.

[222] *Id.*

tive force of nuclear explosions and the possibility of other distur-
bances or abnormal situations occurring in the course of the long
life of the dangerous substances. The costs of averting the risk in
this instance are low—they consist of France providing a full scientifically verifiable environment impact assessment in accordance
with modern environmental practice which demonstrates that the
proposed tests will not result in nuclear contamination.[223]

New Zealand also argued that the Court should reopen the 1974 judgment because of the changes in international law relating to the environment between the period 1974 and 1995. He noted that while the evolution
of international environmental law particularly since the Stockholm
Conference in 1972 has been remarkable, the Court has not contributed
to this development by refining the law. He pointed out that this case gave
the Court this opportunity. Discussing the contribution that the Stockholm
Declaration made to the development of principles of international environmental law, Sir Geoffrey noted that some of the principles have become
part of customary international law, binding on all states. The proliferation
of international conventions and treaties on the global environmental has
been considerable. The Rio Declaration refined, advanced, sharpened and
developed some of the principles adopted at Stockholm. In addition, some
new principles, including Principle 15 dealing with the precautionary
approach and Principle 17 on environmental impact assessment were also
adopted. While the Court has made a contribution in a limited sense to the
development of this field through the cases of *Corfu Channel*,[224] *Nauru*,[225]
and *Nuclear Tests*,[226] authoritative decisions in this area are scarce: "They
certainly lag behind the plethora of conventional law that has sprung into
existence in the more than 20 years spanning the life of this case."[227]

Noting the relationship between technology, development and environmental protection, Sir Geoffrey pointed out:

The obvious and overwhelming trend of these developments from
Stockholm to Rio has been to establish a comprehensive set of
norms to protect the global environment. There is widespread
recognition now that there are risks that threaten our common

---

[223] *Id.* at 405.

[224] United Kingdom v. Albania, 1949 ICJ 4.

[225] Certain Phosphate Lands in Nauru (Nauru v. Australia), 1992 ICJ 240.

[226] Australia v. France and New Zealand v. France, 1974 ICJ 253 and 457.

[227] *Supra* note 202, at 408.

survival. We cannot permit the onward march of technology and development without giving attention to the environmental limits that must govern these issues. Otherwise the paradigm of sustainable development embraced by the world at the Rio Conference cannot be achieved.[228]

Sir Geoffrey Palmer noted that New Zealand had relied, *inter alia*, on the precautionary principle and the obligation to prepare an environmental impact assessment embodied in the Noumea Convention to which both France and New Zealand are parties. New Zealand also sought to apply the emerging international law on environmental impact assessment and the precautionary principle to the facts of the case: "As the law now stands it is a matter of legal duty to first establish before undertaking an activity that the activity does not involve any unacceptable risk to the environment."[229] New Zealand argued that France was under an obligation to show, after preparing an environmental impact assessment, that its activity of carrying out nuclear testing does not cause environmental damage.

With regard to the precautionary principle, New Zealand submitted that it required two things: first, the assessment must be carried out before and not after the activities are undertaken; and second, it is for the state contemplating these activities to carry out the assessment and to demonstrate that there is no real risk. It is not for the potentially affected states to show that there will be a risk. Sir Geoffrey Palmer noted:

The norm involved in the precautionary principle has developed rapidly and may now be a principle of customary international law relating to the environment; . . .

There are obligations based on conventions that may be applicable here requiring environmental impact assessment and precautionary principle to be observed.[230]

While dissenting opinions are only *dicta*,[231] it is clear that the dissenting judges felt the need to discuss the relevant principles of international environmental law, particularly the precautionary principle and the envi-

---

[228] *Id.* at 409.

[229] *Id.* at 411.

[230] *Id.* at 412.

[231] Another dissenting opinion was appended by Judge Koroma. He too referred to environmental impact assessment, the precautionary principle and new developments in the field of environmental law.

ronmental impact assessment process, as they are of direct relevance to the case under consideration. They also felt that the Court let an important opportunity slip by—this would have been a good opportunity to contribute to the development of international environmental law, particularly in relation to nuclear testing, which poses a significant risk to human health and the environment.[232] It also has implications for the rights of future generations[233] and thus becomes an issue of equity.[234] It is a pity that the Court, yet again, passed on an opportunity to deal with an important issue on a mere technicality. As articulated by Sir Geoffrey:

> In this case the Court had an opportunity to make a contribution to one of the most critical environmental issues of our time. It has rejected this opportunity for technical legal reasons which could in my opinion have been decided the other way, fully consonant with proper legal reasoning.[235]

### b. Case Concerning the Gabcikovo Nagymaros Project[236]

In this case, while the Court did not explicitly refer to the precautionary principle, the judgment seems to indicate that the Court was partial toward its application. The Court noted that while no new peremptory norm of environmental law has emerged, "newly developed norms of environmental law are relevant for the implementation of the treaty"[237] and

---

[232] *See The Legality of the Threat or Use of Nuclear Weapons*, Advisory Opinion, 1996 ICJ 226 where the ICJ referred to the obligation of states to respect the environment of other states. *Cf., Legality of the Use by a Sstate of Nuclear Weapons in Armed Conflict*, an advisory opinion requested by the WHO, 1996 ICJ 66 where the ICJ noted that the issue fell outside the scope of WHO's activities.

[233] Both Sir Geoffrey and Judge Weeramantry referred to rights of future generations. According to the former, "In its essence, this case has to be understood as an environmental case. New technology has given humankind massive ability to alter the natural environment. The consequences of these activities need to be carefully analysed and examined unless we are to imperil those who come after us. It is a concern well known to international law," Dissenting Opinion, *supra* note 202, at 419. Judge Weeramantry also quoted from the seminal work of Edith Brown Weiss, *supra* note 213, and noted that the principle of intergenerational equity is "an important and rapidly developing principle of contemporary environmental law," *supra* note 214, at 341. He further articulated that the Court has not pronounced on this issue before and the present case has given a preeminent opportunity to do so as it raised the possibility of damage to generations yet unborn, *id.* at 342.

[234] For an extensive discussion of equity, *see* the separate opinion of Judge Weeramantry in the *Maritime Delimitation in the Area Between Greenland and Jan Mayen (Denmark v. Norway)*, 1993 ICJ 38.

[235] Dissenting opinion, *supra* note 202, at 420.

[236] 1997 ICJ 7. *See* Chapter 2, Section H.1.b, for a discussion of the case.

[237] *Supra* note 236, at para. 112.

noted that the parties could incorporate these norms into the Treaty between them jointly. The Court further recognized that "both Parties agree on the need to take environmental concerns seriously and to take the required precautionary measures"[238] but disagree on the consequences that this has for the project.

The Court further stressed that "the Project's impact upon, and its implications for, the environment are of necessity a key issue."[239] In order to evaluate the environmental risks, current standards have to be taken into consideration. In what seems to be an indirect reference to the precautionary principle, the Court noted:

> The Court is mindful that, in the field of environmental protection, vigilance and prevention are required on account of the often irreversible character of damage to the environment and of the limitations inherent in the very mechanism of reparation of this type of damage.[240]

Despite the criticism that the Court failed to contribute to the development of international environmental law,[241] the Court did, in fact, refer quite extensively to environmental issues—it noted, for example, that many environmental norms have emerged that must be taken into consideration by the parties; that prevention of environmental harm is necessary; reparation of damage plays a limited role in relation to environmental harm given the often irreparable damage to the environment; and in negotiating a new regime under the bilateral treaty between the parties, and most importantly, the project's impact on the environment is the key issue to be taken into consideration. The Court also referred to vigilance, continuous environmental impact assessment and sustainable development as well as the role of ecological necessity in relation to the law of state responsibility.[242]

As noted earlier, Judge Weeramantry appended a separate opinion. Again, his contention was that the majority of the Court did not sufficiently evaluate the application of modern principles of environmental law to the case before it.[243] Judge Weeramantry discussed three issues in relation to

---

[238] *Id.* at para. 113.

[239] *Id.* at para 140.

[240] *Id.*

[241] *See* Dissenting Opinion, Judge Weeramantry, *supra* note 214. *See also* Ida L. Bostian, *Flushing the Danube: The World Court's Decision Concerning the Gabcikovo Dam*, 9 COLO. J. INT'L ENVTL. L. & POL'Y 401 (1998).

[242] Discussed in Chapter 2, Section II.1.b.ii and iv.

[243] *See* Sands, *supra* note 25, who argued that "the Court was concerned with the

the case: the principle of sustainable development in balancing development and environmental protection; the principle of continuing environmental impact assessment; and the applicability of *inter-partes* principles for the resolution of issues with an *erga omnes* character such as environmental damage.[244]

## 2. The European Union

Perhaps the most amount of activity relating to the precautionary principle has taken place in the EU forum. The architects of the precautionary principle (or approach) being a member of the EU—Germany—may have had some influence on this. The precautionary approach has been adopted by the EU in relation to its general activities and constitutes one of its core principles. The Maastricht Treaty incorporates the precautionary principle as the basis for EU policy on the environment.[245] According to Article 174(2):

> Community policy on the environment shall aim at a high level of protection taking into account the diversity of situations in the various regions of the Community. It shall be based on the precautionary principle and on the principles that preventive action should be taken, that environmental damage should as a priority be rectified at source and that the polluter should pay.[246]

Although the precautionary principle is not defined in the European Union Treaty, the Commission considered that it is essentially used by decision makers in the management of risk: "[R]ecourse to the precautionary principle presupposes that potentially dangerous effects deriving from a phenomenon, product or process have been identified, and that scientific evaluation does not allow the risk to be determined with sufficient certainty."[247]

The Commission pointed out that when decision makers are faced with an unacceptable risk, scientific uncertainty and public concerns, they have

---

application of the law as it stood in 1989 when Hungary wrongfully suspended the work on the Project." However, it must be pointed out that the Court noted the emergence of new principles of international environmental law (without actually specifying what they were) and called upon the parties to negotiate a settlement in the light of these new principles.

[244] *See* the discussion in Chapter 2, Section H.1.b.v.

[245] *Available at* http://www.eurotreaties.com/maastrichtext.html.

[246] *Id.*, art. 174(2).

[247] Communication from the Commission on the Precautionary Principle COM (2000) 1 final, Brussels, Feb. 2, 2000, *available at* http://europa.eu.int/.

a duty to find answers. It further pointed out that the decision-making procedure should be transparent. It noted that where action is necessary, measures based on the precautionary principle should be:

- Proportionate to the chosen level of protection—this means that measures to be taken must be commensurate with the level of protection. Since risk cannot be reduced to zero, a total ban may not be proportional to the potential risk in a given situation. In certain situations, however, it is the only response.[248]
- Non-discriminatory in their application;
- Consistent with similar measures already taken;
- Based on an examination of potential benefits and costs of action or lack of action—this entails comparing the overall cost of action as well as lack of action, both in the short and long term. It includes non-economic considerations, and account should be taken of the general principle that the protection of health takes precedence over economic considerations;
- Subject to review in the light of new scientific data;[249] and
- Capable of assigning responsibility for producing the scientific evidence necessary for a more comprehensive risk assessment.[250]

The Commission further provided that where there is no prior authorization procedure, the user or the public authority must demonstrate the nature of the danger and the level of risk: "In such cases, a specific precautionary measure might be taken to place the burden of proof upon the producer, manufacturer or importer, but this cannot be made a general rule."[251] Thus, the Commission accepts that the reversal of the burden of proof should be the exception rather than the rule.

On April 13, 1999, the Council adopted a resolution urging the Commission "to be in the future even more determined to be guided by the precautionary principle in preparing proposals for legislation and in its other consumer-related activities and develop as priority clear and effective guidelines for the application of this principle."[252] The Commission's communication on the subject was prepared in response to this resolution.

---

[248] In this regard, *see* Community response in relation to the genetically modified food, discussed later in this section.

[249] Since new scientific data can emerge, it is necessary to revise action taken periodically in keeping with emerging data.

[250] *Supra* note 247.

[251] *Id.*

[252] *Id.* at 7.

The Commission noted that the precautionary principle goes beyond the short-term and medium-term approach to risks and is concerned with the well-being of future generations. It further provides that decision makers are constantly faced with the dilemma of seeking a balance between the rights of individuals, industry and organizations and the need to reduce or eliminate the risk of adverse effects to the environment or health:

> Finding the correct balance so that proportionate, non-discriminatory, transparent and coherent decisions can be arrived at, which at the same time provide the chosen level of protection, requires a structured decision making process with detailed scientific and other objective information. This structure is provided by the three elements of risk analysis: the assessment of risk, the choice of risk management strategy and the communication of the risk.[253]

The Commission noted that the decision whether to invoke the precautionary principle should be exercised when scientific information is insufficient or inconclusive but where there are indications that the potential impact on the environment, or human, animal or plant health may be potentially dangerous. The Commission, however, warned of unwarranted recourse to the precautionary principle "which in certain cases could serve as a justification for disguised protectionism."[254]

With regard to the status of the precautionary principle in the EU,[255] it has been noted that it has adopted measures in several instances in reliance on the principle, including measures to protect the ozone layer and climate change. The communication seeks to clarify a misunderstanding regarding the distinction between the precautionary principle and the search for zero risk. In other words, reliance on the precautionary principle does not mean that the objective is to search for zero risk, which is rarely to be found. The precautionary principle has been politically accepted as a risk management strategy in several fields.[256]

While Article 174(2) of the Maastricht Treaty mentions the precautionary principle only in relation to environmental protection, the Commission has taken the view that it is not so limited and that it applies in relation to consumer protection as well as protection of human, plant and

---

[253] *Id.*

[254] *Id.* at 8.

[255] *See* Wybe Th. Douma, *The Precautionary Principle in the European Union,* 9 RECEIL 132 (2000).

[256] Communication, *supra* note 247.

animal health.[257] It thus seems to adopt a much wider approach to the precautionary principle than what is envisaged under general international law. Thus, for example, in relation to general principles and requirements of food law, one of the guiding principles of the EU is the precautionary principle.[258]

Tracing the status of the precautionary principle under international law, the Commission noted that it "has been progressively consolidated in international environmental law, and so it has since become a full-fledged and general principle of international law."[259]

The Commission noted that an analysis of the precautionary principle reveals two distinct aspects: (1) the political decision to act or not to act as such; (2) how to act, i.e., the measures resulting from the application of the precautionary principle. With regard to the issue whether the precautionary principle is part of risk assessment or risk management, the Commission is of the view that it belongs in the general framework of risk analysis, and, in particular, risk management. The Communication of the European Commission on the Precautionary Principle[260] refers to four components of risk assessment before precautionary action is to be taken: (1) hazard identification; (2) hazard characterization; (3) appraisal of exposure of the agent under study; and (4) risk characterization—taking into account inherent uncertainties, probability, frequency and severity of known or potential environmental or health effects.[261]

While emphasizing the importance of the precautionary principle, the Commission, however, warns against justifying arbitrary decisions by reference to the precautionary principle. It points out that before a decision is taken whether to apply the precautionary principle, an evaluation of avail-

---

[257]  *Id.* at para. 3.

[258]  Commission of the European Communities, Brussels, Nov. 8, 2000 COM (2000), 716 final. The relevant section on the precautionary principle provides as follows: "The precautionary principle is relevant in those specific circumstances where risk managers have identified there are reasonable grounds for concern that an unacceptable level of risk to health exists but the supporting information and data may not be sufficiently complete to enable a comprehensive risk assessment to be made. When faced with these specific circumstances, decision makers or risk managers, may take measures or other actions to protect health based on the precautionary principle while seeking more complete scientific and other data."

[259]  *Id.* at 10.

[260]  Annex II of the EC Communication, Feb. 2, 2000 (COM (2000)1, *available at* http://europa.eu.int/eur-lex/en/com/cnc/2000/com2000_0001en01.pdf.

[261]  *Id.*

able scientific data must be made. In other words, an assessment of risks based on available data must be undertaken. If such assessment points to serious damage to the environment, human health or plant life, then the precautionary principle can be invoked. In such a situation, the decision makers have to decide whether to act or not.[262]

The precautionary principle has been invoked in several cases. In *Greenpeace v. France*[263] Greenpeace argued that the wording in Article 13(4) of Directive 90/220[264] seemed to give the impression that the competent authority is under an obligation to give its consent although this interpretation is not compatible with the Preamble or the "general scheme of the directive."[265] It was also argued that this interpretation is contrary to the precautionary principle, as new evidence may emerge after an issue has been referred to the competent authority. The Court, however, noted that:

> [o]bservance of the precautionary principle is reflected in the notifier's obligation, laid down in Article 11(6) of Directive 90/220, immediately to notify the competent authority of new information regarding the risks of the product to human health or the environment and the competent authority's obligation, laid down in Article 12(4), immediately to inform the Commission and the other Member States about this information and, secondly, in the right of any Member State, provided in Article 16 of the directive, provisionally to restrict or prohibit the use and/or sale on its territory of a product which has received consent where it has justifiable reasons to consider that it constitutes a risk to human health or the environment.[266]

The Opinion of Advocate General in this case is also important in this regard. With regard to the issue of the precautionary principle being undermined, the Advocate General referred to Principle 15 of the Rio Declaration and noted that: "it does not require an activity to be prohibited or subjected to draconian restrictions whenever it cannot be scientifically proved that there is absolutely no risk attaching to it, since it is

---

[262] *Id.* at 15. The Commission pointed out that the decision not to act may be a response in its own right.

[263] Case 6/99 *(Genetically Modified Maize Case). See* Marielle D. Matthee, *Greenpeace v. France, Case 6/99 (Genetically Modified Maize Case)*, 9(2) RECIEL 192 (2000).

[264] Directive 90/220 was repealed and replaced by Directive 2001/18/EC, *available at* http://europa.eu.int/.

[265] *Supra* note 262.

[266] *Id.*

common knowledge that lawyers have always described proving a negative as *probatio diabolica* and not without reason."[267] It thus seems that the Advocate General has applied a balancing test between the possible impact on the environment of activities of which the full impact is not known, on the one hand, and the possibility of imposing draconian restrictions on activities, on the other, on the ground that science has not proven that those activities are not absolutely safe. Since no activity can be considered as entailing zero risk, this approach has its merits. The EU has taken the view that undue restrictions on activities should not be imposed under the guise of the application of the precautionary principle.

The Advocate General proceeded to point out that Article 11(6) of Directive 90/220 requires the notifier to immediately inform the competent authority if new information becomes available with regard to the risks of the product to human health or the environment. The notifier must also revise the information and conditions specified there as well as take measures to protect human health and the environment. The Advocate General was, therefore, of the opinion that in the circumstances, it cannot be argued that the precautionary principle may not be observed.

In more recent cases involving the use of antibiotics as additives in animal feed, the precautionary principle has again been invoked. In *Pfizer Animal Health SA v. Council*[268] and *Alpharma Inc. v. Council*,[269] the Court of First Instance upheld the decision by the Council to ban the use of certain antibiotics as additives in animal feed.[270] It was held by the Court that despite uncertainty as to the link between the use of these antibiotics and increased resistance to those antibiotics in humans, the ban is not disproportionate given the need to protect public health. At the time the regulation was adopted, it had not been scientifically established that there was a link between the use of antibiotics in question and the development of resistance in humans. Thus, the Council was relying on the precautionary principle when promulgating this regulation.

---

[267] Opinion of Advocate General, delivered on Nov. 25, 1999, Case C-6/99, Association Greenpeace France and Others v. Ministere de l'Agriculture et de la Peche and Others, *available at* http://europa.eu.int/jurisp/cgi-bin/.

[268] Case T-13/99, European Court of Justice, summary available in the official journal of the European Communities, Nov. 23, 2002.

[269] Case T-70/99, *id.*

[270] Council regulation adopted on Dec. 17, 1998, banned the use of four antibiotics as additives in animal feed: virginiamycin, bacitracin zinc, spiramycin and tylosin phosphate.

The Council regulation was challenged by two pharmaceutical companies (producers of two of the banned antibiotics) seeking an annulment of the Council regulation before the Court of First Instance.

The recommendations made in the report on the subject of microbial threat state that resistance to antimicrobial agents is a major public health problem in Europe.[271] This can result in a substantial rise in the number of complications in the treatment of certain diseases including an increased risk of mortality. The reasons for this have not been entirely clarified, although there is broad consensus that this is primarily caused by the excessive and inappropriate use of antibiotics in human medicine. These bodies have also recommended increased research in this field. In addition, they recommended the systematic replacement of all antibiotics used as growth promoters by safer alternatives. Several organizations, including the WHO, have recommended the immediate or gradual discontinuance of them as growth promoters in animals. While it has not been established that the resistance can be transmitted from animals to human beings, it has not been excluded either.

It was noted that "at the time when the measures were adopted, the transfer and development of such resistance had not yet been scientifically established in respect of streptogramins."[272]

Pfizer, on the other hand, argued that scientific literature does not support the conclusion that there could be a transfer of resistance to virginiamycin from animals to human beings. Scientific literature shows that scientific knowledge relating to such transfer "is either totally absent or inadequate"[273] although it is accepted that the issue of antibiotic resistance is an important public health issue.

The Court held that Pfizer failed to establish that the Community regulation was unlawful. In this regard, the Court noted that once the Commission decides to initiate the procedure in Article 24 of Directive 70/524, to carry out at the Community level its own risk assessment in respect of the product concerned, and is independent of the one carried out by national authorities. Only the lawfulness of the Community-level risk assessment is subject to judicial review in this case.

Several conclusions can be drawn from the above survey of the precautionary principle in the EU. First, the approach taken by the EU is that

---

[271] *Supra* note 269, para. 37.

[272] *Id.*, para. 41.

[273] *Id.*, para. 50.

measures taken pursuant to the precautionary principle are *provisional:* i.e., they are valid until such time that scientific data is available. Secondly, it is clear that the EU considers the precautionary principle as a binding principle rather than an approach. Finally, the EU applies the principle to a much broader category of issues than under international law where it has been confined to environmental issues. The EU, by contrast, applies it to food safety, public health and animal and plant health in addition to the environment.[274]

One area of tension between the EU and the United States has arisen in relation to the precautionary principle. They have clashed over the regulation of the number of health and environmental risks "from genetically engineered foods to climate change to beef. Pervading these specific controversies has been a larger debate about the proper stance of government: how should regulators act in the face of uncertainty about risk?"[275] It has been articulated that despite the impression given that the EU is more pro-precautionary principle than the United States, this has not always been the case and that precautionary measures have been part of U.S. law since the early 1970s.[276]

## 3. Other Tribunals

Both the WTO and the International Tribunal for the Law of the Sea (ITLOS) have dealt with the precautionary principle in some disputes before it.

### a. ITLOS

In the *Southern Bluefin Tuna Cases,*[277] which were filed by New Zealand and Australia against Japan, Australia and New Zealand contended that Japan had violated several provisions of the Law of the Sea Convention, the 1993 Convention for the Conservation of Southern Bluefin Tuna[278] and customary international law.

---

[274] *See* Nicolas de Sadeleer, *The Enforcement of the Precautionary Principle by German, French and Belgian Courts,* 9(2) RECIEL 144 (2000); and Peter H. Sand, *The Precautionary Principle: A European Perspective,* 6 HUM. & ECOLOGICAL RISK ASSESSMENT 445–58 (2000).

[275] *See* Wiener & Rogers, *supra* note 45.

[276] *Id.*

[277] Southern Bluefin Tuna Cases (New Zealand v. Japan and Australia v. Japan), Aug. 27, 1999, Nos. 3 and 4, International Tribunal for the Law of the Sea, *available at* http://www.itlos.org. *See* Simon Marr, *The Southern Bluefin Tuna Cases: The Precautionary Approach and Conservation and Management of Fish Resources,* 11 EUR. J. INT'L L. 815–31 (2000).

[278] 1819 UNTS 360, signed May 10, 1993, entered into force May 30, 1994.

Both Australia and New Zealand contended that the parties must act consistently with the precautionary principle when fishing for southern bluefish tuna. The Tribunal noted that:

> [t]he parties should in the circumstances act with *prudence and caution* to ensure that effective conservation measures are taken to prevent serious harm to the stock of southern bluefin tuna;[279]

> Considering that there is scientific uncertainty regarding measures to be taken to conserve the stock of southern bluefin tuna and that there is no agreement among the parties as to whether the conservation measures taken so far have led to the improvement in the stock of southern bluefin tuna.[280]

While the parties seem to have relied on the precautionary principle (Japan denied its relevance), the Tribunal does not refer to it specifically, but refers to *scientific uncertainty* regarding measures to be taken to conserve the stock of southern bluefin tuna as well as to the need to exercise "prudence and caution."

### i. Separate Opinion of Judge Laing

The separate opinion appended by Judge Laing is pertinent in this regard. He specifically referred to the precautionary approach and traced its history in relation to both environmental protection and the management of marine living resources. He noted that the applicants relied on several provisions of the UNCLOS, the 1993 Convention on Southern Bluefin Tuna and their obligations under general international law, in particular, the precautionary principle which they argued:

> [m]ust be applied by States in taking decisions about actions which entail threats of serious or irreversible damage to the environment while there is scientific uncertainty about the effect of such actions. The principle requires caution and vigilance in decision-making in the face of such uncertainty.[281]

Judge Laing noted that the Tribunal's order did not refer to the precautionary principle. Instead, it calls upon the parties to act with "prudence

---

[279] *Supra* note 277, at para. 77 (emphasis added). It may be recalled that the ICJ used similar words in the *Case Concerning the Gabcikovo Nagymaros Project. See supra* note 240 and accompanying text.

[280] *Id.*, para. 79.

[281] Separate Opinion, Judge Laing, *id.*, para. 11.

and caution."[282] The Tribunal also referred to the scientific disagreement about appropriate measures to conserve the fish stocks and noted that the Tribunal's statements are "pregnant with meaning."[283] Looking at the background on environmental precaution, Judge Laing noted that it:

> [l]argely stems from diplomatic practice and treaty making in the spheres, originally, of international marine pollution and, now, of biodiversity, climate change, pollution generally and, broadly, the environment. Its main thesis is that, in the face of serious risk to or grounds (as appropriately qualified) for concern about the environment, scientific uncertainty or the absence of complete proof should not stand in the way of positive action to minimize risks or take actions of a conservatory, preventative or curative nature.[284]

He further noted that two other issues have played a role in the discourse on the precautionary principle: concern for future generations and difficulties relating to proof.[285] The precautionary principle seeks to provide guidance to policymakers and other decision makers and also shifts the burden of proof to the state or the perpetrator. It has been adopted in recent documents relating to environmental protection. Quoting D'Amato and Engel, Judge Laing noted that the notion of precautionary approach has been accepted for international action even if the consequences of its application remain open to interpretation.[286]

Although he concluded that it is not possible to determine that customary international law recognizes the precautionary principle, Judge Laing pointed out that it cannot be denied that the UNCLOS adopts a precautionary approach.[287] He cited several provisions as examples.[288] He further noted that the Tribunal cited possible serious harm to the marine environment as the crucial criterion for the indication of provisional measures. Judge Laing noted that the Tribunal's willingness to base the indication of provisional measures on the language of Article 290 of UNCLOS must be approached with prudence and that Article 194(5) of the Con-

---

[282] *Id.* at para. 77.

[283] *Id.* at para. 12.

[284] *Id.* at para. 13.

[285] *Id.*

[286] *Id.* at para. 14.

[287] *Id.* at para. 16.

[288] Some of the articles he has cited are: Preamble, arts. 63–66, 61, and 116–119, *supra* note 278.

vention is rather equivocal and the reference to precautionary approach is very general:

> It becomes evident that the Tribunal has adopted the precautionary approach for the purposes of provisional measures in such a case as the present. In my view, adopting an *approach*, rather than a principle, appropriately imports a certain degree of flexibility and tends, though not dispositively, to underscore reticence about making premature pronouncements about desirable normative structures.[289]

This case highlights the role that the precautionary principle can play in avoiding serious damage to the environment—in this case, the marine environment. Although no explicit reference was made to the precautionary principle by the Tribunal, it is obvious that the Tribunal was influenced by it. Indeed, the reference to "caution and prudence" in the opinion signifies this influence. The indication of provisional measures is a useful way to avoid significant harm to the environment and this tool has been used in international disputes very often.[290] When used together with the precautionary principle, the remedy of provisional measures becomes even more meaningful. Even in the face of scientific uncertainty, if there is sufficient evidence to suggest the occurrence of significant environmental harm, the indication of provisional measures would be justified and necessary to prevent serious damage to the environment. Judge Laing seems to suggest that even if precaution is not adopted as a legal principle, it provides a flexible approach in avoiding serious damage to the environment.

## ii. Separate Opinion of Judge Treves

Judge Treves also referred to the precautionary principle in his separate opinion. He questioned whether the urgency contended in the present case was such as to warrant the indication of provisional measures.[291] He further noted that:

> While, of course, a precautionary approach by the parties in their future conduct is necessary, such precautionary approach, in my opinion, is necessary also in the assessment by the Tribunal of the urgency of the measures it might take. In the present case, it would seem to me that the requirement of urgency is satisfied only in the light of such precautionary approach. I regret that this is not stated explicitly in the Order.

---

[289] *Supra* note 277, at para. 18.

[290] *See* the cases discussed *infra* note 292.

[291] *See* Separate Opinion, Judge Treves, *supra* note 277, para. 8.

I fully understand the reluctance of the Tribunal in taking a position as to whether the precautionary approach is a binding principle of customary international law. Other courts and tribunals,
recently confronted with this question, have avoided to give an
answer. . . . It is not necessary to hold the view that this approach
is dictated by a rule of customary international law. The precautionary approach can be seen as a logical consequence of the need
to ensure that, when the arbitral tribunal decides on the merits,
the factual situation has not changed. In other words, a precautionary approach seems to me *inherent* in the very notion of provisional measures."[292]

Moreover, Judge Treves noted that the Straddling Fish Stocks Agreement adopts the precautionary principle when it stated that "the absence
of adequate scientific information shall not be used as a reason for postponing or failing to take conservation and management measures."[293]

In the *MOX Plant Case*[294] also before the ITLOS, Ireland argued that
the United Kingdom had failed to cooperate with Ireland in relation to
protecting the marine environment of the Irish Sea, *inter alia*, by refusing
to share information with Ireland and refusing to carry out a proper EIA
of the impacts on the marine environment of the MOX plant.[295] Ireland
also argued that:

[t]he precautionary principle places the burden on the United
Kingdom to demonstrate that no harm would arise from discharges
and other consequences of the operation of the MOX plant,
should it proceed, and that this principle might usefully inform
the assessment by the Tribunal of the urgency of the measures it is
required to take in respect of the operation of the MOX plant.[296]

The United Kingdom, on the other hand, denied that the precautionary principle had any application to the facts of this case.

The Tribunal, while noting that the circumstances of the case did not
warrant the prescription of provisional measures requested by Ireland, it
did, nonetheless, consider that the duty to cooperate is a fundamental prin-

---

[292] *Id.*, para. 9 (emphasis added).

[293] *Supra* note 194, art. 7(2).

[294] Ireland v. United Kingdom, Dec. 3, 2001, International Tribunal for the Law of
the Sea, No. 10 (Request for Provisional Measures), *available at* http://www.itlos.org/.

[295] *Id.*, para. 26.

[296] *Id.*, para. 71.

ciple both under UNCLOS and general international law.[297] It called on the parties to cooperate and enter into consultations in order to exchange further information; monitor risks of the operation of the MOX plant; and devise measures, as appropriate, to prevent pollution of the marine environment as a result of the operation of the MOX plant.[298] However, no reference was made by the Tribunal to the precautionary principle.

Judge Treves in the *Southern Bluefish Tuna Case* made an interesting link between the precautionary principle and the indication of provisional measures. He articulated that a precautionary approach is inherent in the notion of provisional measures. In other words, provisional measures are indicated in order to prevent damage, even if the occurrence of damage or its magnitude is uncertain. The ICJ has held in many cases that provisional measures are indicated[299] to prevent irreparable prejudice[300] or to preserve the rights of the parties until such time that the Court makes a determination on the merits of the case.[301] It would be interesting to see whether parties to future disputes would use this *dicta* and request provisional measures for activities that are likely to cause significant environmental damage to a state or the global commons even though the causal link between the activity and the possible damage has not been conclusively established. Provisional measures would be a good tool to prevent imminent damage to the environment. Such measures would not be a useful tool in relation to contemporary environmental problems that have been caused by the accumulation of certain pollutants in the environment discharged over a long

---

[297] *Id.*, paras. 81 and 82.

[298] *Id.*, para. 89.

[299] Article 41 of the ICJ Statute deals with provisional measures. It provides that:

1. The Court shall have the power to indicate, if it considers that circumstances so require, any provisional measures which ought to be taken to preserve the respective rights of either party.

2. Pending the final decision, notice of the measures suggested shall forthwith be given to the parties and to the Security Council.

[300] In the *United States Diplomatic and Consular Staff in Tehran (Hostages Case) (USA v. Iran)*, 1979 ICJ 7, the ICJ said that "Whereas the power of the Court to indicate provisional measures under Article 41 of the Statute of the Court has as its object to preserve the respective rights of the parties pending the decision of the Court, and presupposes that irreparable prejudice should not be caused to rights which are the subject of disputes in judicial proceedings." *Id.*, para. 36.

[301] In *Military and Paramilitary Activities In and Against Nicaragua (Nicaragua v. USA)*, 1986 ICJ 14, the Court stated that "Whereas the power of the Court to indicate provisional measures under Article 41 of the Statute has as its object to preserve the respective rights of either party pending the decision of the Court." *Id.*, para. 32.

period of time. It can, however, play a useful role in a bilateral context in relation to activities likely to cause a significant impact on the environment.

Judge Treves also referred to the obvious reluctance of international adjudicatory bodies to deal with the legal status of the precautionary principle. Despite the fact that the applicants in this case argued vehemently that the precautionary principle is part of customary international law, the Tribunal simply avoided any reference to the precautionary principle, let alone deal with its legal status. This trend can be seen in the ICJ too. While Hungary relied heavily on the precautionary principle in the *Case Concerning the Gabcikovo Nagymaros Project*, the Court did not make any reference to it except to the need to exercise caution.

This reluctance on the part of tribunals is both disappointing and perplexing. It is almost as if the tribunals feel that they are "interfering" in the process of the evolution of principles and are very hesitant to "take the bull by the horns." A little help from these bodies will go a long way in refining these concepts and better articulating them, particularly when the parties themselves have invoked these concepts. Their reluctance to intervene at all is hindering this process of evolution and could even stultify its development.

### b.  Some National Judiciaries in South Asia

National judiciaries, on the other hand, have been more forthcoming and articulate in dealing with the emerging principles of international environmental law. In the *Vellore Citizens Welfare Forum v. Union of India*,[302] the Indian Supreme Court specifically referred to the precautionary principle, and its counterpart in the neighboring Sri Lanka followed suit in the *Eppawala Phosphate Mining Case*[303] with regard to sustainable development and the precautionary principle. In their opinion these were "principles" which must be followed by government officials.

In the *Eppawala Phosphate Mining Case*, Judge Amerasinghe noted:

It might be noted, particularly by the 4th respondent, that Principle 15 of the Rio De Janeiro Declaration marked a progressive shift from the preventive principle recognized in Principles 6 and 7 of the Stockholm Declaration which was predicated upon the

---

[302]  AIR 1996 SC 2715.

[303]  Tikiri Banda Bulankulama et. al. v. The Secretary, Ministry of Industries et al., SC Application No. 884/99 (FR), *available at* http://www.elaw.org/custom/custompages/resourcesDetail.asp?profile_ID=163.

notion that only when pollution threatens to exceed the assimilative capacity to render it harmless, should it be prevented from entering the environment. . . . The precautionary principle acts to reverse the assumption in the Stockholm Declaration and, in my view, ought to be acted upon by the 4th respondent. Therefore if ever pollution is discerned, uncertainty as to whether the assimilative capacity has been reached should not prevent measures being insisted upon to reduce such pollution from reaching the environment.[304]

If national judiciaries are venturing into the process of articulating these principles, it is difficult to understand why international tribunals are reluctant to do so. It may be because they do not want to upset the status quo, but it also means that they are not contributing to the development of the law, by not even mentioning these emerging principles.

## 4. The WTO—Beef-Hormone Case

The WTO has been confronted with precautionary measures from time to time. In several of the cases before the dispute settlement body, the issue whether precautionary measures justified action by a member state came to the forefront. The issue came to a head in the *Beef-Hormone case* between the EU, on the one hand, and the United States and Canada, on the other.[305] A discussion of the decision of the WTO Appellate Body is instructive in this regard.

This appeal resulted from the legal interpretation in the two Panel Reports on the subject. The Panel dealt with a complaint against the European Communities (EC) relating to an EC prohibition of imports of meat and meat products to which either natural hormones or synthetic hormones identified in the Directives had been administered for growth promotion purposes.[306] Directive 81/602 prohibited placing on the market of both domestically produced and imported meat and meat products that had the substance administered. It provided for two exceptions. Directive 88/146 prohibited the administration of some synthetic hormones to farm animals. It explicitly prohibited both intra-EEC trade and importation from third countries of such meat or meat products. Trade in meat and meat products from animals treated with such substances for therapeutic or zootechnical purposes was allowed under certain conditions.

---

[304] *Id.*

[305] *EC Measures Concerning Meat and Meat Products (Hormones)*, Report of the Appellate Body, WTO, *available at* www.worldtradelaw.net/reports/wtoab/ec-hormones(ab).pdf. Australia, New Zealand and Norway were third participants.

[306] The three Council Directives in question were: 81/602/EEC, July 31, 1981; 88/146/EEC, Mar. 7, 1988; and 88/299/EEC, May 17, 1988.

These three Directives were repealed and replaced in 1997[307] but maintained the prohibition of the administration of hormones to farm animals. This Directive continued to allow members to authorize the administration of such substances for therapeutic or zootechnical purposes. It also allows, under certain conditions, the placing on the market and importation from third countries of meat and meat products from animals to which these substances have been administered for therapeutic and zootechnical purposes.

The U.S. Panel Report and the Canadian Panel Report reached the same conclusions: (1) The EC, by maintaining sanitary measures, which are not based on a risk assessment, has acted inconsistently with Article 5.1 of the SPS Agreement;[308] by adopting arbitrary or unjustifiable distinctions the EC has acted contrary to Article 5.5 of the SPS Agreement;[309] and by maintaining sanitary measures not based on international standards without justification, the EC has acted inconsistently with Article 3.1 of the SPS Agreement.[310]

### a. *Arguments by the EC*

In 1997 the EC notified the Dispute Settlement Body of its decision to appeal certain law issues covered in the Panel Reports. The EC argued that the Panel had erred in the allocation of the burden of proof in three respects: in allocating the burden of proof under Articles 3.3 and 5.1 of the SPS Agreement and under that Agreement in general. The EC also claimed that the Panel erred in law by not according deference to certain aspects of EC measures: first the decision by the EC to apply a higher standard than that recommended by Codex; the EC's scientific assessment and management of the risk from hormones at issue; and third, the EC's adherence to the precautionary principle. Although many interesting arguments were advanced by the parties to the dispute, attention will be paid to their treatment of the precautionary principle. The EC's comments with regard to the precautionary principle are of particular relevance here:

---

[307] Directive 96/22/EC, Apr. 29, 1996.

[308] The WTO Agreement on the Application of Sanitary and Phytosanitary Measures (SPS Agreement), *available at* http://www.wto.org/. Article 5.1 requires members to ensure that their sanitary or phytosanitary measures are based on an assessment of the risks to human, animal or plant life or health.

[309] Article 5.5 requires members to avoid arbitrary or unjustifiable distinctions in the levels it considers to be appropriate in different situations, if such distinctions result in discrimination or a disguised restriction on international trade.

[310] Article 3.1 requires members to base their sanitary and phytosanitary measures on international standards, guidelines or recommendations in order to harmonize these measures.

The European Communities submits that the Panel erred in law in considering that the precautionary principle was only relevant for "provisional measures" under Article 5.7 of the SPS Agreement. *The precautionary principle is already, in the view of the European Communities, a general customary rule of international law or at least a general principle of law, the essence of which that it applies not only in the management of a risk, but also in the assessment thereof.* . . . The European Communities asserts that Articles 5.1 and 5.2 and Annex A.4 of the SPS Agreement do not prescribe a particular type of risk assessment, but rather simply identify factors that need to be taken into account. Thus, these provisions do not prevent Members from being cautious when setting health standards in the face of conflicting scientific information and uncertainty.[311]

The EC also contended that the Panel's interpretation of risk and risk assessment is also flawed. Risk does not mean harm or adverse effect. Risk is the potential for harm, and the mere possibility of risk arising suffices for the purposes of Articles 5.1 and 5.2 of the SPS Agreement. The concept of risk in the SPS Agreement is qualitative, not quantitative.

### b. Arguments by the United States

Several arguments were advanced by the United States including in relation to the precautionary principle. The United States contended that the EC's claim that the precautionary principle is a generally accepted principle of international law is erroneous:

The United States does not consider that the "precautionary principle" represents a principle of customary international law; rather, it may be characterized as an "approach"—the content of which may vary from context to context. The SPS Agreement does recognize a precautionary approach. . . . The EC's invocation of a "precautionary principle" cannot create a risk assessment where there is none, nor can a "principle" create "sufficient scientific evidence" where there is none.[312]

### c. Arguments by Canada

Similar to the United States, Canada was of the view that the precautionary principle is not part of customary international law. It was of the view that the Panel did not take a position on whether it was part of international law:

---

[311] *Id.*, para. 16 (footnotes omitted) (emphasis added).

[312] *Id.*, para. 43.

The "precautionary principle" should be characterized as the "precautionary approach" because it has not yet become part of public international law. Canada considers the precautionary approach or concept as an emerging principle of international law, which may in the future crystallize into one of the "general principles of law recognized by civilized nations," within the meaning of Article 38(1)(c) of the Statute of the International Court of Justice.[313]

### d. Dispute Settlement Body (DSB)

With regard to the controversy surrounding the precautionary principle in international law, the DSB noted that its status under international law continues to be the subject of debate among academics, law practitioners, regulators and judges:

> The precautionary principle is regarded by some as having crystallized into a general principle of customary international *environmental* law. Whether it has been widely accepted by Members as a principle of *general or customary international law* appears less than clear.[314]

The DSB was of the view that it is not necessary for it to take a position on this "important, but abstract,"[315] question. The Panel itself did not do so with regard to the status of the precautionary principle in international law: "The principle, at least outside the field of international environmental law, still awaits authoritative formulation."[316] However, the DSB felt it important to note the relationship between the precautionary principle and the SPS Agreement:

- The principle has not been written into the SPS Agreement as a ground for justifying SPS measures, which are otherwise inconsistent with Members' obligations under the Agreement;
- The precautionary principle is reflected in Articles 5.7 and 3.3 of the SPS Agreement, which recognize the right of members to establish their own appropriate level of sanitary protection that may be higher than international standards;
- With regard to the issue whether sufficient scientific evidence exists to warrant a particular sanitary measure, it is necessary to bear in mind that governments commonly act from pru-

---

[313] *Id.*, para. 60.

[314] *Id.*, para. 123.

[315] *Id.*

[316] *Id.*

dence and precaution where risks of irreversible (e.g., life-ter-
minating) damage to human health are concerned;

- The precautionary principle does not, by itself, relieve the Panel
from the duty of applying the normal principles of treaty interpretation in reading the provisions of the SPS Agreement.[317]

Thus, the DSB agreed with the Panel finding that the precautionary
principle does not override the provisions of Articles 5.1 and 5.2 of the SPS
Agreement.[318] The Appellate Body upheld the decision of the DSB in
January 1998. The EU continues to defend its position that these growth
hormones may be harmful to humans, and the United States continues to
claim that they are not.[319]

The distinction that the Dispute Settlement Body has made in this dispute between the status of the precautionary principle under international
environmental law and the status of the precautionary principle under general international law seems artificial and merits some comment. It does
convey the message that a customary principle can exist under a specialized
field,[320] but not under general international law. If a practice meets the
requirements of Article 38(1) of the Statute of the ICJ,[321] does it matter
whether that practice originated from the environmental field or the
human rights field or any other field? Article 2(4) of the UN Charter deals
with the non-use of force in international relations. Obviously it originated
from the law of armed conflict and may not have any application in some
other fields of international law, but it is nonetheless considered a *customary international law principle.* While there may be customary principles of
general application, such as the principle of good faith, proportionality or
the principle of cooperation, most customary international law principles
originated from a particular field of international law. While international
law has branched out into specialized fields due to their complexity or
sheer volume of material, international law cannot be compartmentalized

---

[317] *Id.,* para. 124.

[318] *Id.,* para. 125.

[319] *See* Wiener & Rogers, *supra* note 45, at 327. The authors also discuss the FDA ban
on blood donors who had spent three months or more in the United Kingdom or five
years or more anywhere in Europe since 1980 on the ground that Bovine Spongiform
Encephalopathy (BSE) could be transmitted not only by eating contaminated beef but
also by transfusions of blood from people who had eaten contaminated beef. This was
titled a "Precautionary Measure" although there have been no studies corroborating this
causal relationship. *Id.* at 332.

[320] This should not be confused with regional customary international law.

[321] As discussed in Chapter 2, Section J, the two requirements are: state practice and
*opinio juris*—the conviction that a practice is binding on states.

into these artificial categories without any overlap. For example, as we saw in Chapter 1, environmental protection has implications for virtually all areas of international law, particularly, human rights, international trade, economic law and now increasingly in relation to security and terrorism.[322] This cross-fertilization is inevitable given the interdependent nature of states in an increasingly globalized world. Thus, to argue that a particular practice has become part of customary law of the environment but not under general international law seems artificial. It must be remembered that these specialized fields exist within a broad framework of general international law.

In the *Beef-Hormone Case*[323] Canada draws a distinction between customary international law and a general principle of law under Article 38(1)(c) of the ICJ Statute and considers that the "precautionary approach" (as opposed to the precautionary principle) is an emerging principle of international law that will crystallize into a general principle under Article 38(1)(c). Canada does not regard it as an emerging customary international law principle. What is the significance of this distinction? Even in the absence of *opinio juris* and state practice, a particular concept can become binding as a general principle. Canada may be implying that consistent state practice and *opinio juris* are lacking in relation to the precautionary principle, but it is being increasingly recognized as a principle under the municipal law of states and hence can become a general principle of international law under Article 38(1)(c).[324] This seems a more plausible argument than the one articulated by the Dispute Settlement Body.

The politics of the precautionary principle reflects a constant tug-of-war between opponents and proponents of the principle, while many states have changed camp at different times or in relation to different issues. For example, the United States did not oppose the adoption of Principle 15 of the Rio Declaration but insisted on the inclusion of cost-effective measures, and opposed it during the Biosafety Protocol negotiations with the Miami Group.[325] The Group of 77 (developing countries), while being wary of it during the Rio Conference, vehemently defended it during negotiations of the Biosafety Protocol with the support of the European Union.[326] Europe, while being largely more pro-precautionary principle than the United States, was divided during the *Nuclear Tests Case* when France argued that

---

[322] *See* NORMAN MYERS, ULTIMATE SECURITY (1993).

[323] *Supra* note 302.

[324] *See* DAMROSCH ET AL., *supra* note 97, at 118.

[325] *See* Sand, *supra* note 51.

[326] *Id.*

the legal status of the precautionary principle was uncertain in response to New Zealand's claim that it was part of customary international law.[327]

The conflict between the EU and the United States over issues ranging from genetically modified food to climate change and to beef reflects the larger debate on how regulators should act in the face of uncertainty about risk.[328] While the EU has expressly adopted the precautionary principle, the United States has not. In the *Benzene Case*,[329] the U.S. Supreme Court stated that the agency must demonstrate "significant risk" before regulating.[330] Thus, the United States adopts a scientific risk assessment as the basis for regulation.[331] However, to say that Europe is more precautionary than the United States is an over-simplification, as the reality is different if looked at different issues. Thus, a case-by-case analysis is necessary.[332]

Precaution does not necessarily mean prohibition. The action taken or mandated would depend on the nature and the probability of risk. However, it is not known for sure whether precautionary measures are effective or whether they tackle the most significant risks. It has been articulated that precaution can be considered as a continuous variable. There is no single accepted version of the precautionary principle. Three main versions of the principle are distinguished here:

*Version 1: Uncertainty does not justify inaction.* In its most basic form, the precautionary principle is a principle that permits regulation in the absence of complete evidence about the particular risk scenario. . . .

*Version 2: Uncertainty justifies action.* This version of the precautionary principle is more aggressive. When an activity raises threats of harm to human health or the environment, precautionary measures should be taken even if some cause and effect relationships are not fully established. . . .

*Version 3: Uncertainty requires shifting the burden and standard of proof.* This version of the precautionary principle is the most aggressive.

---

[327] *See* discussion, in Section E.1.a.

[328] *See* Wiener & Rogers, *supra* note 45.

[329] Industrial Union Dept., AFL-CIO v. API (1980), referred to in Wiener & Rogers, *supra* note 45, at 318.

[330] *Id.*

[331] *Id.*

[332] *Id.*

It holds that uncertain risk requires forbidding the potentially risky activity until the proponent of the activity demonstrates that it poses no (or acceptable) risk.[333]

## F.  RELATIONSHIP BETWEEN PREVENTION, PRECAUTION AND ENVIRONMENTAL ASSESSMENT

As noted above, the principle of prevention emerged upon the realization that the react-after-the-event approach was not the most conducive way to handle environmental issues.[334] While this signified the earlier approach to environmental issues, particularly by developed countries during the time of their industrialization, it is not the best approach to environmental protection. Certainly, species and eco-systems may be lost in the process, which may never be revived in their original form. Moreover, repairing environmental damage may be prohibitively expensive and cannot compensate for lost eco-systems and species. As a result, and faced with growing environmental problems, states started looking at other approaches to environmental protection. They realized that an anticipatory approach to environmental protection was necessary in order to avert serious environmental problems. Principle 21 of the Stockholm Declaration would have contributed to this process. However, Principle 21 discusses the principle of prevention in a transboundary context, not requiring prevention *per se.* Thus, the principle of prevention is wider in scope than Principle 21.

Many environmental instruments embody a preventive approach. The Stockholm Declaration embodies this principle in relation to pollution of the seas:

States shall take all possible steps to prevent pollution of the seas by substances that are liable to create hazards to human health, to harm living resources and marine life, to damage amenities or to interfere with other legitimate uses of the sea.[335]

No comparable provision exists in relation to other forms of pollution. It must be noted, however, that at the time the Stockholm Declaration was adopted, many other forms of pollution were not prevalent. This could be the reason for stressing only the necessity for the prevention of the pollution of the seas.

---

[333]  *Id.,* at 320–21.

[334]  *See* discussion in Chapter 1, Section A.1.

[335]  Principle 7 of the Stockholm Declaration, *supra* note 19.

The draft Earth Charter called upon states to "prevent pollution of any part of the environment and allow no build-up of radioactive, toxic, or other hazardous substances."[336] The Bergen Ministerial Declaration pointed out that "Environmental measures must anticipate, *prevent* and attack the causes of environmental degradation"[337]

It is obvious, that there is a close relationship between sustainable development, the precautionary principle and the principle of prevention. While the ultimate goal is to achieve sustainable development by preventing environmental degradation, the precautionary principle will assist toward that end. Thus, the objective of preventing environmental degradation can be achieved by applying the precautionary principle. The draft Earth Charter notes in this context that prevention of harm is the best method of environmental protection, and, when knowledge is limited, it is necessary to apply a precautionary approach.[338]

The Biosafety Protocol calls upon the parties to ensure that "the development, handling, transport, use, transfer and release of any living modified organisms are undertaken in a manner that *prevents* or reduces the risks to biological diversity, taking also into account risks to human health."[339]

It is thus obvious that the principle of prevention plays an important role in relation to environmental protection. Since it is not practically possible to prevent every kind of environmental damage, international law recognizes the need to at least reduce, limit or control activities that might give rise to serious environmental degradation. States employ various methods to do so under national law, the environmental impact assessment process[340] being one such method. In addition, enactment of environmental legislation,[341] licensing requirements,[342] prior approval requirements for development activities,[343] monitoring requirements,[344] etc., play

---

[336] Draft art. 6(d), *available at* http://www.earthcharter.org/earthcharter/charter. htm.

[337] Ministerial Declaration on Sustainable Development in the ECE Region—United Nations Economic Commission for Europe Conference on Action for a Common Future, Bergen, Norway, May 15, 1990, UN Doc. A/CONF.151/PC/10, Aug. 6, 1990, art. 7.

[338] Draft art. 6, *supra* note 336.

[339] Art. 2, *supra* note 13.

[340] *See* the discussion in Chapter 4, Sections A and B.

[341] The need to adopt national environmental laws was recognized in the Rio Declaration, *supra* note 1 (Principle 11).

[342] *See* discussion in Chapter 6 on the polluter pays principle.

[343] *See* Chapter 4, Sections A, C.1 and C.6.

[344] The role of monitoring was discussed in relation to sustainable development

an important role. Access to information[345] and vigilance by civil society groups[346] also play a significant role in preventing environmental damage or "nipping it in the bud."

According to Philippe Sands:

Closely related to the Principle 21 obligation is the obligation requiring the prevention of damage to the environment, or to otherwise reduce, limit or control activities that might cause such damage. . . . The preventive principle is supported by an extensive body of domestic environmental protection legislation which establishes authorization procedures, as well as the adoption of international and national commitments on environmental standards, access to environmental information, and the need to carry out environmental impact assessments in relation to the conduct of certain proposed activities. The preventive principle may, therefore, take a number of forms, including the use of penalties and the application of liability rules.[347]

The objective of the Framework Convention on Climate Change is to achieve stabilization of greenhouse gas concentrations in the atmosphere at a level that would *prevent* dangerous anthropocentric interference with the climate system.[348] Embodying the precautionary principle it further provides that "The Parties should take precautionary measures to anticipate, prevent or minimize the causes of climate change and mitigate its adverse effects."[349] The use of the word "should" as opposed to "shall" reflects hortatory language and dilutes the effect of Principle 15 of the Rio Declaration.[350]

International decisions also support the principle of prevention. In the much quoted *Trail Smelter Arbitration*, the arbitrator referred to the need to prevent future damage by fumes to the U.S. territory. Similarly, the *Lac Lanoux Arbitration* endorsed the principle of prevention in relation to transboundary water pollution and Australia relied on it in the *Nuclear Tests Cases*.

---

(Chapter 2) and environmental impact assessment (Chapter 4, note 74 and accompanying text).

[345] *See* Chapter 4, Section F.1.a.

[346] *See* Chapter 4, Section F.2.

[347] *See* SANDS, *supra* note 208, at 194, 195.

[348] Art. 2 of the UNFCC, *supra* note 177.

[349] *Id.*, art. 3(3).

[350] Of course, the Rio Declaration, *supra* note 1, itself is a non-binding instrument.

Sands cites an impressive number of treaties endorsing the preventive approach, which he states "provides compelling evidence of the wide support for the principle of preventive action."[351] These range from protection of species of fauna and flora,[352] pollution of the seas by oil,[353] radioactive waste,[354] hazardous substances,[355] river pollution,[356] radioactive pollution of the atmosphere;[357] modification of the ozone layer;[358] loss of biodiversity;[359] and all forms of pollution and degradation of the natural environment.[360] This clearly shows that the principle of prevention is of general application covering all forms of pollution and environment degradation. Given the widespread support it has received, the principle of prevention can be said to have entered the realm of customary international law.

Principle 21 of the Stockholm Declaration applies the principle of prevention in a transboundary context.[361] As noted before, Principle 21 refers to the principle of prevention in a specific context and, as such, is narrower in application. Both these principles are, however, limited by existing sci-

---

[351] *See* SANDS, *supra* note 208, at 249.

[352] Convention Relative to the Preservation of Fauna and Flora in their Natural State, 172 LNTS 241, signed Nov. 8, 1933, entered into force Jan. 14, 1934.

[353] International Convention for the Prevention of Pollution of the Sea by Oil, 327 UNTS 3, signed May 12, 1954, entered into force July 26, 1958.

[354] Convention on Fishing and Conservation of the Living Resources of the High Sea, 559 UNTS 285, signed Apr. 29, 1958, entered into force Mar. 20, 1966.

[355] Convention for the Prevention of Marine Pollution by Dumping from Ships and Aircraft, 932 UNTS 3, signed Feb. 15, 1972, entered into force Apr. 7, 1974; Convention on the Preservation of Marine Pollution by Dumping of Wastes and Other Matter, 1046 UNTS 120, signed Dec. 29, 1972, entered into force Aug. 30, 1975.

[356] Convention Concerning Fishing in the Waters of the Danube, 339 UNTS 23, signed Jan. 29, 1958, entered into force Dec. 20, 1958.

[357] Treaty Banning Nuclear Weapon Tests in the Atmosphere, in Outer Space and under Water, 480 UNTS 43, signed Aug. 5, 1963, entered into force Oct. 10, 1963.

[358] Vienna Convention for the Protection of the Ozone Layer, 26 ILM 1529 (1985), 1513 UNTS 293, signed Mar. 22, 1985, entered into force Sept. 22, 1988 and the Montreal Protocol, *supra* note 173.

[359] Convention on Biological Diversity, *supra* note 179.

[360] Association of South East Asian Nations Agreement on the Conservation of Nature and Natural Resources, 15 EPL 64 (1985), signed July 9, 1985, not in force.

[361] SANDS, *supra* note 208, at 246, notes that Principle 21 derives from the principle of sovereignty whereas the principle of prevention applies to prevention of environmental damage as an objective and extends to prevention within one's jurisdiction. It can be argued that both Principle 21 and the principle of prevention (which is wider than Principle 21) derive from the principle of sovereignty.

entific knowledge on a particular issue—hence the relevance of the precautionary principle.[362]

The environmental assessment process, on the other hand, can be used to realize the principle of prevention, both generally and in a transboundary context. The objective of an environmental assessment report is to anticipate the environmental impact of a particular activity and propose ways to prevent or at least minimize its impact on the environment. As will be discussed in Chapter 4, international law now regulates the environmental assessment process and requires states to evaluate the transboundary impact of activities within their jurisdiction and control.[363]

Thus, taking the principle of prevention as the broad objective of environmental protection (with Principle 21 being applicable in a transboundary context), the EIA can be taken as a tool to achieve that objective, while the precautionary principle is an aid to policymakers as to *when* such action is warranted. If existing evidence point to irreversible or serious damage to the environment, the precautionary principle requires states to take preventive measures, even if there are scientific uncertainties and controversies surrounding the issue. This is the relationship between several related concepts and tools: the principle of prevention, Principle 21, environmental assessment and the precautionary principle. The precautionary principle and the environmental assessment process, in turn, are tools to achieve sustainable development.

## G.  THE PRECAUTIONARY PRINCIPLE AND SUSTAINABLE DEVELOPMENT

As the foregoing discussion revealed, the main objective of the precautionary principle is the prevention of environmental damage. One element of sustainable development is the integration of environmental protection and economic development. The environmental assessment process coupled with the precautionary principle offers a sound tool to achieve such integration. The Bergen Ministerial Declaration[364] is perhaps the only instrument to specifically make a link between the precautionary principle and sustainable development:

> In order to achieve sustainable development, policies must be based on the precautionary principle. Environmental measures must anticipate, prevent and attack the causes of environmental degradation.

---

[362]  *See* Atapattu, *supra* note 168, at 1016, 1017.

[363]  *See* Chapter 4, Section C.1.

[364]  *Supra* note 337.

Where there are threats of serious or irreversible damage, lack of full scientific certainty should not be used as a reason for postponing measures to prevent environmental degradation.[365]

Another aspect of the principle of prevention is to ensure that sufficient resources will be available to future generations to meet their needs. This inter-generational equity principle is another element of sustainable development that can be achieved through the application of the precautionary principle.[366]

It is thus no secret that the precautionary principle can play a significant role in relation to sustainable development. Since it is subject to important caveats, such as the economic capabilities of states, its application should not constitute an undue burden on states, as contended by its opponents. As noted above, its significance lies in the *timing* of action, rather than mandating what kind of action is necessary. In other words, faced with serious threats to the environment, if preventive measures are either postponed or not taken at all, sustainable development will be an unattainable dream, rather than an achievable objective. The problem about postponing action to protect the environment is that, by the time action is taken, it may prove to be too late. Thus, postponing action, particularly in relation to global environmental problems, such as global warming, can entail serious consequences.

The critics of the precautionary principle contend, on the other hand, that if the scientific predictions do not materialize, taking preventive measures would prove to be a wasteful exercise.[367] This argument, however, ignores the restrictions that are embodied in the Rio formulation: there has to be evidence of at least potential serious environmental harm and states are required to take only cost effective measures. However, some have critiqued this restrictive formulation in Principle 15 preferring to adopt a baseline definition of the precautionary principle.[368]

With regard to the relationship between the precautionary principle and sustainable development it has been articulated that:

The precautionary principle is especially important for sustainable development because the carrying capacity of the global environ-

---

[365] *Id.*, art. 1.7.

[366] *See* James Cameron et al., *Precautionary Principle and Future Generations, in* FUTURE GENERATIONS AND INTERNATIONAL LAW, *supra* note 213, at 93.

[367] *See* Cross, *supra* note 52.

[368] *See* Ellis & FitzGerald, *supra* note 47.

ment as well as regional ecosystems is mostly unknown. Although it is generally agreed that the environment can tolerate some abuse, there is a tendency to believe and act as if the environment can tolerate a particular human activity or set of activities unless scientific information demonstrates otherwise. Because the quality of human life ultimately depends on these natural resources, we should be careful to protect them.[369]

It has been further pointed out that the precautionary principle is reinforced by integrated decision making and the polluter pays principle:[370] "Because of the obvious relationship between scientific information and environmental protection, the precautionary approach could have profound consequences for sustainable development decision-making."[371]

Many scientists also favor the application of the precautionary principle.[372] It is noted that the "precautionary principle is actually part and parcel of sound science. . . . Scientific evidence is always incomplete and uncertain. The responsible use of scientific evidence, therefore, is to set precaution."[373] Some have argued that the strict application of the precautionary principle would put an end to technological innovation.[374] This is a misconception. In fact, the precautionary principle is very simple and is based on common sense. It is not a new idea either. It simply means that if we are embarking on something new, we need to think very carefully about its safety and we should not go ahead until we are convinced that it is, in fact, safe. Protecting public health and the environment is the main objective of many laws and regulations worldwide, and the precautionary principle plays a key role here. Those who reject the precautionary principle seem to insist that it is up to the opponents to prove that a particular technology or product is unsafe or dangerous. Furthermore, they refuse to accept liability—if the new technology or product turned out to be hazardous, someone else has to pay the price.[375] This is unacceptable both in terms of fairness and in terms of imposing liability on society and would also be contrary to the polluter pays principle.[376]

---

[369] *See* Dernbach, *supra* note 32.

[370] *Id.*

[371] *Id.*

[372] *See* Peter Saunders, *Use and Abuse of the Precautionary Principle, available at* http://www.ratical.org/co-globalize/MacWanHo/PrecautionP.html.

[373] *Id.*

[374] *See* HUNTER ET AL., *supra* note 2, at 409.

[375] *Id.*

[376] *See* the discussion in Chapter 6, Sections A and B.

While there is no doubt that "the precautionary principle serves as a means for making the principle of sustainable development concrete,"[377] it is perplexing to note that some writers have categorized sustainable development as being an obstacle to the application of the precautionary principle.[378] In other words, it has been argued that these two principles can conflict with each other.[379] The reasoning behind this argument is rather strange:

> To this end, it has been argued that the IWC's moratorium on whales, as well as the world wide ban of large scale pelagic driftnets, could conflict with the principle of sustainable development. However, the precautionary principle, as part of the wider legal principle of sustainable development, constitutes the more specific rule. According to the *lex specialis* rule, it would thus prevail over the latter. This notion, that in a conflict with the principle of sustainable development it is the precautionary principle that prevails is emphasized in the Draft Guidelines for the Ecological Sustainability of Non-Consumptive Uses of Wild Species.[380]

This reasoning is, unfortunately, based on a fundamental misunderstanding of both the precautionary principle and of sustainable development. If it is understood that the precautionary principle is a tool to achieve sustainable development—the Bergen Ministerial Declaration clearly states so[381]—it is hard to see how these two can conflict with each other and that, in the event of a conflict, the precautionary principle, as *lex specialis*, would prevail over sustainable development. It is similar to saying that environmental assessment and sustainable development can conflict with each other, and, in the event of a conflict, the former would prevail over the latter. Both the precautionary principle and the environmental assessment are but tools to achieve the goal of sustainable development, together with other tools such as the polluter pays principle, cost-benefit analysis, strategic environmental assessment, etc. All these tools facilitate the march toward the broad goal of sustainable development. Thus, it is hard to accept the idea that the precautionary principle and sustainable development can be in conflict with one another.

---

[377] *See* MARR, *supra* note 6, at 41.

[378] *Id.*

[379] *Id.*

[380] *Id.*

[381] Bergen Ministerial Declaration, *supra* note 337, states in Article 7: "*In order to achieve sustainable development,* policies must be based on the precautionary principle" (emphasis added).

The following argument articulated by David Wirth seems much more plausible:

> Precautionary approaches are inherent in the concept of sustainable development, presumably because precaution is part of the burden of proof necessary to establish that particular development decisions meet the needs of today while simultaneously satisfying present environmental constraints and preserving the ability of future generations to meet their own needs.[382]

This formulation links the precautionary approach with sustainable development and the inter-generational equity principle. Indeed, if the precautionary principle is a tool to achieve sustainable development, which requires us to take decisions that seeks to ensure the rights of future generations, then the precautionary principle is a tool to achieve inter-generational equity as well. Viewed in this light, the precautionary principle has wide implications.

## H. THE LEGAL STATUS OF THE PRECAUTIONARY PRINCIPLE

Before we discuss the legal status of the precautionary principle, it is necessary to pay attention to the controversy surrounding the nomenclature. While Principle 15 refers to the "precautionary approach," some instruments refer to the "principle of precautionary action."[383] The Third International Conference on the Protection of the North Sea, Ministerial Declaration[384]—the only instrument to do so—notes that signatories "will continue to apply the precautionary principle."[385] In other words, is it a standard, an approach or a principle?[386]

Thus, what is the significance that Principle 15 advocates a precautionary approach as opposed to a precautionary principle? Is there a legal distinction between the two? As a concept guiding the decision making process, the precautionary approach is beyond reproach. Its significance lies in the fact that it allows us to weigh the pros and cons of a new tech-

---

[382] *See* Wirth, *supra* note 40.

[383] Ministerial Declaration of the Second International Conference on the Protection of the North Sea refers to both the precautionary approach and the principle of precautionary action, Nov. 24–25, 1987, 27 ILM 835, 836.

[384] Mar. 8, 1990, *reprinted in* 1 Y.B. INT'L. ENVTL. L. 658, 662–73, *available at* http://www.odin.dep.no/md/html/conf/declaration/hague.html.

[385] *Id.*

[386] *See* de Chazournes, *supra* note 25.

nology or product and proceed if the benefits outweigh the risks. However, the precautionary approach also requires us to continually keep such technology or products under review to ensure that they do not pose a hazard to human health or the environment.

Does this mean that the precautionary approach is a binding principle? Does it convey more than the precautionary approach that is "an integral part of ordinary, everyday risk management"?[387] As has been pointed out "[s]tating that a lack of full scientific certainty cannot by itself justify inaction is very different from stating that action may be required even where no evidence of a causal link exists."[388] Of these, the formulation adopted by the parties in the Ministerial Declaration on the Protection of the North Sea seems to be strongest when requiring action even in the absence of any evidence of a causal link. In the event of such a formulation, authorities may be required to take precautionary measures.

Writers have also delved on the issue of principle versus approach.[389] Simon Marr, for example, notes that, at least with regard to marine activities, the precautionary "approach" is better suited because it implies more flexibility.[390] The term principle "has developed a negative undertone in particular for the high seas fishing nations."[391] The distinction between a "hard principle" and a "soft approach" is important when it comes to regulating activities that could lead to outright bans in relation to the former and a more flexible approach in relation to the latter.

If, on the other hand, the precautionary principle is indeed a principle, the failure to adopt it could be subject to judicial scrutiny. In other words, the failure to apply the precautionary principle would give rise to state responsibility if state agencies are involved. This, in turn, would give rise to reparations. It is, however, doubtful that the precautionary principle, at the present time, is capable of invoking such a legal response.

The precautionary principle has been critiqued for several reasons. It has been argued that the precautionary principle relies on subjective criteria to trigger environmental action.[392] It is pointed out that phrases such

---

[387] *See* Ruessmann, *supra* note 62.

[388] *Id.*

[389] *See* James E. Hickey, Jr. & Vern R. Walker, *Refining the Precautionary Principle in International Environmental Law*, 14 VA. ENVTL. L.J. 423 (1995).

[390] *See* MARR, *supra* note 6 at 17.

[391] *Id.* at 18.

[392] *Id.* at 21.

as "threats or serious or irreversible damage" and "potential adverse effects" are not legal terms, because they are based on subjectivity. Terms such as toxic, hazardous or persistent have been defined, but these definitions can be relative—for example, toxicity can vary from species to species. It has been articulated that there are several fundamental uncertainties in relation to the precautionary principle that must be addressed: it is unclear whether it is a recommendation, an obligation or some intermediate duty; the level of environmental risk that triggers the application of the precautionary principle is unsettled; and the obligation to apply the precautionary principle is rendered imprecise by references to economic considerations.[393]

The precautionary principle is primarily a risk management and decision-making tool: "The inherent character of the precautionary principle is therefore that it is not as concrete as a legal rule."[394] Moreover, the decision makers should apply the principle with caution. It will be subject to a proportionality test that includes a balancing of costs and benefits. This is important, as no decision maker wants to impose an undue burden on the proponent of an activity. The idea is to promote industry and development, while at the same time protecting the environment.[395]

Having surveyed the domestic provisions in several countries, Marr concludes that various countries have incorporated it into their national legislation, and, in most countries, it is implemented as a legal principle. However, the provisions vary from country to country, and countries with a tradition of providing for environmental protection have a sophisticated legal framework while others may only have the bare bones in place.[396] Nevertheless, some common denominators can be identified. It is mostly provided as a deliberation-guiding principle.[397] Moreover, there seems to be a minimum threshold common to all formulations—precautionary action is triggered by irreversible or serious damage to the environment:

> Precautionary action can have various facets ranging from an environmental impact assessment, a licence requirement, the obligation to apply BAT or BEP to measures simply restricting, minimizing or prohibiting the desired activity. In terms of the addressee, the

---

[393] *See* Hickey, Jr. & Walker, *supra* note 389.

[394] *See* MARR, *supra* note 6, at 22.

[395] For a harsh critique of the precautionary principle, *see* Cross, *supra* note 52.

[396] *See* MARR, *supra* note 6, at 99.

[397] *Id.* at 99. Laws of many countries have been surveyed, ranging from the United States to Belgium, from Estonia to Australia and from China to Canada. *See id.* at 80–99.

national laws mostly oblige both individuals and authorities to adhere to pollution prevention under the precautionary principle.[398]

The fact that some form of the precautionary principle has been incorporated into national laws is evidence of state practice. However, given that these are not uniform, it is difficult to prove consistent state practice,[399] although it seems quite widespread. This is quite remarkable, even if the precautionary principle is not part of customary international law, that within a relatively short period of time, the precautionary principle (or some version of it) has found its way into national law and has been subject to judicial decisions.[400]

Philippe Sands, while noting that there is no uniform understanding of the meaning of the precautionary principle among states, points out that:

A more generally accepted view is that the principle requires activities and substances which may be harmful to the environment to be regulated, and possibly prohibited, even if no conclusive or overwhelming evidence is available as to the harm or likely harm that they may cause to the environment.[401]

This suggests that policymakers and those who are entrusted with the task of approving development activities must take risk of harm into account when evaluating the impact of the proposed activity on human health and the environment. Whether there is conclusive proof of such risk is immaterial. What is now relevant, in the light of the precautionary principle, is that a risk exists of serious or irreparable harm. The precautionary principle indicates that policymakers are no longer able to hide behind the "lack of scientific certainty" defense. Similar to sustainable development, the precautionary principle is influencing decision making relating to the environment. A more stringent application of this principle can be mandated by national legislation.

While the precautionary approach is influencing the decision-making process, it is questionable whether non-adherence to the precautionary principle would entail any legal consequences. In other words, if a state

---

[398] *Id.*

[399] The requirement for consistent state practice is discussed in Chapter 2, Section J.

[400] *See supra* notes 302–304 and accompanying text.

[401] *See* Philippe Sands, *"Greening" of International Law: Emerging Principles and Rules,* 1 IND. J. GLOBAL LEGAL STUD. 293 (1994).

does not apply the precautionary principle in relation to its environmental decision making, would that state entail state responsibility under international law? The answer to this would depend on whether the precautionary principle has achieved normative status under international law.[402] If it has, then the failure to apply it would give rise to state responsibility.[403] Otherwise, no sanctions would attach to non-implementation.

Does the precautionary principle meet the rigorous test laid down in the *North Sea Continental Shelf Cases*[404] to establish a customary international law principle? First of all, is state practice sufficiently consistent with regard to the application of the precautionary principle? While international treaties and several non-binding instruments refer to the precautionary principle, it is not possible to come to the conclusion that there is either consistent or widespread practice with regard to the precautionary principle. Part of the problem seems to be the lack of a coherent definition or the lack of understanding of its parameters. Secondly, if it is hard to establish the first element in relation to a custom, then it is even harder to establish the second element: it can even be argued that the reason that there is insufficient state practice is precisely because the second element is lacking—in other words, states are not yet convinced that it is legally binding. While the precautionary approach has certainly influenced the decision-making process, and its normative status seems to be evolving, it cannot yet be concluded that it has entered the sacred portals of customary international law.

It has been articulated that the precautionary principle must be considered as an emerging customary norm:

> Even if it has not yet acquired an unambiguous status in general international law, one should nonetheless consider the precautionary principle as an emerging customary norm. Its inclusion in numerous legal instruments of international and national law, and the fact that it has been taken into consideration by the European Court of Justice as well as by national tribunals bear witness to this.[405]

---

[402] Only a breach of an international obligation would give rise to state responsibility. *See* ILC Draft Articles on State Responsibility, *available at* http://www.un.org/law/ilc/.

[403] *Id.*

[404] The test laid down in this case is discussed in Chapter 2, Section J, note 603 and accompanying text.

[405] *See* de Chazournes, *supra* note 25.

While it is argued that the precautionary principle should be considered as an emerging customary principle, Boisson de Chazournes argues that "The only important obstacle is with regard to its acceptance by the international community as a whole as a principle of general international law."[406] It is not clear what this seeks to convey. Does she, for example, seek to distinguish between a customary norm and a general principle of law, similar to the argument made by Canada in the *Beef-Hormone Case*?[407] There may be more support for the contention that the precautionary principle is a general principle of law rather than a customary principle. Given that both these are primary sources that the ICJ must apply under Article 38 of its Statute, the characterization of the precautionary principle as a custom or a general principle will not be significant.

The general consensus is that the precautionary principle has not yet achieved normative status under international law,[408] although a move towards this seems to be certainly emerging.[409] It has been articulated that the precautionary principle "has become a widely accepted international political practice" and the next step would be to strengthen its content and to refine and develop the substantive obligation to exercise precaution.[410] No doubt it would continue to evolve, and perhaps it will not be long before it does achieve normative status. However, at the present time, its legal status remains rather uncertain.

Some writers, on the other hand, have asserted that it has achieved normative status under international law. Arie Trouwborst, for example, writes that:

In short, as will have become increasingly clear to the reader, a balancing of all preceding considerations on state practice, *opinio juris* and expert opinion allows for the final conclusion that the assumption that nowadays the precautionary principle is a principle of customary international is much better defensible than the contrary.[411]

He relies on his analysis of state practice and international instruments for this conclusion.[412] However, his analysis indicates that state practice is

---

[406]  *Id.*

[407]  *See* discussion in Section E.4.

[408]  *See* HUNTER ET AL., *supra* note 2, at 407.

[409]  *See* de Chazournes, *supra* note 25.

[410]  *See* Hickey, Jr. & Walker, *supra* note 389.

[411]  *See* Trouwborst, *supra* note 167, at 275.

[412]  *Cf.* Atapattu, *supra* note 168.

neither sufficiently widespread nor uniform to warrant his conclusion that the precautionary principle has attained customary international law status.[413] The better view is that it has influenced decision making and that it has entered into the realm of international environmental law, not as a binding principle but rather as a guiding principle.

It has also been articulated that precaution should not be considered as legal rule, but rather as a standard. Thus, it need not fit into the traditional sources of international law but "may derive its legal force from being interpreted as a standard."[414] Whether it is considered a principle or a standard would be immaterial for the purposes of its legal status: in other words, what is necessary would be evidence of its application by states either as a principle, a standard or even an approach in relation to environmental issues. There is no doubt that the precautionary principle has greatly influenced the decision-making process in relation to environmental issues within a relatively short time span. Time will, of course, be a crucial factor in evaluating the legal status of the precautionary principle.

---

[413] *Id.*

[414] *See* Sonia Boutillon, *The Precautionary Principle: Development of an International Standard,* 23 MICH. J. INT'L L. 429 (2002).

## CHAPTER 4
# ENVIRONMENTAL IMPACT ASSESSMENT AND PROCEDURAL RIGHTS

Environmental impact assessment, as a national instrument, shall be undertaken for proposed activities that are likely to have a significant adverse impact on the environment and are subject to a decision of a competent national authority.

Principle 17, Rio Declaration on Environment
and Development, 1992

## A. INTRODUCTION

One of the more established principles of environmental law is the obligation to carry out an assessment of the environmental impact of development activities at the national level. Closely linked to the concept of sustainable development, an environmental impact assessment (EIA) is an invaluable tool to achieve the principle of integration[1]—to integrate environmental concerns into the economic development process.

The United States was the first country in the world to introduce the environmental assessment process into the law.[2] It requires all major federal projects to undergo an environmental assessment. Since then, the environmental assessment process has undergone profound development in many parts of the world, and now constitutes one of the principal tools of environmental protection. Many national systems now incorporate the EA process, which, in some countries, leads to public participation and other procedural rights.

The rationale underlying the environmental assessment process is the principle of prevention, discussed in Chapter 3. In order to prevent environmental degradation, it becomes necessary to understand the environmental consequences of a proposed project as early as possible in the

---

[1] Discussed in Chapter 2, Section E.1.

[2] *See* the National Environmental Policy Act, 1969 (42 U.S.C.A. §§ 4321–4370d), which requires agencies of the U.S. government to prepare an environmental impact statement with respect to "major federal actions significantly affecting the quality of the human environment." *See* DAVID. HUNTER, JAMES SALZMAN & DURWOOD ZAELKE, INTERNATIONAL ENVIRONMENTAL LAW AND POLICY 35 (2d ed. 2002).

project cycle. Once these environmental consequences are identified, mitigatory measures could be taken to minimize the impact on the environment. On the other hand, the decision maker may decide that the impact on the environment is irreversible or that it far outweighs the benefits from the proposed project or that there is no justification for the project to go forward. Thus, the environmental assessment process provides the decision maker with a valuable tool to evaluate a project for its environmental, economic[3] and social consequences,[4] before a decision is taken whether to implement the project or not. Often, EIAs include an analysis of alternatives[5] that are less harmful to the environment, which enables the decision maker to evaluate the alternatives against the proposed activity. Ideally, an EIA should provide the decision maker with a set of options from which the decision maker can choose the best possible one for the proposed activity. In practice, however, this may not happen. Very often, EIA procedures are criticized for coming too late in the decision-making process, where some decisions have already been taken.[6] Sometimes EIAs are prepared to justify a decision that has already been taken. Despite these drawbacks, which are more in relation to the procedure, rather than the process itself, an EIA provides a valuable tool to achieve sustainable development, as it seeks to integrate environmental protection into the development process.

The environmental protection movement at the international level originated from purely cross-border issues such as transboundary pollution. Aside from cross-border issues international law had no role to play in regulating activities that could lead to environmental pollution within national boundaries. Such regulation fell squarely on the shoulders of national agencies that did or did not take much action, depending on the level of interest in relation to environmental issues. As a result, states only had to ensure that activities within their jurisdiction or control did not cause extra-territorial environmental damage.[7] This principle, also referred to as the principle of good neighborliness,[8] was first articulated in the famous *Trail Smelter*

---

[3] *See* the discussion on cost-benefit analysis in Section A.2.

[4] Some countries require the preparation of a separate social impact assessment, *See* discussion in Section A.1.

[5] *See infra* note 73 and accompanying text.

[6] *See* Marceil Yeater & Lal Kurukulasuriya, *Environmental Impact Assessment in Legislation in Developing Countries, in* UNEP'S NEW WAY FORWARD: ENVIRONMENTAL LAW AND SUSTAINABLE DEVELOPMENT 258, at 261 (Sun Lin & Lal Kurukulasuriya eds., 1995).

[7] Now codified in Principle 21 of the Stockholm Declaration, UN Doc. A/CONF.48/14, June 16, 1972, *reprinted in* 11 ILM 1416 (1972). *See* discussion in the Introduction, *supra* note 13 and accompanying text and Chapter 1, *supra* note 329 and accompanying text.

[8] *See* Brian Popiel, *From Customary Law to Environmental Impact Assessment: A New*

*Arbitration,*[9] discussed below. The principle of good neighborliness derives from the principle of sovereignty itself. The sole arbitrator in *The Island of Palmas Case,*[10] Max Huber, articulated a classic definition of sovereignty:

> Territorial sovereignty signifies independence, that is the right to exercise, within a portion of the globe and to the exclusion of other states, the functions of a State. This right has a corollary duty: the obligation to protect within its territory the rights of other States, in particular their right to integrity and inviolability in peace and in war, together with the rights which each State may claim for its nationals in foreign territory.[11]

It is thus clear that the principle of good neighborliness[12] and indeed Principle 21 of the Stockholm Declaration itself are based on the principle of territorial sovereignty, which is not unlimited. In other words, the duty attached to the right to territorial sovereignty requires states to protect the rights of other states. This is particularly pertinent in relation to environmental issues.

The obligation of states to cooperate with their neighbors in relation to international issues is a binding principle of international law and is codified in the UN Charter: "To achieve international co-operation in solving international problems of an economic, social, cultural or humanitarian character."[13] This general duty was further elaborated in the 1970 UN Declaration of Principles of International Law.[14] This obligation in the environmental context is incorporated in Article 24 of the Stockholm Declaration:

> International matters concerning the protection and improvement of the environment should be handled in a co-operative spirit by all countries, big or small, on an equal footing. Co-operation through

---

*Approach to Avoiding Transboundary Environmental Damage Between Canada and the United States,* 22 B.C. ENVTL. AFF. L. REV. 95 (1995).

[9] United States v. Canada, 3 RIAA 1905 (1941).

[10] United States v. Netherlands, 2 RIAA 829 (1928).

[11] *Id.*

[12] *See* Popicl, *supra* note 8.

[13] Art. 1.3, UN Charter.

[14] Declaration of Principles on International Law Concerning Friendly Relations and Cooperation Among States in Accordance with the Charter of the United Nations, GA Res. 2625 (Oct 24, 1970) *reprinted in* 9 ILM 1292 (1972). There is no mention of environmental issues in the Declaration, which is not surprising—the need for international cooperation in relation to the environment was recognized at the Stockholm Conference, *See* HUNTER ET AL., *supra* note 2, at 429.

multilateral or bilateral arrangements or other appropriate means is essential to effectively control, prevent, reduce and eliminate adverse environmental effects resulting from activities conducted in all spheres, in such a way that due account is taken of the sovereignty and interests of all States.[15]

The Rio Declaration formulates this obligation as follows: "States shall cooperate in a spirit of global partnership to conserve, protect and restore the health and integrity of the Earth's ecosystem."[16] Principle 27 is also pertinent in this regard: "States and people shall cooperate in good faith and in a spirit of partnership in the fulfillment of the principles embodied in this Declaration and in the further development of international law in the field of sustainable development."[17] Analyzing these three provisions, several issues of importance can be identified: first, the instruments recognize a general duty on states to cooperate in relation to environmental matters; secondly, the Rio Declaration takes this obligation a step further by requiring states to cooperate in a spirit of global partnership;[18] thirdly, the Rio Declaration also recognizes the duty of non-state actors to cooperate in good faith and in a spirit of partnership to fulfill the principles in the Declaration;[19] finally, states, as well as people, must develop international law in the field of sustainable development.[20]

The Law of the Sea Convention also embodies the good neighborliness principle:

States shall take all measures necessary to ensure that activities under their jurisdiction or control are so conducted as not to cause damage by pollution to other States and their environment, and that pollution arising from incidents or activities under their jurisdiction or control does not spread beyond the areas where they exercise sovereign rights in accordance with this Convention.[21]

---

[15] Principle 24 of the Stockholm Declaration, *supra* note 7.

[16] Principle 7, Rio Declaration, UN Doc. A/CONF.151/26, *reprinted in* 31 ILM 874 (1992), *available at* http://www.un.org/documents/ga/conf151/aconf15126-1annexl.htm.

[17] Principle 27, Rio Declaration, *id.*

[18] Principle 7, Rio Declaration, *id.*

[19] Principle 27, Rio Declaration, *id.*

[20] *Id.*

[21] Art. 194, United Nations Convention on the Law of the Sea, 21 ILM 1261 (1982), 1833 UNTS 3, signed Dec. 10, 1982, entered into force Nov. 16, 1994, *available at* http://www.un.org/Depts/los/index.htm.

However, the threshold that triggered this obligation, now codified in Principle 21 of the Stockholm Declaration, is significant damage. In other words, states are not required to prevent damage that is less than significant, although what constitutes significant damage was subject to interpretation. These fall into the category of "first generation" environmental issues.[22] Damage, causation and state responsibility played an important role in relation to these issues. Transboundary air pollution was a prime example of a first generation environmental issue.

During the second generation (in the 1980s), a different kind of environmental problems started to emerge. These did not have a transboundary component—rather they were global in dimension, threatening to affect every state in the international community, albeit to different degrees.[23] The earlier approach to transboundary damage could not deal with this new category of environmental problems. Thus, waiting for damage to materialize, state responsibility and causation were not very useful in relation to this category of environmental issues. Available evidence suggested that waiting for material damage to manifest itself could prove to be detrimental (and even fatal) for the entire international community. Thus, the regulation of activities of states in order to prevent damage became the norm. This approach signified the action taken in relation to ozone depletion.

Almost simultaneously with this development, we saw the emergence of third generation environmental issues. Here there is neither any transboundary environmental impact nor the entire global community getting affected by a particular issue, but international law sought to regulate various internal policies and activities of states, which had ramifications for environmental regulation. Thus, the very development process became subject to international scrutiny through the notion of sustainable development,[24] and issues that were traditionally outside the realm of international scrutiny began to be subject to international regulation. Protection of biodiversity is a good example of this new process, which is referred to as "internationalization of environmental protection."[25] Furthermore, issues such as poverty became subject to international scrutiny because of its direct impact on sustainable development.[26] The environmental impact assessment process, essentially an internal process, also became subject to

---

[22] *See* HUNTER ET AL., *supra* note 2, 178.

[23] *Id.* at 179.

[24] The process of internationalization is discussed in Chapter 1, Section A.3 and sustainable development is discussed in Chapter 2.

[25] This is discussed in Chapter 1, Section A.3.

[26] Principle 5 of the Rio Declaration, *supra* note 16, endorses the relationship between poverty and sustainable development.

international scrutiny, again because of its relationship with sustainable development. If states are required to prevent environmental damage (with or without extra-territorial damage), then tools have to be developed to evaluate the environmental impact of activities *before* they are undertaken. The EIA is an invaluable tool to do so. Participatory rights, in relation to environmental issues, originated from the EIA process, as most national laws require the EIA report to be a public document subject to public participation. Hence, environmental democracy was born.[27] It must be pointed out that these participatory rights are not confined to activities subject to the EIA process. In other words, participatory rights are wider in scope and apply to any activity likely to cause environmental damage. Given that EIA reports are very expensive to produce, they are usually carried out in relation to activities likely to have a significant impact[28] on the environment. If participatory rights are confined to these activities, a significant proportion of activities that could have a considerable impact, yet may not amount to "significant impact," will not be subject to public scrutiny. People have a right to seek and receive information about activities that may have an impact on the environment irrespective of their magnitude.

This chapter seeks to discuss the emergence of EIA at the international level, the influence of national law, the relevant international instruments on EIA and the content of this principle. It also seeks to discuss procedural rights associated with the EIA process. In this section we will be forging links with international human rights law, as these rights derive from that branch of international law. It also seeks to discuss how this principle can be improved at the international level, which has ramifications for national law. Furthermore, a move toward the adoption of strategic environmental assessment (SEA)[29] at the international level will also be discussed.

## 1. Social Impact Assessment

A closely related and an emerging tool is a social impact assessment, which is used in many countries but this will not be discussed in detail here.

---

[27] *See* SUSTAINABLE DEVELOPMENT LAW: PRINCIPLES, PRACTICES & PROSPECTS (Marie-Claire Cordonier Segger & Ashfaq Khalfan eds., 2004).

[28] What constitutes significant damage is subject to some controversy. It would also depend on the circumstances in each case. Sometimes lists are used to highlight activities that should undergo the EIA process. The Aarhus Convention, discussed later, adopts this approach for activities that should undergo the public participation process.

[29] Some national legislation of some countries already incorporate SEAs. The Netherlands is a good example. In addition, the EU also now requires the preparation of SEAs. *See* Directive 2001/42/EC of the European Parliament and of the Council, June 27, 2001, on the assessment of the effects of certain plans and programs on the environment, *reprinted in* 14 J. ENVTL. L. 131 (2002). *See* discussion in Section E.

A social impact assessment (SIA) has been defined as "the process of assessing or estimating, in advance, the social consequences that are likely to follow from specific policy actions or project development, particularly in the context of appropriate national, state or provincial environmental policy legislation."[30] The SIA needs to be process oriented and seeks to ensure that social needs are included in the project design, planning and implementation.[31] The main purpose of an SIA is to anticipate potential negative impacts of a project and to choose the best option from a variety of options available. The involvement of the local community in this process is imperative. There is a very close relationship between an EIA and an SIA and indeed, many EIAs include the social impact of a project, such as displacement, loss of livelihood, the provision of alternative abode, etc. Both look beyond the mere economic benefits of a project or activity to a wider environmental and social viability of a project, and both involve public participation and the involvement of the affected community in the evaluation process. Both evaluate alternatives to the project or activity. The SIA may be wider in perspective in some respects, as it could involve a gender balance,[32] as well as other cultural nuances that may not be evaluated in an EIA. The SIA will invariably include an analysis of the environment. An SIA will evaluate the changes in one or more of the following areas: people's way of life; their culture; their community; and their environment.[33] While there is an obvious overlap between the two, the emphasis given in them would differ depending on whether an EIA or an SIA is undertaken. For a given project, a combination of the two would be ideal to achieve the best results.

## 2. Cost-Benefit Analysis

It has been articulated that the EIA is essentially a cost-benefit analysis of a planned project.[34] It is submitted that an EIA cannot be equated with a cost-benefit analysis. While some may categorize a cost-benefit analysis as a component of the EIA, others consider that cost benefit is the broadest of the frameworks for assessing regulatory actions and policies

---

[30] *See* Frank Vanclay, *Social Impact Assessment in* ENVIRONMENTAL ASSESSMENT IN DEVELOPING AND TRANSITIONAL COUNTRIES 125 (N. Lee & C. George eds., 2000) *quoting* R.J. Burdge & Frank Vanclay *Social Impact Assessment, in* ENVIRONMENTAL AND SOCIAL IMPACT ASSESSMENT (Frank Vanclay & D.A. Bronstein eds., 1995). *See also* Frank Vanclay, *International Principles for Social Impact Assessment,* 21 IMPACT ASSESSMENT & PROJECT APPRAISAL. (Mar. 2003).

[31] *Id.*

[32] *Id.* at 128.

[33] *Id.* at 129.

[34] *See* Popiel, *supra* note 8.

and include impact assessment, risk assessment and cost-effectiveness.[35] "Formal cost-benefit analysis compares the monetary benefits and costs of government actions aimed at improving public well-being."[36] The problem with the cost-benefit analysis has been quantifying in monetary units public actions that have no private-sector equivalents.[37] It can also lead to some categories being ignored, such as the environment. Thus, early cost-benefit analyses did not quantify the use of public goods, such as water, nor the impact on the environment, such as pollution, deforestation, the public health impact of pollution and the resulting costs, etc. This led to rather distorted cost-benefit analyses, as neither environmental goods nor environmental impacts were reflected in them. However, environmental economics have developed to such an extent that tools are available to quantify these in monetary terms, which enable the decision maker to reach environmentally sound decisions.[38]

Defining a cost-benefit analysis, Moore notes:

Cost-benefit analysis is one way to organize, evaluate, and present information about the actions that governments take to improve public well-being. Because this analytical tool often involves placing monetary values on attributes on human well-being for which no market prices exist, its use is often complicated, expensive, and controversial.

Cost-benefit analysis is a set of procedures to measure the merit of some public sector actions in dollar terms. It is used as a counterpart to private-sector profitability accounting. . . . Cost-benefit analysis attempts to identify the most economically efficient way of meeting a public objective.[39]

Cost-benefit analyses are increasingly used to evaluate projects not only for their economic viability but also for environmental and social viability, thus playing an important role in the decision-making process. Thus, environmental assessment and cost-benefit analyses go hand in hand. It has been articulated that "the spirit of EIA entails making careful, informed

---

[35] *See* John L. Moore, Cost-Benefit Analysis: Issues in its Use in Regulation, CRS Report for Congress, 1995, *available at* http://www.ncseonline.org/NLE/CRSreports/Risk/rsk-4.cfm?&CFID.=46274&CFTOKEN.

[36] *Id.*

[37] *Id.*

[38] *See* Moore, *supra* note 35.

[39] *Id.*

decisions, and taking preventive steps to avoid unnecessary environmental damage."[40]

## B.   THE EMERGENCE OF EIA AT THE INTERNATIONAL LEVEL

It is a customary principle of international law that states must refrain from undertaking or authorizing activities that cause damage to the environment of other states. Its origins can be traced to the *Trail Smelter Arbitration*[41] between the United States and Canada in 1939, which laid down the following principle:

> Under principles of international law and the law of the United States, no state has the right to use or permit the use of its territory in such a manner as to cause injury by fumes in or to the territory of another when the case is of serious concern and the injury is established by clear and convincing evidence.[42]

While this decision does not refer to environmental damage specifically (note the reference to injury to the territory of other states), this is hardly surprising, as, at that time, the notion of environmental damage was not common. The principle enunciated in this arbitration is significant, as Canada was ordered to refrain from causing future damage by way of fumes to the territory of the United States.

A more environment protection-oriented formulation was adopted in 1972 when Principle 21 of the Stockholm Declaration noted thus:

> States have, in accordance with the Charter of the United Nations and the principles of international law, the sovereign right to exploit their own resources pursuant to their own environmental policies and the responsibility to ensure that activities within their jurisdiction or control do not cause damage to the environment of other State or of areas beyond the limits of national jurisdiction.[43]

This formulation was reiterated with a slight modification (albeit a significant one in the context of sustainable development) in the Rio Declaration in 1992[44] and has been incorporated in many international instruments,

---

[40]   *See* Popiel, *supra* note 8.

[41]   *See supra* note 9.

[42]   *Id.*

[43]   Principle 21, Stockholm Declaration, *supra* note 7.

[44]   Principle 2, Rio Declaration, *supra* note 16, where the words "and developmental" was added between the words "environment" and "policies."

both binding and non-binding, adopted since 1972.[45] While several problems remain with this formulation—such as what kind of environmental damage is envisaged under Principle 21, what level of diligence is required to prevent such damage, etc.—it is generally accepted that this principle constitutes customary international law relating to environmental protection.[46] It also received endorsement by the ICJ in its advisory opinion on the *Legality of the Threat or Use of Nuclear Weapons:*

> The existence of the general obligation of States to ensure that activities within their jurisdiction and control respect the environment of other States or of areas beyond national control is now part of the corpus of international law relating to the environment.[47]

While on the face of it, this seems an endorsement of Principle 21, some have criticized it on the ground that the ICJ has diluted the obligation in Principle 21 by referring to the need to "respect" the environment of other states[48] rather than the stricter version of "do not cause damage to the environment." However, what is significant is the Court's endorsement of the obligation, which is now considered as customary law of the environment.

It is generally accepted that the principle embodied in Principle 21 requires due diligence on the part of states to prevent significant extraterritorial damage.[49] In order to do so, the prior evaluation of activities within states for their environmental impact becomes necessary. Thus, Principle 21 constitutes the foundation for transboundary EIA by requiring states to evaluate their activities for their environmental impact to ensure that no significant environmental damage will take place. Where the EIA reveals significant environmental damage, mitigatory measures must be taken to minimize such damage. Thus, while the principle of prevention of environmental damage seems to constitute the foundation for conducting EIAs

---

[45] *E.g.*, Preamble to the Convention on Long-Range Transboundary Air Pollution, 18 ILM 1442 (1979); Preamble to the Vienna Convention for the Protection of the Ozone Layer, 26 ILM 1529 (1985), 1513 UNTS 293, signed Mar. 22, 1985, entered into force Sept. 22, 1988; and Forest Principles, 31 ILM 88 (1992).

[46] PATRICIA BIRNIE & ALAN BOYLE, INTERNATIONAL LAW AND THE ENVIRONMENT 110 (2d ed. 2002). *See also* Chapter 2.

[47] ICJ Advisory Opinion on the *Legality of the Threat or Use of Nuclear Weapons*, 1996 ICJ para. 29.

[48] *See* John H. Knox, *The Myth and Reality of Transboundary Environmental Impact Assessment*, 96 AM. J. INT'L L. 291 (2002).

[49] *See* BIRNIE & BOYLE, *supra* note 46.

at the national level, Principle 21 seems to be the foundation for trans-boundary EIAs.

International environmental law was not concerned with environmental assessment until recently. The Stockholm Declaration, for example, does not contain a provision on EIA, although it embodies the principle of integration in Principle 13, as well as the need for rational planning in Principle 14. Principle 13 reads as:

> In order to achieve a more rational management of resources and thus to improve the environment, States should adopt an integrated and co-ordinated approach to their development planning so as to ensure that development is compatible with the need to protect and improve environment for the benefit of their population.

Principle 14 notes that "rational planning constitutes an essential tool for reconciling any conflict between the needs of development and the need to protect and improve the environment." Taken together, these principles indicate the need to evaluate the environmental impact of development activities. EA constitutes an essential tool in the planning and decision-making process. The lack of reference to EA in the Stockholm Declaration is hardly surprising, given that at the time of the Stockholm Conference, EA had not emerged as an essential tool for rational planning. It is heartening to note that the first seeds of EA were planted in the Stockholm Declaration in its principles on integration and rational planning.

The premise that Principle 21 of the Stockholm Declaration provides the rationale for environmental assessment has been critiqued by some commentators. John Knox notes that Principle 21, while being clear on the face of it, raises more questions than it provides answers. He notes that there is no rationale to conclude that Principle 21 prohibits all trans-boundary harm.[50] In this regard, it must be pointed out there is general consensus that Principle 21 applies in relation to significant or serious damage to the environment. It would be well-neigh impossible to prevent *any* damage to the environment of other states.

John Knox argues that it would be more appropriate to consider trans-boundary EIA as an outgrowth of domestic EIA.[51] His main argument against the first option (that EIA is a corollary of Principle 21) is that it

---

[50] *See* Knox, *supra* note 48.

[51] *Id.* He, however, seems to contradict himself by stating in the same article that "Transboundary EIA does not necessarily follow from domestic EIA."

would require prohibiting significant transboundary harm and would require EIA for all projects that might cause it.[52] He contends that the two regional EIA agreements (the Espoo Convention and the Draft North American Agreement on Transboundary EIA) follow the second path, namely that transboundary EIA is an offshoot of domestic EIA. If, as it is contended, the absence of any reference to Principle 21 in these conventions signifies that significant transboundary environmental damage is not prohibited,[53] this would be contrary to the generally accepted view that Principle 21 is now part of customary international law. In other words, there is no necessity to mention this in the Convention itself. It must be pointed out that the Draft Agreement specifically refers to the principles embodied in Principle 21, although Principle 21 itself is not mentioned there.[54]

Of course, there is no doubt that domestic EIA influenced the development of EIA at the international level. There is no logical contradiction between the two arguments advanced by Knox: that transboundary EIA is a corollary of Principle 21 and that transboundary EIA is an offshoot of domestic EIA. There is nothing strange about the first argument as contended by Knox. Both these positions are correct and can be reconciled with one another.

International law does impose certain procedural requirements on states before activities are undertaken. These are consent, consultation, notification and assessment.[55] While prior informed consent and assessment are of recent origin, notification and consultations are based on the principle of cooperation in good faith, a long entrenched principle of international law. It has also been noted that consent, consultation and notification are contingent upon the implementation of the fourth element—assessment.[56]

There are many definitions of an environmental impact assessment. It can be defined very generally as "the analysis of the likely environmental

---

[52]  *Id.*

[53]  The Preamble to the Espoo Convention does, in fact, refer to the Stockholm Declaration. *See* Convention on Environmental Impact Assessment in a Transboundary Context, 30 ILM 800 (1991), signed Feb. 25, 1991, entered into force Sept. 10, 1997.

[54]  http://www.cec.org/pubs_info_resources/law_treat_agree/. The Preamble specifically refers to the Stockholm Declaration, the Rio Declaration and the sovereign right to exploit resources and the responsibility to ensure that activities within the jurisdiction or control of states do not cause damage to the environment of other states or of areas beyond the limits of national jurisdiction.

[55]  *See* Popiel, *supra* note 8.

[56]  *Id.*

consequences of a proposed human activity."[57] A more specific definition is that "Environmental impact assessment (EIA) is a procedure that seeks to ensure the acquisition of adequate and early information on likely environmental consequences of development projects, on possible alternatives, and on measures to mitigate harm."[58] Effective EIAs depend on three mechanisms: public participation, inter-sectoral coordination and the consideration of alternatives.[59]

The first time that a reference to EIAs appeared in an international instrument was in the World Charter for Nature adopted by the General Assembly in 1982. This is a visionary document that laid the foundation for many other principles and tools that we take for granted today. As noted in the previous chapters, the World Charter for Nature sowed the first seeds of sustainable development and the precautionary principle.

Principle 7 of the Charter reaffirms the principle of integration as follows:

> In the planning and implementation of social and economic development activities, due account shall be taken of the fact that the conservation of nature is an integral part of those activities.[60]

Principle 11 deals with activities that could have an impact on the environment and how to deal with such impacts, depending on the gravity of the impact:

> Activities which might have an impact on nature shall be controlled, and the best available technologies that minimize significant risks to nature or other adverse effects shall be used; in particular:
>
> (a) Activities which are likely to cause irreversible damage to nature shall be avoided;
>
> (b) Activities which are likely to pose a significant risk to nature shall be preceded by an exhaustive examination; their proponents shall demonstrate that expected benefits outweigh potential damage to nature, and where potential adverse effects are not fully understood, the activities should not proceed;

---

[57] *See* Yeater & Kurukulasuriya, *supra* note 6, at 258.

[58] ALEXANDRE KISS & DINAH SHELTON, INTERNATIONAL ENVIRONMENTAL LAW, 236–37 (3d ed. 2004) [hereinafter KISS & SHELTON].

[59] *Id.*

[60] Principle 7, World Charter for Nature, GA Res. 37/7, *reprinted in* 22 ILM 455 (1983).

(c) Activities which may disturb nature shall be preceded by assessment of their consequences, and environmental impact studies of development projects shall be conducted sufficiently in advance, and if they are to be undertaken, such activities shall be planned and carried out so as to minimize potential adverse effects.[61]

This provision, remarkable for the early 1980s, embodies several important principles. First, it calls upon states to use best available technology to minimize the impact of development activities on the environment. Second, it calls upon states to avoid activities that are likely to have an irreversible impact on nature. Third, with regard to activities that are likely to cause significant damage to nature, the Charter requests states to subject the activities to an exhaustive examination of their impact on the environment. Fourth, where the potential impact of activities on nature is not fully understood, the Charter calls upon states not to proceed with such activity.[62] Fifth, those who wish to undertake activities that are likely to have a significant impact on the environment have to demonstrate that the benefits outweigh the potential damage to nature. Finally, environmental impact assessments are to be carried out sufficiently well in advance so that the impact on the environment can be minimized.

The Bergen Ministerial Declaration adopted in 1990 also contains a provision on environmental assessment.[63] It provides that states must undertake the prior assessment and public reporting of the environmental impact of projects that are likely to have a significant effect on human health and the environment and of the policies, programs and plans that underlie such projects. The provisions relating to environmental assessment are included in the section on awareness raising and public participation, which stress the need for democratic decision making. This provision limits the EIA process to activities likely to have a significant effect on human health or the environment.

By the time the Rio Declaration was adopted in 1992, the use of EIA as a tool in decision making at the national level was fairly widespread. However, it is the first universal instrument, adopted by consensus, to embody provisions on environmental assessment. Principle 17 refers to the neces-

---

[61] *Id.*, Principle 11.

[62] This provision embodies the first *Seeds* of the precautionary principle (albeit in its extreme form).

[63] Art. 6, Ministerial Declaration on Sustainable Development in ECE Region—United Nations Economic Commission Future, Bergen, Norway, May 15, 1990, UN Doc. A/CONF.2151/PC/10, Aug. 6, 1990.

sity to prepare an EIA for activities likely to have a significant impact on the environment, but limits it to those activities that are subject to a decision by a national authority.[64] As formulated, Principle 17 does not appear to deal with transboundary EIA but essentially with EIA for activities at the national level. Of course, it could be argued that if states are evaluating their activities for their environmental impact at the national level, it is less likely that such activities will cause extra-territorial environmental damage. While extra-territorial environmental damage is obviously a matter for international regulation, an EIA is essentially a domestic tool, hence the reference to "national instrument" in Principle 17 of the Rio Declaration.

Agenda 21 endorses the importance of prior assessment of activities and decisions within the context of integrated decision making.[65] It calls upon states, *inter alia*, to adopt:

> comprehensive analytical procedures for prior and simultaneous assessment of the impacts of decisions, including the impacts within and among the economic, social and environmental spheres; these procedures should extend beyond the project level to policies and programmes; analysis should also include assessment of costs, benefits and risks.[66]

Agenda 21 seems to refer to strategic environmental assessment (SEA), as reference is made to "the assessment of the impacts of decisions." This is further reinforced by the call to extend the environmental assessment process beyond the project level to policies and programs. Usually, environmental assessment is carried out for projects or activities and not so much in relation to decisions or programs. SEAs are relatively new and will be discussed later. It is, however, significant that Agenda 21 refers to the need to assess the impact of decisions. It is also significant that it calls for the evaluation of impact on the economic, social and environmental spheres and the costs, benefits and risks of the decision be analyzed. This provision shows the relationship between EIAs (or SEAs as the case may be) and sustainable development. In other words, an EIA is a tool to achieve sustainable development as it seeks to integrate environmental protection with economic development.

As noted in earlier chapters, no document containing principles akin to the Stockholm Declaration or the Rio Declaration was adopted at

---

[64] *See* Principle 17 of the Rio Declaration, *supra* note 16.

[65] *See* Agenda 21, UN Doc. A/CONF.156/21, *reprinted in* 31 ILM 874 (1992), ch. 8 on Integrating Environment and Development in Decision-making.

[66] *Id.*

Johannesburg in 2002: instead, a political declaration embodying "a commitment to sustainable development" was adopted. This document does not reiterate any principles of sustainable development. However, the Plan of Implementation adopted at Johannesburg which is similar to Agenda 21 refers to the need to develop and transfer environmentally sound technologies, in particular, to developing countries and countries with economies in transition on favorable terms. It also calls upon states to improve policy and decision making at all levels through improved collaboration between natural and social scientists and between scientists and policymakers, including making greater use of "integrated scientific assessments, risk assessments, and interdisciplinary and intersectoral approaches."[67]

Since its first inclusion in the National Environmental Protection Act in 1969 by the United States,[68] the environmental impact assessment process has progressed considerably. It has evolved from a project-oriented focus to a broader evaluation of policies and programs. While many countries still require the preparation of EIAs for projects that are likely to have a significant impact on the environment, several countries have adopted strategic environmental assessment of policies and programs, which is a much more holistic approach to achieving sustainable development. The project-oriented focus of environmental assessments has been criticized for not taking the broader picture into account—strategic assessment seeks to remedy this problem.[69]

The EIA process is now used worldwide "as an instrument for development planning and control."[70] Over 100 countries now have some kind of national legislation on EIA,[71] while the international provisions on EIA have also expanded. The role of EIA and its relationship with sustainable development and other areas, such as health, have been articulated as:

> At a minimum, EIA provides a systematic process for identifying, predicting and mitigating the adverse ecological and social effects of development projects and activities. More optimally, it has

---

[67] Plan of Implementation, UN Doc. A/CONF.199/20, *available at* http://www.johannesburgsummit.org., para. 109(b).

[68] *See* Kevin Grey, *International Environmental Impact Assessment: Potential for a Multilateral Environmental Agreement*, 11 COLO. J. INT'L ENVTL. L. & POL'Y 83 (2000).

[69] *See* the discussion in Section E.

[70] Australian EIA Network, *International Study of the Effectiveness of Environmental Assessment*, Report of the EIA Process Strengthening Workshop, Canberra Apr. 4–7, 1995, *available at* http://www.ea.gov.au/assessments/eianet/eastudy/aprilworkshop/paper1.html.

[71] *Id.*

become an integrated, planning-oriented approach to ensure development proposals and decisions are consistent with sustainability principles, and take account, wherever necessary, of cumulative effects and socio-economic, human health and other factors.[72]

Many national systems also require the analysis of alternatives to the proposed activity, which would be less harmful to the environment, together with reasons as to why they were rejected. Alternatives constitute the heart of an EIA[73]—it provides the decision maker with several options, in order that he may choose the best option that is economically, environmentally and socially viable.

An EIA should also have mitigatory measures and a monitoring plan, although the latter may not constitute part of the EIA itself. Monitoring or evaluation of a project is important, as the conditions that were originally present may have changed over the years and to ensure that the conditions attached to the approval of the project are being complied with. The need for continuous environmental assessment was recognized by Judge Weeramantry in his separate opinion in the *Case Concerning the Gabcikovo Nagymaros Project*.[74]

Activity at the international level over EIAs can be taken as an instance of internationalization of environmental protection, discussed in Chapter 1. Principle 17 of the Rio Declaration clearly shows that the principle is applicable at the national level. There is no mention of evaluating the transboundary impact of activities, although this could well be implied from the context of the Rio Declaration.

Several trends in EIA practices worldwide have been identified, although each state has tailored its EIA process to meet its environmental needs and socio-economic development:[75]

(1) EIA works in all political systems, whether civil law or common law, whether developing or developed countries, rich or poor.

---

[72] *Id.*

[73] *See* Yeater & Kurukulasuriya, *supra* note 6.

[74] *See* the Separate Opinion of Judge Weeramantry, 1997 ICJ 88, at 111 where he referred to the need for "continuous environmental assessment," which is generally referred to as post-project monitoring.

[75] *See* Nicholas A Robinson, *The 1991 Bellagio Conference on US-USSR Environmental Protection Institution: International Trends in Environmental Impact Assessment*, 19 B.C. ENVTL. AFF. L. REV. 591 (1992).

(2) While EIA is a young analytical tool for decision makers, its use is spreading rapidly. EIA works best when there is an independent authority to oversee the process.

(3) EIA has been effective in providing local people with an opportunity to be heard and to participate in decision making that affects their environment: "EIA facilitates democratic decision-making and consensus building regarding new development."[76]

(4) The EIA is effective in marshalling environmental data for decision makers. It also encourages inter-agency communication and consultation. This is an important development, as many government ministries and departments still operate on a sectoral basis. This is detrimental to environmental decision making, as issues are often interrelated requiring an integrated approach to decision making.

(5) Despite its value, the usefulness of EIAs is not always easy to establish. It has been resisted by all and sundry including decision makers and administrators until they become more familiar with its application.

(6) There is a tendency to use EIAs only for large projects. Many states have lists of projects or activities that should undergo the EIA process: "The tendency to limit EIA to large projects reflects a desire for administrative convenience rather than a mature application of the technique. Similarly, experience suggests that the use of lists as a threshold is evidence of an immature EIA process in which resort to a clear rule of thumb is preferable to a more sophisticated and initially open analysis based on scientific data."[77]

(7) EIA is not uniformly successful. There is a constant need to evaluate the effectiveness of the EIA process: to improve it to streamline it, and weed out its flaws.[78]

Moreover, the EIA procedures in many countries reflect two important facts: the project proponents often have a bias in favor of their proposal; and those who prepare EIAs must have some degree of independence in order to ensure objectivity in relation to identifying the negative impacts of the project as well as alternatives and mitigatory measures. Providing for public disclosure of information and public comments will ensure some degree of objectivity[79] as well as transparency in the process.

---

76  *Id.*

77  *Id.*

78  *Id.*

79  *Id.*

Many illustrations exist, which are evidence of an emerging pattern of state practice in relation to EIAs. Robinson asserts that it is becoming a norm of customary international law that states should undertake an EIA before taking action that could adversely affect either shared natural resources, another state's environment or the global commons.[80] An EIA is a tool to ensure that no state takes action to harm another state's environment, a prohibition embodied in Principle 21 of the Stockholm Declaration. In addition to states, many international organizations have adopted provisions in relation to EIAs, including the World Bank.[81] The Bank has adopted an EIA procedure that involves six steps: screening the proposal; preparing an initial executive project summary; preparing Terms of Reference for an EIA; preparing the EIA; reviewing the EIA and incorporating its findings into the project; and post-project monitoring and evaluation.[82]

It has been articulated that the "legacy of bureaucratic suspicion" can retard the affirmative use of EIA abroad[83] and that the diplomatic community needs education and training in EIA. It is a valuable management tool. With regard to the jurisprudential basis for EIA, Robinson notes:

> EIA reflects the well established duty under international law that each nation must act so as not to harm the environment of any other nation. In order to avert harm, each nation must examine the consequences of its actions and adjust as necessary. This rule of good neighborly relations is an ancient one. EIA can instruct nations on how to protect the environment globally just as it has taught them how to do so locally. EIA is not a linear process, but a feedback loop.[84]

The EIA process works not only in small settings but also on a global scale. Thus, it is a very versatile tool that can be adapted to any situation. It institutionalizes foresight and patience and requires us to give effect to the common sense phrase "look before you leap." Coupled with alternatives, the EIA gives the decision maker guidance as to the best option that is available to him in relation to that project or activity.

It has been noted that "Many international instruments, international institutions and most countries now require some form of EIA."[85] It is

---

[80]   *Id.*

[81]   *See* discussion in Section C.6 and also Chapter 1, Section B.8.

[82]   *See* discussion in Section C.6.

[83]   *See* Robinson, *supra* note 76, at 12.

[84]   *Id.*

[85]   *See* HUNTER ET AL., *supra* note 2, at 432.

increasingly recognized that states are under a general obligation to assess the environmental impacts of their activities, regardless of where those activities are located or where impacts will take place. Thus, this obligation extends to global environmental issues, transboundary environmental impacts and even to activities at the national level that have no apparent extra-territorial effect.[86] It has been adopted by financial institutions in their lending activities, as discussed later.

Despite the assertion that "the international community has recognized the fundamental role of EIA in the decisionmaking process for major development projects,"[87] this development is seen as being confined mainly to developed countries. It has been pointed out that "There is a danger that the advances in environmental protection and enhancement achieved through the use of EIA in developed nations will prove inadequate on a global scale unless a similar level of attention is given to the application of EIA in developing countries."[88] Due to the activities of UNEP, donor agencies, as well as the influence of international instruments such as the Rio Declaration, it has been noted that the EIA is now practiced in more than 100 countries worldwide.[89] However, there is a huge variation in its application in developing countries, just as there is a huge variation in developed countries.[90] While in many developing countries EIA legislation was adopted as a result of development assistance agencies, in some developing countries this initiation resulted from the adoption of a sustainable development agenda.[91] While it is hard to compete with the sophisticated EIA laws and procedure in developed countries, due to lack of resources and trained personnel, it is heartening to note that many developing countries have adopted the EIA process[92] and are beginning to implement public participation associated with it.

---

[86] *Id.*

[87] *See* William Murray Tabb, *Environmental Impact Assessment in the European Community: Shaping International Norms,* 73 TUL. L. REV. 923 (1999).

[88] *See* Christopher Wood, *Environmental Impact Assessment in Developing Countries: An Overview,* Conference on New Directions in Impact Assessment for Development: Methods and Practice, Nov. 24–25, 2003.

[89] *Id.*

[90] *Id.*

[91] *Id.*

[92] For a discussion of some of the developing countries with EIA legislation, *see id.*

## C. SURVEY OF INTERNATIONAL INSTRUMENTS THAT EMBODY PROVISIONS ON EIAs

Several international as well as regional conventions now embody provisions on EIAs: the 1991 Protocol on Environmental Protection to the Antarctic Treaty, 1982 UN Convention on the Law of the Sea, 1992 Convention on Biological Diversity; 1985 ASEAN Agreement and the 1986 Convention for the Protection of the Natural Resources and Environment of the South Pacific Region (Noumea Convention) are some examples. In addition, the 1991 Espoo Convention deals specifically with EIAs. Although geographically limited,[93] its adoption signifies the importance of prior assessment of environmental consequences at the international level. Special attention will be paid to the Espoo Convention as it is the first international convention to adopt provisions on EIAs.

### 1. 1991 Convention on Environmental Impact Assessment in a Transboundary Context [94]

Adopted under the auspices of the UN Economic Commission for Europe, the Espoo Convention refers to several principles in the Preamble:

- the relationship between economic activities and their environmental consequences;
- the need to ensure environmentally sound and sustainable development;
- the need to enhance international cooperation in assessing environmental impact in particular in a transboundary context;
- the need to develop anticipatory policies and of preventing, mitigating and monitoring significant adverse environmental impact; and
- the need to give consideration to environmental factors at an early stage in the decision-making process by applying EIA as a necessary tool to improve the quality of information presented to decision makers so that an environmentally sound decision can be made that, in turn, would minimize significant adverse impacts.[95]

Article 2 of the Convention provides that the parties shall take all appropriate and effective measures to prevent, reduce and control significant adverse transboundary environmental impact from proposed

---

[93] It is limited to the ECE region.

[94] *Supra* note 53.

[95] *Id.*, Preamble

activities.[96] Thus, the primary obligation of the parties is to prevent, reduce and control significant transboundary environmental impact. For activities listed in Appendix I, states are required to establish an environmental impact assessment procedure that permits public participation and preparation of EIA documentation described in Annex II. The party of origin must ensure that an EIA is undertaken prior to a decision to authorize an activity listed in Appendix I that is likely to cause a significant adverse transboundary impact.[97]

Environmental impact assessment has been defined as the "national procedure for evaluating the likely impact of a proposed activity on the environment."[98] The Convention thus makes it clear that what is envisaged is essentially a national procedure, but due to the possibility of transboundary impact, international regulation is necessary. This is a good example of the interaction between international law and national law.

The definition of "impact" is also important in this context. The Convention defines impact as:

> any effect caused by a proposed activity on the environment including human health and safety, flora, fauna, soil, air, water, climate, landscape and historical monuments or other physical structures or the interactions among these factors; it also includes effects on cultural heritage or socio-economic conditions resulting from alterations to those factors.[99]

This definition gives an expansive interpretation to "impacts," and it is obvious that these are not confined to environmental impacts. Moreover, this definition requires the analysis of the impacts on socio-economic conditions. Thus, for example, this definition would require the evaluation of the economic impact of potential ill health caused by a proposed activity.

The Convention emphasizes the importance of anticipatory policies:[100]

> Mindful of the need and importance to develop anticipatory policies and of preventing, mitigating and monitoring significant

---

[96] *Id.*, art. 2.

[97] *Id.*, art. 2(3).

[98] *Id.*, art. 1(vi).

[99] *Id.*, art. 1(vii).

[100] It must be noted that the Convention refers to an anticipatory approach, not a precautionary approach.

adverse environmental impact in general and more specifically in a transboundary context.[101]

It also refers to the need to promote the use of EIA at both the national and the international levels and to take environmental factors into consideration at an early stage in the decision-making process. Toward this end, EIA should be used as a necessary tool to improve the quality of information presented to the decision makers so that an environmentally sound decision can be taken.

The parties to the Convention are under an obligation to take appropriate and effective measures to prevent, reduce and control significant adverse transboundary environmental impact from proposed activities. Each party is required to take necessary legal, administrative or other measures to implement the provisions of the Convention.[102] These measures include the establishment of an EIA procedure in respect of activities listed in Appendix I to the Convention that are likely to cause a significant adverse transboundary impact. The procedure should allow for public participation and the preparation of an EIA as described in Appendix II.

The party of origin is required to ensure that an EIA is undertaken prior to a decision to authorize the activity.[103] It is also required to provide an opportunity to the public in the potentially affected state to participate in the EIA procedure in the same way that an opportunity is provided to the public of the party of origin.[104] This provision gives effect to the principle of non-discrimination initially advanced by the OECD in relation to transboundary environmental damage.[105] The OECD required the potentially affected public in both countries to be provided the same opportunity to be heard. This principle has been extended in relation to transboundary EIAs by the Espoo Convention.

The Convention embodies the obligations of notification and consultation and requires the party of origin to inform any state that could be

---

[101]  Preamble, *supra* note 53.

[102]  *Id.*, art. 2.

[103]  *Id.*, art. 2(3).

[104]  *Id.*, art. 2(6).

[105]  *See* Recommendation of the Council Concerning Transfrontier Pollution, C(74)224, Nov. 14, 1974, *available at* http://www.olis.oecd.org/horizontal/oecdacts.nsf/linkto/C(74)224. *See also* Recommendation of the Council for the Implementation of a Regime of Equal Right of Access and Non-Discrimination in Relation to Transfrontier Pollution, C(77)28/Final, May 17, 1977, *available at* http://www.olis.oecd.org/horizontal/oecdacts.nsf/linkto/C(77)28.

affected by the proposed activity listed in Appendix 1 as early as possible.[106] The purpose of such notification is to ensure adequate and effective consultations with potentially affected states. Some of the activities listed in Appendix I are: crude oil refineries; thermal power stations; installations for the production or enrichment of nuclear fuels; cast-iron smelting; extraction of asbestos; integrated chemical installations; construction of motorways, express roads and lines for long-distance railway traffic and airports; large dams and reservoirs; oil and gas pipelines; ports; pulp and paper manufacturing; major mining; deforestation of large areas; and major storage facilities for petroleum.[107] It is obvious that this list contains activities that can have a significant impact on the environment, hence the necessity for the preparation of an EIA.

Article 4 of the Convention notes that the EIA document should contain, as a minimum, the information contained in Appendix II. Such information should include: (1) a description of the proposed activity and its purpose; (2) a description of reasonable alternatives including the no-action alternative; (3) a description of the environment likely to be affected by the proposed activity and the alternatives; (4) a description of the potential environmental impact of the proposed activity and its alternatives and an estimation of its significance; (5) a description of mitigation measures; (6) an identification of gaps in knowledge and uncertainties encountered in compiling the required information; (7) an outline of monitoring and management programs and any plans for post-project analysis; and (8) a non-technical summary.[108]

Two factors of significance must be highlighted here: the reference to the discussion of alternatives; and the identification of gaps in knowledge. The discussion of alternatives is central to an EIA, and the idea is to present the decision maker with several options to choose from. Without a discussion of alternatives, it is hard to choose the best option. Thus, it has been articulated that alternatives are at the heart of an EIA.[109] However, the wording here, as well as national jurisprudence, suggests that only reasonable alternatives have to be discussed in the EIA.[110]

---

[106] Art. 3, *supra* note 53.

[107] *See* Annex I, *id.*, for a complete list of activities covered by the Convention.

[108] *See* Appendix II, *id.*

[109] *See* Yeater & Kurululasuriya, *supra* note 6.

[110] *See* ROGER FINDLEY, DANIEL FARBER & JODY FREEMAN, CASES AND MATERIALS ON ENVIRONMENTAL LAW (6th ed. 2003).

The requirement that the EIA document must also identify gaps in knowledge is also significant. This seems a reference to the precautionary principle, although it is not mentioned anywhere in the Convention. Since the EIA document essentially seeks to provide the decision maker with options, it is equally important to inform the decision-maker if knowledge on a particular issue was lacking or insufficient. While this may be a factor to prevent the decision maker from approving an activity, it does indicate that it is a factor to be taken into consideration. It is thus possible to see the seeds of the precautionary principle here.

The parties are then required to enter into consultations concerning the potential impact of the proposed activity, including measures to eliminate or reduce its impact, possible alternatives to the proposed activity, including the no-action alternative, possible measures to mitigate the significant transboundary impact and other forms of possible mutual assistance in reducing the transboundary impact.[111] The Convention also embodies, in an Annex, provisions relating to dispute settlement through arbitration.[112]

Appendix III contains general criteria to assist in the determination of the environmental significance of activities not listed in Appendix I. It may be recalled that Article 2 requires the EIA procedure only in relation to activities listed in Appendix I. The criteria to be taken into account are: *the size* of the proposed activity; *the location* (whether it is in close proximity to an environmentally sensitive area or an area of importance (for example, wetlands); and *the effects* (proposed activities with particularly complex and potentially adverse effects, including those likely to cause serious effects on humans or valued species or organisms, etc).[113] In this regard the parties must consider activities located in close proximity to an international border as well as those in a more remote area but are likely to cause significant transboundary effects.

The Convention further provides that the EIAs under the Convention shall, as a minimum, be undertaken at the project level of the proposed activity. The parties shall endeavor to apply these principles to policies, plans and programs.[114] Thus, while the provisions of the Convention should be applied at least at the project level, the parties should endeavor

---

[111] Art. 5, *supra* note 53.

[112] *Id.*, Appendix VII.

[113] *See id.*, Appendix III.

[114] *Id.*, art. 2(7).

to extend these principles to a more macro level. This is an acknowledgement of strategic environmental assessment.

With regard to notification of an activity listed in Appendix I, the party of origin shall notify any party that could be affected as early as possible and not later than when informing its own public about that activity. The notification shall contain, *inter alia:* (1) information on the proposed activity, including any available information on its possible transboundary impact; (2) the nature of the possible decision; and (3) an indication of a reasonable time within which a response is required.[115]

The affected party shall respond to the party of origin within the time frame specified in the notification and indicate whether or not it intends to participate in the EIA procedure.[116] If the affected party indicates that it does not wish to participate in the EIA procedure or does not respond within the specified time limit, provisions in Articles 3(5)–(8) and 4–7 will not apply.[117]

If the affected party responds that it wishes to participate in the EIA procedure, the following procedure shall be followed: the party of origin must provide to the potentially affected party/parties, relevant information regarding the EIA procedure, including an indication of the time schedule for sending comments, as well as relevant information on the proposed activity and its possible transboundary impact. If the party of origin so requests, the potentially affected party shall provide reasonably obtainable information under its jurisdiction that is necessary to prepare the EIA documentation.[118]

Once the EIA documentation has been completed, the party of origin must enter into consultations with the potentially affected party regarding the possible transboundary impact of the proposed activity and the measures that will be undertaken to reduce or eliminate its impact.[119] Consultations may relate to the possible alternatives to the proposed activity, including the no action alternative and possible measures to mitigate the transboundary impact and to monitor the effects of such measures at the expense of the party of origin. They may discuss other forms of possible mutual assistance and shall agree on a reasonable time-frame for the consultations.

---

[115] *Id.*, art. 3.

[116] *Id.*, art. 3(3).

[117] *Id.*, art. 3(4).

[118] *Id.*, art. 3(6).

[119] *Id.*, art. 5.

Furthermore, the parties shall ensure that in the final decision, due account is taken of the outcome of the EIA, including EIA documentation, as well as any comments received and the outcome of the consultations between the parties. The party of origin must provide to the affected party the final decision, as well as the reasons and considerations on which it was based. If additional information becomes available before the commencement of the activity and that could have materially affected the decision, that party shall immediately inform the other parties. Consultations shall be held, if one party requests, as to whether the decision needs to be revised.[120]

The Convention includes provisions on post-project analysis, and the parties are required to determine to what extent such analysis would be carried out given the likely significant adverse transboundary impact of the activity.[121] Also referred to as monitoring, post-project analyses help ensure that the conditions on which approval was granted are being carried out and that any unforeseen consequences are dealt with expeditiously. In some countries, a monitoring plan may be a component of the EIA document.[122] Appendix V contains the objectives of post-project analysis as: monitoring compliance with the conditions set out in the authorization or approval of the activity and the effectiveness of mitigation measures; review of the impact in order to cope with uncertainties; and verification of past predictions so that the same experience can be related to future activities of the same type.

Appendix IV to the Convention establishes an inquiry procedure under which a party can submit the question whether a proposed activity listed in Annex I is likely to have a significant adverse transboundary impact. The Secretariat has to notify immediately all the parties to the Convention of this submission. The inquiry commission shall consist of three members. Both the requesting party and the other party to the inquiry shall appoint a scientific or technical expert who together will designate the third expert who shall be the president of the inquiry. The inquiry committee is to take a decision within two months of the date of its establishment and based on accepted scientific principles. The final opinion shall be transmitted by the commission to the parties as well as to the Secretariat.[123]

---

[120] *Id.*, art. 6.

[121] *Id.*, art. 7.

[122] *See* CHRISTOPHER WOOD, ENVIRONMENTAL IMPACT ASSESSMENT: A COMPARATIVE REVIEW 197 (1995).

[123] Appendix IV, *supra* note 53.

A subsidiary body to the Meeting of the Parties, called the Working Group on EIA, has been established to assist in the implementation of the Convention and the management of the work plan.[124] The report of the fifth meeting of the Working Group on EIA refers to strengthening cooperation with other ECE conventions, prepare guidelines on good practices, strategic environmental assessment (noting that a Protocol on this subject would be open for signature in May 2003), sub-regional cooperation, database on EIA and public participation in EIA in a transboundary context.[125]

The Convention provides that four years after entry into force of the Convention for a particular party, that party may withdraw from the Convention by giving written notification to the Depository.[126] Any such withdrawal shall not affect the provisions of the Convention, where notification has been made before such withdrawal took effect.[127]

The Convention recognizes the importance of research and provides that specific research programs may be established by the parties aimed at: improving existing methods for assessing the impacts of proposed activities; achieving a better understanding of cause-effect relationships; analyzing and monitoring the implementation of decisions on proposed activities with the intention of minimizing or preventing impacts; developing environmentally sound alternatives to proposed activities; and developing methodologies for the application of the principles of environmental assessment at the macroeconomic level.[128] This provision further provides that the parties shall exchange the results of such research programs. Exchange of information in relation to research programs is another important development. This enables parties to collaborate on research and avoid duplication, thereby channeling scarce resources in the right direction. The Convention also

---

[124] Economic Commission for Europe, MP.EIA/WG.1/2003/2, Mar. 3, 2003.

[125] *Id.*

[126] Art. 19, *supra* note 53.

[127] Whether environmental conventions should provide for withdrawal at all is subject to debate and is closely related to the discussion of sovereignty. While it could be argued that environmental treaties should not provide specifically for withdrawal, states, as sovereigns, could withdraw from treaties anytime, as treaties are based on state consent. Having a withdrawal clause would ensure that withdrawal will not take place at the whim and fancy of states. There would be some consistency at least for a period of four years during which time parties cannot withdraw from the treaty. It can be argued, on the other hand, that the principle of *pacta sunt servanda* requires states to fulfill their treaty obligations in good faith. *See* art. 26 of the Vienna Convention on the Law of Treaties, 8 ILM 79 (1969), 1155 UNTS 331, signed May 23, 1969, entered into force Jan. 27, 1980.

[128] Art. 9, *supra* note 53.

indicates that the direction that it should take is towards the adoption of strategic environmental assessment at the macro level.

Appendix VI provides that parties may set up institutional arrangements within the framework of bilateral or multilateral agreements in order to give full effect to this Convention. Such arrangements may include: any additional requirements for the implementation of the Convention, taking into account specific conditions of the sub-region; institutional, administrative or other arrangements to be made on a reciprocal basis; harmonization of policies and measures for the protection of the environment, so that similar standards and methods related to EIA can be used; establishment of threshold levels and criteria; undertaking joint environmental impact assessment, developing joint monitoring programs and harmonizing methodologies.[129]

Two amendments to the Convention have been adopted since its entry into force in 1997. The first amendment allows non-ECE countries to accede to the Convention. By decision taken in 2003,[130] the parties decided to amend the Convention as follows: "Any other State, not referred to in paragraph 2 of this Article, that is a Member of the United Nations may accede to the Convention upon approval by the Meeting of the Parties."[131] This is an important amendment and seeks to expand the geographical scope of the Convention to cover states outside the ECE region. The more states that follow EIA provisions, the more likely it will be universally applied. This amendment also seeks to clarify that the "public" who may participate in EIA procedures includes civil society and in particular, non-governmental organizations.[132]

At its third meeting, the parties adopted the second amendment to the Convention[133] which amended, *inter alia*, Appendix I (by adding more activities that should undergo the EIA process), and also inserting a new article on review of compliance. Adding more activities to the category of activities, which are likely to cause a significant impact on the environment,

---

[129]  *Id.*, Appendix VI.

[130]  Decision II/14, June 2003, *available at* http://www.unece.org/env/eia/amendment.html.

[131]  New art. 17(3), *supra* note 53.

[132]  Decision II/14, *supra* note 130.

[133]  Meeting of the Parties to the Convention on Environmental Impact Assessment in a Transboundary Context, ECE/MP.EIA/6, Sept. 13, 2004, Decision III/17, *available at* http://www.unece.org/env/ eia/amendkjet2.html.

is important, as they have to follow the procedure laid down in the Convention which is subject to public participation.

The Convention also called upon the parties to keep under continuous review the implementation of the Convention, and to, *inter alia:* review the policies and methodological approaches to environmental assessment in order to further improve the procedures; exchange information regarding the experience on bilateral and multilateral agreements on the use of EIAs; and seek the services of competent international bodies and scientific committees.[134]

Despite its geographical limitation, and efforts have been made to expand its scope, the Convention is a significant development under international environmental law, as a hitherto national tool has been used in relation to transboundary environmental harm, thereby elevating the EIA process to the international level.

## 2.  Other Conventions

Several other conventions embody provisions on EIAs. Thus, for example, the Law of the Sea Convention contains several provisions on monitoring and environmental assessment. The Convention calls upon states to endeavor, as far as practicable, to observe, measure, evaluate and analyze the risks or effects of pollution of the marine environment.[135] It requires states to publish reports of the results obtained pursuant to Article 204.[136] The Convention also embodies provisions on the assessment of potential effects of activities:

> When States have reasonable grounds for believing that planned activities under their jurisdiction or control may cause substantial pollution of or significant and harmful changes to the marine environment, they shall, as far as practicable, assess the potential effects of such activities on the marine environment and shall communicate reports of the results of such assessments in the manner provided in Article 205.[137]

This is an example of an early international instrument providing for environmental assessment. The threshold level adopted here is that of substantial pollution damage to the marine environment or significant adverse

---

[134] Art. 11(2), *supra* note 53.

[135] Art. 204, *supra* note 21.

[136] *Id.*, art. 205.

[137] *Id.*, art. 206.

changes to the marine environment. However, the language adopted reflects the hortatory nature of the obligation. Nonetheless, the requirement that the results of such assessments should be disseminated to all states via competent international organizations is an important provision. No other obligations, such as the need for consultations or notification, are tied to the assessment process.

The Protocol to the Antarctic Treaty, adopted in 1991, recognizes the unique nature of the Antarctic environment and provides that activities in the Antarctic Treaty Area shall be planned and conducted so as to limit adverse impacts on the Antarctic environment and dependent ecosystems. The Protocol provides that activities in this area shall be planned on the basis of information sufficient to allow prior assessment of the possible impacts on the Antarctic environment.[138] Such judgments shall take account of: the scope of the activity, duration and intensity; the cumulative impacts of the activity; whether the activity will detrimentally affect any other activity in the area; whether technology and procedures are available to provide for environmentally sound operations; and whether capacity exists to monitor key environmental parameters. It also provides for regular monitoring of activities to assess their impact on the environment as well as to detect any unforeseen effects of the activities.

Article 8 deals with environmental impact assessment and provides that activities must undergo evaluation under the procedure embodied in Annex I. Annex I provides that the environmental impact of an activity must be considered in accordance with the appropriate national procedures and if an activity is likely to have less than a minor impact, the activity can proceed. Unless a comprehensive environmental evaluation is being prepared for a particular activity, an initial environmental evaluation shall be prepared, containing sufficient information to assess whether the activity in question may have more than a minor impact. Such evaluation shall contain a description of the project, alternatives to the proposed activity, and a consideration of cumulative impacts.[139]

If an initial examination reveals that a proposed activity is likely to have more than a minor impact, a comprehensive environmental evaluation shall be prepared. The Annex identifies the information that should go into such an evaluation. These include: a description of the project; direct, indirect, unavoidable and cumulative impacts of the activity; monitoring programs and measures to minimize the impact of the activity; identifica-

---

[138]  30 ILM 1461 (1991), signed Oct. 4, 1991, entered into force Jan. 14, 1998. art. 3.

[139]  *Id.*, Annex I.

tion of gaps in knowledge; and a non-technical summary.[140] A decision whether to proceed with an activity should be based on a comprehensive environmental evaluation and other relevant criteria.

Thus, this Protocol adopts a two-tier process, similar to the procedure adopted in some countries.[141] An initial environmental examination is to be carried out to determine whether a particular activity will have a significant (or more than a minor) impact on the environment. If this initial examination indeed revealed that the consequences are more than minor, a comprehensive environmental assessment has to be carried out. While some may argue that preparing two reports is a waste of money and a duplication of effort, preparing an initial environmental examination (which is less expensive and time consuming than a full-blown EIA) would eliminate some projects from the EIA process. Another approach is to identify activities that should undergo the EIA process because of the potential severity of the environmental impact (identified according to the size of the project or its location) and require other projects to undergo the initial examination process. This would eliminate the need to prepare two documents.

The Convention on Biological Diversity provides an example of environmental assessment in relation to a global environmental issue. It calls upon the parties, as far as possible and as appropriate to:

(1) Introduce appropriate procedures requiring environmental impact assessment of its proposed projects, which are likely to have a significant impact on biodiversity, with a view to avoiding or minimizing such effects. Public participation shall be allowed in such procedures where appropriate.

(2) Introduce appropriate arrangements to ensure that the environmental consequences of its programs and policies,[142] which are likely to have a significant impact on biodiversity, are taken into account.

(3) Promote on the basis of reciprocity, notification and exchange of information and consultation on activities, which are likely to have a significant transboundary impact on the biodiversity

---

[140] *Id.*, art. 3 of the Annex.

[141] Sri Lanka, for example, adopts a two-tier process. *See* Part IV C of the National Environmental Act (No. 47 of 1980 and amendment Act No. 56 of 1988) referred to in Sumudu Atapattu, *Sustainable Development, Myth or Reality?: A Survey of Sustainable Development under International Law and Sri Lankan Law*, 14 GEO. INT'L ENVTL. L. REV. 265 (2001).

[142] This is an example of a strategic environmental assessment. *See* discussion in Section E.

of other states, by concluding bilateral, regional or multilateral arrangements;

(4) In the case of imminent or grave danger to the biodiversity of other states, to notify them immediately and encourage international cooperation.[143]

It must be pointed out that while public participation is envisaged in relation to environmental assessments of projects, no such participation is envisaged for strategic assessment of policies or programs. In relation to possible significant transboundary damage, international principles of notification, exchange of information and consultations are applicable.

Moreover, it must be pointed out that in relation to projects, the Convention provides that public participation shall be allowed, where appropriate. Although the word "shall" indicates a level of compulsion, the words "where appropriate" seems to convey the idea that public participation is not compulsory and shall be provided for only when it is appropriate. This seems to dilute the importance of public participation and is contrary to contemporary international and national practice where public participation is usually provided in relation to all activities that undergo an EIA.

The United Nations Framework Convention on Climate Change, 1992, also provides an example of the use of environmental assessment in relation to a global environmental issue. It requires parties to:

Take climate change considerations into account, to the extent feasible, in their relevant social, economic and environmental policies and actions, and employ appropriate methods, for example, impact assessments, formulated and determined nationally, with a view to minimizing adverse effects on the economy, on public health and on the quality of the environment, of projects or measures undertaken by them to mitigate or adapt to climate change.[144]

The language used here is rather convoluted;[145] while the exact meaning is not clear it does seem to require states to take climate change considerations into account in relevant social, economic and environmental policies. This seems more of an instance of strategic environmental assessment than carrying out EIAs for individual projects.

---

[143] 31 ILM 822 (1992), 1760 UNTS 79, *available at* http://www.biodiv.org/, art. 14.

[144] 31 ILM 849 (1992), 1771 UNTS 107, signed May 9, 1992, entered into force Mar. 21, 1994, *available at* http://www.unfccc.de/, art. 4(1)(f).

[145] *See* PHILIPPE SANDS, PRINCIPLES OF INTERNATIONAL ENVIRONMENTAL LAW 805 (2d ed. 2002).

The Draft North American Agreement on Transboundary Environmental Impact Assessment[146] was drafted within the context of the North American Agreement on Environmental Cooperation between Canada, Mexico and the United States.[147] The Preamble specifically refers to the Stockholm Declaration, the Rio Declaration and the principles encapsulated in Principle 21.[148] The Preamble also refers to the "importance of developing anticipatory policies and of preventing, mitigating and monitoring significant adverse environmental impact in general and more specifically in a transboundary context, in accordance with the precautionary principle."[149]

The parties also refer to the need to give consideration to environmental factors at an early stage in the decision-making process by applying environmental impact assessment so that environmentally sound decisions can be made giving careful attention to minimizing significant environmental impact, particularly in a transboundary context that can limit potential conflicts between the parties.

The Draft Agreement defines an environmental impact as:

Any change caused by a proposed project on human health and safety, flora, fauna, soil, air, water, climate, the current use of lands and resources for traditional purposes by indigenous people or, physical structures, sites or artifacts that are of historical, archaeological, paleontological or architectural significance or, the interaction among these factors; it also includes impacts on cultural heritage or socio-economic conditions resulting from changes to these factors. Impacts include direct, indirect and cumulative impacts.[150]

Transboundary environmental impact assessment means a domestic assessment procedure used to evaluate the transboundary environmental impact of proposed projects. The definition of transboundary environmental impact is to be refined further.[151]

---

[146] *Available at* http://www.cec.org/pubs_info_resources/law_treat_agree/pbl.cfm?varlan=english. This was drafted by a group of experts.

[147] Signed 1993, *available at* http://www.cec.org/pubs_info_resources/law_treat_agree/naaec/index.cfm?varlan=english. *See also* 4 COMMISSION FOR ENVIRONMENTAL COOPERATION, NORTH AMERICAN ENVIRONMENTAL LAW & POLICY (2000).

[148] *Cf.*, Knox, *supra* note 48, who contends that neither the Draft Agreement nor the Espoo Convention refers to Principle 21 of the Stockholm Declaration.

[149] Preamble, *supra* note 147. It is interesting to note that the Preamble specifically refers to the precautionary principle. This could possibly be one reason why this document remains a draft, to date, given the U.S. opposition to the precautionary principle.

[150] Draft art. 1, *supra* note 147.

[151] *Id.*

The party of origin is under an obligation to notify potentially affected states of proposed projects located within 100 kilometers of the Canada-U.S. border or U.S.-Mexico border and falls within the category of projects in Appendix I or determined by the competent government authority to have the potential to cause significant transboundary environmental impacts, taking into account factors in Appendix III irrespective of the distance from the border.[152]

The procedure adopted in the Draft Agreement is very similar to that under the Espoo Convention. The party of origin shall notify the potentially affected party as early as possible, and not later than informing its own public about the proposed project, and early enough so that the public is given a meaningful opportunity to participate in the assessment process.[153]

The notification should contain sufficient information to inform the potentially affected state of the nature of the proposed project and should include elements outlined in Part I of Appendix II and include a reasonable time frame within which the potentially affected party should respond to the notification. If the party of origin has decided to conduct a transboundary EIA, the notification should also include information in Part II of Appendix II. If the potentially affected state does not respond within the time frame or indicates that it does not intend to provide comments, the party of origin has no further obligations under the Agreement.[154]

If a proposed project is likely to cause significant transboundary environmental impacts, the party of origin shall ensure that a transboundary EIA is undertaken, which should include the elements in Appendix IV and notify the potentially affected party, stipulating reasonable timeframes within which to respond. If no response is made or it is indicated that no comments would be provided, the party of origin has no further obligations under the Agreement.[155]

The party of origin shall allow the public of the potentially affected party to submit comments for the transboundary EIA process; participate in any public hearings held by the party of origin within its territory; the potentially affected state must make available relevant information received from the party of origin regarding the proposed project.[156] The draft

---

[152]   *Id.*, draft art. 2.

[153]   *Id.*, draft art. 3.

[154]   *Id.*, draft art. 9.

[155]   *Id.*, draft art. 10.

[156]   *Id.*, draft art. 12.

Convention also requires the party of origin to get close cooperation of the potentially affected state in this process. The party of origin must promptly inform the potentially affected state of the decision whether to allow the proposed project to proceed.[157] The provisions on mitigation, post-project monitoring, dispute settlement etc., are yet to be elaborated on.

### 3. ILC Draft Articles on Prevention of Transboundary Harm from Hazardous Activities[158]

The International Law Commission (ILC) has been grappling with the issue of "liability for lawful activities" for several years and changed its title to the present one.[159] The scope of the draft articles is given in Article 1 as activities not prohibited by international law that involve a risk of causing significant transboundary harm through their physical consequences. Under draft Article 3, the state of origin shall take all appropriate measures to prevent significant transboundary harm or minimize its risk. According to draft Article 6: the state of origin shall require prior authorization for any activity within the scope of these articles carried out in its territory or under its jurisdiction or control; any major changes to such an activity; or any plan to change such an activity. Any decision relating to such authorization shall be based on an assessment of the possible transboundary harm caused by that activity, including any environmental impact assessment.[160]

If the assessment indicates a risk of causing significant transboundary harm, the state of origin shall inform potentially affected states and provide relevant information, including any technical information. No decision to authorize such activity should be taken pending the response from the potentially affected state/s.[161] The state concerned shall enter into consultations at the request of any of them in order to work out an acceptable

---

[157]  *Id.*, draft art. 13.

[158]  Adopted by the Commission at its 53d session, *available at* http://www.un.org/law/ilc/.

[159]  The topic of liability for lawful activities was an offshoot from its work on state responsibility and its original title was "International Liability for Injurious Consequences Arising out of Activities Not Prohibited by International Law." *See* http://www.un.org/law/ilc/. Part of the problem with this topic is that its philosophical basis is rather shaky, and writers are not convinced of the need for a separate regime to govern "injurious consequences of lawful activities." It is submitted that causing injurious consequences to another state is a wrongful act and is covered by the principles of state responsibility.

[160]  Draft art. 7, *supra* note 158.

[161]  *Id.*, draft art. 8.

solution based on an equitable balance of interests in the light of draft Article 10.[162]

The factors to be taken into consideration in an equitable balance of interests are: the degree of risk of significant transboundary harm and the availability of means to prevent or minimize such harm; the importance of the activity; the risk of significant harm to the environment; the degree to which the state of origin and the potentially affected states are prepared to contribute to the costs of prevention; and the economic viability of the activity taking into account prevention costs and the standards of prevention.[163]

The draft articles provide for exchange of information in a timely manner while the activity is proceeding. The states concerned shall provide the potentially affected public relevant information, the risk involved and the harm that might result and seek their views. The parties must apply the principle of non-discrimination and allow access to judicial or other procedures to seek protection or other redress.[164] Articles 16 and 17 deal with emergencies, while Article 19 embodies provisions on dispute settlement.

As can be seen, neither the Draft Agreement on EIA nor the ILC draft articles go as far as the Espoo Convention on Tranboundary EIA. The fate of these two documents remains to be seen.

## 4.    1987 Goals and Principles of EIA Adopted by UNEP[165]

In 1987, UNEP adopted goals and principles of environmental impact assessment for adoption by states for application at the national, regional and international levels. It defines an EIA as "an examination, analysis and assessment of planned activities with a view to ensuring environmentally sound and sustainable development."[166]

It is interesting to note that a link is made between sustainable development and EIA in this document as early as in 1987, the year the WCED published its report *Our Common Future*. The very fact that reference is made to sustainable development is encouraging, given that WCED published its report that very year.

---

[162]  *Id.*, draft art. 9.

[163]  *Id.*, draft art. 10.

[164]  *Id.*, draft art. 12.

[165]  PATRICIA BIRNIE & ALAN BOYLE, BASIC DOCUMENTS ON INTERNATIONAL LAW AND THE ENVIRONMENT 27 (1995).

[166]  *Id.*

The goals of this document are: to ensure that before decisions are taken by a competent authority whether to undertake or authorize activities that are likely to significantly affect the environment, such environmental effects are taken fully into account; to promote the implementation of appropriate procedures in all countries consistent with national laws; to develop reciprocal procedures for information exchange, notification and consultation when proposed activities are likely to have significant transboundary effects.[167]

Thus, the UNEP guidelines apply to activities or projects likely to have a significant impact on the environment. While "significant impact" has not been defined in the guidelines, it is clear that only a fairly high level of potential environmental damage would trigger the application of the EIA procedure. Principle 2 requires states to adopt criteria and procedure, through legislation, regulation or other means, for determining whether an activity is likely to cause significant environmental damage and, therefore, would be subject to the EIA process. Allowing national law to rule on an important issue like this without offering any guidance can give rise to an uncertain situation. Granted that it is ultimately the national law that would govern the EIA procedure, it is, however, necessary to offer some guidance: otherwise, a rather inconsistent and arbitrary situation could arise, as there will be different views of what constitutes "significant" environmental damage. While discrepancies cannot be avoided altogether, some level of harmonization is necessary, particularly where significant transboundary environmental damage is envisaged. Otherwise, while one country may consider an activity to have a significant impact, another country may not consider so, and it would be difficult to apply the EIA procedure in such a situation.

Principle 1 urges states not to undertake or authorize any activities without evaluating, at an early stage, the environmental effects of that activity. If the extent, nature or location of the activity is such that it is likely to cause significant environmental damage, a comprehensive EIA should be undertaken according to the principles laid down in the guidelines.

The information that should be included, at a minimum, in an EIA document is listed in Principle 4. These include a description of the activity, the potentially affected environment, a description of practical alternatives, as appropriate; an assessment of the direct, indirect, cumulative, short-term and long-term effects of the proposed activity and the alternatives; an indication of gaps in knowledge and uncertainties; whether any transboundary environmental impact is likely; and a brief non-technical

---

[167] *Id.*

summary of the information.[168] The provisions here seem to have greatly influenced the Espoo Convention, discussed above, as the information that should be included in an EIA there are remarkably similar to the information listed here.

Principle 7 deals with public participation and provides that before a decision is made on an activity, interested groups and persons should be allowed appropriate opportunity to comment on the EIA. The guidelines further provide that once a decision is made to approve a proposed activity, such activity should be subject to appropriate supervision. This is referred to as post-project analysis in the Espoo Convention.[169]

Principles 11 and 12 deal with transboundary environmental effects and provide that states should endeavor to conclude bilateral, regional or multilateral arrangements, on the basis of reciprocity to provide notification, exchange of information and consultations on activities that are likely to cause significant transboundary environmental damage. Where an EIA indicates that transboundary environmental damage is likely to be caused by an activity, the state in question must notify the potentially affected state/s; provide them with relevant information and enter into timely consultations with one another.

These are important principles that are now part of customary international law. Principles of notification, information and consultation apply with regard to any transboundary damage, and access to information and public participation are significant components of the contemporary EIA process (in addition to being part of international human rights law). Thus, although non-binding in nature, the UNEP guidelines are important in that they have helped shape the law in this area. This is particularly noticeable in relation to the Espoo Convention as many provisions in the UNEP guidelines have been incorporated there.

## 5.  1985 European Community Directive on Environmental Assessment[170]

The Council Directive of June 27, 1985, on the Assessment of the Effects of Certain Public and Private Projects on the Environment[171] notes

---

[168]  Principle 4, *supra* note 165.

[169]  *See* art. 7, *supra* note 53.

[170]  *See* Tabb, *supra* note 87.

[171]  85/337/EEC of 1985, amended by directive 97/11/EC, adopted in 1997, *available at* http://europa.eu.int/comm/environment/eia/full-legal-text/85337.htm. Following signature of the Aarhus Convention, the Community adopted Directive

that general principles for the assessment of environmental effects of public and private projects likely to have a major effect on the environment should be introduced.[172] Article 3 of the Directive requires the EIA to identify, describe and assess the direct and indirect effects of a project on the following: human beings, fauna and flora; soil, water, air, climate and the landscape; material assets and the cultural heritage; and the interaction between these factors. Annex I to the Directive contains a list of projects subject to the EIA procedure under Article 4(1) of the Directive. For those projects listed in Annex II, member states must determine whether the projects shall be made subject to the EIA process. In other words, while subjecting the projects listed in Annex I to the EIA procedure is *mandatory* under the Directive, member states have discretion as to whether to subject the projects listed in Annex II to the EIA procedure.[173]

The Directive further requires the following information to be provided by the developer to the relevant authority in member states:

- a description of the project including, the site, design and size of the project;
- a description of mitigatory measures to avoid, reduce or remedy significant adverse effects;
- an outline of the main alternatives studied by the developer and an indication of the main reasons for his choice;
a non-technical summary of the information.[174]

In addition, member states are required to provide for public participation by specifying the places where the information can be obtained, the way the public may be informed and the manner in which the public would be consulted.[175]

The Directive also provides for transboundary EIA. Where an activity in one state is likely to cause significant effects on the environment of another state, the former state is under an obligation to provide the affected state/s information relating to the project, together with its pos-

---

2003/35/EC amending, *inter alia*, the EIA directive. It sought to align the provisions on public participation with those in the Aarhus Convention.

[172] *Id.*, Preamble.

[173] *See* Tabb, *supra* note 87, who notes that this bifurcated strategy in relation to projects coming within Annexes I and II "was to balance the need for consistency in application with the need for mandatory assessment of projects likely to cause the most significant environmental effects."

[174] Art. 5(3), *supra* note 171.

[175] *Id.*, art. 6.

sible transboundary impact. The would-be affected state may, if it chooses, participate in the EIA procedure in the former state. States are required to enter into consultations on the potential transboundary effects of the project and the measures proposed to reduce or eliminate such effects.[176]

The drawbacks of the EIA Directive have been identified as the lack of reference to alternatives as well as the need to consider the "no-action alternative:"[177]

> The 1997 Directive fails to emphasize, however, the central importance of identifying alternatives as an analytical tool, which would guide the competent authority within the Member State to decide the most desirable method of achieving the purposes of the project in light of environmental impact considerations. . . . Finally, unlike NEPA, the E.C. Directive does not contain a provision for considering taking "no-action" with respect to the proposal.[178]

The lessons that the international community can draw from the European Community law on environmental impact assessment have been identified as follows:

> The recognition of the need for an environmental impact assessment process to evaluate potentially significant effects associated with major development projects has steadily gained momentum in the international community. The historical development of impact assessment practice by the European Community lends insight into the potential future for such procedures as well as highlights some of the inherent difficulties and global ramifications for multinational development projects.[179]

### 6. 1989 World Bank Operational Directive[180]

According to the Operational Policy of the Bank on Environmental Assessment[181] the Bank requires the environmental assessment of projects

---

[176] *Id.*, art. 7.

[177] *See* Tabb, *supra* note 87, who notes that NEPA requires the discussion of the "no action" alternative and that "in NEPA the identification and analysis of alternatives to a proposed action is considered the 'heart' of the entire environmental impact statement process" (footnotes omitted).

[178] *Id.*

[179] *Id.*

[180] *See* Center for International Environmental Law, *A Comparison of Six Environmental Impact Assessment Regimes* (1995), *available at* http://www.ciel.org/publications.

[181] OP 4.01, Jan. 1999, *World Bank Operational Manual, available at* http://wbln0018.

proposed for Bank financing to ensure that they are environmentally sound and sustainable and thereby improve decision making. It states that the Bank favors preventive measures over mitigatory or compensatory measures. Such an assessment must take into consideration the natural environment (air, water and land), human health and safety; social aspects (involuntary resettlement, indigenous peoples and cultural property) and transboundary and global environmental aspects. The environmental assessment considers natural and social aspects in an integrated way.

The borrower is responsible for carrying out the EIA. According to the Bank operational policy, an EIA evaluates a project's potential environmental risks; examines alternatives to the project; identifies ways to improve project selection, siting, planning, design and implementation; provides ways of mitigating and managing adverse environmental impacts through project implementation.

For purposes of the EIA procedure, the Bank classifies projects into four categories: Category A where the proposed project is likely to have significant adverse environmental impacts that are sensitive, diverse or unprecedented. Under Category B, if the environmental impact is less than significant, a narrower EIA would be conducted than for those activities under Category A. For Category C projects—those that are likely to have a minimal impact on the environment—no EIA is necessary. Category F1 projects are projects that involve the investment of Bank funds through a financial intermediary in sub-projects which may result in adverse environmental impacts.

For all Category A and B projects, the borrower must consult would-be affected groups and local NGOs about the project's environmental aspects and take their views into account. For meaningful consultations between the borrower and the affected parties, the borrower must provide relevant information in a timely manner in a form and language understandable and accessible to the groups being consulted. This is an important provision, as often, these documents are made available only in English, which negates the whole purpose of consultation, as the would-be affected groups may not have a sufficient grasp of the language to fully participate in the process.

The International Financial Corporation (IFC) is the World Bank Group entity with the mandate to invest in private sector projects in developing countries. It requires environmental assessment of projects to help

---

worldbank.org/Institutional/Manuals/OpManual.nsf/toc2/9367A2A9D9DAEED385256 72C007D0972?OpenDocument.

ensure that they are environmentally sound and sustainable.[182] Environmental assessment is a process that depends on the nature, scale and potential environmental impact of a proposed project:

> EA evaluates a project's potential environmental risks and impacts in its area of influence; examines project alternatives; identifies ways of improving project selection, siting, planning, design, and implementation by preventing, minimizing, or compensating for adverse environmental impacts and enhancing positive impacts; and includes the process of mitigating and managing adverse environmental impacts throughout project implementation.[183]

IFC favors mitigation over compensation. It must take into account the natural environment, human health and safety; and social aspects as well as transboundary and global environmental factors. The IFC *Operational Policy on Environmental Assessment* notes that an EA considers natural and social aspects in an integrated way; it is initiated as early as possible in project processing; and it is integrated closely with economic, financial, institutional, social and technical analyses of the project. The project sponsor is responsible for carrying out an EA. The policy identifies various environmental assessment instruments that can be utilized in this regard: environmental impact assessment, environmental audit, hazard or risk assessment and environmental action plan (EAP). IFC undertakes environmental screening of each project and classifies it into one of four categories:

(1) Category A—if it is likely to have significant environmental impacts that are sensitive, diverse or unprecedented—for this category of projects, the project sponsor is responsible for preparing a report, normally an EIA;

(2) Category B—those projects whose impact on the environment is less severe than those under category A.

(3) Category C—where the project is likely to have a minimal impact on the environment—beyond screening, no further action is necessary for this category.

(4) Category F1—for projects that involve investment of IFC funds through a financial intermediary in sub-projects that may result in adverse environmental impacts.

For all Category A and for some appropriate Category B projects, the project sponsor must consult with affected groups and local NGOs, which

---

[182] International Finance Corporation, *Operational Policies*, OP 4.01, Oct. 1998, *at* http://www.ifc.org/enviro/EnvSoc/Safeguard/EA/ea/htm.

[183] *Id.*

must be initiated as early as possible. In order to have meaningful consultations, the sponsor must provide all relevant material in a timely manner in a form and language that are understandable and accessible to the groups being consulted.

The environmental assessment reports prepared for Category A projects must include the following information: an executive summary; policy, legal and administrative framework; project description; baseline data; environmental impacts; an analysis of alternatives that compares feasible alternatives to the proposed project site, technology, design and operation including the no-action alternative; an environmental action plan that covers mitigation measures, monitoring and institutional strengthening.[184]

## 7. Equator Principles

Influenced by the EIA provisions adopted by the World Bank, ten leading banks from seven countries[185] adopted the "Equator Principles" in 2003, which is a voluntary set of guidelines developed by the banks for managing social and environmental issues relating to the financing of development projects.[186] The banks will apply the principles globally and to all industry sectors. These principles are based on the policies and guidelines of the World Bank and IFC:

> In adopting the Equator Principles, a bank undertakes to provide loans only to those projects whose sponsors can demonstrate to the satisfaction of the bank their ability and willingness to comply with comprehensive processes aimed at ensuring that projects are developed in a socially responsible manner and according to sound environmental management practices.[187]

The banks will apply these principles to all loans for projects with a capital cost of $50 million or more. The banks will use a screening process for projects based on IFC's environmental and social screening process and will categorize projects as A, B or C (high, medium or low environmental or social risk). For A and B categories, the borrower has to complete an environmental assessment that must be subjected to a consultation process

---

184  *Id.*

185  These banks are: ABN AMRO Bank, N.V., Barclays PLC, Citigroup, Inc., Credit Lyonnais, Credit Suisse Group, HVB Group, Rabobank, Royal Bank of Scotland, WestLB AG, and Westpac Banking Corporation. *See Leading Banks Adopt Equator Principles, at* http://equatorprinciples.ifc.org/ifcext/equatorprinciples.nsf/Content/corepoints.

186  *Id.*

187  *Id.*

with the affected local stakeholders and will prepare environmental management plans addressing mitigation and monitoring of environmental and social risks.[188]

The issues that the environmental assessment must address include: sustainable development and the use of renewable natural resources; protection of human health, cultural properties and biodiversity; major hazards; socio-economic impacts; involuntary settlement; impacts on indigenous peoples and communities; cumulative impacts of existing projects, participation of affected parties in the design, review and implementation of the project and the consideration of environmentally and socially preferable alternatives.[189]

By 2006, the list of banks that have adopted the Equator Principles have grown to about 40, representing about 80 percent of project finance funds worldwide.[190] It has been noted that the Equator Principles are "a huge step forward for responsible banking."[191] As these banks are not empowered to publish derogations from their policies or the Equator Principles and are bound by strict rules of confidentiality, NGOs have argued that there is a lack of transparency.[192] It has been noted, however, that as environmental and social issues play a central role in these principles, "project sponsors must adapt to this new reality if they are to find financing at reasonable rates."[193]

## D. THE APPLICATION OF ENVIRONMENTAL ASSESSMENT BY VARIOUS INSTITUTIONS

### 1. The ICJ and Environmental Impact Assessment

In a few of the cases before the ICJ, issues relating to EIA have come to the forefront. The *Request for an Examination of the Situation in Accordance with Paragraph 63 of the Court's Judgment of 20 December 1974 in the Nuclear Tests (New Zealand v. France) Case*[194] New Zealand relied heavily on environmental impact assessment. According to its written pleadings:

---

[188]  *Id.*

[189]  *Id.*

[190]  *See A New Environment*, LEGAL WEEK, Feb. 2, 2006, *available at* http://www.legal-week.net/ViewItem.asp?Id.=27427.

[191]  *Id.*

[192]  *Id.*

[193]  *Id.*

[194]  1995 ICJ 288.

There is a clear obligation upon France to conduct an Environmental Impact Assessment before carrying out any further nuclear
tests at Mururoa and Fangataufa. This obligation flows, first, from
a specific treaty undertaking and, second, from customary international law derived from widespread international practice.[195]

### a.   New Zealand's Contentions

### i.   Treaty Provisions

New Zealand relied on the Convention for the Protection of the
Natural Resources and Environment of the South Pacific Region (the
Noumea Convention) of 1986 to which both New Zealand and France are
parties and which entered into force on August 22, 1990. Under Article 16
of this Convention, which deals with EIA, the parties have agreed to
develop and maintain technical guidelines and legislation giving adequate
emphasis to environmental and social factors to facilitate balanced development of natural resources and planning of major projects in order to
prevent or minimize harmful impacts on the Convention area. New
Zealand further argued that nuclear testing is not exempt from the
requirements laid down in the Convention and, therefore, there is a clear
obligation on the part of France to carry out an EIA.

New Zealand pointed out that the EIA procedure involves an open
consideration of the issues and provides an opportunity for all interested
parties to present their views. However, the mere carrying out of an EIA
does not entitle the party to proceed with the project: it can only do so if
the project is approved as being environmentally acceptable, giving full
consideration to any objections.

Noting that France has not carried out such an assessment as required
under Article 16 of the Noumea Convention, New Zealand pointed out
that even if it has, it has failed to share the results of the assessment with
the states of the South Pacific Region. Furthermore, it has an obligation
under Article 16 to make such results available to the South Pacific
Commission and, through it, to interested parties.

Responding to France's contention that effects of the tests are carefully
monitored, New Zealand stressed that it is not sufficient that monitoring
takes place after the event:

The requirement of environmental impact assessment is one of conduct *prior to* each test or series of tests. The whole purpose of such

---

[195] Written pleadings of New Zealand (1995), *available at* http://www.icj.org.

assessments is to determine in advance of experiments that they do not entail an unacceptable degree of risk to the environment."[196]

It was further pointed out by New Zealand that the results of investigations should be made public so that any debate can take place in an open and transparent manner. As the threshold that triggers the requirement for an EIA is the likelihood of a proposed activity causing significant environmental damage, there is no doubt that the underground nuclear testing by France fell into this category. Coupled with the precautionary principle, New Zealand argued, the burden would be on France to show that an EIA is not necessary, rather than on New Zealand to show that the preparation of an EIA is necessary. New Zealand also relied on the 1985 European Community Council Directive on EIA[197] (which is applicable to France) that covered nuclear testing.

## ii. Customary International Law

New Zealand contended that even if France were not bound by the provisions of the Noumea Convention, it would still be required by customary international law to carry out an EIA before conducting nuclear tests. New Zealand was of the view that the obligation to carry out such an assessment in relation to activities likely to cause significant damage to the environment, particularly in relation to transboundary damage—and nuclear tests clearly meet such criteria—is supported by a considerable amount of state practice. New Zealand also relied on the UNEP Draft Principles of Conduct,[198] UN Law of the Sea Convention, 1985 ASEAN Agreement,[199] 1985 European Community Environmental Assessment Directive, 1989 World Bank Operational Directive, 1991 Espoo Convention, 1991 Protocol on Environmental Protection to the Antarctic Treaty, the 1992 Convention on Biological Diversity as well as Principle 17 of the Rio Declaration.

Quoting Philippe Sands, New Zealand argued that:

The idea that environmental impact assessment may now be required as a matter of customary law, particularly at the regional level, is capable of being argued, particularly when the project con-

---

[196] *Id.* para. 82 (emphasis added).

[197] *See* Section C.5.

[198] Principle 5, *referred to in* PHILIPPE SANDS, PRINCIPLES OF INTERNATIONAL ENVIRONMENTAL LAW 580 (1st ed. 1995).

[199] Association of South East Asian Nations Agreement on the Conservation of Nature and Natural Resources, signed July 9, 1985, *reprinted in* 15 EPL 64 (1985).

cerned is likely to have very significant effects on the environment and those effects will be transboundary.[200]

New Zealand claimed that "France's consistent refusal to carry out a procedure which is now accepted virtually world-wide as absolutely essential in this class of activity"[201] constituted the first element of illegality of France's conduct.[202]

### b. Decision of the Court

Unfortunately, the Court did not pronounce on the issue, despite having been given a unique opportunity to do so. Just like in 1974 when the issue arose for the first time, 20 years later the Court dismissed the case again on a technicality. It held that since the 1974 application related to atmospheric testing, New Zealand was not entitled to rely on paragraph 63 of the 1974 judgment (upon which New Zealand relied on for jurisdiction)[203] to bring a case against France for underground testing. Thus, the Court did not seize the opportunity to pronounce on the legal status of EIA and the precautionary principle, heavily relied on by New Zealand to establish the illegality of France's conduct.

While Judge Shahabuddeen appended a separate opinion, Judges Weeramantry, Koroma and *ad hoc* judge Sir Geoffrey Palmer appended dissenting opinions.

### c. Dissenting Opinion of Judge Weeramantry

Judge Weeramantry discussed several principles of international environmental law, including the inter-generational equity principle, the precautionary principle, environmental impact assessment and the obligation not to cause damage to the environment of other states.

---

[200] *See* SANDS, *supra* note 145, at 594. Of course, Sands does not unequivocally state that conducting an EIA is part of customary international law for activities likely to cause a significant impact on the environment. He seems to draw a cautious conclusion that it is capable of being so argued, particularly at the regional level.

[201] *See supra* note 195.

[202] New Zealand then relied on Principle 21 of the Stockholm Declaration, Principle 2 of the Rio Declaration as well as art. 4(6) of the Noumea Convention to establish that France has, by conducting nuclear tests, breached the general obligation embodied in those provisions. New Zealand also relied on the precautionary principle.

[203] 1974 ICJ 253. The basis for jurisdiction was discussed in Chapter 3, Section E.1.a. *See infra* note 204 and accompanying text.

With regard to EIA, Judge Weeramantry noted that it was ancillary to the broader principle of precaution and posited that it is "gathering strength and international acceptance, and has reached the level of general recognition at which this Court should take notice of it."[204]

Judge Weeramantry referred to the UNEP Goals and Principles of Environmental Impact Assessment, particularly Principles 1 and 4, and said that on an issue of this magnitude, the principle of EIA would *prima facie* be applicable in terms of the current state of international environmental law. Stating that New Zealand has placed a strong *prima facie* case before the Court, Judge Weeramantry admonished the Court:

> I regret that the Court has not availed itself of the opportunity to enquire more fully into this matter and of making a contribution to some of the seminal principles of the evolving corpus of international environmental law. The Court has too long been silent on these issues and, in the words of ancient wisdom, one may well ask "If not now, when?"[205]

Judge Weeramantry also noted that the Court enjoys a position of special trust and responsibility, particularly in relation to the global commons:

> This Court, situated as it is at the apex of international tribunals, necessarily enjoys a position of special trust and responsibility in relation to the principles of international environmental law, especially those relating to what is described in environmental law as the Global Commons. When a matter is brought before it which raises serious environmental issues of global importance, and a *prima facie* case is made out of the possibility of environmental damage, the Court is entitled to take into account the Environmental Impact Assessment principle in determining its preliminary approach.

> Of course the situation may well be proved to be otherwise and fears currently expressed may prove to be groundless. But that stage is reached only after the Environmental Impact Assessment and not before.[206]

---

[204] Dissenting Opinion, Judge Weeramantry, 1995 ICJ 317, at 344.

[205] *Id.* at 362 (footnotes omitted).

[206] *Id.* at 345.

### d. Dissenting Opinion of Ad Hoc Judge Sir Geoffrey Palmer

Noting that international environmental law has developed remarkably since the Stockholm Conference in 1972, Judge Palmer pointed out: "As the law now stands it is a matter of legal duty to first establish before undertaking an activity that the activity does not involve any unacceptable risk to the environment. An EIA is simply a means of establishing a process to comply with that international legal duty."[207] As noted above, this obligation flows from Principle 21 of the Stockholm Declaration.

Judge Palmer referred to New Zealand's contention that it is unlawful for France to conduct nuclear tests before it has undertaken an environmental impact assessment "according to accepted international standards."[208] Unless such an assessment establishes that the tests will not give rise to radioactive contamination of the marine environment, the rights of New Zealand, as well as of other states, will be violated. Thus, according to New Zealand, the only way to ascertain whether nuclear tests, as contemplated by France, resulted in radioactive contamination is to carry out an environmental impact assessment. New Zealand also argued that if nuclear waste was released into the environment, the effect upon marine natural living resources, particularly fish and plankton, could be significant.[209] This would, in turn, affect the food chain and highly migratory species, including tuna. While the Court is not in a position to make definitive conclusions on the scientific evidence, the submissions show that there were real issues at stake here. The true question is related to the assessment of the level of risk. However, the two states appeared to have very different approaches to this issue. Judge Palmer articulated that there is no doubt that France had engaged in activities that have substantially altered the environment. The nature of the risks inherent in the activity itself would suggest caution. Some way of calculating those risks is necessary to decide whether New Zealand has satisfied the test. Things that should be considered in such an analysis are: the magnitude of the recognizable risk of harm; the probability of the risk materializing; utility and benefits of the conduct; and the cost of measures needed to mitigate the risk. Judge Palmer was of the view that the Court should apply a risk-benefit analysis. There must be a balancing of the risks of the activity, the probability of harm, the utility of the activity and the measures needed to eliminate the risk. The costs of averting the risk in this instance are low—France needs to provide a full scientifically verifiable environmental assessment in accor-

---

[207] Dissenting Opinion, Sir Geoffrey Palmer, 1995 ICJ 381, at 411, para. 87.

[208] *Id.* at 401, para. 59.

[209] *Id.*, paras. 60 and 61.

dance with modern environmental practice. It can be said that New Zealand has made out a *prima facie* case.

Judge Palmer, tracing the evolution of international environmental law, referred to several principles of the Stockholm Declaration and noted that some of these principles have become part of customary international law. The consensus flowing from Rio is itself significant in the context of the arguments advanced in this case: "The Rio Declaration refined, advanced, sharpened and developed some of the principles adopted at Stockholm. Many of the principles were repeated but some new ones make an appearance."[210] Judge Palmer was of the view that the precautionary principle (Principle 15 of the Rio Declaration) and the environmental impact assessment (Principle 17 of the Rio Declaration) as being among the new principles.

Judge Palmer also referred to the ILC draft articles on Prevention of Transboundary Harm from Hazardous Activities,[211] which state that:

A state shall ensure that an assessment is undertaken of the risk of such activity. Such an assessment shall include an evaluation of the possible impact of that activity on persons or property as well as in the environment of other States.[212]

While noting that international environmental law has developed rapidly, Judge Palmer noted that "as the law now stands, it is a matter of legal duty to first establish before undertaking an activity that activity does not involve an unacceptable risk to the environment. An EIA is simply a means of establishing a process to comply with that international legal duty."[213] It was submitted by New Zealand that other parties likely to be affected by the risks have a right to: (1) know what investigations have been carried out; (2) propose additional investigations; and (3) verify for themselves the result of such investigations. This is an important argument and is closely tied to the principles of cooperation, exchange of information and consultation, which are established principles of customary international law.

In conclusion, Judge Palmer noted that the following propositions have been established by principles of international law:

---

[210] *Id.* at 407, para. 78.

[211] *See supra* note 158.

[212] Draft art. 12, *id.*

[213] *Supra* note 207, at 411, para. 87.

(a) international environmental law has developed rapidly and is tending to develop in a way that provides comprehensive protection for the natural environment;

(b) international law has taken an increasingly restrictive approach to the regulation of nuclear radiation;

(c) customary international law may have developed a norm for requiring environmental impact assessment where activities may have a significant effect on the environment;

(d) the norm involved in the precautionary principle has developed rapidly and may now be a principle of customary international law relating to the environment;

(e) there are obligations based on Conventions that may be applicable here requiring environmental impact assessment and the precautionary principle to be observed.[214]

He noted, like Judge Weeramantry, that the legal developments since 1974 are sufficient to meet a *prima facie* test that the legal circumstances have changed sufficiently since the 1974 judgment was rendered to favor an examination of it. He also noted that since nuclear contamination is a continuing harm, the applicable law must be determined at the date the Court is called upon to apply it.

With regard to the development of international environmental law, particularly sustainable development, Judge Palmer noted:

The obvious and overwhelming trend of these developments from Stockholm to Rio has been to establish a comprehensive set of norms to protect the global environment. There is a widespread recognition now that there are risks that threaten our common survival. We cannot permit the onward march of technology and development without giving attention to the environmental limits that must govern these issues. Otherwise the paradigm of sustainable development embraced by the world at the Rio Conference cannot be achieved.[215]

It is regrettable that the Court missed, yet again, an opportunity to contribute to the development of international environmental law; Judge Weeramantry lamented that the Court had not made a contribution "to

---

[214] *Id.* at 412, para. 91.

[215] *Id.* at 409, para. 84.

some of the seminal principles of the evolving corpus of international environmental law."[216]

## 2. Case Concerning the Gabcikovo Nagymaros Project[217]

The facts of this case were discussed in Chapter 2. The Court noted that the parties were entitled to take new environmental norms into consideration when agreeing upon the means to be specified in the Joint Contractual Plan, and indeed this could be done under Articles 15–19 of the Plan. While not specifically stating what these new environmental norms are the Court noted: "The awareness of the vulnerability of the environment and the recognition that environmental risks have to be assessed on a continuous basis have become much stronger in the years since the Treaty's conclusion."[218] While the Court was clearly referring to the principle of environmental impact assessment, it did so in fairly vague language avoiding the issue of its legal status—hence the reference to the recognition of the need to assess the environmental risks as having become "much stronger."

Hungary for its part contended that "a joint environmental impact assessment of the region and of the future of Variant C in the context of the sustainable development of the region" should be carried out.[219]

The Court noted that the project's impact upon the environment is a key issue and in order to evaluate the environmental risks, current standards must be taken into consideration: "The Court is mindful that, in the field of environmental protection, vigilance and prevention are required on account of the often irreversible character of damage to the environment and of the limitations inherent in the very mechanism of reparation of this type of damage."[220] The Court further noted that:

New norms and standards have been developed. . . . Such new norms have to be taken into consideration, and such new standards given proper weight, not only when States contemplate new activities but also when continuing with activities begun in the past. This need to reconcile economic development with protection of

---

[216] *Supra* note 204, at 362.

[217] Hungary v. Slovakia, 1997 I.C.J. 7.

[218] *Id.*, para. 112.

[219] *Id.*, para. 125.

[220] *Id.*, para. 140.

the environment is aptly expressed in the concept of sustainable development.[221]

Despite several references to new norms and standards of environmental protection, the Court failed to enumerate what these new norms and standards are, apart from the reference to sustainable development and the indirect reference to environmental assessment. It was left, yet again, to Judge Weeramantry to elucidate principles of international environmental law.

### a.  Separate Opinion of Judge Weeramantry

In appending a separate opinion, Judge Weeramantry referred extensively to the principle of sustainable development, the principle of continuing environmental impact assessment and the appropriateness of using *inter partes* legal principles for the resolution of problems of an *erga omes* nature.[222]

With regard to EIA, Judge Weeramantry noted that it has assumed an important role in this case and said that it was "gathering strength and international acceptance, and had reached the level of general recognition at which this Court should take notice of it."[223] According to Judge Weeramantry:

> [e]nvironmental impact assessment means not merely an assessment prior to the commencement of the project, but a continuing assessment and evaluation as long as the project is in operation. This follows from the fact that EIA is a dynamic principle and is not confined to a pre-project evaluation of possible environmental consequences. As long as a project of some magnitude is in operation, EIA must continue, for every such project can have unexpected consequences; and considerations of prudence would point to the need for continuous monitoring.[224]

Judge Weeramantry referred here to the need to continually assess the impact of an activity throughout its project cycle. While neither international environmental law nor national law normally mandates "continuing environmental assessment," monitoring of activities post-project is necessary to ensure that conditions attached to the approval of a project are

---

[221]  *Id.*

[222]  *See* Separate Opinion, Judge Weeramantry, 1997 ICJ 88.

[223]  *Id.*

[224]  *Id.*

complied with and to ensure that any unforeseen consequences are addressed. The reference to continuous environmental assessment is important as, in many instances, once an EIA has been carried out prior to the commencement of an activity, not much attention is paid to it when the activity is in operation. Judge Weeramantry emphasized that inasmuch as it is important to evaluate the potential consequences of a proposed activity, it is equally important to continually monitor that activity.

Thus, for activities that are likely to have a significant impact on the environment, the preparation of an EIA is necessary; once a project is in operation, effective monitoring of the activity must be carried out, since it is not possible to anticipate every possible environmental danger which could be caused by the project. Judge Weeramantry noted that "the concept of monitoring and exchange of information has gathered much recognition in international practice"[225] and there is growing international recognition of the concept of continuous monitoring as part of the EIA.[226]

Finally, Judge Weeramantry noted that "EIA, being a specific application of the larger general principle of caution, embodies the obligation of continuing watchfulness and anticipation."[227] He observed that the parties themselves have incorporated environmental considerations into the Treaty of 1979, which meant that the principle of EIA was also built into the Treaty. Judge Weeramantry pointed out that this obligation extends to the continuous monitoring of the project.[228]

Several important principles were articulated by Judge Weeramantry here: There is a general obligation to evaluate the consequences of an activity if there are reasonable grounds to believe that the activity will cause significant environmental damage. This obligation is a continuing obligation—it does not stop the moment the activity is approved or implemented. There is an obligation to ensure that once in operation, the activity does not cause damage to the other states. How does one ensure this? It requires the state to monitor the activity in question—while monitoring by an independent body is the best, often this obligation is passed on to the operator of the activity. In other words, the law can provide for self-monitoring with

---

[225]  *Id.*

[226]  *Id.*

[227]  *Id.*

[228]  Judge Weeramantry noted that over half a century ago, the *Trail Smelter Arbitration* recognized the importance of continuous monitoring. The arbitral tribunal called upon Canada to refrain from causing further damage by fumes to the territory of the United States.

periodic checks by the state authority. Such checks are essential to ensure that no significant damage is being caused by the activity in question. The national law can provide when such monitoring reports have to be furnished to the state agency, what details should be included in them, etc.[229]

Thus, while the ICJ failed to endorse the principle of EIA (although reference was made to the need to continually assess environmental risks), Judge Weeramantry referred to its importance in his separate opinion. Although only *dicta*, it is, as one commentator observed, "a breath of fresh air."[230] It is generally felt that the Court missed a golden opportunity to develop principles of international environmental law in the first ever contentious case involving environmental issues to present before it.[231] It seemed that the Court was more concerned with state responsibility, law of treaties and state succession than with international environmental law: "ultimately, international environmental law ran a poor third to treaty law and international watercourses law as a basis for the court's judgment."[232]

## E. STRATEGIC ENVIRONMENTAL ASSESSMENT

As noted in the foregoing discussion, the environmental impact assessment procedure is usually carried out at the project level. Thus, an EIA is carried out for individual projects and this has, at times, caused problems as the cumulative impact of projects has not been taken into consideration. It can also be *ad hoc* in that it does not take the larger picture into consideration. In an effort to avoid the drawbacks of the EIA procedure, several countries have adopted the assessment of policies and programs for their environmental impact. This is called strategic environmental assessment (SEA).

The adoption of a SEA does not mean that carrying out an EIA for projects would be unnecessary. It means that policies and plans must be evaluated for their environmental impact and that individual projects would be carried out within the framework of these policies or programs. A combi-

---

[229] In his dissenting opinion Judge Oda too referred to the need for environmental assessment: "The Parties should continue the environmental assessment of the whole region and search out remedies of a technical nature that could prevent the environmental damage which might be caused by the new Project," Dissenting Opinion, Judge Oda, 1997 ICJ 158, at 168.

[230] *See* Afshin A-Khavari & Donald R. Rothwell, *The ICJ and the Danube Dam Case: A Missed Opportunity for International Environmental Law?* 22 MELB. U. L. REV. 507 (1998).

[231] *Id. See also* Ida Bostian, *Flushing the Danube: The World Court's Decision Concerning the Gabcikovo Dam*, 9 COL. J. INT'L ENVTL. L. & POL'Y 401 (1998).

[232] *See* A-Khavari & Rothwell, *supra* note 230.

nation of SEAs and EIAs would ensure a holistic approach to policies, programs and projects.

SEAs are a relatively new procedure; therefore, all the intricate details that can arise in practice have not yet been worked out. However, literature on the subject is expanding[233] and there is increasing consensus in relation to SEAs and public participation, particularly in Europe.

The Aarhus Convention recognizes the importance of strategic environmental assessment. Article 7 calls upon parties to make appropriate provisions for the public to participate during the preparation of plans and programs relating to the environment within a transparent and fair framework, having provided the necessary information to the public. The parties are also required to "endeavor" to provide opportunities for public participation in relation to the preparation of policies. Article 8 seeks to extend this procedure in relation to the preparation of regulations and legally binding rules that may have a significant effect on the environment.

A protocol was adopted within the framework of the Espoo Convention on Strategic Environmental Assessment[234] at a meeting held in Kiev in May 2003 at which 35 states plus the EC signed the Protocol. The Protocol recognizes the "importance of integrating environmental, including health, considerations into the preparation and adoption of plans and programs and, to the extent appropriate, policies and legislation."[235]

It also refers to the Aarhus Convention, the Lucca Declaration,[236] Rio Declaration, the third Ministerial Conference on Environment and Health,[237] the WSSD, and the Espoo Convention on Transboundary EIA. Emphasizing the importance of providing for public participation in strategic environmental assessment, the Protocol points out that SEAs should have an

---

[233] *See* SEA and Integration of the Environment into Strategic Decision-Making, Final Report (May 2001); PROCEEDINGS OF INTERNATIONAL WORKSHOP ON PUBLIC PARTICIPATION AND HEALTH ASPECTS IN STRATEGIC ENVIRONMENTAL ASSESSMENT (Jiri Dusik ed. 2000).

[234] Protocol on Strategic Environmental Assessment to the Convention on Environmental Impact Assessment in a Transboundary Context, signed May 21, 2003, *available at* http://www.unece.org/env/eia/sea_protocol.htm.

[235] *Id.*, Preamble.

[236] Lucca Declaration adopted at the first meeting of the Parties held in Lucca, Italy on Oct. 21–23, 2002, ECE/MP.PP/2/Add.1, Apr. 2, 2004, *available at* http://www.unece. org/env/pp/mop1.htm.

[237] *See* Declaration of the Third Ministerial Conference on Environment and Health, 1999, *available at* http://www.euro.who.int/Document/E69046.pdf/.

important role in the preparation and adoption of plans, programs and, to the extent appropriate, policies and legislation.[238]

The Protocol refers to promoting sustainable development, and the parties have based themselves on the conclusions of the Rio Conference, in particular, Principles 4[239] and 10[240] of the Rio Declaration and Agenda 21, the outcome of the Third Ministerial Conference on Environment and Health held in London in 1999[241] and the WSSD.

Stressing the importance of public participation in SEAs, the Preamble acknowledges the benefits to the health and well-being of present and future generations, if the need to protect health is taken into account as an integral part of SEAs. It also refers to the need for enhancing international cooperation in assessing the transboundary environmental impacts of proposed plans and programs as well as policies and legislation. The Protocol places high priority not only on protecting the environment but also the health of the people (including the health of future generations), clearly drawing a link between protecting the environment and people's health. It is clear that a healthy environment is essential for people to enjoy their right to health. While almost all environmental treaties refer to this link,[242] international human rights treaties are yet to draw a link between the enjoyment of human rights and a healthy environment.[243]

The objective of the Protocol is to provide for a high level of protection of the environment, including health, by:

- ensuring that environmental considerations are thoroughly taken into account in the development of plans and programs;
- contributing to the consideration of environmental concerns in the preparation of policies and legislation;
- establishing clear, transparent and effective procedures for strategic environmental assessment;
- providing for public participation in strategic environmental assessment; and

---

[238] Preamble, *supra* note 234.

[239] Principle 4, *supra* note 16, deals with the principle of integration.

[240] Principle 10, *supra* note 16, deals with public participation in environmental issues.

[241] *See supra* note 237.

[242] *See* Chapter 1, Section B.3, for a discussion on environmental protection and health.

[243] *See* the discussion on the right to environment in Chapter 1, Section B.1.a.

- integrating environmental concerns into measures and instruments designed to further sustainable development.[244]

Strategic environmental assessment has been defined as "the evaluation of the likely environmental, including health, effects, which comprises the determination of the scope of an environmental report and its preparation, the carrying out of public participation and consultations and the taking into account of the environmental report and the results of public participation and consultations in a plan or programme."[245]

The Protocol defines "environmental, including health, effect" as "any effect on the environment, including human health, flora, fauna, biodiversity, soil, climate, air, water, landscape, natural sites, material assets, cultural heritage and the interaction among these factors."[246] It is not clear what is meant by material assets here. The inclusion of cultural heritage in an environmental treaty is an innovation, as damage to cultural heritage would not typically fall within the definition of environmental effects. This was probably included to protect the rights of indigenous and native communities. It is pertinent in this context to examine the Convention on the Protection and Promotion of the Diversity of Cultural Expressions, adopted under the auspices of UNESCO in October 2005.[247] It draws a link between, *inter alia*, cultural diversity and sustainable development. According to the Convention:

> Cultural diversity is a rich asset for individuals and societies. The protection, promotion and maintenance of cultural diversity are an essential requirement for sustainable development for the benefit of present and future generations.[248]

The SEA Protocol calls upon each party to take the necessary legislative, regulatory and other appropriate measures to implement the provisions of the protocol within a clear, transparent framework.[249] It further provides that each party shall seek to ensure that officials and authorities assist the public in matters covered by the Protocol. Parties are also required to promote the objectives of the Protocol in international deci-

---

[244] Art. 1, *supra* note 234.

[245] *Id.*, art. 2(6).

[246] *Id.*, art. 2(7).

[247] *Available at* http://www.unesco.org/culture/culturaldiversity/convention_en.pdf.

[248] *Id.*, art. 2(6).

[249] Art. 3, *supra* note 234.

sion-making processes and in international organizations. The public[250] shall be able to exercise its rights without any discrimination as to nationality, citizenship or domicile.

Each party must ensure that a SEA is carried out for plans and programs referred to in paragraphs 2, 3, and 4, which are likely to have significant environmental effects.[251] Strategic environmental assessments are required to be carried out in respect of plans and programs prepared for agriculture, forestry, fisheries, energy, industry, mining, transport, regional development, waste management, water management, telecommunications, tourism, town and country planning or land use, and which set the framework for future development consent for projects listed in Annex I and any other projects listed in Annex II that require the preparation of an EIA under national legislation.

For plans and programs other than those referred to in paragraph 2, a SEA shall be carried out if the party so determines under Article 5(1). The Protocol exempts the following plans and programs from the application of the provisions of the Protocol: those relating to national defense or civil emergencies and financial or budget plans and programs. It is unfortunate that national defense programs and financial programs are excluded from the scope of the Protocol, as these can have significant environmental impacts. There is an increasing recognition under international law of the link between security and environmental degradation, including international terrorism.[252] Similarly, financial programs and plans should be evaluated for their environmental impact. National budgets and financial plans and programs are sometimes screened for their human rights impact.[253] There is no reason why they should not be evaluated for their environmental impact.

Article 5(1) requires the parties to determine whether plans and programs referred to in Article 4 are likely to have a significant environmental impact: (1) through a case-by-case examination; (2) by specifying the type of plans or programs; or (3) a combination of both approaches. To the extent appropriate, parties shall endeavor to provide opportunities for public par-

---

[250] The Protocol defines "the public" as natural or legal persons and their associations, organizations or groups. *Id.*, art. 2(8).

[251] *Id.*, art. 4.

[252] *See* OUR COMMON FUTURE, REPORT OF THE WORLD COMMISSION ON ENVIRONMENT AND DEVELOPMENT (1987).

[253] Thus, sometimes, national budgets are screened to see how much money is allocated for issues such as health, education, women's rights, children's rights, etc.

ticipation in screening plans and programs under this provision, parties are further required to ensure the timely availability of conclusions under Article 5(1) as well as reasons for not requiring a SEA by appropriate means.

Under Article 6 parties are required to establish arrangements for the determination of relevant information to be included in the environmental report under Article 7(2). To the extent appropriate, the parties shall endeavor to provide opportunities for public participation when determining relevant information to be included in the environmental report.

Article 7, which deals with environmental reports, provides that for plans and programs subject to a SEA, parties shall ensure that an environmental report is prepared. The environmental report shall identify, describe and evaluate the likely significant environmental effects of implementing the plan or program and its reasonable alternatives. The report shall contain the information specified in Annex IV taking into account: (1) current knowledge and methods of assessment; (2) the content and level of detail of the plan or program and its stage in the decision-making process; (3) the interests of the public; and (4) the information needs of the decision-making body.

Annex IV contains the information to be included in the reports under Article 7(2). Such information include: the contents and the main objective of the plan or program; current state of the environment and its likely evolution if the plan is not implemented; the environment and health in areas likely to be significantly affected; the environmental problems relevant to the plan or program; environmental objectives established at international, national and other levels that are relevant to the plan or program and the ways in which these objectives and environmental considerations have been taken into consideration during its preparation; measures to prevent, reduce or mitigate any significant adverse effects on the environment; an outline of the reasons for selecting the alternatives, including technical deficiencies or lack of knowledge; monitoring measures; the likely significant transboundary environmental effects; and a non-technical summary.

It is significant that even in relation to SEAs, a discussion of reasonable alternatives is necessary; it should also refer to the current knowledge and methods of assessment. Similar to the Framework Convention, the Protocol requires the parties to discuss the no-action alternative, lack of knowledge in relation to a particular issue, mitigatory and monitoring measures proposed and include a non-technical summary.

Article 8 deals with public participation and provides that parties shall ensure early, timely and effective opportunities for public participation in the SEA of plans and programs. They must make public draft plans or programs and the environmental report in a timely manner. The parties shall further ensure that these reports are available to the public in a timely manner and that the public have the opportunity to express their opinion within a reasonable time frame. They must also determine the arrangements for informing the public and consulting with them, and such arrangements must be publicly available. For this the parties can take into account the elements listed in Annex V to the extent appropriate.

According to Annex V, the following elements may be included in the public participation procedure: the proposed plan or program and its nature; the authority responsible for its adoption; the envisaged procedure including the commencement of the procedure, opportunities for public participation and the time and venue of any envisaged public hearing; the authority from which the relevant information can be obtained; the authority to which comments or questions can be submitted; and what environmental information relating to the plan or program is available. The parties must also indicate the likelihood of the plan or program undergoing a transboundary assessment procedure.

Article 10 embodies provisions on transboundary consultations. Where a party of origin considers that the implementation of a plan or program is likely to have significant transboundary environmental effects, or where a party so requests, the party of origin shall, as early as possible, notify the affected party. This notification shall contain the draft plan or program and the environmental report and information regarding the decision-making procedure, including a reasonable time schedule for receiving comments. The affected party must indicate within the timeframe specified whether it intends to enter into consultations. Where such consultations take place the parties shall agree on the arrangements to ensure that the public and the authorities in the affected party are informed and an opportunity given to forward their comments within a reasonable time frame.

When a decision is taken to adopt a plan or program, due account is taken of the conclusions of the environmental report, the measures to prevent, reduce or mitigate the adverse effects identified in the environmental report and the comments received pursuant to Articles 8–10. The public as well as the authorities and the parties consulted must be informed of the decision, and the plan or program must be made available to them. The parties must also give a statement summarizing how environmental considerations have been integrated into it; how the comments received were taken into account; and the reasons for adopting it in the light of the alternatives considered.[254] Once the plan or program has been adopted, the

---

[254] Art. 11, *supra* note 234.

parties must monitor the significant environmental effects in order to identify, at an early stage, unforeseen adverse effects. The monitoring results shall be made available to the relevant authorities and the public.

Article 13 deals with policies and legislation, and calls upon parties to endeavor to ensure that environmental concerns are considered and integrated, to the extent appropriate, if such policies and legislation are likely to have a significant impact on the environment. Article 25 contains a provision similar to Article 19 of the parent Convention on withdrawal.

Thus, the procedure to be adopted in relation to strategic environmental assessment is similar to that in relation to EIAs. Both envisage a process of public participation in relation to activities likely to have a significant impact on the environment (including health), and both require the documents to be available for public scrutiny. Thus, while SEAs operate at the macro level, EIAs operate at the project level. Unfortunately, neither the Convention nor the Protocol defines significant environmental effects. The Protocol does not make it clear who has the obligation to prepare SEAs, although it requires parties to consult relevant authorities in the preparation. Another clear drawback is that much of the language in the Protocol falls into the realm of "soft law"[255]—many references are made to "endeavor to take" measures "as appropriate."

The European Union has also adopted a Directive on the Assessment of the Effects of Certain Plans and Programs on the Environment.[256] The objective of the Directive is "to provide for a high level of protection of the environment by ensuring that an environmental assessment is carried out of certain plans and programmes and that the results of the assessment are taken into account during the preparation and adoption of such plans and programmes." For the purposes of this Directive, plans and programs refer only to town and country planning plans and programs as well as modifications to existing plans and programs.

The Directive requires the preparation of an environmental assessment before the adoption or submission to the legislative procedure of a plan or program. Minor modifications to existing plans and programs shall require an environmental assessment only where the member states consider that such modifications are likely to have significant negative environmental effects. Where an environmental assessment is required under Article 4,

---

[255] *See* Pierre-Marie Dupuy, *Soft Law and the International Law of the Environment*, 12 MICH. J. INT'L L. 420 (1991).

[256] COM/96/0511 FINAL-SYN 96/0304, *available at* http://europa.eu.int/comm/environment/eia/full-legal-text/96pc511.htm.

the competent authority shall prepare such a statement containing the information referred to in the Annex. The information shall be in such detail as may reasonably be required to assess the significant direct or indirect effects of implementing the plan or program on human beings, fauna, flora, soil, water, air, climate, landscape, material assets and the cultural heritage. The statement must also contain a non-technical summary of the information.[257]

The following details must be included in the environmental statement: the contents of the plan or program and its main objective; environmental characteristics of any area likely to be significantly affected by the plan or program; any existing environmental problems; the likely significant environmental effects of implementing the plan or program; alternatives and the reasons for not adopting those alternatives (such as alternative types of development, or alternative locations); measures envisaged to prevent, reduce and, where possible, offset any significant adverse effects on the environment; and any difficulties encountered in compiling the required information.[258]

The draft plan or program, as well as the environmental statement, shall be made available to the environmental authorities concerned and the public concerned. These bodies and the public must be given the opportunity to express their opinion before its adoption or submission to the legislative procedure. Article 7 deals with transboundary environmental assessment and requires member states to forward a copy of the draft plan or program and the relevant environmental statement to the would-be affected member state who shall indicate whether it wishes to enter into consultations. The parties shall agree on a reasonable time frame for the consultations.

Before taking a decision on the plan or program, the competent authority shall take into consideration, the relevant environmental statement, any opinions expressed under Article 6 and the results of consultations under Article 7.[259] When a plan or program is adopted, the competent authority shall inform the environmental authorities, the public concerned and the member state under Article 7 and make available a copy of the plan or program as well as a statement of how the comments were taken into consideration under Article 8.

---

257 *Id.*

258 *Id.*, Annex.

259 *Id.*, art. 8.

While the European Council Directive does not specifically refer to strategic environmental assessment, it is clear that it seeks to evaluate the environmental impact at the macro level. However, the Directive applies only to a very limited category of plans and programs and hence limits the application of the Directive. Since, however, several individual members have adopted SEAs at the national level, the limited application of the Directive may not be that significant.

Several features of SEAs can be summarized here: they seek to evaluate the environmental impact at the macro level; they require the discussion of alternatives (similar to EIAs); and they are public documents subject to public participation. Where there are potential transboundary effects, the parties are under an obligation to enter into consultations. Transparency thus plays an important role in relation to these procedures.

## F. ENVIRONMENTAL ASSESSMENT AND PARTICIPATORY RIGHTS

A significant feature of the environmental assessment process is that, very often, it is subject to public participation. Thus, EIA documents are considered as public documents open to public comments and participation. This has resulted in democratization of the environmental decision-making process. This is an important feature of the EIA process, and public participation in the decision-making process is a principle of good governance.[260] Thus, it can be said that the EIA procedure promotes good governance.[261] As discussed in Chapter 2, sustainable development envisages both substantive and procedural elements;[262] the right to information,[263] public participation and the right to remedies are considered the procedural elements of sustainable development. Thus, there is a close link between sustainable development, EIAs, participatory rights and good governance.

Why is public participation important? Why is access to information important? It is generally accepted that decisions that are taken with the involvement of those who are likely to be affected by that decision lead to better decisions in the long term. It is only fair that those who are likely to be affected by a decision be heard before a decision is taken. That people

---

[260] KONDRAD GINTHER, ERIK DENTERS & PAUL J.I.M. DE WAART EDS., SUSTAINABLE DEVELOPMENT AND GOOD GOVERNANCE (1995).

[261] *Id.*

[262] *See* Chapter 2, Sections E and F.

[263] *See* Gary Rischitelli, *Developing a Global Right to Know*, 2 ILSA J. INT'L & COMP. L. (1995), who calls for uniform right-to-know requirements at the international level, which is important to protect human health and the environment.

have a right to participate in the decision-making process is a widely accepted principle, both in human rights law[264] and international environmental law[265] (as well as national environmental law).

Participatory rights consist of three pillars: the right to information, the right to participate in the decision-making process and the right to justice. While these rights are established rights under international human rights law, it was only recently that these rights have become part of the international environmental law discourse. It must be noted, however, that although participatory rights first emerged in relation to the EIA process, they need not be tied to the EIA process. In other words, public participation is a broader right, and should be so recognized, irrespective of whether an EIA is being prepared for a particular project. This broader version is recognized in the Rio Declaration.[266] Since an EIA is generally carried out in relation to activities that are likely to have a significant impact on the environment, limiting participatory rights to such a procedure could leave out activities that may still cause considerable environmental damage while falling short of the "significant damage" threshold. Thus, participatory rights should be recognized irrespective of the magnitude of the environmental damage in question. As recognized in Principle 10 of the Rio Declaration:

> Environmental issues are best handled with the participation of all concerned citizens, at the relevant level. At the national level, each individual shall have appropriate access to information concerning the environment that is held by public authorities, including information on hazardous materials and activities in their communities, and the opportunity to participate in decision-making processes. States shall facilitate and encourage public awareness and participation by making information widely available. Effective access to judicial and administrative proceedings, including redress and remedy, shall be provided.[267]

One drawback of this formulation is that environmental information held by private bodies is not covered by it. Moreover, the language used in Principle 10—such as "appropriate access" to information—has been crit-

---

[264] *See* art. 25, ICCPR, *available at* http://www.unhchr.org.

[265] *See* Aarhus Convention, 38 ILM 517 (1999) and Principle 10, Rio Declaration, *supra* note 16.

[266] *See* Principle 10, Rio Declaration, *supra* note 16.

[267] Principle 10, Rio Declaration, *supra* note 16.

icized for being vague.[268] While it has been contended that the reference to the "national level" subordinates the exercise of these rights to domestic law,[269] it is difficult to see how this could be implemented otherwise. It is up to states to implement this right at the national level (sometimes even at the sub-national or local level); except in the context of transboundary environmental damage, an EIA process cannot be implemented at the international level. Even then, documentation must be prepared at the national level. Public participation must necessarily take place at the national level and, hence, subject to national law.[270] What international law seeks to do is to provide a common standard upon which national laws can be formulated.

Despite its drawbacks,[271] Principle 10 is important in many respects. It requires states not only to facilitate public awareness and participation, but also to *encourage* such participation. Thus, the mere provision of an opportunity to participate or the mere availability of information is not sufficient. States will have to ensure that information is accessible to the public; it is in a language that is widely understood by people; the information is not technical; and that people are aware of their right to make comments and participate in the decision-making process. States may also have to, through its public bodies, conduct awareness and public education programs on environmental issues to ensure that the members of the public fully understand the issues involved. It also requires states to provide effective access to judicial and administrative remedies. Thus, Principle 10 goes beyond the mere provision of information and participation. Given the increasing convergence between environmental law and human rights law, and the advent of international sustainable development law,[272] the non-rights language employed in Principle 10 may not be significant. Indeed, sustainable development also envisages public participation and, to that extent, overlaps with good governance.[273] It can thus be said that partici-

---

[268] *See* Marc Pallermaerts, *International Environmental Law From Stockholm to Rio: Back to the Future?, in* GREENING INTERNATIONAL LAW 1, at 11–12 (Philippe Sands ed., 1994).

[269] *Id.* at 12.

[270] *See* the discussion in Section C.1 of the provisions in the Espoo Convention on public participation in relation to activities likely to cause transboundary environmental harm.

[271] *E.g.,* Principle 10 requires *appropriate* access to information. It is not clear what "appropriate" means in this context. In addition, Principle 10 does not employ rights language—it does not state that people have a *right* to information or the *right* to participate in the decision making process. *See id.*

[272] *See* Chapter 2, Section K and also Chapter 7.

[273] *See* discussion in Chapter 1, Section B.1 and Chapter 2, Section F.

patory rights are essential components of both good governance and sustainable development.

The importance of public participation in the environment context was recognized at the international level when the Aarhus Convention was adopted in 1998 under the auspices of the ECE. This is an important step for the realization of environmental rights, as these rights were hitherto confined to the human rights field. Although geographically limited in its application (confined to ECE states), it has ramifications for the entire international community and is the first international environmental convention to adopt environmental procedural rights. In this context, the Convention breaks new ground in international environmental law.

## 1.   Aarhus Convention on Access to Information, Public Participation in Decision Making and Access to Justice in Environmental Matters, 1998[274]

As noted above, the Aarhus Convention breaks new ground in international environmental law as being the first international environmental instrument, albeit regional, to adopt participatory rights in relation to the environment, in addition to recognizing a substantive right of people to a healthy environment. It was also the first time that NGOs were actually involved in the drafting and negotiation process.[275] This probably led to a better overall product.

The Preamble to the Convention refers to Principle 1 of the Stockholm Declaration, Principle 10 of the Rio Declaration, the General Assembly resolution on the need to ensure a healthy environment for the well-being of individuals[276] and the European Charter on Environment and Health.[277] It affirms the need to protect, preserve and improve the quality of the environment and to ensure sustainable and environmentally sound development and recognizes that adequate protection of the environment is essential for the enjoyment of basic human rights, including the right to life itself.

---

[274]   *Supra* note 265 [hereinafter the Aarhus Convention].

[275]   *Human Rights and the Environment: The Role of Aarhus Convention,* submission by the UN Economic Commission for Europe provided as input to the report being prepared by the Office of the High Commissioner for Human Rights pursuant to Res. E/CN.4/RES/2003/71, Dec. 2003, *available at* http://www.unece.org/, para. 9.

[276]   GA Res. 37/7, Oct. 28, 1982.

[277]   *Available at* http://www.who.dk/eprise/main/WHO/AboutWHO/Policy/20010827 _3.

The Preamble further recognizes every person's right to live in an environment adequate to his or her health and well-being and the duty to protect and improve the environment for the benefit of present and future generations. It further notes that in order to assert this right and observe this duty, people must have participatory rights. It seeks to further the accountability of and transparency in decision making and to strengthen public support for decisions on the environment. The Convention notes the important role that individual citizens, non-governmental organizations, as well as the private sector can play in protecting the environment. It acknowledges that public authorities hold environmental information in the public interest and that effective judicial mechanisms should be accessible to the public. Moreover, environmental concerns should be fully integrated into the governmental decision-making process, and public authorities must be in possession of accurate, comprehensive and up-to-date information on the environment.

The objective of the Aarhus Convention is as follows:

> In order to contribute to the protection of the right of every person of present and future generations to live in an environment adequate to his or her health and well-being, each Party shall guarantee the rights of access to information, public participation in decision-making, and access to justice in environmental matters in accordance with the provisions of this Convention.[278]

It is thus clear from Article 1 that the main objective of the Convention is the realization of the right of every person of present and future generations to live in a healthy environment. This is the first time that the right of future generations to a healthy environment has been included in a binding instrument. The Convention recognizes participatory rights as a way of realizing the right to environment.[279] The explicit link made in the Convention between the right to environment and participatory rights is a significant development.[280] Thus, the Convention indicates that without providing for public participation, it would be difficult to realize the right

---

[278] Art. 1, *supra* note 265.

[279] *See* the discussion in Chapter 1, Section B.1.a on current debate on the right to environment.

[280] The Report prepared for the Third Ministerial Conference on Environment and Health, 1998, notes that the Convention includes a general obligation to guarantee access to information, public participation and access to justice in order to contribute to the protection of the right to environment: "In doing so, it sets a new precedent in international environmental legislation."

to environment. In other words, the right to environment and participatory rights go hand in hand.

### a. Access to Information

Access to information is one of the three pillars of rights recognized in the Convention, which can be considered as the foundation for other rights. The Convention defines "environmental information" as any information in written, visual, aural, electronic or any other material form on: (1) the state of elements of the environment including the interaction among these elements; (2) factors, activities or measures, including administrative measures, environmental agreements, policies, legislation, plans and programs affecting or likely to affect the elements of the environment, and economic analyses and assumptions used in environmental decision making; and (3) the state of human health and safety, conditions of human life, cultural sites and structures.

Article 3 requires each party to take necessary legislative, regulatory and other measures to establish and maintain a clear, transparent and consistent framework to implement the provisions of the Convention. Each party shall endeavor to ensure that officials and authorities assist and provide guidance to the public in seeking access to information, in facilitating participation and seeking access to justice. Here the language reflects the soft nature of the obligation as parties only need to "endeavor to ensure."

Parties are also required to promote environmental education and awareness among the public especially in relation to how to obtain information, participate in decision making and to obtain justice. The Convention does not preclude the right of parties to adopt broader provisions than that are envisaged under the Convention. The Convention shall not require any derogation from any existing rights to information, participation and access to justice. It further provides that the public shall have access to information, to participate in decision making and have access to justice without discrimination on the basis of citizenship, nationality or domicile.

Article 4 provides that the public authorities in each state party must make environmental information available, within the framework of national legislation, in response to a request for such information. The party requesting such information need not have an actual interest in the information sought. Such information must be provided as soon as possible and, in any event, within one month of the request, unless an extension up to two months is justified given the volume and the complexity of the information sought. In that event, the applicant must be informed of the delay and the reasons for it.

Information can be refused on several grounds:

- where the public authority does not hold the information requested;
- where the request is manifestly unreasonable or formulated too generally;
- where it concerns material in the course of completion or concerns internal communications of public authorities;
- where the disclosure would adversely affect the confidentiality of the proceedings of public authorities;
- where it affects international relations, national defense or public security;
- where it affects the confidentiality of commercial and industrial information;
- where it affects intellectual property rights;
- where it affects interests of a third party that has supplied the information;
- where it affects the environment to which the information relates, such as breeding sites of rare species;
- where it affects the confidentiality of personal data or files relating to a natural person where that person has not consented to the disclosure.[281]

However, the Convention requires these grounds to be interpreted in a restrictive manner, taking into account the public interest served by disclosure. Where information exempted from disclosure can be separated without prejudice to its confidentiality, public authorities shall make remainder of information available to the public. A refusal of a request, together with reasons for refusal, shall be in writing if the request was in writing or if the applicant so requests. Such refusal shall be made as soon as possible and at least within a month, unless an extension is justified. Public authorities may charge a reasonable fee for supplying information.

This long list of exceptions to the right to information gives the impression that the Convention gives with one hand and takes away with the other.[282] However, these are standard grounds on which information can be refused—grounds such as national defense, industrial secrecy, intellectual property rights, etc., are common. It must be noted that, as far as the Convention is concerned, dissemination of information is the rule, not the exception. This is an important development, as the earlier practice

---

[281] Art. 4, *supra* note 265.

[282] *See* Atapattu, *supra* note 141.

has been the reverse: refusal of information was the norm, rather than the exception. It is noteworthy that access to environmental information—the cornerstone of the other rights in the Convention—is recognized as a basic right.

Article 5 of the Convention relates to the collection and dissemination of environmental information. It provides that parties must ensure that: (1) public authorities possess and update environmental information relevant to their functions; (2) mandatory systems are established to ensure an adequate flow of information about proposed and existing activities that may significantly affect the environment; (3) in the event of any imminent threat to human health or the environment, all relevant information that could enable the public to take measures to prevent or mitigate the harm is disseminated immediately to members of the public who may be affected.

Within the framework of national law, each party shall ensure that public authorities make environmental information available in a transparent manner and is effectively accessible by: (1) providing information to the public about the type of information held by the relevant public authority, terms and conditions under which such information is made accessible and the process for obtaining such information; (2) establishing practical arrangements such as registers; and (3) providing access to information in publicly accessible lists or registers free of charge.

The parties must also ensure that environmental information become progressively available in electronic databases and publish, at regular intervals, a national report on the state of the environment and disseminate legislation and policy documents, international treaties and other significant international documents on environmental issues.

Parties are required to encourage operators whose activities have a significant impact on the environment, to inform the public regularly of the environmental impact of their activities and products through voluntary eco-labeling or eco-auditing or by other means. Parties are also required to take steps to establish pollution inventories or registers at the national level. While it is desirable to encompass activities of private persons within the ambit of the provisions on access to information, these are only envisaged to be voluntary—no penalty will attach to non-compliance.

### b. Public Participation

Articles 6–8 of the Convention deal with public participation. While access to information is important, public participation can influence the decision-making process, which can be even more important. Inasmuch as it is not possible to participate in an effective manner without having access to information, if no proper forum is available for public participation, the mere provision of information is insufficient. Thus, these two rights go hand in hand.

With regard to the decisions on whether to permit activities listed in Annex I, the parties shall apply the provisions in Article 6 of the Convention. The parties can, in accordance with national law, decide whether to apply the provisions of the Convention to those activities not listed in Annex I but that may, nevertheless, have a significant effect on the environment. The parties have the discretion as to whether to subject activities serving national defense purposes to this process.

The Convention requires the public concerned to be informed of the proposed activity early in the environmental decision-making procedure in an adequate, timely and effective manner.[283] The public shall also be informed of the public authority responsible for making the decision; the envisaged procedure; the time and venue for any public hearing; what environmental information pertaining to the activity is available; the relevant public authority to which comments can be submitted; and whether the activity is subject to national or transboundary EIA procedure.[284] The public participation procedure shall include reasonable timeframes—it should allow sufficient time to inform the public, and for the public to prepare and participate during the environmental decision making. Public participation must be provided early in the decision-making process when options are open. Competent authorities must give the public concerned relevant information for examination free of charge. Relevant information shall include: (1) a description of the site and the physical and technical characteristics of the proposed activity; (2) a description of the effects on the environment; (3) measures proposed to prevent or reduce the effects; (4) a non-technical summary; (5) an outline of the alternatives studied by the applicant; and (6) the main reports and advice issued to the public authority.[285]

The public shall be allowed to submit in writing or at a public hearing any comments that it considers relevant to the proposed activity. When making the decision, due account shall be taken of the outcome of public participation. The public shall be promptly informed of the decision. The text of the decision shall be accessible along with the reasons and considerations on which the decision was based.

---

[283] Art. 6(2), *supra* note 265.

[284] *Id.*

[285] *Id.*, art. 6(6).

The "public concerned" has been defined as the public affected or likely to be affected by or having an interest in the environmental decision making and includes NGOs promoting environmental protection.[286] Thus, the Convention makes a distinction between access to information and public participation: while anybody can request environmental information without having to show a special interest in the issue, public participation is limited to those who are either affected or likely to be affected by the proposed activity or have an interest in the issue. This includes non-governmental organizations.

Each party is required to provide for early public participation, when all options are open and effective public participation can take place. Article 7 seeks to extend the public participation procedure to plans and programs relating to the environment. This procedure extends to "the public" within a transparent and fair framework. The public that may participate shall be identified by the relevant public authority. The parties are required to endeavor to provide for public participation to the extent appropriate in the preparation of policies relating to the environment. Thus, while on the face of it, this provision is applicable to the public, a closer look reveals that the public authority concerned can decide who should participate in the process. Article 7 thus provides for public participation and access to information in relation to strategic environmental assessment. However, the scope for public participation in relation to plans, programs and policies is more restrictive than that envisaged under Article 6 dealing with public participation in relation to activities listed in Annex I.

With regard to executive regulations and other legally binding rules, parties shall strive to promote effective public participation at an appropriate stage by fixing timeframes; publishing draft rules; and giving the public the opportunity to comment. The results of public participation shall be taken into account as far as possible.

Public participation can be provided through various means: there will be a period of public comments during which the public may provide written comments to the relevant authority; with regard to some activities, public hearings may be held, at which the public concerned can make comments orally; there could be a combination of both written comments and a public hearing for some activities. If a public hearing is held, it is important to follow a transparent and fair procedure so that the proceedings are not one-sided or biased against one group (usually, the pubic), and both sides must be given an opportunity to be heard.

---

[286] *Id.*, art. 2(5).

## c. *Access to Justice*

Access to justice forms the last, but nonetheless an important, pillar of participatory rights. While a state may provide access to information and facilitate public participation, without access to justice, the public may not have any forum to seek redress in the event their rights are violated. Thus, all three pillars discussed in this chapter form the basis of participatory rights envisaged under the Convention that are now considered part of customary international law.[287]

Article 9 deals with access to justice and requires each party to ensure that any person whose request for information under Article 4 has been ignored or wrongfully refused, shall have access to a review procedure before a court of law or other independent body under its national legislation. Similarly, any member of the public concerned, having a sufficient interest or maintaining an impairment of a right[288] has access to a review procedure before a court or other independent body, to challenge the substantive or procedural legality of any decision, act or omission under Article 6[289] and, to the extent permitted by national law, of other relevant provisions of this Convention. Parties must also ensure that there are adequate and effective remedies, including injunctive relief. The procedures must be fair, equitable, timely and not prohibitively expensive. The parties must also ensure that information is provided to the public about access to administrative and judicial review procedures.

Article 9 thus makes a distinction in relation to access to information and public participation as far as remedies are concerned: in relation to the latter, the public concerned has to establish that he/she has a sufficient interest or has suffered an impairment of a right, while there is no need to establish that in relation to a violation of access to information. The aggrieved person only has to establish that information was wrongfully denied or that the request for information was ignored. No doubt, much would depend on the national legislation and procedure in place, which the aggrieved parties will have to abide by.

The significance of the Aarhus Convention has been noted as:

This emphasis on process rather than the outcome provides an innovative model of multilateral policy making which promises to create a new operating environment for pubic agencies and the

---

[287] *See* discussion in Section II.

[288] This will be defined under national law.

[289] Article 6, *supra* note 265, deals with the right to participate.

corporate world. . . . The Convention integrates environmental protection and governance norms. This integration is bound to benefit both the environment and democratic governance. It promotes citizen involvement as a key to combating environmental mismanagement. Its principles of transparency and accountability are integral to the meaningful practice of democratic governance.[290]

The Convention further promotes "horizontal accountability" by governments and corporations to NGOs and citizens.[291] It has been articulated that the Aarhus Convention has transformed Principle 10 of the Rio Declaration into a legally binding instrument.[292] As noted above, it has three pillars: access to information, public participation in decision making and access to justice. The second pillar encompasses public involvement in three kinds of decisions: (1) decisions regarding specific development activities included in Annex I; (2) public plans, programs and policies that relate to the environment; and (3) decisions about executive regulations and legislation and agreements—the Convention recognizes a limited right of participation in relation to this category. It is accepted that the Aarhus Convention has the potential to become a powerful instrument in the ECE region. However, several challenges remain:

(1) Several governments, particularly the United States and Russia refused to sign the Convention. NGOs in these countries must promote the principles embodied in the Aarhus Convention domestically in order to build political momentum for their countries' accession;

(2) Signatories must ensure that their national legislation as well as institutional framework are on par with their obligations under the Convention in order for the Convention to become effective; and

(3) Regional institutions, such as the EU, should revise and adjust their disclosure policies and participation mechanisms in order to comply with the provisions in the Convention.

The involvement of the NGO community right through the drafting process is a significant development in international environmental law. It is thus necessary to promote these principles globally to ensure environmental democracy at the global level.

---

[290] *See* Elena Petkova & Peter Veit, *Environmental Accountability Beyond the Nation-State: The Implications of the Aarhus Convention, at* http://www.wri.org/governance/publications.html.

[291] *Id.*

[292] *Id.*

## 2. Significance of Public Participation

The significance of public participation has been increasingly recognized in many international instruments, as well as at the national level. It has been recognized that:

> When governments enable the public to participate in decision-making, they help meet society's goal of sustainable and environmentally sound development. . . . As a result of public participation, the process of decision-making, up to and including the final decision, becomes more transparent and legitimate.[293]

As discussed earlier, transparency and legitimacy are important features of good governance.

The right of participation has also been recognized in relation to indigenous communities. The ILO Convention Concerning Indigenous and Tribal Peoples in Independent Countries[294] embodies this right as follows:

> The peoples concerned shall have the right to decide their own priorities for the process of development as it affects their lives, beliefs, institutions and spiritual well-being and the lands they occupy or otherwise use, and to exercise control, to the extent possible, over their own economic, social and cultural development. In addition, they shall participate in the formulation, implementation and evaluation of plans and programmes for national and regional development which may affect them directly.[295]

The Convention further provides that studies should be carried out "in co-operation with the peoples concerned," to assess the social, spiritual, cultural and environmental impact of planned activities.[296] It is significant that the Convention requires these studies to be carried out with the cooperation of indigenous groups.

A similar right to participate is recognized in the UN Draft Declaration on the Rights of Indigenous Peoples.[297] Draft Article 19 provides that:

---

[293] Guidance on Public Participation, *at* http://www.unece.org/env/eia/public-part_guidance.htm.

[294] ILO Convention No. 169 of 1989, entered into force, Sept. 5, 1991, *available at* http://www.unhchr.ch/html/menu3/b/62.htm.

[295] *Id.*, art. 7.

[296] *Id.*

[297] Draft UN Declaration on the Rights of Indigenous Peoples, 1994/45, *available at*

> Indigenous peoples have the right to participate fully, if they so
> choose, at all levels of decision-making in matters which may
> affect their rights, lives and destinies through representatives
> chosen by themselves in accordance with their own procedures,
> as well as to maintain and develop their own indigenous decision-
> making institutions.[298]

The importance of public participation has been identified as follows:
public participation leads to better decisions, decisions that better meet the
needs of the public and, as a result, decisions that will last longer and decisions more likely to withstand scrutiny: "Involving the public at an early
stage in the decision-making process, and finding ways for their views to be
heard and taken into account, helps to build consensus."[299] The *Handbook*
prepared in relation to the Aarhus Convention on public participation cautions against giving the impression that the decision has already been
made, as it is very damaging to the public participation process.[300] The
process must be open and honest and seek to encourage trust, which may
not be an easy task, particularly where the process is relatively new or where
there have been previous bad experiences.[301] In addition, the *Handbook*
proposes a trust-building phase with the public, NGOs and the business
community and a training phase for both decision makers and the public.
It is important to inform the public about the process that will be followed
and how the decision makers will evaluate the public comments etc.[302]

It is also necessary to involve the public at an early stage in the decision-making process, as it is important to get the public's input as early as
possible and, in any event, before a final decision is imminent. This can
avoid unnecessary challenges to the decision or even litigation at a later
stage. It is not always easy to get the public to participate in the decision-
making process. They may not participate due to apathy or because they
feel that it will not make any difference to the decision. While building

---

http://www.unhchr.ch/hurId.ocda/hurId.oca.nsf/(Symbol)/E.CN.4.SUB.2.RES.1994.45.
En?OpenDocument.

[298] *Id.*, draft art. 19.

[299] *Public Participation in Making Local Environmental Decisions,* THE AARHUS CONVEN-
TION NEWCASTLE WORKSHOP, GOOD PRACTICE HANDBOOK (2000), *available at* http://
www.unece.org/env/pp/ecases/handbook.pdf/ [hereinafter GOOD PRACTICE HAND-
BOOK].

[300] *Id.*

[301] *Id.*

[302] *Id.*

trust is a long-term exercise, each participation process can help achieve that goal.

An important point to remember is that the "public" is not a homogenous body with common interests and objectives.[303] They often have conflicting interests. Thus, this realization has led to the use of the word "stakeholders" instead of the word "public." Stakeholders are social groups, organizations or individuals whose interests may be affected by a proposed project.[304]

Four types of consultation and public participation have been identified: (1) information dissemination; (2) consultation; (3) collaboration and partnerships; and (4) empowerment and local control.[305] Of these, only the last two categories can be identified as true instances of participation. At the international level, consultation has been the most commonly used method. It is generally accepted that "there is a definite momentum towards giving the public more control over the conduct of EAs."[306]

While there is no doubt that the general trend is toward getting the public more involved in the EA process, how and when this should be done has given rise to problems. It is generally accepted that the preparation of an EIA and public participation should take place as early as possible in the project cycle and certainly before any decision regarding the project is taken.[307]

It is necessary to explain why the public should be involved, as is the need to make the process interesting. Information is essential for effective participation—information relating to both the process and the proposal must be supplied. In addition, information must be complete, easy to understand (avoiding technical language) and must be easily accessible to the public.[308]

Once a decision has been made, it is necessary to provide the public with feedback to show that their comments were considered in making the

---

[303] Ron Bisset, *Methods of Consultation and Public Participation, in* ENVIRONMENTAL ASSESSMENT IN DEVELOPING AND TRANSITIONAL COUNTRIES: PRINCIPLES, METHODS AND PRACTICE 149, 151 (Norman Lee & Clive George eds., 2000).

[304] *Id.*

[305] *Id.*

[306] *Id.* at 150.

[307] *See* GOOD PRACTICE HANDBOOK, *supra* note 299.

[308] *Id.* at 18.

decision. If this is not done, the public is less likely to participate in the future. It also shows that their comments helped in evaluating the project. Moreover, it is important to show that it is not possible to take all comments into account when making a decision. Some comments, however relevant they may seem to those who made them, may have to be rejected. When this is done, it is always best to provide reasons why those comments were rejected. Evaluating the public participation process in a given situation can be helpful in improving the process for future projects. The public too can be involved in this exercise.[309] It is also good to remind the public that no two public participation instances may be alike, although the same procedure is followed, given that the issues at stake are different.

The public participation process could vary depending on whether the activity in question is likely to give rise to transboundary environmental damage. The guidance on public participation prepared under the Espoo Convention[310] notes that Article 2.2 of the Convention requires parties to establish a national EIA procedure that permits pubic participation. It also provides that "public participation forms an essential part of transboundary environmental impact assessment."[311] The Guidance recommends that, as a minimum, national EIA provisions should include:

(1) The public are informed on any proposals relating to an activity with potential adverse environmental impacts in cases subject to an EIA procedure;
(2) The public, in the areas likely to be affected, are entitled to express comments on the proposed activity when all options are open;
(3) Reasonable timeframes are provided allowing sufficient time for public participation at different stages in the EIA procedure; and
(4) In making the final decision, due account is taken of the results of public participation.[312]

The Guidance notes that "The essence of public consultation is the communication of a genuine invitation to give advice and a genuine con-

---

[309] *Id.* at 19.

[310] UN Economic Comission for Europe, *Guidance on Public Participation in Environmental Impact Assessment in a Transboundary Context*, Decision III/8, ECE/MP.EIA/6, Feb. 2001, *available at* http://www.unece.org/env/eia/publicpart_guidance.htm [hereinafter Guidance].

[311] *Id.* Preamble.

[312] *Id.*

sideration of that advice."[313] Giving sufficient information is essential for
this process to be successful. While sufficient time[314] must be given to the
public to provide comments, sufficient time must be available for the government body to consider them. In a transboundary context, the country
of origin must provide an opportunity to the public in the affected state
equivalent to that offered to the public in the country of origin, if the
affected state has expressed an interest in participating in the transboundary EIA procedure.[315] While what is equivalent is not defined in the
Convention, in a given situation, the party of origin will have to decide this
in accordance with the provisions of its national law. Difference in language, socio-economic context, and other circumstances may be taken into
consideration in deciding how to provide equivalent opportunity for public participation in the affected state. The Convention does not require
identical opportunity to be provided.[316] However, Article 3.8 of the
Convention requires both the party of origin and the affected party to
ensure public participation in the affected state.

The other issue to be taken into consideration is the financial aspect
of the process. Thus, for example, costs relating to the translation of the
EIA document into the language of the affected party, translating comments into the language of the party of origin and organizing public hearings and meetings in the affected country are some of the costs involved in
the public participation process in a transboundary context. The question
that arises here is who should be responsible for the costs of participation
by the public in the affected state? The Convention is silent on this issue.
While the party of origin may be generally responsible for such costs, the
cost of public participation in a transboundary context can be covered by:
the developer; the party of origin; the affected party; an international financial institution; or a combination.[317] It may be recommended that the proponent of an activity should have financial responsibility for public
participation in both states, including payment for translation and dissemination of EIA materials to the public.[318]

As with all EIAs, the availability of adequate information about the proposed activity is key to effective public participation. This becomes chal-

---

[313]  *Id.* at 4.

[314]  The Guidance notes that sufficient time does not mean ample time, but enough
to enable the purpose to be fulfilled. *Id.*

[315]  *Id.*

[316]  *Id.* at 5.

[317]  *Id.* at 8.

[318]  *Id.*

lenging when the EIA has to be translated into the language of the affected party, and a poor translation can impede the process if key information is lost or nuances are not properly translated. Given that EIA reports are often technical, it is more than likely that this would happen. Those responsible for organizing public hearings must ensure that at least the non-technical summaries are properly translated, clear, and easily understood by the community. While the proponent may assume responsibility for the translations, when the activity is a joint project, the costs are usually shared.[319] At the very least, the non-technical summary of the EIA should be translated, as translating the whole EIA can be a very expensive undertaking.

As noted above, timing of notification is crucial to effective participation. Article 3.1 of the Convention requires the party of origin to notify the affected party as early as possible about the proposed activity and not later than when informing its own public. The purpose of the notification is to enable the potentially affected state to decide whether it wants to participate in the EIA procedure. The Convention does not specify a time period that must be allowed for the affected party to respond to the party of origin. The party of origin must set a timeframe according to its national procedure. However, it must bear in mind that the law of the affected party may require it to consult with its environmental authorities or even its public before deciding whether to participate in the EIA procedure of the party of origin. In this event, the affected party may request additional time to convey its decision. Having analyzed several case studies, the Guidance notes that the public participation procedure in affected parties was most effective where it began during discussion of the EIA program and continued, as the results of the EIA reports were discussed.

Where the affected party responds affirmatively to the notification of the party of origin, there is joint responsibility to ensure public participation of the affected party in a transboundary EIA. The concerned parties are expected to make arrangements for such public participation. The Guidance makes the following recommendations:

(1) The party of origin should be responsible for the translation of all relevant documents, for providing the information and for receiving comments;
(2) Affected parties may handle the distribution of information via particular organizations;
(3) Both parties must make arrangements for collecting the comments from the public and sending them to the party of ori-

---

[319] This was done, for example, in the case of the bridge over River Danube between Bulgaria and Romania. *Id.*, case study 2, at 10.

gin. There may be a need to translate the comments so that the party of origin can understand them;

(4) The party of origin may be able to recover the costs from the proponent of the activity.

If the public of the affected party sends its comments to the competent authority of the party of origin, it should also send copies to the competent authority of the affected party. The methods used for effective public information, distribution and receipt of comments could vary from country to country and from region to region. Developed countries increasingly make use of the Internet for this purpose. Some of the frequently used methods are:

- development of Web sites or Web pages with EIA information on the Internet;
- dissemination of EIA information and receipt of responses from public by email;
- notification of stakeholders in the region likely to be affected and national and international NGOs by mailing a questionnaire;
- organizing points of contact with the public in and around the proposed site;
- organizing public hearings and meetings with all stakeholders;
- publishing and disseminating booklets and other materials with EIA information including a questionnaire;
- advertising in local, regional and national newspapers;
- informing the television and the radio;
- posters in and around the proposed site; and
- a combination of these methods, which may be most effective, depending on the circumstances in each case.[320]

Having analyzed several case studies, the Guidance notes that the effectiveness of public participation may be enhanced through several means:

(1) Preliminary work with potential participants—to maximize the time available and to ensure effective participation the following preliminary measures may be useful—to establish effective relations with national focal points of the Convention; to inform potential proponents about the need for transboundary EIA with public participation and to recommend to them to include in their budgets adequate resources for financing measures for public participation; to recommend to the proponents to be in contact with competent authorities from the very beginning; to understand which

---

[320] *Id.*

NGOs and groups of the public may be interested in and have the relevant skills for participation.

(2) Contacts with potentially affected parties: bilateral and multi-lateral agreements; joint bodies—in regions where direct communication between countries is politically sensitive or difficult, it is sometimes effective to use an impartial third party or joint body to help with the notification. It might be prudent for parties to consider establishing joint bodies where joint EIAs are common.

(3) Organizing points of contact for the public—in practice it might be useful to establish a point of contact for each specific project and thereby increasing the effectiveness of public involvement overall. The main benefit here is that the public can act quickly and effectively so that the procedure does not get held up.

(4) The role of the public—"The public should participate fully in transboundary EIA in order to make both the process of environmental decision-making on projects with transboundary effects and the final decisions on such projects more transparent and legitimate."[321]

The Guidance calls upon the public to organize itself for effective participation by: developing contacts and cooperation with relevant NGOs and experts; organizing and participating in activities of national and international public networks and public centers on EIAs; taking part in training programs on EIAs; and supporting the dissemination of information about the implementation of the Convention, case studies and other relevant information.[322]

Where an activity with transboundary impacts is likely to take place, but no notification under the Convention has taken place, the public should be able to request the competent authority to request public participation under the Convention. It is important that the public, particularly NGOs, play this watchdog role in order to prevent any transboundary environmental impacts that could arise as a result of an activity in another state.

## 3. Difficulties in Implementing Public Participation

The importance of providing for public participation and its merits were noted above. Despite its merits, there are many difficulties in getting the public involved. Since many stakeholders are involved, sometimes it

---

[321] *Id.* at 20.

[322] *Id.*

could be difficult to reach a consensus. In addition, public authorities are cynical about public participation, and people may only participate if their immediate interests are at stake, not otherwise. It could also slow down the decision, and it does involve resources that could be scarce, particularly in developing countries. Public participation can also give the impression that everything will be changed very quickly, and it can lead to frustration and mistrust when this does not happen. It is thus necessary to be honest about the process and to be clear about the process involved, outcomes and time-lines.[323] In addition, cultural barriers may prevent certain stakeholders from participating. For example, women in some societies are debarred from taking part in public life. In addition, the public authorities will have to deal with illiteracy and linguistic and cultural diversity in many societies.[324] Moreover, in societies where there are more pressing issues, such as abject poverty or gross human rights violations, it is unlikely that people will be interested in participating in decisions relating to the environment.[325]

Given the difficulties involved in public participation, the question has been raised whether it is just a hollow promise.[326] It has been pointed out that in order for public participation to be truly meaningful, a specific procedural mechanism must be developed to guide the developer and the decision maker to evaluate the comments.[327] At the international level this difficulty becomes compounded, as there is no effective enforcement mechanism to force compliance. On the one hand, the public should not have a veto right over the international environmental assessment process. On the other hand, giving member states the right to tailor the forum and evaluation of public comments without limits could also be detrimental: "The solution must be to build into the equation a notion of reasonableness."[328]

## a. Significance of the Aarhus Convention

It has been noted in recent years that participatory democracy has gained increasing support and recognition.[329] Involving the public in the

---

[323] *Id.* at 21–22.

[324] *See* Bisset, *supra* note 303, at 154.

[325] *See* Michael Burger, *Bi-polar and Polycentric Approaches to Human Rights and the Environment*, 28 COLUM. J. ENVTL. L. 371 (2003).

[326] *See* Tabb, *supra* note 87.

[327] *Id.*

[328] *Id.*

[329] *See Human Rights and the Environment: The Role of Aarhus Convention, supra* note 275, at para. 1.

decision-making process will improve the quality of the decision and will strengthen the public belief in the credibility of the decision-making process. The emergence of participatory democracy is reflected in a multitude of national measures and to a lesser extent in global instruments, the most far reaching example of the latter being the Aarhus Convention.[330] This Convention seeks to link environmental rights and human rights and acknowledges that we owe an obligation to future generations. It further notes that sustainable development can be achieved only through the involvement of all stakeholders; moreover, it links government accountability and environmental protection: "The Convention is therefore not only an environmental agreement; it is also a Convention about government accountability, transparency and responsiveness."[331] Moreover, the key elements of public participation in the Convention are widely recognized as providing a benchmark for environmental democracy.[332] In addition to the three pillars of rights included in the Convention,[333] several other features of the Convention must be noted: it adopts a rights-based approach; it adopts minimum standards but does not prevent any party from adopting higher standards; it prohibits discrimination; the main obligations in the Convention is towards "public authorities," which are broadly defined; and the Convention is open to accession by non-ECE members with the approval of the meeting of parties.[334] Although it is primarily a regional convention, its global significance is widely recognized,[335] particularly since it is now open for accession by non-ECE member states. The Convention draws a crucial link between environmental rights and human rights and, as the then UN High Commissioner for Human Rights articulated, "The Convention is a remarkable achievement not only in terms of protection of the environment but also in terms of the promotion and protection of human rights."[336]

## 4. Participation in SEAs

Public participation also extends to plans and programs, as noted by Article 7 of the Aarhus Convention and the Protocol on SEA adopted under the Espoo Convention. Some examples of such plans are: a national

---

[330] *Id.* at para. 2.

[331] *Id.* at para. 3.

[332] *Id.* at para. 5.

[333] As noted, these are the right to information, the right to participate and the right to remedies.

[334] *Supra* note 275, paras. 14–17.

[335] *Id.*, para. 38. It is further noted that the Convention is the leading example of the implementation of Principle 10 of the Rio Declaration, *supra* note 16.

[336] *Id.*, para. 38.

environmental health action plan, a biodiversity action plan, a water supply strategy for a city or a tourism master plan. Unlike Article 6 of the Aarhus Convention, Article 7 does not specify the steps that should be taken in relation to public participation. This gives the public authority some flexibility in adopting the procedure appropriate for each activity.[337] Thus, the preparation phase is important, and the authorities need to show that the process will be transparent and fair from the start.[338] A participation strategy needs to be developed to suit the kind of plan being prepared and the local conditions. What works in one area may not work in another. In some cases, it might be helpful to develop a strategy in partnership with another organization, perhaps a local NGO. As with Article 6 exercises, being flexible and responsive to the public is necessary. Sometimes the strategies used to encourage the public to participate may come from the people themselves.[339]

The main purpose of public participation under Article 7 is to ensure that the public's opinions are taken into account in the final plan or program. The key aims are: to inform the public that the plan or program is being prepared; help them form an informed opinion; collect their opinions and ideas; and prepare a plan/program that takes account of their opinions.[340] There could be other aims of public participation, such as involving the local community in nature protection and tourism, or to enable different groups to build mutual understanding, etc. In all cases, however, the authorities need to be clear what the process is before it starts, if it wants to involve the public effectively.[341]

Article 7 requires the relevant public authority to decide who should participate. It is conducive to make the process open to everyone including those who oppose the plan or program. This could include community groups, local authorities, business and industry, residents' organizations, women's groups, universities and experts from research institutions. It must be remembered, however, that those most willing to participate may not be representative of the public's views. Thus, it is important to involve ordinary people as well as specialist groups.[342]

Involving the public as early as possible in the process helps the authority to develop a better strategy and to understand public perception; iden-

---

[337] *See* GOOD PRACTICE HANDBOOK, *supra* note 299, at 38.

[338] *Id.*

[339] *Id.*

[340] *Id.* at 39.

[341] *Id.* at 40.

[342] *Id.*

tify their priorities; raise awareness; and encourage community ownership of the plan. A range of methods can be used to encourage the public to participate, including writing to local organizations offering workshops; holding public meetings with videos; publishing information in local newspapers; sending information to local schools; and public exhibitions in local libraries and local events. All this, however, takes prior and careful planning and requires the public authority to be creative and use opportunities as they arise.[343]

In order to participate effectively, people must have information and need to know that the process is taking place. Thus, publicity is necessary and the authorities need to think of ways to inform the public that will reach as many people who may be affected as possible. In addition, it is necessary to keep people informed of the process. For the public to participate effectively, information needs to be complete, easy to understand and accessible. The information should explain the possible environmental impacts of the different options being studied. The failure to provide all the information can result in distrust of the process and of the authority.[344] It is important that the information is presented in a form that can be easily understood. Providing a non-technical summary is a good way of doing this. Depending on the local situation, the language in which the information is provided is also an important issue.[345]

The next crucial issue would be how the public comments are handled by the authorities. It is important to be open about this process. Publishing a summary of the public's comments can help people understand the different issues involved and can help build consensus.[346] Once a draft plan is in place incorporating public comments, one option available to the authority is to hold a public meeting to ensure that it has incorporated the comments properly. Once the decision has been made about the final plan or program, it is necessary to inform the public of this as soon as possible. It is also necessary to explain how the plan would be implemented. Maintaining links with the public would be good for future activities and also for the involvement of the public in implementation or monitoring. It is also a good exercise to evaluate how successful the process was. Some issues to be discussed are: Did all of the affected public knew about the plan? Were they able to participate in the preparation? Do they feel that their views were taken into account? Do they understand the

---

[343] *Id.* at 42.

[344] *Id.* at 44.

[345] *Id.*

[346] *Id.* at 46.

reasons for the final plan? Depending on the answers to these questions, the authorities may want to review their process for the next public participation exercise.[347]

## G. CONCLUSION

Environmental impact assessment has come a long way since its adoption at the national level by the United States in 1969. It has been extended to activities having a transboundary environmental impact as well as in relation to global environmental issues such as biodiversity and climate change. It has also progressed from its project-oriented focus to a more comprehensive assessment of plans, policies and programs. The rationale underlying EIAs is the need to prevent environmental harm, rather than repair damage later. This has given rise to the need to develop tools to evaluate the environmental impact before undertaking an activity (or implementing a policy or program) in order to take mitigatory measures to minimize the damage on the environment, whether or not there are transboundary environmental impacts.

With regard to its legal status, Philippe Sands contends that:

There is considerable support for the view that environmental impact assessments are required as a matter of customary law, particularly in respect of activities which may cause transboundary effects. Most multilateral development banks now require some form of environmental impact assessment, and they are now required by international law also to assess the environmental consequences of potentially damaging projects into which they consider putting financial resources.[348]

Given the scientific uncertainty surrounding some environmental issues, it would be necessary to use the tool of environmental assessment together with the precautionary principle, as the former is necessarily limited by existing scientific knowledge. Indeed, some international conventions require the environmental impact assessment report to identify and document any gaps in knowledge.

The participatory rights associated with EIA have also developed considerably and are increasingly recognized as having become part of customary law relating to the environment. The procedural requirements of provision of information, public participation and access to justice are con-

---

[347] *Id.* at 47–48.

[348] *See* SANDS, *supra* note 145, at 824.

sidered the three pillars of procedural rights, which are also part of good governance and sustainable development. By balancing environmental, social (to a limited extent) and economic factors of a given activity, there is no doubt that EIA is a valuable tool to achieve sustainable development.

The Aarhus Convention adopts an expansive right to information concerning the environment and extends the right to participation to non-governmental organizations promoting environmental protection. State parties are under an obligation to inform the public concerned early in the decision-making process in an adequate, timely and effective manner.

The rights to information and participation are increasingly being recognized as part of principles of democratic governance that require, *inter alia*, transparency and accountability. These also constitute principles of sustainable development.[349] The importance of public participation in the context of sustainable development was articulated by the Supreme Court of Sri Lanka in a case before it: "Public participation, transparency and fairness are essential if sustainable development is to be achieved."[350] The importance of the Aarhus Convention and Principle 10 of the Rio Declaration is that these procedural rights are not tied to the EIA process. Rather, these rights come into play where a particular activity is likely to have a significant impact on the environment. It is nothing but fair that those who are likely to be affected by a particular activity be informed of such activity and an opportunity be given to voice their opinion on the issue. Since sustainable development requires the balancing of competing claims, it is essential that people be given a chance to voice their opinion on an issue likely to have an impact on their lives. In order to do so, however, timely and accurate information is necessary, and there is an obligation on the part of states to facilitate the provision of such information.

EIA, being an essential tool to achieve the principle of integration, is a tool to achieve sustainable development. It would be very hard for states to deny the need to carry out an EIA for activities likely to cause a significant impact on the environment, whether within states or extra-territorially. As noted, participatory rights seek to emphasize the process rather than the outcome—in other words, if the process is satisfactory, the outcome would be too. There is no doubt that democratic governance through the provision of participatory rights is crucial to achieving sustainable development.

---

[349] *See* discussion in Chapter 2, Section F.

[350] V.D.S. Gunaratne v. Homagama Pradeshiya Sabha and five others, 5(2) & (3) SOUTH ASIAN ENVTL. L. REP. 28 (1998).

# COMMON BUT DIFFERENTIATED RESPONSIBILITY PRINCIPLE

States shall co-operate in a spirit of global partnership to conserve, protect and restore the health and integrity of the Earth's ecosystem. In view of the different contributions to global environmental degradation, States have common but differentiated responsibilities. The developed countries acknowledge the responsibility that they bear in the international pursuit of sustainable development in view of the pressures their societies place on the global environment and of the technologies and financial resources they command.

Principle 7, Rio Declaration on Environment and Development

## A. INTRODUCTION

One of the cardinal principles of international law is sovereign equality of states. It constitutes one of the principles on which the United Nations is established.[1] Sovereign equality is a juridical concept, because the law treats each state as being sovereign and equal, similar to the principle of equality at the national level:[2] the law treats each person similarly, despite various differences that may exist. A corollary of the sovereign equality principle is that international legal obligations are based on the principle of reciprocity, binding each signatory in the same way.[3] However, sovereign equality does not mean that all states are equal in substantive terms. They vary in size, power, level of development population, etc. Thus, to talk in terms of equality can be misleading in some instances. Given the diversity of states with different cultures, languages, level of development and resources at their disposal, it is difficult to speak of equality in substantive terms. Differentiation becomes inevitable in some spheres of inter-

---

[1] Article 2.1 of the UN Charter states that the "Organization is based on the principle of sovereign equality of all its members."

[2] See Article 26 of the ICCPR, *available at* http://www.unhchr.org, which states that "All persons are equal before the law and are entitled without any discrimination to the equal protection of the law."

[3] See PHILIPPE CULLET, DIFFERENTIAL TREATMENT IN INTERNATIONAL ENVIRONMENTAL LAW 57 (2003).

national law, although juridical equality has been, and should continue to be, the main bedrock of international society.

With the expansion of the international community after decolonization, international law underwent some challenges. The international community itself became much more heterogeneous, and the newly independent states with their developing economies came to test the very legal foundations of international law:[4]

> It became, for instance, more and more evident that a strict reliance on the concept of legal equality could not be upheld in all circumstances within a growing community whose members had different economic, political and military capacities. These changes and the ensuing developments reflected to a certain extent the broader forces influencing international law whose function slowly changed from that of ensuring the peaceful coexistence of states to ensuring broad-ranging cooperation on a number of socio-economic issues.[5]

While the first wave of differentiation originated with the call by developing countries for a New International Economic Order (NIEO),[6] the second wave of differential treatment commenced with the emergence of global environmental problems, which is "largely devoid of controversial ideological undertones."[7] Interdependence of states and the fact that these global environmental problems do not respect national boundaries led to this development. Another issue that has given rise to differential treatment is that the emphasis placed by developing and developed countries on global environmental issues has varied significantly: developing countries have paid more attention to immediate pressing problems such as poverty, the provision of basic needs and economic development while developed countries, with the resources they command, are more concerned with environmental issues. However, without the involvement of developing countries, with their alarmingly expanding populations and fast industrializing economies, it is difficult for developed countries to take measures to address global environmental problems alone: "In practice, differential treatment has thus become the price to be paid to ensure universal participation in environmental agreements concerned with global problems."[8]

---

4 *Id.* at 59.

5 *See id.* at 59 *quoting* Georges Abi-Saab, *Whither the International Community?*, 9 EUR. J. INT'L L. 248 (1998).

6 *See id.* at 62.

7 *Id.* at 69.

8 *Id.*

Thus, in some fields, such as environmental protection, it became necessary to take into account differentiations that are inherent in contemporary international society. The main distinction that has been taken into consideration is between developed and developing countries, although it is hard to consider developing countries as a homogenous group, given the vast differentiation visible within that group. Thus, distinctions have been made between small island states,[9] countries with economies in transition,[10] Annex I countries,[11] non-parties to conventions,[12] etc. It has become necessary to take these differentiations into consideration, as they have a direct bearing on the implementation of international obligations or whether states would decide to ratify an international convention at all. Thus, based on the formal equality principle, many regimes of differentiation have been born because it is no longer possible to speak only in terms of formal equality without taking these differentiations into account on a more pragmatic level.

While the emergence of the common but differentiated responsibility principle is rather new in the field of international environmental law, differentiation is not new to international law.[13] In several instances, differentiation has been adopted—in the UN Security Council, the five permanent members enjoy the veto power that none of the other members enjoy.[14] In some financial institutions, weighted voting has been adopted based on the income of states.[15] With the emergence of many newly inde-

---

[9] *E.g.*, The Kyoto Protocol to the United Nations Framework Convention on Climate Change, FCCC/CP/1997/L.7/Add.1, entered into force Feb. 16, 2005. *reprinted in* 36 ILM 22 (1998), *available at* http://www.unfccc.de/ [hereinafter Kyoto Protocol].

[10] This categorization is made in the Stockholm Convention on Persistent Organic Pollutants, UN Doc. UNEP/POPS/CONF/4, 40 ILM 532 (2001), signed May 22, 2001, entered into force May 17, 2004, *available at* http://www.pops.int/, discussed in Section C.2. *See infra* note 171 and accompanying text.

[11] "Annex I countries" have the main obligations under the Kyoto Protocol, *supra* note 9.

[12] Several conventions ban trade with non-parties, *see* Montreal Protocol, 26 ILM 1541 (1987), 15 UNTS 3, signed Mar. 22, 1965, entered into force Sept. 22, 1988, Basel Convention, 1673 UNTS 57, signed Mar. 22, 1989, entered into force May 5, 1992, *available at* http://www.basel.int/, discussed in Section C.2. *See infra* notes 174 and 151 and accompanying text.

[13] *See* Christopher D. Stone, *Common but Differentiated Responsibilities in International Law*, 98 AM. J. INT'L. L. 276 (2004).

[14] *See* Article 27(3) of the UN Charter which provides that: "Decisions of the Security Council on all other matters shall be made by an affirmative vote of nine members including the concurring votes of the permanent members." All other matters here refers to non-procedural matters.

[15] *See* Cullet, *supra* note 3, at 74.

pendent states after decolonization in the early 1970s, these states started the move toward a new international economic order in order to establish new rules to govern them on the ground that they were not involved in the formation of old obligations, which were negotiated by their colonial masters. There was considerable opposition to this movement, which subsequently failed to make any significant impact on the international legal order.[16]

Another instance of unequal treatment is the application of the notion of affirmative action under human rights law.[17] This is also called reverse or positive discrimination.[18] In order to correct past imbalances and to provide every player with a level playing field, certain groups of individuals who have been subject to years of discrimination have been given special protection under the law. Thus, although all are equal before the law, some groups may enjoy special protection under the law in order to redress past discrimination. Women, those with disabilities or certain ethnic groups may enjoy special protection under special legislation, which will not be contrary to the principle of equality.

It has been articulated that differential treatment can take two main forms: allocation of rights and entitlements; and redistribution of resources.[19] With regard to the former, the starting point is equal treatment under the law, which is the universal rule. However, in order to provide rights and entitlements for certain groups, differential treatment leads to positive (or reverse) discrimination.[20] As noted, at the domestic level, various policies to redress existing inequalities have been used in different countries in the form of affirmative action.[21] While affirmative action policies have been controversial, even the opponents accept that "there is a need for measures targeting the poorest and enhancing the status of disfavoured communities."[22] Positive discrimination has been successful in highlighting existing deprivation and redressing inequalities in general and can be transferred

---

[16] *See* DAVID HUNTER, JAMES SALZMAN & DURWOOD ZAELKE, INTERNATIONAL ENVIRONMENTAL LAW AND POLICY (2d ed. 2002).

[17] *See* ANITA MARGRETHE HALVORSSEN, EQUALITY AMONG UNEQUALS IN INTERNATIONAL ENVIRONMENTAL LAW 28 (1999), and Donald W. Jackson, *Affirmative Action in Comparative Perspective: India and the United States, in* NON-DISCRIMINATION LAW: COMPARATIVE PERSPECTIVES 249 (Titia Loenen & Peter R. Rodrigues eds., 1999).

[18] *See* Cullet, *supra* note 3, at 70.

[19] *Id.* at 32.

[20] *Id.*

[21] *Id.*

[22] *Id.* at 33.

to the international sphere to deal with inequalities because the issues are broadly similar.[23] Several international instruments recognize that differential measures or positive discrimination measures do not violate the principle of equality.[24]

While most obligations at the international level are based on reciprocity, which in turn is based on the principle of sovereign equality, differentiation constitutes an exception to this notion. In most cases, while obligations formally apply to all parties in the same manner, the treaty regime could provide for some flexibility based on need,[25] geographic location[26] or vulnerability.[27] This is not true differentiation. These clauses are still based on reciprocity. True differential norms are those that actually provide different obligations for different groups identified on particular criteria.[28] These different norms could either be in relation to the end result[29] or the obligation itself.[30] Obligations, whether based on reciprocity

---

[23] *Id.*

[24] *E.g.*, Art. 4 of the Convention on the Elimination of All Forms of Discrimination against Women, 1979, *available at* http://www.unhchr.ch/, which states that adoption of temporary special measures aimed at accelerating *de facto* equality between men and women shall not be considered discrimination. These measures shall be discontinued when the objectives of equality of opportunity and treatment have been achieved. Another example is Protocol No. 12 of the European Convention on Human Rights which reaffirmed that the principle of non-discrimination is not incompatible with positive discrimination as long as those measures are based on objective and reasonable grounds, Preamble of Protocol No. 12 to the Convention for the Protection of Human Rights and Fundamental Freedoms, Rome, Nov. 4, 2000, ETS No. 177, *referred to in* Cullet, *supra* note 3, at 34.

[25] As discussed later, some treaties require the special situation of developing countries to be taken into account. The Stockholm Convention on Persistent Organic Pollutants, *supra* note 10, refers to developing countries, least developed countries and countries with economies in transition.

[26] The Law of the Sea Convention, 21 ILM 1261 (1982), 1833 UNTS 3, signed Dec. 10, 1982, entered into force Nov. 16, 1994, *available at* http://www.un.org/Depts/los/index.htm, for example, discusses the special situation of land-locked countries. *See* discussion in Section C.1. *See infra* notes 133–138 and accompanying text.

[27] The Kyoto Protocol, *supra* note 9, refers to the special situation of small island states that are particularly vulnerable to any change in the sea level caused by the greenhouse effect.

[28] The Montreal Protocol on Substances that Deplete the Ozone Layer, *supra* note 12, is a good example.

[29] This could be a situation where a different compliance regime is given to developing countries.

[30] This could be where different obligations apply to different groups of states, such as under the Kyoto Protocol, *supra* note 9.

or differentiation, are binding on the parties. They are no less rigorous than general obligations.

## B. THE RATIONALE FOR THE ADOPTION OF THE COMMON BUT DIFFERENTIATED RESPONSIBILITY PRINCIPLE

In the environmental field, many factors must be taken into consideration when drafting obligations for states. Until the early 1980s, international environmental treaties did not differentiate between various players or actors in relation to their environmental obligations. In other words, the principle of juridical equality was applied without taking into account the various differentiations that are present in the international community. However, this formal adoption of treaties, without taking various differentiations into account, became problematic as developing countries were unwilling to accept obligations that entailed a huge financial burden on them. The net result of this was that developing countries failed to participate in environmental treaties that they felt were one-sided: developed countries were responsible for most of the present-day environmental problems, and no concessions were given to developing countries to participate in these treaties. The issue came to a head with negotiations on the Ozone Convention. It was obvious that if the support of developing countries was to be harnessed, some kind of incentives had to be offered to them to participate in the process. India and China, two countries with the biggest population and fast growing economies, said outright that they will not participate in the treaty regime unless there were economic incentives to do so.[31] This ultimately led to the adoption of the ozone fund.

The rationale underlying the common but differentiated responsibility principle is the principle of equity[32] or justice.[33] Equity requires us to take "other" considerations into account. Equity is one of the oldest principles of international law and has been consistently applied by tribunals in many contexts.[34] It requires us to hold those who caused damage to be responsible for repairing that issue, not hold everybody responsible to pay for that damage. In the environmental field, the principle of equity dictates us to hold those who caused the environmental problem to take more

---

[31] *See* HUNTER ET AL., *supra* note 16, at 550.

[32] *Id.* at 402.

[33] *See* Cullet, *supra* note 3, at 36.

[34] In the *Tunisia/Libya Continental Shelf Case*, 1982 ICJ 18, the Court stated that "Equity as a legal concept is a direct emanation of the idea of justice." In the *Maritime Delimitation in the Area Between Greenland and Jan Mayen (Denmark v. Norway)*, 1993 ICJ 38, Judge Weeramantry referred extensively to equity and equitable principles. *See* discussion in Section B.1 and note 72 and accompanying text.

responsibility than others, although every state has the general obligation not to cause significant environmental damage. While an effort can be made to achieve a level playing field for the players, the players themselves are not equal by any means. Thus, how does one take into account this differentiation in the players? This differentiation gave rise to the common but differentiated responsibility principle, which was specifically adopted as a principle for the first time in the Rio Declaration, although several instruments refer to the special needs of developing countries.[35]

While its adoption as a "principle" signifies the recognition of the vast disparity between developing countries and developed countries and the bigger contribution the developed countries had historically made to pollution, it can be argued that it imposes an unfair and disproportionate burden on developed countries. On the other hand, it is no secret that developed countries contributed much more to pollution than developing countries; that developed countries have much more resources at their disposal to expend on environmental protection; that developing countries require all the resources they can muster to deal with poverty and underdevelopment; that technology transfer and an environmental fund are necessary if present-day environmental problems are to be addressed in a meaningful manner. While it has been argued that "poverty is the biggest polluter,"[36] the situation is not so simple, as people in developed countries consume much more resources than those in developing countries: thus, for example, a person in the United States consumes about 50 percent more resources than a person in a developing country.[37] Moreover, developed countries, with a little over 20 percent of the world's population, consume 80 percent of the world's energy.[38] Thus, over-consumption of resources is as a big an issue as poverty when it comes to environmental degradation. This issue requires urgent attention.[39]

The principle of justice has also been put forward as a rationale for differential treatment, which includes concerns with regard to protecting the

---

[35] *E.g.*, the Vienna Convention for the Protection of the Ozone Layer, 26 ILM 1529 (1985), 1513 UNTS 293, signed Mar. 22, 1985, entered into force Sept. 22, 1988, refers to the circumstances and particular requirements of developing countries (Preamble) and the Montreal Protocol, *supra* note 12, acknowledges that "special provision is required to meet the needs of developing countries" (Preamble).

[36] *See* Chapters 1 and 2.

[37] *See* David Pimentel et al., *Will Limits of the Earth's Resources Control Human Numbers?*, Cornell University (1999), *available at* http://dieoff.org/page174.htm.

[38] *See* OUR COMMON FUTURE, REPORT OF THE WORLD COMMISSION ON ENVIRONMENT AND DEVELOPMENT 32 (1987).

[39] *Id.*

weak and the disadvantaged, compensation for past injustices and social justice.[40] Except for the first category, the other categories have not received much support (indeed the second category has been very contentious) and will not be discussed in detail. Protecting the weak and the disadvantaged, particularly in relation to meeting the basic needs of peoples, has been incorporated in various instruments in various forms.[41]

It has been noted, with regard to the adoption of Principle 7 of the Rio Declaration, that:

> Recognition of differentiated responsibilities was at the political heart of the UNCED synthesis because developing countries were unwilling to have global environmental problems impede their development. Differentiated responsibilities also reflect equitable norms concerning the use of resources and the treatment of nations with varying capabilities.[42]

Principle 7 recognizes the need for a global partnership to address environmental problems. It notes that international cooperation in a spirit of global partnership is necessary. This means that developing countries and developed countries alike must work together toward the common goal of protecting the global environment. Solidarity,[43] considered as a principle of international law,[44] implies a sense of partnership[45] among all actors in solving issues that are of concern to the community as a whole. The principle of global partnership[46] in Principle 7 "reflects the ecological

---

[40] *See* Cullet, *supra* note 3, at 36.

[41] *See,* for example, Principle 5 of the Rio Declaration, UN Doc. A/CONF.151/26, *reprinted in* 31 ILM 874 (1992), *available at* http://www.un.org/documents/ga/confl51/aconf15126-lannexl.htm, on reducing poverty; and Article 69(2) of the UN Law of the Sea Convention, *supra* note 26, which refers to the nutritional needs of the populations of respective states.

[42] *See* John Dernbach, *Sustainable Development as a Framework for National Governance,* 49 CASE W. RES. L. REV. 1 (1998) (footnotes omitted).

[43] It is posited that the principle of solidarity is codified in Article 55 of the UN Charter, which requires states to cooperate with one another to achieve the goals of economic and social development. *See* Cullet, *supra* note 3, at 44. The UN Convention to Combat Desertification in Countries Experiencing Serious Drought and or Desertification, particularly in Africa, 1954 UNTS 3, signed Oct. 14, 1994, entered into force Dec. 26, 1996, also refers to international solidarity and partnership. Art. 3(b).

[44] *See* Cullet, *supra* note 3, at 42.

[45] The UN Desertification Convention also refers to the need for cooperation in a spirit of partnership. *See* Article 3(c), *supra* note 43, which is considered as a guiding principle.

[46] *See* Marion Wilson, *The New Frontier in Sustainable Development: World Summit on*

interdependence of all states, and the need for broad North-South cooperation and compromise to resolve global environmental issues."[47] Principle 7 further provides that while states have the common responsibility to protect the environment, they have a differentiated responsibility as to how to achieve that common objective. This differs from universalism.[48] Developing states have different and diminished responsibilities in relation to certain environmental treaty regimes. In other words, the developed countries bear the major burden of environmental protection while developing countries' obligations are significantly less onerous.

When Principle 7 was being negotiated, developing countries wanted developed countries to take legal responsibility for past environmental harm on the basis of Principle 7.[49] This was obviously resisted by developed countries; hence no reference was made in Principle 7 to legal responsibility for past environmental damage. It does, however, recognize the greater responsibility that developed countries have in relation to environmental protection.

Despite the rather vague language adopted in Principle 7, there is little doubt that it has broken new ground in international environmental law. While it is open to debate whether it is a legal principle or a guiding principle, it could lead to significant legal implications, as more and more environmental treaties adopt differential obligations for states.

Differential treatment is a deviation from the strict application of the principle of sovereign equality.[50] It takes other factors, such as the level of economic development, geographic location, etc., into account. Differential treatment refers to "non reciprocal arrangements which seek to foster substantive equality in the international community."[51]

The reaction to Principle 7 has been rather mixed. Some consider that the concept remains very controversial.[52] It could require developed coun-

---

*Sustainable Development Type II Partnerships*, 36 VICTORIA U. WELLINGTON L. REV. 389 (2005).

[47] *See* HUNTER ET AL., *supra* note 16, at 403–04.

[48] *See* Duncun French, *Developing States and International Environmental Law: The Importance of Differentiated Responsibilities*, 49 ICLQ 35 (2000).

[49] *See* Lavanya Rajamani, *The Principle of Common but Differentiated Responsibility and the Balance of Commitments under the Climate Regime*, 9(2) RECIEL 120 (2000).

[50] *See* Philippe Cullet, *Equity and Flexibility Mechanisms in the Climate Change Regime: Conceptual and Practical Issues*, 8 RECIEL 168 (1999).

[51] *Id.* at 169.

[52] *See* HUNTER ET AL., *supra* note 16, at 402.

tries to provide financial assistance to developing countries, transfer technology[53] or allow developing countries less rigorous compliance regimes.[54] All three aspects are reflected in the Montreal Protocol on Substances that Deplete the Ozone Layer.[55] As discussed later, it established a multilateral fund to help developing countries to achieve their obligations, it contains provisions on technology transfer and developing countries were given a longer phase-out period for ozone depleting substances. However, the precise issue gave rise to controversy during the Kyoto negotiations, and the lack of binding commitments on developing countries was a major reason why the United States pulled out of the Kyoto negotiations in 2001.[56]

Principle 7 has several components: (1) it lays down the general obligation of states to cooperate[57] to protect and conserve the ecosystem; (2) this obligation is to be discharged in a spirit of global partnership; (3) due to different contributions to global environmental degradation, states have common but differentiated responsibilities; (4) developed countries acknowledge the responsibility they bear in the pursuit of sustainable development given the pressures their societies have placed on the global environment and the technologies and resources at their disposal.

Thus, it can be said that Principle 7 reiterates the principle of cooperation in the environmental field,[58] which is common to all states. They are required to cooperate in a spirit of global partnership highlighting the interdependency of the global environment.[59] However, it is not clear what "global partnership" really seeks to convey. Principle 27 of the Rio Declaration, which also refers to cooperation, does not contain the word "global," although reference is made to "partnership."[60] Principle 27 confers this obligation on both states and people, while Principle 7 refers only to states. It is significant that Principle 27 refers to both states and people

---

[53] *See* Gaetan Verhoosel, *Beyond the Unsustainable Rhetoric of Sustainable Development: Transferring Environmentally Sound Technologies,* 11 GEO. INT'L ENVTL. L. REV. 49 (1998).

[54] *See* HUNTER ET AL., *supra* note 16, at 402.

[55] *See supra* note 12. *See* discussion in Section C.2.

[56] *See* HUNTER ET AL., *supra* note 16, at 403.

[57] *See* Chapter 4. *See also* Rajamani, *supra* note 49, at 121.

[58] It may be recalled that Principle 24 of the Stockholm Declaration, UN Doc. A/CONF.48/14, June 16, 1972, *reprinted in* 11 ILM 1416 (1972), and Principle 27 of the Rio Declaration, *supra* note 41, also refer to the principle of cooperation.

[59] *See* HUNTER ET AL., *supra* note 16, at 403.

[60] Principle 27 reads: "States and people shall cooperate in good faith and in a spirit of partnership in the fulfillment of the principles embodied in this Declaration and in the further development of international law in the field of sustainable development."

and confers on them the general obligation to cooperate in good faith and in a spirit of partnership to fulfill the principles contained in the Declaration. The word "partnership" conveys the impression that parties are equal at least formally. Principle 27, by conferring the obligation on both states and people, gives the impression that states must cooperate with other entities in order to achieve sustainable development.

Principle 7 refers to two forms of differentiation: the first form is based on the different contribution of states to *global* environmental problems. The second form is based on the different capacities of states:[61]

> Together, these two elements of differentiated responsibility provide the beginnings of a philosophical basis for international cooperation in the fields of environment and development. It is a basis that allows the characterization of transfer of resources from developed to developing countries as "obligation" rather than as "aid" or assistance and provides a theoretical basis to justify different environmental standards, in view of the different capacities of States and their different contributions to environmental degradation.[62]

It is, however, doubtful whether developed countries would consider technology transfer and transfer of resources as an obligation under international law, rather than providing aid.[63] Thus, when signing the Rio Declaration, the United States attached an interpretative statement to Article 7 stating that it entailed no legal responsibility for global environmental problems, and that acceptance of Article 7 did not mean that developing countries had diminished responsibility in relation to global environmental problems.[64]

The main caveat in Principle 7 is that the common but differentiated responsibility principle applies only to global environmental problems. For a regional environmental problem, such as acid rain, for example, it would seem that this principle will not be applicable even if there are various categories of players. Given the rather controversial nature of the concept, restricting its application to global environmental problems seems logical, so that the number of issues encompassed by this concept can be limited. Of the several global environmental threats, two regimes have

---

[61] *See* Ileana Porras, *The Rio Declaration: A New Basis for International Cooperation, in* PHILIPPE SANDS, GREENING INTERNATIONAL LAW 20, at 29 (1994).

[62] *Id.*

[63] *See supra* notes 119–124 and accompanying text.

[64] *See* HUNTER ET AL., *supra* note 16, at 403.

already applied this concept—depletion of the ozone layer and the greenhouse effect.

It has been articulated that issues regarding differentiated responsibilities arise in at least three major areas: environmental responsibilities, financial and other assistance and consumption of materials and energy.[65] Because developed countries have primarily contributed to global environmental problems, and because they have the ability to address them, Principle 7 calls upon them to take a lead role. The Rio Declaration calls upon developed states to provide financial, technical and other assistance to developing countries in order to meet the goal of sustainable development. Although diminished responsibility for developing countries is not universally supported,[66] for global environmental problems, it is hard for developing countries to fulfill their obligations without assistance from developed countries. Financial assistance and technological transfer are common features of modern environmental treaties.[67]

## 1. The Role of Equity

As noted earlier, Principle 7 is based on the principle of equity.[68] Given the differing contributions of states to global environmental problems, it is inequitable to hold all of them responsible to adopt and implement the same obligations. Two notions of equity have been put forward.[69] Where one party has taken unfair advantage of others by imposing costs on them without their consent, those disadvantaged are entitled to demand that in the future, the offending party should shoulder a bigger burden at least to the extent of unfair advantage previously taken. The issue of climate change can be cited as an example. Industrial countries have benefited disproportionately from the industrialization process, which, in turn, led to the accumulation of greenhouse gases in the atmosphere. However, the effects of the damage are global, and the costs are borne by every member of the international community. It is thus contended that those who contributed to the problem should bear a bigger burden in addressing the problem.[70]

---

[65] *See* Dernbach, *supra* note 42.

[66] *See* in this regard, the interpretative statement attached to Principle 7 by the United States, in HUNTER ET AL. *supra* note 16, at 403.

[67] *See* discussion in Section C.2.

[68] *See* Paul Harris, *Common But Differentiated Responsibility: The Kyoto Protocol and United States Policy*, 7 N.Y.U. ENVTL. L.J. 27 (1999) who notes that "this principle is grounded in shared notions of fairness."

[69] *See* Rajamani, *supra* note 49, *quoting* Henry Shue, *Global Environment and International Inequality*, 75(3) INT'L AFF. 531 (July 1999).

[70] *Id.*

The second notion of equity is the formulation articulated by Justice Jimenez de Arechaga in the *Tunisia-Libya Case:*

> The resort to equity means, in effect, to appreciate and balance the relevant circumstances of the case, so as to render justice, not through the rigid application of general rules and principles and of formal legal concepts, but through an adaptation and adjustment of such principles, rules and concepts to the facts, realities and circumstances of each case.[71]

An extensive discussion of equity and its role can be found in the separate opinion of Judge Weeramantry in the *Maritime Delimitation in the Area Between Greenland and Jan Mayen (Denmark v. Norway) Case.*[72] He looked at equitable principles, equitable procedures, equitable methods and equitable results, as well as the different origins of the principle.[73] He then identified several methods of operation of equity—through balancing the interests of parties; through an equitable interpretation of a rule of law or of a treaty or set of facts; through the choice of an equitable principle; through the use of judicial discretion; through filling in gaps and interstices in the law; through following equitable procedures; through the application of equitable principles already embedded in the law; and through its use in a negative fashion to test a result.[74]

Of these various applications, equity has been used most commonly to balance the interests of the parties, to fill a gap in the law or to soften the outcome that may result from the rigid application of a particular law.[75] Judge Weeramantry quotes a renowned international lawyer that "true equity consists in holding in the best equilibrium the considerations of equity invoked by both parties."[76] Equity also "demands reasonableness and good faith in the interpretation and application of treaties."[77]

Thus, while there are many applications and functions of equity, it primarily seeks to achieve an equitable result. This aspect of the principle of

---

[71]  1982 ICJ 106, 109.

[72]  *See supra* note 34.

[73]  *Id.*

[74]  *Id.*

[75]  *See* Cullet, *supra* note 3, at 27.

[76]  *See supra* note 34, at 247, para. 122, *quoting* BIN CHEN, GENERAL PRINCIPLES OF LAW AS APPLIED BY INTERNATIONAL COURTS AND TRIBUNALS 48–49 (1987).

[77]  *Supra* note 34, at 249, para. 129, *quoting* Georg Schwarzenberger, *Equity in International Law,* Y.B. WORLD AFF. 346, at 357 (1972).

equity is relevant to the present discussion. It could be contended that the common but differentiated responsibility principle seeks to achieve an equitable result by adopting differential obligations based on the level of development of a particular state, as well as the contribution that a particular state has historically made to the environmental issue in question. Furthermore, the notion of fairness is inherent in the concept of equity and is another argument made by developing countries in favor of the common but differentiated responsibility principle.

## 2. Various Forms of Differentiation

It has been advocated that the principle brings together several strands of thought.[78] First it establishes the common responsibility of states to protect the global environment. Second, it acknowledges that industrial countries bear the primary responsibility for dealing with global environmental problems. Third, it recognizes broad distinctions between states, based on economic development, vulnerability or consumption levels. Finally, it emphasizes the ability of states to respond to environmental crises and gives a leadership role to developed countries.[79] It is further contended that the notion of differential responsibility derives from both the *differing contributions* of states and the *differing capacities* of states.[80] Since it has been more or less accepted that developed countries have, at least historically, contributed more to global environmental problems, it has been contended that the legal basis for the transfer of technology and financial resources is founded on entitlement and not need.[81]

Differentiation can be applied at two levels.[82] First, in the case of obligations, different obligations can be adopted in relation to different categories of states. A good example of this approach is the Kyoto Protocol, which does not contain any quantified emission limitations for developing countries, whereas Annex I countries have emission limitation and reduction commitments.[83] The second level of differentiation takes place at the implementation level. At this level, all states accept the same obligations, but different groups of states are given incentives to implement their commitments. This can take the form of deferred compliance regimes, tech-

---

[78] *See* Rajamani, *supra* note 49.

[79] *Id.*

[80] *Id.*

[81] *Id.*

[82] *See* Cullet, *supra* note 50, at 169.

[83] *See* Article 3 of the Kyoto Protocol, *supra* note 9, which lays down general obligations for Annex I countries.

nology transfer or financial mechanisms, such as the Global Environment Facility.[84]

Duncun French argues that there are different types of differentiation: setting different standards; permitting grace periods for implementation; providing flexibility in approach; and providing for international assistance.[85] An example of the first approach can be found in the Kyoto Protocol, while the second approach signifies the obligations under the Montreal Protocol. It also provides for a fourth approach by establishing an international fund. Related to the fourth approach is technology transfer, which is envisaged under both the Kyoto Protocol and the Montreal Protocol. Another example of providing for technology transfer is the Convention on Biological Diversity.

Christopher Stone identifies several dimensions of differential terms in existing conventions:[86] those that make differential substantive requirements;[87] those that have more favorable compliance timetables;[88] those permitting special defenses;[89] those that make non-compliance overlooked;[90] yet others afford qualified states financial and technical assistance, either to absorb costs of compliance[91] or as a pre-condition for their participation.[92]

Daniel Magraw notes that since much of the world's population increase is taking place in developing countries, and since they do not have adequate resources at their disposal to expend on environmental protection, it is vital that international environmental protection measures involve the continuous participation of developing countries.[93] This is one of the pri-

---

[84] *E.g.*, the Montreal Protocol, *supra* note 12.

[85] *See* French, *supra* note 48.

[86] *See* Stone, *supra* note 13.

[87] Examples cited are the Conference on the Limitation of Armament, Treaty Between the United States of America, the British Empire, France, Italy, and Japan (Washington Treaty of 1922), signed, Washington, Feb. 6, 1922, *available at* http://www.ibiblio.org/pha/pre-war/1922/nav-lim.html; Treaty on Non-Proliferation of Nuclear Weapons, 729 UNTS 161 (1970), *available at* http://www.fas.org/nuke/control/npt/text/np2.htm; and the Kyoto Protocol, *supra* note 9.

[88] The Montreal Protocol (amendments) is cited as an example.

[89] UNCLOS Convention, art. 71, *supra* note 26.

[90] *See* Stone, *supra* note 13. This double standard is discussed mostly in the human rights area.

[91] This is the function of the international fund established under many treaties.

[92] UNFCC, art. 4(7), *supra* note 9.

[93] *See* Daniel Barstow Magraw, *Legal Treatment of Developing Countries: Differential, Contextual and Absolute Norms*, 1 COLO. J. INT'L ENVTL. L. & POL'Y 69 (1990).

mary reasons for adopting the common but differentiated responsibility principle. Without the participation of developing countries in environmental treaties, many environmental goals would fail, even where the past and present contributions of developing states to environmental issues are negligible. Given that 89 percent of the world's population live in developing countries, and that many of these developing countries are fast industrializing, without their participation, many environmental treaty regimes would become meaningless. Magraw further notes that since an effort must be made to deal with absolute poverty, it is clear that fairness issues must be taken into consideration seriously when dealing with international environmental obligations.[94]

Magraw differentiates between three general types of international norms: differential norms, contextual norms and absolute norms.[95] According to him, differential norms are those norms that provide more advantageous standards for one set of states than for another set of states and cites the Montreal Protocol on Substances that Deplete the Ozone Layer as an example.[96] Contextual norms, on the other hand, provide, on the face of it, identical treatment to all states, but the application of the norms requires the consideration of characteristics that might vary from country to country. This involves the balancing of multiple interests and characteristics. In other words, this will require taking into account the socio-economic conditions, vulnerability to environmental degradation, etc. These norms have certain advantages: it is often easier to reach agreement on these norms than on more definite norms. They are also good for problems that are clouded with uncertainty. Moreover, flexibility allows a contextual norm to adapt to changed circumstances. It also eliminates the need to renegotiate the standard in question, which can be time consuming and expensive. Given the range of factors that may be considered, however, contextual norms can allow states to escape compliance. Examples of general contextual norms that have been cited include the reference to "just and equitable" and "reasonable" in the 1972 Space Liability Convention[97] while the World Heritage Convention of 1972[98] provides an example of a limited contextual norm: "to the utmost of its own resources."[99]

---

[94] *Id.*

[95] *Id.*

[96] *Id.* He states that the Montreal Protocol is highly unusual, perhaps "unique" because it defines "developing countries."

[97] Convention on International Liability for Damage Caused by Space Objects, signed Mar. 29, 1972, entered into force Sept. 1, 1972, 961 UNTS 187.

[98] Convention for the Protection of the World Cultural and Natural Heritage, signed Nov. 16, 1972, entered into force Dec. 17, 1975, 11 ILM 1358 (1972), *available at* http://www.wcmc.org.uk/igcmc/convent/wh/wh_atls.html.

[99] *Id.*, art. 4.

Absolute norms, on the other hand, are norms that provide identical treatment to all countries and do not permit the consideration of factors that could vary between states (socio-economic conditions, for example).[100] Unlike the previous two norms, these norms are very precise and allow for more predictable outcomes. Because of their precision, it is much easier to apply these norms. One major disadvantage, however, is its inflexibility.[101]

It is interesting to note the progression of environmental treaties according to the type of obligations contained in them. Early environmental treaties, such as the Geneva Convention on Long-Range Transboundary Air Pollution,[102] contained contextual norms in that it contains phrases, such as using "the best available technology," which is "economically feasible."[103] The Protocols adopted under the Framework Convention,[104] on the other hand, contained, for the most part, absolute norms. However, even within these rigid regimes, it is possible to identify several contextual norms, as well as differential norms. The 1984 Protocol to the Geneva Convention,[105] for example, differentiates parties on the basis of, *inter alia,* the total land area and the amount of annual sulfur emissions.[106] Examples of truly differential norms can be found in the Montreal Protocol and the Kyoto Protocol.

Starting with the Stockholm Declaration, most environmental instruments refer to the needs of developing countries. In addition to the reference to developing countries in the Preamble, Principles 9–12 and 23 of the Stockholm Declaration refer to developing countries in one form or other. This has led Magraw to articulate the possibility that a "soft law" principle or a customary norm is emerging to the effect that "international conventional regimes should, as a general matter, take the interests of developing countries into account in achieving sustainable development."[107]

---

[100] *See* Magraw, *supra* note 93.

[101] *Id.*

[102] 18 ILM 1442 (1979), 1302 UNTS 217, signed Nov. 13, 1979, entered into force Mar. 16, 1983, *available at* http://www.unece.org/env/lrtap/lrtap_h1.htm.

[103] *Id.,* art. 6.

[104] Eight protocols have been adopted under the Framework Convention, 31 ILM 849 (1992), 1771 UNTS 107, signed May 9, 1992, entered into force Mar. 21, 1994, *available at* http://www.unfccc.de/. *See* http://www.unece.org/leginstr/cvenvi.htm for a complete list of the protocols and their texts.

[105] Protocol to the 1979 Convention on Long-Range Transboundary Air Pollution on Further Reduction of Sulphur Emissions, UN Doc. EB.AIR/R. 84, signed June 14, 1994, entered into force Aug. 5, 1998.

[106] *Id.,* art. 2(3).

[107] *See* Magraw, *supra* note 93. *Cf.* discussion in Sections E and F.

Despite these references to developing countries as early as 1972 and the recognition that their needs and obligations toward the environment are distinct from those of developed countries, specific differential obligations were not adopted until the 1987 Montreal Protocol. Contextual norms are more abundant than differential norms. An example where differential norms deadlocked negotiations is the Kyoto Protocol.[108]

While it is doubtful that developed countries have a customary law obligation to assist developing countries meet their international environmental obligations, environmental treaties increasingly refer to this obligation. The Rio Declaration, where this obligation was referred to in Principle 7, seems to be the beginning of this trend. Although the Montreal Protocol pre-dated this, no specific reference was made to the common but differentiated responsibility principle.

Principle 7 of the Rio Declaration has several important components. First, it affirms the principle of cooperation. It recognizes that in view of the different contributions to global environmental degradation by states, they have common but differentiated responsibilities. Further, developed countries have accepted their role toward the realization of sustainable development given the pressures they place on the global environment and the technology and financial resources that are at their disposal. Principle 7 also refers to the concept of "global partnership." It is not clear whether this is a stand alone principle, or whether it is a component of the principle of cooperation.

The role of the common but differentiated responsibility principle in the context of climate change has been articulated as:

> While the CBDR principle emphasizes the different responsibilities and capabilities of states, it also seeks to bring all states together to cooperate in solving international environmental problems. Another dimension of the CBDR principle is thus its emphasis on partnership to avoid further environmental harm. In other words, it strives to find a solution to the problem of finding who has the resources to pay for climate change mitigation and who has the responsibility to do so.[109]

While states have the common responsibility (obligation) to protect the global environment,[110] Principle 7 makes it clear that different coun-

---

[108] As noted, one of the main reasons why the United States pulled out of the Kyoto regime in 2001 was because there were no binding obligations for developing countries.

[109] *See* Cullet, *supra* note 50, at 169.

[110] *See* Stone, *supra* note 13, who notes that the word "common" suggests that certain risks affect and are affected by every nation on earth.

tries will have different obligations toward achieving this common objective. These differential obligations are based on social, economic and ecological considerations. An earlier version of Principle 7 required developed countries to accept legal responsibility for their past contributions to global environmental problems.[111] This was strongly opposed by developed countries, and the compromise language adopted at the Rio Conference avoids any reference to historic responsibility for past environmental wrongs.

Despite the recent move to embody differential norms in treaties, uniform obligations or universalism remain the rule and differentiation, the exception.[112] It has been articulated that "the real puzzle about differentiation is not why we have them, but why they emerged so late and appear no more frequently then they do."[113] There are several reasons why differentiation is the exception: some treaties are too morally ambiguous to permit them; the lowest common denominator standard would be unacceptable for many; and where the participation of weak countries is desirable, cooperation may be obtained through other means without diluting the obligations under the treaty.[114]

Differentiated responsibility can take many forms. It could entail differential obligations (for example, like in the Montreal Protocol, developing countries have a grace period of ten years to comply with their obligations under the Protocol), technology transfer or the establishment of a fund to assist developing countries. The Montreal Protocol adopts all three approaches.

Christopher Stone argues that Principles 6 and 7 of the Rio Declaration taken together provide at least three arguments for differentiation: (1) differentiation in accordance with needs; (2) differentiation based on the pressures that each country places on the environment; and (3) differential capabilities in terms of wealth and technology.[115] While Principle 6 focuses on the need of developing countries, particularly, the least developed, Principle 7 focuses on the burden that developed countries place on the environment.[116] In other words, the developed nations are being held accountable for the damage they have caused to the global environment. This, according to Stone, is no more controversial than the polluter pays principle.[117]

---

[111] *See* Porras, *supra* note 61, at 28.

[112] *See* Stone, *supra* note 13.

[113] *Id.*

[114] *Id.*

[115] *Id.*

[116] As noted by Stone, *supra* note 13, Principle 7 "shifts the focus from Poor's needs to Rich's wrongs."

[117] *Id.*

The adoption of differentiated responsibilities "as a principle" has given rise to much controversy.[118] Developed states did not like the idea of having to provide technology and resources as a "legal obligation." The provision of aid and other resources has never been done on the basis of a legal obligation. In this context, it is interesting to note the statement issued on November 21, 2005, by several UN Experts to the donor community in relation to providing aid to the survivors of the South Asian earthquake.[119] The joint statement was issued by the Representative of the Secretary-General on the Human Rights of Internally Displaced Persons; the Special Rapporteur on Adequate Housing; the Special Rapporteur on the Right to Health; the Special Rapporteur on the Right to Education; and the Special Rapporteur on the Right to Food.[120] It called upon the donor countries to deliver the $5.4 billion pledged by them, "which are in accordance with States' international human rights responsibilities."[121] It further stated that "Governments which are in a position to do so *have a responsibility to provide international assistance* and cooperation. This responsibility derives from the Charter of the United Nations, the Universal Declaration of Human Rights, the Millennium Declaration, and other international instruments."[122] It also referred to the World Summit Outcome Report of September 2005,[123] which expressed the commitment of the international community to respond rapidly to natural disasters and mitigate their impact.[124]

This statement implies that there is a legal obligation on the part of states, which can afford to do so, to provide international assistance and cooperation. The fact that this obligation, according to the UN Experts' statement, derives from, *inter alia*, the UN Charter and international human rights law is noteworthy. The UN Charter is the supreme document of the international community and primacy is given to this instrument by Article 103 of the Charter.[125] Couched in these terms, it would be hard for

---

[118] *See* HUNTER ET AL., *supra* note 16, at 402. *Cf.* Stone, *supra* note 13, who notes that this concept is receiving increasing recognition in international law.

[119] UN Press Release: *Donors Must Meet International Responsibilities to Survivors of South Asia Earthquake, UN Experts Warn*, Nov. 21, 2005, *available at* http://www.unhchr.ch/huricane/huricane.nsf/view01/F6B122567B509E1CC1257 0C1003245AD?.

[120] *Id.*

[121] *Id.*

[122] *Id.* (emphasis added).

[123] *See infra* note 237 and accompanying text.

[124] UN General Assembly, 2005 World Summit Outcome, UN Doc. A/RES/60/1, Oct. 24, 2005, *available at* http://www.un.org/summit2005/documents.html, para. 69.

[125] Article 103 provides that in the event of a conflict between the obligations under

the donor countries to deny that there is a legal obligation on them to provide international assistance. However, the real question is, will the failure to provide aid amount to a breach of an international obligation giving rise to international responsibility?[126] Additionally, can the developing country or the victim state demand that such aid be provided by the international community? These issues are increasingly coming to the forefront, and the international community will have to deal with these challenging questions.

### 3. Common but Differentiated Responsibility and Sovereign Equality: Contradiction or Conciliation?

It can be questioned whether the principle of common but differentiated responsibility contradicts the cardinal principle of international law of sovereign equality of states. One of the fundamental principles of public international law is that all states are sovereign and equal, whatever their size, the population, the military power or the economic status. This principle has been necessary for the harmonious relations among states and is codified in the UN Charter. Article 2.1 emphasizes that "The organization is based on the principle of the sovereign equality of its Members."[127] This is also reflected in the "one-member, one-vote" policy of the UN General Assembly.[128] Thus, according differential treatment to developing countries seems, on the face of it, contrary to the principle of equality.

On a practical level, however, things are very different. It is no secret that states differ vastly according to their economic status and military prowess. According equal treatment in a world plagued by differences seems impractical and, in some instances, unjust, to say the least. This is particularly true with regard to environmental issues. Most environmental problems that the international community faces today have been created by developed countries in the pursuit of "development." While a handful of states have created these problems, the entire international community has to bear the brunt of the repercussions. In order to address these issues, every state has had to take measures that, in some instances, entail prohibitive costs. Grappling with high levels of poverty and disease, many of

---

the UN Charter and another international instrument, the obligations under the Charter would prevail.

[126] *See* ILC Draft Articles on State Responsibility, *available at* http://www.un. org/law/ilc/.

[127] UN Charter art. 2.1.

[128] Art. 18.1 of the UN Charter: "Each member of the General Assembly shall have one vote." The World Bank, on the other hand, has adopted a system of weighted voting, which depends on the per capita income of member states. *See* Cullet, *supra* note 3, at 74.

the developing countries cannot afford to divert much-needed funds to environmental protection. Without their assistance, however, many environmental protection regimes would fail. Thus, what is the solution to this problem?

Recognizing this dilemma, the international community's response was to adopt differing standards for developing countries. In some instances, developing countries have demanded that they be given some concessions if they were to comply with an environmental protection regime. The ensuing section discusses the application of this principle in environmental treaties.

## C. OPERATIONALIZATION OF THE COMMON BUT DIFFERENTIATED RESPONSIBILITY PRINCIPLE IN INTERNATIONAL INSTRUMENTS

International conventions adopt many kinds of differential treatment.[129] Of these, the conventions that refer to the need to take the special situation of developing countries into account are probably the most prevalent. While the common but differentiated responsibility principle was first articulated in the Rio Declaration, differential treatment is by no means confined to the environmental field, nor is it new.[130]

### 1. General Treaties

Many treaties outside the environmental protection field embody provisions on differential treatment. Some of the early examples are the Treaty Establishing the ILO[131] and the General Agreement on Tariff and Trade (GATT).[132] The Law of the Sea Convention[133] refers to giving developing countries preferential treatment:

Developing States shall, for the purposes of prevention, reduction and control of pollution of the marine environment or minimiza-

---

[129] *See* Stone, *supra* note 13, where he refers to the Treaty of Versailles establishing the ILO, which recognized that "differences of climate, habits and customs, of economic opportunity and industrial tradition, make strict uniformity in the conditions of labor difficult of immediate attainment." Similarly, the GATT added provisions to encourage nonreciprocal trade concessions in favor of developing countries.

[130] Stone, *id.*, articulates that "the environment is emerging as the most fertile field for nonuniform obligations."

[131] Constitution of the International Labour Organisation, June 28, 1919, 49 Stat. 2712, 2733–34, 225 CONSOL. T.S. 188.

[132] General Agreement on Tariffs and Trade, signed Oct. 30, 1947, 55 UNTS 187.

[133] *See supra* note 26.

tion of its effects, be granted preference by international organizations in:

(a) the allocation of appropriate funds and technical assistance; and

(b) the utilization of their specialized services.[134]

Article 202 refers to scientific and technical assistance to developing countries. States are required, directly or through competent international organizations, to promote programs of scientific, educational, technical and other assistance to developing countries for the protection of the marine environment and the prevention and reduction of marine pollution. They are also required to provide appropriate assistance, especially to developing countries, for the minimization of the effects of major incidents which may cause serious marine pollution; and for the preparation of environmental assessments.[135]

While Article 202 refers to the need to give assistance to developing countries, Article 203 confers them preferential treatment. These are two different approaches to the notion of differentiation. Article 140 dealing with the Area, notes that activities in the Area shall be carried out for the benefit of mankind as a whole, irrespective of the geographical location of states, whether coastal or land-locked, and taking into consideration the interests and needs of developing states. The Authority shall provide for the equitable sharing of financial and other economic benefits derived from activities in the Area through any appropriate mechanism on a non-discriminatory basis.[136]

Further, the Convention has provisions on transfer of technology and provides that the Authority shall take measures to acquire technology and scientific knowledge relating to the activities in the Area and to promote and encourage the transfer to developing states of such technology and scientific knowledge so that all parties will benefit from them. It also refers to the need to train personnel from developing states in marine science and technology.[137] The Convention further provides for the promotion of effective participation of developing states in activities in the Area, having due regard to their special needs and interests.[138]

---

[134] *Id.*, art. 203.

[135] *Id.*, art. 202.

[136] *Id.*, art. 140.

[137] *Id.*, art. 144.

[138] · *Id.*, art. 148.

Similarly, the UN Convention on the Law of the Non-Navigational Uses of International Watercourses[139] refers both to the importance of international cooperation and good neighborliness, as well as the special situation and needs of developing countries. It also refers to the Rio Declaration and Agenda 21.[140]

The Preamble to the Agreement Establishing the World Trade Organization[141] also distinguishes between developed countries and developing countries and further identifies least developed countries. It refers to the need to take positive efforts to ensure that developing countries, and especially least developed countries, "secure a share in the growth in international trade commensurate with the needs of their economic development."[142] Although one of the principles of the WTO is non-discrimination,[143] it does recognize the need to accord special and differential treatment for developing countries.[144] The Doha Ministerial Declaration of 2001[145] also refers to the need to give particular attention to the effect of environmental measures on market access, especially in relation to developing countries, in particular the least developed among them in relation to the work of the Committee on Trade and Environment.[146]

The Doha Ministerial Declaration also affirms the principle of special and differential treatment and notes that it is an integral part of the WTO Agreements.[147] It further refers to the proposal by some members to adopt a Framework Agreement on Special and Differential Treatment. The Ministers have agreed that such provisions shall be reviewed with a view to strengthening them and making them more precise, effective and operational and endorsed the work program on special and differential treatment.[148]

---

[139] UN Doc. A/51/869, signed May 21, 1997, not yet in force.

[140] *Id.*, Preamble.

[141] *Available at* http://www.wto.org.

[142] *Id.*, Preamble.

[143] *See* the discussion in Chapter 1.

[144] Vice Yu, *Special and Differential Tratement (SDT) and Common but Differentiated Responsibility (CDR): Principles in Favor of Developing and LDS Countries in the Trade and Environment Negotiations, at* http://www.tradeobservatory.org/library.cfm?reflD=25707.

[145] Doha Ministerial Declaration, *available at* http://www.wto.org/english/thewto_e/minist_e/min01/mindecl_e.htm.

[146] *Id.*, para. 32.

[147] *Id.*, para. 44.

[148] *Id.*

Similarly, the least developed countries were recently granted an extension until July 1, 2013, to provide for an intellectual property regime under the TRIPS Agreement.[149] The WTO Council for TRIPS decided to extend the transition period for least developed countries by seven and a half years. This transition period was due to expire on January 1, 2006. The Preamble to the Decision recognizes "the special needs and requirements of least-developed country Members, the economic, financial and administrative constraints that they continue to face, and their need for flexibility to create a viable technological base." It further notes:

> Recognizing the continuing needs of least-developed country Members for technical and financial cooperation so as to enable them to realize the cultural, social, technological and other developmental objectives of intellectual property protection.[150]

Article 2 of the decision calls upon least developed country members to provide to the Council as much information as possible on their individual priority needs for technical and financial cooperation in order to assist them to take steps necessary to implement the TRIPS Agreement. Developed country members shall provide technical and financial cooperation in favor of least developed countries in accordance with Article 67 of the TRIPS Agreement.[151]

This is a very intriguing provision as it confers an obligation on developed countries to provide financial and technical cooperation to least developed countries so that they can meet their obligations under the TRIPS Agreement. However, the text refers to technical and financial *cooperation*, and not technical and financial *assistance*, as it is usually referred to in environmental treaties. Whatever the wording is, it is clear that this provision seeks to convey a sense of obligation to provide such assistance to least developed countries. Many of the environmental treaties, discussed below, do not use such clear language.

## 2. Environmental Instruments

While many treaties recognize the need for differential treatment, it is really in the field of environmental protection that this principle has gained the most ground. Several environmental treaties, particularly those

---

[149] Decision of the Council of TRIPS, Nov. 29, 2005, extension of the transition period under Article 66.1, *available at* http://www.wto.org/english/news_e/pres05_e/pr424_e.htm.

[150] *Id.*, Preamble.

[151] *Id.*, art. 2.

adopted since the Montreal Protocol on Substances that Deplete the Ozone Layer, have adopted differential treatment mainly for developing countries, although other categorizations are also visible. The starting point, as with many other issues, is the Stockholm Declaration:

> Resources should be made available to preserve and improve the environment, taking into account the circumstances and particular requirements of developing countries and any costs which may emanate from their incorporating environmental safeguards into their development planning and the need for making available to them, upon their request, additional international technical and financial assistance for this purpose.[152]

Principle 23 refers to the need to take account of the systems of values in each country and notes that standards in developed countries may be inappropriate for developing countries. Principle 24 refers to the need for cooperation by all countries, big or small, on an equal footing, in relation to international environmental issues. This seems to affirm the notion of equality, rather than differentiation.

The Rio Declaration is the first instrument to specifically adopt the common but differentiated responsibility principle. Principle 7, which embodies this principle, was already noted. In this regard the provisions in Principle 6 of the Rio Declaration are also relevant, which is a clear acceptance of the need for differentiation:

> The special situation and needs of developing countries, particularly the least developed and those most environmentally vulnerable, shall be given special priority. International actions in the field of environment and development should also address the interests and needs of all countries.[153]

The Basel Convention on the Control of Transboundary Movement of Hazardous Wastes and Their Disposal[154] provides an example of taking the needs of developing countries into consideration, although it contains no specific obligations towards them. The Preamble recognizes the limited capabilities of developing countries to manage hazardous waste and also the need to promote the transfer of technology for the sound management of hazardous wastes in accordance with the Cairo Guidelines[155] and UNEP

---

[152] *See supra* note 58, Principle 12.

[153] *See supra* note 41, Principle 6.

[154] *See supra* note 12.

[155] Cairo Guidelines and Principles for the Environmentally Sound Management of Hazardous Wastes, *available at* http://www.unep.org/.

Governing Council Decision.[156] Article 10 requires parties to cooperate with each other to achieve environmentally sound management of hazardous waste and calls on parties to cooperate actively in the transfer of technology and management systems.[157] They are also required to cooperate in developing the technical capacity among parties, especially those countries which may request such assistance. Cooperation between parties and international organizations is encouraged, taking into account the needs of developing countries, to promote public awareness, the development of sound management of hazardous wastes and the adoption of low-waste technologies.

The UN Convention on Desertification is interesting in many respects. It is the first treaty to give preferential treatment to a whole continent. It refers to developing countries and least developed countries in many instances. Indeed, the whole convention actually discusses the special situation of Africa. It refers to the necessity of international cooperation and partnership in combating desertification[158] and the need to develop, in a spirit of partnership, cooperation among all levels of government, communities, non-governmental organizations and landholders.[159] It also states that "Parties should take into full consideration the special needs and circumstances of affected developing country Parties, particularly the least developed among them."[160]

Article 5 deals with obligations of affected parties, while Article 6 deals with obligations of developed country parties. Under Article 6 developed country parties have undertaken, *inter alia*, to provide substantial financial resources and other forms of support to assist affected developing countries, particularly those in Africa, effectively to develop and implement their plans and strategies to combat desertification and mitigate the effects of drought. They have also agreed to promote the mobilization of new and additional funding pursuant to Article 20(2)(b) and to promote and facilitate access to appropriate technology, knowledge and know-how.[161] The Convention gives priority to Africa in implementing the Convention, in the light of the particular situation prevailing in that region, while not neglecting affected developing country parties in other regions.[162]

---

[156] Decision 14/30 on Environmentally Sound Management of Hazardous Wastes, *available at* http://www.unep.org/.

[157] *Id.*, art. 10(2)(d). This provision, however, does not refer specifically to developing states.

[158] *See supra* note 43, Preamble.

[159] *Id.*, art. 3(c).

[160] *Id.*, art. 3(d).

[161] *Id.*, art. 6.

[162] *Id.*, art. 7.

Article 18 of the Convention applies to transfer, acquisition, adaptation and development of technology, while Article 19 applies to capacity-building, education and public awareness. Article 20 refers to financial resources, while Article 21 refers to financial mechanisms. These provisions seek to ensure that developed country parties, while giving priority to affected African parties without neglecting other affected developing countries, mobilize substantial financial resources in order to support the implementation of programs under the Convention; facilitate, through international cooperation, the transfer of technology, knowledge and know-how; explore innovative methods and incentives for mobilizing and channeling resources, particularly debt swaps by reducing the external debt burden of affected developing countries, particularly those in Africa.[163]

The Convention further notes that the full implementation by affected developing countries, particularly those in Africa, of their obligations under the Convention will be greatly assisted if developed countries would fulfill their obligations under the Convention, particularly those relating to financial resources and transfer of technology.[164] The Conference of Parties, established under Article 22 of the Convention, is required to promote the availability of financial mechanisms for affected developing countries, particularly those in Africa, to implement the Convention. The establishment of a fund is one of the mechanisms envisaged in the Convention.[165]

This is probably the first time that an international convention accords preferential treatment to a particular continent[166] within the category of developing countries, due to the particular situation prevailing in that region. The Convention itself does not elaborate on what factors were taken into account in deciding on the "particular situation" except to note that Africa is experiencing particularly tragic consequences of serious drought and desertification.[167] While developing countries facing desertification have been identified as a group to be given special assistance, including financial assistance and transfer of technology, the Convention accords special status to Africa, giving it preferential treatment. Thus, if a choice is to be made between a developing country facing drought and/or desertification in another part of the world and a country in Africa, the

---

[163] *Id.*, art. 20.

[164] *Id.*, art. 20(7).

[165] *Id.*, art. 21.

[166] This must be distinguished from regional treaties which are applicable to a particular region. The Desertification Convention, by contrast, is a universal treaty, which accords preferential treatment to Africa.

[167] *See supra* note 43, Preamble.

Convention requires that the country in Africa be given assistance under the Convention. The Convention, however, is not an example of providing different obligations for different groups such as under the Kyoto Protocol. While the basic obligations remain the same, developed country parties have more burdensome obligations in relation to financial mechanisms, transfer of technology and know-how.

The Rotterdam Convention on Prior Informed Consent Procedure for Certain Hazardous Chemicals and Pesticides in International Trade[168] provides another example of differential treatment. It takes into account "the circumstances and particular requirements of developing countries and countries with economies in transition, in particular the need to strengthen national capabilities and capacities for the management of chemicals, including transfer of technology, providing financial and technical assistance and promoting cooperation among the Parties."[169] The Convention also provides for technical assistance to developing countries:

> The parties shall, taking into account in particular the needs of developing countries and countries with economies in transition, cooperate in promoting technical assistance for the development of the infrastructure and the capacity necessary to manage chemicals to enable implementation of this Convention. Parties with more advanced programs for regulating chemicals should provide technical assistance, including training, to other Parties in developing their infrastructure and capacity to mange chemicals throughout their life-cycle.[170]

It is noteworthy that while the general obligation to cooperate is laid down in mandatory language ("shall cooperate"), hortatory language is used ("should provide") in relation to providing technical assistance including training.

Similarly, the Stockholm Convention on Persistent Organic Pollutants[171] refers to the particular requirements of developing countries. It distinguishes between developing countries, least developed countries and countries with economies in transition:

---

[168]  38 ILM 1 (1999), signed Sept. 11, 1998, entered into force Feb. 24, 2004, *available at* http://www.pic.int/en/ViewPage.asp?id=104.

[169]  *Id.*, Preamble.

[170]  *Id.*, art. 16.

[171]  *See supra* note 10.

Taking into account the circumstances and particular requirements of developing countries, in particular least developed
among them, and countries with economies in transition, especially the need to strengthen their national capabilities for the
management of chemicals, including through the transfer of technology, the provision of financial and technical assistance and the
promotion of cooperation among the Parties.[172]

Article 12 provides for technical assistance. It notes that the parties recognize that giving timely and appropriate technical assistance in response
to requests from developing countries and parties with economies in transition is essential to the successful implementation of the Convention. The
parties are required to cooperate toward this end, to assist developing
countries and parties with economies in transition, taking into account
their particular needs, to develop and strengthen their capacity to implement their obligations under the Convention. Technical assistance shall
include assistance for capacity-building relating to the implementation of
the obligations under the Convention. Further guidance in this regard is
to be provided by the Conference of the Parties. The parties are also
required to establish arrangements for the purpose of providing technical
assistance and promoting transfer of technology, including regional and
sub-regional centers for capacity-building and transfer of technology.
Furthermore, the parties are required to take full account of the specific
needs and the special situation of least developed countries and small
island developing states in their actions with regard to technical assistance.

Article 13 deals with financial resources and mechanisms and provides
that developed countries shall provide new and additional financial
resources to enable developing countries to meet the agreed full incremental costs of implementing the obligations under the Convention. It
provides further that:

The extent to which the developing country Parties will effectively
implement their commitments under this Convention will depend
on the effective implementation by developed country Parties of
their commitments under this Convention relating to financial
resources, technical assistance and technology transfer. The fact
that sustainable economic and social development and eradication
of poverty are the first and overriding priorities of the developing
country Parties will be taken fully into account, giving due consideration to the need for the protection of human health and the
environment.[173]

---

[172] *Id.*, Preamble.

[173] *Id.*, art. 13(4).

The Convention provides for the establishment of a financial mechanism to assist developing country parties to fulfill their obligations under the Convention, which will function under the authority of the Conference of Parties. Under Article 14, the Global Environment Facility has been used on an interim basis as the principal entity entrusted with the operations of the financial mechanism.

The provisions in the Stockholm Convention are significant for many reasons: unlike many other conventions, discussed above, which seem merely to pay lip service to the special needs of developing countries, the Stockholm Convention actually establishes a financial mechanism to assist developing countries. It also clearly acknowledges that developing country parties will be unable to discharge their obligations under the Convention, unless a financial mechanism is established to help them. It also seeks to balance the overriding priorities of developing countries, such as eradication of poverty with the need for protecting human health and the environment.

Although these conventions do not specifically mention the common but differentiated responsibility principle, they provide for other forms of special treatment, including technology transfer, providing technical assistance, capacity-building and establishing a financial mechanism. The Stockholm Convention is by far the most comprehensive of the conventions discussed so far. None of these conventions, however, provides for differential obligations or different compliance regimes.

True differential obligations are found in the Kyoto Protocol while the Montreal Protocol is the first environmental treaty to adopt different compliance regimes. Although the Stockholm Declaration makes reference to developing countries in several of its principles, the first binding instrument to adopt differential obligations is the Montreal Protocol. It is noteworthy, however, that neither the Vienna Convention nor the Montreal Protocol explicitly refers to the common but differentiated responsibility principle.

The Vienna Convention notes in the Preamble that the parties to the Convention have taken into account the circumstances and particular requirements of developing countries. Apart from this recognition, the Vienna Convention contains no further reference to developing countries. The Montreal Protocol, on the other hand, has extensive provisions on developing countries. It acknowledged that "special provision is required to meet the needs of developing countries for these substances."[174] Article 5 deals specifically with the special situation of developing countries. It allows developing countries to delay its compliance under the Protocol by ten years, provided its annual calculated level of consumption of the "con-

---

[174] *See supra* note 12, Preamble.

trolled substances"[175] is less than 0.3 kilograms per capita on the date that the Protocol entered into force and does not exceed 0.3 kilograms annually. The parties have undertaken "to facilitate access to environmentally safe alternative substances and technology for Parties that are developing countries and assist them to make expeditious use of such alternatives."[176] Furthermore, they undertake to facilitate the provision of subsidies, aid, credits, guarantees or insurance programs to developing country parties for the use of alternative technology and for substitute products.

Article 10 is also relevant in this regard. Parties are required to cooperate in promoting technical assistance to facilitate participation in the Protocol, taking into account the needs of developing countries and in the context of the provisions of Article 4. Article 4 bans trade in controlled substances with non-parties to the Protocol. Any party can submit a request to the secretariat for technical assistance to implement the Protocol.

Several amendments to the Protocol have been adopted over the years. The London amendments to the Protocol were adopted in 1990. These amendments, *inter alia*, replaced the ninth preambular paragraph of the Protocol as follows:

Considering the importance of promoting international cooperation in the research, development and transfer of alternative technologies relating to the control and reduction of emissions of substances that deplete the ozone layer, bearing in mind in particular the needs of developing countries.[177]

Article 5 of the Amendments deals with the special situation of developing countries and replaces Article 5 of the Protocol referred to above. Paragraph 5 of the Amendments is the most important for the present discussion. It clearly states that developing countries' capacity to fulfill the obligations under Article 5 will depend on the effective implementation of financial cooperation as provided under Article 10 and transfer of technology as provided under Article 10A.

Any party can inform the Secretariat that it is unable to implement its obligations under paragraph 1 or other obligations in Articles 2A-2E because of the inadequate implementation of Articles 10 and 10A. The

---

[175] Defined in Art. 1(4) of the Protocol, *id.*

[176] *Id.*, art. 5(2).

[177] London Amendments to the Montreal Protocol on Substances that Deplete the Ozone Layer, UNEP/Oz.L.Pro.2/3, signed June 29, 1990, entered into force Aug. 10, 1992.

Secretariat will transmit a copy of the notification to the parties who will decide, at their next meeting, the appropriate action to be taken.

Article 10 of the amendments provides that the parties shall establish a mechanism to provide financial and technical cooperation, including the transfer of technology, to parties operating under Article 5(1) of the Protocol[178] to enable them to comply with their measures set out in Articles 2A-2E of the Protocol. Contributions to the mechanism will be in addition to other financial transfers to parties operating under Article 5(1). The mechanism established under this provision shall include a multilateral fund. The fund shall meet the agreed incremental costs, on a grant or concessional basis as appropriate, and according to criteria to be decided upon by the parties. It shall also finance clearinghouse functions to assist parties operating under Article 5(1), through country specific studies and other technical cooperation, to identify their needs for cooperation, facilitate technical cooperation and distribute information and relevant materials and hold workshops and other training sessions for the benefit of developing country parties. It shall also finance the Secretariat services of the multilateral fund. It shall operate under the authority of the parties who shall decide on its overall policies. The fund shall be financed by contributions from parties other than those operating under Article 5(1).

Article 10A deals with the transfer of technology. It provides that each party shall take every practicable step to ensure that the best available, environmentally safe substitutes and related technologies are expeditiously transferred to parties operating under Article 5(1) and that such transfer shall occur under fair and most favorable conditions. Further amendments to the Protocol were adopted in 1992, 1997 and 1999.

Thus, the Montreal Protocol provides a classic example of differential obligations. It adopts a wide range of differential obligations, starting with a grace period of ten years for developing countries to comply with their obligations. Thus, while the basic obligation remains the same for all the parties to the Protocol (to phase out ozone depleting substances), the time table for the implementation of this obligation varies depending on whether the party is a developed country or a developing country. Furthermore, the Protocol also requires technology transfer, making substitutes available to developing countries and also establishes a multilateral fund to help developing countries fulfill their obligations under the Protocol. This provides a comprehensive "package" to developing countries and is considered a very successful global environmental treaty.[179]

---

[178] These are essentially developing countries.

[179] *See* HUNTER ET AL., *supra* note 16, at 300.

The first treaty to specifically embody the common but differentiated responsibility principle is the United Nations Framework Convention on Climate Change. It acknowledged that "the global nature of climate change calls for the widest possible cooperation by all countries and their participation in an effective and appropriate international response, in accordance with their common but differentiated responsibilities and respective capabilities and their social and economic conditions."[180] The Convention lays down the principles that the parties shall be guided by in order to achieve the objective of the Convention:

> 1. The Parties should protect the climate system for the benefit of present and future generations of humankind, on the basis of equity and in accordance with their common but differentiated responsibilities and respective capabilities. Accordingly, the developed country Parties should take the lead in combating climate change and the adverse effects thereof.

> 2. The specific needs and special circumstances of developing country Parties, especially those that are particularly vulnerable to the adverse effects of climate change, and of those parties, especially developing country Parties, that would have to bear a disproportionate or abnormal burden under the Convention, should be given full consideration.[181]

In addition, Article 3 refers to the need to take precautionary measures as well as to sustainable development. It states that the parties have a right to, and should, promote sustainable development. No definition of sustainable development is contained in the Convention.

The enumeration of principles in an environmental treaty is a major step forward, particularly because some of these do not enjoy the status of a legal principle. These are more guiding principles than those having a binding quality. It is also noteworthy that Article 3 employs the word "should," rather than "shall," indicating the hortatory nature of the "principles" embodied there. Nonetheless, the inclusion of these provisions under the caption "principles" conveys the intention of parties to the Convention.

The commitments adopted by the parties are laid down in Article 4. While these are not specific commitments, developed country parties are under an obligation to provide new and additional financial resources to meet the agreed full costs incurred by developing countries in complying

---

[180] *See supra* note 104, Preamble.

[181] *Id.*, art. 3.

with their obligations under Article 12(1). They shall also provide financial resources, including the transfer of technology, needed by the developing country parties to meet the agreed full incremental costs of implementing measures covered by Article 4(1) of the Convention. They shall also assist those developing country parties that are particularly vulnerable to the adverse effects of climate change in meeting costs of adaptation to those adverse effects.

Furthermore, developed country parties are required to take all practicable steps to promote, finance and facilitate the transfer of or access to environmentally sound technologies to other parties, particularly developing country parties, to enable them to implement the provisions of the Convention. They are also required to support the development and enhancement of endogenous capacities and technologies of developing country parties.

The Convention also recognizes that, as did the Montreal Protocol, the extent to which developing country parties will effectively implement their commitments under the Convention shall depend on the effective implementation by developed country parties of their commitments under the Convention relating to financial resources and transfer of technology. It also notes that the overriding priorities of developing countries are economic and social development and poverty eradication.

Specific commitments in relation to global warming are contained in the Kyoto Protocol[182] adopted under the auspices of the UNFCC, and the Protocol constitutes an example of true differential treatment for different categories of parties. The Protocol specifically refers to Article 3 of the Convention, which lays down the guiding principles for the purposes of the Convention. It may be recalled that these principles include the common but differentiated responsibility principle.[183] Thus, by referring to Article 3 of the Convention, the Protocol has endorsed those principles. The specific commitments detailed in the Protocol are mainly in relation to the parties listed in Annex I to the Convention. These parties are essentially developed countries and countries with economies in transition. No developing countries are included in Annex I.

Under Article 3 of the Protocol, the parties included in Annex I of the Convention are required to individually or jointly ensure that their aggregate anthropogenic carbon dioxide emissions of greenhouse gases, listed in Annex A of the Protocol, do not exceed their assigned amounts as laid

---

[182]   *See supra* note 9.

[183]   Principle 3.1 of the UNFCCC, *supra* note 104.

down in Annex B with a view to reducing their overall emissions by at least 5 percent below 1990 levels in the period between 2008–2012. Thus, the obligations under this category are only in relation to Annex I countries.

Article 12 of the Protocol deals with the clean development mechanism (CDM) and notes that the purpose of that mechanism is to assist parties not included in Annex I (essentially developing countries) to achieve sustainable development and to contribute to the ultimate objective of the Convention. It also seeks to assist parties included in Annex I to achieve compliance with their quantified emission limitations and commitments under Article 3.

Under the CDM, parties not included in Annex I[184] will benefit from project activities resulting in certified emission reductions; Annex I parties may use the certified emission reductions accruing such project activities to contribute to compliance with part of their quantified emission limitation and reduction commitments under Article 3. The CDM is subject to the authority of the Conference of the Parties (COP) and may be supervised by an executive board. The CDM shall also assist in arranging funding of certified project activities as necessary. The COP shall ensure that a share of the proceeds from certified project activities is used to cover administrative expenses, as well as to assist developing country parties that are particularly vulnerable to climate change to meet the costs of adaptation. Thus, the Kyoto Protocol distinguishes between Annex I countries, Annex II countries and developing countries and provides a good example of differential obligations for different groups of countries.

Another convention that addresses concerns of developing countries is the Convention on Biological Diversity.[185] It acknowledged that "special provision is required to meet the needs of developing countries, including the provision of new and additional financial resources and appropriate access to relevant technologies"[186] and noted the "special conditions of the least developed countries and small island states."[187] The Preamble also recognized that economic and social development and poverty eradication are the first and overriding priorities of developing countries.

The Convention advances, for the first time in the history of environmental protection, the concept of benefit sharing. It lays down the objec-

---

[184] Parties not included in Annex I are essentially developing countries.

[185] 31 ILM 822 (1992), 1760 UNTS 79, signed June 5, 1992, entered into force Dec. 29, 1993, *available at* http://www.biodiv.org/.

[186] *Id.*, Preamble.

[187] *Id.*

tives of the Convention as: conservation of biological diversity; sustainable use of its components; and fair and equitable sharing of benefits arising out of the utilization of genetic resources, including appropriate access to genetic resources. It also refers to the need to transfer relevant technology as well as provide appropriate funding.[188]

Similar to the leverage obtained in relation to climate change, developing countries also played a significant role in the negotiations leading up to the adoption of the Biodiversity Convention. This time they were able to call the shots, as they were rich in biodiversity while being poor in terms of resources and technology. This is also reflected in the provisions on benefit sharing.

Article 15 deals with access to genetic resources. It recognizes the sovereign rights of states over their natural resources and that the authority to determine access to genetic resources rests with national governments and is subject to national legislation. The influence of developing countries in including this provision in the Convention is obvious. They insisted that recognition must be given to the principle of sovereignty over natural resources.[189] It further provides that access to genetic resources shall be subject to the prior informed consent of the contracting party providing such resources. The principle of prior informed consent (PIC) first appeared in the Basel Convention on the Control of Transboundary Movements of Hazardous Wastes and Their Disposal[190] and can be found in subsequent environmental treaties.[191]

Article 16 deals with access to and transfer of technology. Each contracting party, recognizing that access to and transfer of technology (including biotechnology) are essential to realize the objectives of the Convention, has undertaken to provide and facilitate access and transfer to other contracting parties of relevant technologies. It further provides that such transfer to developing countries shall be provided under fair and most favorable terms.

The Convention deals with distribution of benefits arising from biotechnology. Each contracting party is under an obligation to take all prac-

---

[188]  *Id.*, art. 1.

[189]  *See* HUNTER ET AL., *supra* note 16, at 932–34.

[190]  Art. 6, *supra* note 12.

[191]  *E.g.*, the Rotterdam Convention on Prior Informed Consent Procedure for Certain Hazardous Chemicals and Pesticides in International Trade, *supra* note 168, and the Stockholm Convention on Persistent Organic Pollutants and the Protocol, *supra* note 10, discussed *supra* notes 168 and 171 and accompanying text.

ticable measures to promote and advance priority access on a fair and equitable basis by contracting parties, particularly developing countries, to the results and benefits arising from biotechnologies based on genetic resources provided by those contracting parties.[192]

A financial mechanism is established for the provision of financial resources to developing country parties which functions under the authority of the Conference of Parties (COPs).[193] The COPs shall also determine the policy, strategy, program priorities and eligibility criteria relating to access to and utilization of resources. The COPs shall review the effectiveness of the mechanism, including the criteria and guidelines, not less than two years after the Convention enters into force.[194]

## 3. Analysis

The above survey illustrates the influence that the common but differentiated responsibility principle has had on environmental treaties, particularly since its inclusion in the Rio Declaration. This principle has ensured the participation of developing countries, which would otherwise not have had any incentive or the necessary resources to participate in the treaty regime. In other words, the principle has ensured universal participation in environmental treaties. In this light, the common but differentiated responsibility principle is a significant principle somewhat akin to the affirmative action principle in human rights law,[195] which has ensured that traditionally marginalized groups (for example, women, disabled people or minorities) are given special protection to wipe out the effects of discrimination. Since affirmative action measures are usually temporary, the question arises whether the common but differentiated responsibility principle should also be considered a temporary measure. Some writers have articulated that this should be so, until developing countries are in a position to address environmental issues themselves, without the need for incentives or technology transfer.[196] Given the ground reality, as well as the fact that these issues are intrinsically linked to the development process itself, how soon the majority of developing countries would be able to stand on their own feet is anybody's guess right now.

---

[192] Art. 19, *supra* note 12.

[193] *Id.*

[194] The Cartagena Protocol on Biosafety to the Convention on Biological Diversity, 39 ILM 1027 (2000), signed Jan. 29, 2000, entered into force Sept. 11, 2003, *available at* http://www.biodiv.org/ adopted in Montreal in 2000 was one the most contentious environmental treaties ever adopted. *See* HUNTER ET AL., *supra* note 16, at 953–56.

[195] *See* Jackson, *supra* note 17.

[196] *See* HALVORSSEN, *supra* note 17.

Different applications of the principle in treaties have been identified by Halvorssen as: (1) norms that differentiate among states with regards to core obligations; (2) financial assistance—financing the implementation of the agreements; (3) joint implementation; and (4) technical assistance, including access to technology and capacity building.[197] Under the first category, which gives developing countries less stringent commitments or obligations, treaties adopt different approaches, such as delayed compliance schedules or different targets and timetables.[198]

Halvorssen has distinguished between positive incentives and negative incentives.[199] She has identified asymmetrical norms, financial mechanisms and joint implementation as methods of participation; technical assistance falls into the former category, while trade sanctions and non-compliance procedures fall into the latter category.[200] She articulates the advantages of using differential treatment as follows:

> The advantages of using differential treatment rather than uniform environmental norms include compensation for lack of reciprocal state interest, avoiding the least-common-denominator problem, promoting participation in the environmental treaties at an earlier stage, and facilitating harmonization of national environmental standards.[201]

In certain instances, developing countries contend that since they did not contribute to a particular environmental problem, they should not be burdened with obligations that they can ill afford to fulfill. Thus, they could either opt out of the whole treaty regime by not participating in the treaty negotiating process, or they could participate and demand that very low obligations be adopted, resulting in the least common denominator problem. Differential treatment is a way to get around that problem.[202] In order to have as many states as possible participating in the process and to satisfy the requirements of a multitude of states with varying interests, the earlier environmental treaties invariably adopted the lowest common denominator. The ensuing result was a very weak regime with almost no teeth at all. In the words of Anita Halvorssen:

---

[197] *Id.*

[198] *Id.*

[199] *Id.* at 70.

[200] *Id.*

[201] *Id.* at 71

[202] *See* PETER H. SAND, LESSONS LEARNED IN GLOBAL ENVIRONMENTAL GOVERNANCE 6 (1990), *referred to in* HALVORSSEN, *supra* note 17, at 71.

In order to satisfy the most reluctant party in the negotiation of a treaty, compromise is often arrived at by lowering the standards for all parties to the treaty. By using incentives the higher standards would be maintained, yet the developing countries would be given special treatment, differential treatment, in order to facilitate their participation at an earlier stage. In effect, the incentives would create double standards, but the idea is that most often they are only meant to be temporary.[203]

"Temporary incentives" are justified by special circumstances in developing countries. These include their low technical and regulatory capabilities, lack of funding as well as low contribution to global environmental problems. It can be contended that even with differential regimes, the core obligations remain the same. Thus, for example, under the Montreal Protocol, the core obligation of reducing and ultimately eliminating controlled substances remains for all states. What the developing countries have obtained under the Montreal Protocol regime is a temporary respite to comply with their obligations under the Protocol. Once the grace period is over, their obligations will be on par with those of developed countries.

As the above survey of environmental instruments illustrated, these instruments have adopted differential regimes, delayed compliance schedules as well as financial mechanisms and technology transfer in order to encourage developing countries to participate in environmental treaties. For example, India and China insisted that they be provided with financial incentives to participate in the ozone protection regime.[204]

As with any multilateral regime, there are disadvantages in adopting differential regimes. These include higher administrative costs; distortions in trade as a result of lower environmental standards in some states resulting in competitive advantage for them; and could be counter-productive in the long term.[205] While all these allegations are true, they must be weighed against the advantages of adopting differential obligations for developing countries.

Having analyzed different schools of thought, Anita Halvorssen concludes that:

[d]ifferential treatment is more effective to promote the participation of developing countries because they are specifically men-

---

[203] *See* HALVORSSEN, *supra* note 17, at 71.

[204] *See supra* notes 178 and 179 and accompanying text.

[205] *See* HALVORSSEN, *supra* note 17, at 72.

tioned as the beneficiaries, whereas contextual norms, allowing for consideration of characteristics that might vary from country to country, require an interpretation to decide which countries are encompassed by the provisions.[206]

Alternative approaches to differential norms for developing countries have also been identified.[207] Two such approaches are using NGOs, including businesses and development agencies to induce developing countries to participate in multilateral environmental agreements and to use uniform norms but provide developing countries with compensation for lost opportunity costs.[208] While the latter approach might encourage states to participate in multilateral environmental treaties, the former approach might only encourage them to opt out, if no incentives are offered. With regard to providing "compensation" it is likely to be vehemently opposed by developed countries, as it could imply that they are taking responsibility for creating environmental problems and are compensating developing countries for the damage caused by them. This would no doubt rekindle the opposition to the common but differentiated responsibility principle.

## 4.  Negative Incentives

In addition to positive incentives to induce developing countries to participate in a particular treaty regime, there are negative incentives (or disincentives) in place too. These come mainly in the form of trade sanctions. Although a negative incentive, it does not discriminate between states and applies to both developing and developed states alike, as long as they are non-parties to the environmental treaty.

The first time that trade sanctions were used in the environmental context was in the CITES Convention.[209] It bans trade in certain species (usually endangered species) and regulates trade in a number of other species. Since then, several environmental treaties have used the same approach to induce non-parties to join the regime and also to ensure that non-parties do not jeopardize the entire regime. These treaties include the Montreal Protocol and the Basel Convention on Hazardous Wastes. Article 4 of the Montreal Protocol requires each party to ban the import of controlled substances from any non-party one year after the Protocol enters into force. After January 1, 1993, no party may export any controlled substance to any

---

[206]  *Id.* at 76.

[207]  *Id.*

[208]  *Id.* at 77.

[209]  Convention to Regulate International Trade in Endangered Species of Flora and Fauna, 12 ILM 1085 (1973), 993 UNTS 243, signed Mar. 3, 1973, entered into force July 1, 1975, *available at* http://www.cites.org/.

non-party. Parties are also discouraged from exporting, to any non-party, any technology for producing and for utilizing controlled substances.

Anita Halvorssen discusses the advantages of trade restrictions in the context of ozone depletion as follows:

> By promoting universal participation, such prohibitions also indirectly address the free rider problem and "pollution havens." Trade restrictions would ensure that the goal of the Protocol which is to reduce or eliminate ozone-depleting substances, would not be defeated by a few non-party States establishing themselves as havens where obligations accepted by the rest of the international community could be evaded. Developing countries not happy with the financial aid offered by a new treaty would not necessarily be able to stay outside trade sanctions without suffering any disadvantages.[210]

The issue whether such trade restrictions are contrary to the obligations under the GATT is subject to some controversy. While these measures are not discriminatory in the sense that they do not discriminate between non-parties,[211] whether states are entitled to restrict trade on environmental grounds has not yet been settled by any forum. While the WTO Dispute Settlement Panel has shown increasing sensitivity to sustainable development and has referred to it in a few cases,[212] whether trade restrictions could be justified on environmental grounds is yet to be seen.

The issue has also arisen whether having differential regimes for different states would undermine the legitimacy of the treaty regime and also give rise to monitoring problems. For example, when should these differential obligations cease to exist? Or should they be there as long as developing countries cannot meet their obligations without outside assistance? If we take the Montreal Protocol as the model, we could come to the conclusion that once the grace period is over, all parties have the same obligations. In other words, differential treatment is temporary, giving developing states the chance to "catch up" with other states. Whether this can happen in reality depends on a multitude of factors.

Christopher Stone categorizes three possible versions of the common but differentiated responsibility (CDR) principle—rational bargaining

---

[210] *See* HALVORSSEN, *Supra* note 17, at 104.

[211] *See* Chapter 1, Section B.2.a.

[212] *Id.*

CDR; equitable CDR; and inefficient CDR.[213] He notes that differential norms are not new—they pre-date the Rio Declaration, although its formal recognition in environmental treaties is a recent phenomenon.[214] He defines rational bargaining CDR as some non-uniformities that come as the natural outcome of mutually bargaining negotiators pursuing their own advantage in a narrowly self-interested manner. The second category goes a step further and introduces constraints on unbridled bargaining. The third category goes a step still further in advantaging one group—generally the poor.[215]

Reading Principles 6 and 7 of the Rio Declaration together, one can advance at least three forms of differentiation: (1) differentiation in accordance with needs; (2) differentiation in accordance with the harm caused; and (3) differentiation in accordance with the availability of technological and financial resources.[216] Montreal Protocol, discussed above, seems to adopt at least (1) and (3). Approach (2) seems to be the most controversial as far as developed countries are concerned. It seems to imply that developed countries accept responsibility for past conduct which they have opposed consistently.

In the words of Christopher Stone:

> Rio Principle 7, in calling for the assignment of heavier contributions to developed countries in response to "the pressures their societies place on the global environment," shifts the focus from Poor's needs to Rich's wrongs. If we agreed to put the principle into action, it would mean that the Rich (and everyone else) should be confronted with the full social costs of their emissions. Thus understood, the principle is no more controversial, or peculiarly equitable than declaring that the polluter should pay.[217]

What is the distinction between the CDR and the polluter pays principle?[218] The latter does not distinguish between the different types of polluters—it applies to all polluters. Having differential obligations/norms means that one state's obligations under the same treaty regime would be different than the other/s, depending on the economic and social conditions of that state. Thus, CDR and the polluter pays principle, while sharing simi-

---

[213] *See* Stone, *supra* note 13.

[214] *Id.*

[215] *Id.*

[216] *Id.*

[217] *Id.*

[218] *Id.*

larities, do not mean the same thing. Nonetheless, the two principles can be applied together.

Some have contended that the exclusive application of differential norms in relation to greenhouse gas emissions "suffers from nearsighted bias with potentially devastating consequences."[219] It is further contended that a modified approach to CDR must be adopted in order to address the climate issue and that absolute and universal norms can be achieved without unduly burdening the economies of developing states.[220] The writer is silent as to how this can be achieved.

## D. RELATIONSHIP WITH OTHER CONCEPTS

### 1. Common but Differentiated Responsibility Principle and the Inter-Generational Equity Principle

Whether the present generation should be held responsible for past conduct is a hotly debated issue. On the one hand, it can be argued that in the same way that the present generation should be held accountable for the impact of its activities on future generations, the present generation should be held responsible for past activities.[221] As one writer argues, "If we dismiss historical responsibility, what is to prevent future generations from doing so as well?"[222] While there is much merit in this argument, accountability for past contributions has been the main reason for the opposition to the CDR principle itself. During negotiations, developed countries insisted on removing all references to historic responsibility for past contributions to environmental problems from the wording of Principle 7 of the Rio Declaration.

It has also been contended that "reliance on historical responsibility enriches the principle of common but differentiated responsibility, for over time it results in an even-handed treatment of states."[223] The contention here is that, at some point in the future, the contribution of developing countries today becomes historic, and, hence, they too will be held responsible for their contributions.

---

[219] *See* Michael Weisslitz, *Rethinking the Equitable Principle of Common but Differentiated Responsibility: Differential Versus Absolute Norms of Compliance and Contribution in the Global Climate Change Context*, 13 COLO. J. INT'L ENVTL. L. & POL'Y 473 (2002).

[220] *Id.*

[221] *See* Rajamani, *supra* note 49, at 122.

[222] *See* K.R. Smith *quoted in* Rajamani, *supra* note 49 at 122, n.20.

[223] *See* Rajamani, *supra* note 49, at 122.

One of the components of sustainable development is the inter-generational equity principle.[224] It requires the present generation to evaluate the impact of its activities on future generations when taking decisions today. Similarly, the common but differentiated responsibility principle implicitly refers to the responsibility of the present generation for past polluting activities—in this instance, the responsibility of developed states for causing much of the global environmental problems. Although Principle 7 does not specifically refer to this in terms of legal responsibility, it does refer to the greater pressures that developed countries have placed on the global environment. As articulated by Christopher Stone, Principle 7 has a temporal quality.[225]

Both the CDR principle and the inter-generational equity principle are based on equity. It is the principle of equity that dictates us to take the special situation of developing countries into account when formulating environmental obligations. It is also the principle of equity that dictates us to evaluate the impact of our activities on future generations. Thus, while much of international law and obligations are based on the principle of reciprocity and equality,[226] in some instances states have opted to apply the principle of equity and adopt differential norms, as otherwise, the result will not be equitable.

## 2. Sustainable Development and the Common but Differentiated Responsibility Principle

The main rationale behind the common but differentiated responsibility principle is to ensure as wide a participation in international treaties as possible. The main argument advanced by developing countries not to join a particular environmental protection regime is that it would require developing countries to invest a considerable amount of resources in order to comply with their obligations under these regimes—resources that they can ill afford. The other argument behind this is based on equity. Developing countries also argued that they were not responsible for creating these global environmental problems and, therefore, it would be unfair to subject them to rigid obligations under environmental treaties. On the other hand, it was obvious to developed countries that without the participation of developing countries, these environmental regimes would fail. Thus, in order to ensure global participation in treaties, on the one hand, and to respond to the argument about equity, on the other, the international community adopted the common but differentiated responsibility

---

[224] *See* the discussion in Chapter 2, Section C.1.d.

[225] *See* Stone, *supra* note 13.

[226] *See* Cullet, *supra* note 3, at 57.

principle. Without the participation of developing countries, many treaty regimes, such as those governing climate change or biodiversity, would have failed. Thus, through the participation of the international community—in other words, by ensuring that as many states as possible are parties to global environmental treaties—the common but differentiated responsibility principle seeks to give effect to sustainable development. There is no doubt that without the different mechanisms adopted in these treaties, such as differential treatment, different compliance regimes, differed compliance regimes, technology transfer and an environmental fund, developing countries would not be able to fulfill their obligations under these global treaties, which would have placed a huge financial burden on them.

### 3. The Polluter Pays Principle and the Common but Differentiated Responsibility Principle

As the above discussion revealed, the common but differentiated responsibility principle is also closely related to the polluter pays principle, which will be discussed in the next chapter. In basic terms, the polluter pays principle requires states to internalize the costs of pollution control measures and reflect such costs in the goods and services provided to the consumer. The idea here is that the more demand there is for a polluting product, the more the consumer will have to pay for it. While on the face of it the common but differentiated responsibility principle and the polluter pays principle do not share common features, one aspect of the common but differentiated responsibility principle—namely the aspect that requires developed countries to take the lead role in abating environmental problems, given the pressures those countries place on the environment—is similar to the polluter pays principle. This will be discussed in Chapter 6.

### E. LEGAL STATUS OF THE COMMON BUT DIFFERENTIATED RESPONSIBILITY PRINCIPLE

While differential norms have been in existence as early as the ILO Convention and later the General Agreement on Tariffs and Trade (GATT), the term "common but differentiated responsibility" first appeared in the Rio Declaration of 1992, which falls into the realm of soft law. The first multilateral treaty to adopt the term was the UN Framework Convention on Climate Change. The Kyoto Protocol adopted five years later also refers to the principle. While the Montreal Protocol, as discussed above, contains extensive provisions on differential norms, no reference is actually made to CDR. What does this reveal about the legal status of the concept?

In order for a practice or a concept to become part of customary international law, it must satisfy the two elements embodied in Article 38 of the Statute of the ICJ: state practice and *opinion juris*. In the *North Sea*

*Continental Shelf Cases*[227] the ICJ noted several criteria that must be satisfied for a provision to become part of customary international law: (1) the provision in question should be of a fundamentally norm-creating character and could be regarded as forming the basis of a general rule of law; (2) there should be widespread and representative participation in the convention (or in relation to state practice), including the participation of states whose interests were specially affected; and (3) although a particular duration is not required, state practice in question should be extensive and virtually uniform and should be the result of a conviction that such practice is required by law.[228]

It can be questioned whether customary international law has become less important given the plethora of treaties now in existence. To the extent that some states have not ratified treaties, customary law serves as a backup. Its relevance was particularly evident in the *Nicaragua v. USA*[229] case where the Court was unable to apply treaty law, including the UN Charter, because of the multilateral treaty reservation entered into by the United States when accepting the compulsory jurisdiction of the Court under the optional clause.[230] Thus, the Court applied customary international law on non-use of force and intervening in internal affairs of states and held that the United States had breached its obligations under customary international law. It is interesting to note that the Court actually looked at the UN Charter (although it could not apply its provisions to the case before it) in order to establish *opinio juris* in relation to non-use of force.

Thus, the issue before the international community is whether there is sufficiently widespread state practice in relation to the common but differentiated responsibility principle to constitute a customary international law norm, so that even states that have not ratified the relevant treaties would be bound to apply it. It is submitted that it is premature to evaluate state practice at this juncture. Although it is 13 years since the adoption of the Rio Declaration, state practice during this period, in relation to the common but differentiated responsibility principle, has been anything but

---

[227] 1969 ICJ 3. The question that arose in this case was whether the provisions on the continental shelf in the Geneva Convention of 1958 had become part of customary international law. One of the parties to the dispute—Germany—had not ratified the Convention, hence, it was not bound by its provisions. Thus, other parties sought to establish that the particular provisions in the Convention had become part of customary international law as a result of subsequent state practice.

[228] *Id.*

[229] 1986 ICJ 14.

[230] In protest for the Court proceedings, the United States withdrew its acceptance of the Court's jurisdiction and has not accepted its jurisdiction since.

uniform or widespread. The general consensus seems to be that "the practice of differentiating responsibilities has not, despite occasional claims by its proponents, been elevated to the status of a customary principle of international law."[231]

According to Christopher Stone "the real puzzle about differentiations is not why we have them, but why they emerged so late and appear no more frequently than they do."[232] He noted several reasons as to why differentiations cannot be admitted generally. In relation to issues that require universalism, differentiations cannot be allowed. Thus, for example, treaties on genocide or torture cannot allow differentiation based on, for example, the level of economic development. The level of economic development, on the other hand, constitutes an "excuse" in relation to economic and social rights. Article 2 of the ICESCR provides as follows:

Each State Party to the present Covenant undertakes to take steps, individually and through international assistance and co-operation, especially economic and technical, to the maximum of its available resources, with a view to achieving progressively the full realization of the rights recognized in the present Covenant by all appropriate means, including particularly the adoption of legislative measures.[233]

No comparable limitation exists in the ICCPR. In other words, the obligations in the ICCPR are subject to immediate implementation. By contrast, the rights enshrined in the ICESCR are limited by resources and are subject to progressive realization. This is an example where uniform standards are adopted (as opposed to the differential norms in the Kyoto Protocol), but the parties are given leeway in implementing those standards at the domestic level depending on the resources available to the state party in question. This does not, however, mean that state parties can postpone the implementation of their obligations indefinitely. As General Comment No. 3 adopted by the Committee on Economic, Social and Cultural Rights pointed out, several obligations toward achieving full realization are of *immediate effect:* the guarantee that the right will be exercised without discrimination and the obligation to take steps toward full realization of the rights in the Covenant.[234] The General Comment also stressed that:

---

[231] *See* Stone, *supra* note 13.

[232] *Id.*

[233] Art. 2, ICESCR, 1966, *available at* http://www.unhchr.org.

[234] *The Nature of States Parties Obligations (Art. 2, para. 1),* General Comment No. 3, adopted by the Committee on Economic, Social and Cultural Rights at its fifth session, Dec. 14, 1990, *available at* http://www.unhchr.org/.

Thus, while the full realization of the relevant rights may be achieved progressively, steps towards that goal must be taken within a reasonably short time after the Covenant's entry into force for the States concerned. Such steps should be deliberate, concrete and targeted as clearly as possible towards meeting the obligations recognized in the Covenant.[235]

The Comment further noted that the term "progressive realization" is used to describe the intent of Article 2:

The concept of progressive realization constitutes a recognition of the fact that full realization of all economic, social and cultural rights will generally not be able to be achieved in a short period of time. . . . It is on the one hand a necessary flexibility device reflecting the realities of the real world and the difficulties involved for any country in ensuring the full realization of economic, social and cultural rights. On the other hand, the phrase must be read in the light of its overall objective of the Covenant which is to establish clear obligations for States parties in respect of the full realization of the rights in question. It thus imposes an obligation to move as expeditiously and effectively as possible towards that goal.[236]

States must demonstrate that every effort was made to use all resources that are at their disposal to satisfy the minimum obligations in the Covenant. Even with limited resources, states are required to strive to ensure the enjoyment of rights recognized in the Covenant. In their periodic reporting to the Committee, states are required to include information that shows progress over time with respect to the effective realization of the relevant rights. Both qualitative and quantitative data are required to make an adequate assessment of the situation in a given state.

Thus, the General Comment indicates that, while state parties have been given certain leeway in implementing the provisions under the ICE-SCR based on their level of economic development, they cannot postpone their obligations indefinitely. At least initial steps must be taken to implement the provisions in the Covenant, and the country reports to the Committee must indicate how these rights are being realized, given the limited amount of resources at the disposal of the state. They must show why and on what criteria these resources have been allocated for a given issue/project. Above all, their action cannot be discriminatory.

---

[235] *Id.*, para. 2.

[236] *Id.*, para. 9.

Giving preferential treatment to developing countries was endorsed recently in the World Summit Outcome Report of September 2005.[237] The world leaders have reiterated their commitment to sustainable development and to taking action through "practical international cooperation" in relation, *inter alia:*

> [t]o continue to assist developing countries, in particular small island developing States, least developed countries and African countries, including those that are particularly vulnerable to climate change, in addressing their adaptation needs relating to the adverse effects of climate change.[238]

Reference was also made to the implementation of the UN Convention on Desertification through, *inter alia,* "the mobilization of adequate and predictable financial resources, the transfer of technology and capacity-building at all levels."[239] The world leaders also resolved to continue to negotiate an international regime to promote and safeguard the fair and equitable sharing of benefits arising out of the utilization of genetic resources within the framework of the Convention on Biological Diversity.

The world leaders have also pledged to assist developing countries' efforts to prepare integrated water resources management and water efficiency plans[240] and to accelerate the development and dissemination of affordable and cleaner technology for energy efficiency and conservation and to transfer such technologies to developing countries on favorable terms.[241] They have also identified the need to support developing countries in strengthening their capacity for the sound management of chemicals and hazardous wastes by providing technical and financial assistance.[242]

The report further identified the importance of science and technology in relation to achieving development goals and that international support can help developing countries to benefit from technological advancements. The world leaders committed themselves to address "the special needs of developing countries in the areas of health, agriculture, conservation, sustainable use of natural resources and environmental man-

---

[237] *See supra* note 124.

[238] *Id.,* para. 55.

[239] *Id.,* para. 56.

[240] *Id.,* para. 56(h).

[241] *Id.,* para. 56(i).

[242] *Id.,* para. 56(k).

agement, energy, forestry and the impact of climate change."[243] They have also pledged to promote and facilitate access to and transfer of technologies including environmentally sound technologies, and know-how to developing countries.[244] It has also identified several categories of states as having special needs: least developed countries;[245] landlocked developing countries;[246] small island developing states;[247] and Africa.[248]

Thus, this report highlights how the international community has identified the special needs of several categories of developing countries and the need to transfer technology, as well as to give financial assistance within a framework of international cooperation in support of their pursuit of sustainable development. Thus, while not endorsing differentiation *per se,* the 2005 World Summit report is a good example of preferential treatment of several categories of developing countries.

While the emergence of the common but differentiated responsibility principle is relatively recent,[249] differential norms and preferential treatment is not new to international law. Even where no explicit reference has been made to the common but differentiated responsibility as a principle, a particular trend in recent environmental treaties is to adopt differential obligations for developing countries in relation to global environmental issues. This trend is likely to continue as long as a vast disparity remains between developing countries and developed countries. Given the vast differentiations within the category of developing countries, further categorization is likely depending on the issue at hand. Thus, references may be made to small island states, least developed countries or, as we saw in relation to the Desertification Convention, the whole continent of Africa.

While universalism is the norm in relation to most treaties, in the field of environmental protection, differential norms have become increasingly common, as it is virtually impossible to have absolute norms for all parties, given the vast disparities in states. The main objective of having differential norms is to include all the players in the treaty regime, rather than exclude them by having uniform norms. While some treaty regimes have success-

---

[243] *Id.,* para. 60(a).

[244] *Id.,* para. 60(b).

[245] *Id.,* para. 64.

[246] *Id.,* para. 65.

[247] *Id.,* para. 66.

[248] *Id.,* para. 68.

[249] *See* Harris, *supra* note 68, referring to this principle as a nascent principle.

fully done this, some regimes have become very contentious, as we saw in relation to the Kyoto Protocol.

In discussing the influence of differential treatment on the development of international law, Philippe Cullet notes that:

> Examples analyzed in this chapter show that differentiation has been widely used in different contexts. It is noteworthy that the form through which differentiation is carried out is not in itself a mark of differentiation. Indeed, both reciprocal and non-reciprocal arrangements can amount to differential treatment depending on the aim and intent of the provision or regime. . . . Differential treatment examined here is thus not linked to particular forms or procedures but to the intent to remedy existing or potential inequalities.

> The various forms taken by differential treatment reflect the complexity of the problems at stake and the numerous factors which must be taken into account to have rules which effectively promote substantive equality. The furtherance of substantive equality sometimes comes at the cost of complicating the legal system. However, the fact that the international community is constantly looking for ways to adapt the standard formula of legal equality so that adopted regimes foster substantive equality demonstrates that on the whole the disadvantages of complexity do not outweigh the benefits that can be gained through differential measures.[250]

It has been articulated that, given the rather frequent references to differential norms, the international community seems to recognize that the application of the principle of formal equality is limited in a community that encompasses subjects with varying sizes and populations, different economic and political prowess and with access to unequal quantity of natural resources.[251] Differential treatment can constitute the very basis of a legal regime, such as in relation to deep seabed mining, which is based on the concept of common heritage of mankind.[252]

Two main justifications have been made in relation to the adoption of differential norms: first, weaker states have been able to secure differential

---

[250] *See* Cullet, *supra* note 3, at 83–84.

[251] *Id.* at 84.

[252] *See* the discussion of this concept/principle in Chapter 2 Section E.2. The common heritage of mankind principle has been rather controversial, despite its inclusion in the Law of the Sea Convention. *See* HUNTER ET AL., *supra* note 16, at 393. *See also* Harris, *supra* note 68, for the view that the common but differentiated responsibility principle evolved from the notion of common heritage of mankind.

norms in situations where their bargaining power has been stronger; secondly, differential regimes have been adopted where it has been in the stronger states' interests to do so.[253] Global environmental problems have provided the forum for differentiation in both these instances.

Differential norms have greatly influenced the development of international law, a system of law based traditionally on equality and universalism. Its influence on international environmental law has been particularly significant and has enabled the participation of a greater number of states in treaty regimes, which would probably not have participated in the regime otherwise. From that point of view, the influence of the common but differentiated responsibility principle is significant in the field of environmental law.

While differential treatment has become "a common feature of international law,"[254] at least with respect to environmental issues, its legal status remains unclear. Thus, whether there is a customary international obligation to adopt differential obligations where the players are not equal is subject to controversy. It has been articulated that in agreements in the fields of international trade, economic development and environmental protection, differential obligations have been used extensively.[255] Another writer concludes that "CBDR has moved from being a "soft" international legal principle . . . to a nascent but increasingly robust component of international law."[256]

Having analyzed the developments over the past 20 years, Philippe Cullet draws out several conclusions:

- Differentiation to enhance the economic situation of poorer countries has been upheld to date.
- Differential treatment has developed rapidly in international environmental treaties in recent years: "It is remarkable that there has been a consistent practice of granting differential treatment in global environmental agreements since the adoption of the Montreal Protocol in 1987."[257]
- The techniques for differentiation have also diversified. An innovative approach has been to make the implementation of developing countries' obligations contingent upon devel-

---

[253] *See* Cullet, *supra* note 3, at 84.

[254] *Id.* at 86.

[255] *Id.*

[256] *See* Harris, *supra* note 68.

[257] *See* Cullet, *supra* note 3, at 86.

oped countries fulfilling their own obligations in relation to finances etc.[258]

It has been contended that the principle that encapsulates the essence of differential treatment is the common but differentiated responsibility principle.[259] It differentiates on the basis of both the past and present contribution to environmental problems as well as the capacity to address them:

> The principle of CBDR has been applied both to the question of the responsibility of states for the creation of specific global environmental problems and to the responsibility for solving international environmental problems on the basis of differing capacity to provide resources to address these problems. While CBDR focuses on the allocation of responsibilities, it also seeks to bring all states together to cooperate in solving international environmental problems. The essence of the principle of CBDR is thus its twin emphasis on partnership and differential treatment.[260]

While it is true that the principle of common but differentiated responsibility principle is based on the twin pillars of partnership and differential treatment, which are not necessarily mutually supportive (could even be contradictory), it is not correct that it has been applied in relation to the responsibility of states for creating global environmental problems. As has been discussed earlier, this issue has been vehemently opposed by developed countries. A watered-down version of this principle was included in the Rio Declaration, which does not refer to legal responsibility for past acts on the part of developed countries.

In this regard, the interpretive statement attached to Principle 7 by the United States when signing the Rio Declaration is reflective of the sentiment of many developed countries:

> The United States understands and accepts that principle 7 highlights the special leadership role of the developed countries, based on our industrial development, our experience with environmental protection policies and actions, and our wealth, technical expertise and capabilities.

> The United States does not accept any interpretation of principle 7 that would imply a recognition or acceptance by the United

---

258  *E.g.*, the Convention on Biological Diversity, *supra* note 185.

259  *See* Cullet, *supra* note 3, at 87.

260  *Id.*

States of any international obligations or liabilities, or any diminution in the responsibilities of developing countries.[261]

Not only did the United States categorically reject responsibility for historic contribution to global environmental problems, it also specifically rejected giving developing countries differential treatment by way of adopting less stringent obligations for them.[262] This interpretive statement is, however, silent on the section of Principle 7, which indicates that the enhanced responsibility of developed countries in protecting the global environment is due in part to the pressures that developed societies place on the global environment. Instead, the statement refers to the "leadership role" that developed countries play in the international community.

Philippe Cullet argues that the common but differentiated responsibility principle is an economic principle:

The principle of CBDR is in large part an economic principle, as illustrated by the emphasis on the temporal dimension of each nation's responsibility in the creation of international environmental problems. . . . The economic dimension of the principle CBDR is extremely important since it highlights continuity with differential treatment in economic instruments.[263]

As noted above, this principle does not refer to each nation's responsibility in creating global environmental problems. Although developing countries were very keen to include this in Principle 7, due to the opposition of developed countries, no reference was made to historic responsibility for the creation of global environmental problems. Thus, it is submitted that Philippe Cullet's argument here is erroneous, although it is true that, reading between the lines, one can come to this conclusion. The common but differentiated responsibility principle is also not an economic principle similar to the polluter pays principle, for example, although economic aspects of transfer of technology and the establishment of funds are very much part of it. Neither does Principle 7 make any reference to the temporal dimension of the creation of global environmental problems that, again, may be arrived at by reading between the lines.

While some have contended that the common but differentiated responsibility principle recognizes the primary responsibility of developed

---

[261] *See* HUNTER ET AL., *supra* note 16, at 403.

[262] *Cf.* Harris, *supra* note 68, who contends that the United States is not against the common but differentiated responsibility principle. Rather, it actually supports it.

[263] *See* Cullet, *supra* note 3, at 88.

countries by causing environmental problems through over-consumption of resources,[264] this is not strictly correct.

With regard to the legal status of the common but differentiated responsibility principle, it has been contended that:

> Recent state practice with regard to the CBDR indicates that there is no clear consensus on the issue of differentiated responsibilities and the principle of CBDR is clearly not yet part of customary law. However, the increasing recognition of differentiated responsibilities in different contexts read together with the development of differentiated treatment generally may at some point in the future lead to the recognition of CBDR as a general principle of international environmental law. Despite a rather disjointed history, the practice of granting differential treatment may be slowly finding stronger roots in the specific context of international environmental law.[265]

Thus, the general consensus seems to be that it is premature to consider the CBDR as being a customary international law principle. It is, at the same time, contended that it is being increasingly applied in the environmental field (although it is by no means confined to that field) and that it has become a robust principle. It is likely that the trend of adopting differential norms will continue in the environmental protection field, although how much differentiation will be adopted will depend on the issue in question. Thus, for example, the Montreal Protocol did not adopt differential obligations for developed and developing countries although it gave a grace period to developing countries to comply with their obligations. The Kyoto Protocol, on the other hand, did adopt differential norms for developing countries and Annex I countries. The twin pillars in Principle 7—cooperation and differentiation are important to achieve sustainable development.

## F.  CONCLUSION

Differential treatment of developing countries has become increasingly common in international law and has become a common feature of international environmental treaties governing global issues. Given the fact that these differential regimes have to be expressly included in treaties, the

---

[264] International Environmental Governance: Some Issues from a Developing Country Perspective, Working Paper by Third World Network, Sept. 2001, at http://www.twnside.org.sg/title/iefg.htm.

[265] *See* Cullet, *supra* note 3, at 88–89.

question arises whether the common but differentiated responsibility principle has any application outside these treaty regimes. In other words, can a developing country party to a treaty, which has not fulfilled its obligations under that treaty, invoke the common but differentiated responsibility principle to contend that its economic status should be taken into account when evaluating its compliance, although the treaty itself does not grant preferential treatment? It is submitted that while there may be other "defenses"[266] that a state may be able to invoke, the common but differentiated responsibility principle cannot be applied in this manner. It is contended by the present writer that the common but differentiated responsibility principle has no general application, and preferential treatment and differentiated regimes have to be explicitly included in treaties. It also has implications for other concepts or tools that have emerged, particularly sustainable development and the polluter pays principle. However, given the contention that the common but differentiated responsibility principle must be expressly included in treaties, it would seem that this principle will have no application outside these treaty regimes governing global environmental issues.

However, the question arises whether this principle can be applied by international tribunals when evaluating the conduct of a particular state. In other words, in a dispute before an international tribunal in which one party alleges non-compliance of obligations by the other, can the tribunal apply the common but differentiated responsibility principle to the dispute to evaluate non-compliance? If this was, in fact, possible, the common but differentiated responsibility principle would become a defense that a developing state can invoke, and the "economic development status" itself would become a defense in such a situation. Needless to say, this would become a very contentious issue.

It is also contended that differential norms are temporary in nature,[267] similar to affirmative action under human rights treaties. Thus, given its temporary nature, can the common but differentiated responsibility principle become a generally applicable principle outside treaty regimes?

While it is easy to concentrate only on the common but differentiated responsibility principle, Principle 7 of the Rio Declaration is not confined to it. It also embodies the concept of global partnership that many contend

---

[266] *See* ILC Draft Articles on State Responsibility, *supra* note 126, for a list of defenses available to states under international law. For the defense of "ecological necessity" advanced by Hungary in the *Case Concerning the Gabcikovo Nagymaros Project, see* Chapter 2, Section II.1.b.ii.

[267] *See* Cullet, *supra* note 3, at 85.

has given rise to a new kind of partnership in relation to global environmental problems. This idea of global partnership is very important particularly in relation to global environmental problems, and it is hoped that the international community would continue to work together on these issues in a spirit of global partnership.

# CHAPTER 6
# THE POLLUTER PAYS PRINCIPLE

National authorities should endeavour to promote the internalization of environmental costs and the use of economic instruments, taking into account the approach that the polluter
should, in principle, bear the cost of pollution, with due regard
to the public interest and without distorting international trade
and investment.

Principle 16, Rio Declaration on Environment and Development

## A. INTRODUCTION

Environmental protection has come a long way since the adoption of
the Stockholm Declaration in 1972. The focus of environmental protection
has changed to encompass sustainable development, and several new concepts or tools such as the precautionary principle, the polluter pays principle and the common but differentiated responsibility principle have
emerged with some enjoying the status of customary law. This is the case
with procedural rights of information, participation and access to remedies
that were transposed from international human rights law to international
environmental law. This cross fertilization of norms across disciplines is a
significant feature of contemporary international law. Indeed, the entire system of international law itself has undergone profound change, encompassing novel concepts and actors. This has led some writers to claim that
international legal order is being fragmented.[1] In reality international law
has become more complex, and it has encompassed many specialized areas
that were not part of the international legal order several decades ago.
Environmental protection and trade issues are good examples. Because
these issues are complex and often impact on other areas, it has become virtually impossible for international lawyers to keep abreast of these developments—hence the necessity to specialize. This is not fragmentation; rather,
it is diversification that is necessary for any legal system that is maturing.[2]

---

[1] Keynote address by Professor Pierre Marie Dupuy at the Canadian Council of
International Law Annual Conference, Ottawa, Oct. 2005 (to be published in the
Proceedings of the Canadian Council of International Law).

[2] *See* Sumudu Atapattu, *Sustainable Development, Environmental Protection, and Human
Rights: A Necessary Linkage?*, Proceedings of the Canadian Council of International Law
(forthcoming).

Compared to the international legal order, international environmental law is a relatively new development. Its modern foundation can be traced to the Stockholm Declaration. As noted, since then, its development has been rapid, and many concepts and principles have been adopted within its framework. We now turn to another tool that has been utilized in the environmental field and that can be utilized to achieve sustainable development—the polluter pays principle.

The atmosphere and the oceans were treated, until recently, as a huge receptacle for the disposal of waste matter by the international community. Indeed, the oceans were particularly vulnerable with the atmosphere also being the recipient of huge emissions of pollutants. The situation was exacerbated by the fact that these areas—constituting the global commons—were considered *free* disposal areas for the large amounts of pollutants generated by the international community. Thus, the person who created the pollution emitted the pollutants regardless of its impact on other people or, indeed, the environment itself. Since absorption of waste was considered a free service provided by the environment, no internalization of costs of pollution took place. Needless to say, this led to the present environmental problems that loom large over not only the present generation, but also the generations to come.

It thus became obvious that internalizing the costs of pollution and imposing the duty on the polluter to bear the costs of pollution without passing them onto society was necessary. Thus, generators of pollution were no longer able to emit their waste into the environment freely. As a result, the polluter pays principle was born. While it essentially developed as an economic tool, it has found its way into legal documents.

There is no doubt that internalization of environmental costs is a sound economic as well as environmental principle. As past experience has shown us, it is precisely the non-internalization of costs that led to the present day environmental problems. Natural resources were considered free goods, and the utilization of these resources were not reflected in the cost benefit analyses prepared for projects. By the same token, the emission of pollution was considered a free exercise as a result of which the environment was used as a large receptacle for the discharge of pollutants. Thus, the environment was not valued at all. Until the economists started valuing the environment, little or no thought went into the need to protect the environment, as people thought that the services provides by the environment were "free" services that were at the disposal of human beings. The moment, however, a price tag was attached to natural resources, as well as for the emission of pollutants, attitudes began to change. While economic estimates may not be very precise, it served as an eye opener. No longer were people allowed to pollute the environment or use its natural resources without having to pay for it. This meant that people would start economizing, which, in turn, meant that it would promote efficiency in exploiting resources. While economists were quick to grasp this, international lawyers have lagged behind, as the Rio Declaration has clearly demonstrated. This is also evident in academic writings. While it is possible to find more than 1,000 articles on sustainable development—which by and large emerged only after 1987—or the precautionary principle, which again was a rather recent addition to the principles on international environmental law, by contrast, the polluter pays principle—one of the oldest principles of international environmental law—has attracted only a few articles, the majority of which deal with the polluter pays principle in the context of international trade. This step-motherly treatment of the polluter pays principle is hard to fathom, given that it goes to the very core of environmental protection and is a tool to achieve sustainable development.

## B. EVOLUTION OF THE POLLUTER PAYS PRINCIPLE

The origin of the polluter pays principle lies in the OECD.[3] It is one of the oldest principles of international environmental law and dates back to the early 1970s. Despite its early emergence, it did not receive universal acceptance, and the first international instrument of universal application to mention the polluter pays principle is the Rio Declaration. Thus, a period of 20 years elapsed without the principle gaining any significant ground in international environmental law, outside the OECD region.

Despite this, the principle itself makes sound economic sense.[4] Originally adopted as an economic principle, it has found its way into legal instruments, and despite the rather vague language that Principle 16 embodies, its inclusion in the Rio Declaration is a significant development.

The exact definition of the polluter pays principle is subject to some controversy. In its original form, the polluter pays principle meant that polluters should internalize costs of pollution prevention as mandated by public authorities, and such costs should be reflected in the price of goods and services that are provided to the public.[5] In this form, the polluter pays

---

[3] Organization for Economic Cooperation and Development (originally called the OEEC). *See* discussion in Section C.1, and http://www.oecd.org.

[4] *See* John Dernbach, *Sustainable Development as a Framework for National Governance*, 49 CASE W. RES. L. REV. 1 (1998) who notes that this principle would result in greater efficiency.

[5] *See* Recommendation of the Council on the Implementation of the Polluter-Pays principle, *in* THE POLLUTER PAYS PRINCIPLE: DEFINITION, ANALYSIS, IMPLEMENTATION, (OECD, 1975).

principle is an efficiency principle and seeks to ensure that costs of pollution are not passed onto society at large. Since then, however, the definition has undergone change and has been extended to cover compensation for environmental damage.[6] It must be mentioned at the outset that the polluter pays principle and liability for environmental damage are two distinct principles and should not be treated synonymously.[7] According to the 1972 formulation of the OECD, the polluter pays principle means:

1.  The Polluter-Pays Principle constitutes for Member countries a fundamental principle for allocating costs of pollution prevention and control measures introduced by the public authorities in Member countries.
2.  . . . that the polluter should bear the expenses of carrying out the measures, as specified in the previous paragraph, to ensure that the environment is in an acceptable state. In other words, the cost of these measures should be reflected in the cost of goods and services which cause pollution in production and/or consumption.[8]

This definition clearly states that the polluter pays principle applies in relation to pollution prevention and control measures that are mandated by public authorities. Thus, for example, where the law of a particular member state requires all industries to ensure emissions below a particular level, the costs to reduce such emissions to the level acceptable under the law must be borne by the industry in question. To illustrate this further, if the cost of the production of a particular product is x, and the cost of pollution control is y, then the proper cost of the product would be x+y. According to the polluter pays principle, this cost may be passed on to the consumer, although it is not mandatory to do so.

It has been articulated that the "polluter-pays principle is necessary to ensure that social, economic and environmental goals are realized harmoniously; it is essential to integrated decision-making."[9] Since economic development should not come at the expense of either social development or natural resources protection, it is necessary to ensure that the polluter does not pass the costs on to others or the environment. It also prevents

---

[6] *See* the discussion on liability in Section G.1.

[7] *Id.*

[8] *See supra* note 5.

[9] *See* Dernbach, *supra* note 4. With regard to integrated decision making, *see* Chapter 2, Section E.2.

involuntary wealth distribution that can take place when some benefit at the expense of others.[10]

Thus, if one takes a close look at the OECD definition of the polluter pays principle, nowhere does the definition refer to environmental damage. Indeed, the idea behind the polluter pays principle is to avoid environmental damage by ensuring that pollution remains at an acceptable level. Liability for environmental damage, although interrelated, is not the same as the polluter pays principle and occurs only after environmental damage has taken place.[11] While the two can be used together (that means the polluter would be liable to compensate for environmental damage), they cannot be used synonymously.[12] Thus, the polluter pays principle is not the same as paying compensation for environmental damage. While the polluter pays principle refers to *consumers* of products and services, liability refers to *victims* of environmental damage.[13]

Sanford Gaines notes that the polluter pays principle "strives for the twin goals of efficiency in using economic resources to achieve environmental standards and equity between nations in uniformly allocating the costs of compliance to the polluter sources."[14] Thus, efficiency and equity can be said to be the twin pillars of this principle.

It must be noted that the reference to this as a "principle" does not seek to convey any idea about its legal status under international law. It was always referred to as the "polluter pays principle" and the same name will be used throughout for easy reference.

---

[10] *See* Dernbach, *supra* note 4.

[11] *See* Sanford Gaines, *The Polluter-Pays Principle: From Economic Equity to Environmental Ethos*, 26 TEX. INT'L L.J. 463 (1991).

[12] *Cf.* Dernbach, *supra* note 4, who contends that in practice, "it is difficult to properly allocate costs without also asserting liability against particular entities for those costs. The principle is thus broadly understood to include both cost-and liability-allocation." However, this is not necessarily true. As discussed later, it is possible to apply the polluter pays principle without resorting to liability. Liability is *ex post facto* and is not the preferred method for environmental protection.

[13] *See* Scott N. Carlson, *The Montreal Protocol's Environmental Subsidies and GATT: A Needed Reconciliation*, 29 TEX. INT'L L.J. 211 (1994), in which he confuses the polluter pays principle with the issue of liability: "This principle [referring to the polluter pays principle] . . . calls upon polluters to bear the liability for the damage caused by pollution they produce." It is interesting that he refers to Sanford Gaine's article on the polluter pays principle (*supra* note 11) to support his contention. As noted, Sanford Gaines makes a clear distinction between the polluter pays principle and liability. *See* discussion in Section G.1.

[14] *See* Gaines, *supra* note 11, at 481.

## C. APPLICATION OF THE POLLUTER PAYS PRINCIPLE

Under the polluter and user pays principle "States should take those actions necessary to ensure that polluters and users of natural resources bear the full environmental and social costs of their activities."[15] It is thus designed to internalize environmental externalities. It seeks to integrate environmental protection and economic activities and thus, plays an important role in achieving sustainable development. The main objective behind the principle is to ensure that full environmental and social costs are reflected in the ultimate market price for goods and services. In other words, environmentally harmful goods will cost more and, over time, consumers will switch to less polluting goods and services that will result in a more efficient and sustainable allocation of resources.

It has been articulated that the application of the polluter pays principle "is still highly controversial,"[16] because in developing countries internalizing environmental costs is considered as being too high a burden.[17] However, it provides sound economic logic and seeks to harmonize standards. Agenda 21 also endorses the polluter pays principle, although the phrase itself is missing there: it calls upon business and industry to use "free market mechanisms in which the prices of goods and services should increasingly reflect the environmental costs of their input, production, use, recycling and disposal."[18] Not internalizing the costs and not reflecting the environmental costs in the price of goods and services will lead to a distortion in the marketplace. Natural resources are not free goods, as was earlier perceived by states and individuals. Thus, the polluter pays principle is an important principle, although its application outside the OECD area remains rather sparse.

However, the OECD formulation of the polluter pays principle does not require all environmental costs to be internalized.[19] The polluter should bear the expenses of preventing and controlling pollution to ensure that the environment is in an acceptable state. Here the emission standards set by the public authorities will play an important role, as does monitoring by them to ensure that these standards are being met. As long as the environment is in an acceptable state, all pollution costs need not be internalized.

---

[15] *See* DAVID HUNTER, JAMES SALZMAN & DURWOOD ZAELKE, INTERNATIONAL ENVIRONMENTAL LAW AND POLICY, 412 (2d ed. 2002).

[16] *Id.*

[17] *See* OECD Recommendation, *supra* note 5.

[18] Agenda 21, UN Doc. A/CONF.151/26, *reprinted in* 31 ILM 874, para. 30.3.

[19] *See* HUNTER ET AL., *supra* note 15, at 414.

There are various ways that the polluter pays principle can be implemented. Imposing liability is one such method.[20] This, however, is not the preferred method, as liability is typically incurred once damage has taken place.[21] Other forms include user fees or taxes, elimination of subsidies, environmental pollution standards and greener accounting systems.[22] Methods to inform the consumer include green labeling[23] and ISO standards.[24] The provision of information plays an important role here and the Aarhus Convention, discussed in Chapter 4, is significant in this regard. Under the Aarhus Convention, the parties are required to provide information relating to the environment[25] to enable the public to make informed environmental choices. Thus, in relation to the polluter pays principle, particularly in relation to green labeling and ISO standards, access to information is an important tool that the public can use to make informed choices. If such information is not available, the public cannot make an informed choice relating to products and services. Thus, it is important to ensure access to relevant information in a timely manner, if the polluter pays principle is to be properly implemented.

## 1.   The OECD and the Polluter Pays Principle

The first time that the polluter pays principle appeared in an instrument on environmental protection was in 1972 in the "Guiding Principles Concerning the International Economic Aspects of Environmental Policies"[26] adopted by the OECD. With regard to the polluter pays principle, this document stated:

> The principle to be used for allocating costs of pollution prevention and control measures to encourage rational use of scarce environmental resources and to avoid distortions in international trade and investment is the so-called "Polluter-Pays Principle." The Principle means that the polluter should bear the expenses of carrying out

---

[20]   *Id.*

[21]   *See* discussion in Section G.1.

[22]   *See* HUNTER ET AL., *supra* note 15, at 412. *See also* PHILIPPE SANDS, PRINCIPLES OF INTERNATIONAL ENVIRONMENTAL LAW 863 (2d ed. 2002).

[23]   *See* SANDS, *supra* note 22, at 861. This is also referred to as "eco-labeling."

[24]   *See* Eric Thomas Larson, *Why Environmental Liability Regimes in the United States, the European Community and Japan Have Grown Synonymous with the Polluter Pays Principle,* 38 VAND. J. TRANSNAT'L L. 541 (2005).

[25]   Arts. 4 and 5, Aarhus Convention, 38 ILM 517 (1999).

[26]   Recommendation of the Council on Guiding Principles Concerning International Economic Aspects of Environmental Policies, C(72)128, May 26, 1972, *available at* http://www.olis.oecd.org/horizontal/oecdacts.nsf/linkto/C(72)128.

the above mentioned measures decided by public authorities to ensure that the environment is in an acceptable state. In other words, the cost of these measures should be reflected in the cost of goods and services which cause pollution in production and/or consumption. Such measures should not be accompanied by subsidies that would create significant distortions in international trade and investment.[27]

This provision contains several important components of the polluter pays principle. First, it is essentially a cost allocation principle. Second, the costs in question relate to those that are incurred in the course of pollution prevention and control measures mandated by public authorities. Third, the objective of the polluter pays principle is to encourage the rational use of scarce environmental resources and to avoid distortions in international trade and investment. Fourth, the costs of pollution prevention and control should be reflected in the cost of goods and services that cause pollution in production and/or consumption. Fifth, such measures should not be accompanied by subsidies. Finally, the polluter should bear these costs to ensure that the environment is in an acceptable state.

The OECD, while noting that no subsidies should be offered,[28] recognizes that there may be exceptions or special arrangements, particularly for transitional periods. Exceptions could also be made for research and development of technological innovation and for countries or regions that are economically depressed.[29] It has been noted that providing exceptions for transitional periods and for economically depressed countries is consistent with the principle of differentiated responsibilities.[30] These exceptions, however, should not lead to significant distortions in international trade and investment.[31]

---

[27] *Id.*

[28] *See* Candice Stevens, *Interpreting The Polluter Pays Principle In The Trade And Environment Context*, 27 CORNELL INT'L L.J. 577 (1994), who notes that "the Polluter Pays Principle in the OECD context is a non-subsidization principle, meaning that governments should not as a general rule give subsidies to their industries for pollution control. Its intent is to guide the cost allocation between the government and the private sector in paying for domestic pollution abatement or protecting their national environments. It concerns who should pay, not how much should be paid." (footnotes omitted).

[29] *See* Dernbach, *supra* note 4.

[30] *Id.*

[31] *See* Principle 16 of the Rio Declaration, UN Doc. A/CONF.151/26, *reprinted in* 31 ILM 874 (1992), *available at* http://www.un.org/documents/ga/confl21/aconfl5126-lannexl.htm.

In a further Note on the Implementation of the Polluter Pays Principle,[32] the OECD points out that it is no more than an efficiency principle for allocating costs and does not involve bringing pollution down to an optimum level of any type. The Note provides that it is desirable that consumers and producers would adjust to the total social costs of the goods and services they are buying and selling. For the purposes of the polluter pays principle, however, it does not matter whether the polluter passes on some or all of the environmental costs or absorbs them. It further provides that the polluter pays principle may be implemented by various means ranging from processes and product standards, individual regulation and prohibitions to levying various kinds of pollution charges. A combination of these instruments can also be used.[33]

The Note recognized that a speedy or a sudden and very extensive implementation of environmental policy would be helped or even speeded up, if existing polluters are given aid in their efforts to reduce their emissions. It warns, however, that such aid payments would be valid only if it formed part of transitional arrangements and do not lead to significant distortions in international trade and investment. Another exception that the OECD recognizes is when steps to protect the environment jeopardize the social and economic policy objectives of a country. However, the provision of aid by the government to promote research and development is not inconsistent with the polluter pays principle.[34]

The OECD recognized further that "the PPP does not imply that the polluter necessarily hands over any payment to anybody—either to victims of pollution or to some State agency." Despite what its name implies, the polluter pays principle does not mean that the polluter pays anything to anybody. It is also irrelevant whether the polluter passes on some or all of the costs of pollution abatement in the form of higher prices. The OECD refers to three main forms of price mechanisms that can be used in relation to the polluter pays principle: pollution charges (tax), a payment to producers based on the amount of pollution they abate, and the sale of a given quantity of pollution rights. The report points out that while, in the short term, all three tools have the same resource allocation effects, in the long run, the second method ("bribe method") would be undesirable.[35]

---

[32] OECD, Recommendation of the Council on the Implementation of the Polluter Pays Principle, C(74)223, Nov. 14, 1974, *available at* http://www.olis.oecd.org/horizontal/oecdacts.nsf/linkto/C(74)223.

[33] *Id.*

[34] *Id.*

[35] Wilfred Beckerman, *The Polluter-Pays Principle Interpretation and Principles of Application, in* OECD, *supra* note 5.

In the OECD, the polluter pays principle mirrors the free trade principle—that government interventions that might affect trade should be minimized. It has been argued that it is an efficiency principle for allocating costs for domestic pollution and "does not involve reducing pollution."[36] It is submitted that this argument is erroneous. The OECD definition of the polluter pays principle clearly notes that the polluter should internalize the costs of pollution prevention mandated by the government so that the environment is in an acceptable state and reflect the costs of abatement in the price of goods or services. Thus, it is difficult to agree with the view that the polluter pays principle does not lead to reducing pollution. The whole idea of this principle is to reduce pollution and to hold those who cause such pollution accountable for such pollution. The writer then goes on to argue, contradicting her previous statement, that "The private sector should bear the expense of preventing and controlling pollution to ensure that the environment is in an acceptable state."[37] The public authorities will, through environmental regulations, decide on what constitutes an acceptable state.[38] The adoption of emission standards and discharge levels for various pollutants,[39] as well as for the receiving environment,[40] will be necessary here.

In 1989, the OECD adopted the Recommendation on the Application of the Polluter-Pays Principle to Accidental Pollution,[41] while in 1990 the European Community moved toward finalizing a directive on Civil Liability for Damage Caused by Waste.[42] Both these instruments mark a departure from the earlier formulation of the polluter pays principle in that they seek to cover liability as well. The earlier formulation of the polluter pays principle was quick to point that it does not cover liability, rather it covers only the costs of pollution prevention as mandated by public authorities. As Sanford Gaines notes, "These recent initiatives open the door to a fundamental

---

[36] *See* Stevens, *supra* note 28.

[37] *Id.*

[38] *Id.*

[39] Many countries have adopted ambient air quality and water quality standards for various pollutants.

[40] These emission standards could be different depending on the receiving environment—thus, for example, a wetland of ecological significance; protected areas etc., may have more stringent emission standards than other receiving environments.

[41] Recommendation of the Council Concerning the Application of the Polluter-Pays Principle to Accidental Pollution, C(89)88/Final, July 7, 1989, *available at* http://web-domino1.oecd.org/horizontal/oecdacts.nsf/linkto/C(89)88.

[42] COM (89)(282), Oct. 4, 1989, which the Commission withdrew in favor of the White Paper on Environmental Liability.

redesign of the PPP which will adapt it to the issues of the 1990s."[43] He also refers to the Guiding Principles Relating to Accidental Pollution as a definitive OECD interpretation and expansion of the polluter pays principle.[44]

These guiding principles are significant because they require polluters to pay response costs as well as prevention costs for pollution. For the first time, the high priests of the PPP have interpreted it to include an *ex post* obligation to pay for harms caused as well as the *ex ante* obligation to pay for preventive pollution control. In so interpreting the PPP, the OECD moved the principle a considerable distance along the continuum from pure precaution to pure liability for compensation.[45]

The OECD notes that since its adoption in 1972, the polluter pays principle has evolved very significantly. Originally perceived as the internalization of costs of pollution abatement (polluter pays principle in a strict sense), the polluter pays principle has come to encompass compensation for environmental damage, taxes and charges and all pollution-related expenditure (polluter pays principle in a broader sense).[46] The OECD notes that "This evolution is in line with the efficiency objective of both environmental as well as economic policy."[47]

In OECD countries, several members have adopted the broader interpretation of the polluter pays principle. A Belgian statute, for example, states: "The polluter-pays principle means that the costs of pollution prevention, abatement and control, and the costs of repairing any damage inflicted, shall be borne by the polluter."[48] Liability issues are usually covered by the domestic law of member states.[49]

---

[43]  *See* Gaines, *supra* note 11, at 482-83.

[44]  *Id.*

[45]  *Id.*

[46]  OECD, Joint Working Party on Trade and Environment, The Polluter-Pays Principle as it Relates to International Trade, COM/ENV/TD(2001)44/FINAL, Dec. 23, 2002, Executive Summary.

[47]  *Id.*

[48]  Act of March 12, 1999 on the protection of the marine environment in seas under Belgian jurisdiction, referred to in OECD, Joint Working Party on Trade and Environment, *supra* note 46.

[49]  *Id.*

## 2. The European Community and the Polluter Pays Principle

Apart from the OECD, the polluter pays principle has received attention by the European Community and is incorporated in the EC Treaty. According to Article 174(2) of the EC Treaty:

> Community policy on the environment shall aim at a high level of protection taking into account the diversity of situations in the various regions of the Community. It shall be based on the precautionary principle and on the principles that preventive action should be taken, that environmental damage should as a priority be rectified at source and that the polluter should pay.[50]

The European Commission prepared a White Paper to explore how the polluter pays principle can best serve the aims of the Community in relation to its environmental policy, one of which is to avoid environmental damage.[51] Thus, the White Paper notes that "environmental liability aims at making the causer of environmental damage (the polluter) pay for remedying the damage that he has caused."[52] It further notes that without liability, the failure to comply with existing standards may result in administrative or penal sanctions but not compensation for the damage caused.

It must be noted here that the White Paper on Environmental Liability departs from the traditional definition of the polluter pays principle and deals with one application of it—in relation to environmental damage that has been caused by the polluter. It seems to acknowledge this when it states thus: "Environmental liability is a way of implementing the main principles of environmental policy enshrined in the EC Treaty (Article 174(2)), above all the 'polluter pays' principle."[53]

Article 174(2) embodies several principles: the precautionary principle; the principle of preventive action; the principle that environmental damage should be rectified at the source; and the polluter pays principle. Environmental liability does not feature on this list of principles. According to the White Paper, environmental liability is a way of *implementing* the prin-

---

[50] Consolidated Version of the Treaty Establishing the European Community, C 325/33, Official Journal of the European Communities, Dec. 24, 2002, *available at* http://europa.eu.int/.

[51] European Commission, White Paper on Environmental Liability, COM (2000) 66 final, Feb. 9, 2000, *available at* http://europa.eu.int/comm/environment/liability/el_full.pdf.

[52] *Id.* at 13.

[53] *Id.* at 14.

ciples embodied in Article 174(2). Most of the principles therein are aimed at preventing environmental damage: indeed Article 174(1) clearly refers to "preserving, protecting and improving the quality of the environment."[54] Since the basic objective of the EU in relation to the environment, as enshrined in Article 174, is prevention of environmental damage, it is difficult to see how this objective or the principles therein could be implemented through the imposition of environmental liability, as the latter necessarily relies on the existence of environmental damage. The precautionary principle, the preventive principle and even the (original definition of the) polluter pays principle all seek to prevent environmental damage. A liability regime will come into play only when these principles have failed to protect the environment.[55] As noted above, the utility of a liability regime to prevent environmental damage is minimal, as it relies on the existence of environmental damage. Thus, while environmental liability may be one application of the polluter pays principle, a liability regime cannot be applied in relation to the precautionary principle, or the preventive principle. This drawback of the White Paper must be borne in mind when analyzing it.

The White Paper notes that in order to be effective, there needs to be an identifiable polluter/s; quantifiable damage; and the causal link to be established between the damage and the pollution. In other words, it must be established that it was the act of the polluter that caused the damage in question. It notes, however, that liability is not a suitable instrument to deal with pollution of a widespread and diffuse character. In this case, it is difficult to establish the causal link, as well as identify the polluter/s with precision.[56]

According to the White Paper, an initial objective is to make the polluter liable for the damage he has caused. It notes that if the polluter has to pay for any damage caused, he will cut back pollution so that compensation can be avoided: "Environmental liability results in prevention of damage and in internalization of environmental costs. Liability may also lead to the application of more precaution, resulting in avoidance of risk and damage."[57] While the existence of a liability regime can prevent environmental damage *indirectly* as a deterrent, a liability regime comes into play only when there is environmental damage—in other words, where a preventive regime has failed. It cannot thus be said that environmental lia-

---

[54] Article 171(1) of the EC Treaty, *supra* note 50.

[55] *See* discussion in Section G.1.

[56] *See* White Paper on Liability, *supra* note 51.

[57] *Id.* at 14.

bility leads to the prevention of damage and in internalization of environmental costs. The latter takes place as a result of the polluter pays principle, not because of the liability regime. This distinction is important —liability and the polluter pays principle cannot be, and should not be, used synonymously. The White Paper is based on the premise that environmental liability is necessary to implement the polluter pays principle (and indeed, the precautionary principle). As noted above, however, the two concepts are not synonymous.

The White Paper notes that: "The European Community believes that allocating environmental waste abatement costs to the private sector will force market prices to represent more closely the social costs of production."[58] The idea is that this will reduce the consumption of pollution intensive products, thereby encouraging pollution abatement[59] and less demand for such products.

According to the Commission, codifying an environmental liability regime is a way of implementing the main principles of environmental law as laid down in Article 174(2) of the European Community Treaty, which includes the polluter pays principle.[60] The main objective of the Commission is to hold the polluter liable for the damage it causes. In other words, the European Commission has chosen to operationalize the polluter pays principle through a regime of liability. According to the Commission, the environmental liability regime covers damage to health and property and "traditional damages." Whether a system of fault based or strict liability applies depends on the activity in question, but the modern trend is to rely on strict liability as it is increasingly difficult to establish fault on the part of the polluter.[61] The Commission notes that the polluter pays principle demands that the person who operates an inherently dangerous activity bears the risk of damage caused by that activity, rather than the victim or society at large.[62] The position of the European Union with regard to its environmental liability regime has been summarized as follows:

> The introduction of liability for damage to the environment, as proposed by the White Paper, is expected to generate a change of attitude in the European Community that should result in an increased level of prevention and precaution. The new environ-

---

[58] *See* Larson, *supra* note 24.

[59] *Id.*

[60] *Id.*

[61] *Id.*

[62] *Id.*

mental liability regime aims at making the polluter pay for reme-diating the damage that he has caused. Environmental regulation aims at establishing norms and procedures through which the environment is preserved, and it will allow the European Community to challenge potential polluters to comply, or to restore and compensate for, the damage that they have caused according to the polluter pays principle.[63]

It must be noted here that the regime of liability that the EU envisages is civil liability and not international responsibility. The latter could arise as a result of transboundary environmental damage, but not otherwise. The White Paper proposes the extension of the liability regime to damage to biodiversity whether caused by a dangerous activity or not. If the damage is caused by a non-dangerous activity, liability will be based on fault.[64]

With regard to defenses that are available to the defendant, the White Paper accepts that commonly accepted defenses, such as acts of God, con-tribution or consent by the plaintiff and intervention by a third party should be allowed. With regard to the burden of proof, the White Paper recommends the adoption of a regime that eases the burden of proof on the plaintiff, as it is often difficult for the plaintiff in cases of pollution dam-age to establish causation.[65]

## 3. The Polluter Pays Principle Outside the OECD

While the polluter pays principle has remained confined mainly to the OECD, its inclusion "in the most important and far-reaching international statement of the fundamental principles of environmental law demon-strates its significance on the international stage."[66] Despite its inclusion in the Rio Declaration its definition has been somewhat elusive:

The polluter pays principle is a normative doctrine of environ-mental law. Although its precise legal definition remains elusive, the core of this principle stems from the fundamental, logical, and fair proposition that those who generate pollution, not the gov-ernment, should bear pollution costs. The principle that underlies much of modern environmental law, and in recent years, has

---

[63]  *Id.*

[64]  *Id.* at 18.

[65]  *Id.*

[66]  Jonathan Remy Nash, *Too Much Market? Conflict Between Tradable Pollution Allowances and the "Polluter Pays" Principle*, 24 HARV. ENVTL. L. REV. 465 (2000).

become increasingly important in guiding environmental policy, especially at the international level.[67]

It is generally the case that outside of the OECD, the polluter pays principle has not received much attention,[68] although economic instruments such as pollution charges, taxes on pollution emissions and incentives for pollution control have been used throughout the world.[69] Specific incorporation of the polluter pays principle, however, is rare. The adoption of emission standards for industries is a common practice in many countries.[70] This is usually implemented through the issuance of a license or permit that will allow industries to emit certain pollutants into the environment, provided they adhere to certain standards. They are also required to comply with pollution abatement and treatment of pollutants before discharging into the environment. The polluter is responsible for complying with emission standards, which means that the polluter must pay for such pollution abatement.[71] In some instances, the polluters may be able to avail themselves of a fund that has been created to help them with the initial costs of pollution abatement.[72] While this may be a distortion of the polluter pays principle in the long term, the OECD guidelines recognize that, in the short term, providing aid is not contrary to the polluter pays principle.[73]

The Stockholm Declaration, apart from referring to the need to safeguard natural resources for the benefit of present and future generations through careful planning and management,[74] makes no reference to the

---

[67]  *Id.*

[68]  *Id.*

[69]  *See* SANDS, *supra* note 22, at 861.

[70]  *See* HUNTER ET AL., *supra* note 15, at 131, who notes that "By far the most common way to internalize costs is indirectly, through 'command-and-control' regulations aimed specifically at controlling pollution through emission, technology, or process standards."

[71]  *Id.* Although these command-and control regulations are widespread, economists and industry have criticized them as being inefficient and unwieldy. For example, once these standards are met, there is often no incentive for industry to reduce pollution further or to opt for pollution prevention strategies or develop new technologies.

[72]  OECD, THE POLLUTER PAYS PRINCIPLE: DEFINITION, ANALYSIS AND IMPLEMENTATION (1975).

[73]  OECD, *The Polluter-Pays Principle: Note on the Implementation of the Polluter-Pays Principle* (1974); Recommendation of the Council on the Implementation of the Polluter-Pays Principle, C(74)223, Nov. 14, 1974, *available at* http://www.olis.oecd.org/horizontal/oecdacts.nsf/linkto/C(74)223.

[74]  Principle 2, UN Doc. A/CONF.48/14, June 16, 1972, *reprinted in* 11 ILM 1416 (1972).

polluter pays principle. Despite the developments in the OECD, UNEP or other UN agencies have made no attempt to adopt the principle. Thus, it has largely remained a "European" concept, with little or no application in other parts of the world. It received universal recognition only in 1992 when it was incorporated into the Rio Declaration. Despite the vague language it employs, its incorporation in the Rio Declaration is a significant development. Even for a non-binding document, the language utilized in Principle 16 is vague and hortatory. It provides that national authorities should (not "shall" like in many other Principles in the Rio Declaration) *endeavor to promote* the internalization of environmental costs and the use of economic instruments. It further provides that the polluter should (again, not shall), *in principle*, bear the cost of pollution, without distorting international trade and investment. It is difficult to envisage language vaguer than this. Drafters seem to have gone into great lengths to ensure that only hortatory language will be used in discussing the polluter pays principle. Moreover, the language in Principle 16 gives the impression that there would be circumstances in which a person, other than the polluter, would bear the cost of pollution. It also provides that the polluter pays principle will not be used if it results in distorting international trade and investment. Does this mean that international trade and investment have been given priority over environmental protection?

The Plan of Implementation adopted at the WSSD also makes reference to the polluter pays principle. It discusses this principle under the heading "Changing unsustainable patterns of consumption and production" and notes that all countries should take action, taking into account the development needs and capabilities of developing countries, through the mobilization of financial and technical assistance and capacity-building for developing countries. It notes that this would require action at all levels to "adopt and implement policies and measures aimed at promoting sustainable patterns of production and consumption, applying, *inter alia*, the polluter-pays principle, described in principle 16 of the Rio Declaration on Environment and Development."[75]

The Plan of Implementation has endorsed Principle 16 of the Rio Declaration verbatim in paragraph 19. It calls upon relevant authorities at all levels to take sustainable development considerations into account in decision making and notes that this would include action at all levels, *inter alia*, to:

[c]ontinue to promote the internalization of environmental costs and the use of economic instruments, taking into account the

---

[75] Plan of Implementation, Sept. 4, 2002, UN Doc. A/CONF.199/20, para. 15(b).

approach that the polluter should, in principle, bear the costs of pollution, with due regard to the public interest and without distorting international trade and investment.[76]

Thus, by reproducing Principle 16 verbatim, the Johannesburg Plan of Implementation has also endorsed its weaknesses, particularly, the hortatory language utilized in Principle 16. This is regrettable, as even ten years after the Rio Declaration, no attempt has been made to refine the principle or to remove objectionable language found in Principle 16. Thus, an opportunity has been lost, and it may well be the case that we would have to wait for the next world summit ten years later to elaborate on the definition of the polluter pays principle.

The polluter pays principle has different meanings in different contexts, and its parameters are not clear.[77] In its original version, it was essentially an economic term, and it has been noted that the OECD recommendation embodies the "weak" form of the polluter pays principle.[78] While it can have a broader application, the recommendation has been interpreted as requiring only that the government should not subsidize pollution costs. Today, however, given the global nature of environmental problems, its interpretation has expanded to call governments to require cost internalization in order to achieve the optimal level of pollution.[79]

The polluter pays principle was meant to apply within states, not between states.[80] While, as a goal of domestic policy, it has been only partially realized in practice, Principle 16 sought to bring it outside the developed country context to be applied globally.[81] While developed countries have consistently used economic instruments in their national legislation, developing countries and countries with economies in transition have begun to use them only recently. Some of these instruments are: deposit/refund schemes, pollution fines, eco-management schemes and eco-label-

---

[76] *Id.* para. 19(b).

[77] *See* Nash, *supra* note 66. *See also* Stevens, *supra* note 28, who articulates that "The Polluter Pays Principle has come to mean all things to all people, and, in this, it has been rendered somewhat meaningless."

[78] *See* Nash, *supra* note 66.

[79] *Id.*

[80] *Rio Declaration on Environment and Development: Application and Implementation,* Report of the Secretary-General, Commission on Sustainable Development, 5th Session, E/CN.17/1997/8, Feb. 10, 1997, para. 87, *available at* http://www.un.org/esa/documents/ecosoc/cn17/1997/ecn171997-8.htm.

[81] *Id.*

ing systems.[82] "In most States, the polluter pays principle is established as a direct obligation for citizens and companies included in general environmental protection regulations which are specified by provisions in sectoral laws."[83]

It has been noted that "The Polluter-Pays Principle (PPP) is the oldest, most durable, and arguably the most important doctrine bridging environmental and trade policies."[84] The polluter pays principle is not explicitly mentioned in the GATT. Although durable and widely referenced, "the PPP is not without its ambiguities and idiosyncratic interpretations."[85] Originally, the polluter pays principle referred to cost allocation for reasons of efficiency: "Specifically, the costs of pollution abatement activities undertaken in the private sector should be borne by the private sector and not offset by government grants or subsidies."[86] Both the OECD and the EC were clear on this issue and recognized that by allocating abatement costs to the polluter, market prices would closely reflect social costs of production.[87] At the international level, the adoption of the polluter pays principle would avoid distortions in international trade arising from differential pollution abatement financing methods: "Thus, the PPP supports improved efficiency in the allocation of natural and environmental resources—it helps correct externality-distorted product prices."[88] If the costs are passed on to the consumer—and the polluter pays principle does not mandate this—the polluter pays principle becomes consistent with the consumer pays principle.[89] Furthermore, residual pollution costs may continue to be borne by the victim—leading to the victim pays principle.[90]

How much the polluter should pay depends on the pollution abatement instruments adopted by the government—mandated technology, emission standards, pollution charges and taxes are some of the instruments at the disposal of governments.[91] One hundred percent pollution

---

[82] *Id.*, para. 89.

[83] *Id.*, para. 90.

[84] *See* Charles S. Pearson, *Testing the System: GATT+PPP=?*, 27 CORNELL INT'L L.J. 553 (1994).

[85] *Id.*

[86] *Id.*

[87] *Id.*

[88] *Id.*

[89] *Id.*

[90] *Id.*

[91] *See* HUNTER ET AL., *supra* note 15, at 130, where different policy options for internalizing external environmental costs are discussed.

abatement is rarely required by governments. The socially optimal level of pollution[92] leaves some residual pollution. Under the polluter pays principle, should the polluter also pay for residual pollution? The general consensus is that the polluter pays principle does not require this, although an extended polluter pays principle can require compensation for damage caused by pollution.[93] With regard to accidental pollution, the OECD has drawn a distinction between (1) measures taken prior to an accident to prevent or mitigate the damage; (2) measures taken after an accident to limit damage and to rehabilitate the environment; and (3) compensation to victims of accidental pollution.[94]

In actual fact, "polluter pays" is a misnomer as there is really no "polluter" in the strict sense of the word, and he/she does not "pay" anybody. The 1972 OECD recommendation noted that: "The principle to be used for allocating costs of pollution prevention and control measures to encourage rational use of scarce environmental resources and to avoid distortions in international trade and investment is the so-called 'Polluter-Pays Principle.'"[95] Thus, the polluter pays principle seeks to allocate costs of pollution prevention measures. If pollution is prevented or controlled, there is really no "polluter," and that person does not have to pay anybody.[96]

## D. ECONOMIC TOOLS AND THE POLLUTER PAYS PRINCIPLE

Economic tools play a major role in influencing consumer behavior. Because these tools encourage, or in some instances mandate, that the price of goods or services reflect environmental and social costs that went into producing them, the consumers are in a position to take informed decisions about these goods and services. This way, it promotes both integrated decision making as well as the polluter pays principle:

> Economic tools oblige producers or users to incur the environmental and social costs of their activities through the price they

---

[92] Defined as the level that minimizes total social costs of pollution control and pollution damages. *See* Pearson, *supra* note 84.

[93] *Id.*

[94] While the earlier OECD documents did not refer to compensation for damage, in the 1990s, the OECD increasingly referred to this aspect, thereby clearly departing from the earlier notion of internalizing pollution abatement costs.

[95] Recommendation of the Council on Guiding Principles Concerning International Economic Aspects of Environmental Policies, C(72)128, OECD, 1972, referred to in Joint Working Party on Trade and Environment, *supra* note 46.

[96] *Id.* It is noted that "this definition of the PPP does not imply that the polluter actually has to 'pay' anything to anyone."

pay, thus directly affecting the financial accounting inherent in private and much governmental decision making. Economic instruments can thus facilitate both integrated decision-making and the polluter-pays principle.[97]

These economic tools have become increasingly sophisticated and include fees, taxes and trading systems for pollutants.[98] Green (eco) labeling and green auditing are other tools that have been used to inform the consumer of how "green" a product is.[99] While licensing fees and, to a lesser extent, taxes have been used in developing countries, most of these economic tools have been confined to developed countries.

The usefulness of economic tools has been articulated by Dernbach as:

> Economic tools are particularly useful as a supplement to regulatory and other tools. Because sustainable development would change the dynamic and direction of our economic life, industrial and other economic activity must become an agent of sustainable development. Economic tools can harness the powerful and creative energy of the market system on behalf of social and environmental goals within a regulatory structure.[100]

Another role that economic tools play is to place a price tag on natural resources such as water, forests, minerals, etc.[101] While for short-term gain, people might indulge in unsustainable practices, this can be minimized if a price tag can be attached to these natural resources and the service that they render to human beings: "Legal and policy instruments should recognize, and create economic incentives for the protection of, these and other natural resources."[102] Agenda 21 suggests that governments should share information about the effectiveness of economic instruments and

---

[97] *See* Dernbach, *supra* note 4.

[98] *Id.*

[99] *See* SANDS, *supra* note 22, at 861–64 and PATRICIA BIRNIE & ALAN BOYLE, INTERNATIONAL LAW & THE ENVIRONMENT 719 (2d ed. 2002).

[100] *See* Dernbach, *supra* note 4.

[101] *See* HUNTER ET AL., *supra* note 15, at 127, where it is noted that many environmental amenities such as clean air and water, are "public goods" and because they are not exchanged in markets "no price signals indicate scarcity and environmental degradation." This type of market failure applies to open access resources where no rules govern their use and is described as "the tragedy of the commons."

[102] *See* Dernbach, *supra* note 4.

gain a better understanding of pricing policies, environmental taxation and other aspects of economics.[103]

A variety of policy instruments is available to achieve pollution abatement. These can be broadly categorized into two instruments: (1) command-and-control measures; and (2) economic instruments. While mandated technology and effluent and emission standards fall into the first category, pollution charges, distributive charges,[104] pollution abatement subsidy schemes[105] and tradable permits[106] fall into the latter category.[107] Pearson notes that to the extent that command and control measures are not financed by government assistance, they are compatible with the polluter pays principle; however, they may not be the most efficient.[108]

Although the label "polluter pays" is not visible, many environmental policies that rely on emission standards for pollutants[109] or that require certain technology[110] to be used are, in fact, implementing the polluter pays principle. Thus, for example, most countries have emission standards for various pollutants, and industries have to obtain a license (or similar procedure) before they can engage in an activity that may cause pollution. This license or similar mechanism will lay down the conditions on which the industry can operate.[111] One condition would be to abide by the ambient air quality or water quality standards set by the government. In order to abide by these standards, the industry in question will have to ensure that certain technology is used, so that its emissions remain within the stan-

---

[103] Agenda 21, *supra* note 18, paras. 8.36–8.38.

[104] These are an incentive charge for pollution imposed by governments and return the revenue as subsidies for further pollution abatement. Although the OECD considers these as being consistent with the polluter pays principle, it is not very clear that they are.

[105] *See* Pearson, *supra* note 84.

[106] For tradable permits, a maximum flow of pollution is established for an air shed or watershed, at a level deemed appropriate. The maximum flow is divided into units or permits, and the permit price is determined by the market forces. They can be auctioned or sold by governments or distributed without charge. *See* HUNTER ET AL., *supra* note 15, at 133.

[107] *See* Pearson, *supra* note 84.

[108] *Id.*

[109] Air quality or water quality standards are very common all over the world.

[110] *E.g.*, Installing scrubbers for coal powered power plants in order to limit the amount of sulfur being discharged into the atmosphere, which is responsible for causing acid rain. Catalytic converters are another example.

[111] *See supra* notes 70 and 71 and accompanying text.

dards prescribed by the government. By installing technology, the industry (the polluter) is internalizing the costs of pollution abatement that he will very likely pass on to the consumer. The earlier approach of not having emission standards meant that the government was actually subsidizing pollution. Thus, although the label is not used, many countries actually adopt the polluter pays principle in their day-to-day activities.

Two further extensions of the principle are visible. The first application is where multiple actors are present. Thus, in the case of aggregate pollution loading, where pollution is caused by multiple polluters, the polluter pays principle requires the proper allocation of costs among polluters and apportions costs in accordance with each polluter's contribution for the aggregate problem.[112] The second application is where it is impossible to identify the victims. Here the government serves as a proxy for the victims, and each polluter is required to internalize the costs of residual pollution by reimbursing the government for its expenses in addressing the problem.[113]

It has also been articulated that by requiring polluters to internalize abatement costs, the polluter pays principle creates incentives to reduce the waste output and to develop new technology.[114] Such technology could either reduce the amount of waste produced or reduce the harmful effects of waste or use fewer resources in the production process. It also leads to the acceptance of individual responsibility for the pollution that is produced, which, in turn, sends the signal to society that even multi-national companies will be held accountable for pollution damage they cause: thus, "the polluter pays principle, aside from providing a normative guide for developing environmental regulatory policy, may also shape the norms of society when implemented."[115]

Noting that the polluter pays principle means "all things to all people," one writer argues that what is needed is to expand its operation to global environmental problems: "What is needed is an interpretation of the Polluter Pays Principle to guide cost internalization and cost allocation for protecting shared environments."[116]

Different approaches have been adopted by governments, in relation to pollution control, that indirectly apply the polluter pays principle. One

---

[112] *See* Nash, *supra* note 66.

[113] *Id.*

[114] *Id.*

[115] *Id.*

[116] *See* Stevens, *supra* note 28.

such approach is the command-and-control regime under which governments set standards for a particular pollutant.[117] Under this, two options are available to governments: to adopt either performance-based standards or technology-based standards.[118] While the former would set a ceiling on the amount of pollution that a manufacturer can discharge, the latter would require the adoption of certain technology. Various forms of this have been used in treaties, and the commonest phrase is the use of "best available technology."[119]

The other approach is to adopt market-based regimes and allow the market to regulate pollution. These regimes fall into two categories: effluent taxes and tradable pollution permits.[120] With regard to the former, the government imposes a tax based either on the amount of pollution created or on the product to ensure that pollution is at an acceptable level. Under tradable pollution permits, the government will issue allowances "which authorize the holder to emit a certain amount of pollution over a given time. Companies buy and sell these allowances subject to certain constraints."[121] It has been opined that tradable pollution permits could be inconsistent with the polluter pays principle, as these permits allow the emission of certain amount of pollution over a given period of time.[122] While tradable permits do allow the emission of pollution to a certain extent, it is not incompatible with the polluter pays principle, as the latter does not require the internalization of costs of all pollution. It is understood that even with emission standards, some level of pollution is inevitable. With regard to tradable permits, the government sets the standard for an acceptable level of pollution, allocates the allowances and allows trading.[123] Viewed in this light, there is hardly any incompatibility between the polluter pays principle and tradable pollution permits.

---

[117] *See* Nash, *supra* note 66.

[118] *Id.*

[119] *E.g.,* the Convention on Long-Range Transboundary Air Pollution, 18 ILM 1442 (1979), 1302 UNTS 217, signed Nov. 13, 1979, entered into force Mar. 16, 1983, *available at* http://www.unece.org/env/lrtap/lrtap-h1.htm, which requires parties, *inter alia,* to "develop the best policies and strategies including air quality management systems, and as part of them, control measures compatible with balanced development, in particular by using the *best available technology which is economically feasible* and low-and non-waste technology" (emphasis added).

[120] *See* Nash, *supra* note 66.

[121] *Id.*

[122] *Id.*

[123] *Id.*

## E. EXCEPTIONS TO THE POLLUTER PAYS PRINCIPLE

From an international trade standpoint, the costs borne by a polluter in a developed country may be very different from a polluter in a developing country. Whereas those in developed countries may have to abide by very strict emission standards, pay high pollution taxes and incur no-fault liability in the event of damage, for those in a developing country, the situation can be very different, with lax environmental standards, regulations not enforced properly and where no pollution taxes exist. This can lead to a distortion in international trade. Even within the OECD, different standards can lead to trade distortions. While harmonization of environmental laws and policies is imperative in this regard, it is hard to achieve given the vast disparity that exists in the world today.

As a result, the polluter pays principle recognizes exceptions, as the rigid application of the polluter pays principle can lead to problems. At the same time, these exceptions themselves should not lead to a distortion in international trade and investment. Three exceptions have been explicitly adopted: "the establishment of new environmental protection measures might be accelerated if existing pollution sources are given assistance in their transitional efforts."[124] Such transitional assistance must be limited to a reasonable amount and time period. Secondly, exceptions may be justified to avoid increasing regional imbalances within a country, to avoid adjustment costs to industry and to allow attrition over time to moderate labor adjustment costs.[125] Third, because of its public good character, assistance may be given for research and development of pollution abatement technology.[126] While the OECD recognized several exceptions to the implementation of the polluter pays principle,[127] it recommended limited assistance to industries; the adoption of well-defined transitional periods; and that assistance should not lead to significant distortions in international trade and investment. The European Community followed suit and adopted exceptions very similar to those permitted by the OECD. However, it is not clear to what extent the polluter pays principle or its exceptions have been followed either in the OECD or the EC, as no empirical studies are available.[128]

---

[124] *See* Pearson, *supra* note 84.

[125] *Id.*

[126] *Id.*

[127] *See* POLLUTER PAYS PRINCIPLE, *supra* note 5.

[128] *See* Pearson, *supra* note 84. He notes that: "A thorough study of the implementation of the PPP in OECD members might be useful if changes in the GATT are to be seriously considered, but such a study would surely be a tedious affair."

In 1974, the OECD recognized that government assistance may be given in exceptional circumstances, if the rapid implementation of the polluter pays principle leads to socio-economic problems in the member states.[129] However, such assistance—whether by means of subsidies or tax advantages—should be strictly controlled and be subject to conditions: it should be selective and restricted to those parts of the economy where severe difficulties would otherwise occur; it should be limited to a well-defined transitional period; and it should not create significant distortions in international trade and investment.[130]

## 1. Environmental Subsidies

The initial activity in the OECD with regard to the polluter pays principle centered on the notion that governments should not offer subsidies for polluting activities. While this was not an absolute prohibition, as some exceptions were provided,[131] subsidies were generally considered unfavorable, as they could create significant distortions in international trade and investment.

The issue of environmental subsidies has arisen mainly in the context of international trade. During the Uruguay Round of the GATT in 1995 the pros and cons of adopting environmental subsidies were debated. It was finally agreed that "environmental subsidies would be placed in the non-actionable category along with subsidies for research activities and subsidies to disadvantaged regions."[132] They covered only industrial sector subsidies and not those in agriculture or natural resource sectors.[133]

However, some have argued that environmental subsidies should not be used and that a strict application of the polluter pays principle should be used fearing that government assistance for pollution control would give an unfair advantage to some industries,[134] thereby distorting international trade. It has been articulated that one of the issues here is lack of data on government subsidies:

---

[129] *See* Recommendation of the Council on the Implementation of the Polluter-Pays Principle, *supra* note 5.

[130] *Id.*

[131] These exceptions were generally considered temporary.

[132] *See* Stevens, *supra* note 28.

[133] *Id.* The Agreement on Agriculture covers agriculture sector environmental subsidies, *available at* http://www.wto.org.

[134] *See* Stevens, *supra* note 28.

Environmental subsidies might be more generally accepted if it were easier to monitor their use and to ensure that they were not violating the exceptions to the OECD Polluter Pays Principle. Establishing such a monitoring system might ensure that environmental subsidies do not go beyond the new rules set by the GATT; otherwise, they will be subject to countervailing duties if the subsidized exports cause injury to competing industries in other countries.[135]

## 2. Environmental Funds

The establishment of international funds under various environmental treaties has become quite a common phenomenon of recent years. The Montreal Protocol on Substances that Deplete the Ozone Layer, the Kyoto Protocol, the Biodiversity Convention, etc., all envisage the establishment of an environmental fund. Of these, the most notable is the Global Environment Facility (GEF) jointly administered by UNEP, UNDP and the World Bank.[136] It provides funds to developing countries and countries with economies in transition to enable them to fulfill their obligations under the specific treaty in question. The GEF was established in 1991 initially to fund activities in relation to ozone depletion. It has since been expanded to support projects in six focal areas: biodiversity; climate change; ozone depletion; international waters; land degradation; and persistent organic compounds.[137]

The question then arises, what is the relationship between the polluter pays principle and these financial mechanisms? On the face of it, such mechanisms seem to be contrary to the polluter pays principle. It has been articulated that, in a sense, these financial mechanisms "invert the polluter pays principle—the polluter is paid not to pollute."[138] Here, of course, it is not strictly correct to talk of polluters, as the idea is to avoid pollution. Thus, it could be said that the idea behind funds, such as the GEF, is to ensure that pollution (or other environmental damage such as climate change) will not take place by providing financial assistance to parties to implement their obligations under various treaties. Thus, these mechanisms play a preventive role, rather than a remedial role.

---

[135] *Id.*

[136] *See* discussion in Chapter 1, Section B.9.

[137] For information on the GEF, *see* http://www.gefweb.org/Projects/Focal_Areas/focal_areas/html.

[138] *See* Pearson, *supra* note 84.

These funding mechanisms can also be analyzed in the light of the common but differentiated responsibility principle. They are a way to implement the common but differentiated responsibility principle, given that without such a funding mechanism, many developing countries will be unable to fulfill their environmental obligations under various treaties.[139]

## F.  OPERATIONALIZING THE POLLUTER PAYS PRINCIPLE

Unlike the other principles discussed in the previous chapters, explicit reference to the polluter pays principle in global environmental treaties is not very common. As pointed out earlier, the polluter pays principle was confined to the OECD region until recently. The first universal instrument to refer to it was, in fact, the Rio Declaration. Perhaps the only binding universal instrument that refers to the polluter pays principle is the Stockholm Convention on Persistent Organic Pollutants.[140] Several regional treaties, on the other hand, embody this principle.

The Stockholm Convention on Persistent Organic Pollutants refers to the health effects, especially in developing countries, caused from local exposure to persistent organic pollutants.[141] It affirms several principles of international environmental law including Principle 21,[142] the precautionary principle,[143] the common but differentiated responsibility principle[144] and the polluter pays principle.[145] The Convention reaffirms Principle 16 of the Rio Declaration verbatim. In other words, the weak formulation of the polluter pays principle adopted under Principle 16 has been transferred directly into the text of this Convention. The Preamble interestingly refers to the importance of manufacturers of these pollutants taking responsibility for reducing adverse effects caused by their products and for providing information to users, governments and the public on the hazardous properties of those chemicals. This refers to product liability,[146] as

---

[139]  *See* the discussion in Chapter 5, Section B.3 and C.2.

[140]  UN Doc. UNEP/POPS/CONF/4, signed May 22, 2001, entered into force May 17, 2004 *available at* http://www.pops.int/.

[141]  *Id.*, Preamble.

[142]  The Preamble adopts the version in Principle 2 of the Rio Declaration, *supra* note 31. *See also* Chapter 1, note 20 and accompanying text.

[143]  The Preamble refers to "precaution" while Article 1 refers to the precautionary approach as set forth in Principle 15 of the Rio Declaration, *supra* note 31. *See also* Chapter 3.

[144]  Preamble. *See* discussion in Chapter 5.

[145]  Preamble.

[146]  Product liability differs from the polluter pays principle because the former holds

well as the importance of public disclosure of information relating to these chemicals.[147]

The UNECE Convention on the Transboundary Effects Industrial Accidents,[148] opened for signature in 1992, refers to the polluter pays principle in the Preamble. The parties have taken account of the polluter pays principle as a general principle of international environmental law. The other principles referred to in the Preamble are the principles of good neighborliness, reciprocity, non-discrimination and good faith, which the parties consider are "principles of international law and custom."[149] Apart from a cursory reference to the polluter pays principle, which is referred to as "a general principle of international environmental law,"[150] no other reference is made to the polluter pays principle in the main body of the Convention. Thus, it is not clear what definition of the polluter pays principle has been adopted in this Convention.

The UNECE Convention on the Protection and Use of Transboundary Watercourses and International Lakes[151] also refers to the polluter pays principle. Under Article 2 of the Convention, the parties are required to take all appropriate measures to prevent, control and reduce any transboundary impact on any watercourses and international lakes. In taking such measures to prevent any transboundary impact, the parties shall be guided by the precautionary principle, the polluter pays principle "by virtue of which costs of pollution prevention, control and reduction measures shall be borne by the polluter"[152] and the inter-generational equity principle. Both conventions call upon parties to support international rules to elaborate rules and criteria in the field of responsibility and liability.

---

the manufacturer liable for any damage arising from its products. *See* Nicole C. Kibert, *Extended Producer Responsibility: A Tool for Achieving Sustainable Development*, 19 J. LAND USE & ENVTL. L. 503 (2004). The writer argues that the extended producer responsibility principle utilizes the polluter pays principle to extend responsibility for a product throughout the product lifecycle rather than up to the time of sale.

[147] Access to information is an important feature of modern international environmental law, as well as a procedural component of sustainable development. *See* Chapter 2, Section F and Chapter 4, Section F.

[148] 31 ILM 1330 (1992), signed March 17, 1992, entered into force Apr. 19, 2000, *available at* http://www.unece.org/env/teia/text.htm.

[149] *Id.*, Preamble.

[150] *Id.*

[151] Opened for signature on Mar. 17, 1992, entered into force Oct. 6, 1996, *available at* http://www.unece.org/env/.

[152] *Id.*, art. 2.

A Protocol on Civil Liability and Compensation for Damage Caused by the Transboundary Effects of Industrial Accidents on Transboundary Waters[153] was adopted within the framework of both conventions. The Protocol reiterated "the polluter pays principle as a general principle of international environmental law, accepted also by the parties to the above-mentioned Conventions."[154] The Protocol applies to damage caused by the transboundary effects of an industrial accident on transboundary waters.[155]

Article 4 provides for strict liability. It notes that the operator shall be liable for the damage caused by an industrial accident. However, no liability shall attach to the operator, if he proves that the damage was: the result of an act of armed conflict, hostilities, civil war or insurrection; the result of a natural phenomenon of exceptional, inevitable, unforeseeable and irresistible character; wholly the result of compliance with a compulsory measure of a public authority; or wholly the result of the wrongful intentional conduct of a third party. If two or more operators are liable, the claimant shall have the right to seek full compensation from any or all of the operators liable. However, the operator who proves that only part of the damage was caused by an industrial accident shall be liable for that part of the damage only.[156]

Claims for compensation under the Protocol must be brought within 15 years from the date of the industrial accident. Such claims must be brought within three years from the date that the claimant knew or ought to have known of the damage. Where the industrial accident consists of a series of occurrences, the time limit shall run from the date of the last occurrence. Where the industrial accident consists of a continuous occurrence, the time limit shall run from the end of that occurrence.[157]

The Protocol defines "damage" as loss of life or personal injury; loss of or damage to property; loss of income directly deriving from an impairment of a legally protected interest; cost of measures of reinstatement of the impaired transboundary waters; and the cost of response measures.[158] Under Article 11, the operator is required to ensure that liability under

---

[153] Signed May 2003, not yet in force, *available at* http://www.unece.org/env/civilliability/documents/protocol_e.pdf.

[154] *Id.*, Preamble.

[155] *Id.*, art. 3.

[156] *Id.*

[157] *Id.*, art. 10.

[158] *Id.*, art. 2.

Article 4 for amounts not less than the minimum limits for financial securities in Annex II (part II) and shall remain covered by financial security. Article 12 further provides that the Protocol shall not affect the rights and obligations of parties under rules of general international law with regard to international responsibility. Thus, while the Protocol provides for civil liability of operators, it does not preclude states from being held responsible under general international law, if the criteria required are satisfied.[159]

Although reference is made to the polluter pays principle in the Preamble to the Protocol, it is, in fact, an example of the application of civil liability for damage caused by industrial accidents on transboundary waters. It provides for compensation to victims—it does not provide for the internalizing of costs that the original version of the polluter pays principle sought to convey. This Protocol is an example of the application of the polluter pays principle through liability.

The Convention on the Protection of the Marine Environment of the Baltic Sea Area, 1992[160] also refers to the polluter pays principle. The parties are determined to embody developments in international environmental policy and law into a new Convention to extend, strengthen and modernize the legal regime for the protection of the marine environment of the Baltic Sea Area.[161] The objective of the parties is to take relevant measures to prevent and eliminate pollution in order to promote the ecological restoration of the Baltic Sea Area and the preservation of its ecological balance.[162] The Convention further provides that they shall apply the precautionary principle;[163] use best environmental practice and best available technology;[164] and apply the polluter pays principle.[165] While the Convention defines the precautionary principle, there is no definition of the polluter pays principle. The parties have undertaken to develop rules concerning liability for damage resulting from acts or omissions in contravention of the Convention, including limits of liability, criteria and procedures and available remedies.[166]

---

[159] *See* Chapter 1, Section B.5, on the discussion on state responsibility.

[160] Signed Apr. 9, 1992, entered into force Jan. 17, 2000, *available at* http://www.helcom.fi/Convention/en_GB/text/.

[161] *Id.,* Preamble.

[162] *Id.,* art. 3(1).

[163] *Id.,* art. 3(2).

[164] *Id.,* art. 3(3).

[165] *Id.,* art. 3(4).

[166] *Id.,* art. 25.

The Convention for the Protection of the Marine Environment of the North-East Atlantic (OSPAR Convention)[167] was also opened for signature in 1992. The Preamble refers to both the Stockholm Conference and the Rio Conference and also the relevant provisions of customary international law reflected in Part XII of UN Convention on the Law of the Sea and in particular Article 197. The OSPAR Convention calls upon the parties to take all possible measures to prevent and eliminate pollution and to protect the maritime area against the adverse effects of human activities so as to safeguard human health and to conserve marine ecosystems.[168] The parties shall apply the precautionary principle, the polluter pays principle and use best available techniques and best environmental practices including clean technology.[169]

Unlike other conventions surveyed above, this Convention actually contains a definition of the polluter pays principle. It is used in the sense that the costs of pollution prevention, control and reduction measures are to be borne by the polluter. This is the traditional definition of the polluter pays principle. The parties are required to take steps to prevent and eliminate pollution from land based sources,[170] from dumping or incineration,[171] from offshore sources[172] and pollution from other sources.[173] Thus, this Convention does not seek to provide compensation for any damage caused; rather it seeks to prevent damage from taking place—hence the present definition of the polluter pays principle. It follows that the operator of a particular activity will be required to internalize the costs of pollution prevention. This obligation would pass on to the state parties in the event of transboundary damage.

The only convention outside Europe to refer to the polluter pays principle is the ASEAN Agreement on the Conservation of Nature and Natural Resources.[174] It provides for the conservation and development of natural resources in the ASEAN region and adopts several principles in this regard.

---

[167] 32 ILM 1068 (1993), signed Sept. 22, 1992, *available at* http://www.ospar.org/eng/html/convention/ospar_conv1.htm.

[168] *Id.*, art. 2(1).

[169] *Id.*, art. 2(2).

[170] *Id.*, art. 3.

[171] *Id.*, art. 4.

[172] *Id.*, art. 5.

[173] *Id.*, art. 7.

[174] Signed July 9, 1985, *reprinted in* 15 EPL 64 (1985), *available at* http://www.ocean-law.net/texts/asean.htm.

The parties have undertaken to prevent, reduce and control degradation of the natural environment and endeavored to take measures to promote environmentally sound agricultural practices; to promote pollution control and the development of environmentally sound industrial processes and products; to promote adequate economic or fiscal incentives; and, as far as possible, to consider the originator of the activity causing environmental degradation responsible for the prevention, reduction and control as well as for rehabilitation and remedial measures.

This definition of the polluter pays principle seems to encompass both the preventive aspect as well as the remedial aspect. It seeks to hold the originator liable to prevent environmental degradation, and where this is not possible, the originator will be responsible for rehabilitation and remedial measures. It is not clear whether compensation is included in this formula. However, it is clear that the definition encompasses both aspects of the measures and has a wider application than the OSPAR Convention, discussed above. It is interesting that the Convention refers to the "originator" of pollution rather than the "polluter." It seems a better word than the word "polluter," as in the strict sense of the word, there is no polluter, since the objective is to prevent pollution from taking place.

The OECD notes that there are no international instruments that adopt the broader formulation of the polluter pays principle:

> From a formal standpoint, however, there is no binding instrument of international law that lays down a clear and precise basis for the PPP "in a broad sense." For example, there are provisions of international law that govern compensation, but there are no international provisions in force, other than agreements on discharge from ships in Europe, that institute an obligation to pay charges or taxes for environmental pollution.[175]

Thus, at the present time, the only formulation of the polluter pays principle we have at the international level is the formulation embodied in Principle 16 of the Rio Declaration, which, at best, is full of hortatory language and incorporates only the strict version of the polluter pays principle. The OECD seems one step further by having adopted the broader version of the polluter pays principle.

---

[175] *See* Joint Working Party on Trade and Environment, *supra* note 46.

## G. RELATIONSHIP WITH OTHER DISCIPLINES, CONCEPTS AND PRINCIPLES

### 1. The Polluter Pays Principle and Liability for Damage

Sometimes the polluter pays principle has been confused with liability for environmental damage. While the latter can certainly be an extension of the polluter pays principle, or the way it has been operationalized, they are by no means synonymous.[176] A distinction must also be made between civil liability and international responsibility. While the former refers to liability of non-state actors within states, the latter refers to liability between states at the international level.

International law has long recognized that states are responsible under international law for any extra-territorial damage they may cause by pollution. This principle, articulated in the *Trail Smelter Arbitration*[177] is now a customary international law principle in the field of environmental protection. That states must refrain from carrying out activities that can cause damage by pollution to the environment of other states or in areas beyond the limits of national jurisdiction is a well established principle of international environmental law and is now codified in Principle 21 of the Stockholm Declaration. Principle 21 was reproduced almost verbatim in Principle 2 of the Rio Declaration.[178]

Much has been written on the subject.[179] It is a general principle of international law that a violation of an international obligation gives rise to state responsibility.[180] According to ILC Draft Article 1, "Every internation-

---

[176] *See* Gaines, *supra* note 11.

[177] USA v. Canada, 3 RIAA 1905 (1941).

[178] *See* Chapter 1, note 20 and accompanying text.

[179] The International Law Commission (ILC) has been working on the topic of state responsibility since its inception. It was only in 2003 that a draft was finalized and submitted to the UN General Assembly. While the draft articles themselves are not binding on states, it is generally accepted that the ILC draft articles on state responsibility reflect, for most part, customary international law. *See generally* IAN BROWNLIE, SYSTEM OF THE LAW OF NATIONS I: LAW OF STATE RESPONSIBILITY (1983); James Crawford, *The ILC's Articles on Responsibility of States for Internationally Wrongful Acts: A Retrospect*, 96 AM. J. INT'L L. 874 (2002); Edith Brown Weiss, *Invoking State Responsibility in the Twenty-First Century*, 96 AM. J. INT'L L. 798 (2002); James Crawford et. al., *The ILC's Articles on Responsibility of States for Internationally Wrongful Acts: Completion of the Second Reading*, 12 EUR. J. INT'L L. 963 (2001); and *Symposium: Assessing the Work of the International Law Commission on State Responsibility*, 13 EUR. J. INT'L L. 1053 (2002).

[180] In the *Chorzow Factory Case (Jurisdiction)*, 1927 P.C.I.J., Ser. A, No. 9, 21, the Permanent Court of International Justice stated that:

It is a principle of international law that a breach of an agreement involves an obligation to make reparation in an adequate form. Reparation therefore is the

ally wrongful act of a State entails the international responsibility of that State."[181] An internationally wrongful act is further elaborated in Draft Article 2:

> There is an internationally wrongful act of a State when conduct consisting of an action or omission:
> (a) Is attributable to the State under international law; and
> (b) Constitutes a breach of an international obligation of the State.[182]

Thus, two criteria have to be satisfied in order to hold a state responsible under international law: (1) there has to be a breach of an international obligation; and (2) the conduct in question has to be imputed to the state.[183] It is a general principle that a state is responsible only for the wrongful acts or omissions of state officials or organs even if they had acted *ultra vires*.[184] As a general rule, a state is not responsible for the activities of private individuals unless the state failed to control the activities of the private individual or failed to take steps to punish the wrongdoer.[185] In the context of pollution or environmental damage, a state would be held responsible under international law if it failed to control the activities of the polluter. If, however, the state has discharged its due diligence obligation,[186] it will not entail responsibility. In this context, the victim state has to establish that there was a violation of the due diligence obligation embodied in Principle 21 of the Stockholm Declaration.

In addition to these two criteria identified by the ILC, the question has arisen whether the traditionally required criteria, such as negligence and damage, have to be proved in order to establish liability. While ILC Draft Article 2 does not refer to either negligence or damage, much would depend on the primary obligation undertaken by the states in question. If

---

indispensable complement of a failure to apply a convention and there is no necessity for this to be stated in the convention itself.

[181] Draft Articles on Responsibility of States for Internationally Wrongful Acts, adopted by the ICL at its 53d session (2001), *available at* www.un.org/law/ilc/.

[182] ILC draft art. 2.

[183] Draft Articles 4–11 deal with principles of attribution.

[184] *See* draft art. 7.

[185] *See* IAN BROWNLIE, PRINCIPLES OF PUBLIC INTERNATIONAL LAW, 455 (5th ed. 1998).

[186] It is generally accepted that states have only a due diligence obligation, unless under treaties a regime of strict liability has been accepted. *See* BIRNIE & BOYLE, *supra* note 99, at 112.

the primary obligation requires proof of either negligence or damage or both, it is necessary to prove them in order to establish responsibility. In the environmental protection field, proof of significant damage will go a long way in establishing liability—however, this can lead to problems where damage is either long term[187] or cumulative.[188] Establishing causation[189] is another problem in the environment field, particularly where there are multiple sources of pollution emanating from different states.[190]

While state responsibility principles can be valuable in relation to seeking compensation for damage already caused, it cannot provide relief to those who seek to prevent such damage from occurring. In the context of state responsibility, the polluter pays principle dictates that the polluter state should pay the necessary compensation for the damage caused by pollution. The general application of the polluter pays principle does not deal with pollution damage. It seeks to ensure that the polluter internalizes the costs for pollution abatement so that the environment would be in an acceptable state.[191] This must be distinguished from paying compensation for any damage caused. The polluter in this instance would be the state (or if it is a private individual or company, its activities must be attributable to the state), and the damage is transboundary in nature. If there is no transboundary environmental damage, issues of state responsibility will not arise. Thus, liability in the context of the polluter pays principle will arise only in the event of transboundary environmental damage.

However, the polluter pays principle can be extended to cover the situation where environmental damage is caused to a person in another state. If the person who causes environmental damage is under an obligation to repair that damage, then it logically follows that it is the polluter who must repair that damage, although, in some circumstances, identifying the polluter may be difficult. It might have to be channeled to the operator, the owner or other person depending on who was in charge of the activity. In some circumstances, of course, the victim too has contributed to the damage and hence must bear part of the costs himself. The concept of contributory negligence is a well established principle of tort law.

---

[187] Damage caused by radiation is a good example.

[188] Acid rain is a good example.

[189] Caution must be distinguished from attributability. Caution requires linking the act in question with the damage in question. Attributability requires linking the act in question with the state in question. Both issues must be established for the purposes of state responsibility.

[190] Again, acid rain is a good example.

[191] *See* Nash, *supra* note 66.

It could also be argued that the polluter pays principle can be implemented through the liability principle, although this would not find favor with environmentalists. As is well known, international environmental law has moved away from imposing liability for environmental damage to a regulatory regime with prevention of damage as the objective. Adopting the liability principle as a vehicle for the implementation of the polluter pays principle would be contrary to this trend and will not promote the preventive principle.

The polluter pays principle in the context of extraterritorial damage can be seen in Principle 21 of the Stockholm Declaration, which deals with liability for such damage. This is strictly not an application of the polluter pays principle but an extension of it. Sanford Gaines notes this distinction thus:

> As originally propounded, the PPP is *not* a liability principle, but rather is a principle for the allocation of the costs of pollution control. To have a clear understanding of the PPP and what it stands for as a matter of official international law and policy, one must maintain the distinction between the assessment of liability for the abatement of specific harms on the one hand and the allocation of the costs of broad preventive measures on the other (emphasis in original).[192]

> The liability principle not only imposes on the source of pollution a legal liability to pay for the damage caused to innocent victims, but may also require the source, at its own expense, to abate the pollution in order to reduce its effects on innocent neighbors to a socially and legally acceptable level.[193]

Sanford Gaines notes that the polluter pays principle has its ideological roots in economics—not law. It is only recently (in fact, 20 years after it was first adopted by the OECD) that it was included in a legal instrument.[194] Even then, it is so full of hortatory language that it is difficult to discern its status under international law. Its importance in the field of environmental protection and sustainable development, however, is not in doubt.

Thus, while a liability regime can be one of the modes in which the polluter pays principle can be operationalized, it is not its main objective. The main objective of the polluter pays principle is to *prevent* environmen-

---

[192] *See* Gaines, *supra* note 11, at 463 (emphasis added).

[193] *Id.* at 469.

[194] The Rio Declaration, *supra* note 31.

tal damage by ensuring that pollution remains at accepted levels—levels prescribed by the government. However, the liability regime has a role to play in two scenarios: (1) where there is residual damage; and (2) where there is accidental damage.

It is argued that "distortions in international trade and investment arising from differential pollution abatement financing methods could be eliminated through the adoption of the polluter pays principle."[195] If this principle is not applied, polluters would simply make decisions based on the market price alone, ignoring environmental and social costs.[196] It is further noted that:

> Because decision makers prefer the least expensive goods and services when given a choice among goods and services of comparable quality, the polluter pays principle makes it more likely that the choices they make in their self-interest also will further sustainable development and environmental responsibility.[197]

## 2. The Polluter Pays Principle and International Trade

The main aim of the polluter pays principle is to ensure that no distortions in international trade and investment will arise as a result of subsidies that may be given to the polluter in some instances. However, the WTO agreements do not specifically mention the polluter pays principle. Nonetheless, the general idea behind the polluter pays principle, and, in particular, the restrictions on pollution prevention subsidies, is broadly consistent with WTO principles. Thus, "although distinct concepts, the PPP and the WTO's disciplines on subsidies are often closely related."[198]

A number of WTO provisions allow subsidies for pollution prevention and control that may be contrary to the strict application of the polluter pays principle. The three main WTO agreements dealing with subsidies are: The General Agreement on Tariffs and Trade (GATT), the Agreement on Subsidies and Countervailing Measures (ASCM), and the Agreement on Agriculture (AA).[199]

---

[195] *See* Larson, *supra* note 58.

[196] *Id.*

[197] *Id.*

[198] *See* OECD, Joint Working Party on Trade and Environment, *supra* note 46.

[199] *Id. See also* Pearson, *supra* note 84 and Kibert, *supra* note 146.

With regard to the GATT, exceptions to its obligations are available under its general exceptions clause, which provides that measures "necessary to protect human, animal or plant life or health"[200] or those "relating to the conservation of exhaustible natural resources"[201] may be taken by states. However, such measures must meet the requirements in the *chapeau*—it should not constitute a means of "arbitrary or unjustifiable discrimination between countries where the same conditions prevail, or a disguised restriction on international trade."[202]

The Agreement on Subsidies and Countervailing Measures prohibits certain subsidies (Articles 3 and 4), makes others actionable (Articles 5–7) and identifies non-actionable subsidies (Articles 8 and 9). This latter category includes environmental subsidies.[203] As these were not renewed after 1999 when they lapsed, the non-actionable subsidies category no longer includes environmental subsidies.

The primary aim of the Agreement on Agriculture is to progressively reduce agricultural support and protection in order to prevent distortions in world agricultural markets.[204] The Agreement applies to both domestic support measures as well as export subsidies on agricultural products. Exceptions are available for pollution prevention and control subsidies.

The polluter pays principle was invoked in the dispute relating to the *US—Taxes on Petroleum and Certain Imported Substances* (1987).[205] The issue raised involved the financing of the U.S. Superfund by a tax on pollution-causing chemicals. Because imported products, unlike domestic products, caused no pollution in the United States, the EEC challenged the tax invoking the polluter pays principle. It alleged that the tax financed an environmental protection program from which U.S. producers alone can benefit. The Panel did not consider whether the tax was inconsistent with the polluter pays principle, but held that "the General Agreement's rules

---

[200] Art. XX(b), 55 UNTS 194, signed Oct. 30, 1947, *available at* http://www.wto.org.

[201] *Id.*, art. XX(g).

[202] *Id.*, art. XX.

[203] These provisions lapsed five years after its adoption. The OECD report noted that the issue of environmental subsidies was discussed by the negotiating group on subsidies during the Uruguay Round. It was agreed that environmental subsidies should be included in the non-actionable category, which was introduced for a period of five years (until end of 1999) and has not been renewed. *See* OECD, Joint Working Party on Trade and Environment, *supra* note 46, at 20.

[204] Preamble, *available at* http://www.wto.org.

[205] 13ISD 345/136, *available at* http://www.wto.org/english/.

on tax adjustment thus give the contracting party in such a case the possibility to follow the Polluter-Pays Principle, but they do not oblige it to do so."[206] The Panel further noted that the EEC could refer its issue to the Working Group on Environmental Measures and International Trade.

Three issues relating to the polluter pays principle in relation to international trade have been raised.[207] The first issue is whether the polluter pays principle set a higher standard in limiting government financial assistance than does the GATT. If so, is it desirable to bring them on par with the polluter pays standards? Even if the case can be made that the polluter pays principle adopts a more stringent standard than the GATT, there is no evidence to suggest that financial subsidies for pollution abatement are a significant distortion of international trade:[208] "While these rules [WTO provisions] may not be perfect, it would seem unnecessary, disruptive, and counter-productive to create a special, more stringent regime for pollution abatement financial subsidies."[209]

While a strong argument can be made that the attractive features of the polluter pays principle should be extended beyond the OECD—and indeed, the Rio Declaration has sought to do so—the problem is which interpretation of the polluter pays principle should be adopted? If it were introduced into the GATT, the polluter pays principle would become universal. However, rather than attempting to rewrite the GATT provisions, it has been articulated that the better approach would be to persuade these countries to adhere to the polluter pays principle voluntarily.[210]

The second issue that arises is where countries set artificially low environmental standards or fail to enforce environmental standards in order to get a comparative advantage in international trade ("pollution haven" issue).[211] It is clear that this would violate both the polluter pays principle, as well as principles of international trade. Where countries have set environmental standards below the level appropriate to their social and economic conditions, the OECD requires polluters to pay for abatement costs to ensure that the environment is in an acceptable state, which is to be decided by public authorities.[212]

---

[206] *See* OECD, Joint Working Party on Trade and Environment, *supra* note 46, *referred to in* n.31.

[207] *See* Pearson, *supra* note 84.

[208] *Id.*

[209] *Id.*

[210] *Id.*

[211] *Id.*

[212] *Id.*

The final issue is whether the GATT should play a more central role in relation to transnational pollution and, if so, how this should relate to the polluter pays principle. It has been articulated in this regard that: "Surely the preferable route is to seek international agreements outside the GATT, perhaps through some new international environmental organization."[213] These measures may include trade restrictions, as have been adopted in many environmental treaties;[214] however, their consistency with GATT provisions will have to be resolved. The better approach would be, as we saw in Chapter 5, to provide financial mechanisms or facilitate technology transfer[215] to enable developing countries to comply with their environmental obligations.

In the 1972 Recommendation, the OECD specified that its Guiding Principles did not cover problems related to developing countries.[216] This could lead to distortions in international trade, if official development assistance helped the producers in those countries to comply with national or international pollution standards.[217] With regard to local pollution, there is a distortion of the polluter pays principle, as the enterprises that use the pollution control facilities financed by development assistance do not pay the full cost of abatement measures.[218] As regards global environmental issues, international conventions seem to move towards the adoption of international funds (for example, the GEF) to enable developing countries to fulfill their environmental obligations under these treaties.[219] Without such mechanisms, it would be difficult for developing countries to participate in these multilateral environmental agreements.[220] This is a significant development given that some developing countries are becoming major polluters at the global level with their expanding populations and increasingly industrializing economies. The effect of such mechanisms on international trade, however, requires closer scrutiny.

## 3. The Polluter Pays Principle and Sustainable Development

As was discussed in Chapter 2, sustainable development encompasses several components, both procedural and substantive. One such component is the principle of integration—ensuring that environmental protec-

---

[213] *Id.*

[214] *See* Carlson, *supra* note 13.

[215] *Id.*

[216] Rec. C(72)128, *supra* note 26.

[217] *See* OECD, Joint Working Party on Trade and Environment, *supra* note 46.

[218] *Id.*

[219] *Id.*

[220] *See* Carlson, *supra* note 13. *See* Chapter 5, Section B and C.2.

tion and economic development are integrated. How does the polluter pays principle contribute to this process of integration? The polluter pays principle seeks to ensure that pollution costs are not passed on to the government or to society at large. According to the polluter pays principle, the polluter should ensure that costs of pollution abatement are internalized and that the environment is at an optimal level. In other words, the role of this principle is to balance economic development with environmental protection, an essential component of sustainable development. It can thus be contended that the polluter pays principle is an essential tool to achieve sustainable development. As noted by Dernbach, "The polluter-pays principle is necessary to ensure that social, economic and environmental goals are realized harmoniously; it is essential to integrated decision-making."[221] In other words, economic development should not come at the expense of social development or the protection of the environment.

While there are various ways in which this principle has been implemented, a very common approach is the command-and-control approach through the adoption of emission standards for pollutants. These standards are set by the government in question or by international organizations to ensure that pollution remains at acceptable levels and that there is no danger to human health[222] or the environment. Industrial operators ("polluters") must ensure that appropriate technology is installed to keep emissions below these standards. The costs associated with such technology must be internalized and borne by the operator or could be passed on to the consumer. The idea behind this is to reduce demand for highly polluting products or services, as they would be more expensive. By reducing demand for highly polluting products or services, the environment would become less polluted.

As noted above, without the polluter pays principle, private actors will tend to ignore environmental and social costs, making decisions based simply on the market price. This will lead to distortions in international trade. When the price of goods and services reflects their environmental and social costs, it is not necessary to engage in a separate task of gathering such information and then weighing that information against the economic price of goods and services:

> Because decision makers prefer the least expensive goods and services when given a choice among goods and services of compara-

---

[221] *See* Dernbach, *supra* note 4.

[222] Protecting human health is an important objective of environmental legislation. *See* EU White Paper, *supra* note 51. *See also* HUNTER ET AL., *supra* note 15, at 131, for the drawbacks of this approach.

ble equality, the polluter pays principle makes it more likely that the choices they make in their self-interest also will further sustainable development and environmental responsibility.[223]

As noted, outside the OECD, the polluter pays principle has not been explicitly adopted or applied. However, many developing countries require industries to comply with emission standards, environmental laws and regulations, which include obtaining licenses for operation. Thus, for example, Sri Lanka's National Environmental Act (as amended) requires industries to obtain an "environmental protection license" in order to operate.[224] This license has certain conditions attached to it, which include complying with emission standards.[225] The failure to fulfill these conditions can lead to the revocation of the license or non-renewal.[226] While the term "polluter pays" is not mentioned in the Act, the government has actually implemented it by subjecting industries to emission standards.

Although the polluter pays principle has not penetrated into legal texts in developing countries, their judiciaries have been keenly following international developments. In his seminal judgment in the *Eppawala Phosphate Mining Case*[227] in Sri Lanka, Judge Amerasinghe noted in relation to the polluter pays principle:

> Today, environmental protection, in the light of the generally recognized "polluter pays" principle (e.g. see Principle 16 of the Rio Declaration), can no longer be permitted to be externalized by economists merely because they find it too insignificant or too difficult to include it as a cost associated with human activity. The costs of environmental damage should, in my view, be borne by the party that causes such harm, rather than being allowed to fall on the general community to be paid through reduced environmental quality or increased taxation in order to mitigate the environmentally degrading effects of a project.[228]

---

[223] *See* Larson, *supra* note 58 *quoting* Dernbach, *supra* note 4.

[224] National Environmental Act No. 47 of 1980 as amended by Act No. 56 of 1988. *See* Sumudu Atapattu, *Sustainable Development, Myth or Reality?: A Survey of Sustainable Development Under International Law and Sri Lankan Law*, 16 GEO. INT'L ENVTL. L. REV. 265 (2001).

[225] National Environmental Act, *id.*, sec. 23B.

[226] *Id.*, sec. 23D.

[227] *Tikiri Bankda Bulankulama et al. v. The Secretary, Ministry of Industrial Development et al.*, SC Application No. 884/99 (FR), SC Minutes, June 2, 2000.

[228] *Id.*

The Indian judiciary, by far the most activist in the South Asian region, has handed down several judgments on this issue. In the *Vellore Citizens Welfare Forum v. Union of India,*[229] the Supreme Court of India noted that although the leather industry is a major foreign exchange earner for India and provided employment, it cannot destroy the ecology, degrade the environment and create health hazards. In this context, the Court noted that "Sustainable development, and in particular the polluter pays principles and the precautionary principle, have become a part of customary international law."[230] It further noted that:

> If a polluter refuses to pay compensation, his industry will be closed, and the compensation recovered as arrears of land revenue. If an industry sets up necessary pollution control devices now, it is still liable to pay for the past pollution it has generated.[231]

This lays down the principle that industry will be held accountable for past pollution despite it having installed pollution control devices now. The judgment seems to refer to the polluter pays principle in the context of liability, as reference is made to compensation.

In *M.C. Mehta v. Kamal Nath and Others,*[232] the Supreme Court of India ordered the respondent to pay compensation to restore the environment and to remove the various constructions along the bank of the river. The Court further ordered the respondent to show why a pollution fine should not be imposed on it, pursuant to the polluter pays principle.[233]

## 4. The Polluter Pays Principle and the Common but Differentiated Responsibility Principle

In Chapter 5 we discussed the evolution and the application of the common but differentiated responsibility principle embodied in Principle 7 of the Rio Declaration. In this context it has been contended by Christopher Stone that:

> Rio Principle 7, in calling for the assignment of heavier contributions to developed countries in response to "the pressures their

---

[229] AIR 1996 SC 2715, Supreme Court of India.

[230] *Id.*

[231] *Id.*

[232] (1997) 1 Supreme Court Cases 388.

[233] The Court also referred to the public trust doctrine and noted that the government is the trustee of all natural resources which are by nature meant for public use and enjoyment.

societies place on the global environment," shifts the focus from Poor's needs to Rich's wrongs. If we agreed to put the principle into action, it would mean that the Rich (and everyone else) should be confronted with the full social costs of their emissions. Thus understood, the principle is no more controversial, or peculiarly equitable than declaring that the polluter should pay.[234]

According to Christopher Stone, Principle 7 shifts the focus from the needs of the poor countries to the wrongs of the rich countries. In actual fact, Principle 7 does not refer either to the wrongs of rich countries or to the needs of poor countries. Rather, it refers to the greater responsibility of developed countries as a result of (1) the pressure they place on the global environment and (2) greater capacity in terms of technology and financial resources to deal with such environmental problems. Principle 7 further provides that in view of the different contributions to global environmental problems, there shall be common but differentiated responsibilities. If there was an acknowledgement of responsibility for past pollution acts, there would be a recognition of the polluter pays principle. However, the above formulation does not explicitly promote the responsibility of developed countries for past polluting activities or for creating present-day global environmental problems. As can be seen, there is a close nexus between the polluter pays principle, and the common but differentiated responsibility principle and the latter seeks to promote the polluter pays principle implicitly.

John Dernbach contends that the common but differentiated responsibility principle is an off-shoot of the polluter pays principle,[235] as the former principle requires those who caused global environmental problems to bear responsibility for such damage:

> The principle of differentiated responsibilities is largely an outgrowth of the polluter-pays principle. Because they have made the greatest contribution to most global environmental problems, developed countries should pay for the cleanup. The equitable considerations intrinsic to the polluter-pays principle also suggest that it is appropriate for developed countries, whose development is imposing significant negative externalities on the environment of both developed and developing countries, to help developing countries meet their environmental obligations.[236]

---

[234] *See* Christopher Stone, *Common but Differentiated Responsibilities in International Law*, 98 AM. J. INT'L L. 276 (2004).

[235] *See* Dernbach, *supra* note 4.

[236] *Id.*

## 5. The Polluter Pays Principle and the User Pays Principle

Related to the polluter pays principle is the "user pays principle," which is considered as the natural resources equivalent of the polluter pays principle. While the polluter pays principle concerns itself with pollution or environmental damage (where a liability regime is used), the user pays principle deals with the pricing of natural resources. The OECD has endorsed the user pays principle; nonetheless, it is a more difficult principle to operationalize.[237] Under the user pays principle, governments have to find social prices and charge users for the cost of using natural resources, such as water, forests, minerals and land resources. The charge would depend on whether they are renewable or non-renewable resources. For the former, costs would include, in addition to the standard cost of extraction, environmental damage costs and depletion costs. For the latter, costs imposed on future generations will be included, as that resource will not be available in the future.[238]

## H. CONCLUSION—LEGAL STATUS

While specific incorporation of the polluter pays principle outside the OECD and the EU is rare, it has been implemented through various means all over the world, particularly, through emission standards, pollution taxes and tradable permits. While legislation in developing countries may not explicitly incorporate the polluter pays principle, their judiciaries have not been immune to these international developments and have, on many occasions, referred to the polluter pays principle, the precautionary principle and, more commonly, sustainable development.

With regard to the application of the polluter pays principle, it has been articulated that:

> Despite its ambiguities, the Polluter-Pays Principle has stood up surprisingly well over the past two decades. It is sufficiently flexible to accommodate a range of interpretations, a variety of environmental protection approaches, and reasonable derogations and exceptions. Indeed, it is consistent with a Consumer-Pays Principle, a User-Pays Principle, and a Victims-Pays Principle, while maintaining its core meaning of no government subsidies for pollution abatement. Most likely, the PPP has improved environmental and economic efficiency with the OECD, helped avoid trade distortions, and prevented trade disputes.[239]

---

[237] *See* Pearson, *supra* note 84.

[238] *Id.*

[239] *Id.*

While the polluter pays principle may fall short of a customary international law principle, in the field of environmental protection applicable to the entire international community, it is more widely applied than was previously contended. Given its extensive application in OECD countries, it would be good contender for a regional custom.[240] While its specific incorporation outside the OECD and the EU is not widespread, it has been implemented mainly through the command-and-control approach by way of emission or effluent standards. The contention that its application is limited to a regime of liability cannot be accepted, because the very idea of the polluter pays principle (despite its nomenclature) is to avoid damage to the environment. By contrast, liability arises only in the event of damage to the environment. While it is possible to implement the polluter pays principle through a regime of liability, this is not the preferred method, as this approach does not lead to prevention of damage, rather to remediation.

The lack of a universally accepted definition of the polluter pays principle may be a problem for its implementation. The OECD definition has ranged from a simple version, where no government subsidies should apply to pollution, to a more extended version of paying compensation for environmental damage. The polluter pays principle has implications for international trade, as the application of the polluter pays principle should not lead to distortions in international trade and investment. It is really the application of exceptions to the polluter pays principle that can lead to such distortions.

The polluter pays principle is an important tool to achieve sustainable development. It seeks to reconcile economic development with environmental protection and, as such, seeks to give effect to the principle of integration, an important component of sustainable development.[241] As such, it must be universally implemented.[242] It also has implications for the common but differentiated responsibility principle and the precautionary principle.

---

[240] *See Asylum Case (Colombia v. Peru)*, 1950 ICJ 266, which dealt with a regional custom relating to diplomatic asylum in Latin America. *See also* LORI DAMROSCH, LOUIS HENKIN, RICHARD DUGH, OSCAR SCHACHTER & HANS SMIT, INTERNATIONAL LAW: CASES AND MATERIALS, 88 (4th ed. 2001).

[241] *See* discussion in Chapter 2, Section E.1.

[242] *See* Pearson, *supra* note 84, who argues that while the harmonization of the polluter pays principle with GATT provisions is necessary, the GATT should not become the forum to settle environmental disputes.

# CHAPTER 7
# FUTURE OF INTERNATIONAL SUSTAINABLE DEVELOPMENT LAW

The influence that sustainable development has had on international environmental law within a fairly short time span is quite remarkable. From a rather broad and imprecise definition, it has developed into an umbrella term encompassing different components—both substantive and procedural. It is now possible to identify the distinct components that comprise the umbrella. While the WCED report succeeded in popularizing the term "sustainable development," it was the Rio Declaration that was instrumental in expanding and refining it and placing it firmly on the international agenda. Moreover, the Rio Declaration identified tools to achieve sustainable development, as well as linkages, such as poverty, security, war and peace, that have a direct bearing on sustainable development. The WSSD further reinforced the importance of sustainable development and reiterated the international community's commitment to sustainable development. It also identified the three pillars of sustainable development as economic development, social development and environmental protection. The next few years would be crucial in further refining the components of sustainable development, as well as fine-tuning the tools to achieve it, such as the precautionary principle, environmental impact assessment process and the polluter pays principle. The procedural components of sustainable development, which forge a link with international human rights law, have a crucial role to play in democratizing sustainable development.

Sustainable development has had a considerable impact at the national level too. In fact, national judiciaries in some countries have been much more forthcoming than their international counter-parts, handing down judgments that refer specifically to sustainable development, the precautionary principle, environmental impact assessment and the polluter pays principles and applying these concepts and principles to domestic environmental cases, thereby contributing to the development of general principles of international law. As with any international principle or norm, the success of sustainable development and other principles depends on the extent to which they are internalized and applied at the national level. As discussed in Chapter 2, it has been articulated that sustainable development provides the framework for governance at the national level.[1]

---

[1] *See* John Dernbach, *Sustainable Development as a Framework for National Governance*, 49 CASE W. RES. L. REV. 1 (1998).

Sustainable development has slowly but surely influenced international law and policy as no other norm has done in recent years. Despite definitional problems and rather hesitant views about its legal status, it would not be wrong to say that sustainable development "came of age" with the adoption of the Rio Declaration. It has not only influenced states and their activities, it has also influenced the work of international organizations and specialized agencies. Moreover, it has been embraced by NGOs, both national and international. Firmly based on the concept of equity, sustainable development contains a temporal element and strongly urges us to take a long-term view of development instead of concentrating on short-term gain.

During its rather short journey of evolution, sustainable development has acquired an identity of its own and has developed into a separate branch of international law called "international sustainable development law." It has been articulated that:

> Sustainable development law is both an emerging body of legal principles and instruments, as well as an "interstitial norm," a concept that serves to reconcile conflicting environmental, social and economic development norms in international law, in the interest of present and future generations.[2]

Of course, sustainable development is not a cure for all evils. Because it lacks a precise definition, states and other actors can manipulate its definition to suit their needs at a give time. Because virtually anything can come within the rubric of sustainable development, it seems to have "come to mean all things to all people."[3] However, despite the lack of clarity, there is a fairly widespread understanding of what sustainable development would entail for states:

> [A]lthough international law may not require development to be sustainable, it does require development decisions to be the outcome of a process which promotes sustainable development. Specifically, if states do not carry out EIAs, or encourage public participation, or integrate development and environmental considerations in their decision-making, or take account of the needs of intra- and inter-generational equity, they will have failed to implement the main elements employed by the Rio Declaration

---

[2] SUSTAINABLE DEVELOPMENT LAW: PRINCIPLES, PRACTICES AND PROSPECTS 365 (Marie-Claire Cordonier Segger & Ashfaq Khalfan eds., 2004).

[3] *Id.* at 367.

and other international instruments for the purpose of facilitating sustainable development. There is . . . ample state practice to support the normative significance of most of these elements.[4]

In other words, international law requires certain steps to be followed in the decision-making process,[5] and it is very likely that the failure to do so would result in a violation of an international obligation resulting in state responsibility. It is interesting to note that Ireland complained, *inter alia*, of U.K.'s failure to cooperate in the *MOX Plant Case*[6] before the ITLOS. It is, therefore, obvious that the components of sustainable development, particularly the procedural elements, are playing an important role in relation to environmental issues. Thus, it has been articulated that components of sustainable development, rather than the concept itself, will be very relevant when courts or tribunals have to interpret, apply or develop the law:[7]

> Whether or not sustainable development is a legal obligation, and as we have seen this seems unlikely, it does represent a goal which can influence the outcome of cases, the interpretation of treaties, and the practice of states and international organizations, and it may lead to significant changes and developments in the existing law. In that very important sense, international law does appear to require states and international bodies to take account of the objective of sustainable development, and to establish appropriate processes for doing so.[8]

Thus, sustainable development seems to have permeated every activity and every subject at the international level; has received support at the national level in every region of the world;[9] and has been identified as an established international legal concept.[10] It is thus obvious that while sus-

---

[4] PATRICIA BIRNIE & ALAN BOYLE, INTERNATIONAL LAW & THE ENVIRONMENT 96 (2d ed. 2002).

[5] It has been articulated that the ICJ implied that "the process of decision-making the key legal element of sustainable development" in its decision in the *Case Concerning the Gabcikovo Nagymaros Project. See* BIRNIE & BOYLE *id.*

[6] *See* Chapter 3, note 293 and accompanying text.

[7] *See* BIRNIE & BOYLE, *supra* note 4, at 96 *quoting* Vaughn Lowe, *Sustainable Development and Unsustainable Arguments, in* INTERNATIONAL LAW AND SUSTAINABLE DEVELOPMENT: PAST ACHIEVEMENTS AND FUTURE CHALLENGES 26 (Alan Boyle & David Freestone eds., 1999).

[8] *Id.* at 97.

[9] PHILIPPE SANDS, PRINCIPLES OF INTERNATIONAL ENVIRONMENTAL LAW 253 (2d ed. 2003).

[10] *Id.* at 252.

tainable development may lack normative status under international law,[11] it is not wholly devoid of any legal effect.

Thus, sustainable development has "graduated" from a "slippery concept" to an "international legal concept," and just as the decade of the 1990s was crucial in articulating the norm of sustainable development, the current decade would be crucial as to how the international community refines it and applies it to increasingly complex environmental issues that it now faces. Global warming would be the litmus test for many of these principles and tools. The precautionary principle would, no doubt, continue to influence the decision-making process as to when decisions should be taken to prevent environmental damage in the absence of scientific certainty. The environmental impact assessment process, which originated from national law, is being increasingly applied in relation to transboundary environmental problems. The procedural rights attached to the EIA process is now being applied to environmental issues generally, thus forging a link with international human rights law. The common but differentiated responsibility principle, developed as a response to the vast disparity between developed and developing countries, is likely to continue to influence future international environmental treaties. The polluter pays principle must be adopted by all states at the national level and implemented through various means at their disposal, whether it is through the imposition of liability (not the preferred method), or the adoption of environmental standards or green labeling, or a combination of them.

International environmental lawmaking has also undergone profound change. From its rather timid origins of purely cross-border environmental issues (which were mainly bilateral) to which existing international law principles were adapted, international environmental law has proceeded to encompass, within its ambit, highly complex environmental issues, such as ozone depletion, global warming, biotechnology and genetic engineering. The proliferation of multilateral treaties on the subject is another feature of modern international environmental law, and the international community has increasingly moved toward adopting these treaties through consensus. Soft law instruments continue to play an important role in this area. The international community has also adopted innovative methods to ensure participation of developing countries in treaty regimes, through the adoption of the common but differentiated responsibility principle within a framework of global partnership.

---

[11] *Cf.* the reference to sustainable development as a principle of customary international law. *See* Graham Mayeda, *Where Should Johannesburg Take Us?, Ethical and Legal Approaches to Sustainable Development in the Context of International Environmental Law*, 15 COLO. J. INT'L ENVTL. L. & POL'Y 29 (2004) and Separate Opinion of Judge Weeramantry in the *Case Concerning the Gabcikovo Nagymaros Project, supra* note 5.

Of course, many obstacles still remain. Many of these environmental issues are enmeshed in politics, and international cooperation (let alone a global partnership) is lacking in relation to global environmental issues with a constant tug-of-war between the European Union and the United States, whether it is global warming, genetically modified foods or the precautionary principle. The future remains rather bleak in relation to global warming without the participation of the United States, the world's largest contributor of greenhouse gases to the atmosphere, in the Kyoto Protocol regime.[12] If the predicated consequences of global warming materialize, they will be sufficient to upset the very core of international order present today, giving rise to a massive influx of refugees, disruption of the global economy and an enormous threat to national and international security.

While there is no doubt that international environmental law has come a long way since the Stockholm Conference in 1972 and even branched out into a new field of international law called international sustainable development law, there are significant challenges posed to its realization by, *inter alia*, abject poverty and civil strife. These issues require the urgent attention of the international community as there is a vicious cycle of poverty breeding conflict and conflict breeding poverty[13] that must be addressed. In addition, governance issues[14] and institutional reform will play an important role in the march toward sustainable development. As has been articulated, "Sustainable development law is clearly becoming one of the most important and intellectually challenging areas of international law and policy."[15] Because it is inter-linked with so many other issues, such as poverty and conflict, sustainable development will remain elusive if these interrelated issues are not addressed together. Thus, as the WCED pointed out, an integrated approach to development must be adopted that must be economically, socially and environmentally viable. The present and the next generation have a crucial role to play in articulating, applying and refining the components of sustainable development as well as other tools to achieve sustainable development, such as the precautionary principle, environmental impact assessment and the polluter pays principle. The procedural rights of information, participation and remedies should be rigorously applied so that environmental democracy will give rise to the further reinforcing of sustainable development.

---

[12] *See* Jutta Brunnee, *The United States and International Environmental Law: Living with an Elephant*, 15 EUR. J. INT'L L. 617 (2004).

[13] *See* Sumudu Atapattu, *Sustainable Development and Terrorism: International Linkages and a Case Study of Sri Lanka*, 30 WILLIAM & MARY ENVTL. L. REV. 273 (2006).

[14] *See* Daniel Bodansky, *The Legitimacy of International Governance: A Coming Challenge for International Environmental Law*, 93 AM. J. INT'L L. 596 (1999).

[15] *See* Dernbach, *supra* note 1, at 372.

As articulated by the WCED:

We came to see that a new development path was required, one that sustained human progress not just in a few places for a few years, but for the entire planet into the distant future. *Thus, "sustainable development" becomes a goal not just for the "developing" nations, but for industrial ones as well.*[16]

---

[16] OUR COMMON FUTURE, REPORT OF THE WORLD COMMISSION ON ENVIRONMENT AND DEVELOPMENT 4 (1987) (emphasis added).

# BIBLIOGRAPHY

*A New Environment*, LEGAL WEEK, Feb. 2, 2006, *available at* http://www.legal-week.net/ViewItem.asp?id=27427.

Abi-Saab, Georges, *Whither the International Community?*, 9 EUR. J. INT'L L. 248 (1998).

Agenda 21: A Blueprint for Action for Global Sustainable Development into the 21st Century (1992).

AGIUS, EMMANUEL ET AL. EDS., FUTURE GENERATIONS AND INTERNATIONAL LAW (1998).

A-Khavari, Afshin & Donald R. Rothwell, *The ICJ and the Danube Dam Case: A Missed Opportunity for International Environmental Law?*, 22 MELB. U. L. REV. 507, 534 (1998)

ALSTON, PHILIP & MARY ROBINSON EDS., HUMAN RIGHTS AND DEVELOPMENT (2005).

———— *A Third Generation of Solidarity Rights: Progressive Development or Obfuscation of International Human Rights Law?*, 29 NETH. INT'L L. REV. 307 (1985).

———— *Conjuring Up New Human Rights: A Proposal for Quality Control*, 78 AM. J. INT'L L. 607 (1984).

———— *Conjuring up New Human Rights: A Proposal for Quality Control*, 78 AM. J. INT'L L. 607 (1984) *and in* RIGHTS OF PEOPLES (James Crawford ed., 1988).

———— *Making Space for New Human Rights: The Case of the Right to Development*, HARV. HUM. RTS. Y.B. 3 (1988).

Annan, Kofi, "In Larger Freedom: Towards Development, Security and Human Rights For All", A/59/2005, *available at* http://www.un.org/.

———— "We the Peoples: The Role of the United Nations in the 21st Century" (New York, 2000), *available at* http://www.un.org/millennium/sg/report/full.htm.

Applegate, John S. & Alfred C. Aman, Jr., *Syncopated Sustainable Development*, 9 IND. J. GLOBAL LEGAL STUD. (2001).

Araujo, Robert John, *Rio+10 and the World Summit on Sustainable Development: Why Human Beings Are at the Center of Concerns*, 2 GEO. J.L. & PUB. POL'Y 201 (2004).

ASBJORN EIDE, CATARINA KRAUSE & ALLAN ROSAS EDS., ECONOMIC, SOCIAL AND CULTURAL RIGHTS (1995).

Atapattu, Sumudu, Book Review, *Evolution and Status of the Precautionary Principle in International Law, by Arie Trouwborst*, 96 AM. J. INT'L L. 1016, 1017 (2002).

———— *International Human Rights Law and Poverty Eradication*, in SUSTAIN-
ABLE JUSTICE: RECONCILING ECONOMIC, SOCIAL AND ENVIRONMENTAL
LAW, 355 (Marie-Claire Cordonier Segger & C.G. Weeramantry eds.,
2005).

———— *Sustainable Development and Terrorism: International Linkages and a Case
Study of Sri Lanka*, 30 WILLIAM & MARY ENVTL. L. & POL'Y REV. 273 (2006).

———— *Sustainable Development and the Right to Health*, in SUSTAINABLE JUS-
TICE: RECONCILING ECONOMIC, SOCIAL AND ENVIRONMENTAL LAW, 355
(Marie-Claire Cordonier Segger & C.G. Weeramantry eds., 2005).

———— *Sustainable Development, Myth or Reality?: A Survey of Sustainable
Development under International Law and Sri Lankan Law*, 14 GEO. INT'L
ENVTL. L. REV. 265, 273 (2001).

———— *The Right to a Healthy Life or the Right to Die Polluted?: The Emergence of
a Human Right to a Healthy Environment Under International Law*, 16
TULANE ENVTL. L. REV. 65 (2002).

———— *Sustainable Development, Environmental Protection, and Human Rights:
A Necessary Linkage?*, Proceedings of the Canadian Council of International Law (forthcoming).

Australian EIA Network, *International Study of the Effectiveness of Environmental Assessment*, Report of the EIA Process Strengthening Workshop,
Canberra Apr. 4–7, 1995, *available at* http://www.ea.gov.au/assess-
ments/eianet/eastudy/aprilworkshop/paper1.html.

AXELROD, REGINA S. ET AL. EDS., THE GLOBAL ENVIRONMENT: INSTITUTIONS,
LAW AND POLICY (2004).

BASLAR, KEMAL, THE CONCEPT OF THE COMMON HERITAGE OF MANKIND IN
INTERNATIONAL LAW (1998).

Bastmeijer, Kees & Ricardo Roura, *Current Development: Regulating Antarctic
Tourism and the Precautionary Principle*, 98 AM. J. INT'L L. 763.

Basu, Paroma, *Third World Bears Brunt of Global Warming Impacts*, *available at*
http://www.news.wisc.edu/11878.html.

Baxi, Upendra, *The Development of the Right to Development*, in HUMAN RIGHTS:
NEW DIMENSIONS AND CHALLENGES, 99 (Janusz Symonides ed., 1998).

Beckerman, Wilfred, *The Polluter-Pays Principle: Interpretation and Principles of
Application*, in OECD, THE POLLUTER PAYS PRINCIPLE: DEFINITION,
ANALYSIS, IMPLEMENTATION (1975).

Bernabe-Riefkohl, Alberto, *"To Dream the Impossible Dream": Globalization and
Harmonization of Environmental Laws*, 20 N.C. J. INT'L & COMP. REG. 205
(1995).

BIRNIE, PATRICIA & ALAN BOYLE, BASIC DOCUMENTS ON INTERNATIONAL LAW
AND THE ENVIRONMENT 27 (1995).

———— INTERNATIONAL LAW & THE ENVIRONMENT (2d ed. 2002).

Bisset, Ron, *Methods of Consultation and Public Participation in* ENVIRONMEN-
TAL ASSESSMENT IN DEVELOPING AND TRANSITIONAL COUNTRIES: PRIN-
CIPLES, METHODS AND PRACTICE 149, 151 (Norman Lee & Clive George
eds., 2000).

Bodansky, Daniel, *Customary (and Not so Customary) International Environmental Law*, 3 IND. J. GLOBAL LEGAL STUD. 105 (1995).

———— *New Developments in International Environmental Law*, 85 AM. SOC. INT'L L. PROC. 413, at 414 (1991).

———— *What's So Bad about Unilateral Action to Protect the Environment?*, 11 EUR. J. INT'L L. 339 (2000).

———— *The Legitimacy of International Governance: A Coming Challenge for International Environmental Law?*, 93 AM. J. INT'L L. 596 (1999).

Bostian, Ida, *Flushing the Danube: The World Court's Decision Concerning the Gabcikovo Dam*, 9 COLO. J. INT'L ENV'L L. & POL'Y 401 (1998).

Boutillon, Sonia, *The Precautionary Principle: Development of an International Standard*, 23 MICH. J. INT'L L. 429 (2002).

Boutros-Ghali, Boutros, *An Agenda for Peace*, United Nations, New York (1992) *in* SUSTAINABLE DEVELOPMENT AND GOOD GOVERNANCE 1 (Konrad Ginther et al. eds., 1995).

Boutros-Ghali, Boutros, Report on the Work of the Organization from the 46th to the 47th session of the General Assembly, UN, New York (1992), *referred to in* SUSTAINABLE DEVELOPMENT AND GOOD GOVERNANCE 1 (Konrad Ginther et al. eds., 1995).

BOYLE, ALAN & DAVID FREESTONE EDS., INTERNATIONAL LAW AND SUSTAINABLE DEVELOPMENT: PAST ACHIEVEMENTS AND FUTURE CHALLENGES (1999).

———— & MICHAEL ANDERSON EDS., HUMAN RIGHTS APPROACHES TO ENVIRONMENTAL PROTECTION (1996).

———— *Protecting the Marine Environment: Some Problems and Developments in the Law of the Sea* 16 MARINE POL'Y 79–85, 84–85 (1992).

Brock, Paige J., *A Change in the "Trade-Winds:" World Trade Organization Places Human Health Before Free-Trade*, COLO. J. INT'L ENV'L. L. & POL'Y 85 (2000).

BROWN WEISS, EDITH, IN FAIRNESS TO FUTURE GENERATIONS: INTERNATIONAL LAW, COMMON PATRIMONY AND INTERGENERATIONAL EQUITY (1989).

———— *Invoking State Responsibility in the Twenty-First Century*, 96 AM. J. INT'L L. 798 (2002).

———— *Opening the Door to the Environment and to Future Generations, in* INTERNATIONAL LAW, THE INTERNATIONAL COURT OF JUSTICE AND NUCLEAR WEAPONS, 338, at 340 (Laurence Boisson de Chazournes & Philippe Sands eds., 1999).

BROWNLIE, IAN ED., BASIC DOCUMENTS ON HUMAN RIGHTS (1992).

———— SYSTEM OF THE LAW OF NATIONS: STATE RESPONSIBILITY—PART I (1983).

———— THE RULE OF LAW IN INTERNATIONAL AFFAIRS (1998).

———— PRINCIPLES OF PUBLIC INTERNATIONAL LAW (5th ed. 1998).

*Brundtland starts new movement to address environmental crisis affecting children's health, at* http://www.who.int/mediacentre/news/releases/who66/en/.

Brunnee, Jutta, *Of Sense and Sensibility: Reflections on International Liability Regimes as Tools for Environmental Protection*, 53 ICLQ 351 (2004)

——— *The United States and International Environmental Law: Living with an Elephant*, 15 EUR. J. INT'L L. 617 (2004)

Bryner, Gary C., *Implementing Global Environmental Agreements in the Developing World*, COLO. J. INT'L ENVTL. L. Y.B. 1 (1997).

Bunn, Isabella D., *The Right to Development: Implications for International Economic Law*, 15 AM. U. INT'L L. REV. 1425 (2000).

Burger, Michael, *Bi-polar and Polycentric Approaches to Human Rights and the Environment*, 28 COLUM. J. ENVTL. L. 371 (2003).

Cameron, James et. al., *Precautionary Principle and Future Generations, in* FUTURE GENERATIONS AND INTERNATIONAL LAW 93 (Emmanuel Agius et al. eds. 1998).

Carlson, Scott N., *The Montreal Protocol's Environmental Subsidies and GATT: A Needed Reconciliation*, 29 TEX. INT'L L.J. 211 (1994).

CARSON, RACHEL, SILENT SPRING (1962).

Center for International Environmental Law, *A Comparison of Six Environmental Impact Assessment Regimes* (1995), *available at* http://www.ciel.org/publications.

Charney, Jonathan I., *Universal International Law*, 87 AM. J. INT'L L. 529 (1993).

CHEN, BIN, GENERAL PRINCIPLES OF LAW AS APPLIED BY INTERNATIONAL COURTS AND TRIBUNALS (1987).

*Children in the New Millennium: Environmental Impact on Health, available at* http://www.unep.org/ceh/.

*Children's Environmental Health, available at* http://www.who.int/ceh/en/.

CHURCHILL, ROBIN & DAVID FREESTONE EDS., INTERNATIONAL LAW AND GLOBAL CLIMATE CHANGE (1991).

Climate and Health, Fact Sheet No. 266, Dec. 2001, *available at* http://www.who.int/inf-fs/en/fact266.html.

COMMISSION FOR ENVIRONMENTAL COOPERATION, NORTH AMERICAN ENVIRONMENTAL LAW & POLICY (VOL. 4, 2000).

Communication from the Commission on the Precautionary Principle COM (2000) 1 final, Brussels, Feb. 2, 2000, *available at* http://europa.eu.int/.

CORDONIER SEGGER, MARIE-CLAIRE & C.G. WEERAMANTRY EDS., SUSTAINABLE JUSTICE: RECONCILING ECONOMIC, SOCIAL AND ENVIRONMENTAL LAW (2005).

——— & KHALFAN, ASHFAQ, SUSTAINABLE DEVELOPMENT LAW: PRINCIPLES, PRACTICES & PROSPECTS (2004).

Crawford, James et al., *The ILC's Articles on Responsibility of States for Internationally Wrongful Acts: Completion of the Second Reading*, 12 EUR. J. INT'L L. 963 (2001).

——— *The ILC's Articles on Responsibility of States for Internationally Wrongful Acts: A Retrospect*, 96 AM. J. INT'L L. 874 (2002).

———— RIGHTS OF PEOPLES (1988).

Cross, Frank B., *Paradoxical Perils of the Precautionary Principle*, 53 WASH & LEE L. REV. 851 (1996).

CULLET, PHILIPPE, DIFFERENTIAL TREATMENT IN INTERNATIONAL ENVIRON-MENTAL LAW (2003).

———— *Equity and Flexibility Mechanisms in the Climate Change Regime: Conceptual and Practical Issues*, 8 RECIEL 168 (1999).

DAMROSCH, LORI, LOUIS HENKIN, RICHARD PUGH, OSCAR SCHACHTER & HANS SMIT, INTERNATIONAL LAW: CASES AND MATERIALS 59 (4th ed. 2001)

de Chazournes, Laurence Boisson & Philippe Sands, *Introduction, in* INTERNATIONAL LAW, THE INTERNATIONAL COURT OF JUSTICE AND NUCLEAR WEAPONS 338, at 340 (Laurence Boisson de Chazournes & Philippe Sands eds., 1999).

———— & PHILIPPE SANDS EDS., INTERNATIONAL LAW, THE INTERNATIONAL COURT OF JUSTICE AND NUCLEAR WEAPONS (1999).

———— *Unilateralism and Environmental Protection: Issues of Perception and Reality of Issues*, 11 EUR. J. INT'L L. 315 (2000).

———— *The Precautionary Principle, in Precaution from Rio to Johannesburg*, Proceedings of a Geneva Environment Network Roundtable (2002).

de Sadeleer, Nicolas, *The Enforcement of the Precautionary Principle by German, French and Belgian Courts*, 9(2) RECIEL 144 (2000).

Declaration on the Tenth Anniversary of the World Summit for Social Development, Commission for Social Development, Report on the Forty Third Session, E/2005/26, E/CN.5/2005/7.

Dernbach, John C., *Achieving Sustainable Development: The Centrality and Multiple Facets of Integrated Decisionmaking*, 10 IND. J. GLOBAL. LEGAL STUD. 247 (2003).

———— *Sustainable Development as a Framework for National Governance*, 49 CASE W. RES. L. REV. 1 (1998).

———— *Symposium: Globalization and Governance: The Prospects for Democracy: Part II" Globalization, Democracy and Domestic Law: Achieving Sustainable Development: The Centrality and Multiple Facets of Integrated Decision-making,"* 10 IND. J. GLOBAL LEGAL STUD. 247 (2003).

———— *Targets, Timetables and Effecting Implementing Mechanisms: Necessary Building Blocks for Sustainable Development*, 27 WM. & MARY ENVTL. L. & POL'Y REV. 79 (2002).

DESAI, BHARAT H., INSTITUTIONALIZING INTERNATIONAL ENVIRONMENTAL LAW (2004).

Desgagne, Richard, *Integrating Environmental Values into the European Convention on Human Rights*, 89 AM. J. INT'L L. 263 (1995)

Di Leva, Charles E., *International Environmental Law and Development*, 10 GEO. INT'L ENVTL. L. REV. 501 (1998).

Diaz, Carolina Lasen, *Biotechnology and the Cartagena Protocol, in Precaution from Rio to Johannesburg*, Proceedings of a Geneva Environment Network Roundtable (2002).

Dobos, Daniel, *The Necessity of Precaution: The Future of Ecological Necessity and the Precautionary Principle*, 13 FORDHAM ENVTL. L.J. 375 (2002).

Dolzer, Rudolf, *Global Environmental Issues: The Genuine Area of Globalization*, 7 TRANSNAT'L L. & POL'Y 157 (1998).

———— *The World Bank and the Global Environment: Novel Frontiers?*, in SCHLEMMER-SCHULTE, SABINE & KO-YUNG TUNG EDS., LIBER AMICORUM IBRHIM F.I. SHIHATA: INTERNATIONAL FINANCE AND DEVELOPMENT LAW 141 (2001).

Dommen, Caroline, *Claiming Environmental Rights: Some Possibilities Offered by the United Nations' Human Rights Mechanisms*, 11 GEO. INT'L ENVTL. L. REV. 1 (1998)

Douma, Wybe Th., *The Precautionary Principle in the European Union*, 9 RECEIL 132 (2000).

Downs, Jennifer A., *A Healthy and Ecologically Balanced Environment: An Argument for a Third Generation Right*, 3 DUKE J. COMP. & INT'L L. 351 (1993).

Dupuy, Pierre Marie, Keynote Address at the Canadian Council of International Law Annual Conference, Ottawa, Oct. 2005 (to be published in the Proceedings of the Canadian Council of International Law).

———— *Soft Law and the International Law of the Environment*, 12 MICH. J. INT'L L. 420 (1991).

Dusik, Jiri ed., *Proceedings of International Workshop on Public Participation and Health Aspects in Strategic Environmental Assessment* (2000).

Eaton, Joshua, *The Nigerian Tragedy, Environmental Regulation of Transnational Corporations, and the Human Right to a Healthy Environment*, 15 B.U. INT'L L.J. 261 (1997).

Ebbesson, Jonas, *Information, Participation and Access to Justice: the Model of the Aarhus Convention*, Background Paper No. 5, Joint UNEP-OHCHR Expert Seminar on Human Rights and the Environment (2002).

*EC Measures Convening Meat and Meat Products (Hormones)*, Report of the Appellate Body, WTO, *available at* www.worldtradelaw.net/reports/wtoab/ec-hormones(ab).pdf.

Eide, Asbjorn, *The Right to an Adequate Standard of Living Including the Right to Food*, in ECONOMIC, SOCIAL AND CULTURAL RIGHTS, 89 (Asbjorn Eide, Catarina Krause & Allan Rosas eds., 1995).

Ellis, Jaye & FitzGerald Alison, *The Precautionary Principle in International Law: Lessons from Fuller's Internal Morality*, 49 MCGILL L.J. 779 (2004).

ENVIRONMENTAL PROTECTION AND SUSTAINABLE DEVELOPMENT: LEGAL PRINCIPLES AND RECOMMENDATIONS adopted by the Experts Group on Environmental Law of the World Commission on Environment and Development (R.D. Munro & J.G. Lammers eds., 1986).

EU Sustainable Development Strategy: A Test Case for Good Governance (2001), *available at* http://europa.eu.int/comm/env/forum/susdevs-tra.pdf.

European Commission, White Paper on Environmental Liability, COM (2000) 66 final, Feb. 9, 2000, *available at* http://europa.eu.int/comm/environment/liability/el_full.pdf.

Fabra, Adriana & Eva Arnal, *Review of Jurisprudence on Human Rights and the Environment in Latin America,* Background Paper No. 6, Joint UNEP-OHCHR Expert Seminar on Human Rights and the Environment (2002).

—————— *The Intersection of Human Rights and Environmental Issues: A Review of Institutional Developments at the International Level,* Background Paper No. 3, Joint UNEP-OHCHR Expert Seminar on Human Rights and the Environment (2002).

Fernando, Jude, *Rethinking Sustainable Development: Preface: The Power of Unsustainable Development: What is to be Done?,* 590 ANNALS AM. ACADEMY POL. & SOC. SCI. 6 (2003).

FIJALKOWSKI, AGATA & MALGOSIA FITZMAURICE eds, THE RIGHT OF THE CHILD TO A CLEAN ENVIRONMENT (2000).

Final Report Prepared by Mrs. Fatma Zohra Ksentini, Special Rapporteur, UN Doc. E/CN.4/Sub.2/1994/9 (1994).

FINDLEY, ROGER, DANIEL FARBER & JODY FREEMAN, CASES AND MATERIALS ON ENVIRONMENTAL LAW (6th ed. 2003).

First Progress Report Prepared by Mrs. Fatma Zohra Ksentini, Special Rapporteur, UN Doc. E/CN.4/Sub.2/1992/7 and Add. 1 (1992).

*Follow-up to Johannesburg and the Future Role of the CSD—The Implementation Track,* Report of the Secretary-General, E/CN.17/2003/2, Feb. 18, 2003.

FREESTONE, DAVID & ELLEN HEY EDS., THE PRECAUTIONARY PRINCIPLE AND INTERNATIONAL LAW: THE CHALLENGE OF IMPLEMENTATION (1996).

—————— & Ellen Hey, *Origins and Development of the Precautionary Principle, in* THE PRECAUTIONARY PRINCIPLE AND INTERNATIONAL LAW: THE CHALLENGE OF IMPLEMENTATION 13 (David Freestone & Ellen Hey eds., 1996).

—————— & T. IJLSTRA EDS., THE NORTH SEA: PERSPECTIVES ON REGIONAL ENVIRONMENTAL CO-OPERATION (1990).

—————— *Implementing Precaution Cautiously, in* DEVELOPMENTS IN INTERNATIONAL FISHERIES LAW 287, at 306 (Ellen Hey ed., 1999).

—————— *The Precautionary Principle, in* INTERNATIONAL LAW AND GLOBAL CLIMATE CHANGE 21, at 36 (Robin Churchill & David Freestone eds., 1991).

French, Duncan, *Developing States and International Environmental Law: The Importance of Differentiated Responsibilities,* 49 ICLQ 35 (2000).

Fullem, Gregory D., *The Precautionary Principle: Environmental Protection in the Face of Scientific Uncertainty,* 31 WILLAMETTE L. REV. 495 (1995).

Gaines, Sanford, *The Polluter-Pays Principle: From Economic Equity to Environmental Ethos,* 26 TEX. INT'L L.J. 463 (1991).

Ghai, Yash, *Whose Human Right to Development?*, Human Rights Unit Occasional Paper, 5–6 (Commonwealth Secretariat, Nov. 1989).

Gibson, Noralee, *The Right to a Clean Environment*, 54 SASK. L. REV. 5 (1990)

GINTHER, KONRAD, ERIK DENTERS & PAUL J.I.M. DE WAART EDS., SUSTAINABLE DEVELOPMENT AND GOOD GOVERNANCE (1995).

Globalization and its Impact on the Full Enjoyment of all Human Rights, Preliminary Report of the Secretary-General, A/55/342, 55th Session of the UN General Assembly, Aug. 31, 2000.

*Globalization and its Impact on the Full Enjoyment of Human Rights*, Progress Report Submitted by J. Oloka-Onyango and Deepika Udagama, E/CN.4/Sub.2/2001/10, Aug. 2, 2001.

GORMLEY, PAUL, HUMAN RIGHTS AND ENVIRONMENT: THE NEED FOR INTERNATIONAL CO-OPERATION (1976).

Grey, Kevin, *International Environmental Impact Assessment: Potential for a Multilateral Environmental Agreement*, 11 COLO. J. INT'L ENVTL. L. & POL'Y 83 (2000).

Guidance on Public Participation, *available at* http://www.unece.org/env/eia/publicpart_guidance.htm.

Gundling, Loather, *The Status in International Law of the Principle of Precautionary Action, in* THE NORTH SEA: PERSPECTIVES ON REGIONAL ENVIRONMENTAL CO-OPERATION, 23–30 (David Freestone & T. Ijlstra eds., 1990).

Guruswamy, Lakshman D., *Energy, Environment & Sustainable Development*, 8 CHAP. L. REV. 77 (2005).

HALVORSSEN, ANITA MARGRETHE, EQUALITY AMONG UNEQUALS IN INTERNATIONAL ENVIRONMENTAL LAW (1999).

Handl, Gunther, *Human Rights and Protection of the Environment: A Mildly "Revisionist" View, in* HUMAN RIGHTS, SUSTAINABLE DEVELOPMENT AND THE ENVIRONMENT (Antonio Trindade ed., 1992).

——— *The Legal Mandate of Multilateral Development Banks as Agents for Change Toward Sustainable Development*, 92 AM. J. INT'L L. 642.

Hans-Joachim Priess & Christian Pitschas, *Protection of Public Health and the Role of the Precautionary Principle Under WTO Law: A Trojan Horse Before Geneva's Walls?*, 24 FORDHAM INT'L L.J. 519 (2000)

HARREMOES, POUL ET AL. EDS., THE PRECAUTIONARY PRINCIPLE IN THE 20TH CENTURY (2002).

Harris, Paul, *Common But Differentiated Responsibility: The Kyoto Protocol and United States Policy*, 7 N.Y.U. ENVTL. L.J. 27 (1999).

HEY, ELLEN ED., DEVELOPMENTS IN INTERNATIONAL FISHERIES LAW (1999).

Hickey, James E. Jr. & Vern R. Walker, *Refining the Precautionary Principle in International Environmental Law*, 14 VA. ENVTL. L.J. 423 (1995).

Hodas, David, *The "Rio" Environmental Treaties Colloquium: The Climate Change Convention and Evolving Legal Models of Sustainable Development*, 13 PACE ENVTL. L. REV. 75 (1995).

Hossain, Kamal, *Evolving Principles of Sustainable Development and Good Governance, in* GINTHER, KONRAD, ERIK DENTERS & PAUL J.I.M. DE WAART EDS., SUSTAINABLE DEVELOPMENT AND GOOD GOVERNANCE 15 (1995).

*Human Rights and the Environment: The Role of Aarhus Convention,* Submission by the UN Economic Commission for Europe provided as input to the report being prepared by the Office of the High Commissioner for Human Rights pursuant to Resolution E/CN.4/RES/2003/71, Dec. 2003, *available at* http://www.unece.org/.

HUNTER, DAVID, JAMES SALZMAN & DURWOOD ZAELKE, INTERNATIONAL ENVIRONMENTAL LAW AND POLICY (2d ed. 2002).

Intergovernmental Panel on Climate Change, Climate Change 2001: Synthesis Report, Summary for Policy Makers, *available at* http://www.ipcc.ch/pub/un/syreng/spm.pdf.

International Finance Corporation, Operational Policies, OP 4.01, Oct. 1998, *at* http://www.ifc.org/enviro/EnvSoc/Safeguard/EA/ea/htm.

International Law Commission, Draft Articles on State Responsibility, *available at* http://www.un.org/law/ilc/texts/State_responsibility/responsibility_articles(e).pdf.

IUCN, *World Conservation Strategy, 1980*

———— DRAFT INTERNATIONAL COVENANT ON ENVIRONMENT AND DEVELOPMENT (2d ed. 2001).

Jackson, Donald W., *Affirmative Action in Comparative Perspective: India and the United States, in* NON-DISCRIMINATION LAW: COMPARATIVE PERSPECTIVES 249 (Titia Loenen & Peter R. Rodrigues eds., 1999).

JAYAWICKRAMA, NIHAL, THE JUDICIAL APPLICATION OF HUMAN RIGHTS, (2002).

JEWELL, TIM & JENNY STEELE, LAW IN ENVIRONMENTAL DECISION-MAKING, NATIONAL, EUROPEAN AND INTERNATIONAL PERSPECTIVES (1998).

Joint Working Paper on Trade and Environment, *The Polluter-Pays Principle as it Relates to International Trade,* COM/ENV/TD(2001)44/ FINAL.

Katz, Deborah, *The Mismatch Between the Biosafety Protocol and the Precautionary Principle,* 13 GEO. INT'L ENVTL. L. REV. 949 (2001).

Kibert, Nicole C., *Extended Producer Responsibility: A Tool for Achieving Sustainable Development,* 19 J. LAND USE & ENVTL. L. 503 (2004).

Kiss, Alexandre, *The Right to the Conservation of the Environment, in* LINKING HUMAN RIGHTS AND THE ENVIRONMENT 31, 36 (Romania Picolatti & Jorge Daniel Taillant eds., 2003).

———— & DINAH SHELTON, INTERNATIONAL ENVIRONMENTAL LAW 236–37 (3d ed. 2004).

Knox, John H., *The Myth and Reality of Transboundary Environmental Impact Assessment,* 96 AM. J. INT'L L. 291 (2002).

KUOKKANEN, TUOMAS, INTERNATIONAL LAW AND THE ENVIRONMENT: VARIATIONS ON A THEME (2002).

Lafranchi, Scott, *Surveying the Precautionary Principle's Ongoing Global*

*Development: The Evolution of an Emergent Environmental Management Tool*, 32 B.C. ENVTL. AFF. L. REV. 678 (2005).

Larson, Eric Thomas, *Why Environmental Liability Regimes in the United States, the European Community and Japan Have Grown Synonymous with the Polluter Pays Principle*, 38 VAND. J. TRANSNAT'L L. 541 (2005).

*Leading Banks Adopt Equator Principles*, available at http://equatorprinciples.ifc. org/ifcext/equatorprinciples.nsf/Content/corepoints.

Lee, John, *The Underlying Legal Theory to Support a Well-Defined Human Right to a Healthy Environment as a Principle of Customary International Law*, 25 COLUM. J. ENVTL. L. 283 (2000)

LEE, NORMAN & CLIVE GEORGE EDS., ENVIRONMENTAL ASSESSMENT IN DEVELOPING AND TRANSITIONAL COUNTRIES: PRINCIPLES, METHODS AND PRACTICE (2000).

LIN, SUN & LAL KURUKULASURIYA EDS., UNEP'S NEW WAY FORWARD: ENVIRONMENTAL LAW AND SUSTAINABLE DEVELOPMENT (1995).

Lindroos, Anja, *The Right to Development*, The Erik Castren Institute of International Law and Human Rights Research Reports 2/1999 (Helsinki, 1999).

LOENEN, TITIA & PETER R. RODRIGUES EDS., NON-DISCRIMINATION LAW: COMPARATIVE PERSPECTIVES (1999).

LOMBORG, BJORN, THE SCEPTICAL ENVIRONMENTALIST, MEASURING THE REAL STATE OF THE WORLD (2001).

Lowe, Vaughn, *Sustainable Development and Unsustainable Arguments, in* INTERNATIONAL LAW AND SUSTAINABLE DEVELOPMENT: PAST ACHIEVEMENTS AND FUTURE CHALLENGES 26 (Alan Boyle & David Freestone eds., 1999).

Magraw, Daniel Barstow, *Legal Treatment of Developing Countries: Differential, Contextual and Absolute Norms*, 1 COLO. J. INT'L ENVTL. L. & POL'Y 69 (1990).

MAHONEY, KATHLEEN E. & PAUL MAHONEY EDS., HUMAN RIGHTS IN THE TWENTY-FIRST CENTURY: A GLOBAL CHALLENGE (1993).

Malanczuk, Peter, *Sustainable Development: Some Critical Thoughts in the Light of the Rio Conference, in* GINTHER, KONRAD, ERIK DENTERS & PAUL J.I.M. DE WAART EDS., SUSTAINABLE DEVELOPMENT AND GOOD GOVERNANCE 23 (1995).

Marks, Stephen, *Emerging Human Rights: A New Generation for the 1980s?*, 33 RUTGERS L. REV. 435 (1980–81).

Marong, Alhaji B.M., *From Rio to Johannesburg: Reflections on the Role of International Legal Norms in Sustainable Development*, 16 GEO. INT'L ENVTL. L. REV. 21 (2003).

MARR, SIMON, THE PRECAUTIONARY PRINCIPLE IN THE LAW OF THE SEA: MODERN DECISION MAKING IN INTERNATIONAL LAW (2003).

Marr, Simon, *The Southern Bluefin Tuna Cases: The Precautionary Approach and Conservation and Management of Fish Resources*, 11 EUR. J. INT'L L. 815–831 (2000).

Matthee, Marielle D., *Greenpeace v. France, Case 6/99 (Genetically Modified Maize Case)*, 9(2) RECIEL 192 (2000).

Mayeda, Graham, *Where Should Johannesburg Take Us? Ethical and Legal Approaches to Sustainable Development in the Context of International Environmental Law*, 15 COLO. J. INT'L ENVTL. L. & POL'Y 29 (2004).

McCloskey, Michael, *The Emperor has no Clothes: The Conundrum of Sustainable Development*, 9 DUKE ENVTL. L. & POL'Y F. 153 (1999).

*MEA Database: Matrix on Trade Measures Pursuant to Selected Multilateral Environmental Agreements (MEAs), available at* http://www.wto.org/english/tratop_e/envir_e/mea_database_e.htm.

Meeting of the Parties to the Convention on Environmental Impact Assessment in a Transboundary Context, ECE/MP.EIA/6, Sept. 13, 2004. Decision III/17, *available at* http://www.unece.org/env/eia/amendkjet2.html.

Moore, John L., *Cost-Benefit Analysis: Issues in its Use in Regulation*, CRS Report for Congress, 1995, *available at* http://www.ncseonline.org/NLE/CRSreports/Risk/rsk-4.cfm?&CFID=46274&CFTOKEN.

Nanda, Ved P., *Sustainable Development, International Trade and the Doha Agenda for Development*, 8 CHAP. L. REV. 53 (2005).

Nash, Jonathan Remy, *Too Much Market? Conflict Between Tradable Pollution Allowances and the "Polluter Pays" Principle*, 24 HARV. ENVTL. L. REV. 465 (2000).

Nherere, Pearson, *Conditionality, Human Rights and Good Governance: A Dialogue of Unequal Partners, in* GINTHER, KONRAD, ERIK DENTERS & PAUL J.I.M. DE WAART EDS., SUSTAINABLE DEVELOPMENT AND GOOD GOVERNANCE 289 (1995).

Note Prepared by Mrs. Fatma Zohra Ksentini pursuant to Sub-Commission decision 1989/108, UN Doc. E/CN.4/Sub.2/1990/12 (1990).

OBERTHUR, SEBASTIAN & HERMANN E. OTT, THE KYOTO PROTOCOL: INTERNATIONAL CLIMATE POLICY FOR THE 21ST CENTURY (1999).

OECD, THE POLLUTER PAYS PRINCIPLE: DEFINITION, ANALYSIS, IMPLEMENTATION (1975).

OECD, *The Polluter-Pays Principle: Note on the Implementation of the Polluter-Pays Principle* (1974).

Oloka-Onyango, Joe, *Human Rights and Sustainable Development in Contemporary Africa: A New Dawn, or Retreating Horizons?*, 6 BUFF. HUM. RTS. L. REV. 39 (2000).

OUR COMMON FUTURE, REPORT OF THE WORLD COMMISSION ON ENVIRONMENT AND DEVELOPMENT (1987).

Pallemaerts, Marc, *International Environmental Law From Stockholm to Rio: Back to the Future? in* GREENING INTERNATIONAL LAW 1, 5 (Philippe Sands ed., 1994).

———— *The Future of Environmental Regulation: International Environmental Law in the Age of Sustainable Development: A Critical Assessment of the UNCED Process*, 15 J. L. & COM. 623 (1996).

Palmer, Geoffrey, *New Ways to Make International Law*, 86 AM. J. INT'L L. 259 (1992).

Paul, James C.N., *The United Nations Family: Challenges of Law and Development: The United Nations and the Creation of an International Law of Development*, 36 HARV. INT'L L.J. 307 (1995).

Pearson, Charles S., *Testing the System: GATT+PPP=?*, 27 CORNELL INT'L L.J. 553 (1994).

Petkova, Elena & Peter Veit, *Environmental Accountability Beyond the Nation-State: The Implications of the Aarhus Convention*, *available at* http://www.wri.org/ governance/publications.html.

PICOLATTI, ROMANIA & JORGE DANIEL TAILLANT EDS., LINKING HUMAN RIGHTS AND THE ENVIRONMENT (2003).

Pimentel, David et al., *Will Limits of the Earth's Resources Control Human Numbers?*, Cornell University (1999), *available at* http://dieoff.org/page174.htm.

Popiel, Brian, *From Customary Law to Environmental Impact Assessment: A New Approach to Avoiding Transboundary Environmental Damage Between Canada and the United States*, 22 B.C. ENVTL. AFF. L. REV. 95 (1995).

Popovic, Neil, *In Pursuit of Environmental Human Rights: Commentary on the Draft Declaration of Principles on Human Rights and the Environment*, 27 COLUM. HUM. RTS. L. REV. 487 (1996).

Porras, Ileana, *The Rio Declaration: A New Basis for International Cooperation*, *in* PHILIPPE SANDS, GREENING INTERNATIONAL LAW 20, at 29 (1994).

Preliminary Report Prepared by Mrs. Fatma Zohra Ksentini, Special Rapporteur, UN Doc. E/CN.4/Sub.2/1991/8 (1991).

Pring, George (Rock), *The 2002 Johannesburg World Summit on Sustainable Development: International Environmental Law Collides with Reality, Turning Jo'Burg Into Joke'Burg*, 30 DENV. J. INT'L L. & POL'Y 410 (2002).

*Public Participation in Making Local Environmental Decisions*, The Aarhus Convention Newcastle Workshop, Good Practice Handbook (2000), *available at* http://www.unece.org/env/pp/ecases/handbook.pdf/.

Rajamani, Lavanya, *The Principle of Common but Differentiated Responsibility and the Balance of Commitments under the Climate Regime*, 9(2) RECIEL 120 (2000).

Razzaque, Jona *The Environment: The National Experience in South Asia and Africa*, Background Paper No. 4, Joint UNEP-OHCHR Expert Seminar on Human Rights and the Environment (2002).

Report of a Consultation on Sustainable Development: The Challenge to International Law, convened by the Foundation for International Environmental Law and Development (FIELD), 2:4 RECIEL r1, r5 (1993).

Report of the Expert Group Meeting on Identification of Principles of International Law for Sustainable Development, Geneva, September 1995 and prepared by the Division for Sustainable Development for the Commission on Sustainable Development, 4th session, 1996, *available at* http://www.un.org/gopher-data/esc/cn17/1996/background/law.txt.

Report of the Working Group on the Right to Development on its Sixth Session, E/CN.4/2005/25, Mar. 3, 2005.

Rich, Ronald, *The Right to Development as an Emerging Human Right*, 23 VA. J. INT'L L. 287 (1983).

*Rio Declaration on Environment and Development: Application and Implementation*, Report of the Secretary-General, Commission on Sustainable Development, 5th Session, E/CN.17/1997/8, Feb. 10, 1997.

Rischitelli, Gary, *Developing a Global Right to Know*, 2 ILSA J. INT'L & COMP. L. (1995).

Robinson, Nicholas A., *The 1991 Bellagio Conference on US-USSR Environmental Protection Institution: International Trends in Environmental Impact Assessment*, 19 B.C. ENVTL. AFF. L. REV. 591 (1992).

———— *Legal Structure and Sustainable Development: Comparative Environmental Law Perspectives on Legal Regimes for Sustainable Development*, 3 WID. L. SYMP. J. 247 (1998).

Roch, Philippe & Franz Zaver Perrez, *International Environmental Governance: The Strive Towards a Comprehensive, Coherent, Effective and Efficient International Environmental Regime*, 16 COLO. J. INT'L ENVTL. L. & POL'Y 1 (2005).

ROLEN, MATS ET AL. EDS., INTERNATIONAL GOVERNANCE ON ENVIRONMENTAL ISSUES (1997).

Rosas, Allan *So-called Rights of the Third Generation in* ECONOMIC, SOCIAL AND CULTURAL RIGHTS 244 (Asbjorn Eide, Catarina Krause & Allan Rosas eds., 1995).

Ruessmann, Laurent A., *Reflections on the WTO Doha Ministerial: Conference: Putting the Precautionary Principle in Its Place: Parameters for the Proper Application of a Precautionary Approach and the Implications for Developing Countries in Light of the Doha WTO Ministerial*, 17 AM. U. INT'L L. REV. 905 (2002).

Sachs, Albie, *Enforcing Socio-Economic Rights, in* SUSTAINABLE JUSTICE: RECONCILING ECONOMIC, SOCIAL AND ENVIRONMENTAL LAW, 355 (Marie-Claire Cordonier Segger & C.G. Weeramantry eds., 2005)

SAND, PETER H., LESSONS LEARNED IN GLOBAL ENVIRONMENTAL GOVERNANCE (1990).

———— *The Precautionary Principle: A European Perspective*, 6 HUM. & ECOL. RISK ASSESSMENT 445–458 (2000).

SANDS, PHILIPPE ED., GREENING INTERNATIONAL LAW (1994).

———— *"Greening" of International Law: Emerging Principles and Rules*, 1 IND. J. GLOBAL LEGAL STUD. 293 (1994).

———— CHENOBYL: LAW AND COMMUNICATION (1988).

———— *International Courts and the Precautionary Principle, in Precaution from*

*Rio to Johannesburg,* Proceedings of a Geneva Environment Network Roundtable (2002).

———— *International Environmental Law: An Introductory Overview, in* GREENING INTERNATIONAL LAW (Philippe Sands ed., 1994)

———— *International Environmental Litigation and its Future,* 32 U. RICH. L. REV. 1619 (1999).

———— *International Law in the Field of Sustainable Development,* 65 BRIT. Y.B. INT'L L. 303 (1994).

———— PRINCIPLES OF INTERNATIONAL ENVIRONMENTAL LAW (2d ed. 2002).

Sathkunanathan, Ambika, *Bribery and Corruption, in* SRI LANKA: STATE OF HUMAN RIGHTS 2001 (Law & Society Trust, Colombo, 2001).

Saunders, Peter, *Use and Abuse of the Precautionary Principle, available at* http://www. ratical.org/co-globalize/MaeWanHo/PrecautionP.html.

Schachter, Oscar, *United Nations Law,* 88 AM. J. INT'L L. 1 (1994)

SCHLEMMER-SCHULTE, SABINE & KO-YUNG TUNG EDS., LIBER AMICORUM IBRHIM F.I. SHIHATA: INTERNATIONAL FINANCE AND DEVELOPMENT LAW (2001).

Schorn, Timothy, *Drinkable Water and Breathable Air: A Livable Environment as a Human Right,* 4 GREAT PLAINS NAT. RES. J. 121 (2000).

Schultz, Jennifer, *The GATT/WTO Committee on Trade and the Environment— Toward Environmental Reform,* 89 AM. J. INT'L L. 423 (1995).

Schwarzenberger, Georg, *Equity in International Law,* Y.B. WORLD AFF. 346, 357 (1972).

Scott, Shirley V., *How Cautious is Precautious? Antarctic Tourism and the Precautionary Principle,* 50 ICLQ 953 (2001).

Second Progress Report Prepared by Mrs. Fatma Zohra Ksentini, Special Rapporteur, UN Doc. E/CN.4/Sub.2/1993/7 (1993).

Shelton, Dinah, *Human Rights and Environment Issues in Multilateral Treaties Adopted Between 1991 and 2001,* Background Paper No. 1, Joint UNEP-OHCHR Expert Seminar on Human Rights and the Environment (2002).

———— *Human Rights and the Environment: Jurisprudence of Human Rights Bodies,* Background Paper No. 2, Joint UNEP-OHCHR Expert Seminar on Human Rights and the Environment (2002).

———— *Human Rights, Environmental Rights and Right to Environment,* 28 STAN. J. INT'L L. 103 (1991).

———— *Human Rights, Health & Environmental Protection: Linkages in Law & Practice,* A Background paper for the World Health Organization (2002).

———— *International Decisions: Decision Regarding Communication 155/96 (Social and Economic Rights Action Center/Center for Economic and Social Rights v. Nigeria). Case No. ACHPR/COMM/A044/1, at* http://www.umn.edu/humanrts/africa/comcases/allcases.html African Commission on Human and People's Rights, May 27, 2002, *reprinted in* 96 AM. J. INT'L L. 937 (2002).

———— Symposium: Globalization & the Erosion of Sovereignty in Honor of Professor Lichtenstein: *Protecting Human Rights in a Globalized World*, 25 B.C. INT'L & COMP. L. REV. 273 (2002).

———— *What Happened in Rio to Human Rights?*, 3 Y.B. INT'L ENVTL. L. 75 (1992)

Shue, Henry, *Global Environment and International Inequality*, 75(3) INT'L AFFAIRS 531 (July 1999).

Silveira, Mary Pat Williams, *International Legal Instruments and Sustainable Development: Principles, Requirements, and Restructuring*, 31 WILLAMETTE L. REV. 239 (1995).

SIPRI YEARBOOK 2003: ARMAMENTS, DISARMAMANET & INTERNATIONAL SECURITY (2003).

Sonia Boutillon, *The Precautionary Principle: Development of an International Standard*, 23 MICH. J. INT'L L. 429 (2002).

Sripati, Vijayashri, *Toward Fifty Years of Constitutionalism and Fundamental Rights in India: Looking Back to See Ahead (1950–2000)*, 14 AM. U. INT'L L. REV. 413 (1998).

Stevens, Candice, *Interpreting The Polluter Pays Principle In The Trade And Environment Context*, 27 CORNELL INT'L L.J. 577 (1994).

Stone, Christopher D., *Common but Differentiated Responsibilities in International Law*, 98 AM. J. INT'L L. 276 (2004).

SYMONIDES, JANUSZ ED., HUMAN RIGHTS: NEW DIMENSIONS AND CHALLENGES (1998).

Symposium on Trade and Sustainable Development held in Oct. 2005.

*Symposium: Assessing the Work of the International Law Commission on State Responsibility*, 13 EUR. J. INT'L L. 1053 (2002).

Tabb, William Murray, *Environmental Impact Assessment in the European Community: Shaping International Norms*, 73 TUL. L. REV. 923 (1999).

Taillant, Jorge Daniel, *A Rights-based Approach to Analysing International Financial Institutions*, in SUSTAINABLE JUSTICE: RECONCILING ECONOMIC, SOCIAL AND ENVIRONMENTAL LAW, 355 (Marie-Claire Cordonier Segger & C.G. Weeramantry eds., 2005).

Tarlock, Dan, *Ideas without Institutions: The Paradox of Sustainable Development*, 9 IND. J. GLOBAL LEGAL STUD. (2001).

Taylor, Prudence E., *From Environmental to Ecological human Rights: A New Dynamic in International Law?* 10 GEO. INT'L ENVTL. L. REV. 309 (1998).

Taylor, Prudence, *Testing Times for the World Court: Judicial Process and the 1995 French Nuclear Tests Case*, 8 COLO. J. INT'L ENVTL. L. & POL'Y 199 (1997).

———— AN ECOLOGICAL APPROACH TO INTERNATIONAL LAW: RESPONDING TO CHALLENGES OF CLIMATE CHANGE (1998).

*The Relationship Between Trade and MEAs, available at* http://www.wto.org/english/tratop_e/envir_e/envir_backgrnd_e/c5s1_e.htm.

Third report of the Independent Expert on the Right to Development, Mr.

Arjun Sengupta, submitted in accordance with Commission resolution 2000/5, E/CN.4/2001/WG.18/2, Jan. 2, 2001.

Third World Network, *International Environmental Governance: Some Issues from a Developing Country Perspective*, Working Paper, Sept. 2001, *available at* http://www.twnside.org.sg/title/iefg.htm.

Thornton, Justine & Stephen Tromans, *Human Rights and Environmental Wrongs: Incorporating the European Convention on Human Rights: Some Thoughts on the Consequences for UK Environmental Law*, 11 J. ENVTL. L. 35–58 (1999).

TICKNER, JOEL, CAROLYN RAFFENSPERGER & NANCY MYERS, THE PRECAUTIONARY PRINCIPLE IN ACTION: A HANDBOOK (1st ed. 1999).

Tolentino, Amado S., *Good Governance through Popular Participation in Sustainable Development, in* KONRAD GINTER ET AL. EDS., SUSTAINABLE DEVELOPMENT AND GOOD GOVERNANCE 137 (1995).

Tomasevski, Katrina, *Health Rights in* ECONOMIC, SOCIAL AND CULTURAL RIGHTS, 125 (Asbjorn Eide, Catarina Krause & Allan Rosas eds., 1995).

TOMUSCHAT, CHRISTIAN, HUMAN RIGHTS BETWEEN IDEALISM AND REALISM (2003).

TRINDADE, ANTONIO ED., HUMAN RIGHTS, SUSTAINABLE DEVELOPMENT AND THE ENVIRONMENT (1992).

———— HUMAN RIGHTS, SUSTAINABLE DEVELOPMENT AND THE ENVIRONMENT (2d ed. 1995).

TROUWBORST, ARIE, EVOLUTION AND STATUS OF THE PRECAUTIONARY PRINCIPLE IN INTERNATIONAL LAW (2002).

Tung, Ko-Yung, *Sustainable Development and the Global Role of International Financial Institutes, in* SUSTAINABLE JUSTICE: RECONCILING ECONOMIC, SOCIAL AND ENVIRONMENTAL LAW 355 (Marie-Claire Cordonier Segger & C.G. Weeramantry eds., 2005).

Turlock, Dan, *Ideas Without Institutions: The Paradox of Sustainable Development*, 9 IND. J. GLOBAL LEGAL STUD. (2001).

Uhlmann, Eva M. Kornicker, *State Community Interests, Jus Cogens and Protection of the Global Environment: Developing Criteria for Peremptory Norms*, 11 GEO. INT'L ENVTL. L. REV. 101 (1998).

UN Economic Commission for Europe, *Guidance on Public Participation in Environmental Impact Assessment in a Transboundary Context*, Decision III/8, ECE/MP.EIA/6, Feb. 2001, *available at* http://www.unece.org/env/eia/publicpart_guidance.htm.

UNDP, HUMAN DEVELOPMENT REPORT (2005).

UNEP, *From Globalization to Sustainable Development: UNEP's work on Trade, Economics, and Sustainable Development*, Background Paper No.1, submitted by UNEP to the Commission on Sustainable Development, DESA/DSD/PC4/BP1.

———— *Understanding Environment, Conflict and Cooperation* (2004), *available at* http://www.unep.org/PDF//ECC.pdf.

United Nations Press Release: *Donors Must Meet International Responsibilities to Survivors of South Asia Earthquake, UN Experts Warn*, Nov. 21, 2005, *available at* http://www.unhchr.ch/huricane/huricane.nsf/view01/F6B122567B509E1CC1257 0C1003245AD?

U.S. Comments to the Right to Development Working Group (Feb. 25–Mar. 8, 2002), *at* http://www.state.gov/s/1/38654.htm.

U.S. Environmental Protection Agency, Acid Rain, *at* http://www.epa.gov/airmarkets/acidrain/index.html.

Vanclay, Frank, *International Principles for Social Impact Assessment*, 21 IMPACT ASSESSMENT & PROJECT APPRAISAL (Mar. 2003).

———— *Social Impact Assessment in* ENVIRONMENTAL ASSESSMENT IN DEVELOPING AND TRANSITIONAL COUNTRIES 125 (N. Lee & C. George eds., 2000).

Verhoosel, Gaetan, *Beyond the Unsustainable Rhetoric of Sustainable Development: Transferring Environmentally Sound Technologies*, 11 GEO. INT'L ENVTL. L. REV. 49 (1998).

Vig, Norman J., *Introduction: Governing the International Environment, in* THE GLOBAL ENVIRONMENT: INSTITUTIONS, LAW AND POLICY 6 (Regina S. Axelrod et al. eds., 2004).

Wadrzyk, Mark E., *Is It Appropriate for the World Bank to Promote Democratic Standards in a Borrower Country?* 17 WIS. INT'L L.J. 553 (1999).

Wahlstrom, Bo, *Precaution and the Stockholm Convention, in Precaution from Rio to Johannesburg*, Proceedings of a Geneva Environment Network Roundtable (2002).

Weeramantry, Christopher, *Right to Development*, 25 INDIAN J. INT'L L. 482 (1985).

WEHAB Working Group (Aug. 2002).

Weisslitz, Michael, *Rethinking the Equitable Principle of Common but Differentiated Responsibility: Differential Versus Absolute Norms of Compliance and Contribution in the Global Climate Change Context*, 13 COLO. J. INT'L ENVTL. L. & POL'Y 473 (2002).

Werksman, Jacob, *Greening Bretton Woods, in* GREENING INTERNATIONAL LAW 65 (PHILIPPE SANDS ED., 1994).

Wiener, Jonathan B. & Michael D. Rogers, *Comparing Precaution in the United States and Europe*, 5(4) J. RISK RESEARCH 317 (2002).

WILDAVSKY, AARON, BUT IS IT TRUE? (1995).

Wilson, Marion, *The New Frontier in Sustainable Development: World Summit on Sustainable Development Type II Partnerships*, 36 VICTORIA U. WELLINGTON L. REV. 389 (2005).

Winter, Ryan L., *Reconciling the GATT and WTO with Multilateral Environmental Agreements: Can We Have Our Cake and Eat it Too?*, 11 COLO. J. INT'L ENVTL. L. & POL'Y 223 (2000).

Wirth, David, *The Rio Declaration on Environment and Development: Two Steps Forward and One Back or Vice Versa?*, 29 GA. L. REV. 599 (1995).

Wolfe, Karrie, *Greening the International Human Rights Sphere? Environmental Rights and the Draft Declaration of Principles on Human Rights and the Environment*, 9 APPEAL: REV. CURRENT L. & L. REF. 45 (2003).

WOOD, CHRISTOPHER, ENVIRONMENTAL IMPACT ASSESSMENT: A COMPARATIVE REVIEW (1995).

—— *Environmental Impact Assessment in Developing Countries: An Overview*, Conference on New Directions in Impact Assessment for Development: Methods and Practice, Nov. 24–25, 2003.

World Bank Operational Manual, Operational Directive—Poverty Reduction (OD 4.15, Dec. 1991).

—— Operational Manual, Operational Policies, Environmental Assessment OP 4.01 (Jan. 1999).

—— *Focus on Sustainability 2004* (2004) *available at* http://Inweb18.worldbank.org/ESSD/sdvext.nsf.

—— *Globalization, Growth, and Poverty: Building an Inclusive World Economy*, A World Bank Policy Research Report (2002) *available at* www.econ.worldbank.org/.

—— *Johannesburg and Beyond: An Agenda for Action* (2002).

—— *Making Sustainable Commitments: An Environment Strategy for the World Bank* (2001).

—— Sustainable Development (ESSD) Vice Presidency, Reference Guide.

—— *Sustainable Development in the 21st Century, available at* http://Inweb18.worldbank.org/ESSD/sdvext.nsf.

—— *World Development Report 2000/2001: Attacking Poverty, available at* http://web.worldbank.org/WBSITE/EXTERNAL/TOPICS/EXTPOVERTY/.

Yeater, Marceil & Lal Kurukulasuriya, *Environmental Impact Assessment Legislation in Developing Countries, in* UNEP'S NEW WAY FORWARD: ENVIRONMENTAL LAW AND SUSTAINABLE DEVELOPMENT 257, at 261 (Sun Lin & Lal Kurukulasuriya eds., 1995).

Yu, Vice, *Special and Differential Treatment (SDT) and Common but Differentiated Responsibility (CDR): Principles in Favor of Developing and LDS Countries in the Trade and Environment Negotiations, at* http://www.tradeobservatory.org/library.cfm?reflD=25707.

Yu, Vicente Paolo B. III, *Briefing Paper on the WTO Committee on Trade and Environment* (2002), *available at* http://www.tradeobservatory.org/library.cfm?reflD=25583.

# TABLE OF TREATIES AND INTERNATIONAL INSTRUMENTS

## Treaties and Other Binding Instruments

**1934**

Convention Relative to the Preservation of Fauna and Flora in their Natural State, 172 LNTS 241, signed November 8, 1933, entered into force January 14, 1934

**1945**

United Nations Charter, *reprinted in* INTERNATIONAL INSTRUMENTS OF THE UNITED NATIONS 405 (Irving Sarnoff ed., 1997), *available at* http://www.un.org/aboutun/charter/

Statute of the International Court of Justice, *reprinted in* INTERNATIONAL INSTRUMENTS OF THE UNITED NATIONS 419 (Irving Sarnoff ed., 1997), *available at* http://www.icj-cij.org/icjwww/ibasicdocuments/ibasictext/ibasic-statute.htm

**1946**

International Convention for the Regulation of Whaling, 161 UNTS 72, 10 UST 952, signed December 2, 1946, entered into force November 10, 1948

**1947**

General Agreement on Tariff and Trade (GATT), 55 UNTS 194, signed October 30, 1947, *available at* http://www.wto.org

**1952**

International Convention of the High Seas Fisheries of the North Pacific, *available at* http://www.oceanlaw.net/texts/nphs.htm (The Convention was replaced by the Convention for the Conservation of Anadromous Stocks in the North Pacific Ocean in 1992, 205 UNTS 65, signed February 11, 1992, entered into force February 16, 1993, *available at* http://www.oceanlaw.net/texts/npas.htm

**1954**

International Convention for the Prevention of Pollution of the Sea by Oil, 327 UNTS 3, signed May 12, 1954, entered into force July 26, 1958

**1958**

Convention Concerning Fishing in the Waters of the Danube, 339 UNTS 23, signed January 29, 1958, entered into force December 20, 1958

**1963**

Treaty Banning Nuclear Weapon Tests in the Atmosphere, in Outer Space and under Water, 480 UNTS 43, signed August 5, 1963, entered into force October 10, 1963

**1966**

International Covenant on Civil and Political Rights, *reprinted in* INTERNATIONAL INSTRUMENTS OF THE UNITED NATIONS 93 (Irving Sarnoff ed., 1997), *available at* http://www.unhchr.org

International Covenant on Economic, Social and Cultural Rights, *reprinted in* INTERNATIONAL INSTRUMENTS OF THE UNITED NATIONS 88 (Irving Sarnoff ed., 1997), *available at* http://www.unhchr.org

First Optional Protocol to the ICCPR, GA Res. 2200A (XXI), December 16, 1966, entered into force March 23, 1976, *reprinted in* INTERNATIONAL INSTRUMENTS OF THE UNITED NATIONS 101 (Irving Sarnoff ed., 1997), *available at* http://www.ohchr.org/english/law/ccpr-one.htm

Convention on Fishing and Conservation of the Living Resources of the High Sea, 559 UNTS 285, signed April 29, 1958, entered into force March 20, 1966

**1969**

Vienna Convention on the Law of Treaties, 8 ILM 679, 1155 UNTS 331, signed May 23, 1969, entered into force January 27, 1980, *available at* http://www.taiwandocuments.org/vienna01.htm

**1972**

Convention for the Protection of World Cultural and Natural Heritage, 11 ILM 1358 (1972), signed in 1972 under the auspices of UNESCO, *available at* http://www.wcmc.org.uk/igcmc/convent/ wh/wh_atls.html

Convention for the Prevention of Marine Pollution by Dumping from Ships and Aircraft, 932 UNTS 3, signed February 15, 1972, entered into force April 7, 1974

Convention on the Preservation of Marine Pollution by Dumping of Wastes and Other Matter, 1046 UNTS 120, signed December 29, 1972, entered into force August 30, 1975.

## 1973

Convention to Regulate International Trade in Endangered Species of Flora and Fauna (CITES), 12 ILM 1085 (1973), entered into force July 1, 1975

Convention on the Conservation of Migratory Species of Wild Animals, 19 ILM 15 (1980)

## 1976

Convention for the Protection of the Marine Environment and the Coastal Region of the Mediterranean, 15 ILM 290 (1976), formerly known as the Barcelona Convention, amended extensively (including the name), signed on February 16, 1976, entered into force February 12, 1978, *available at* http://www.oceanlaw.net/texts/unepmap.htm and www.unep.ch/region-alseas/

## 1977

Convention on the Prohibition of Military or other Hostile use of Environmental Modifications Techniques (ENMOD Convention), 1108 UNTS 151 (1977), signed May 18, 1977, entered into force October 5, 1978

Protocol I Additional to the Geneva Conventions of 12 August 1949 and Relating to the Protection of Victims of International Armed Conflicts, December 12, 1977, 16 ILM 1391 (1977), 1125 UNTS 3, signed June 8, 1977, entered into force December 7, 1978

## 1979

Geneva Convention on the Long-Range Transboundary Air Pollution, 18 ILM 1442 (1979), 1302 UNTS 217, *available at* http://www.unece.org/env/lrtap

Convention on the Elimination of All Forms of Discrimination Against Women, *available at* http://www.unhchr.ch/

## 1981

African Charter on Human and People's Rights, 21 ILM 58 (1982), signed June 27, 1981, entered into force October 21, 1986, *reprinted in* BASIC DOCUMENTS ON HUMAN RIGHTS 557 (Ian Brownlie ed., 1992), *available at* http://www.unhchr.org/docs/Banjul/afrhr.html

## 1982
UN Convention on the Law of the Sea, 21 ILM 1261 (1982), 1833 UNTS 3, *available at* http://www.un.org/Depts/los/index.htm

## 1985
Vienna Convention for the Protection of the Ozone Layer (1985), 26 ILM 1529 (1995), 1513 UNTS 293, signed March 22, 1985, entered into force September 22, 1988

Association of South East Asian Nations Agreement on the Conservation of Nature and Natural Resources (ASEAN), signed July 9, 1985, 15 EPL 64 (1985)

European Community Directive on Environmental Assessment, Council Directive of 27 June 1985 on the Assessment of the Effects of Certain Public and Private Projects on the Environment, 85/337/EEC, of 1985 amended by directive 97/11/EC adopted in 1997, *available at* http://europa.eu.int/comm/environment/eia/full-legal-text/85337.htm

## 1986
Convention for the Protection of the Natural Resources and Environment of the South Pacific Region (Noumea Convention), 26 ILM 38 (1987), signed November 25, 1986, entered into force August 22, 1990

Convention on Early Notification of a Nuclear Accident, entered into force October 27, 1986, 25 ILM 1370 (1986), signed September 26, 1986, entered into force October 27, 1986, *available at* http://www.iaea.org/Publications/Documents/Infcircs/Others/inf335.shtml

Convention on Assistance in the Case of a Nuclear Accident or Radiological Emergency, 25 ILM 1377 (1986), signed September 26, 1986, entered into force February 26, 1987, *available at* http://www.iaea.org/Publications/Documents/Infcircs/Others/inf336.shtml

## 1987
Montreal Protocol on Substances that Deplete the Ozone Layer (1987), 26 ILM 1541 (1987), 1522 UNTS 3, signed September 16, 1987, entered into force January 1, 1989, *available at* http://www.unep.org/ozone/index.html (amended several times since its adoption)

## 1988
Additional Protocol to the American Convention on Human Rights in the Area of Economic, Social and Cultural Rights (Protocol of San Salvador), 28 ILM 156, November 14, 1988

Protocol Concerning the Control of Nitrogen Oxides or their Transboundary Fluxes, entered into force February 14, 1991

### 1989
Basel Convention on the Control of Transboundary Movements of Hazardous Wastes and Their Disposal, 1673 UNTS 57, signed in Mar. 22, 1989, entered into force May 5, 1992, *available at* http://www.basel.int./

Convention on the Rights of the Child, *available at* http://www.unhchr.org

ILO Convention No. 169 Concerning Indigenous and Tribal Peoples in Independent Countries, entered into force September 5, 1991, *available at* http://www.unhchr.ch/html/menu3/b/62.htm

### 1990
London Amendments to the Montreal Protocol on Substances that Deplete the Ozone Layer, UNEP/Oz.L.Pro.2/3, signed, June 29, 1990, entered into force August 10, 1992

### 1991
Convention on Environmental Impact Assessment in a Transboundary Context, 30 ILM 800 (1991)

Protocol on Environmental Protection to the Antarctic Treaty, 30 ILM 1461, entered into force January 14, 1998

Protocol Concerning the Control of Emissions of Volatile Organic Compounds or Their Transboundary Fluxes, signed November 1991, entered into force September 29, 1997, *available at* http://www.unece.org/env/lrtap/vola_h1.htm

### 1992
UN Framework Convention on Climate Change, 31 ILM 849 (1992), 1771 UNTS 107, signed May 9, 1992, entered into force March 21, 1994, *available at* http://www.unfccc.ed/

UN Convention on Biological Diversity, 31 ILM 822 (1992), 1760 UNTS 79, signed June 5, 1992, entered into force December 29, 1993, *available at* http://www.biodiv.org/

Convention on the Protection and Use of Transboundary Watercourses and International Lakes, 31 ILM 1312 (1992), signed March 17, 1992, entered into force October 6, 1996, *available at* www.unece.org/env/water/

Convention for the Protection of the Marine Environment of the North-East Atlantic (OSPAR), 32 ILM 1068 (1993), signed September 22, 1992, entered into force March 25, 1998, *available at* http://www.ospar.org

UNECE Convention on the Transboundary Effects of Industrial Accidents, 31 ILM 1330 (1992), signed March 17, 1992, entered into force April 19, 2000, *available at* http://www.unece.org/env/teia/text.htm

Convention on the Protection of the Marine Environment of the Baltic Sea Area, signed April 9, 1992, entered into force January 17, 2000, *available at* http://www.helcom.fi/Convention/en_GB/text/

Maastricht Treaty on European Union, *available at* http://www.eurotreaties. com/maastrichtext.html

### 1993
Convention for the Conservation of Southern Bluefin Tuna, 1819 UNTS 360, signed May 10, 1993, entered into force May 30, 1994

### 1994
United Nations Convention to Combat Desertification in Countries Experiencing Serious Drought and/or Desertification, Particularly in Africa, 33 ILM 1328 (1994), 1954 UNTS 3, signed October 14, 1994; entered into force December 26, 1996

Protocol to the 1979 Convention on Long-Range Transboundary Air Pollution on Further Reduction of Sulphur Emissions (Oslo Protocol), 33 ILM 1540 (1995), signed June 14, 1994, entered into force August 5, 1998

Agreement Establishing the World Trade Organization, *available at* http:// www.wto.org

Agreement on Trade-Related Aspects of Intellectual Property Rights (TRIPS Agreement), *available at* http://www.wto.org/english/tratop_e/ trips_e/t_agm0_e.htm

Agreement on the Application of Sanitary and Phytosanitary Measures (SPS Agreement), *available at* http://www.wto.org/

Agreement on Subsidies and Countervailing Measures, *available at* http:// www.wto.org/

Agreement on Agriculture, *available at* http://www.wto.org

North American Agreement on Environmental Cooperation, signed 1993, *available at* http://www.cec.org/pubs_info_resources/law_treat_agree/ naaec/ index.cfm?varlan=english

### 1995
United Nations Conference on Straddling Fish Stocks and Highly Migratory Fish Stocks: Agreement for the Implementation of the Provisions of

the United Nations Convention of the Law of the Sea of 10 December 1982, Relating to the Conservation and Management of Straddling Fish Stocks and High Migratory Fish Stocks, UN Doc. A/CONF.164/37, *reprinted in* 34 ILM 1542 (1995), signed August 4, 1995, entered into force December 11, 2001

## 1996

Protocol to the Convention on the Prevention of Marine Pollution by Dumping of Wastes and other Matter, 36 ILM 1 (1997), signed November 7, 1996, *available at* http://www.londonconvention.org and http://www.imo.org

## 1997

UN Convention on the Law of the Non-Navigational Uses of International Watercourses, UN Doc. A/51/1869, *reprinted in* 36 ILM 700 (1997), signed May 21, 1997

Kyoto Protocol, FCCC/CP/1997/L.7/Add.1, *reprinted in* 36 ILM (1997), signed December 11, 1997, entered into force February 16, 2005, *available at* http://www.unfccc.de/

## 1998

Convention on Access to Information, Public Participation in Decision-making and Access to Justice in Environmental Matters (the Aarhus Convention), 38 ILM 517 (1999)

Rotterdam Convention on Prior Informed Consent Procedure for Certain Hazardous Chemicals and Pesticides in International Trade, 38 ILM 1 (1999), signed September 11, 1998, entered into force February 24, 2004

## 1999

Protocol on Water and Health, UN Doc. UNEP/POPS/CONF/4, *reprinted in* 38 ILM 1708 (1999), signed May 22, 2001, not yet in force, *available at* www.unecc.org/env/water/

## 2000

Biosafety Protocol to the Convention on Biological Diversity (Cartegena Protocol), 39 ILM 1927 (2000), signed January 29, 2000, entered into force September 11, 2003

Protocol No. 12 to the Convention for the Protection of Human Rights and Fundamental Freedoms, Rome, ETS No. 177, November 4, 2000

## 2001

International Treaty on Plant Genetic Resources for Food and Agriculture, not yet in force, *available at* http://www.fao.org/biodiversity/cgrfa/

European Council Directive on the Assessment of the Effects of Certain Plans and Programs on the Environment, COM/96/0511 FINAL-SYN 96/0304, *available at* http://europa.eu.int/comm/environment/eia/full-legal-text/96pc511.htm

## 2002

Stockholm Convention on Persistent Organic Pollutants, UN Doc. UNEP/POPS/CONF/4, 40 ILM 532 (2001), signed May 22, 2001, entered into force May 17, 2004, *available at* http://www.pops.int/

## 2003

Protocol on Strategic Environmental Assessment to the Convention on Environmental Impact Assessment in a Transboundary Context, signed May 21, 2003, *available at* http://www.unece.org/env/eia/sea_protocol.htm

Protocol on Civil Liability and Compensation for Damage Caused by the Transboundary Effects of Industrial Accidents on Transboundary Waters, Signed May 2003, not yet in force, *available at* http://www.unece.org/env/civilliability/documents/protocol_e.pdf

## 2005

Convention on the Protection and Promotion of the Diversity of Cultural Expressions, adopted under the auspices of UNESCO in October 2005, *available at* http://www.unesco.org/culture/culturaldiversity/convention_en.pdf

### Non-Binding Instruments

## 1948

Universal Declaration of Human Rights, GA Res. 217 A (III), UN Doc. A/810, December 10, 1948, *reprinted in* INTERNATIONAL INSTRUMENTS OF THE UNITED NATIONS 85 (Irving Sarnoff ed., 1997), *available at* http://www.un.org/Overview/rights.html

## 1970

Declaration of Principles on International Law Concerning Friendly Relations and Cooperation Among States in Accordance with the Charter of the United Nations, GA Res. 2625, October 24, 1970, *reprinted in* 9 ILM 1292 (1972)

**1972**

Stockholm Declaration, UN Doc. A/CONF.48/14, June 16, 1972, *reprinted in* 11 ILM 1416 (1972).

Recommendation of the Council on Guiding Principles Concerning International Economic Aspects of Environmental Policies (OECD), C(72) 128, May 26, 1972, *available at* http://www.olis.oecd.org/horizontal/oec-dacts.nsf/linkto/C(72)128

**1974**

OECD, Recommendation of the Council on the Implementation of the Polluter Pays Principle, C(74)223, November 14, 1974, *available at* http://www.olis.oecd.org/horizontal/occdacts.nsf/linkto/C(74)223

**1978**

UNEP Principles on Conservation and Harmonius Utilization of Natural Resources Shared by Two or More States, May 19, 1978, *reprinted in* PATRICIA BIRNIE & ALAN BOYLE, BASIC DOCUMENTS ON INTERNATINOAL LAW AND THE ENVIRONMENT 21 (1995)

**1980**

World Conservation Strategy (IUCN), synopsis *available at* http://www.unep.org/geo/geo3/ english/049.htm

**1982**

World Charter for Nature, GA Res. 37/7, *reprinted in* 22 ILM 455 (1983)

**1985**

UNEP, Montreal Guidelines on the Protection of the Marine Environment Against Pollution from Land-Based Sources (1985), *reprinted in* INTERNATIONAL ENVIRONMENTAL LAW: PRIMARY MATERIAL 29 (Michael R. Molitor ed., 1991)

**1986**

UN General Assembly Resolution on the Right to Development, GA Res. 41/128, December 4, 1986

**1987**

London Declaration of the Second International North Sea Conference, *available at* http://odin.dep.no/md/nsc/declaration/022001-990245/index-dok000-b-n-a.html

UNEP Goals and Principles of Environmental Impact Assessment, *available at* http://www.unep.org/Documents.multilingual/Default.asp?DocumentID =100&ArticleID=1658

Cairo Guidelines and Principles for the Environmentally Sound Management of Hazardous Wastes, *available at* http://www.unep.org/

### 1989
World Bank Operational Directive on Environmental Assessment, OP 4.01, January 1999, World Bank Operational Manual, *available at* http://wbln0018.worldbank.org/Institutional/Manuals/OpManual.nsf/toc2/9367 A2A9D9DAEED38525672C007D0972?OpenDocument

### 1990
Draft Earth Charter, *available at* http://www.earthcharter.org/earthcharter/charter.htm

Ministerial Declaration on Sustainable Development in the ECE Region (Bergen Declaration), Bergen, Norway, May 15, 1990

IUCN Draft Articles on Environment and Development, *reprinted in* IUCN, DRAFT INTERNATIONAL COVENANT ON ENVIRONMENT AND DEVELOPMENT (2d ed. 2001)

General Comment No. 3 of the UN Committee on Economic, Social and Cultural Rights, December 14, 1990, *available at* http://www.unhchr.org/

### 1992
Rio Declaration on Environment and Development, UN Doc. A/CONF.15/ 26, *reprinted in* 31 I.L.M. 874 (1992), *available at* http://www.un.org/documents/ga/confl21/aconf15126-1annex1.htm

Agenda 21, UN Doc. A/CONF.151/26, *reprinted in* 31 ILM 874 (1992)

Non-legally Binding Authoritative Statement of Principles for a Global Consensus on the Management, Conservation and Sustainable Development of All Types of Forests, UN Doc. A/CONF.151/26, *available at* http://www.un.org/documents/ga/confl51/aconf15126-3annex3.htm

### 1993
Vienna Declaration on Human Rights, UN Doc. A/CONF.157/23, *available at* http://www.unhchr.ch/huridocda/huridoca.nsf/(Symbol)/A.CONF. 157.23.En?OpenDocument

**1994**

Draft Declaration on Principles on Environment and Human Rights, appended to the Final Report Prepared by Mrs. Fatma Zohra Ksentini, Special Rapporteur, UN Doc. E/CN.4/Sub.2/1994/9 (1994), *available at* http://www.worldpolicy.org/globalrights/environment/envright.html

Draft UN Declaration on the Rights of Indigenous Peoples, GA Res. 1994/45, *available at* http://www.unhchr.ch/hur*Id*.ocda/hur*Id*.oca.nsf/ (Symbol)/E.CN.4.SUB.2.RES.1994.45.En?OpenDocument

WTO Ministerial Decision on Trade and Environment, *available at* http://www.wto.org/english/tratop_e/envir_e/envir_e.htm

Draft Guidelines for the Ecological Sustainability of Non-Consumptive Uses of Wild Species, *available at* http://www.iucn.org

**1995**

Copenhagen Declaration on Social Development, adopted at the World Social Summit in 1995, *available at* http://www.visionoffice.com/socdev/wssdco-0.htm

Fourth World Conference on Women—Beijing Declaration and Platform for Action, *available at* http://www.unhchr.ch/

FAO Code of Conduct for Responsible Fisheries, *available at* http://www.fao.org/documents/show_cdr.asp?url_file=/DOCREP/005/v9878e/v9878e00.htm

**1997**

Draft North American Agreement on Transboundary Environmental Impact Assessment, *available at* http://www.ccc.org/pubs_info_resources/law_treat_agree/pbl.cfm?varlan=english

**2000**

UN Millennium Declaration, A/res/55/2, *available at* http://www.un.org/millennium/declaration/ares552e.htm

General Comment No. 14 of the UN Committee on Economic, Social and Cultural Rights, E/C.12/2000/4, July 4, 2000, *available at* http://www.unhchr.org/

**2001**

Doha Ministerial Declaration, *available at* http://www.wto.org/english/thewto_e/minist_e/ min01/mindecl_e.htm

ILC Draft Articles on State Responsibility, adopted in 2001, *available at* http://www.un.org/law/ilc/texts/State_responsibility/responsibility_articles(e).pdf

ILC Draft Articles on Prevention of Transboundary Harm from Hazardous Activities, *available at* http://www.un.org/law/ilc/

**2002**

Johannesburg Declaration on Sustainable Development and Plan of Implementation, UN Doc. A/CONF.199/20 (2002)

General Comment No. 15 of the UN Committee on Economic, Social and Cultural Rights, *available at* http://www.unhchr.ch/html/menu2/6/gc15.doc

ILA New Delhi Principles on Sustainable Development, Res. 3/2002

UNEP Governing Council Decision on Environmentally Sound Management of Hazardous Wastes, Dec. 14/30, *available at* http://www.unep.org/

# TABLE OF CASES

Permanent Court of International Justice and International Court of Justice

# INDEX